KUMĀRAJĪVA
PHILOSOPHER AND SEER

KUMĀRAJĪVA
PHILOSOPHER AND SEER

Edited By
SHASHIBALA

Indira Gandhi National Centre For The Arts
New Delhi

KUMĀRAJĪVA
PHILOSOPHER AND SEER

ISBN: 978-93-80935-61-4
Sale Price: Rs. 1500/-

First Published in 2015 by:
Indira Gandhi National Centre for the Arts
Central Vista Mess, Janpath, New Delhi- 110 001 (India)

Distributor:
D.K. Printworld (P) Ltd.
Regd. Office: Vedaśrī, F-395, Sudarshan Park
(Metro Station: Ramesh Nagar)
New Delhi-110 015-11
Phones: (011) 2545 3975, 2546 6019; Fax: 2546 5926
e-mail: indology@dkprintworld.com
Web: www.dkprintworld.com

Designed and Printed in India by
Nutech Print Services, New Delhi

Foreword

India and China both are ancient civilizations of the world. Buddhism with its origin in India became the major cultural link between these two oldest continuing civilizations. Buddhist savants from India travelled to China, risking their own lives by crossing deserts and oceans to spread the spiritual message. Many from China also took pilgrimage to India on the quest of the Dharma and collected Buddhist scriptures. By this, these savants and pilgrims contributed not only to the spread of Buddhism but also facilitated understanding of social and economic relations of Indian civilization to Central Asia and China. Though the ancient records of India are silent about them but there are large number of documents preserved in Chinese and Central Asian languages in which a few Chinese records have been discovered narrating the lives and works of eminent Buddhist monks and scholars.

Kumārajīva was one of the most eminent Buddhist scholars who broke political, geographical, cultural and linguistic barriers with a long cherished mission of the propagation of true spirit of Buddhism. His father was an Indian (Kashmiri) brahmin and mother a Kuchean princess. He studied Buddhist doctrines in Kucha, Kashmir, and in Kashgar under great teachers. Thus, he developed himself as a brilliant monk who was well versed in the Buddhist learning of the schools, then current in northern India. With his thorough study of Chinese language while in captivity, taking up the translation of Buddhist scriptures sponsored by the state, presiding over a team of Chinese specialists before an audience of hundreds of monks, he translated a large number of Buddhist texts into Chinese. In the collection of his translated works some are the most important texts now available only through his translations.

Kumārajīva's legacy is preserved in thousands of monasteries in China, Korea and Japan in his translations of sacred Sanskrit texts copied over last sixteen centuries. His works have inspired members of imperial houses, Emperors, writers, artists, pilgrims and philosophers. The canvas covering his life and legacy spans from Kashmir to Japan running through mountains, snow covered hills, barren deserts and green valleys.

Indira Gandhi National Centre for the Arts organised an International seminar on "Kumārajīva : Philosopher and Seer" in February 2011 to study closely the life and contributions of Kumārajīva in enhancement of India-China cultural relations. It is gratifying to place in the hands of scholars this collection of research papers that throws significant light on various aspects related to the life and works of Kumārajīva.

I am grateful to the Chinese and Indian scholars, as well as the scholars from other countries for their contribution to this volume. My gratitude to Dr. Shashibala for editing this volume. She was also the coordinator of the seminar along with the exhibition on Kumārajīva. I am thankful to Dr. Advaitavadini Kaul, Chief Editor, IGNCA for her careful handling of the publication and seeing it through press.

I hope the volume will inspire more scholars and readers of the two countries to strengthen existing contacts and enhance the cordial understanding and co-operative relationship between the two countries.

Chinmaya R. Gharekhan
President, IGNCA Trust

Contents

Contributors

Advaitavadini Kaul
akaul@ignca.nic.in
Chief Editor & Head of Publication Unit
Klakosa Division
Indira Gandhi National Centre for the Arts
11, Mansingh Road, New Delhi-110001
Tel.: 011 23388438

Bachchan Kumar
bachchan_kumr@yahoo.com
In Charge, South East Asian Studies
Indira Gandhi National Centre for the Arts
11, Mansingh Road, New Delhi-110001
Tel.: 011 23388241

Barbara Meisterernst
bmeisterernst@googlemail.com
Researcher,
Humboldt-University,
Berlin, Seminary for Sinology
Invalidenstrasse 118, 10115 Berlin
Private Address:
Geygerstrasse 3, 12043 Berlin

Bill M. Mak
bill.m.mak@gmail.com
University of Kyoto
Graduate School of Humanities,
Faculty of Letters
Department of Indological Studies
Yoshida-Honmachi, Sakyo-ku,
Kyoto, 606-8501, Japan

B.R. Deepak
deepak110@yahoo.com
Associate Professor of Chinese
Managing Editor *'Think India'* Quarterly
Centre of Chinese and Southeast Asian Studies
Jawaharlal Nehru University, New Delhi,
India 110067
Tel: 011 26704282

Chrles Willemen
chrleswillemen@yahoo.com
Lifelong Member Belgian Royal Academy of Sciences
(Overseas Sciences).
Add: PB 656. 8400 Oostende, Belgium.
Tel.: 00.32.478616799

Chongfeng Li
tflee@pku.edu.cn,
Associate Professor of Buddhist Archaeology
Deptt. of Archaeology
Peking University
Beijing 100871
PR China
Tel.: 86.10.6276.5713(O), 6275, 5912,
Fax: 6275.1667

Elsa Legittimo
elsa.legittimo@gmail.com
Faculté des Lettres UNIGE
Unité d'Histoire des Religions
Ètudes Bouddhiques
Uni Bastions Aile Jura bureau 311
Rue de Candolle 5
CH-1211 Genéve 4, Switzerland
Phone Office: +41-22-379-7312

Fan Jingjing
fanjingjing@pku.edu.cn
Researcher
Peking University
Beijjing
China

Gensei Ito
President, A.S.C.A. Overseas Cultural Exchange
6-5-23, Honkomagome, Bunkyo-ku,
Tokyo, 113-0021,
Japan

Guilaine Mala
guilaine.mala@wolfson.oc.ac.uk
Associate of the Sub-Faculty of East Asian Studies
University of Oxford
Add: 11 Hanborough Close,
Eynsham/Witney OX29 4NR (U.K.)
Tel.: [0]1 865 882 446

Har Prasad Ray
haraprasadray@rediffmail.com
Senior Fellow and Scholar Supervisor
The Asiatic Society,
Flat -3, Onobin Aptts.,
64 Santoshpur Avenue,
Kolkata-700075.

Jing Nan
jinchinese@gmail.com
Assistant Researcher
Oriental Literature Research,
Institute of Foreign Literature, CASS
Beijing-100732, China

Katsuhisa Yamada
Emeritus Professor
The University of Osaka Kyoiku
Vice President of Koshien University and Researcher in Charge of Silk Road Studies, IOP,
1-13 Momijigaoka
Takarazuka City
Hyogo 665-0006
Japan

Kimiaki Tanaka
kimiaki_tanak@livedoor.com
Research Fellow
Eastern Institute Inc. Tokoy,
Chief Curator
Toga Meditation Museum
3-14-4 Minami-yukigaya
Ota-ku
Tokyo 145-0066
Japan
Tel.: 81-3-3729-5573

Dr. Kin-Tung Yit
Assistant Professor
National Sun Yat-Sen University (NSYSU)
Center for general Education/Institute of Philosophy
No. 70, Lianhai Rd., Gushan District,
Kaohsiung City 804,
Taiwan (R.O.C.)
Tel.: +886-7-525-200 ext. 5867
(O) +886-916276056

Liu Cheng-you
chengyoul@yahoo.com.cn
Professor
Department /School of Philosophy & Religiours Studies,
Minzu University
No. 27, Zhongguancum South St.,
Haidian, Beijing-100081
P.R.C. China

Liu Yingsheng
liuys@nju.edu.cn
Director of the Institute of Asian Studies,
Professor
Dept. of History, Nanjing University,
China Nanjing University, China
Tel.: 025-83593162

Paula Tizzano Fernández
paulatizzano@gmail.com
Jaume I Universitat (Universitat Jaume I)
Castellón (city), Spain (Country)
Bartolomé Mitre 3743, Ap.A
Buenos Aires
CI201AAS-Argentina
Ph.: (+5411) 6380-2699

Pokan Chou
pkchou@mail.edu.tw, phchou@ntu.edu.tw
Professor, Department of Buddhist Studies
Fo Guang University
Taiwan (Republic of China)
Fl.4, No. 21, Alley 14, Lane 208, Rui An St.
Taipei, Taiwan (Republic of China) 106
Tel.: 886-3-9871000 ext. 27212 (Office)

Saroj Kumar Chudhuri
sroj.chudhuri_18arojkumar67crp@yahoo.com
J-1867, Chittranjan Park
New Delhi-19
Ph.: 011-41603452

Shashibala
drshashibl@yhoo.com
Research Professor,
International Academy of India Culture,
New Delhi
38 Naya Ganj, Ghaziabad, UP
Ph.: 01202835098

Sylvie Hureau
sylvie_hureau@hotmail.com
Maître de conférences
Ecole Pratique des Hautes Etudes
EPHE, 46 rue de Lille
7507 PARIS, FRANCE

Yao-ming Tsai
tsaiyt@ntu.edu.tw
Associate Professor
Dept of Philosophy, National Taiwan University
Department of Philosophy
National Taiwan University
Taipei, Taiwan, 106 ROC
Office Ph.: (886-2) 3366-3381

Yoichi Kawada
Director
The Institute of Oriental Philosophy
2-10-8 Yamato-cho
Nakano-ku, Tokyo 165-0034

Yu Inoue
Shiga Prefecture Research Institution
Kamo, Tabashima City in
Japan

Zhu Qingzhi
qingzhi@ied.edu.hk
Head of Department of Chinese
Chair Professor of Chinese Language
Hong Kong Institute of Education
Tai Po, NT, HK
852-2948-8049

Preface

Indira Gandhi National Centre for the Arts (IGNCA) had organised a three-day international conference on 3rd-5th February 2011 on the life and legacy of Kumārajīva, an outstanding Buddhist master of the 4th-5th century CE, whose mission in life was the promotion of universal human values which arise from within, evolving from a blend of individual experiences and collective consciousness. Born out of royal blood from his mother's side, and an aristocratic lineage from his father's, he inherited his spiritual doctrine from both. His impeccable pedigree and rigorous education made him an icon of wisdom and sacrifice, gave him *vajra* like determination and spurred him to constant effort. His life was unique in all aspects - from parentage and education to old age and nirvāṇa.

He saw many vicissitudes in his eventful life, starting from being a hostage of war to becoming *Rājyaguru.* Through his translations of Buddhist texts from Sanskrit into Chinese he established ethical and aesthetical, physical and spiritual value systems for the people of East Asia. His translations are recited in monasteries to this day. With him, secular became sacred and sacred became secular. Under his tutelage, politically divided China was united for the first time. His teachings continue to be relevant in this age of globalization.

The research papers presented during the conference covered several areas concerning his life and legacy. The paper by **Sylvie Hureau** deals with the question of the date of Kumārajīva's birth which has a considerable significance as it could be helpful in fixing the date of his arrival in Ch'ang-an as well as to understand his relations with his disciples. The documention presented by **Katsuhisa Yamada** is based on his visits to the towns and villages associated with Kumārajīva – Kashgar, Tumushuk, Kucha, Loulan, Dunhuang, Liangzchou and Ch'ang-an – the various places where Kumārajīva was born, educated, travelled and translated many texts from Sanskrit into Chinese. He was taken as booty of war by the Chinese and raised to the status of *Rājyaguru.* **BR Deepak's** paper traces the history of "Kumārajīva in China: from war booty to *Rājyaguru*", exploring civilizational dialogue between India and China.

Harprasad Ray's paper is titled "Kumārajīva and his contemporaries". It outlines the political circumstances of the period and explains the Buddhist philosophical scenario preceding the time of Kumārajīva. The earlier masters gained faith and confidence of the rulers by taking recourse to the supernatural resorting to magical powers.

The first image of the Buddha ever made in India, believed to have been brought to China by Kumārajīva and his father, copied by monk Chōnen from

Japan, was either destroyed during the Boxer Rebellion or was carried off to Russia as booty. In his paper **Kimiaki Tanaka** presents his findings on the sandalwood image.

The paper on "Early Mahāyāna according to Kumārajīva's Upadeśa" by **Elsa Legittimo** talks about the denomination Mahāyānā in the Upadeśa, the metaphor of the Mahāyāna Ocean, Karuṇā as the foundation of Mahāyāna, Mahāyāna as the world's most supreme eloquence etc. According to the paper the Bodhisattva is the main protagonist of the Upadeśa.

Saroj Kumar Chaudhary discusses if Sanskrit taught by Kumārajīva played any role in innovation or dissemination of the Fan-ch'ieh spelling method, and if it was in any way associated with the invention of 'Recent Style Poetry' (Chin-t'i-shi). Kumārajīva's translation of the Lotus Sūtra, is the central scripture for T'ien T'ai Buddhists in China and Tendai and Nichiren Buddhism in Japan. **Yoichi Kawada** studies the journey "From Kumārajīva to Nichiren – connected through Myoho-Renge-Kyō". **Yao-ming Tsai** in his paper "Soteriological unfolding of the mind, body and abiding places in the 'Sāmantamukhaparivarta' of the Lotus Sūtra" employs it as the main source to discuss with a philosophical approach the possibility of the most superlative unfolding of three concepts, namely mind, body and abiding-places in practice and application of Mahāyāna Buddhism.

Barbara Meisterernst brings to light peculiarities of the language of Kumārajīva's translation of the Lotus Sūtra. Her analysis of the language of the Lotus Sūtra is based on a previous and more general investigation of the temporal and aspectual structures of early Buddhist texts. Kumārajīva is evidently more conservative in his grammatical structure than the original Chinese text written by Fahien. "The added topic-shift markers in the Chinese translations of Buddhist scriptures: A Sanskrit-Chinese comparative analysis of the Lotus Sūtra" by **Jiang Nan** is based on a Chinese-Sanskrit comparative analysis of the Lotus Sūtra and a comparative study of its different Chinese translations. The paper explores the structural features of the texts in Chinese translations of Buddhist scriptures.

"Kumārajīva and Abhidharma" by **Charles Willemen** states that although the Sarvāstivādins were the most influential school in Gandhāran cultural area – certainly in Bactria - during the first centuries CE, the reality was more complex. He talks about the texts which give an idea about Kumārajīva's knowledge of Abhidharmic traditions in his time. **Bill M. Mak** throws light on "Kumārajīva and Prajñāpāramitā in China". He addresses a number of issues concerning these texts: Lesser and Greater and Vajracchedikā, and the important commentary *Prajñāpāramitopadeśa*, attributed to Nāgārjuna, from both, a philological as well as historical perspective.

Kin Tung Yit in "Two Traditions of Śrāvaka Meditation: Kumārajīva's Zuo chan san mei jing and Buddhaghoṣa's Visuddhimagga", has done a comparative study of Kumārajīva's "Sitting Meditation Samādhi Sūtra" and Buddhaghosa's Visuddhimagga, and he aims to explore the main practices of the Śrāvaka meditation in these two Buddhist meditation manuals. The tradition of Dhyāna by Buddhist monks in northern China during 4th-6th centuries has been reflected in many cultural spheres. Dhyāna-sūtras translated by Kumārajīva became the basis of Buddhist cave temples. **Chongfeng Li** in "Kumārajīva and early cave-temples of China: the case of the Dhyāna-sūtras", co-relates art, literature and history.

Liu Cheng-you has discussed "Kumārajīva's influence on humanstic Buddhism from Yim Shun's conversion". Many Chinese intellectuals shouldered responsibility for the promotion of nationalism and withstood great pain. The contemporary Buddhist movement was always led by Yinshun's thought in China which had its roots in the thought of Nāgārjuna which was translated by Kumārajīva.

Po-kan Chou in his paper "Defining a new road for Mahāyāna Buddhism in China" refutes the earlier research on the history of Mahāyāna, presenting his argument that laity is indeed the main driving force in China rather than in India. According to him it was mainly defined by the Lotus Sūtra rather than any other Buddhist text. **Zhn Qingzhi's** paper focuses on Kumārajīva's contribution in creation of Chinese Budhism and the Chinese culture.

Paula Tizzano Fernandez offers a detailed research on "Kumārajīva's visibility: research in translation studies". He relied on biographical markers which facilitate exploration of his translation theories from a hermeneutic-philosophical approach, the cognitive acquisition of his translating competence, his sense of mission and purpose, and the singularities of his forerunning translators' school. Lastly, from an action-theory paradigm, she investigates the extent to which his methodology of "oral translation-master class-collective workshop" could be applied today in the training of specialized translators.

Liu Yingsheng's paper examines the materials written during 13th and 14th centuries CE. "History of the Sixteen Kingdoms" is the first that mentions Kumārajīva's translations. Shortly thereafter, it was repeated by Hui Jiao 慧皎 (497—554 CE) in his "Biographies of the Famous Monks".

Guilaine Mala has searched references to "Kumārajīva in 18th century Tibetan Sources", another valuable contribution to the works on Kumārajīva. **Fan Jingjing's** paper is on Kumārajīva's contribution to Chinese literature focusing on his translation of Vimalakīrtinirdeśasūtra which is one of the most popular sūtras that has exerted a great influence on Chinese literature since Six Dynasties.

In Japan, sūtras were copied for presenting as offerings at temples in large numbers. When these piled up, they were tied into bundles and immersed in flowing water. Many of them were unearthed from river banks or dried up beds. A report on such sūtras translated by Kumārajīva is presented by **Yu Inoue** in "The third case unearthed Kokera Sūtra copy of Diamond Wisdom Sūtra translated by Kumārajīva..." "The influence of Sūtras translated by Kumārajīva on the development of Mahāyāna Buddhism in Japan" by **Gensei Ito,** traces the history of Mahāyāna Buddhism in Japan from its official advent to the present day, stating that 62,000 temples out of the existing 75,000 belong to the sects based on the sūtras translated by Kumārajīva. **Bachchan Kumar's** paper focuses on "Kumārajīva and Mādhyamaka school of thought". Kumārajīva was a Kashmirian from his father's side. His mother took him to Kashmir for studies. **Advaitavadani Kaul** in her paper on "Kumārajīva: his connections with Kashmir and the development of Buddhist lore" attempts to trace the state of Buddhism in Kashmir during the 4th-5th century CE and the impact of the Buddhist scholars of Kashmir outside Kashmir.

The present volume is an excellent collection of research papers adding insight and new dimensions to the body of works done on great masters and pilgrims who contributed towards cultural advancement through transcendence in life.

I am grateful to IGNCA for giving me an opportunity to organize this international conference and curate an exhibition on the 'Life and Legacy of Kumārajīva' whose memories have gone into amnesia. On behalf of IGNCA, I sincerely thank all those who contributed towards making this conference successful. Moreover I am grateful to all those who contributed their documentation for a photo exhibition on "Life and Legacy of Kumārajīva" from remote areas in China especially from the Silk Route and various collections from Japan, making the event rewarding and memorable.

Shashibala

1

Kumārajīva's date of birth

Sylvie Hureau

Whereas many biographies of monks give precise indications of the dates of their death and of their age, those of Kumārajīva 鳩摩羅什, in the *Chu sanzang jiji* 出三藏記集, the *Gaoseng zhuan* 高僧傳 and the *Jinshu* 晉書,[1] give only imprecise information on his death and none on his date of birth.

If the question of his date of death has been often debated, that of his date of birth has been less often discussed, probably because it has been thought to be of less interest to the extent that it has little impact on the authenticity of the translations he carried out at the end of his life in Chang'an 長安.

Nevertheless, this question is not without importance, because from the date of his birth we can deduce the age at which he arrived in Chang'an and better comprehend one of the possible keys to his success in China: whether he was a man whose advanced age commanded respect, like the image that stands at the entrance to the grottoes at Kizil, showing him as an old, emaciated sage, or whether, on the contrary, he was a young master who dazzled audiences with his presence. Knowing his age, we would also better understand his relations with his disciples.

If this question has already been discussed, it has not been definitively answered. In the following lines I will begin by presenting the two main dates between which researchers have been divided, CE 344 and 350, along with the arguments in their favour. I will then argue that neither of them is compatible with what is said in Kumārajīva's biographies and that the biographies have been composed in such a way that they do not permit any firm conclusion.

---

[1] In order: T. 2145 (14), 55.100a-102a; T. 2059 (2), 50.330a-333a; *Jinshu* (95), 8.2499-2502. References to Buddhist texts are given according to the *Taishō* edition of the canon, *Taishō Shinshū Daizōkyō* 大正新脩大藏経 (T.) and the Shinsan edition of the Complement to the Buddhist canon, *Shinsan Zokuzōkyō* 卍新纂續藏經 (X.).

However, if these official and canonical biographies are the main documents on which we rely to know about the life of Kumārajīva, they are not the only ones. There exist other narratives which were circulated in the same period and which competed with them. I will present these narratives and, based more precisely on two biographies found in the Dunhuang 燉煌 manuscripts, I will consider the possibility that Kumārajīva was born in the second half of the 360s, a date which is compatible with what the biographies say.

Before beginning, I will recall several events that marked the life of Kumārajīva and of which mention will be made in this paper.

Kumārajīva was born in Kucha. His father was a native of India and his mother apparently was from a royal family in this small kingdom bordering the northern edge of the desert of Taklamakan. While he was leading, one may suppose, the peaceful life of a member of the Buddhist community, Fu Jian 苻堅 (338-385) of the Former Qin, who reigned over a small area in northern China, planned to extend his realm by conquering areas to the west. His troops, led by the General Lü Guang 呂光 (337-399), conquered Kucha in 384. A year later, they returned to China, carrying spoils of war, among which was Kumārajīva. But on the way back, Lü Guang learned of the death of Fu Jian. He halted in Liangzhou 涼州 (in today's Gansu province), where he founded his own kingdom. Sixteen years later, in 401, this kingdom was overthrown by Yao Xing 姚興 (366-416), king of the Later Qin, and Kumārajīva was once again carried away as a war trophy, this time to Chang'an. He lived there till the end of his life, translating the works that would prove extremely important in Buddhist thought and practice in China in the coming centuries.

1. The dates- CE 344 and 350; the sources on which they are based and the problems they raise:

The date CE 344 is indirectly written in a posthumous eulogy for Kumārajīva that would have been composed by his disciple Sengzhao 僧肇 (374-414)[2] in honor of his deceased master: the "Jiumoluoshi Fashi Lei" 鳩摩羅什法師誄 (hereafter "Lei"). The "Lei" says that Kumārajīva died in 413 (a *guichou* 癸丑 year) and that he was seventy years old.[3] By implication, then, the "Lei" assigns him the date of birth of 344.

Attributed to one of Kumārajīva's closest disciples, and by this fact stamped with the highest possible authority, the "Lei" and its dates were

---

[2] I follow Tsukamoto's demonstration (1955, pp. 120-121) that Sengzhao was 41 years old when he died, in 414, and not 31 as is said in his biography in the *Gaoseng zhuan*, T. 2059 (6), 50.366a29.

[3] T. 2103 (23), 52.264c18-19:癸丑之年。年七十。四月十三日薨于大寺. Age in China was, and is still, calculated from conception, not birth, and a newborn starts at one year of age. In order to convert into Western terms, the reader has to count one year less than what the Chinese text says.

uniformly accepted by scholars[4] until, in 1954, Tsukamoto Zenryū 塚本善隆 called them into question and, based on indications given in the biographies of Kumārajīva, proposed a date of birth of CE 350 and a date of death of 409.[5] Tsukamoto's argument continued to be accepted by a number of scholars,[6] although it was also criticised, notably by Arthur Robinson, who preferred to return to the dates of the "Lei", 344-413, a position that was also taken by some other scholars.[7] Nevertheless, Saitō Tatuya 斉藤達也 has recently returned to the question of the date of Kumārajīva's death and has given a detailed analysis of the "Lei" in which he has proved irrefutably that its author was describing past events and therefore it could have been written neither by Sengzhao nor by any other contemporary of Kumārajīva.[8] From this, the contents of the "Lei" can be called into question, particularly the dates it gives.[9]

To determine whether Kumārajīva's date of birth was 350, Tsukamoto based his argument on an analysis of Kumārajīva's biographies. It says that Kumārajīva entered the monastic order at the age of seven and that, two years later, he left Kucha in the company of his mother to go to study in Jibin, where he stayed three years, then returned to Kucha. On the way back to Kucha they encountered an arhat who said these words to his mother:

> *Be constantly attentive to this śrāmaṇera. If he reaches the age of thirty-five without having broken the regulations, he will propagate the Buddhist law and save myriads of beings, as many as did Upagupta. But if he does not respect them*

---

4 Pelliot 1912:.392 n.; Lévi 1913:335; Nobel 1927:207; Tang Yongtong 1938:196; Uehara 1949:123.

5 Before Tsukamoto took a position on reopening the question of the dates given in the "Lei", Paul Pelliot voiced a reservation concerning not the date of death but that of birth. In notes that were published only in 2002 by Antonino Forte, Pelliot not only reviewed Nobel's study of the biography of Kumārajīva, published in 1927, but also provided an analytical study of the biographies of Kumārajīva in which he compared them in detail, looking for divergences and filiations among them and seeking to distinguish the true from the false. He admitted having at first followed the birth date proposed by the "Lei", but he added that, in view of the contradictions this would create, and "despite the authority of the text [of Sengzhao]", he suggested "lowering" this date by a decade.

6 Hurvitz 1962:64; Ōchō Enichi and Suwa Gijun 1982:113-117; Kamata Shigeo 1983:225; Wang Wenyan 1984: 218; Itô Takatoshi 1996: 68.

7 Robinson 1967: n. 1:244-247; Zheng Yuqing 1988:23.

8 Saitō T. begins by pointing out that the "Lei" equally credits both rulers of the Qin kingdoms, Fu Jian and Yao Xing, for their contribution to the expansion of Buddhism, although these two families were implacable enemies. Sengzhao, member of a community protected by the Yao family, would not have dared hold such a position on the Fu family. Further, the "Lei" speaks plainly of the fact that Kumārajīva had relations with courtesans, something of which neither Sengzhao nor a contemporary of Kumārajīva would have dared to write. For Saitō T., the author describes past events, so he cannot have been Sengzhao.

9 Having questioned the authority of the dates, Saitō proceeds to give a study of the date of Kumārajīva's death, proving that a death occurring in 409 could not be sustained and arriving at the conclusion that Kumārajīva died in 411 at the earliest. In my doctoral dissertation, I also arrived at the conclusion that the date 409 is not acceptable and offered as a hypothesis a date of death no earlier than 411, perhaps in that year or in 412; cf. Hureau, 2003, p. 358.

completely, he will do none of that and will be a master of the law who is surely very talented but who will not surpass [this quality].[10]

Tsukamoto assumes that the regulation in question was the vow of chastity. That Kumārajīva broke this vow is a well known fact. His biography recounts that in Chang'an, Yao Xing, wanting to ensure that Kumārajīva had descendants, forced him into unions with his own concubines.[11] The meeting with the arhat is, for Tsukamoto, a fiction created by the Chinese Buddhist community to vindicate the fact that Kumārajīva had broken his vow of chastity. It was a means of making the event seem ineluctable.

To determine on what date this breaking of the vow took place, Tsukamoto based himself once again on the biographies of Kumārajīva. They recount that after seizing Kucha, in the seventh month of CE 384, Lü Guang met Kumārajīva. He mocked him, and one day after having forced him to drink, he locked him in a room with a princess and compelled him to break his vow. Based on the arhat's prediction of the year when the sad affair would take place, Tsukamoto concludes that if Kumārajīva was in his thirty-fifth year in CE 384, one can deduce a date of birth of CE 350.[12]

Although Tsukamoto's argument is persuasive, one of its weaknesses is that it does not account for all the contents of the biographies of Kumārajīva. In particular, it does not take account of the fact that the biographies say that Kumārajīva was a young man when Lü Guang forced him to break his vow. The paragraph in question says, in fact:

[Lü] Guang was of a distant nature and did not see the extent of Kumārajīva's knowledge. Seeing that he was still of a young age (qinian shangshao 其年尙少), some vulgar men mocked him and forced him to unite with a princess of Kucha, but Kumārajīva obstinately did not accept [to do it], excusing himself from this baleful outcome. Lü Guang said to him: "The proper conduct of a monk is not to offend his father. Why do you cling to this dolorous proposition?" He got him drunk and shut him in [with the princess] in a room, so that Kumārajīva was constrained to comply and lost his chastity.[13]

It would appear unlikely that a man of thirty-five would have been mocked because of his youth, even if he seemed to be quite young. But it is precisely the words "young man" (*shaonian* 少年) that is in question in this passage. The expression *shaonian* 少年 applies to a child or adolescent but not to

[10] T. 2145 (14), 55.100b23-26; T. 2059 (2) 50.330b22-25; the paragraph is missing in the biography in the *Jinshu*.

[11] T. 2145 (14), 55.101c23-24; T. 2059 (2), 50.332c12; *Jinshu* (95), 8.2502.

[12] Tsukamoto 1954: 578.

[13] T. 2145 (14), 55.100c29-101a4; T. 2059 (2), 50.331c3-7 says *nianchi shangshao*年齒尙少; *Jinshu* (95), 8.2500 repeats the *Gaoseng zhuan*.

an adult in his thirties. As Kamata Shigeo 鎌田茂雄 has remarked, if Kumārajīva had been thirty-five years old, it would have been the epithet *zhuangnian* 壯年 that would have been applied to him.[14]

Another source seems to confirm that Kumārajīva was effectively a youth, or at least a young man, in CE 384. Several Vinaya extracts that two Chinese monks had brought from Kucha were translated in Chang'an in 379. In the preface to one of these, the monks report having seen a young man whom they recognized as Kumārajīva. This preface, which relates the circumstances in which the text was acquired in Kucha, reads as follows:

> *The new saṅghārāma of the king (wang xin sengqielan* 王新僧伽藍*) has ninety monks. Among them is a young śramaṇa (nianshao shamen* 年少沙門*) named Kumāra* 鳩摩羅*, who shines in his study of the Greater Vehicle. A disciple of [Fotu]shemi, he studies the Āgama.*[15]

That the young *śramaṇa* named Kumāra, mentioned in this preface, was none other than Kumārajīva would concur with the fact that it is stated in his biography in the *Chu sanzang jiji* that Kumārajīva was installed in the "new monastery of the King Bo Chun" (*Bo Chun wang xinsi* 帛純王新寺) after his return from Jibin.[16] One has the feeling that the Chinese monks are remarking on the prodigy precisely because he was so young. If Kumārajīva had been born in 350, as Tsukamoto believes, he would have been twenty-nine years old in 379. Would he then have been described as a "young *śramaṇa* "? Would the author of the preface not simply have remarked on a brilliant *śramaṇa* who excelled in the study of the Greater Vehicle? Should we not construe that he intends to indicate that Kumārajīva is younger than that? For the content of this notice to be compatible with the date of birth determined by Tsukamoto, it would be necessary for the Chinese monks to have gone to Kucha quite a few years earlier and that on returning to Chang'an they would have waited for favourable circumstances for translating manuscripts, so that the author of the notice would have been recalling old memories. If, on the contrary, we consider that the texts were translated into Chinese upon their arrival in Chang'an, in 379, then we must shift the date of Kumārajīva's birth toward the 360s to make the content of the preface coincide with his age. Only on this condition can we understand why the biographies again characterized Kumārajīva as a young man in 384.

However, the fact that Kumārajīva was a young man in 384 does not accord with the arhat's prediction, according to which Kumārajīva would lose his chastity at thirty-five. In other words, there is an inconsistency when the

[14] Kamata 1983:224.

[15] "Biqiuni jieben suochu ben moxu" 比丘尼戒本所出本末序, T. 2145 (11), 55.79c16-17.

[16] T. 2145 (14), 55.100c9. The *Gaoseng zhuan* simply says "new monastery" (*xinsi* 新寺): T. 2059 (2), 50.331a13.

biographies say on the one hand that Kumārajīva would lose his chastity at thirty-five and on the other hand that he broke his vow of chastity while he was still a young man.

This incoherence leaves us with two possibilities: the first, that a biographer has added the detail about Kumārajīva's young age, in order to dramatize the fact that he was constrained to break his vow, and the second, that the biographer added the story of his loss of chastity to dramatize the horror of the brutality that the young man suffered.[17]

That any biography is reworked is a well known fact. In this context, the example of Kumārajīva is instructive. It would suffice to merely compare the biographies in the *Chu sanzang jiji* and the *Gaoseng zhuan* to notice additions, suppressions, rewritten passages, and so on. In addition, comparing the treatment of sources which were elaborated in the biographies shows that the way in which they were used was not neutral. A biography is not a neutral account, confined to reporting the facts as they really unfolded in the times and places indicated. It consists of malleable material that a biographer may choose to lengthen, shorten, or shape according to his purposes, working and arranging the material as he sees fit.[18]

The first possibility must be rejected because of the mention of the young Kumāra in the preface dated 379. On the other hand, the second hypothesis is reinforced by an idea raised by Asada Nobuhisa 浅田信久, that the one responsible for the brutalities against Kumārajīva was not Lü Guang but his son, Lü Zuan 呂纂, who ruled the kingdom after his father's death and who was acquainted with Kumārajīva.[19] Indeed, Lü Guang is presented in his biography as a man who, although certainly not interested in Buddhism, was generous and magnanimous,[20] as opposed to Lü Zuan, whom the historical sources uniformly present as a brutal man, uncultivated and debauched, who constantly turned a deaf ear to the remonstrances of the dignitaries at his court.[21] Asada cites one of the sources that was used in the preparation of what

[17] It is this incoherence on the basis of which Pelliot proposes to lower the date of death of 344 to a decade earlier (cf. Forte 2002:17-18). Pelliot comments on the absurdity of the history's saying that Lü Guang forced Kumārajīva to break his vow of chastity, because the biographies say that Lü Guang had been sent by Fu Jian to retrieve Kumārajīva. "Singuliére façon d'observer les recommandations de Fu Jian qui soi-disant avait organis, l'expédition pour profiter des enseignements de ce maître éminent !" (p. 15).

[18] See Lu Yang 2004, specifically on passages concerning Kumārajīva's mother, Māra Pāpīyan and the conversion of the master who instructed Kumārajīva in Jibin, Bandhudatta.

[19] Several passages in the Lü Zuan's biography as well as in Kumārajīva's biographies show how the latter tried to give him advises, warning him about abnormal events and exhorting him to rectify his conduct: *Jinshu* (122), 10.3067 for Lü Zuan's biography; T. 2145 (14), 55.101a26-b6; T. 2059 (2), 50.332a5-15; *Jinshu* (95), 8.2501 for Kumārajīvas'.

[20] *Kuanjian you daliang* 寬簡有大量: Jinshu (122), 10.3053; translation by Mather 1959:28.

[21] *Jinshu* (122), 10.3067.

is now the *Jinshu*, the *Qinji* 秦紀 of Pei Jingren 裴景仁 (fl. 450),[22] which leaves no doubt when it comes to the difference in the sort of relations the two Lüs, father and son, had with Kumārajīva: "When Lü Guang attacked Kucha, he protected Kumārajīva. After his death, his son Lü Zuan assumed the throne. He taunted Kumārajīva."[23]

For Asada, Kumārajīva was forced to break his vow of chastity not by Lü Guang in Kucha, in 384, but rather by Lü Zuan in Liangzhou in 398, the year in which he considers Lü Zuan to have assumed the throne. Therefore, as Kumārajīva would have been in his thirty-fifth year in 398, Asada concludes that he was born in 364.

Asada's idea implies that the biographies of Kumārajīva link two events which occurred at a certain distance from one another: one, that Kumārajīva was taunted on account of his youth in 384, and the second that he broke his vow of chastity several years later, at the age of thirty-five. It is interesting because it accords with the hypothesis according to which a biographer would have inserted the paragraph on Kumārajīva's loss of chastity, constrained by Lü Guang, but it is flawed on two points. First, the date of accession of Lü Zuan to the throne was not 398 but 399. This accession occurred after the death of his father, which the sources unanimously attribute to the twelfth month of 399.[24] Lü Zuan did not succeed him immediately. Power would have devolved to his half-brother Lü Shao 呂紹, who had been designated heir-apparent in 396, when Lü Guang was proclaimed emperor.[25] However, several days after his father's death, Lü Zuan mounted a coup d'état and forced Lü Shao to commit suicide. He then took the title of celestial king (*tianwang* 天王) and changed the name of the reign era from the Longfei 龍飛 of Lü Guang to Xianning 咸寧, inaugurating a new reign-era. These events took place, again, in the twelfth month of 399.[26]

The second flaw in Asada's reasoning is that if one is prepared to accept the idea that it was under Lü Zuan's reign that Kumārajīva broke his vow, one does not see why this event should have taken place right at the beginning of his reign and only then. It would be justified to admit a certain latitude and presume that those events would have transpired between 400 and 401 (one cannot count the 12th month of 399, since Lü Zuan reigned only from the end of this month). For Kumārajīva to have been in his thirty-fifth year in 400 or 401, he would have to be born in 366 or 367.

---

[22] Rationale for Pei Jingren in Hureau 2003: pp. 102-103.

[23] *Taiping yulan* (754/2b), 4.3345b.

[24] Cui Hong's *Shiliuguo Chunqiu, quoted in the Taiping yulan* (125/2b), 1.604b11; *Zizhi tongjian* (111), 4.3504. Lü Guang's biography in the *Jinshu* gives only the year of his death, not according to Lü Guang's era name, but to its equivalent in the Jin dynasty era name, that is the third year of the Long'an 龍安 reign period of Emperor An 安, i.e. 399: *Jinshu* (122), 10.3064.

[25] *Jinshu* (122), 10.3059. The date is given in the Zizhi tongjian (108), 4.3429.

[26] *Jinshu* (122), 10.3065. *Jinshu* (10), 1.252.

2. The limits of the biographies; the existence of parallel facts:

We understand that thirty-five was a pivotal age in his life and if we know in what year he was this age, we will have determined his year of birth. But we see that his biography has been reworked in one way or the other, certainly more than once. His story has been rewritten so as to minimize an aspect of his life seen as shameful, to an extent whereby the biographical sources that survive do not permit us to resolve this question.

We know that these biographical sources on which we base our reasoning do not constitute the "final" word concerning the person of Kumārajīva. The biography reported in the *Chu sanzang jiji* is the oldest one extant, but before it there were already some sources in circulation, dealing with the life of Kumārajīva.

We find, in the biographies of Kumārajīva, traces of some of these earlier sources. Among them are prefaces to Kumārajīva's translations,[27] an essay by Sengzhao,[28] and some historical chronicles.[29] But it is not possible to identify them all, and in particular we do not know if there existed a biography earlier than that in the *Chu sanzang jiji* and, if it did, what it may have said. Pelliot advanced the idea of the existence of a primitive biography, perhaps a *biezhuan* 別傳, which the biographies of Kumārajīva would have followed faithfully

---

[27] These are the "Dapin jing xu" 大品經序, "Pimoluojieti jing yishu xu" 毘摩羅詰堤經義疏序, "Weimojie jing xu" 維摩詰經序 and "Dazhi shilun xu" 大智釋論序.

A passage in the biographies in the *Chu sanzang jijii* (p. 101b13-15) and the *Gaoseng zhuan* (p. 332a26-28), which shows Kumārajīva's dissatisfaction with the translations done by his predecessors, combines two statements extracted from the • Pimoluotieji jing yishu xu • (T. 2145 [8], 55.59a1-2) and the • Weimojie jing xu • (*ibid.* 58b9-10) which shows Kumārajīva dissatisfied only with previous translations of the *Vimalakīrti sūtra*. The narrative in the *Chu sanzang jiji* (p. 100c9-15) and *Gaoseng zhuan* (p. 331a13-18) recounting the temptation of Māra is inspired by a sentence in the • Dapin jing xu • (T. 2145[8], 55.53a20-21). The narrative in the *Gaoseng* (p. 331a21-b8), showing Kumārajīva converting to Mahāyāna his former master Bandhudatta, is inspired by another proposition in the • Dapin jing xu • (*ibid.* p. 53a21).

[28] The passage in the biography in the *Gaoseng zhuan* (p. 330c24-27), theatrically showing Kumārajīva emerging victorious from a debate with a monk in the Wensu kingdom, seems to have been inspired by a sentence in the • Banruo wuzhi lun • 般若無知論 saying that Kumārajīva vanquished heretical monks (T. 1858, 45.153a11). It is absent from the biography in the *Chu sanzang jiji.* A sentence in the *Chu sanzang jijii* (p. 101b7-8) and the Gaoseng zhuan (p. 332a16-17) saying that he kept the teaching of the scriptures hidden during his stay in Liangzhou is similar to another proposition in the • Banruo wuzhi lun • (T. 1858, 45.153a12).

[29] We recognize at least borrowings from Yao Hedou's (fl. 410) 姚和都 *Qinji* 秦紀, and Pei Jingren's 裴景仁 *Qinji.* We may also surmise a borrowing from Duan Guilong's (fl. 391-397) 段龜龍*Liangji* 涼記. *Rationale for the dates of Duan Guilong and Yao Hedou in Hureau 2003: pp. 100-102.*

Concerning the borrowing from Yao Hedou's *Qinji:* compare the sentence from *Qinji* cited in *Taiping yulan* (977/1b), 4.4328a21 to the sentence in *Chu sanzang jiji*, 55.101b11 and *Gaoseng zhuan*, 50.332a21-22. It speaks of the appearance of an auspicious sign (the transformation of onions into fragrant flowers) in Chang'an some months prior to Kumārajīva's arrival. We note that the sentence in *Qinji* connects to the victory of the Qin armies, while *Gaoseng zhuan* adds an interpretation to it that is favorable to

for the most part, omitting bits from time to time.[30] Further, other written sources would have circulated alongside these biographies at certain times and places, and we cannot rule out the possibility that some of them would have contained contrary indications or even conveyed a different image of the life of Kumārajīva. We also cannot rule out the possibility that the image of Kumārajīva was progressively reduced to a few legendary facts, among which the breaking of his vow figured.

Some of these sources that circulated parallel to the biographies are known to us only from their titles; but in some cases we also have citations from them. I will cite them in the order of their supposed date of appearance.

Kumārajīva had a biography in the *Sapoduo shizi zhuan* 薩婆多師資傳, a work on the history of the transmission of the Vinaya of the Sarvāstivāda school, composed during the Qi dynasty (479-502) by Sengyou 僧祐.[31] The work was lost and no citation has been preserved, and so we know nothing of its possible relation to the biography of Kumārajīva of which Sengyou was also the author and which is preserved in the *Chu sanzang jiji*. Were they identical or were they composed some years apart? Nothing prevents us from surmising that one of them might have contained information that had appeared in the interim.

Kumārajīva also had a biography in the *Mingseng zhuan* 名僧傳, compiled between CE 514 and 519 by Baochang 寶唱, a disciple of Sengyou. In a general way, the usage of the *Mingseng zhuan* was limited due to the appearance of the *Gaoseng zhuan* only a few years later, and no author refers to this work in speaking of the life of Kumārajīva. Six sentences from this biography were copied by the Japanese monk Shūshō 宗性 (ca. 1235) and can thus be compared

Kumārajīva, in the way of concluding: "This was taken as a fortunate sign and it was said that a sage would arrive".

Concerning the borrowing from Pei Jingren's *Qinji*, regarding Kumārajīva and Lü Zuan playing chess and Kumārajīva predicting that Lü Zuan would soon be beheaded, compare the quotation in the Taiping yulan (754/2b), 4.3345b with *Chu sanzang jiji*, p. 101b4-6 and *Gaoseng zhuan*, p. 332a11-15.

Concerning the borrowing from Duan Guilong's (fl. 391-397) 段龜龍*Liangji* 涼記, compare *Jinshu* (122), 10.3067/5-6 to *Chu sanzang jiji* and *Gaoseng zhuan*. It describes abnormal phenomena appearing during the reign of Lü Zuan, which Kumārajīva interpreted as inauspicious signs. The idea that this is a borrowing from *Liangji* is a supposition, based on the fact that in the *Jinshu*, the passage figures among a set of four anecdotes, the three others of which figure also in the *Liangji*. We know that the *Liangji* was one of the works used in the compilation of the *Shiliuguo chunqiu*, which was used next for chapters devoted to the Sixteen Kingdoms in the *Jinshu*. For the first passage, compare *Jinshu* (122), 10.3067/3-4 with *Liangji* quoted in *Taiping yulan* (581/2a), 3.2620b and *Chuxue ji* (22), 3.540. For the second passage, compare *Jinshu* (122), 10.3067/7-12 with *Liangji* quoted in *Taiping yulan* (454/10a), 2.2091b. For the third passage, compare *Jinshu* (122), 10.3067/12-13 with *Liangji* quoted in *Chuxue ji* (18), 2.439. More in Hureau 2003: pp. 176-178.

[30] Forte 2002:7.

[31] The preface and the table of contents of the *Sapoduo shizi zhuan* are copied in the *Chu sanzang jiji*, T. 2145 (12), 55.88c-90b; cf. p. 90a12 for the reference of Kumārajīva's biography. On the structure of the *Sapoduo shizi zhuan*, see Funayama, 2000, pp. 326-337.

with the two other biographies.[32] If four of these sentences have an equivalent in the *Chu sanzang jiji* and/or the *Gaoseng zhuan*, two are different: one announcing the number of his translations and, above all, a sentence without any equivalent in either of these two biographies and which fits in no obvious way into either of them, reminding us, again, that a biography is a narrative which is based both on sources and an author's invention.[33]

The *Jiumoluoshi fashi dayi* 鳩摩羅什法師大義 and the *Zhaolun shu* 肇論疏 of Huida 慧達,[34] both composed during the Chen dynasty, cite a document titled *Fushu* 苻書 in speaking of the life of Kumārajīva.[35] In both, the little that is cited from the *Fushu* is clearly being summarized from a longer text. If the two biographies I just mentioned, from the *Sapoduo shizi zhuan* and the *Mingseng zhuan*, can be considered as possible sources for the *Chu sanzang jiji* and the *Gaoseng zhuan*, this is not the case with the *Fushu*, whose date of composition falls between CE 550 and 589. The content of the citations bears no fundamentally new or divergent information when compared to familiar sources (with the exception of a passage saying that upon the birth of Kumārajīva a ray of light appeared, and a passage mentioning his disciples), but what is important for our purpose is knowing that the *Chu sanzang jiji* and the *Gaoseng zhuan* were not the only documents of reference concerning Kumārajīva and that certain authors in the second half of the 6th century preferred to refer to contemporary sources.

The "Shi Lao zhi" 釋老志 of the *Weishu* 魏書 (completed in 565) speaks of Kumārajīva and his disciples in a paragraph showing a difference, though slight, with the *Gaoseng zhuan*, and a similarity with the *Fushu*, or a source used in its redaction.[36]

Jizang 吉藏 (549-623) speaks of the date of death of Kumārajīva as well as the presence of his descendants, in a way attesting that he had other sources at his disposal and that he was not strictly following the orthodoxy of the *Gaoseng zhuan*.[37]

---

[32] X. 1523, 77.359c6-13.

[33] X. 1523, 77. 359c 7-10. Lu Yang, 2004, n. 61 p. 27 gives a translation and surmises a significance of the sentence.

[34] Respectively T. 1856, 45.122b23-28; X. 866 (2), 54.62c6-63a19.

[35] The source is titled differently in the two works: *Jiumoluoshi fashi dayi* cites *Fushu* 苻書, while Huida cites Fu Xi苻喜. The content of the citations being the same, at least at the outset, they are certainly citing the same document. I choose to adopt the reading *Fushu* and not Fu Xi for the following reasons: no Fu Xi is cited in Buddhist or historical sources; the title *Fushu* is parallel to a text called *Yaoshu*姚書 (Book of the Yao, or *History of the Yao*), which is mentioned for the first time in the "Erjiao lun" 二教論 of Dao'an 道安, which appeared in 569 (T. 2103 [8], 52.140c23); a Japanese author, Anchō安澄 (763-814), also cites the Fushu, written 苻書, in speaking of the life of Kumārajīva: T. 2255 (3), 65.92c6.

[36] Compare *Weishu* (114), 8.3031 lines 6-9 with T. 1856, 45.122b26-27, notably in mentioning Daorong as the first in Kumārajīva's disciples list.

[37] The source(s) on which Jizang relies are unknown. We just know that he cites the *Mingseng zhuan* concerning one of Kumārajīva's close collaborators, Daorong 道融: *Fahua xuanlun*, T. 1720 (1), 34.363c8-14. This, of course, is not enough to assume that for Kumārajīva's biography he was also relying on the *Mingseng zhuan*.

The biography of Kumārajīva in the *Jinshu* 晉書 (that appeared between 644 and 648) is distinct from its Buddhist models in having two passages that lack any equivalent elsewhere. While the biographies in the *Chu sanzang jiji* and *Gaoseng zhuan* say that Yao Xing forced Kumārajīva to copulate with palace women so as to leave descendants, the *Jinshu* says that Kumārajīva had in fact encouraged Yao Xing's offer. Further, it adds that Kumārajīva's disciples took to imitating their master, but he recalled them to the order.[38] Here too, the presence of these passages shows the existence of a transmission that was effectively parallel, oral or in writing, to the tradition conveyed in the canonical biographies. The existence of this parallel transmission is confirmed by the fact that the "Shi Lao zhi" and Jizang also spoke of the descendants of Kumārajīva.[39]

Anchō 安澄 (763-814), Japanese author of a commentary on the essays of Sengzhao, presents Kumārajīva by way of citing two documents: "a biography" (*zhuan* 傳) and the *Fushu*.[40]

Finally, as additional proof of a transmission parallel to the biographies, we must also note the existence of two Dunhuang manuscripts that contain a succinct biography of Kumārajīva: S 381 and S 3074.[41] S 381 bears an indication of the date at which it was written: the 26th day of the 4th month of 873. S 3074 is not dated so precisely, but it speaks anachronistically of the arrival of Kumārajīva in the territory of the "Great T'ang", with a space preceding the characters *da tang* 大唐, as a sign of respect, and not in the territory of Qin, as one would expect.

These two narratives are structured in the same way: they begin with a very standard biography of Kumārajīva (on the origin of his parents, his entry into the order at age seven; his ability to defeat heretical masters in debate; the respect shown to him by the King of Jibin; his arrival in Chang'an) and then report, as none of the above-mentioned sources do, a discussion between

---

38 *Jinshu* (95), 8.2501-2502.

39 *Weishu* (114), vol. 8, p. 3040 ; T. 1827 (1), 42.235c4-5.

40 T. 2255(3), 65.92c6sq, where *Fushu* is written 符書. The citation of the biography, on which Anchō is silent concerning the source and the author, diverges on one point from sources known to us, saying that Kumārajīva and his mother entered the religion after the death of his father, while the *Gaoseng zhuan* says that his mother asked permission to enter religion of her husband who refused, and that she had to carry out a hunger strike in order for her entourage to allow her to fulfill her vow.

41 In S 381 the narrative comprises around 295 characters distributed over 18 columns; it follows an anecdote concerning a monk named Zhixing and precedes a miracle tale involving devotion to Vaiśvaraṇa at Longxing 龍興 monastery. In S 3074 the narrative comprises around 220 characters distributed over 11 columns; it follows upon a narrative concerning Kang Senghui 康僧會 and is followed in turn by stories about Zhu Daocheng 竺道生 Faxian 法顯 and Fotudeng 佛圖澄.
See images of the manuscripts in *Yingzang dunhuang wenxian* 英藏敦煌文献 *(Dunhuang Manuscripts in British Collections)*, Sichuan People's Publishing House, Chengdu, vol. 1, 1990, p. 166 for S 381; vol. 5, 1992, p. 6 for S 3074. The texts can also be seen at this url: www.idp.bl.uk.

Kumārajīva and Yao Xing on the meaning of a phrase in the *Weimojie jing* 維摩詰經 that Kumārajīva was in the process of translating.[42] Both describe Kumārajīva's arrival in Chang'an in a way that is not found elsewhere.

S 381 reads: "*He was thirty-five when he arrived in [the territory of] Qin.*"[43]

S 3074 reads: "*He was thirty-five when he brought the fan texts to the Great Tang.*"[44]

One could object that the phrases "in [the territory of] Qin" and "to the Great Tang" are ambiguous, and might signify that Kumārajīva had arrived not in Chang'an, but in Liangzhou, since Liangzhou was a part of Qin/Chinese territory. The sentence would indicate an event that occurred in 385, when Kumārajīva was brought back from Kucha by Lü Guang. This objection does not hold. In S 381, the sentence "He was thirty-five when he arrived in [the territory of] Qin" follows a sentence about the many years he spent detained by Lü Guang. If the author of these lines had wanted to say that Kumārajīva was thirty-five when Lü Guang brought him to Liangzhou, he would have said it beforehand. Further, just after this sentence the text moves on to discuss a prodigy that appeared in a park in Chang'an before Kumārajīva's arrival, which, for the author establishes a link between the premise of his arrival in Qin, that is to say, Chang'an, and the arrival.

In S 3074, it is not a question of Lü Guang, but the sentence "He was thirty-five when he brought the *fan* texts to the Great Tang" is immediately followed by a sentence saying that the King of Qin invited him to translate sūtra and śāstra. The author of these lines implies that the territory of the Great T'ang is the territory of Qin, or more precisely the region of Chang'an.

The first striking particularity here is the mention of the age of thirty-five years, as is the case in the arhat's prediction. Must we understand, if we conjoin the prediction and the content of these manuscripts, that it was only at this time that Kumārajīva broke his vow of chastity? Did he do this in the year of his arrival in Chang'an? Was he constrained by Lü Zuan or by Yao Xing? Did he already have children when he arrived in Chang'an? Was it for this reason that the passage on Lü Guang was added in his biographies, so as to create a precedent with the fact that Kumārajīva broke his vow? Is there not another way to read the arhat's prediction? Might it not have meant that Kumārajīva would break his vow not precisely *at the age of thirty-five* but *after thirty-five years*? In other words, that it would be after his arrival in Chang'an that he would do this?

---

[42] It is a sentence from the chapter *Bu siyi pin* 不思議品 of the *Weimo jie jing* 維摩詰經, saying that a mustard seed contains the mount Sumeru; T. 475 (2), 14.546b25-26.

[43] 年卅五方達秦中.

[44] 至卅五將梵本届大唐.

The other particularity, and not the least, is that this indication allows us to deduce the year of birth of Kumārajīva, because the date of his arrival in Chang'an is known with precision: the 20th day of the 12th month of 401. Consequently, if Kumārajīva was in his thirty-fifth year in 401,[45] he was born in 367. If one takes this date as correct, the year of his departure for Jibin is 375 and that of his return to Kucha is 379. It would then have been a boy of 12 that the two Chinese monks noticed in the new *saṅghārāma* of the king, and a boy of 17 whom Lü Guang took from the city of Kucha in 384. He would still have been a very young man.

One could remark that this date of birth does not correspond with the assertion in the *Gaoseng zhuan* that Kumārajīva received complete ordination (*shoujie* 受戒) at the age of twenty, this being before 384,[46] for if he was born in 367, he would not have been twenty until the year 386. Nonetheless, Kumārajīva's full ordination and his apprenticeship in the Vinaya are points on which the biographies contradict each other. Not only does the *Chu sanzang jiji* not say either where or when Kumārajīva received complete ordination, but also this sentence in the *Gaoseng zhuan* appears in a corpus where everything concerning his apprenticeship in the discipline has been totally rewritten: the name of the *ācārya* and the place where Kumārajīva received instruction have been modified.

One could also say that this date, which would infer that Kumārajīva died before reaching the age of 50, is in contradiction with a statement that figures in the biography of Buddhabhadra. The latter says that one day when the two

[45] According to statements made in the biographies (*Chu sanzang jiji*, p. 101b9; *Gaoseng zhuan*, p. 332a17-18), Yao Chang 姚萇, father of Yao Xing, had already heard of Kumārajīva's reputation and had expressed the desire to meet him. The biographies (*Chu sanzang jiji*, p. 101b10-11; *Gaoseng zhuan*, p. 332a19-20) also say that Yao Xing, upon succeeding his father, at once sent an emissary to find him. Sengzhao, the young student of Kumārajīva, went so far as to say that Yao Xing planned the invasion of Liangzhou in order to cause Kumārajīva to come (T. 1858, 45.153a13), but these statements seem exaggerated when one compares them to indications in the historical sources, and one may ascribe them to Sengzhao's young age and the admiration he held for his master.
According to historical sources, in the fifth month of 401 Yao Xing sent his uncle, Yao Shuode 姚碩德, to Liangzhou (*Shiliuguo chunqiu quoted in Taiping yulan* [123/3b], 1.595a). Lü Long abdicated in the ninth month (*Jinshu* [10], 1.254). Yao Shuode returned to Chang'an followed by fifty deported families, including the parents and descendants of Lü Long, men of letters, soldiers, and senior high officials. They arrived in the eleventh month. By all indications, Kumārajīva was among these fifty persons close to the Lü family, who arrived in Chang'an at the end of 401. Kumārajīva's arrival is mentioned in the biography of Yao Xing in the *Shiliuguo chunqiu* and is dated to the eleventh month, precisely when Yao Shuode returned (*Taiping yulan* [123/3b], 1.595a26-27). Also, the biographies of Kumārajīva directly recount his coming upon the surrender of Lü Long, even though they give as the date for this the same date that figures in the three prefaces to his translations: the twentieth day of the twelfth month. This indication is given in "Dapin jing xu" 大品經序 (T. 2145 [8], 55.53a23-24), "Dazhi shilun xu" 大智釋論序 (*ibid.*, 75a5), and "Guanzhong chu chanjing xu" 關中出禪經序 (*ibid.*, 65a23) ; *cf.* his biographies: *Chu sanzang jiji*, p. 101b12-13; *Gaoseng zhuan*, p. 332a24-25. This date is, precisely, 8th February 402.

[46] T. 2059 (2), 50.331a5-6.

men met in Chang'an, Buddhabhadra asked Kumārajīva the reason for his success. The latter replied that it was due to his advanced age (吾年老).[47] To this objection one could respond that the biographies are quite imprecise, when on the one hand they present Kumārajīva as a young man in 384 and on the other they present him twenty years later as an old man.

Nonetheless, this last remark underlines the question of how much credit should we give to the content of these manuscripts. Do they merely reflect a baseless rumour, or, on the contrary, do they perhaps reflect a well-grounded story? Did this rumour, if such it was, circulate locally or more widely? Where did it come from, and when did it originate? Does it reflect the content of a *biezhuan*? These are questions which, given the current state of knowledge, we are unable to answer.

We will perhaps never know the date of Kumārajīva's birth, and it may be that this intimate detail of the life of this great man will remain forever hidden. Even if other manuscripts come to light that either reinforce the notion seen in these two manuscripts or contradict it, the existence of these two texts nevertheless shows that in the Dunhuang region, in the 9th century, Kumārajīva was remembered as a man who arrived, still young, in China, and not as a middle aged man, which would have been the case if he was born in CE 350, or *a fortiori* in 344. They remind us also that biographies are, above all, stories that one tells.

[47] T. 2145 (14), 55.103c19; T. 2059 (2), 50.335a6.

BIBLIOGRAPHY

Asada, Nobuhisa. 1959. 浅田信久, *Kumarajū no shoshutsu nendai suitei ni kansuru ichi kōsatsu* 鳩摩羅什の生卒年代推定に関する一考察. *Ōtani shigaku*大谷史學 7, pp. 16-20.

*Chuxue ji*初學記. 1962 (rpt.1989). *Xu Jian* 徐堅 (659-729). Beijing. Zhonghua shuju. 3 vol.,

Forte, Antonino. 2002. [Notes sur Kumārajīva] de Paul Pelliot, in *A Life Journey to the East, Sinological Studies in Memory of Giuliano Bertuccioli (1923-2001).*

Forte, Antonino and Masini Federico (ed.). Kyōto. Istituto Italiano di Cultura. Scuola di Studi sull'Asia Orientale. pp. 1-19.

Funayama, Tōru 船山徹, 2000. *Ryō no Sōyūū sen 'Sappata shishiden' to Tōdai bukkyōō* 梁の僧祐撰『薩婆多師資伝』と唐代仏教, in *Tōdai no shūkyō* 唐代の宗教. Hōyū Shoten. pp. 325-354.

Hureau, Sylvie. 2003. *Kumārajīva (env. 344-413), conseiller des princes, traducteur et instigateur d'une orthodoxie bouddhique en Chine*. Paris. Institut des Langues et Civilisations Orientales. 2 vols.

Hurvitz, Leon. 1962. *Chih-I (538-597), An Introduction to the Life and Ideas of a Chinese Buddhist Monk, M,langes Chinois et Bouddhiques* XII. Bruxelles. Institut Belge des Hautes Études Chinoises.

ItḌ Takatoshi. 1996. *The Formation of Chinese Budhism and 'Matching the Meaning'* (*geyi* 格義), *Memoirs of the Research Department of the Toyo Bunko* 54. Tōkyō. pp. 65-91.

Jinshu 晉書. 1974, reed. 1991. Fang Xuanling 房玄齡 (578-648) *et al.*. Beijing. Zhonghua shuju. 10 vols.

Kamata, Shigeo 鎌田茂雄. 1983. *Chūgoku bukkyō shi* 中國佛佛教史. Tōkyō. Tōkyōōdaigaku shuppankai. 2 vol.

Lévi, Sylvain. 1913, *Le 'tokharien B', langue de Koutcha. Journal Asiatique* sér. 11, t. 2. pp. 311-380.

Lu, Yang. 2004. *Narrative and Historicity in the Buddhist Biographies of Early Medieval China: The Case of Kumārajīva*. Asia Major 17-2. pp. 1-43.

Mather, Richard B. 2004. *Biography of Lü Kuang*. Berkeley and Los Angeles University of California Press.

Nobel, Johannes. 1927. *Kumārajīva*. Berlin, *Sitzungsberichte der Preussischen Akademie der Wissenschaften*. pp. 206-233

ŌchŌ Enichi 横超慧日. 1982. Suwa Gijun 諏訪義純, *Rajū* 羅什. Daizōō shuppan.

Pelliot, Paul. 1912. *Autour d'une traduction sanskrite du Tao tö king. T'oung Pao* sér. II. vol. 13. pp. 351-430.

Robinson, Richard H, 1967. *Early Mádhyamika in India and China*. New York. Samuel Weiser.

Saitō, Tatuya 斉藤達也. 2000. *Kumarajū no botsunen mondai no saikentō* 鳩摩羅什の没年問題の再検討, *Journal of the International College for Advanced Buddhist Studies* III. pp. 125-154.

Taiping yulan 太平御覽. 1960. *Li Fang* 李昉 (925-996). Shanghai. Zhonghua shuju. 4 vol.

Tang, Yongtong 湯用彤. 1938 (rpt. 1983). *Han Wei liang Jin nanbei chao fojiao shi* 漢魏兩晉南北朝佛教史. Beijing. Zhonghua shuju. 2 vols.

Tsukamoto, Zenryū 塚本善隆. 1954. *The Dates of Kumārajīva and Seng-chao reexamined*. Kyōto. *Silver Jubilee Volume of the Jimbun Kagaku Kenkyūsho*. pp. 568-584.----*Jōron kenkyū* 肇論研究, 1955. Kyōto. Hōzōkan.

Uehara, Senroku 上原専禄. 1949. *Kumarajū kō* 鳩摩羅什考. *Nihon Hyōronsha* 日本評論社 22-1. pp. 120-149.

Wang, Wenyan 王文顏. 1984. *Fodian hanyi zhi yanjiu* 佛典漢譯之研究. Taipei. Tianhua chuban.

Weishu 魏書. 1974, reed. 1992. Wei Shou 魏收 (506-572). Beijing. Zhonghua shuju. 8 vol.

Zheng, Yuqing 鄭郁卿. 1988. *Jiumoluoshi yanjiu* 鳩摩羅什研究. Taipei. *Wenjin chubanshe.*

Zizhi tongjian 資治通鑑. 1956. *Sima Guang* 司馬光 *(1019-1086)*. Beijing. Guji chubanshe. 10 vol.

2

A report on Kumārajīva's life and the towns associated with him: Kashgar, Tumushuk, Kucha, Loulan, Dunhuang, Liangzchou and Ch'ang-an

Katsuhisa Yamada

Introduction

Life is a journey. I started my journey from Kucha, Kumārajīva's birth place, and followed his footprints. I spent 45 years travelling on foot from the Pamirs over 4,000 meters high to Taklamakan Desert. In the process, I visited twelve countries including Samarkand, Palmyra, Nepal of Śākyamuni, Macedonia of Alexander the Great, etc. completing 52 journeys in all. In this paper I would like to examine Kumārajīva's brilliant life, showing the past and current circumstances of towns and villages associated with him in comparison with the paths of Faxian and Xuanzang.

The statue of Kumārajīva in the front garden of Qizil Thousand Buddha Caves

1. Kumārāyaṇa, Father of Kumārajīva

Kumārajīva came from a distinguished family, whose members had served as prime ministers of a kingdom for generations. It is easy to guess the kingdom was in north India, since his father Kumāradatta was a well-known Buddhist scholar of the Sarvāstivāda school. Like his father, Kumārāyaṇa was a person of noble mind, intelligent and self-controlled. At around forty years of age, he renounced his right to the position and became a

Buddhist monk instead. Thereafter he set out on a journey to China in order to transmit Buddha's teachings.

Kumārāyaṇa made his way over the difficult plateaus of Pamir more than 4,000 meters high, the roof of the world, shining in the snow and from there to Tash Kurghan, "castle of stone" in old Turkish, in south Xinjiang. He then arrived at Yarkand. After that, he travelled eastward by way of Kashgar on the southern path of the Tianshan mountains.

Baichun, the King of Kucha, respecting him deeply, went out in person to the outskirts of the capital to greet him. Appointed as a State-adviser due to his distinguished ability and rich humanity, he carried out his duty well as expected.

An Indian village reminding us of the birth place of Kumārāyaṇa

Jīvā, the king's sister, was then twenty years old, with a strong will and noble mind like a white lily. As soon as she laid eyes on Kumārāyaṇa, she expressed her desire to become his wife. He also became a layperson in order to marry her. In 350 CE, a boy was born, who was named Kumārāyaṇa, after the names of his parents. Since he was a boy of great talent, he was considered an infant prodigy. Though Jīvā was loved very much by her husband and spent a happy life, yet she is said to have strongly wished to renounce the world, after having watched old human bones scattered around in a graveyard. She went on a six-day fast, ready for death unless her brother Baichun and husband Kumārāyaṇa would grant her wish. In the end she could fulfill her cherished objective.

2. Kumārajīva leaves for Peshawar

Mol Pagoda in Kashgar built in the age of Kumāraīva

Kumārajīva left the secular life and entered the Buddhist Order when he was seven years old. It was in 359 CE that Kumārajīva set out with his Mother on a journey to Peshawar. They left Kucha for Peshawar passing by Gumo, Wenxiu and Qilan old castle and stayed at Tukuzsalai Temple in Tumushuk.

After leaving Kashgar, they set off for the southeast, passing by Akotao, Yingchisha, Yigekongye and Qiareke to Yarkand, from where they turned westward to take a rest at Tash Kurghan, a border town. Then they seemingly set out southwestward travelling over the plateaus of Pamir and Karakorum through Khujerab Pass for the Hunza valley by way of Basu and Gurmit. Hunza is 160 kilometres away from the Pass, and Gilgit, where a manuscript of the Lotus Sūtra was found, is another 110 kilometers away from there. They moved along the Indus 130 kilometres to Chilas, and 245 kilometres to Takot.

In Peshawar, Kumārajīva became a disciple of Bandhudatta, a cousin of the king. He acknowledged Kumārajīva to be a genius and even the king himself paid special attention to him. Once the king held a discussion on some religious questions with a Brāhmaṇa who showed an attitude of arrogance towards young Kumārajīva. The book, *Biographies of Eminent Priests* says the former was out-argued completely by Kumārajīva and was consumed by terrible shame and could not say a word.

In 361 CE at the age of 12, Kumārajīva returned to Kucha with his mother. On the way, he stayed at Kashgar for one year to study further. Kashgar was an oasis and a strategic point with a population of about 20,000, located at the farthest end of the Silk Road. The castle of the kingdom is supposed to be Hanoi old castle, then a centre of nine branch castles. The Mol Pagoda there stirs our imagination about its past splendour.

The best outcome of his stay there was an encounter with Sūryasoma, a teacher of the Mahāyāna doctrine. According to *The Afterword to the Lotus Sūtra* (Translation by Sengzhao), Sūryasoma entrusted Kumārajīva with the Sanskrit text of the Lotus Sūtra in his left hand and with his right hand patted the head of Kumārajīva, and said, *The sun of the Buddha has set in the west, but its lingering rays shine over the north-east. This text is destined for the north-east. You must make certain that it is transmitted there.*

3. Tukuzsalai Temple in Tumushuk, brilliant Buddhist ruins

Tukuzsalai Buddhist Temple in Tumushuk

Tumushuk is located between Kucha and Kashgar. Once it was a busy town where a great number of official tributaries and Sogdian merchants with valuable goods would come and stay. The relics of these goods, such as flowery silk products, painted pottery, old Chinese coins, glass beads, Kuchean and Chinese documents, excellent handicrafts etc, reveal how rich its culture was.

We can see some ruins of the Tukuzsalai Temple built in Donghan. When Kumārajīva visited the temple, a number of pagodas stood there. Many Buddhists came to pray and the voices of the monks reading the Buddhist Sūtras never stopped. There were six statues of Buddha and Bodhisattva carved on the rock wall, as much as thirty metres high.

In 364 CE at the age of fourteen, he left Tumushuk and visited Qilan to take a short rest with his mother. It was located 75 kilometres northeast of Tumushuk and was a branch castle of the Gumo kingdom, stretching about 1.5 kilometres from east to west and about 2 kilometres from north to south.

The ruins of the monastery in Qiran Castle where Kumārajīva might have rested

The view tower in the northwest was thirteen metres high. The gates were located in the north, east and south of the castle. Inside the castle, the houses were lined close together and the main street stretched from north to south. There were watercourses connected to the Datiao, a tributary of the Kashgar River. A Buddhist pagoda, which was built on a square measuring about 12 meters a side, was located on the west side was confirmed to have eight small towers. A gate in the Indian fashion, some 7 metres high still remains. The true teaching of Śākyamuni Buddha seems to have been preserved without the corruption of Buddhist monks, when Kumārajīva visited the area of south Xinjiang.

4. Remarkable activities in Kucha

Kucha was a great oasis kingdom located on the south foot of the Tianshan mountains. *A Liang* records that the scale of the outer castle was as big as that of Chang'an, and the buildings were beautiful. *A Jin* records that the palace shone brilliantly like the abode of the Gods. There may have been a large number of people resentful of Kumārajīva, as he preached the doctrine of Mahāyāna Buddhism, since the people in Kucha were believers in Hīnayāna Buddhism. Numerous monks, however, flocked to him from many different countries to receive his instruction; the *Biographies of Eminent Priests* records that nobody could match him in preaching, and that the listeners could not hear his discourses without crying and regretting that they had not met him earlier.

Jīvā, the mother of Kumārajīva, meanwhile left Kucha for India. At the

The ruins of Subashi Castle where Kumārajīva seems to have been born

time of parting, she urged him to spread the profound teachings of Mahāyāna Buddhism in China. She said that he alone was capable of carrying out such a big task. He answered that the goal of an ambitious person drove him to perform his duty devotedly. After listening to his words, she set off on her journey to India with peace of mind. They were never to meet again.

Bandhudatta, his master in Peshawar, happened to come to Kucha. Kumārajīva was pleased to see him and preached to his master the doctrine of Mahāyāna Buddhism in gratitude for his kindness. Bandhudatta was very pleased with his success, and was so impressed by the doctrine that he became Kumārajīva's disciple.

Kumārajīva lived in Kucha until he was thirty-five years old (384 CE). The *Collection of Records concerning the Tripitaka* says that Kumārajīva accepted Mahāyāna Buddhism under the initiation of Buddhayaśas in Kashgar, during his second visit there after coming back to Kucha from Peshawar. On the other hand *Biographies of Eminent Priests* records that he became a believer in Mahāyāna Buddhism during his one year's stay in Kashgar on the way to Kucha from Peshawar under the initiation of Sūryasoma. It is true that Kumārajīva's conversion from Hīnayāna to Mahāyāna Buddhism took place in Kashgar, an oasis kingdom located at the southern route of the Western regions, although the two records are completely contradictory.

In the new year of 377 CE, a secretary of Former Liang sent a report to Fu Jian, the King of Former Liang that he had found a star in a foreign field, and that he was a person of great virtue and wisdom worthy of being invited to China. Fu Jian replied that he had heard of Kumārajīva in the Western regions (*Biographies of Eminent Priests*), and immediately sent a mission to Kucha to request Kumārajīva to visit China.

The Taklamakan Desert through which Kumārajīva passed (South of Peacock River)

It was in September 382 CE that the king sent a big army solely to bring Kumārajīva over. On the departure of his army, he declared that the wise were the great treasure of a nation, and that after overcoming the King of Kucha, Kumārajīva should be escorted back as soon as possible, without resting at staging points. It is easy to imagine how eagerly the King was waiting for Kumārajīva's arrival.

The expeditionary army of 70,000 soldiers lead by General Lü Guang marched westward, and the Loulan army etc. joined the expedition. It was in December 383 CE that they took up a position in the suburbs of Kucha after a 15-month long expedition passing through deserts. There, General Lü Guang waited for the capitulation of Kucha's king for seven months. Kumārajīva advised him to accept Lü Guang's demand and not to fight against his army. Baichun, the King of Kucha, however, gave orders for attacking the enemy in July 384 CE. He was defeated and killed and Baizhen, his brother, was enthroned as a puppet.

5. In Loulan, a phantom kingdom

The expeditionary army was stationed in Kucha until August 385 CE. Kumārajīva strongly advised Lü Guang to return home, as the latter had a keen desire to settle in Kucha. Accepting Kumārajīva's advice, the army left Kucha for Loulan, marching southeast to the Peacock River, the lower course of the Tarim River, and reached the Loulan kingdom passing by the graveyard of Xiaohe. Another record says that they entered Dunhuang via Turfan through Yonqi.

Loulan is one of the oases in the Western regions. The description of Western regions in the *Book of Former Han* records that the kingdom was an

The Pagoda 12 meters high of Loulan Old Castle, which Kumārajīva might have seen

international city with 14,100 people and 2,912 soldiers, where many travellers from the east and west, as well as Sogdian merchants came every day.

The King was an enthusiastic follower of Buddhism and the Queen was from Khotan, another Buddhist kingdom. From the beginning to the middle of 4th century, it maintained its great national strength, extending its territory to 300 kilometres in width and 900 kilometres in length.

On March 2, 2003, I watched a news story titled "Discovery of the Century" televised by Xinhua News Agency, reporting that a large number of coloured wall paintings had been discovered in Loulan. I immediately left for Loulan to research the wall paintings in the tomb located in the north-northeast of the Buddha Bone Pagoda. I saw the wall paintings of Sogdian merchants with Iranian moustaches enjoying a feast along with the nomads.

They were originally Zoroastrians, but might have converted to Buddhism while living in Khotan, since I saw some thirty paintings of Dharmacakras of Buddhism on the walls and pillars. I can imagine that Kumārajīva, accompanying the expeditionary army, may have enjoyed the sight of Lake Lop Nor, a phantom lake, and turned his thoughts to the unseen city of Chang'an, filled with a sense of anticipation.

6. White Horse Pagoda towering in the sky of Dunhuang

Dunhuang was at first a military base in the Dunhuang county set up in 111-110 BCE by Wu, Emperor (Liuche) of Former Han dynasty. As time passed, it changed into a cultural city, often visited by Sogdian people with deep green eyes, hooked noses and thick moustaches .

The Yumen Pass of the Han Dynasty through which Kumārajīva passed

There are 8 Buddhist sites in Dunhuang such as Mogao Caves, Western Caves of the Thousand Buddhas, Yungang Grottoes, etc. The largest and the oldest site is Mogao Caves of the Thousand Buddhas.

In 385 CE, at the age of 36, Kumārajīva entered the fortress of Dunhuang through the Yumen Pass in June or July when his beloved white horse died. The White Horse Pagoda was built there in its memory. The history of Kumārajīva and his white horse that came to Dunhuang crossing the desert is depicted in the signboard in front of the pagoda.

White Horse Pagoda related to Kumārajīva

The expeditionary army left Dunhuang, and fought against the army from Liangzchou, having 50,000 soldiers, at Jiuquan just east of Liangzchou, which resisted the entry of General Lü Guang to the fortress of Liangzchou. The army was quickly defeated by the victorious troops from Kucha. Thereafter, all the powerful clans in the Hexi district obeyed General Lü Guang.

When the General entered the fortress of Liangzchou, he read a report from Chang'an and was informed that Fu Jian, his master, had died during the battle at Feishui. He unwillingly settled in Liangzchou, as he had no place to go. Kumārajīva also was forced to live in this frontier town for 17 long years from the age of 36 to 52, from September 385 CE to December 401 CE, since no one would have welcomed him in Chang'an which was full of upheavals.

Dayun Temple in Liangzchou which Kumārajīva might have visited

Possibly, he might have exposed himself to danger of death, instead of translating Buddhist scriptures.

7. 17 years custody in Liangzchou

Liangzchou was an important base for supplying food for Hexi regions, as it had been said that Zhangye is goldwhile Wuwei (Liangzchou) is silver. It was the very first place where Buddhism was transmitted from India and where a unique Buddhist culture flourished. Kumārajīva's sojourn of 17 years in Liangzchou almost coincides with the reign of Lü Guang of Later Liang dynasty. Since he had a peaceful time in this country, compared with his stay in other regions which were full of upheavals, he could devote himself to the study of Buddhist scriptures and Chinese books and in mastering the Chinese language.

In Liangzchou, there remains a temple called Hongzang built by Zhang Tianxi, King of Former Liang dynasty (reign 363-376 CE), which was later named Dayun in the reign of Zetian Wuhou. Its bell tower built at that time, still stands. Kumārajīva might have visited it. On December 20th 401 CE, he left Liangzchou for Chang'an by way of Gulang, Yongdeng and Lanzhou.

8. At Bingling temple in Lanzhou

Lanzhou is a historical town, also called Jincheng, located on the upper reaches of the Yellow River, at the junction of an agriculture belt and a pasture

Statues of Śākyamuni Buddha and Many Treasures Buddha sharing one seat with each other in Bingling Temple

belt. It is also at the crossroads of the Tibetan plateau and the Western regions. Behind the rocks in the valley of the mountain called Jishi, is the Bingling temple, which stands for thousand or ten thousand Buddhas in Tibetan. The old name is Longxing, also known as Lingyan. We can read some writings in China ink on the wall painting made by the Qifus in the era of Jianhong of Western Chin dynasty. We see the statues of Śākyamuni Buddha and Many Treasures Buddha sharing a seat. I found a clay statue of the Fasting Buddha about one metre tall on the upper left of the great image of Buddha on the rock surface, thrity-five metres above the ground. The Fasting Buddha, with only skin and bones, created a loving and sublime atmosphere, as if he was saying ''No cross, no crown'' with a smile on his lips and around the eyes. We can see Fahsien's writing in China ink on the wall of the 167th cave. Kumārajīva might have visited this temple too.

9. Daily translation of Buddhist texts in Chang'an

The Stone Pagoda of Kumārajīva at Caotang temple in Ch'ang-an

In May 401 CE, Yao Xing, the Emperor of Later Qin sent his army of 67,000 soldiers to Liangzchou to bring Kumārajīva to Ch'ang-an. Lü Lung, the King of Liangzchou surrendered to the enemy in September, after 10,000 soldiers died and 25,000 deserted. Kumārajīva was among the hostages captured and taken away, also comprising of the king's mother, brother, children and some fifty senior statesmen. It was on the 20th December 401 CE, in the winter, at the age of 52, that Kumārajīva was welcomed and treated as a teacher of the State by the Emperor, who had assumed the throne at an age of twenty-nine. He appointed many wise men to responsible positionsandhadsomeinfluenceonDunhuang in far away Gansu. Kumārajīva must have been lucky to be welcomed at such a prosperous time of the dynasty, which could afford to fund the project of

The beginning of the 7th volume of the Lotus Sūtra by Kumārajīva in Zhangye

translating Buddhist texts.

Sengjui, his disciple, records in the introduction of *Larger Wisdom Sūtra* that he would take a Sanskrit text in his hand and would expound on it orally in Chinese. His translations were elegant, precise and accurate enough to satisfy the Chinese people who thought highly of poetry. The *Biographies of Eminent Priests* records that he would make complete sentences without changing or eliminating a word. His expressions of metaphors would be beautiful, simple and replete with deep meanings.

It was, however, not likely that all the attendants would appreciate Kumārajīva's translations and respect him, although Sengjui records that the members of the group, on receiving the new translations, were filled with delight, feeling as though they were standing on the summit of the Kunlun Mountains on a clear day and gazing at the world below. Some attendants broke their promise with the master, fled southwards and joined the group of Huikuan of Daochang temple in Jiankang. Others, like Zhimeng and Tanzuan, conspired against Kumārajīva and slandered him.

Chu Taosheng, one of his disciples, in contrast, never gave up following his master's teaching, even though he was exiled to the Su Mountain by the State rulers. Sengjui propagated his teaching around the country until his death, to prove the greatness of his master. Daorong, another disciple of Kumārajīva, moved to Peng castle and kept the faith of oneness of master and disciple until his death at the age of seventy-four, leading some 7,000 pupils who held him in deep respect.

On 20th August in the year of Hongshi 11 during the reign of Later Qin dynasty (409 CE), Kumārajīva passed away at Ch'ang-an Dasi at the age of sixty. He led a great life in which he fulfilled his mission of achieving the correct translation of the Buddhist texts. According to Sengchao's *Praises of Kumārajīva,* the date of his death was 30th April of the year Guichou (413 CE) at Ch'ang-an Dasi at the age of 70. Sengchao was also one of the best disciples of Kumārajīva. The year of his death can be calculated as 344 CE based on the record, which was also adopted in *Records of Kaiyuan* by Chihsheng in Tang. I personally would like to adopt the year of 409 CE recorded in *Biographies of Eminent Priests*.

Biographies of Eminent Priests records that only Kumārajīva's tongue was found unaltered by the flames after his corpse had been reduced to ashes on the funeral pyre. The description has been handed down today to indicate how accurate his translation was.

There are different records about the number of his translation works:

- *Record of religious precepts for Bodhisattva* some 50 parts
- *Collection of Records concerning the Tripitaka* 35 parts 297 volumes
- *Catalog of Sengyu* 32 parts some 300 volumes
- *Biographies of Eminent Priests* some 300 volumes

Some Chinese fragments of the 25th chapter in the Lotus Sūtra titled *"The Universal Gateway of the Bodhisattva: Perceiver of the World's Sounds"*, were found in the Thousand Buddha Caves at Bezeklik in Turfan in Xinjiang Weiwu'er.

Lotus Sutra translated by Soka Gakkai International into different languages

This seems to be proof of the phrase "Westward Transmission of Buddhism". The fragments are very precious and are celebrated relics in China, since they were copied only 153 years after the completion of Kumārajīva's translation. It used simplified Chinese characters, which were popular among people of that time, such as 万, 无, 尔, 号 instead of 萬, 無, 爾, 號. We cannot find the verses at the end of the Chapter. It is also a notable fact that the contents of the text are close to that of B manuscript of Sanskrit Lotus Sūtra Fragments from the Lushun Museum Collection. This Chinese document was copied in 559 CE. This fact provides evidence that the Lotus Sūtra was transmitted westward to Turfan on the Silk Road.

As Kumārajīva wished, Chinese Buddhism made remarkable developments in the course of time, and was transmitted to the Korean

Peninsula, Japan and other regions. Even in the 21st century, 1,600 years after his death, his translation of the Lotus Sūtra remains the king of the Buddhist texts that has been worshipped and read uniterruptedly by people ever since, regardless of race, language or nationality.

The Soka Gakkai International has recently published Kumārajīva's Lotus Sūtra, translated into nine modern languages, i.e. English, Italian, Greek, German, Thai, Laotian, Modern Chinese, French and Korean. They are now attracting more and more people and are expected to be revered and read even more widely.

3

Kumārajīva in China: from war booty to *Rājyaguru*

B R Deepak

India and China, the two giants of Asia, are two of the oldest living civilizations of the world. While the Sindhu and Ganges gave birth to the Indian civilization, and influenced South and Southeast Asia, the Huanghe and Yangtze rivers gave birth to the Chinese civilization that influenced Northeast and Southeast Asia.

Being neighbours, India and China had established intimate trade and cultural relations since time immemorial. The legendry 'Silk Route' along with other routes of communication between India and China has been well recorded in Chinese historical texts, and reminds us of this magnificent interface. It has been established by historical records that the India-China interaction was a two-way traffic and the two most important elements of this traffic were material and spiritual exchanges.

Buddhism was the world's earliest missionary religion, missionary in the context of austerity and not the present day ostentation, and it was natural that this missionary zeal would take it to boundaries beyond India; equally important for its success was the Chinese response, which altogether revolutionized the entire movement. Both the missionary nature of Buddhism as well as the Chinese response resulted in a number of waves of Indian scholar monks going to China and Chinese monks coming to India. Since this paper deals with Kumārajīva, I will restrict myself to briefly touching on these Buddhist waves to China and then taking up the Kumārajīva episode in China.

The earliest wave perhaps started with Kāśyapa Mātaṅga and Dharamrakṣa reaching Loyang in the 1st century CE, and continued till the end of the 3rd century. Some of the leading personalities of this missionary zeal were Dharmakāla (reached China in 249-50) and Kangsenghui, Weizhinan and Zhuluyan (reached Wuhan in 224). The second wave stretched between the 4th and 5th centuries. During this period, personalities such as Saṅghabhadra and Saṅghadīpa (reached Ch'ang-an in 381), Kumārajīva (reached Ch'ang-an in 401) reigned supreme on the Buddhist horizon. The third major wave passed through the 6th and 7th centuries, and the most prominent figures of the times were Bodhidharma, Amoghvajra and Vajrabodhi. Of all the Indian scholar monks or cultural ambassadors to China, Kumārajīva, 鸠摩罗什 (in Chinese), was undoubtedly the brightest of them all, whose brilliance and impeccable memory, apart from reducing this great monk to a booty of war, also made him the Rājyaguru of Later Qin dynasty in China.

Sources

As regards the sources pertaining to Kumārajīva, there are primarily three of his biographies still to be found in China. One, written by Seng You (445-518) could be found in 出三藏记集 (Collected Accounts of Tripiṭaka). The second, was written by Hui Jiao (497-554) in his book entitled 僧传 (Biographies of Eminent Monks), and the third was the Biography of Kumārajīva by Guanxiu enshrined in 晋书·艺术传 (Jin Annals: Art Biography) of 7th century (T'ang) vintage. The third biography could be termed as a synthesis of Hui Jiao and Seng You's biographies of Kumārajīva. A contemporary of Hui Jiao, 宝唱 (Name in English not given by author) (464-514) also incorporated the biography of Kumārajīva in his 名僧传 (Biographies of Famous Monks), but unfortunately the book is lost and unavailable. Fortunately, a Japanese monk named 宗性 (Name in English not given by author) (1202-?) copied its contents and provides us some details about the work. Due to my handicap of the Japanese language, I have not consulted the source. In 资治通鉴 (A general mirror for the reference of government administration) compiled during Song dynasty by Si Maguang (1019-1086), a chapter on Kumārajīva was carried in volume 114. Besides, there are also some translations of Kumārajīva's biography. One by a German Buddhist scholar, Johannes Nobel is available in German. Of all the sources, Hui Jiao's 慧皎 biography of Kumārajīva in the Biographies of Eminent Monks remains the most credible source for Kumārajīva's feats in China. Some edited works such as Collection of South Asian Historical Materials from Chinese Sources by the Institute of South Asian Studies of Peking University, Geng Yinzeng's book 'Historical Data of South Asia' (1991) from Chinese sources also reproduce these biographies with their annotations and comments.

Kumārajīva in Kucha

Kumārajīva (344-413) was born in Kucha (present day Kuche in Xinjiang), to an Indian father Kumārāyaṇa 鸠摩罗炎 and a Kuchean mother Jīvā 耆婆. Before describing his mother, Hui Jiao's biography of Kumārajīva gives an account of his father Kumārāyaṇa and his ancestry. It says that his ancestors were descendants of a line of Prime Ministers. Kumārāyaṇa discarded the prime ministerial post and traveled from Kashmir to Kucha, where the king enthroned him as *Rājyaguru*.[1]

As regards his mother Jīvā, she was the sister of Kucha King Bai Chun 白纯王. It was love at first sight for Jīvā when she met Kumārāyaṇa, and both got married as per the wishes of Jīvā and Bai Chun, even though Kumārāyaṇa was a bit reluctant. Kumārajīva's mother was a wise woman, who could understand the sūtras being recited, according to the biographies of eminent monks. Their son Kumārajīva shared his parents' interest in religion and became a monk at the age of seven. Like his mother, Kumārajīva could also recite a thousand sūtras/verses from memory. Prior to entering the monastery, the child prodigy had already memorized many Buddhist scriptures. By the time he was twenty, Kumārajīva's name was well-known in Central Asia and China. Before Jīvā left Kucha for India, she encouraged the twenty year old Kumārajīva to go to China to further Mahāyāna Buddhism. But it was not until many years later that Kumārajīva was able to fulfill his mother's wish through a tumultuous and circuitous route.

Jīvā, who chose to be a nun when Kumārajīva was just seven, desired him to be a great monk and asked him to go Kashmir, the centre of the Sarvāstivāda 说一切有部. He went with his mother to learn āgama sūtras and other Hīnayāna scriptures under the noted monk Bandhudatta 盘头达多 in Kashmir and Buddhayaśas 佛陀耶舍 in Kucha. It was under her influence that Kumārajīva was influenced by Mahāyāna Buddhism. Later, the Prince of Yarkand called Sūryasoma 须立耶苏摩 not only taught Kumārajīva Anavatapta Sūtra 阿耨达经 but also introduced *śūnyavāda* etc. theories of Mahāyāna Buddhism. Kumārajīva had said, "I thought Hīnayāna Buddhism was the best teaching before I studied Mahāyāna Buddhism. I was like a man who does not know of gold, and thinks brass is the best (Hui Jiao: 53)."

Kumārajīva became a fully ordained monk at the age of twenty, acquiring the precepts that Buddhist monks followed. Kumārajīva was well known in his country Kucha and in neighbouring countries. Later, he invited his former teacher Bandhudatta to study Mahāyāna Buddhism. However, his mother encouraged Kumārajīva to carry the true teachings of Buddhism to China.[2] The famous Chinese monk Dao An 道安 had also invited him to China.

[1] Hui JIao: 51

[2] Hui Jiao: 53

Kumārajīva as war booty

In CE 379, Chinese Buddhist monks returning from Kucha praised the impeccable memory and wisdom of Kumārajīva to Fu Jian of Former Qin. Dao An 道安, the eminent Chinese scholar monk had also urged Fu Jian to invite Kumārajīva to China. Fu Jian had reasons to agree, as he was apprised by his court historian in 377 that 'a brilliant star has been sighted over foreign horizon, which was an omen of the arrival of a great sage to assist his rule in China.' Fu Jian had replied that "he was aware of the presence of Kumārajīva in western region."[3] In 382, Fu Jian dispatched over 70,000 troops under the command of Lü Guang 吕光 to invade the Central Asian kingdoms including Kucha, and ordered the capture of Kumārajīva for his extremely invaluable political capital.

In CE 384, Lü Guang entered Kucha, King Bai Chun was put to death and Kumārajīva taken as a captive. It is recorded in Hui Jiao and Seng You's biographies that Lü Guang not only sought to make fun of Kumārajīva by forcing him to ride on cows and untamed horses, but also forced him to destroy his *śīla* of celibacy. He was forced to drink heavy doses of liquor and locked with the Kucha princess in a room. Lü Guang even retorted that "Your conduct has not surpassed that of your father, so why are you so reluctant?"[4] It is said that initially Kumārajīva put up a strong resistance. However, he gave in under the influence of liquor. Even though Kumārajīva was subjected to various humiliations, he was calm. On the way back to China, Lü Guang set up his camp in the foothills, but Kumārajīva warned him that "it was not wise to rest at the foothills, there could be dangers." Lü Guang did not pay any heed to the warning. As it happened, torrential rains in the night caused flash floods and drowned thousands of troops.[5] It was after this incident that Lü Guang took Kumārajīva's words more seriously.

While still in Liangzhou (present day Gansu), Lü Guang heard the news that Fu Jian had been defeated and killed by the rival king Yao Chang, the founder of Later Qin, who went on to found his own dynasty, the Later Liang. Kumārajīva was forced to stay in Liangzhou for the next sixteen years. Yao Chang also repeatedly invited Kumārajīva to his court, but Lü Guang was resolute in not handing over Kumārajīva to his rivals. After the death of Lü Guang and Yao Chang, Yao Chang's son Yao Xing dispatched forces against Lü Long, the son of Lü Guang. Lü Long suffered defeat and Kumārajīva was brought to Chang'an in CE 401 CE at the age of fifty-eight, yet again as 'war booty'. While in Lü Guang's captivity, Kumārajīva had used this opportunity to learn Chinese and mastered the language to perfection.

---

[3] Hui Jiao: 54

[4] Huai Jiao: 55

[5] Hui Jiao: 55

Sūtra translation

Once in Hou Qin, Yao Xing treated Kumārajīva with respect and appointed him as his *Rājyaguru*. Both of them deepened and nurtured this relationship of priest and patron with great care, and established a translation bureau headed by Kumārajīva, who in turn was assisted by over 800 scholar monks[6]. The King himself sometimes participated in the activities.

Thus started the biggest ever project of translation in the history of mankind. Between the 2nd and 13th centuries some 6000-7000 fascicles of the sūtras were disseminated to China and translated into Chinese, primarily from Sanskrit. Among all the translators, Kumārajīva undoubtedly was the most prominent. He was perhaps only rivalled by Xuan Zang, yet another scholar monk and cultural ambassador during the 7th Century.

Hui Jiao tells us that over 300 Buddhist scriptures were translated from Sanskrit to Chinese under Kumārajīva's leadership. The quality and clarity of Kumārajīva's translation surpassed the quality of previous translations. Much of Kumārajīva's translation have survived the vagaries of time and are still available in China. Before Kumārajīva died, he proclaimed that if his translation was in accord with the genuine principles of Buddhism, his tongue would be intact on the funeral pyre and not turn into ash. As prophesized, Hui Jiao says that after cremation of his mortal remains, the tongue remained intact and was not damaged[7].

Between CE 401-413, Kumārajīva translated 74 scriptures in 384 fascicles in total; some of these are given below:

Time	Sūtra	Chinese name	Fascicles
402-412	*Satyasiddhi-śāstra* (Treatise on the Completion of Truth)	成实论	20
408	*Śatasāhasrikā-prajñāpāramitā-sūtra* (The Perfection of Wisdom Sūtra)	小品般若波罗蜜经	10
402-412	*Vajracchedikā-prajñāpāramitā-sūtra* (The Diamond Sūtra)	金刚般若经	1
	Saddharmapuṇḍarīka-sūtra (Lotus Sūtra)	妙法莲华经	7/8
402	*Smaller Sukhāvatī-vyūha* (Amitabha Sūtra)	阿弥陀经	1
409	*Mādhyamaka-śāstra* (Treatise on the Middle)	中论	4
404	*Śatikā-śāstra* (Treatise in One Hundred Verses)	百论	2

[6] Hui Jiao: 56

[7] Hui Jiao: 58

409	*Dvādaśamukha-śāstra* (Treatise on the Twelve Gates)	十二门论	1
404-09	*Sarvāstivāda-vinaya* (Ten-Category Vinaya)	十诵律	61
402-05	*Mahāprajñāpāramitā-upadeśa* (Treatise on the Great Perfection of Wisdom Sūtra)	大智度论	100
404	*Pañchavimśatisāhasrikā-prajñāpāramitā-sūtra* (Perfection of Wisdom Sūtra in Twenty-five Thousand Lines)	摩诃般若波罗蜜经or 大品般若	27
406	*Vimalakīrtinirdeśa-sūtra* (Vimalakīrti-sūtra)	维摩诘经	3
	Kāruṇikarāja- prajñāpāramitā-sūtra	大品般若	2
	Maitreyavyākaraṇa-sūtra		1
	Sūrangama-samādhi-sūtra	禅法要解	2
	Brahmajāla sūtra (Brahma net sūtra)	思益梵天所问经	2/4
	Daśabhūmikavibhāśa	十住毗婆沙论	14/17

Kumārajīva's greatest contribution to translation was that he changed the erstwhile technique of literal translation, and emphasized more on meaning. He thoroughly studied previous translations, and made a number of criticisms. Kumārajīva used innovative methods, such as transliteration, and avoided the terminology that invoked the popular mysticism prevalent in China at that time. He sought unity of words and avoided using synonyms. Moreover, Chinese was an acquired language for him; problems must have been in plenty. The assistance from thousands of his disciples and contemporary scholar monks would have been invaluable in surmounting any problems that were encountered.

Kumārajīva: a layman or a monk?

Yao Xing who 'treated Kumārajīva like a god', wanted the latter to have progeny so that the genius of Kumārajīva could be cloned and preserved. He often used to tell Kumārajīva[8], 'The great master is unmatchable genius under heaven. If you pass away one day [in celibacy], how can we allow no posterity to this dharma seed?' Hence, against the wishes of Kumārajīva, Yao Xing selected ten pretty maids to serve Kumārajīva. He put the monk in a new house especially built for him away from the monastery. In the words of Tan[9] ' Kumārajīva's devotion to the holy discipline was thus impaired by

[8] Hui Jiao: 57

[9] 1995:25

his Chinese host with a sinister design but with a noble idea behind it, for the improvement of the intellectual quality of humanity.'

Kumārajīva was forever apologetic for his conduct of not observing the *śīla* of celibacy. Every time he preached, he would start with the words, 'Like a lotus is born from filthy mud, you should pluck the lotus without touching the filthy mud.'[10] In other words, he asked his disciples that numbered over 3000 to emulate his spiritual heights, rather than a few aberrations in his personal conduct. Kumārajīva perhaps never came to terms with what he had done; however, he vowed to his disciples that what he had preached was the truth, and would be proven by the fact that his tongue would remain intact even after his cremation, which did happen according to his biography. Kumārajīva died in the year 409, and thus ended the memorable journey of an exceptionally gifted genius in China.

Prof. Tan calls the breaking of *śīla* as a 'frivolous episode'. However, he reminds us about the cultural differences between India and China vis-à-vis Buddhism and Buddhist personalities. I agree with his postulations that the Indian cultural tradition attached utmost importance to 'spiritual loftiness without being impaired and polluted', contrary to 'practical utility' sought by the Chinese ruling elites in order to 'strengthen their regimes, and to overcome social instability, confrontation, greed etc.' According to Tan, 'it was this utilitarian perspective which led to the scrambling for eminent Indian monks among Northern Chinese warlords' and Kumārajīva was no exception. He further asserts that it was perhaps beacuse of the utilitarian nature of the Chinese culture that Mahāyāna Buddhism flourished in Chine while it could not survive in India. In his words, 'the way Mahāyāna Buddhism prospered in China was the result of China's nursing not only the lotus, but also the mud that went along with it.'

Legacy of Kumārajīva

During the civilizational interaction between India and China, there were hundreds of scholar monks who went to China from India and who came from China to India. Amongst all these cultural ambassadors, Kumārajīva was undoubtedly the most outstanding. Yao Xing, of Later Qin has called him an 'unmatchable genius under heaven" and it was for Kumārajīva's intellectual supremacy that he ended up as a war booty between various Chinese rulers; it was for the same reason that Yao Xing made Kumārajīva break his *śīla* so that the genius of this great scholar monk could be reproduced and preserved.

Kumārajīva's greatest contribution is that he was responsible for the core of East Asian Buddhist literature. It was he who introduced the 'Three

[10] Hui Jiao: 57

Treatises School' to China. His translation of Nāgārjuna's *Mādhyamaka-śāstra* 中论，*Dvādaśanikṣya-śāstra* 十二门论, Śata-śāstra 百论 was greatly responsible for the Chinese form of the Mādhyamika School. He is also responsible for Five Lineages of Transmission 五种传承 in China. These are the lineage of *Vinaya* or discipline (律传承); lineage of Tantra 密宗; lineage of vast conduct 广大行宗/法相宗；lineage of profound view 甚深观派/法性宗；and lineage of quintessential meaning 禅宗.

Kumārajīva's feats as a translator is unrivalled. Hui Jiao tells us that over 300 Buddhist scriptures were translated from Sanskrit to Chinese under Kumārajīva's leadership. The quality and clarity of Kumārajīva's translation surpassed the quality of previous translations, for he abandoned the prevalent method of concept matching in favour of meaning and substance. His translation project under Yao Xing was a mix of oral, collective, in depth knowledge of Buddhist doctrine that reached the pinnacles of accuracy, fluency and elegance.

Kumārajīva laid a solid foundation for the India-China civilizational dialogue. His efforts not only made Buddhism universal in China but also enabled Indian philosophical traits to make inroads into or amalgamate with Chinese philosophical thought. The concept of *naraka* (hell), Chinese literature about ghosts and spirits, as well as other literary genres such as *bianwen* and *Chuanqi* could be attributed to the synthesis of the Indian and Chinese civilizations.

BIBLIOGRAPHY

DGK. 2010. 鸠摩罗什法师*Dharma Guru Kumārajīva*. http://www.lingshh.com/16-a/4.htm. November 18, 2010.

Geng, Yinzeng. 耿引曾. 1990. 汉文南亚史料学 *Historical data of South Asia from Chinese sources*. Beijing. Peking University Press.

Huang Shumei黄淑美（2010）«浅谈鸠摩罗什的佛经翻译理论» *On the Buddhist Sūtra translation theory of Kumārajīva*. http://www.buddhismmiufa.org.hk/buddhism/special/Theory A.htm.

Huijiao's 1994. 慧皎 "鸠摩罗什传 *Biography of Kumārajīva*, produced from Hui Jiao's Biographies of Eminent Monks. Institute of South Asian Studies Peking University in 中国载籍中南亚史料汇编 Collection of South Asian Historical Materials from Chinese sources. Vol. I. Shanghai. Shanghai Guji Publishing House.

Ji, Xianlin. 1991. 中印文化交流史 History of Sino-Indian cultural contacts. Beijing New China bookshop.

Lu Yang 陆扬. 2009. 解读《鸠摩罗什传》：兼谈中国中古早期的佛教文化与史学 *Decoding the Biography of Kumārajīva: A discussion on early Buddhist culture and historiography in China*. http://www.foyuan.net/plus/view.php?aid=101066&pageno=15. accessed on November 20, 2010.

Tan Cung. 1994. *Cultural ambassadors: Buddhist monks from India to China and from China to India*. Paper presented at the First seminar on India and China: Looking at each other, organized by Indira Gandhi National Centre for the Arts and the Institute of Chinese Studies. New Delhi. November 15 and 18, 1995.

4

Kumārajīva (CE 344-409 or 413) and his Contemporaries

Haraprasad Ray

A lot of controversy has been generated around the arrival of Buddhism into China. Without further delving into the subject, we may safely state on the basis of Hui Jiao's (6th Century CE) Gao Sengzhuan (Biographies of the Eminent Monks) written during the 6th century CE, that till his time at least six Indian monk-scholars had arrived in China to preach Buddhism. These include Kāśyapa Mātaṅga, Dharmaratna, Dharmakāla, Kang Senghui, Weizhinan (probably Vijñāna, Indian) and Zhulian.[1] There must be many more who came unofficially, unnoticed in the official records and authors like Hui Jiao. This leads one to assume that China initially embraced Buddhism only indirectly from India via Central Asia during the early centuries of our common era. Such an impression goes against the ground reality, as around the time of Christ, while on the one hand there was already a strong movement in India with a large number of Buddhist scholars leaving their country, on the other hand, there was a keen desire in China to embrace Buddhism - as Emperor Ming's (58-75 CE) dream in the 1st century CE symbolises.[2] We can say for certain that these two dynamic forces must have resulted in the rendezvous of a large number of Indian and Chinese Buddhist intellectuals on the soil of China and other countries. Unfortunately, recovering their names and deeds has not been possible due to historical ups and downs. This was the first wave of Indian travellers to China as cultural envoys.

During the 4th and 5th centuries there was a second wave of Indian Buddhist monks arriving in China, followed by a counter-wave of Chinese

1 Hui Jiao cites the examples of other monks like Kang Senghui and others mentioned here.

2 Tan Chung, 'Ageless neighborliness between India and China: Historical perspective and future prospects,' China Report, 15.2, 1979, p. 21-2.

Buddhists coming to India for advanced knowledge and training in Buddhism. This second wave was headed among others, by two Kashmiris whose names in Chinese are recorded as Sengjia Badeng and Sengjia Tipo whose likely equivalents are Saṅghabhadra and Saṅghadeva.[3] Saṅghabhadra arrived in Ch'ang-an, the northern capital of China in CE 381 while Saṅghadeva had arrived there several years earlier, and both were received by the court of the northern warlord Fujian (351-357) who proclaimed himself as the Emperor of the Former Qin dynasty (Qianqin) (350-394).[4]

To mention some remarkable facts related to the story, the Former Qin was founded in CE 351 with its capital in Ch'ang-an by the Di tribesman, Fujian who was succeeded by another Fujian (357-384) (jian written differently) as the third emperor, while Later Zhao (Hou Zhao) (319-351) was set up in 319 by Shi Le (CE 319-339), a Jie tribesman and previously General of Liu Yuan (of Former Zhao) with his capital at Ch'ang-an; its capital was first at Xiangguo (in Hebei), and then at Ye (southwest of present day Linzhang county in Hebei).

Fujian (the third Emperor) was keen to invite eminent monks to his court to boost its morale. In 377, he received reports that an unusually brilliant star was sighted over the foreign horizon, and he was told that this was the augury of the arrival of a great sage to assist him to reign. Fujian was keen to have that sage, besides Saṅghabhadra and Saṅghadeva, in his court. This great sage was none other than Kumārajīva. We shall not go into the details of the life of this great son of a Kashmiri Brāhmaṇa Kūmārāyaṇa and a Kuchcan princess Jīvā (his name being amalgamation of the names of his parents, and thus, Kumārajīvā). Kumārajīva followed his mother into the Buddhist order and studied Hīnayāna Buddhist texts under one of the most famous masters, Bandhudatta. He earned a reputation very early in his life all over Central Asia. Fujian immediately singled him out as the cynosure of his dream. As a ruthless soldier, he was bent on bringing Kumārajīva as a treasure, a war booty, and nothing more than that. So Fujian sent his general Lü Guang with a contingent of troops to Kuca (Kucha) to invite Kumārajīva. Upon resistance by the Kuchan King, Lü Guang put him to the sword and took away Kumārajīva; in this uncouth manner was the invitation executed, and a new leaf in India - China interface was opened with the arrival of Kumārajīva in North China in 382 (at Guzang in Gansu).

However, before we recount Kumārajīva's work in China, let us focus on another Indian monk who as a precursor of our hero, exercised tremendous influence on China and had also made history in China before the arrival

[3] Ibid.

[4] Daisaku Ikeda, The flower of Chinese Buddhism tr. Burton Watson, New York, Tokyo, W e a t h e r hill, 1976, pp. 44-5; see also, Haraprasad Ray, Chinese Sources of South Asian History in Translation: Data for study of India- China Relations through History, vol. 3 "Buddhist Trilogy" pp, 36-7.

of Kumārajīva. His name is recorded as "Fotudeng" which may be the transcription of Buddhaatuṅga (some scholars read it as Buddhaatuṅga which does not seem to be correct)[5]. His native place is not exactly known, but it is certain that he was of Central Asiatic origin who had arrived in North China in circa CE 310 for setting up a religious centre in Loyang. According to some sources, he was surnamed Bo in which case he was from the kingdom of Kucha where the royal surname was Bo. By his display of magic, such as using spirits as his messenger, producing a lotus out of a bowl of water, and drawing water from dried-up wells with toothpicks, he gained the confidence of Shi Le of Later Zhao dynasty who ruled from 319-33, and served him for more than two decades as an imperial advisor.

He was a versatile man apart from being a devout Buddhist. He first cured Shi Le's troops of an infectious disease, and then converted the warlord and all his soldiers *en masse* to Buddhism. He could correctly predict the sudden change of weather which greatly helped the movement of troops and strategies for fighting. His wisdom helped Shi Le to rise from strength to strength; he was declared a Rāṣṭguru (Guoshi, also translated as Rājyaguru) of Later Zhao (Hou Zhao) (319-351) by Shi Le. In 334, Shi Le's nephew Shi Hu (335-348) usurped the throne, and treated Buddhatuṅga (Fotu Deng) with even greater reverence. When the Emperor rose in court, Fotu Deng would be escorted to the stage by the side of the Emperor, with the courtiers chanting «the Great Monk" (Da Heshang). Never before had any foreigner been accorded such imperial honour in China. Significantly, the recipient of such unprecedented honour was an Indian.

Kumārajīva was thus the second Rāṣṭraguru (or Rājyaguru) in Chinese history. His contribution to the development of Buddhism in China far exceeded that of Fotu Deng or any other Indian preceding or following him, and the hospitality accorded to him by his Chinese host was also most extraordinary.

When Kumārajīva reached Ch'ang-an, his original solicitor, Fujian (357-384) had already been overthrown; Lü Guang who declared himself in 386 as the Emperor of Hou Laing (Later Liang, 386- 405), kept Kumārajīva as his close advisor. After Lü Guang's death, his successor, Lü Long (401-403), suffered a defeat in 401 at the hands of another Northern Chinese warlord, Yao Xing (394-415), the Emperor of Hou Qin (Later Qin) (384-420). Kumārajīva was the main cause of this conflict as Lü Guang had been consistently refusing the request of Yao Chang (Yao Xing's predecessor) to part with the Indian monk. He, thus, made history of being twice treated as war booty in China. However,

[5] See complete translation of his life from Gaoseng Zhuan (Biographies of the Eminent Monks) in Ray, ibid., pp. 109-36; see also, Kenneth K.S. Chen, Buddhism in China, A Historical Survey, Princeton, New Jersey, Princeton University Press, 1964, pp.79- 80.

the second transfer of Kumārajīva from the possession of the Hou Liang ruler to the government of the Hou Qin marked a historic transition. Kumārajīva's genius and scholarship became fully utilized in the changed circumstamces.[6]

Shi Daoan[7]

Here we may introduce a contemporary of Kumārajīva whom he never met but spoke of him. He is the Saint of the East; and this Saint is none other than Shi Daoan (CE 312-385). Surnamed Wei, Shi Daoan was from Fuliu district in Changshan commandery of Hebei province and belonged to a family of eminent scholars. The life of Shi Daoan primarily reflects the period of growth of Chinese Buddhist thought during the 4th century CE when Hīnayāna Buddhism, preoccupied with ascetic practices (*yoga*) and acquisition of esoteric power through various processes of meditation *(dhyāna)*, yielded place to Mahāyāna Buddhism which stressed transcendental insight *(prajñā)* and ontological problems. Daoan zealously studied and commented on many of the early translations of *dhyāna* texts authored by An Shikao, a Parthian monk (arrived in Loyang in CE 148), and made teaching of the Prajñāpāramitā literature the final goal of his life in his later years. He was the founder of the Benwuzong, the school of Original Non-existence, a school profoundly influenced by Taoist thought. His many expositions and debates led to the establishment of the first Chinese Buddhist schools.

It is worth mentioning here that before Daoan, a method of translation called "matching meanings" (geyi) was used by the Chinese to explain the Buddhist works. This involved systematic explanation of Indian terms and concepts by expressions which were culled from classical works like Laozi, Yijing and Zhuangzi. This technique was quite effective in the initial stage of analysis and exegesis of the texts, but it gradually became a hindrance to the proper understanding of Buddhist ideas. This problem became quite apparent to Daoan and his contemporaries, who thought that the method of "matching meanings" frequently did injustice to the Indian Buddhist texts. Daoan boldly abandoned this method[8] although it was universally in vogue during his time. He then laid the foundation of the translation technique that insisted on exact translation and a clear differentiation between the original Indian and the Chinese exegetical strands in Buddhist thought. This method was successfully used by Kumārajīva and his followers.

Daoan compiled the first critical bibliography of the Chinese Tripiṭakas, translated before and during his own time; he also adumbrated the rules of discipline (*vinaya*) regulating the monastic life of the Chinese Buddhist monks.

---

6 For translation of Kumarajiva's biography see, Ray, op. cit., pp. 31-42.

7 For translation of Daoan's biography, see ibid, pp. 56-78.

8 For a short discussion on this issue ibid; pp. 55-6.

As remarked by Arthur E. Link "his tireless example and zeal in instructing disciples extended his influence far beyond his own times, some of his precepts adumbrating the doctrines of the Pure Land and the cult of Maitreya"[9].

Although he remained far away from Kumārajīva, Daoan always had great respect and admiration for him. Being very intimate with Emperor Fujian of Former Qin dynasty (CE 350-394), he often exhorted the king to bring Kumārajīva to China. Fortunately for historians, he was brought to China, and thus we have these detailed narratives about the Buddhist scholars who went to spread Buddhism, thanks to the unique Chinese tradition of putting down everything in writing. Along with his Indian collaborators like Saṅghadeva (Sengjia tipo), Dharmanandin (Tanmonanti) and Saṅghabhadra (Sangjiaba cheng), Shi Daoan translated more than a million words of sūtras.

Kumārajīva arrived at Ch'ang-an sixteen years after Shi Daoan's death. He regretted that he could not meet Daoan before his death, and his grief knew no bounds.

Shi Huiyuan[10]

Shi Huiyuan (CE 334-416) is another outstanding personality without whom this discussion will remain incomplete. Originally surnamed Jia, he was from Yanmen commandery in Northern Shanxi. He was inspired by Shi Daoan's exposition of Prajñāpāramitā (Boruojing) that led to his initiation into Buddhism. His vast knowledge, superior consciousness and enlightenment endeared him to all - both the laity and the nobility, including rulers. Huiyuan was instrumental in acquainting South China with the genuine texts of Buddhism. In the words of Hui Jiao, "Buddhist scriptures in the region east[11] of the Yangtse were not comprehensive. The *dhyāna (chan)* methods were not yet heard of, and the Collection of Statutes (Vinaya Piṭaka) were deficient ".[12] Huiyuan sent his disciples like Faling and others in search of Buddhist texts which were collected in large numbers after a long search in Central Asia and beyond and thus the gap was filled.

Kumārajīva's arrival in Ch'ang-an was warmly welcomed by Huiyuan in his letter in 402. Kumārajīva's reply was also very significant, because among other things it showed that he had not mastered Chinese till then. He said, "In expressing my feelings and transmitting (my feelings of) friendship (to you), I have to communicate my ideas by means of translation"[13] But Kumārajīva's

[9] Arthur E. Link, "Biography of Shih Tao-an", T' oung Pao, 46, 1958, p.2; see also, E.Zurcher, The Buddhist Conquest of China the spread and adaptation of Buddhism in early medical China, Leiden, E.J. Brill, 1956, pp.194-206.

[10] For biography of Shi Huiyuan, see Hui Jiao, Gaoseng Zhuan (Lives of Eminent Monks), Taisho Tripitaka edn, vol 50, no 2059, pp. 357c- 361, for translation see, Ray, op. cit. pp. 85-100

[11] Should be 'south'

[12] See Ray, op. cit. p.91

[13] Ibid., p.92

immense output leaves us in no doubt that he took no time in fully mastering Chinese, so as to be able to guide his disciples and also to translate the scriptures himself, which till today remains unchallenged.

To continue with Huiyuan, there are several supernatural stories about his spiritual power like causing rainfall in a year of drought after his recitation of Sāgaranāgarāja-paripṛchhā in Chinese (Hailongwang Jing). The other famous monk Shi Daoan had great faith in him; he admired him and remarked that Huiyuan was the person who would make Buddhism (Dao) spread all over China (which he called the Eastern country).

Hui Yuan had not only thoroughly mastered the tenets of Buddhism, but was also thoroughly conversant with all other branches of literature. When he was twenty-one, he came across Shi Daoan and after hearing the latter's exposition of the Prajñāramitā (Boruojing), suddenly realized and exclaimed, "Confucianism, Taoism and the Nine Schools (jiu liu) are all nothing more than husks[14], and then got himself initiated into the path of the Buddha along with his younger brother. His treatises, prefaces, inscriptions, eulogies, poems and letters, which were highly valued by his generation of Buddhist scholars, were collected into fifty works (plan).[15]

Apart from Kumārajīva, Shi Daoan and Shi Huiyuan, Hui Jiao has provided us the details of other lesser known monks like Shi Sengguang, Shi Daohu, Zhu Faya and Shi Fayu. Zhu Faya together with Kang Falang, Fatai as well as Shi Daoan used to discuss and explain to each other the difficult points which they encountered during their study of the Buddhist canons. It was at this time that the principles of «matching the meanings» was evolved by this group, under which, terms from secular canons of China were picked up and matched with Buddhist terms.

Shi Sengguang from the area north of Huang He river, was also a friend of Shi Daoan. (Both of them promised to follow the path of the Buddha, and help each other in order to make their understanding stronger and to advance the cause of Dharma). It was during his discussion with Sengguang that Daoan realized the shortcomings of «matching the meanings» and developed the new method of translation which laid stress on grappling with the original Buddhist concepts underlying the faulty translations of scholars like An Shih-kao. Thus, independent of Kumārajīva, Daoan had set foot on a path that led him much beyond the contracted vision of his contemporaries like Shi Sengguang who did not deviate from the inadequate method of 'matching of meaning' in translation.

---

[14] Ibid., 86

[15] Ibid; for further details see Zürcher, op. cit., p.412n. 132

Shi Fayu was one of the many disciples of Shi Daoan who was inspired by the latter to become a Buddhist. Shi Daohu, who met Shi Daoan in a secluded abode on the famous Feilong Shan mountain, took an oath with Daoan to move down to the plains to preach Buddhism among the populace.

Kumārajīva received his instruction in Mahāyāna from the then famous scholar Sūryasoma[16] after which he said he was able to «savour the taste of true understanding (of Mahāyāna)''. He continues, ''He (Sūryasoma) entrusted his Sanskrit texts to me and charged me with the propagation of the sūtras, saying, 'The sun of the Buddha has gone into hiding behind the Western mountains, but its lingering rays shine over the Northeast. These texts are destined for the lands of the Northeast. You must make certain that they are transmitted to them'[17].

According to Hui Jiao, twenty-three voluminous works were translated by Kumārajīva. These translations totalled more than three hundred volumes (juan).[18] Though Kumārajīva himself passed away many centuries ago, his translation of the Lotus Sūtra and other scriptures remain an imperishable treasure to be passed down through the ages.

When we think of Kumārajīva we are sure to be inspired to compare him with the great monk Swāmī Vivekānanda. Both these supermen dared the Himalayan barriers of conservatism and fundamentalism, triumphed over the rough and tumble of life, and striding the world's stage fearlessly, endeared themselves to the laity and elite alike.

[16] Ikeda has Sutyasoma, op. cit., p. 42; perhaps it is a printing mistake.

[17] Ikeda, loc. cit.

[18] See Gaoseng Zhuan, op.cit, p.332C

5

Kumārajīva and the Sandalwood image

Kimiaki Tanaka

1. What is the Sandalwood Image (Tib. Tsan dan jo bo)?

When he was thirty-eight years old, the Buddha Śākyamuni is said to have ascended to the Trayastriṁśa Heaven in order to pay his respects to his deceased mother Māyā Devī, and he spent the three-month summer retreat there instructing Indra, his mother, and the gods in the Dharma. Deeply missing Śākyamuni during his absence, King Udayana of Kosambī (Skt. Kauśāmbī) had made a sandalwood image of Śākyamuni, and this is believed to have been the first image of the Buddha. It became known as the Sandalwood Image on account of its material and as 'King Udayana's image of yearning' on account of its origins, and it is known from the *Da T'ang xiyuji* 大唐西域記 by Xuanzang 玄奘 (602–664) and other works to have been long and widely revered in India.

In China there evolved a belief that this sandalwood image had been brought to China by the translator Kumārajīva and his father, Kumārayaṇa, and a cult centred on it began to flourish during the period of the Five Dynasties and Ten Kingdoms (10th cent.). In 983, the Japanese monk Chōnen 奝然 visited Kaiyuansi 開元寺 Temple in Yangzhou 揚州 where the sandalwood image was enshrined during the T'ang dynasty. However, the statue had been moved to Kaifeng 開封, the capital of the Northern Song. The following year, he worshiped the sandalwood image at the Imperial Palace in Kaifeng. Deeply inspired by the image, Chōnen made a replica at Taizhou 台州 in 985, which he brought back with him to Japan the following year, and it was then enshrined at Seiryūji 清凉寺 Temple in Kyoto and became known as the Seiryūji Śākyamuni image. Meanwhile, after the fall of the Northern Song, the original sandalwood image was installed in the capital cities of successive dynasties and continued to be widely worshipped. During the Qing dynasty a temple called Zhantansi 旃檀寺 (Sandalwood Temple) was built in Beijing to house this image, resulting in an upsurge of devotion. The emperor Kangxi 康熙, for example, sent a special message of felicitation[1] to the temple and many pilgrims from Tibet and Mongolia also came to worship here. Accordingly, this type of standing image of Śākyamuni is known in Tibet as the 'Venerable Sandalwood Image' (Tib. tsan dan jo bo) and was an object of special devotion.

The sandalwood image remained in Beijing until the final years of the Qing dynasty, but during the Boxer Rebellion in 1900, Zhantansi suffered shelling by foreign forces and was destroyed by fire, and the sandalwood image is said either to have shared the temple's fate or to have been carried off to Russia as booty. Today there is a sandalwood image in Ulanude in the Buryat Republic, and some local Buddhists maintain that this is the original sandalwood image, which was presented to them by the Russian Czar. The former USSR Academy of Sciences conducted an examination of this sandalwood image in Ulanude, and Dr. Andrey Terentyev, one of the researchers, gave a short lecture on the sandalwood image in Buryat at Otani University in March 2008.[2]

2. Text Recording the Legend of the Sandalwood Image

Although not based on historical fact, the sandalwood image exerted enormous influence not only on Chinese but also on Japanese, Tibetan and Mogolian Buddhist art. In this paper, after briefly mentioning the preceding studies on the sandalwood image in Japan, China and Europe, I will present the results of my own research on it.

Scientifically speaking, the first historical record clearly stating that the sandalwood image enshrined in Kaiyuansi in Yangzhou was brought to China by Kumārajīva and his father is the "Chronicle of the Sandalwood Image of Śākyamuni Produced by King Udayana" ("Youtian wangzhantan Shijia ruixiang liji" 優塡王所造栴檀釋迦瑞像歷記),[3] which was brought back to Japan together with the sandalwood image by Chōnen. This text was originally compiled in 932 during the rule of Wu 吳, one of the Ten Kingdoms, although

---

[1] Wakamatsu, Hiroshi 1979

[2] Regarding Terentyev's study on the Sandalwood Image, see Andrey Terentyev, Udayana Buddha Statue: Its Fate in Russia,*Buddhist and Pali Studies in Honour of The Venerable Professor Kakkapalliye Anuruddha,* Hong Kong, 2009, pp.473-500.

[3] Dai Nihon bukkyō zensho 大日本佛教全書,vol.114, pp.310-320.

it was enlarged in the Northern Song.

However, when the Japanese monk Ennin 圓仁 visited Kaiyuansi in 838, he recorded an entirely different account of the image in the renowned record of his travels[4]. According to Ennin, the image had flown from India during the reign of Yangdi 煬帝 of the Sui dynasty.

The Chinese monk Daoxuan 道宣, on the other hand, explains that the image was brought back to China as booty by Wudi 武帝 of the Song, one of the Southern dynasties, from Funan 扶南, an ancient pre-Angkor kingdom.[5]

It becomes evident, at any rate, that the view that would attribute the arrival of the sandalwood image to Kumārajīva and his father was not very widespread during the T'ang dynasty.

However, after the Song dynasty, tales like the aforementioned "Chronicle of the Sandalwood Image of Śākyamuni Produced by King Udayana" became very popular in China. Moreover, Tibetan Buddhists translated into Tibetan a chronicle of the sandalwood image, entitled the *Tsan dan gyi sku rgya nag na bźugs pa'i byon tshul,*[6] and it was included in the Tengyur.

This chronicle contains several errors in chronology, since it was translated from Chinese into Tibetan through Uyghur. The Chinese scholar Huang Mingxing 黄明信 a.k.a bSod nams rgya mtsho wrote an article entitled the "Tsan dan jo bo'i lo rgyus bod skad skyoṅ sel"[7] in which he corrected the errors in the chronology of the Sandalwood Image.

We thus learn that the Sandalwood Image of Tibetan Buddhism is none other than the statue that was enshrined in Kaiyuansi in Yangzhou during the T'ang dynasty and is also the same as the original of the Japanese Seiryūji Śākyamuni image, although Huang Mingxing does not seem to have been aware of the existence of the "Chronicle of the Sandalwood Image of Śākyamuni Produced by King Udayana."

---

4 *Nittō guhō junrei kōki* 入唐求法巡禮行記, vol.1, 11th month of Kaicheng 開成 3.

5 *Daoxuan lushi gantong lu* 道宣律師感通錄, Taishō no.2107, vol.52, p.437c.

6 Peking No.5090.

7 *sBraï* char, Feb. 1986.

The Tibetan hitorian, Tshal pa, Kun dga' rdo rje (1309-1364) also mentions the story of the sandalwood image in his *Deb ther dmar po.*[8] Kun dga' rdo rje changes the homeland of Kumārajīva (Tib. Kumara chuï ba) from Kucha to a small country between India and lJaṅ (present-day Yunnan).

[8] *Deb ther dmar po*, Beijing, 1981, pp.13-15.

3. The Prototype of the Sandalwood Image

Unfortunately, the sandalwood image was lost in 1900. However, we can reconstruct its style and iconography from various materials.

The sandalwood image enshrined in Zhaofolou 照佛樓 of the Yonghegong 雍和宫 in Beijing is a replica of the image of Zhantansi.[9] This statue was created by the Emperor Qianlon's 乾隆 mother, an ardent devotee of Tibetan Buddhism. It seems to me to be the most reliable replica among statues of this kind[10] because of the geographic closeness between Zhantansi and Yonghegong and its creation under imperial sponsorship.

Another remarkable piece of material is a painting now kept in gNas rniṅ monastery near Gyantse (Tib. rGyal rtse) in Central Tibet.[11] In this picture, there is inscribed an eulogy to the sandalwood image composed by the Emperor Yongle 永樂 himself (1412).

In addition, a thangka held by the Hahn Cultural Foundation in Seoul also depicts the sandalwood image.[12] In this thangka, Tsoṅ kha pa is shown above the image, flanked by two figures, who probably represent the Dalai Lama and Panchen Lama, while the image itself is flanked by the Eight Great Bodhisattvas (Tib. Ñe ba'i sras chen) in accordance with the traditions of Tibetan Buddhism. It is not surprising to find Tsoṅ kha pa and the Eight Great Bodhisattvas in the present thangka since Zhantansi was under the supervision of the dGe lugs pas throughout the Qing dynasty. Therefore, this thangka must be depicting the image enshrined in Zhantansi during the Qing Dynasty.

Furthermore, in both these paintings, the sandalwood image wears a red garment adorned with small flower patterns. Generally speaking, the hair, eyes, and lips of images made of sandalwood were usually painted, while the rest of the statue was left with its natural surface to release the fragrance of the wood. However, traces of red pigment and patterns of golden foil have recently been discovered on the garments of the Japanese Seiryūji Śākyamuni image.

As regards the prototype of the sandalwood image, several Japanese scholars, including I, have taken note of a Buddha statue dated Taihe 太和 10 (486 CE) in the possession of the Metropolitan Museum of Art.[13] Oku Takeo 奥健夫 of the Japanese Agency of Cultural Affairs, on the other hand, has

---

[9] Tanaka Kimiaki 田中公明, "Chibetto to Nihon no bukkyō" チベットと日本の仏教, in *Zusetsu Nihon no bukkyō* 図説日本の仏教, Tokyo, 1988.

[10] On other replicas of the Sandalwood Image, see Jin shen 金申, "Zanghan foqiao zhongde zhantan ruixiang" 藏漢佛教中的旃檀瑞像, *Wenwu chunqiu* 文物春秋 2005-4.

[11]. David Jackson, *A History of Tibetan Painting* (Vienna, 1996), fig. 42.

[12] Tanaka Kimiaki: *Art of Thangka,* vol.2 (Seoul, 1999), pl. 18.

[13] John Steward Kennedy Fund, 1926 (26.123)

pointed to a copper statue dated Taipingzhenjun 太平眞君 4 (443 A.D.) in the possession of Kyūshū ational Museum, Japan.[14] Both statues, although created as Maitreya, show the gesture of granting fearlessness (Skt. abhayaprada) with the right hand and show the wish-granting gesture (Skt.varada) with the left hand, as does the sandalwood image. Moreover, their manner of wearing three garments an undergarment (qun 裙), an intermediary piece and a robe (Skt. saṅghāṭī) shows a close resemblance to the sandalwood image.

In addition, several Japanese and Western scholars have already pointed out the influence of Indian and Central Asian Buddha statues on these statues. If Chinese Buddhists from the 5th to 8th centuries saw such statues for the first time, it is not surprising that they would have thought that they had been brought from India.

4. Why was the Sandalwood Image Attributed to Kumārajīva?

As we have already discussed, there existed many views in T'ang China concerning the date and route of arrival of the sandalwood image. However, after the Song, only the legend that Kumārajīva and his father had brought this image to China survived, and this story was ūtransmitted to Japan, Tibet and Mongolia. Next, I wish to consider the reason that the image was attributed to Kumārajīva.

As has already been pointed out by several Japanese and Chinese scholars, the other great translator Xuanzang, ranked with Kumārajīva, brought back to China copies of seven statues revered in India. This is not a legend but a historical fact, and King Udayana's image of yearning was included among Xuanzan's seven statues.

Moreover, according to a recent study, it has came to light that after Xuanzang's return to China, several statues with the inscription "King Udayana's image of yearning" were created in China, particularly in the suburbs of Chang'an 長安 and Loyang 洛陽, the Western and Eastern capitals of the T'ang.[15]

However, the size, style and iconography of "King Udayana's image of yearning" attributed to Xuanzang are fundamentally different from the sandalwood image enshrined in Kaiyuansi. Moreover, the influence of Xuanzan's images did not last long.

Xuanzang studied Vijñāvāda philosophy under Śīlabhadra at Nālandā

[14] Oku, Takeo, *Seiryōji shaka nyoraizō* 清凉寺釈迦如来像, Nihon-no bijutsu 日本の美術 513 (Tokyo, 2009), p.37.

[15] Hida Romi 肥田路美, "Shotō jidai ni okeru Udennōzō" 初唐時代における優塡王像, Bijutsushi 美術史 120 (1986); Hamada Tamami 濱田瑞美, "Chūgoku shotō jidai no Rakuyō shūhen ni okeru Udennōzō ni tsuite" 中国初唐時代の洛陽周辺における優塡王像について, Bukkyō geijutsu 佛教藝術287 (2006).

and his theories became the basis of the Faxiang 法相 school. For a time, this school became the main current of Buddhism in T'ang China. However, the predominance of the Faxiang school also did not last long.

After the death of Xuanzang, Fazang 法蔵 (643–712) systematized the Huayan 華厳 school on the basis on the *Garland Sūtra* (Skt. *Buddhāvataṁsakasūtra*). During the reign of Empress Wu, this school flourished and became the mainstream of Chinese Buddhism.

After the Huayan school, Esoteric Buddhism was transmitted to China by Śubhākarasiṁha, Vajrabodhi and Amoghavajra. Esoteric Buddhism came into vogue during the reign of Xuanzong 玄宗 and his successors. When Śubhākarasiṁha translated the *Vairocanābhisambodhisūtra* into Chinese, Yixing 一行 (683–727), a Chinese monk, helped him and edited his lectures on the *Vairocanābhisambodhisūtra.* Yixing belonged to the Tiantai 天台 school, which had been established by Zhiyi 智顗 (538-597) during the Chen 陳 and Sui. This school was revived by Zhanran 湛然 (711-782) in the middle of T'ang, and through Yixing Tiantai theories were introduced into Chinese and Japanese Esoteric Buddhism.

After the T'ang, Tiantai and Huayan became the two main schools in Chinese Buddhist doctrine, and their influence surpassed that of the Faxiang school.

The Faxiang school asserts that there are three kinds of sentient beings. The first kind has no possibility of emancipation from cyclic existence, and the best course for such beings is to be reborn in good destinies, namely, the realms of gods and humans, The second kind of beings are vessels for the Hīnayāna doctrine, and they are suited to becoming an arhat or a pratyekabuddha. The last kind is those who are the vessels for the Mahāyāna doctrine, and they alone can become fully enlightened Buddhas. This theory is based on the *Mahāyānasūtrālaṅkāra* translated by Xuanzang.

Faxiang's theory, which recognizes the real existence of the three vehicles, is contrary to the one vehicle (Skt. ekayāna) theory of the *Saddharmapuṇḍarīkasūtra* translated by Kumārajīva. The *Saddharmapuṇḍarīkasūtra,* which asserts that all sentient beings can become fully enlightened Buddhas, had, moreover, already captivated Buddhists in East Asia, including Korea and Japan. Furthermore, Huayan, Tiantai and Esoteric Buddhism all recognize the one vehicle theory, and Tiantai, which is directly based on the *Saddharmapuṇḍarīkasūtra* translated by Kumārajīva, styled the Faxiang school as the Provisional Mahāyāna (quan dacheng 權大乗).

The legend of Kumārajīva's sandalwood image seems to have arisen againt this background as a way of dealing with King Udayana's image of yearning brought back by Xuanzang. However, Kumārajīva himself never visited India except for a period of study in Kashmir. Therefore, Kumārajīva's father who came from India, was supposed to have brought the sandalwood image from India to Kucha, the birthplace of Kumārajīva.

In this context, an episode that appears in the aforementioned *Deb ther dmar po*[16] just after the story of the sandalwood image is suggestive. When the Chinese monk Zon klu sri fell from a cliff, he was rescued by a heavenly being, the son of Vaiśravaṇa. Zon klu sri asked him about Kumāraśrī (i.e. Kumārajīva). He replied that Kumāraśrī was a Bodhisattva who had attained the *darśanamārga* and was now listening to Maitreya's preaching after having been miraculously reborn on a lotus filament in the Tuṣita Heaven. Next, Zon klu sri asked him about Thaṅ dzam tshaṅ (the translator of T'ang= Xuanzang). The heavenly being replied that Xuanzang had reached the *bhāvanāmārga* and was now outside the enclosure of the Tuṣita Heaven, and although he could not see Maitreya's body, he was listening to him preaching.

BIBLIOGRAPHY

Wakamatsu, Hiroshi 若松寛. 1979. "Kōki gyosei sendanbutsu sairai rekidai denshukuki to chankya hutukutu" 康熙御製栴檀佛西來歴代傳祝記と章嘉呼圖克圖), in *Sōgendai no shakai to shūkyō no sōgōteki kenkyū* 宋元代の社会と宗教の総合的研究. Kyoto

[16] *Deb ther dmar po*, (Beijing, 1981), pp.16-17.

6

Early Mahāyāna according to Kumārajīva's Upadeśa

Elsa Legittimo

1. The sources

We have in the Chinese Canon a complete translation of a lost Indian work entitled *Da zhi du lun* 大智度論.[1] The translation was completed by Kumārajīva (and his team) and represents the only extant version of the *Mahāprajñāpāaramitopadeśa*, the *Large Prajñāpāramitā Commentary* attributed to Nāgārjuna, appropriately called 'large' since (in Chinese) it has a hundred scrolls. Late Professor Étienne Lamotte from Belgium translated the first third of the oeuvre into French between 1944 and 1980,[2] while the other two thirds are not yet translated. The huge compendium is also known by its short names *Upadeśa* as well a *Traité* , as Lamotte called the work: *Le Traité de la Grande Vertu de Sagesse.*

Let us literally begin with the end, with the very last few lines of the *Upadeśa:* the postscript:

> "The dharmācarya Kumārajīva 究摩羅耆婆法師,[3]arrived in Chang'an 長安 in the 3rd year of the period Hong-shi 弘始 of the Qin 秦, in the Xinchou year 歲在辛丑, on the 20th day of the 12th moon (8th February 402). During the

[1] *Taishō edition* (T), vol. 25, no. 1509, p. 57c-756c. *Taishō Shinshū Daizōkyō* 大正新脩大藏經 : ed. TAKAKUSU 高楠 et WATANABE 渡邊, vol. I-LV, Tokyo 1924-1929.

[2] LAMOTTE, Etienne, *Trait, de la Grande Vertu de Sagesse,* 5 vol., Louvain 1944-1980.

[3] Noteworthy is the transcription used here for Kumārajīva's name: Jiumoluoqipo 究摩羅耆婆. The pinyin is far from the ancient pronunciation, as is generally the case with Buddhist transcriptions in Chinese, but the characters correspond to Ku-ma-ra-ji-va. Despite the fact that it is a very accurate transcription, it is very rare. It only appears in this postscript, three more times in the *Chu san zang ji ji,* T55, no. 2145, p. 61c, 75a and 75b, and in a later dictionary like work on Sanskrit vocabulary, the *Fan fan yu* 翻梵語, T54, no. 2130, p. 994a.

summer of the 4th year (402) [working in] the pavillon of the Western gate of the Xiao-yao 逍遙 park, he published for the Emperor Yao 姚, this *Upadeśa* 釋論. The translation was completed on the 27th day of the 12th moon of the 7th year (1st February 406). [...] The first chapter of the *Upadeśa* fills the first 34 scrolls and only comments on one chapter of the sources text fully. From chapter two onwards, the dharma master has summarized [the commentary], and thus we obtained this large commentary in hundred scrolls. Had it been translated fully, it would have been ten times larger."[4]

The work is a commentary on the *Mahāprajñāpāramitā-sūtra*, and although there are a great number of versions in different lengths with the same title, Kumārajīva refers to that sūtra which he translated at the same time as the *Upadeśa:* The *Pañcaviṁśatisāhasrikā-prajñāpāramitā / Mo he ban ruo bo luo mi jing* 摩訶般若波羅蜜經 in twenty-seven scrolls.[5] To be more precise this text might have been expounded by Kumārajīva, translated by Zhu Fonian and written down by Hui Zhao. The *Li dai san bao ji* 歷代三寶紀 says that the Sanskrit text was expounded by Kumārajīva 什執梵文, translated by Zhu Fonian 竺佛念傳語 and written down by Hui Zhao 叡肇筆受.[6] We do not know where the author of the *Li dai san bao ji* obtained this information from, but if the data is correct, it is the only clear mention of a collaboration between Kumārajīva and Zhu Fonian. In any case, the *prajñāpāaramitā-sūtra* in question was translated between 403 and 404, parallel to the *Upadeśa,* which was a large amount of work. Since Zhu Fonian had already translated a five scroll long *prajñāpāaramitā* text[7] and a sūtr*a* on the ten stages of the bodhisattva career in ten scrolls,[8] it cannot be denied that he was worthy and capable of the task of also translating the *Pañcaviṁśatisāhasrikāprajñāpāramitā* .

Both texts, *Prajñāpāramitā sūtra* and its commentary the *Upadeśa* are divided into ninety chapters; the postscript explains that, in fact the first chapter of the commentary was translated in full and fills thirty-four scrolls (corresponding, by the way, to the part translated by Lamotte), and the other eighty-nine chapters were summarized in the following sixty-six scrolls.

4 The translation into French by LAMOTTE is found in the introduction to vol. III of the Trait,. (LAMOTTE 1970: XLV). The postscript is found at the end of the hundredth scroll of the Chinese translation of the Upadeśa (T25, no. 1509, p. 756c), as well as in the Chu san zang ji ji 出三藏記集 (T55, no. 2145, p. 75b). This work is the oldest existing catalogue on Buddhist scriptures. It was composed in the year 515 by Seng You 僧祐 (445-518) and it contains a lot of precious data (biographies, prefaces and postscript to translations, the actual catalogue, etc.) and it also draws information from various older, presently lost works..

5 T8, no. 223, p. 217a-424a.

6 I am grateful to Sylvie Hureau for having pointed out this passage to me. Cf. the Li dai san bao ji 歷代三寶紀 (T49, no. 2034, p. 77b-79a).

7 The Mo he ban ruo chao jing 摩訶般若鈔經, Aṣṭasāharikā-prajñāpāramitā, (T8, no. 226), expounded by Dharmapriya and translated by Zhu Fonian in the year 382.

8 The Shi zhu duan jie jing 十住斷結經 (T 10, no. 309) was translated by Zhu Fonian in the last quarter of the fourth century.

2. A note on the denomination *Mahāyāna* 大乘 in the *Upadeśa*

The *Upadeśa* being a commentary of *Prajñāpāsamitā a* literature is of course a compendium on Buddhist science and knowledge from a Mahāyāna perspective, but from a rather early or slightly later state of development. The present investigation focuses on the linguistic and terminological aspects of this doctrinally very important term. We want to know where the Great Vehicle was placed within this huge commentary. In which context does its denomination circulate and who was driving or riding the vehicle? Metaphors for the Great Vehicle are numerous. We will see a few examples later, but this aspect of the metaphor that a vehicle can in fact be driven and ridden - was brought to international attention by Harrison.[9]

Mahāyāna 大乘 appears under this most frequent translation 161 times in the *Upadeśa.* This amounts to more than one and less than two times in every scroll. In the following sections, I will try to give an overview of its most frequent usages and also present interesting passages.

3. The metaphor of the Mahāyāna Ocean 大乘海

This highly figurative expression is very rare. It appears only once in the *Upadeśa* and once in four other sūtras. In the *Upadeśa* it is found at the beginning of a commentarial explanation:

"The commentary says: Like there are all kinds of treasures and pearls in the great ocean, there can also be killing poisons, monsters (ghosts), one can become sick and ill, get a fever or starve [...] in the same way there are immeasurable and countless treasures and pearls. In the Mahāyāna Ocean it is also like this. There are all sorts of bodhisattva treasures, there are bodhisattvas who can destroy the three evil paths (destinies), who can open the three good/ beneficial gates and produce the five eyes."[10]

4. Mahāyāna and *sarvajña* 薩婆若

If Mahāyāna is a vehicle, then omniscience might be its fuel. What is interesting is that the *Upadeśa* has this particular transcription of *sarvajña*, 薩婆若 more than any other scripture. The transcription is found 1966 times

[9] Paul HARRISON, "Who Gets to Ride in the Great Vehicle? Self-image and Identity Among the Followers of the Early Mahāyāna", Journal of the International Association of Buddhist Studies (JIABS), vol. X, no. 1, 1987, p. 67-89

[10] Translated from T25, no. 1509, p. 352a-352b. The five eyes are the physical eye, the divine eye that sees everything, the wisdom eye that sees the emptiness of all dharmas, the dharma eye that distinguishes all dharmas, and the Buddha eye of omniscience that includes the preceding four at the most supreme level.

in the whole Chinese Canon, and 1521 times in translations (the first thirty-two volumes of the *Taishō*). Among these translations, it occurs only 11 times in the largest Chinese *Mahāprajñāpāramitā-sūtra* (within the 600 scrolls of this enormous work the transcription only appears between scrolls 544 to 561),[11] 325 times in the afore-mentioned *Prajñāpāramitā-sūtra* translated by Kumārajīva and Zhu Fonian. Here, the transcription is found abundantly in all the twenty-seven scrolls, except that it only appears once in scroll 25 and not at all in scrolls 23, 24, 26 and 27.

But the *Upadeśa* outnumbers these other texts by mentioning the transcription for *sarvajña* a total of 506 times. Several passages are set in direct connection with Mahāyāna. In percentages, 5.75% of this *sarvajña* transcription appears in close relation with Mahāyāna. On the other hand ca. 12.5% of all Mahāyāna appearances are in close relation with *sarvajña*.

Sarvajña is also often related to *Mahāyāna dharma* 大乘法, to the primary *pāramitā*: the *Prajñāpāramitā* 般若波羅蜜 and to the bodhisattva's start in the Mahāyāna 菩薩摩訶薩發趣大乘.

5. *Karuṇā* as the foundation of Mahāyāna

When Buddhas and bodhisattvas interfere with living beings they make use of the four *apramāṇas: maitrī, karuṇā, muditā and upekśā*. Now, the *Upadeśa* has a unique formulation that underlines the foremost importance of compassion *(karuṇā)* out of the four: 四無量心中大悲是大乘之本.[12] In this same context the passage discusses also sarvajña, emptiness, and the *prajñā-pāramitā*. Also, the path is an important component in that passage, as well as elsewhere in passages which mention Mahāyāna.

6. Mahāyāna is the foremost path (in emptiness)

In a commentarial passage the hypothetical questioner asks about the most supreme and perfect awakening, *anuttara-samyak-saṁbodhi* 阿耨多羅三藐三菩提 and about the most supreme path. The answer is:

Mahāyāna is the most supreme path 答大乘無上. Here the three vehicles are also briefly discussed and it is said that in fact such distinctions are also empty.[13]

---

[11] T6/7/8, no. 220.

[12] T25, no. 1509, p. 601a. Cf. the only complete study on the subject of the ethic significance of these concepts by Mudagamuwe Maithrimurthi: Wohlwollen, Mitleid, Freude und Gleichmut: eine ideengeschichtliche Untersuchung der vier apramāṇas in der buddhistischen Ethik und Spiritualität von den Anfängen bis hin zum frühen Yogācāra, Stuttgart, 1999.

[13] T25, no. 1509, p. 567c.

7. Mahāyāna is the world's most supreme eloquence

Because it can explain each and everything in the world, the most supreme eloquence is that of Mahāyāna.[14] This statement is fully embedded in the context of *Prajñāpāramitā* .

8. Mahāyāna and *Prajñāpāramitā* 般若波羅蜜

To throw away the small profit/gain and get the great vehicle, that is called *Prajñāpāramitā* .[15] Many passages correlated in one way or the other *Prajñāpāramitā* to Mahāyāna, so that it cannot be dissociated, but there is a particularly noteworthy passage where *Prajñāpāramitā* is called a mantra 咒 by the hypothetical questioner and the author takes up the challenge. The core of the explanation is that *Prajñāpāramitā* is a mantra that can separate the people from old age, illness and death, and that it can establish the living beings in the Great Vehicle.[16]

There are further passages in which these terms correlated in close context, that cannot all be mentioned here.[17]

9. The Mahāyāna people

Certain terms, such as the Mahāyāna disciples 大乘弟子) are very rare. This formulation, for example, is unique to the *Upadeśa* and only mentioned once. The author says that the Mahāyāna disciples teach the emptiness of *dharma*, in contrast to the disciples of the Hīnayāna that teach the emptiness of the living beings.[18] Also unique is the mention that all the Buddhas are "Mahāyāna persons" 諸佛大乘人,[19] but, there are other passages with (only) "Mahāyāna person" 大乘人.[20]

10. The engagement part

When the bodhisattva hears the profound meaning of the Mahāyāna,[21] he sets out on the journey of Mahāyāna 發趣大乘. In Sanskrit this expression corresponds to *Mahāyānasaṃprasthita and/or Mahāyāna-saṃprasthāna.* This is a primary step for the bodhisattva, thus the formulation is not rare.[22] When the

[14] T25, no. 1509, p. 450c-451a.
[15] T25, no. 1509, p. 394b-394c.
[16] T25, no. 1509, p. 469a-469c.
[17] Cf. for example T25, no. 1509, p. 477c-478a, p. 551c-552a, p. 650b and p. 746b.
[18] T25, no. 1509, p. 287b-288a.
[19] T25, no. 1509, p. 488b-488c.
[20] Cf. for example: T25, no. 1509, p. 85b-85c, p. 345c-346a and 662a-662b.
[21] T25, no. 1509, p. 668c.
[22] T25, no. 1509, p. 393b, p. 411a, p. 419c and 893c-894a.

bodhisattva makes up his mind, he practices the six *pāramitās* and rides this Mahāyāna 發心行六波羅蜜乘是大乘.[23]

11. Expressing the intention of Mahāyāna

A lot of effort is used to underline the importance of taking the vows and taking up the decision to follow the bodhisattva path. Various expressions involving Mahāyāna are used, the most common ones are: a) the above-mentioned "setting out on the journey of Mahāyāna" 發趣大乘 and "expressing the intention of Mahāyāna" 大乘意. This formulation appears a total of 27 times in the *Upadeśa*. A bodhisattva can also be said to express his Mahāyāna mind or heart 發大乘心者, an expression that is only found four times in the *Upadeśa*.[24]

12. The Mahāyāna *dharma* 大乘法

This expression is sometimes, but not always, set in contrast with the Hīnayāna, and only once is it set in contrast with the Hīnayāna *dharma* 小乘法.[25] Mahāyāna *dharma* is found all together 27 times in the commentary.

13. Mahāyāna being criticised

When Mahāyāna is attacked (literally or hypothetically) and accused of having no base, the author of the *Upadeśa* argues that it is nonsense to say only this or that has or does not have a base, since all such distinctions are empty. The fact is that Mahāyāna is founded in *sarvajña*.[26] This passage is very closely following the *Prajñāpāramitā-sūtra*.[27]

Another noteworthy passage is where the hypothetical opponent asks: "Why is it said at the beginning of the *Mahāyānasūtras* 大乘經 that there were two assemblies: that of the bodhisattvas and that of the Śrāvakas, whereas at the beginning of the sūtras of the Śrāvakas only the monks" assembly are mentioned and not that of the bodhisattvas? "The answer: "It is for distinguishing the two vehicles: the vehicle of the Buddha and the vehicle of the Śrāvakas. [...]" The author explains that the latter is narrow and self-centred, whereas the former is large and for the benefit of all, an argument that has become a standard value in Mahāyāna Buddhism.[28] But let us note that Hīnayāna 小乘, appears only 82 times in the commentary, thus half as often as Mahāyāna.

[23] T25, no. 1509, p. 387a-389a.
[24] T25, no. 1509, p. 263b-263c, p. 281b-281c, p. 531a and p. 610a-610b.
[25] T25, no. 1509, p. 540b-540c.
[26] T25, no. 1509, p. 421a-421b.
[27] Cf. T8, no. 223, p. 260b-c.
[28] T25, no. 1509, p. 85b. For the French cf. vol. I (LAMOTTE 1944 : 238).

14. The bodhisattva is the main active hero of the *Upadeśa*

It is, of course, not possible to distillate the information that relates to the bodhisattva or the bodhisattvas. It is however possible to investigate particular topics that are related to the propagation of his Mahāyāna ideals. In the same way that emptiness is omnipresent when it comes to bodhisattvas they have similar intrinsically connected features such as the aforementioned qualities. Certainly the bodhisattva himself rides the great vehicle and in case there was any doubt about this, the *Upadeśa* has an explicit mention.[29] And when the bodhisattva-vehicle is mentioned this is always done in the sense of Mahāyāna; actually the bodhisattva vehicle is Mahāyāna.[30] Prajñāpāramitā is its fuel.

15. A great variety of vehicles

Other vehicles, or the expressions used, are the śrāvaka-yāna 聲聞乘, the pratyekabuddhayāna 辟支佛乘and of course the bodhisattva-yāna 菩薩乘. These two 二乘or three vehicles 三乘 are also mentioned in close connection with Mahāyāna.[31] Noteworthy is that the *Upadeśa* never mentions the concept of ekayāna 一乘.

BIBLIOGRAPHY

Taishō edition (T), vol. 25, no. 1509, p. 57c-756c. *Taishō Shinshū Daizōkyō* 大正新脩大藏經 : ed. Takakusu 高楠 et Watanabe 渡邊, vol. I-LV, Tokyo 1924-1929.

Lamotte, Etienne, *Trait, de la Grande Vertu de Sagesse,* 5 vol., Louvain 1944-1980.

Noteworthy is the transcription used here for Kumārajīva's name: Jiumoluoqipo 究摩羅耆婆. The pinyin is far from the ancient pronunciation, as is generally the case with Buddhist transcriptions in Chinese, but the characters correspond to Ku-ma-ra-ji-va. Despite the fact that it is a very accurate transcription, it is very rare. It only appears in this postscript, three more times in the *Chu san zang ji ji,* T55, no. 2145, p. 61c, 75a and 75b, and in a later dictionary like work on Sanskrit vocabulary, the Fan fan yu 翻梵語, T54, no. 2130, p. 994a).

The translation into French by Lamotte is found in the introduction to vol. III of the *Trait,.* (Lamotte 1970: XLV). The postscript is found at the end of the hundredth scroll of the Chinese translation of the *Upadeśa* (T25, no. 1509, p. 756c), as well as in the *Chu san zang ji ji* 出三藏記集 (T55, no. 2145, p. 75b). This work is the oldest existing catalogue on Buddhist scriptures. It was composed in the year 515 by Seng You 僧祐 (445-518) and it contains a lot of precious data (biographies, prefaces and postscript to translations, the actual catalogue, etc.) and it also draws information from various older, presently lost works..

T8, no. 223, p. 217a-424a.

I am grateful to Sylvie Hureau for having pointed out this passage to me. Cf. the *Li dai san bao*

29 T25, no. 1509, p. 704b-704c.

30 Cf. T25, no. 1509, p. 567a-567b, p. 385c and p. 389b-390a.

31 See for example T25, no. 1509, p. 321c and p. 487a-487b.

ji 歷代三寶紀 (T49, no. 2034, p. 77b-79a).

The Mo he ban ruo chao jing 摩訶般若鈔經, *Aùñasāharikā-prajñāpāramitā,* (T8, no. 226), expounded by Dharmapriya and translated by Zhu Fonian in the year 382.

The *Shi zhu duan jie jing* 十住斷結經 (T 10, no. 309) was translated by Zhu Fonian in the last quarter of the fourth century.

Paul Harrison, "Who Gets to Ride in the Great Vehicle? Self-image and Identity Among the Followers of the Early Mahāyāna", *Journal of the International Association of Buddhist Studies (JIABS),* vol. X, no. 1, 1987, p. 67-89

Translated from T25, no. 1509, p. 352a-352b. The five eyes are the physical eye, the divine eye that sees everything, the wisdom eye that sees the emptiness of all dharmas, the dharma eye that distinguishes all dharmas, and the Buddha eye of omniscience that includes the preceding four at the most supreme level.

T6/7/8, no. 220.

T25, no. 1509, p. 601a. Cf. the only complete study on the subject of the ethic significance of these concepts by Mudagamuwe Maithrimurthi: *Wohlwollen, Mitleid, Freude und Gleichmut: eine ideengeschichtliche Untersuchung der vier apramāõas in der buddhistischen Ethik und Spiritualität von den Anfängen bis hin zum frühen Yogācāra,* Stuttgart, 1999.

T25, no. 1509, p. 567c.

T25, no. 1509, p. 450c-451a.

T25, no. 1509, p. 394b-394c.

T25, no. 1509, p. 469a-469c.

Cf. for example T25, no. 1509, p. 477c-478a, p. 551c-552a, p. 650b and p. 746b.

T25, no. 1509, p. 287b-288a.

T25, no. 1509, p. 488b-488c.

Cf. for example: T25, no. 1509, p. 85b-85c, p. 345c-346a and 662a-662b.

T25, no. 1509, p. 668c.

T25, no. 1509, p. 393b, p. 411a, p. 419c and 893c-894a.

T25, no. 1509, p. 387a-389a.

T25, no. 1509, p. 263b-263c, p. 281b-281c, p. 531a and p. 610a-610b.

T25, no. 1509, p. 540b-540c.

T25, no. 1509, p. 421a-421b.

Cf. T8, no. 223, p. 260b-c.

7

Kumārajīva and the Chinese academic world

Saroj Kumar Chaudhuri

1. Introduction

Very few foreign monks attained real mastery over Chinese during the millennium of Sino-Indian Buddhist contacts. One of them was Kumārajīva. This paper will explore whether Kumārajīva (a) taught Sanskrit, (b) played any role in the innovation or dissemination of the *fan-ch'ieh* 反切 spelling method, and (c) was in any way connected with the invention of the Recent Style Poetry (*Chin-t'i-shi* 近體詩).

2. Intellectual Background

2.1. Early Contacts

The Later Han administration (CE 235-220) was heading towards disintegration when Buddhist monks from the West started translating Buddhist sūtras. It was a time of great political and social turmoil. The Emperor Wu-ti 武帝 (156-87 BCE) of the Former Han Dynasty 前漢 had established a highly centralised bureaucratic state, and shortly afterward a national central university was set up to train future recruits to the civil services. This became the leading centre of learning during the Later Han period (CE 25-220). The intense intellectual activity at the university gave birth to scholarly circles where anti-establishment ideas also brewed. The government retaliated by proscribing the scholarly circles. Some arrests were also made.[1]

[1] Yoshikawa, Tadao. 1991. *Scholarship in Ching-chou at the End of the Later Han Dynasty*. Tokyo. Acta Asiatica. V. 60. Tōhō Gakkai. pp. 1-3.

The Han bureaucratic model was based on Confucian ideals. All philosophical schools other than Confucianism were ignored. The Wei 魏 and Chin 晉 periods (CE 220-420) that followed the Han collapse freed the Chinese intellectual world from the fetters of Confucianism. A hundred flowers bloomed in the intellectual arena during this period. One of these was Buddhism. Some of the intellectuals were attracted to the new religion from the West, obviously out of curiosity. At least in Lo-yang 洛陽 the monks from the West were attracting attention in society as early as around CE 100, as can be deduced from a poem called "Hsiching fu" 西京賦 (Ode to the Western Capital) by a poet named Chang Heng (CE 78-130). Describing the seductive beauty of the women of Ch'ang-an, the poet says that even the virtuous śramaṇas would be captivated by them.[2]

2.2. Academic Level of the Chinese Collaborators

As stated above, towards the end of the Later Han dynasty, the university was a centre of anti-establishment elements. As can be expected, many brilliant students failed in the civil services examination. Later on, one hundred flowers would bloom in the intellectual arena. In this potent brew, it is quite natural that a few of the intellectuals would evince interest in the monks from the West. There was another reason for this. Although the monks were considered as barbarians, they were the barbarians with a difference. Unlike the barbarians they were accustomed to see, these barbarians from the West had a script, and were as educated as they were. Again, the strict monastic discipline and adherence to celibacy must have created a great impression.

It may not be wrong to assume that some of the Chinese who evinced interest in the monks came forward to collaborate with the monks in translating sūtras. Translation, especially of sūtras, is an intellectual activity that calls for a high level of education of the translators. If we see the level of education of the collaborators of An Shih-kao 安世高, the first authentic translator of sūtras, who worked around CE 150, one glance at the variety of characters used in the translations is enough to show the high level of education of the collaborators.

3. Kumārajīva and Sanskrit

3.1. Tao-an and Sanskrit

It is natural that some of the collaborators, being highly educated, would evince interest in Sanskrit, the language of the scripture they were translating. The first step in learning a language is to pick up its letters. Early Chinese texts dealing with Sanskrit mention its script as *hsi-t'an* 悉曇, a corruption of *siddham*.

---

[2] Ch'en, Kenneth K.S.. 1973. *Buddhism in China, A Historical Survey*. Princeton. Princeton University Press. p. 42.

It is a loose term meaning both the language and the script. One attraction for learning the language was the phonetic information embedded in its script, a revolutionary new concept for Chinese intellectuals. Although there is no material of that period available on the topic, what is notable is the presence of *Hsi-t'an-mu* 悉曇慕 (Adorable Siddham) in two fascicles in Tao-an's 道安 (312-385) catalogue.[3] It may be that the character *mu* here is a copying mistake for the character *mo* 副 that means 'exercise book'. Scores of foreign monks, and far more number of Chinese were involved in translation up to the time of Tao-an. It was natural that the Chinese collaborators would discuss among themselves the novel ideas and the language that carried it, and a textbook of the script appeared, as the first step for learning the new language. This perhaps is the *Hsi-t'an-mu*. The contents of *Hsi-t'an-mu* are not known as the book is lost, and no quotes from the work have been found so far. However, it is generally assumed that it is a primer of *siddham* script. If this assumption is correct, then it suggests that some Chinese studied at least the Sanskrit script around the time of Tao-an. The presence of the word *hsi-t'an* in the title suggests that the Chinese called this script *Hsi-t'an* or Siddham. The primers of Sanskrit script usually started with the word *siddham* meaning 'let there be success'.[4] From this, the Chinese students probably started calling the script as *Hsi-t'an*, the Chinese form of the word *siddham*, perhaps as a joke, and this stuck. Based on the date given by Diringer, it is unlikely that the script of Tao-an's *Hsi-t'an-mu* was the same as the Siddhamātṛkā script that was current in India around the 6th century. It is difficult to identify the script of *Hsi-t'an-mu* at this stage, but a hypothesis can be considered to explain how the word *hsi-t'an* or siddham got attached to it. Considering the textbooks mentioned above, it is likely that the earliest textbooks of the Sanskrit script had the word *siddham* in the very beginning. This was either written or read. This ultimately became the synonym for the Sanskrit script, and by extension the Sanskrit language, in China and Japan.

3.2. Kumārajīva's Sanskrit Textbook

The presence of *Hsi-t'an-mu* 悉曇慕 (Adorable Siddham), probably a Siddham textbook, in the 4th century catalogue of Tao-an has been mentioned above. The biography of Kumārajīva, who came to the capital Chang-an about fifteen years after the death of Taoan, in *Ch'u-san-ts'ang-chi-chi* 出三藏記集 says that he discussed literary styles of the West with his talented disciple Hui-jui 叡. He explained the similarities and dissimilarities.[5] Kumārajīva was a strong candidate to teach Sanskrit, although his biography is silent on

[3] Seng-yu 雌童. *Ch'u-san-tsang-chi-chi* 出三欟記集, *Taishō Shinshū Daizōkyō* 大正新修藏經 (TSDK), V. 55, 2145, p. 18M22.

[4] For instance, Chih-kuang 智廣, *Hsi-t'an-tzu-chi* 悉曇字記, TSDK, V. 54, p.1186M2

[5] Seng-yu 僧童, p. 101B7-11.

this point. It is likely that some of those who had studied *Hsi-t'an-mu* were around. Indeed there is evidence to suggest that Kumārajīva actually taught Sanskrit. A catalogue entitled *Shosha Shōrai Hōmontō Mokuroku* 書寫招来法門等目録 (Catalogue of Scriptures Copied in China and Brought Back to Japan) by the Japanese monk Shūei 宗叡 (809-884) mentions a *Nieh-p'an-ching-hsi-t'an-chang* 涅槃經悉談章 (Parinirvāṇa-sūtra, Siddham Chapter) in one fascicle translated by Kumārajīva on nine sheets of paper.[6] A Japanese monk Gyōgan 行願 printed this in the fifth year of the Hōreki 寶暦 era (1755).[7] The *Nieh-p'an-ching-hsi-t'an-chang* of Kumārajīva, better known as *Hsi-t'an-chang* (Siddham Chapter), can be dated between 401 and 413, when he lived in Ch'ang-an.

There is a handwritten text entitled *Chiu-mo-lo-shih-fa-shih-t'ung-yün* 鳩摩羅什法師通韻 (Comprehensive Rhymes of the Monk Kumārajīva) found in Tun-huang 敦煌 that is now in the Stein Collection of the British Museum (No. S1344). The notable point here is that the same name *Hsi-t'an-chang* 悉談章 appears in this manuscript. The manuscript opens with the statement: "Originally there are fifty-two letters from which one hundred and eighty-two symbols are produced. If these are harmonized with the fourteen traditional sounds (vowels) and combined with the five groups of plosives, the total number will be four million and eighty thousand."[8] Now, there are sixteen vowels from *'a'* to *'ah'*, and thirty-three consonants from *'ka'* to *'ha'*. Along with *'llam'* and *'ksa'* they make fifty-one letters. It is not known what the fifty-second letter of Kumārajīva was. Even then, the presence of the name *Hsi-t'anchang* in this Dun-huang text corroborates that he prepared this textbook to teach the script and probably some elements of grammar to his disciples.

4. Kumārajīva and the *Fan-ch'ieh* Spelling Method

4.1. The *Fan-ch'ieh* Spelling

One of the reasons for some Chinese intellectuals to evince interest in the Siddham letters is the phonetic information embedded in them. By the time Buddhism arrived, the number of Chinese characters had proliferated to such an extent that they desperately needed some means to indicate their readings. The *tu-jo* 讀若 system they evolved for giving the reading of a character with the help of another was found to be thoroughly inadequate. Then came the phonetic spelling method called *fan-ch'ieh* 反切, where two characters gave the reading of a character. The first one gave the initial consonant, and the second one gave the rest, called final or rhyme. For example, the word *tung* 東 was

6 Shūei 宗叡, *Shosha Shōrai Hōmontō Mokuroku* 書寫樽怯法門等日札, TSDK, V. 55, No. 2174A, p. 1110M.

7 Jao Tsung-i, "The Four Liquid Vowels, R, Q, L, Ḷ, of Sanskrit and their Influence on Chinese Literature – Notes on Kumārajīva's *T'ung Yun*", *The Adyar Library Bulletin*, Nos. 3132, 1967-68, pp. 582-83.

8 Jao Tsung-i, p. 582.

expressed with the two characters *te* 德 and *hung* 紅 with the character *fan* 反 or *ch'ieh* 切 added below as a technical term to tell the reader that the initial /t-/ should be taken from *te* and the final /-ung/ should be taken from *hung*, and the character should be read as *tung*. This method worked remarkably well and has remained in vogue ever since. The mechanism of *fan-chieh* discussed above shows that the concept of consonants is vitally important here.

The role of Sanskrit in the invention of *fan-chieh* has been a highly disputed topic for a very long time, some acknowledging and some totally denying its role. Yen Chih-t'ui 顏之推 (CE 531-591) is the earliest scholar to take up the question of the origin of *fan-ch'ieh*. He associates Sun Yen 孫炎, who lived towards the end of the Han period (early 3rd century) with the origin of *fan-ch'ieh* in his *Yen-shih-chia-hsün* 訓.[9] He does not mention Sanskrit at all. The 9th century Japanese monk Annen, however, writes in his *Shittanzō* that the system was first devised by Fu Ch'ien, who flourished around 168.[10] As against this, the Sung 宋 period (9601279) scholars attribute Western origin to *fan-ch'ieh*. For instance, Shen Kua 沈括 writes in his *Meng-hsi-pi-t'an* 談 that the science of *fan-ch'ieh* came from the Western Regions.[11]

Some modern scholars, however, dispute the hypotheses of Yen Chih-t'ui and Annen saying that the periods they mention are too early. They suspect that the earliest instances of *fan-chieh* were additions of a later date. At present, it is generally thought that the Chinese had already hit upon the idea of *fan-chieh* when Sanskrit arrived on the scene, and that Sanskrit provided the theoretical basis for refining it and its general acceptance.[12]

It is generally agreed that *fan-chieh* was used extensively during the Six Dynasties period (222-589). An important attribute in *fan-chieh* is the addition of the character *fan* 反 to the spelling. This practice started in the North-South dynasties period (420-589), first in conversation, and then in writing.[13]

Thus, it is very clear that the concept of consonants is vitally important for *fan-chieh*. As we know, the Varṇamālā gives the letters in two separate categories, vowels and consonants, and a student is likely to form a good concept of consonants from this work. The concept of *fan-chieh* that was nebulous got a concrete theoretical basis. Kumārajīva's students must have

---

[9] Yen Chih-t'ui 顏之推, *Yen-shih-chia-hsün* 顏氏家訓; Utsunomiya, Kiyoshi 宇都宮清吉, tr., *Ganshi Kakun* 顏氏家訓, Chūgoku Koten Bungaku Taikei 中国古典文学大系, V. 9, Heibonsha 平凡社, Tokyo, 1977, pp. 568T, 580B-581T.

[10] Annen 安然, *Shittanzō* 悉曇藏, TSDK, V. 84, p. 382T.

[11] Shen Kua 沈括, *Meng-his-pi-t'an* 夢渓筆談, Umehara, Kaoru 梅原郁, tr., *Mukei Hitsudan* 夢渓筆談, V. 2, Heibonsha 平凡社, Tokyo, 1989, p. 107.

[12] Konishi, Jinichi 小西甚一, *Bunkyō Hifuronkō* 文鏡秘府論考, V. 1, Daihachishu Shuppan Co. Ltd. 第八洲出版, Kyoto, 1948, pp. 179, 187.

[13] Konishi, p. 184.

discussed the novel idea with their academic friends, and they all played a major role in its acceptance and dissemination.

Let us see the concept of consonants from the angle of the Mantra of Forty-Two Letters that appears in *Mo-ho-po-jo-po-lo-mi-ching* translated by Kumārajīva in 403.[14] A look at the first few letters *a, ra, pa, ca, na,* - of the mantra will show that they are syllables consisting of a consonant and a vowel. The Chinese also had similar syllables. It is likely that Kumārajīva, with his command over Chinese could explain the concept of consonants to his disciples, and they disseminated the concept to others.

5. Kumārajīva and Chinese Prosody

5.1. Recent Style Poetry

The Recent Style Poetry (*Chin-t'i-shi* 近體詩) is a special genre of poems based on the tonal prosody initiated by Shen Yüeh 沈約 (441-513) and his associates, and perfected by successive generations of poets. Its importance can be judged from the fact that it became an important component of the Chinese civil service examination. It is popular even today.

5.2. Literary Discussions of Kumārajīva

Kumārajīva's biography says that he discussed literary styles of the West with his disciples. After explaining the similarities and dissimilarities, he says that in India, the common people consider the poetical rhythms that can be played on stringed instruments to be better. In the ceremony of visiting the Buddha, it is considered to be a noble thing to sing in his praise. All the *gāthās* in the sūtras are also in this form. He also composed ten poems.[15] It can be well imagined that some of his disciples, being highly educated and engaged in translating *gāthās*, the verses in the sūtras, evinced interest in Sanskrit poetics. Because of his command over Chinese he was most suited to explain Sanskrit prosody to his disciples. This may have been one of the sources of the Recent Style Poetry. However, it should be kept in mind that about a century separates youthful Shen Yüeh from Kumārajīva.

5.3. Eastern and Western Prosodies

Kao-seng-chuan 高雎傳 of Hui Chiao 慧皎 (c. 530) makes a brief comparison of Sanskrit and Chinese poems while discussing recitation of Buddhist hymns and *gāthās*, known by the name *fan-pai* 梵唄 in its thirteenth fascicle. Here it says that poems in the Eastern countries are made up of a succession of rhyming finals (*chi-y n* 結韻), whereas in the Western Regions, the hymns are made up of harmonizing sounds (*ho-sheng* 和聲). Sanskrit words are polysyllabic (*ch'ung-*

14 Kumārajīva, *Mo-ho-po-jo-po-lo-mi-ching* 摩訶般若波羅蜜經, TSDK, V. 8, p. 256T-M.

15 Seng-yu, p. 101B7-15.

fu 重複), while Chinese is monosyllabic (*tan-ch'I* 單奇單奇). Chanting Chinese poems with a Sanskrit accent sounds cumbersome to Chinese ears. Finals get shortened and phrases get elongated when Chinese song forms are used to chant Sanskrit texts.[16] The time period mentioned here is from around 345 to 494. In short, a section of Chinese literati was exposed to Sanskrit poetics up to the time when Shen Yüeh (441-513) proposed his Recent Style Poetry.

5.4. Changes in Chinese Prosody

Traditionally, Chinese poems consisted of a variable number of syllables per line and a variable number of lines per poem. Again, they were meant for singing; so they were set to music. Two important changes occurred in Chinese poetry around the time the Recent Style Poetry appeared.

One is that the pentasyllabic verse became the dominant form. In this style, each line consisted of five syllables, and the number of lines in a poem consisted of multiples of two. Pentasyllabic verse was just one of the styles at the time of Kumārajīva. A study of the *gāthās* in the Lotus Sūtra of Kumārajīva shows that they come in two styles, pentasyllabic and hexasyllabic, the vast majority being in the pentasyllabic form. The number of lines in Kumārajīva's translations of *gāthās* are multiples of two. The Lotus Sūtra was enormously influential during the period that followed Kumārajīva. Perhaps, the Lotus Sūtra played an important role in championing the pentasyllabic style.

The other is the switch over from singing to reciting. The *gāthās* were chanted. In short, the preference around the time tonal prosody appeared, was to recite poems rather than singing them.[17] Did the disciples of Kumārajīva play an important role in bringing about this change also?

5.5. Characteristics of Recent Style Poetry

One of the basic features of the Recent Style Poetry is the bifurcation of the four tones into two prosodic categories, level (*ping* 平) and deflected (*ts^* 仄). Level is the level tone (*pingshn̂g* 平聲), and it is long. Deflected is made up of three tones, rising (*shang-shn̂g* 上聲), departing (*ch'u-shn̂g* 去聲), and entering (*ju-shn̂g* 入聲), and it is short.[18] This was done to introduce into Chinese prosody the concept of metres of Sanskrit prosody, where the opposition between long and short syllables, called *laghu* (short) and *guru* (long), plays a cardinal role. These two terms were translated literally as *chi'ng* 輕 and *chung* 重 by Chinese

---

[16] *Kao-seng-chuan* 高雎傳, TSDK, V. 50, 414B24-25, 415T10-12.

[17] For instance, Chung Yung says as follows: Let me try to make it clear. What in ancient times were called poems and hymns were all accompanied on instruments of metal or bamboo. ... This meant that they emphasised music and rhyme. ... I say that literary creations should be chanted. ...

[18] Bodman *Poetics and Prosody in Early Mediaevel China: A Study and Translation of Kukai's Bunkyo Hifuron*, UMI issertation Services, Michigan, 1999, pp. 121-22. Bodman mentions "Chüan hsia" of *Nan-ch'ih-shu* (or *Nan-shih* ?), p. 1a, SPPY ed., as the source.) Chung Yung flourished during the Southern Ch'i period (479-502).

prosodists. The object was to bring Sanskrit-like euphonic effects in Chinese poems that was lacking till then.

An example of application of *laghu* (level) and *guru* (deflected) in Recent Style Poetry will be seen here. The Recent Style Poetry comes in a number of forms. In the form called 'changing the head' (*huan-t'ou* 換頭), the first two characters in the first line are level, the first two characters in the second line are deflected; the first two characters in the third line are deflected, the first two characters in the fourth line are level; and this format goes on. The third and the fourth lines are a mirror image of the first and the second lines.[19]

Another important feature of the Recent Style Poetry is poetic defect, the inspiration of which can be traced to yamaka (repetition of sounds in the feet) and *dośa* (poetic blemish) of Sanskrit prosody. Shen Yüeh 沈約 mentions eight defects, some of which have striking similarity with *yamaka* and *doṣa*. These ideas are also totally new in Chinese prosody, and it is difficult to identify the sources from which Shen Yüeh got these ideas. One is discussed below.

Shen Yüeh says that in a pentasyllabic verse, the first and the sixth syllables should not be in the same tone. In other words, the first syllables of two successive lines should not be in the same tone. Shen Yüeh called this Level Head (*p'ing-t'ou* 徘頭) defect.[20] In *Nāṭyaśātra*, Bharata defines the *pādādi* (beginning of a foot) *yamaka* as the case where a similar word or syllable occurs at the beginning of two successive feet.[21]

6. Study

China, around the time when the monks started translating the scripture, had some highly educated Chinese who were curious to know about the new ideas brought by the barbarian monks from the West. Some of them came forward to collaborate in translating the scripture.

Kumārajīva was one of the very few foreigners who gained real mastery over the Chinese language. His translation of the *Saddharma-puṇḍarīka-sūtra* is considered to be a masterpiece of Chinese literature. He had a paramount position in the Chinese Buddhist establishment. It may be assumed that his activities created a surge of interest in Sanskrit. The earliest indication of learning Sanskrit by the Chinese is suggested by *Hsi-t'an-mu* 悉曇慕 (Admirable Siddham) listed in Tao-an's catalogue. Unfortunately the book is lost. The repeated mention of *Hsi-t'an-chang* 悉談章 of Kumārajīva strongly suggests that he actually taught Sanskrit to his disciples.

---

19 Liu T'ao 劉滔 who flourished around 547 CE says that the level tone is long and drawn-out and is used most frequently. Compared with the other three, the syllables of this tone constitute a majority. This statement shows that the Chinese prosodists considered level tone to be long and the deflected tones to be short.

20 Kōzen Hiroshi 興膳宏, Tr., *Bunkyō Hifuron* 文鏡秘府論, *Kōbō Daishi Kūkai Zenshū* 弘法大師空海全集, V. 5, Chikuma shobō, 1986, Tokyo, p. 601; Bodman, p. 126.

21 *Bunkyō Hifuron*, p. 42-43; Bodman, 202-03.

Although about a century separates Shen Yüeh from Kumārajīva, the likelihood of Shen Yüeh's inspiration dating back to Kumārajīva cannot be ruled out. While translating sūtras, Kumārajīva (401-413) discussed Sanskrit poems with his disciples. Being prolific writers, some of collaborators may have written whatever they understood, and these circulated among the interested. If this is correct, then a small group appeared with interest in Sanskrit prosody. Next comes Hui Chiao's discussion of Sanskrit and Chinese poetics. The time period is from around 345 to 494. Then came Recent Style Poetry of Shen Yüeh (441-513) with features bearing striking similarities with those of Sanskrit poems. The three dates are so close to each other that a continuum cannot be ruled out.

It is likely that the Chinese wrote about their experiences with Tao-an's *Hsi-t'an-mu* and Kumārajīva's *Hsi-t'an-chang*. These remained confined to a limited circle, and being outside the scope of mainstream academic activities, they failed to attract the attention of mainstream scholars, and soon went into oblivion. The apathy of the Chinese academic world towards barbarian ideas, however important they may be, is illustrated by the Recent Style Poetry. The Chinese wrote about the technicalities involved in the Recent Style Poetry that can be readily associated with Sanskrit prosody, but no such writings survived in China. It was another barbarian from the East, the famous monk Kūkai, to whom we owe our information on the indebtedness of Recent Style Poetry to Sanskrit prosody. He copied the Chinese writings on Recent Style Poetry around CE 806 and brought it back to Japan. This is the only information we have today.

7. Conclusion

China had a highly developed academic society when the Buddhist monks started their translation activities. Some of the intellectuals evinced interest in the ideas of the new creed of the monks, and collaborated in translating its scripture. While translating, some of the collaborators became interested in the language of the scripture. Thereafter, textbooks of the language appeared, and the linguistic information carried by the script proved to be highly attractive. This information was important for devising the *fan-ch'ieh* spelling method for the Chinese characters. The Recent Style Poetry borrowed heavily from Sanskrit prosody. It is certain that the Chinese wrote about their experiences with foreign academic ideas, but very little of these writings has survived because of the apathy of the Chinese academic world towards foreign academic ideas.

BIBLIOGRAPHY

1. Yoshikawa, Tadao. 1991. *Scholarship in Ching-chou at the End of the Later Han Dynasty.* Tokyo. Acta Asiatica. V. 60. Tōhō Gakkai. pp. 1-3.
2. Ch'en, Kenneth K.S.. 1973. *Buddhism in China, A Historical Survey.* Princeton. Princeton University Press. p. 42.
3. Seng-yu 雌童. Ch'u-san-tsang-chi-chi 出三欟記集, *Taishō Shinshū Daizōkyō* 大正新修藏經 (TSDK), V. 55, 2145, p. 18M22.
4. For instance, Chih-kuang 智廣, *Hsi-t'an-tzu-chi* 悉曇字記, TSDK, V. 54, p.1186M2
5. Seng-yu 僧童, p. 101B7-11.
6. Shūei 宗叡, *Shosha Shōrai Hōmontō Mokuroku* 書寫樽怯法門等目札, TSDK, V. 55, No. 2174A, p. 1110M.
7. Jao Tsung-i, "The Four Liquid Vowels, R, Q, L, of Sanskrit and their Influence on Chinese Literature – Notes on Kumārajāāva's *T'ung Yun", The Adyar Library Bulletin,* Nos. 31-32, 1967-68, pp. 582-83.
8. Jao Tsung-i, p. 582.
9. Yen Chih-t'ui 顔之推, *Yen-shih-chia-hsün* 顔氏家訓; Utsunomiya, Kiyoshi 宇都宮清吉, tr., *Ganshi Kakun* 顔氏家訓, Chūgoku Koten Bungaku Taikei 中国古典文学大系, V. 9, Heibonsha 平凡社, Tokyo, 1977, pp. 568T, 580B-581T.
10. Annen 安然, *Shittanzō* 悉曇藏, TSDK, V. 84, p. 382T.
11. Shen Kua 沈括, *Meng-his-pi-t'an* 夢渓筆談, Umehara, Kaoru 梅原郁, tr., Mukei Hitsudan 夢渓筆談, V. 2, *Heibonsha* 平凡社, Tokyo, 1989, p. 107.
12. Konishi, Jinichi 小西甚一, *Bunkyō Hifuronkō* 文鏡秘府論考, V. 1, Daihachishu Shuppan Co. Ltd. 第八洲出版, Kyoto, 1948, pp. 179, 187.
13. Konishi, p. 184.
14. Kumārajāāva, *Mo-ho-po-jo-po-lo-mi-ching* 摩訶般若波羅蜜經, TSDK, V. 8, p. 256T-M.
15. Seng-yu, p. 101B7-15.
16. *Kao-seng-chuan* 高雌傳, TSDK, V. 50, 414B24-25, 415T10-12.
17. For instance, Chung Yung says as follows: Let me try to make it clear. What in ancient times were called poems and hymns were all accompanied on instruments of metal or bamboo. … This meant that they emphasised music and rhyme. … I say that literary creations should be chanted. …

    Bodman *Poetics and Prosody in Early Mediaevel China: A Study and Translation of Kukai's Bunkyo Hifuron,* UMI issertation Services, Michigan, 1999, pp. 121-22. Bodman mentions *"Chüan hsia"* of *Nan-ch'ih-shu* (or *Nan-shih* ?), p. 1a, SPPY ed., as the source.) Chung Yung flourished during the Southern Ch'i period (479-502).
18. Liu T'ao 劉滔 who flourished around 547 CE says that the level tone is long and drawn-out and is used most frequently. Compared with the other three, the syllables of this tone constitute a majority. This statement shows that the Chinese prosodists considered level tone to be long and the deflected tones to be short.

    Kōzen Hiroshi 興膳宏, Tr., *Bunkyō Hifuron* 文鏡秘府論, *Kōbō Daishi Kūkai Zenshū* 弘法大師空海全集, V. 5, Chikuma shobō, 1986, Tokyo, p. 601; Bodman, p. 126.
19. *Bunkyō Hifuron,* p. 42-43; Bodman, 202-03.
20. *Bunkyō Hifuron,* p. 580; Victor H. Mair, Tsu-lin Mei, p. 462.
21. Bharata, *The NāTyaśātra of Bharatamuni,* Tr., A Board of Scholars, Sri Satguru Publications, India Book Centre, Delhi, 2000, 248; Victor H. Mair, Tsu-lin Mei, p. 465.

8

From Kumārajīva to Nichiren - connected through Myoho-Renge-Kyō

Yoichi Kawada

1. Introduction: From Indian Buddhism to Chinese Buddhism traditionally, Indian Buddhism is said to have been transmitted to China during the Later Han dynasty under the rule of Emperor Ming (67 CE)[1]. Although there is debate about the historical accuracy of this account, it can be said that without a doubt that Buddhism had entered China by the 1st century.

For Buddhism, which originated in the 5th century BCE upon a foundation of the wide expanse of Indian spirituality, to enter and be accepted by Chinese civilization is in literal terms, a defining moment in the history of the world.

Indian and Chinese civilizations have from ancient times been the two major influences in the Eastern world, each with its own unique thinking, philosophy, and culture. So naturally, when Buddhism was transmitted from India to China, the fundamental principles of Indian Buddhism were kept, but were also coloured by elements that made Chinese Buddhism unique in itself.

Indispensable to the transmitting of Buddhism from India to China are the monk-translators who traversed the Western Region to arrive in China. Historically speaking, the first monk- translator was An Shigao from Parthia, and the next was Lokakṣema from Yuezhi. An Shigao principally translated the Theravāda Sūtras, whereas Lokakṣema translated the early Mahāyāna Sūtras such as the Aṣṭasāhasrikā-prajñāpāramitā Sūtra and the Pratyutpañña Sūtra.

---

[1] *Taishō Tripitaka,* vol.49, p.329.

There were many others that followed, but it was Zhu Fahu from Dunhuang who translated the Lotus Sūtra, Wisdom Sūtra, Vimalakīrti Sūtra and the Buddha Infinite Life Sūtra.

From the end of the Han Dynasty to the Six Dynasties era in China, Buddhism was accepted alongside Taoism, and Buddhist philosophy co-existed with the teachings of Laozi and Zhuangzi as complementary ideas. For example, the Taoist principle of *wu*, or nonbeing, is used to explain the concept of *Sūnyatā*, or non-substantiality, in the Wisdom Sūtra. In other words, this was called the "matching the meaning" method of describing Buddhism.

However, this method of interpreting Buddhism had its limits, as it could not explain the true meaning of the underlying principles. Daoan (314-85), the foremost disciple of Buddhaciṅga (ca.235-348) of Kucha, was one Chinese Buddhist leader who sought a more correct understanding of the teachings. It was Daoan who suggested inviting Kumārajīva to Ch'ang-an, where Fu Jian (338-85) of Former Qin had his capital. When Kumārajīva finally arrived in Ch'ang-an in 401, the Later Qin held power. For the next eight years, he translated approximately thirty-five works totaling three hundred volumes of Buddhist texts into Chinese under the patronage of the king, Yao Xing (366-416), according to the *Collection of Records concerning the Tripitaka*[2]. This period of time was when Buddhist concepts in their true form entered China.

Soka Gakkai International President Ikeda gives the following explanation as to why Kumārajīva's translations became widely regarded as superior to others in a book entitled, *The Flower of Chinese Buddhism*. Not only did he produce works that were noted for their skill and beauty of language, but he based himself squarely upon the philosophy of the Indian scholar Nāgārjuna, whose teachings represent the orthodox line of Mahāyāna doctrine. Thus, Kumārajīva carried out a task of inestimable merit in making certain that the Buddhist teachings were correctly transmitted to the Chinese. At the same time, we should recognize that the fact that such basic Mahāyāna texts as the Lotus Sūtra, the Great Wisdom Sūtra, and the Vimalakīrti Sūtra came to be so widely studied and revered throughout China was due not only to the superior nature of the ideas expressed in these texts but also to the fact that Kumārajīva's translations of them are couched in such powerful and compelling language.[3]

In his explanation, there are three reasons presented, with the first being Kumārajīva's mastery of languages. The language of Indian Buddhism, Sanskrit, and the Chinese language are fundamentally different in many aspects. Therefore, understanding the structure and nuances of both languages

[2] *Taishō Tripitaka*, vol.55, p.11.

[3] Daisaku Ikeda, *The Flower of Chinese Buddhism*, translated by Burton Watson, (Los Angeles: Middle Way Press, 2009), p.30.

was essential. In addition to these two languages, Kumārajīva was also well versed in the languages of the Western Region.

The second reason was the fact that Kumārajīva correctly transmitted the core philosophical concepts of Mahāyāna Buddhism, namely the concept of the Middle Way as described by Nāgārjuna. Kumārajīva translated *The Treatise on the Great Perfection of Wisdom* which is a commentary explaining *The Fundamental Verses on the Middle Way* and the Wisdom Sūtra. In *The Treatise on the Great Perfection of Wisdom*, many passages from the Lotus Sūtra are used. Other works such as *The One-Hundred Verse Treatise, The Treatise on the Twelve Gates, The Commentary on the Ten Stages Sūtra,* and *The Treatise on the Establishment of Truth* were also rendered in Chinese. In this way, a range of teachings from Theravāda Buddhism's Sarvāstivāda to the Wisdom Sūtra, and the concept of the Middle Way were introduced in China, forming the foundation for what later develops into Chinese Buddhism.

The third reason was the fact that a large number of Sūtras were translated by Kumārajīva, including the Lotus Sūtra, Larger Wisdom Sūtra, Smaller Wisdom Sūtra, Vimalakīrti Sūtra, as well as other Mahāyāna Sūtras like The Sūraṣ Ṣūraṅgama Samadhi Sūtra, The Amida Sūtra, and other texts such as *The Ten Divisions of Monastic Rules*. Taking these and other important works from Indian Buddhism, Kumārajīva's translations greatly impacted the development of Chinese Buddhism, also known as Sectarian Buddhism. One of the leading schools of this period is the Tiantai School, which based its teachings on the Kumārajīva translation of the Lotus Sūtra. In order to further explain this Sūtra, the founder of the school, Tiantai Zhiyi, developed the theory of three thousand realms in a single moment of life.

Sectarian Buddhism of China was transmitted to the Korean peninsula, and from there to Japan. In Japan, the Kumārajīva's translation of the Lotus Sūtra, whose title is pronounced *Myoho-renge-kyō* in Japanese, was revered by Prince Shotoku and became the central Sūtra for the Japanese Tendai Sect, and helped contribute to the development of Heian culture.

In Japan, the person who most fully internalized the teachings of the Lotus Sūtra translated by Kumārajīva was a priest by the name of Nichiren (1222-1282) in the 13th century. Following in the tradition of Śākyamuni and his enlightenment under the Bodhi tree to Nāgārjuna's philosophy of the Middle Way and to Tiantai's theory of three thousand realms in a single moment of life, Nichiren took on Kumārajīva's translation of the Lotus Sūtra as his core Buddhist scripture and established a new Buddhist sect.

In the 20th century, the Soka Gakkai has continued this tradition and the Soka Gakkai International (SGI) has developed the movement on a global scale. This paper will focus on Nichiren and his appraisal and analysis of

Kumārajīva's translation of the Lotus Sūtra. In addition, this paper will examine just how the Soka Gakkai and SGI have realized Nichiren's philosophy for humankind in the 21st century.

2. Kumārajīva in Nichiren's writings: References to Kumārajīva appear forty-three times throughout Nichiren's writings. In this part of the paper, I would like to discuss three particular aspects of the historical view of Kumārajīva, and introduce passages in Nichiren's writings related to these aspects. Then, in the section following, I will discuss an analysis of the Lotus Sūtra from the standpoint of Nichiren Buddhism. The first aspect is Sūryasoma's prediction of Kumārajīva's mission. In the writing entitled, "The Sūtra of True Requital," Nichiren states:

Some two hundred or more years after Buddhism was brought to China, a man known as the Tripiṭaka Master Kumārāyaṇa lived in a country called Kucha, located between India and China. His son, Kumārajīva, journeyed from Kucha to India, where he received instruction on the Lotus Sūtra from the Tripiṭaka Master Sūryasoma. On entrusting Kumārajīva with the Sūtras, Sūryasoma said to him, "This Lotus Sūtra has a deep connection with a country to the northeast."

With these words in mind, Kumārajīva set out to carry the Sūtras to the region east of India, to the land of China.[4]

Another passage, entitled "On the Five Guides for Propagation," reads:

Seng-chao's Afterword to the Lotus Sūtra Translation states, "The Great Teacher Sūryasoma held the Lotus Sūtra in his left hand and with his right patted Kumārajīva on the head and charged him as follows, saying, 'The sun of the Buddha has set in the west, but its lingering rays shine over the northeast. This text is destined for the lands of the northeast. You must make certain that it is transmitted there.'"

When I respectfully peruse this passage from Seng-chao's text, my eyes overflow with cascades of tears and my whole body is filled with joy. "This text is destined for the lands of the northeast," it says. India, the land of the western sky, lies in the southwest, while Japan, the land of the eastern sky, lies in the northeast. If someone in India speaks of something being "destined for the lands of the northeast," how can this fail to refer to the country of Japan?[5]

Both passages, refer to a quote from *The Afterword to the Lotus Sūtra Translation*[6] written by Seng-chao (384-414), who is one of the foremost disciples of Kumārajīva. The quote is referring to the story when Sūryasoma entrusts the Lotus Sūtra to a young Kumārajīva, and tells him of a future vision in

[4] Nichiren, *The Writings of Nichiren Daishonin* vol.1, (Tokyo: Soka Gakkai, 1999), p.928.

[5] Nichiren, *The Writings of Nichiren Daishonin* vol.2, (Tokyo: Soka Gakkai, 2006), pp.557-8.

[6] *The Afterword to the Lotus Sutra Translation* in the *Taishō Tripitaka*, vol.51, p.54.

which Kumārajīva transmits this teaching to the people of the northeast, as they have a deep connection with the Lotus Sūtra. Sūryasoma's words are quoted in both passages, "The sun of the Buddha has set in the west, but its lingering rays shine over the northeast," and "You must make certain that it is transmitted there." The meaning contained within these quotes are that the sun, i.e. the Buddha and his wisdom, had fallen behind the western mountains, but the remaining light still shines on in the lands in the northeast, in other words, symbolizing the fact that this message of the Buddha must be transmitted there. This is the reason Kumārajīva gives for travelling from the Western Region to China and translating the Lotus Sūtra into Chinese.

Nichiren interprets the land northeast of India from this passage in *The Afterword* as meaning Japan. In a different writing, entitled, "On Protection of the Nation," he states, "The word 'northeast' refers to Japan, because Japan is situated to the northeast of India, which is in the southwest,"[7] and in yet another passage from "The Meaning of the Sacred Teachings of the Buddha's Lifetime," he states, "I would like to note that Japan is in the region that lies northeast of India."[8] Nichiren took the Kumārajīva translation of the Lotus Sūtra as the embodiment of the Buddha's will, and took it upon himself as his personal mission to spread this teaching from Japan to the rest of the world.

The second historical aspect mentioned in Nichiren's writings about Kumārajīva is the illuminating power of Kumārajīva's translation. In the writing entitled, "Attaining Buddhahood in One's Present Form," Nichiren states:

There were 176 persons who conveyed the Sūtras and treatises of Buddhism from India to China. Among these, Kumārajīva alone passed along the Sūtra texts of Śākyamuni, the lord of teachings, just as they were without adding any private opinions of his own. Among the remaining 175 persons, 164 lived shortly before or after the time of Kumārajīva, and their work can be judged in the light of Kumārajīva's wisdom. In fact, his work brought to light the errors of these 164 men and also the errors of the eleven translators who later produced the so-called new translations, though they were somewhat cleverer than the earlier translators because they had Kumārajīva's work to guide them.[9]

And in the writing entitled, "On Reprimanding Hachiman," he states:

It should be noted, however, that there was a total of 187 translators who carries out the task of transmitting the Sūtras from India to the land of China. With the exception of one man, the Tripiṭaka Master Kumārajīva, all the other 186, when

[7] *The Writings of Nichiren Daishonin* vol.2, p.143.
[8] *The Writings of Nichiren Daishonin* vol.2, p.57.
[9] *The Writings of Nichiren Daishonin* vol.2, p.587.

they produced their translations, added water to the milk of the teachings and mixed poison with the medicine.[10]

According to the *The Kaiyuan Era Catalog of the Buddhist Canon*[11] there were 176 people who worked on the old and new translations, and according to the *The Zhenyuan Era Catalog of the Buddhist Canon*[12] there were 187 people who were translators of Buddhist scriptures.

Borrowing from the explanations in these two documents, Nichiren stresses the fact that Kumārajīva was the only translator that "alone passed along the Sūtras texts of Śākyamuni, the lord of teachings, just as they were without adding any private opinions of his own," and that the others, "added water to the milk of the teachings and mixed poison with the medicine." However, Nichiren was not the only person that thought Kumārajīva was the only translator that maintained the integrity of the Buddha's true intent. Daoxuan (596-667) of the T'ang Dynasty also speaks of Kumārajīva's illuminating power in *The Record of Miraculous Instruction on Matters of Monastic Rules*.

The translations of the Sūtras by Kumārajīva are unsurpassed even now despite the newer translations. The reason being, Kumārajīva had great mastery of the Mahāyāna teachings, whereas others only had a shallow understanding, demonstrating fading in later ages, illuminating former ages.[13]

In this passage, the illuminating power of Kumārajīva's translation is explained from two perspectives. One perspective is that in the translations that follow Kumārajīva's, there is none that can compare in skillfulness. This is what is meant by "fading in later ages." The other perspective is that the translations previous to Kumārajīva, i.e. translations made during the Later Han to Later Qin era, become clear as if a light had been shone on them, hence, "illuminating former ages." In other words, the errors made in earlier translations came to light when compared to Kumārajīva's translations, and translations that came later used Kumārajīva as a base, therefore lack originality. Because Kumārajīva kept his personal opinion out of his translations, Śākyamuni's enlightenment was transmitted in its entirety and without error in Chinese.

The Sūtras are an expression from various perspectives of the fundamental law of the universe (Dharma) that Śākyamuni discovered within his own inner cosmos when sitting under the Bodhi tree. Because of the various ways in which the Buddha explained his enlightenment, the Sūtras are said to number 80,000.

---

[10] *The Writings of Nichiren Daishonin* vol.2, pp.921-2.

[11] *Taishō Tripitaka*, vol.55, p.477.

[12] *Taishō Tripitaka*, vol.55.

[13] Translation from Japanese. *The Record of Miraculous Instruction on Matters of Monastic Rules* in the *Taishō Tripitaka*, vol. 44. Note: Another translation of the title of this writing which appears in *The Writings of Nichiren Daishonin* vol.2, p.587 is *On Questions about the Practical Aspect of Precepts*.

As explained in the introduction of this paper, in order to correctly understand the Buddha's intent within these teachings and to be able to accurately translate them from Sanskrit to Chinese, Kumārajīva's skills were invaluable. That is, in order to correctly translate the Sūtras, it was first necessary to have mastered both Sanskrit and Chinese, which are so linguistically different; second, to have a correct understanding of the Buddha's will by having studied both Theravāda and Mahāyāna Sūtras; and third to have fully understood the significance of Nāgārjuna's philosophy of the Middle Way.

Lacking knowledge of either Sanskrit or Chinese would compromise the translation process, creating misunderstandings and losing the intended message of the Buddha. Furthermore, lacking a correct understanding of the philosophy of the Middle Way would lead to a distorted view of the system of Mahāyāna and Theravāda teachings, giving undue emphasis to one particular Sūtra or concept, which would in turn promote a misguided or personal interpretation, warping the correct view of Śākyamuni's teachings. Nichiren expresses these misunderstandings, prejudices, and personal interpretations as "adding water to the milk" and "mix[ing] poison with the medicine."

Nichiren, taking these points into account and compiling various sources of information about the translators of the Sūtras, concluded that Kumārajīva was the only one that faithfully conveyed Śākyamuni's enlightenment from Sanskrit into Chinese.

Kumārajīva himself must have undoubtedly realized this fact, and to attest to this, Nichiren focuses on the legend of Kumārajīva's tongue not being consumed by the flames during his cremation.

The third aspect that Nichiren mentions about Kumārajīva is the legend of his unburned tongue. In the writing entitled, "A Sage and an Unenlightened Man," Nichiren states: "...Hence the Tripiṭaka Master Kumārajīva of the Later Ch'in dynasty always used to say: 'When I examine the Buddhist teachings as they exist in China, I find that in many cases they differ from the Sanskrit originals. If the Sūtra translations that I have produced are free from error, then, after I am dead and cremated, my body, since it is impure, will no doubt be consumed by the flames, but my tongue alone will not be burned.' And when he was finally cremated, his body was reduced to a pile of bones, but his tongue alone remained, resting on top of a blue lotus blossom and emitting a brilliant light that outshone the rays of the sun. What a wonderful thing!

"Thus it came about that the translations of the Lotus Sūtra made by the Tripiṭaka Master Kumārajīva in particular spread easily throughout China."[14]

[14] *The Writings of Nichiren Daishonin* vol.1, p.113.

This story appears in *The Biographies of Eminent Priests*[15] and *The Kaiyuan Era Catalog of the Buddhist Canon*[16]. Nichiren, by introducing this legend, is providing support for the position that Kumārajīva himself felt, that his translation of the Sūtras from Sanskrit into Chinese express Śākyamuni's enlightenment just as it was. In particular, Nichiren wanted future generations to widely know that Kumārajīva's translation of the Lotus Sūtra most accurately portrays the fundamental law of the universe (Dharma) discovered by Śākyamuni. Because of its accuracy, this version of the Lotus Sūtra, sometimes called the Lotus Sūtra of the Wonderful Law, became known as the best translation of the Lotus Sūtra and spread throughout China, Japan, and Eastern Asia, and as I will discuss further in the following section, adopted by Nichiren as the core text for Nichiren Buddhism.

In *The Flower of Chinese Buddhism*, SGI President Ikeda also contemplates this legend from a contemporary perspective, and explains it in the following way:

> *To a person committed to rational thought, this story may be rather difficult to accept, yet Kumārajīva's disciples claimed to have witnessed the event and took care to record it as proof to later ages that Kumārajīva's numerous translations of the sacred texts were free from error.*
>
> *....there is no doubt that Kumārajīva's translations mark the pinnacle of Chinese Buddhist translation and continue to shine with undimmed luster even today. In particular, his translation of the Lotus Sūtras, a work that represents the highest expression of the Buddhist teachings, has over the millennium and a half since its appearance been read and admired by more people than any other translation of the Sūtras. The story of the tongue that survived the flames may be taken as symbolic of his achievement. Though Kumārajīva himself passed away many centuries ago, his translation of the Lotus Sūtra remains an imperishable treasure to be passed down through the ages.*[17]

3. Kumārajīva's Lotus Sūtra of the Wonderful Law and Nichiren Buddhism: In the fifth century B.C., Śākyamuni sat under a Bodhi tree and deeply meditated until the light of wisdom shined to reveal the great cosmos within, and ultimately to the fundamental law of the universe (Dharma). The moment the Dharma became manifest is recorded in the *Udāna*:

> *When things become manifest*
>
> *To the ardent meditating brāhmaṇa,*
>
> *He abides scattering Māra's host*
>
> *Like the sun illumining the sky.*[18]

[15] *Taishō Tripitaka*, vol.50, p.333.
[16] *Taishō Tripitaka*, vol.55, p.513.
[17] *The Flower of Chinese Buddhism*, p.51-2.
[18] See *Udana* http://www.accesstoinsight.org/tipitaka/kn/ud/ud.1.01.irel.html

The "things [that] become manifest" mentioned here refers to the fundamental law of the universe. Śākyamuni's enlightenment was the realization of the inner cosmos within the life of one human being as the fundamental law of the universe. The grand state of life that manifested when realizing this law was like the sun rising to dispel the fundamental darkness that lies within all living things (the devil's army), and crushing all earthly desires.

This Dharma becomes the "Thus Come One" and forms the basis of Mahāyāna Buddhism, which teaches that the cause which allows all people to attain enlightenment is the Buddha nature or Storehouse of the Thus Come One contained within the depths of all life.

Institute of Oriental Philosophy researcher Hiroshi Kanno says:

> *It is said that under the Bodhi tree is where Śākyamuni was awakened to the Dhamma and the Saddharma. The compliers of the Lotus Sūtra took name of the Saddharma in Sanskrit equivalent to its Pali counterpart to use as the name of the Sūtra, calling it, Saddharma-puṇḍarīka-sūtra (Lotus Sūtra), and placing it as the ultimate law preached by all the Buddhas.*[19]

The Lotus Sūtra proclaims that it teaches the entrance of the path to enlightenment and *anuttara-samyak-sambodhi* to Bodhisattvas, and aims to help people achieve the state of *anuttara-samyak-sambodhi* by manifesting the Dharma like the sun described in the *Udāna*.

Nichiren believed that only Kumārajīva accurately translated Śākyamuni's enlightenment as it was from Sanskrit into Chinese. So how then was his enlightenment to the fundamental law of the universe described in the Lotus Sūtra of the Wonderful Law? Using Nichiren's writings as wisdom to guide us, let us take a look at (1) the title and (2) the philosophical content of Kumārajīva's translation.

The Title

The title of the Lotus Sūtra in Sanskrit is *Saddharma-puṇḍarīka-sūtra*. The first word "Sat" means "correct," therefore Zhu Fahu translated it as "correct law" (正法). However, Kumārajīva translated it as "mystic law" (妙法). The meaning of "mystic" (Jpn. *myo*) is explained by Dr. Lokesh Chandra in a dialogue with Ikeda entitled, *Buddhism: A Way of Values*.

Laozi's philosophy, which was very popular in China at that time, propounded that the fundamental truth of the universe was like a gate from which many mystic things appeared. In other words, things given birth to by

[19] Hiroshi Kanno, *Hokekyō Nyumon* [Introduction to the Lotus Sutra], (Tokyō: Iwanami, 2001), p.18.

the fundamental truth are "mystic" in nature.... meaning so mysterious that our minds are not able to comprehend it.[20]

Nichiren talks about the meaning of "mystic" in a writing entitled, "On Attaining Buddhahood in This Lifetime":

> *What then does myo signify? It is simply the mysterious nature of our life from moment to moment, which the mind cannot comprehend or words express.... It is the mystic entity of the Middle Way that is the ultimate reality. Myo is the name given to the mystic nature of life, and ho, to its manifestations.*[21]

Myo is the single mind, that is, the name given to the mysterious and fundamental cosmos within an individual, and the "mystic entity of the Middle Way" that expands within the depths of all life, which makes up the life of the universe itself, and is at one with the Dharma that pulsates through all. This deeper meaning could not be encompassed if translated as "correct law," therefore Kumārajīva translated it as "mystic law."

Next, *puṇḍarīka* literally means white lotus (白蓮華), but again in "On Attaining Buddhahood in this Lifetime," referring to the meaning contained within this phrase, Nichiren says, "*Renge* which means lotus flower, is used to symbolize the wonder of this law."[22] He explains that the "mystic law" is difficult to understand, so the metaphor of a white lotus is used. The unique features of the white lotus are fit to describe the "mystic law."

The first unique feature of the lotus blossom is its purity, as described in the fifteenth chapter of the Lotus Sūtra, "unsoiled by worldly things like the lotus flower in the water."[23] However, another feature that is represented by the lotus flower is the aspect of cause and effect. That is, the law of cause and effect is contained within the "mystic law" which is the fundamental life of the universe at one with the Dharma. In *The Record of the Orally Transmitted Teachings*, Nichiren states, "*Renge* stands for the two elements of cause and effect. Cause and effect are also a single entity."[24] Herein, he also explains that the nine worlds signify cause and that effect signifies the world of Buddhahood. Whereas other plants only produce fruit after they shed their leaves, the lotus plant flowers and bears fruit at the same time, so that by the time the flower petals fall, the fruit is also ripe. This flower is used to symbolize the single mind of the mystic law, which simultaneously contains the cause, i.e. the nine worlds, as well as the effect, i.e. the world of Buddhahood.

---

[20] See Lokesh Chandra and Daisaku Ikeda, *Buddhism: A Way of Values*, Eternal Ganges Press: New Delhi, 2009.

[21] *The Writings of Nichiren Daishonin* vol.1, p.4.

[22] *Ibid.*

[23] *The Lotus Sūtra*, translated by Burton Watson, New York: Columbia University Press, 1993, p.222.

[24] Nichiren, *The Record of the Orally Transmitted Teachings*, translated by Burton Watson, Tokyō: Soka Gakkai, 2004, p.4.

The translation of *Sūtra* is *kyō* (経), as the teachings of the Buddha are referred to as *kyō*. In *The Record of the Orally Transmitted Teachings*, Nichiren states:

> *Kyō* represents the words and voices of all living beings. A commentary [On "The Profound Meaning," volume one] says, "The voice carries out the work of the Buddha, and it is also called *kyō*." *Kyō* may also be defined as that which is constant and unchanging in the three existences of past, present, and future.[25]

Kyō represents the voice of the Buddha, conveying his enlightenment in his own words, and later, when recorded into a written form, has the power to save all living things for all eternity.

In this way, *myoho*, or the mystic law of cause and effect, *renge*, is expressed in linguistic form, *kyō*. Kumārajīva's translation of the title of the Lotus Sūtra of the Wonderful Law (妙法蓮華経) contains all of the deeper meanings mentioned above. The content of the Buddha's enlightenment, explained by the vast system of Buddhist philosophy, is encapsulated in its title: *Myoho-renge-kyō*.

The Philosophical Content

The Lotus Sūtra of the Wonderful Law is made up of twenty-eight chapters. However, when Kumārajīva originally translated this Sūtra, it only had twenty-seven and did not include the Devadatta chapter. This chapter was translated into Chinese by another person and added later to the Kumārajīva translation. By the time this Sūtra reached Tiantai, the full twenty-eight chapter version, including the Devadatta chapter, was available.

In his explanation of the Lotus Sūtra as a whole, Tiantai divides the Lotus Sūtra into two parts—viewing the first fourteen chapters as the provisional teachings and the latter fourteen chapters as the essential teachings. Borrowing from this analysis, Nichiren expresses Kumārajīva's intent in the following passage from *The Record of the Orally Transmitted Teachings*.

> Question: In the present text of the Lotus Sūtra, the "Introduction" chapter begins with the word, *nyo* (如), "this" or "like this," and the "Universal Worthy" chapter, the last chapter, ends with the word *ko* (去), "departed." This arrangement was made on purpose by the Tripiṭaka Master Kumārajīva, but what doctrinal principle is he attempting to express thereby?
>
> Answer: The essence of the teachings expressed in the Lotus Sūtra lies in the two principles of the true aspect of all phenomena and Śākyamuni Buddha's original enlightenment in the distant past. These constitute its

[25] *The Record of the Orally Transmitted Teachings*, p.4.

essential doctrines. The first word in the Sūtra, *nyo*, expresses the true aspect of all phenomena, while the last word, *ko*, expresses the event in the remote past. Hence, we may say that the true aspect of all phenomena represents the theory or principle (理 Jpn. *ri*) underlying the teaching, while the event in the remote past represents the factual realization (事 Jpn. *ji*) of the principle.[26]

The "Introduction" chapter of the Lotus Sūtra of the Wonderful Law begins with the words, "This is what I heard," and ends with the phrase, "they bowed in obedience and departed" in the final Universal Worthy chapter. Nichiren states the significance of the Lotus Sūtra starting with *nyo*, or this, and ending with *ko*, or departed.

The entity of the law expressed in the Lotus Sūtra contains both the provisional teaching of the true aspect and the essential teaching of the distant past. In addition, the first word, *nyo* (如), represents the true aspect of the provisional teaching and the last word, *ko* (去), represents the time without beginning of the essential teaching. In the second chapter of the Lotus Sūtra, The Expedient Means chapter, the phrase "true aspect of all phenomena" (諸法実相) appears. This refers to the fact that all phenomena, or everything that we see around us, is an embodiment of the Lotus Sūtra rooted in the true aspect. From a different perspective, this is an expression of the law that all living things that exist in the phenomenal nine worlds (九界) are all latently endowed with the world of Buddhahood (仏界).

However, this teaching is provisional, because it only states the theoretical possibility of realizing the world of Buddhahood within all life. Therefore, the true aspect represented by *nyo* is strictly theoretical.

In the sixteenth chapter, the Life Span of the Thus Come One chapter, which is in the essential teachings, Śākyamuni reveals the true nature of his enlightenment, and his identity as the Eternal Buddha from the distant past. Not only that, he conveys that he is the Eternal Savior Buddha who yearns to save all living things throughout time. In this way, using the life of Śākyamuni as an example, the way to realize Buddhahood within one's life is revealed, making the distant past represented by *ko*, a real application of the theory.

Basing the principle of the law on the provisional and essential teachings contained within the Lotus Sūtra of the Wonderful Law, Nichiren expounds on three central principles.

He talks first about the enlightenment of all living beings (万人成仏), second, the Eternal Buddha (久遠仏), and third, the practicing of the Bodhisattva Way (菩薩道). In regard to the first principle of the enlightenment of all living beings, Nichiren points to a quote in the Lotus Sūtra from the Expedient Means

[26] *The Record of the Orally Transmitted Teachings*, p.193-4.

Chapter which states, "[this] is the one great reason for which the Buddhas appear in the world."[27] As the principle of the true aspect of all phenomena explains, all people have a Buddha nature in the depths of their lives. To open the path and show the way to enlightenment (開示悟入) is the reason why the Buddha appears in this world. From the fact that all living beings have a Buddha nature and that it is possible to manifest it, forms the Buddhist rationale for the dignity of all life. As examples of the universality of this fact, the people of the two vehicles (二乗) and women are shown to be able to attain enlightenment in the Lotus Sūtra.

In other words, all people, regardless of race, sex, occupation, culture, ethnicity, birth, mental and physical condition, are endowed with a Buddha nature, and therefore are equally worthy of respect and dignity. This principle of enlightenment of all living beings establishes a basis for overcoming all discrimination and prejudices, to respect differences and create a society that supports mutual cooperation (共生). This is a model for a harmonious society. In addition, the endowment of a Buddha nature is not restricted to only human beings, but all living things as well, so this extends to a philosophy of dignity for all life. In the Parable of the Medicinal Herbs Chapter of the Lotus Sūtra, the symbiosis of all living things is described in a metaphor of the three kinds of medicinal herbs and two kinds of trees[28].

The second principle is the Eternal Buddha, which forms the basis for the harmonious society of humanity within the universe.

In the sixteenth chapter of the Lotus Sūtra, Śākyamuni reveals that he is the Eternal Buddha (久遠仏)[29], with the passage from the Life Span of the Thus Come One chapter indicating that he achieved enlightenment in the far distant past, and that he will continue to live on for twice the amount of time that has passed from the time that he achieved this original enlightenment to the present, which in effect means that he will live on for eternity. The Eternal Buddha is Śākyamuni at one with the fundamental law of the universe. That is why the Eternal Buddha is also the Eternal Saviour Buddha (永遠の救済仏). The Life Span chapter also states, "Sometimes I speak of myself, sometimes I speak of others."[30] The Second President of the Soka Gakkai, Josei Toda talks about the Universal Buddha (宇宙仏) who compassionately works to save all people in his *Theory of Compassion*, "This universe is the entity of the Buddha and all phenomena are manifestations of the Buddha's compassion."[31] Supported by

[27] *The Lotus Sutra*, p.31.
[28] *The Lotus Sutra*, p.98.
[29] *The Lotus Sutra*, p.225.
[30] *The Lotus Sutra*, p.226.
[31] Josei Toda, *Jihiron* [Theory of Compassion]. In *Toda Josei Zenshu* [The Collected Works of Josei Toda] vol. 3, Tokyō: Seikyō Shimbunsha, 1983, p.44.

the workings of compassion of this Universal Buddha, humanity is able to build a harmonious society.

The third principle of practicing the Bodhisattva Way directly supports the Universal Buddha's work by increasing the number of individuals who take on the same mission to save all living beings. These individuals are bodhisattvas. In the Lotus Sūtra, there are many bodhisattvas who are introduced, but the Bodhisattvas of the Earth, who appear in the Emerging from the Earth chapter, pledge to carry on the teachings of the Sūtra after the Buddha's passing. And in the Teacher of the Law chapter, they are referred to as the "envoy(s) of the Thus Come One"[32]. Bodhisattvas contribute their unique skills in different areas. For example, Medicine King is active in the field of medicine, Wonderful Sound symbolizes the areas of music and the arts and is a force for creativity, Universal Worthy and Mañjuśrī contribute to the fields of academics, science and philosophy.

Bodhisattva Perceiver of the World's Sounds gives people the strength to become fearless while acknowledging their secular desire to gain a profit in this lifetime.

In the twelfth or Never Disparaging chapter, a bodhisattva of that name appears. Never Disparaging respects all people and uses dialogue and non-violence to draw forth from people their Buddha nature and good will. To those who disparage, speak ill of, or even attack with weapons, Never Disparaging recites the twenty-four word Lotus Sūtra saying, "I have profound reverence for you,"[33] and continues his practice of equally showing all he encounters the same respect, believing that someday they will become Buddhas.

The Soka Gakkai and the SGI are Buddhist organizations that strive to actualize these three important principles contained in Kumārajīva's translation of the Lotus Sūtra in current society for the sake of lasting peace and happiness of all humankind—carrying out the Bodhisattva Way in the 21st century.

The conception of the Soka Gakkai and SGI

November 18, 1930 is when the Soka Gakkai was established by Tsunesaburo Makiguchi, the first President, and Josei Toda (who was general director at the time, and later became the second President of the organization).

The first volume of *The System of Value-Creating Pedagogy* is a crystallization of the concept of the creation of value which pursues the happiness of the common people and the flourishing of society. The publication of this volume

[32] *The Lotus Sutra*, p.162.
[33] *The Lotus Sutra*, p.266.

is dated November 18, 1930, and its publication commemorates the day that the Soka Gakkai was established. Soka is a shortened form of the Japanese word *kachisouzou*, which translates to "creation of value."

Makiguchi came to realize the deeper meaning behind the principles of Soka education through his study of the Lotus Sūtra and the teachings of Nichiren, and endeavored to widely promote Nichiren's teachings which covet the universal values of the human being.

The year 1939 was when the First General Meeting was held, but was also the same year that the Second World War began. The Japanese Army undertook military expansion in China and Korea and other South-East Asian countries.

During that time, in order to spiritually unify the nation behind the war effort, State Shinto was imposed and a majority of Buddhist sects in Japan complied with the government's agenda. However, unwilling to compromise the religious principle of pacifism, Makiguchi refused to lend support.

In December of 1941, the war in the Pacific began. Makiguchi was put under surveillance by the Special Higher Police. He was imprisoned in July 1943, along with Toda.

After being imprisoned for several years together with Makiguchi, Toda was released on July 3, 1945. Toda, who had a momentous religious experience while in prison, set out to rebuild the organization after his release.

Toda's awakening is described in the novel, *The Human Revolution*, written by Ikeda. Toda read and reread the Lotus Sūtra, trying to grasp its essence and the reason it was expounding. One morning, when focussed in thought, he realizes that he himself was among the Bodhisattvas of the Earth who appeared in the Ceremony in the Air as described in the Lotus Sūtra.

In the Emerging from the Earth chapter, there is a description of the appearance of thousands of millions of bodhisattvas from deep underground—the Bodhisattvas of the Earth. The leader of these bodhisattvas is Bodhisattva Superior Practices. *The Human Revolution* provides us with insight into this momentous event.

In an instant, Toda found himself in the air, in a huge crowd of people—numbering as many as the sands of sixty thousand Ganges Rivers—all worshipping the Gohonzon.

It was neither dream nor illusion. It seemed as if it lasted only a few seconds, or perhaps a few minutes, or again as long as several hours. It was to Toda a firm reality that he was experiencing for the first time. As supreme jubilation filled his body, he cried to himself that the experience was without falsity and that he had actually been part of it all…

...With tears streaming down his face, he read the passage: "The assembly on Eagle Peak has not yet been dispersed"[34]

This passage was transmitted from China and is also mentioned in writings by Nichiren[35].

This experience bolstered Toda's belief that Nichiren was a reincarnation of Bodhisattva Superior Practices as described in the Sūtras, and that his religious mission lay in the salvation of the people of the Latter Day of the Law through Buddhism centered on the Lotus Sūtra. This realization motivated Toda to rebuild the organization, and clearly defined the direction for the activities of the Soka Gakkai and SGI.

On May 3, 1951, Toda became the second President of the Soka Gakkai, and until his death on April 2, 1958, he progressively expanded the membership to over 750,000 households.

Following the death of Toda, Daisaku Ikeda became the third President of the Soka Gakkai (currently honorary President) on May 3, 1960, carrying on the second President's legacy, further expanding the membership beyond the borders of Japan. On January 26, 1975, representatives from throughout the world gathered in Guam to establish Soka Gakkai International (SGI) with President Ikeda as the first President of the SGI. Now, the SGI has organizations in 192 countries and territories throughout the world, and is working at many levels as a Buddhist organization dedicated to creating a peaceful society.

The Soka Gakkai and the SGI have revived the philosophy and practice of humanism from Śakyamuni to the Lotus Sūtra and Nichiren for the current century. Our mission in society is to actualize the salvation of humanity and reform society through peace, culture and education.

[34] Daisaku Ikeda, *The Human Revolution*, abridged edition, book 1, vol.4, World Tribune Press, 2004, p.411.

[35] *The Record of the Orally Transmitted Teachings*, p.135.

9

Soteriological unfolding of the Mind, body and abiding-places in the "Samanta-mukha-parivarta" of the Lotus Sūtra

Yao-ming Tsai

1.1. Thesis

This paper employs "Samanta-mukha-parivarta" of the *Lotus Sūtra* as the main literary source to discuss, from a philosophical perspective, the most superlative unfolding possibility of the three concepts of mind, body and abiding-places in the practice and application of Mahāyāna Buddhism. The paper will first identify the limitations of ideation formed by the three concepts as well as by attachments in practice. It will then attempt to reveal the creativity in the teachings of Mahāyāna Buddhism and the characteristics by which they break limitations and attachments.

1.2. Literary Sources

In order to focus on the literary sources used, so as to offer an interpretation drawn from context among various Mahāyāna Buddhist *sūtras,* "Samanta-mukha-parivarta" is chosen to be the major source for the present paper. It is a chapter of the *Saddharma-puṇḍarīka-sūtra.* In addition to various Sanskrit manuscripts, annotated versions, and editions translated into other languages, there are three extant Chinese translations of the *Lotus Sūtra.* We will not repeat references, widely available elsewhere, to the substantial body of work on the collation, introduction and analysis of the *Lotus Sūtra*. In this article, the quotations of the *Lotus Sūtra* are mainly from the most popular Chinese translation by Kumārajīva and also from Ueki Masatoshi's *Comparative Edition.*

1.3. Research Approach

The present paper intends to offer some philosophical reflections on the Bodhisattva Avalokiteśvara's endeavours that aim toward the "possible superlative" state. Accordingly, on the one hand, it will not fall into mediocre and repetitive preoccupations or parlance. On the other hand, it can best exemplify a philosophical speciality, namely deliberation.

1.4. Outline of the Sections

This article comprises six sections. Section 1 offers a broad outline of the paper's argument and a breakdown of its individual sections. Section 2 summarizes the main thesis of "Samanta-mukha-parivarta," including the structure, title, style, and key concepts of the text to serve as the context for the argument contained within the paper. Section 3 establishes that the message conveyed by "Samanta-mukha-parivarta" is an unfolding religious operation. In Section 4, three sub-sections elucidate how the topics of mind, body and abiding-places systematically construct unfolding thinking and practice. Section 5 investigates different kinds of unfolding practised by Bodhisattva and best exemplified by Bodhisattva Avalokiteśvara. This section also reflects on the scope of the Bodhisattva practices from a philosophical perspective and questions the possibility of unfolding them to as superlative a state as possible. Section 6 concludes and summarizes the main points of the article.

2. Main Points in "Samanta-mukha-parivarta"

It is necessary to summarize the main points of "Samanta-mukha-parivarta" to serve as the context for this research, since it is the kernel of the present paper, and to provide a more complete picture of its Buddhist principles.

The main points of "Samanta-mukha-parivarta" can be delineated according to the structure of the text, the title of the text, the style of operation, the key concepts, and the foundational ideas.

2.1. Structure of the Text

Both the extant Sanskrit manuscripts and the one translated by Kumārajīva show that there are two *genres* in "Samanta-mukha-parivarta," the prose discourse and verse discourse. In terms of the structure, it can be roughly categorized into five segments according to the discourse and genre.

In the first segment, Bodhisattva Akṣayamati asks the Buddha for what reason (*kena kāraṇena*) Bodhisattva Avalokiteśvara got his name.

In the second segment, Bodhisattva Akṣayamati further asks the Buddha about how Bodhisattva Avalokiteśvara goes forward in this Sahā world (*asyām sahāyām loka-dhātau pravicarati*), how he teaches the Dharma for the sake of sentient beings (*sattvānām dharmam deśayati*), as well as the range of skill-in-means he obtains.

The third segment states how, upon comprehending the profound and lofty qualities Bodhisattva Avalokiteśvara had achieved as an exemplar, Bodhisattva Akṣayamati made an offer to Bodhisattva Avalokiteśvara.

The fourth section reiterates the main thesis of the previous three sections in verse form.

After the verse, in the fifth section, Bodhisattva Dharaṇī-dhara construes the title of this chapter and reveals the uncommon virtuous roots resulting from hearing this chapter.

In conclusion, the structure of "Samanta-mukha-parivarta" centers around the particularly excellent qualities and achievements created by Bodhisattva Avalokiteśvara. The reason for his title, why he roams this world, how he preaches to sentient beings, and the domain and state of his skilful means are the linkages to this main axis.

2.2. Title of the Text

The main theme of "Samanta-mukha-parivarta," which is also the main focus of this chapter, is the all-encompassing, wisdom-laden observation and manifestations of Bodhisattva Avalokiteśvara. This recurrent theme appears in the title, permeates the whole chapter, and is asserted again in the conclusion.

"Samanta-mukha-parivarta" is in fact a shortened version of the title. According to the extant Sanskrit version, the complete title is *Samanta-mukha-parivarto nāmāvalokiteśvara-vikurvaṇanirdeśaś catur-viṃśatimaḥ*, which means "the 24th chapter with the title of 'samanta-mukha,' and [the main theme] expounds the manifestations by [Bodhisattva] Avalokiteśvara." In the last paragraphs, Bodhisattva Dharaṇī-dhara confirms the title of this chapter as "the chapter from the *dharma-paryāya* [of the *Saddharmapuṇḍarīka-sūtra*] [that focuses] on Bodhisattva-Mahāsattva Avalokiteśvara" (*Avalokiteśvarasya bodhisattvasya mahāsattvasyêmam dharmaparyāya-parivartam*), or "the title is the chapter of 'samanta-mukha' which expounds the manifestations of Bodhisattva-Mahāsattva Avalokiteśvara, [i.e.,] the supernatural transformations and manifestations of Bodhisattva-Mahāsattva Avalokiteśvara" (*Avalokiteśvarasya bodhisattvasya mahāsattvasya vikurvā-nirdeśam samanta-mukha-parivartam nāmāvalokiteśvarasya bodhisattvasya vikurvaṇa-prātihāryam*).

Therefore, the title of the chapter, "Samanta-mukha-parivarta," which is also the main theme of this chapter, can also be referred to as "the samanta-mukha that explicates Bodhisattva-Mahāsattva Avalokiteśvara's supernatural manifestation." The main purpose of this chapter is to build at least two pillars. The first one is Bodhisattva Avalokiteśvara, who acts as the pillar to the agent in question while *samanta-mukha* is the pillar in content. The ultimate exemplification of *samanta-mukha* entails supernatural transformations and manifestations.

Here, it is necessary to explain the two concepts of samanta-mukha and supernatural transformations and manifestations in order to comprehend the title and theme of "Samantamukha-parivarta" .

The first word of this compound "*samanta-mukha*" can be further dissected into "*sam* (together; entire)+*anta* (end)." The literal meaning of this word is "universal," "on all sides," "in all directions," "all," or "entire." The word "*mukha*" can mean mouth, face, facade, door, or entrance. When putting these two words together, there are four inter-connected meanings in this compound, "*samanta-mukha:*" all-sided face(s), facing all directions, (becoming the) universal door or gateway (to something), and the gateway to every direction. In short, initially, the compound "*samanta-mukha*" meant "facing all directions," and later developed into "the gateway universally leading to every direction."

Buddhist *sūtras* employ various terms, such as *ṛddhi/ abhijñā* (extraordinary insight/extraordinary knowledge), *ṛddhi-bala* (extraordinary power), *prātihārya* (extraordinary transformation/transformational appearance), *vikurvaṇa/ vikurvā* (miraculous transformation), *vikurvaṇa-prātihārya* (extraordinary transformational manifestation), *nirmita* (created through transformation), and *vidarśana* (manifestation), to express a similar idea. Setting aside the interchangeability of synonyms, composite usage, and rhetoric, and focusing on the meaning of the idea itself, then the supernatural transformations and manifestations means the superlative ability developed as counter reaction to the missions to deal with and actively solve problems in all directions, so as to metamorphose into numerous different physical and facial appearances. In this context, this "supernatural power to manifest" can be comprehended as the ultimate demonstration of the "universal gateway." In other words, it is the superlative endeavour of facing all directions, or even becoming the gateway to every direction so as to be able to transform into countless physiques or facial likenesses in order to accomplish tasks in all directions.

2.3. Style of Operation

Obviously, the message delivered by "Samanta-mukha-parivarta" is an unfolding religious process, which is being considered under the fundamental perspective of exegesis in the present paper. Therefore, the details of this issue will be discussed in full in the next section.

2.4. Key Concepts

In a text, the so-called key concepts are derived from certain words or phrases. They are like the keys that can open the content of the text, express the major concepts of the text, or define the text. This section covers the structure, title, style, and the major concepts of this text, including "Avalokiteśvara," "Bodhisattva-Mahāsattva," "samanta-mukha," "supernatural transformations and manifestations," and "unfolding," which can be considered the key concepts of "Samanta-mukha-parivarta." In addition, topics being focussed on in this text, such as "mind," "body," and "abiding-places (or world)," can also be taken as the key concepts of "Samanta-mukha-parivarta."

Many related concepts constitute an inventory of key concepts. As a result, it is possible to formulate the following two statements to delineate the main thesis of the text in question with the help of the inventory of key concepts. First of all, the main thesis of "Samantamukha-parivarta" lies in the "samanta-mukha" of Bodhisattva Avalokiteśvara. In other words, Bodhisattva Avalokiteśvara faces all directions and further becomes the gateway toward all possible directions. Secondly, by ways of unfolding the mind, body and abiding-places to a superlative state, the universal gateway of Bodhisattva Avalokiteśvara will be able to save various sentient beings through skilful supernatural transformations and manifestations.

2.5. Foundational Ideas

After unlocking the foundational ideas of a text, it is then possible to comprehend the meaning of the text more profoundly. Among all the possible and relevant representations of a text, it is those concepts that are situated at the lower level that enable the various embodiments, make them applicable, or entail further development, which are the foundational concepts.

As a result, at least one series of interconnected foundational concepts can be decoded from the diverse narratives elucidated in "Samanta-mukha-parivarta." The series of five foundational concepts-mental, ontological, practical, bodily, and in-reality, can be described roughly as follows:

First, the inquiry into mental foundation: The most fundamental reasons for Bodhisattva Avalokiteśvara's actions are his *karuṇā* (compassion), *kṛpā/ kṛpaṇa* (commiseration/sympathy), and *maitra/ maitrī* (kindness/benevolence), which make up the idea of benevolence/compassion.

Secondly, the inquiry into ontological foundation: From Bodhisattva Avalokiteśvara's perspective, the most significant among countless predicaments of sentient beings is the idea of "the possibility of liberation." In Sanskrit, this idea is presented with *pari* in front of the optative mood of the verb that means 'to liberate', √*muc*. In other words, if it were not for the possibility of liberating sentient beings under any circumstance, then there would be no need for Bodhisattva Avalokiteśvara to try to arrange a series of reactions to help such beings to be liberated from their predicaments.

Thirdly, the inquiry into practical foundation: The major reason for Bodhisattva Avalokiteśvara's behaviour is the idea of "the possibility of salvation." Conceptually, if it were not possible for sentient beings to be rescued, then Bodhisattva Avalokiteśvara would not have been busy rescuing sentient beings in all respects, and be the world's saviour or protector. In Sanskrit, this idea is presented by *trātṛ/trātā/trātāru* (savior/rescuer/protector), the agent of action of √*trā*, which means to save from, to rescue, or to protect.

Fourthly, the inquiry into bodily foundation: The major idea that enables Bodhisattva Avalokiteśvara to appear in different forms and shapes so as to rescue sentient beings from sufferings by adopting an appropriate form lies in "transformation." What the Buddha strives to teach is that all things in the world, including the body, are illusions (*māyā*) or emanated constructions/ fabrications *(nir-mita/nir-māṇa)*. However, Bodhisattva Avalokiteśvara does not only passively recognize or comprehend that the body is merely an illusion. On the contrary, he actively manipulates the illusory body to its highest degree in order to rescue sentient beings.

Fifthly, the inquiry into in-reality foundation : The major reason why Bodhisattva Avalokiteśvara's most distictive behaviour forms the universal gateway lies in the idea of the "thoroughly unimpeded." So-called reality cannot be limited to immediate, surrounding, revealed, or segmented appearances; it encompasses the comprehensive, true or meaningful items throughout the process of ever-changing causes and conditions. The so-called foundation in-reality focuses on the reality that can unlock and probe into the foundations of items. What the universal gateway advocates is to disregard differences or segregations in time, direction, life form, sex, society, culture, or religion or even between appearances and foundations created by the discourse. "Samanta-mukha-parivarta" treats all elements described above as a fundamental principle, and puts this into practice in salvation. Therefore, the act of thoroughly seeking the reality behind all superficial appearancesand differences made by parlance or segregation, and yet always staying grounded in-reality can be called "the thoroughly unimpeded."

To sum up, the study of the text reveals at least one set of foundational ideas: the main mental foundation is benevolence-compassion; the main ontological foundation is the possibility of liberation; the main foundation in practice is the possibility of salvation; the main foundation in body is illusion/ transformation; and the main foundation in-reality is the thoroughly unimpeded.

3. Unfolding as a Style in Religious Operation

Based mainly on "Samanta-mukha-parivarta," the present paper particularly focusses on the topics of mind, body and abiding-places. Considering "Samanta-mukha-parivarta" as a religious text, it is necessary to clarify how it operates in a religious sense in order to decipher the meanings and operations in mind, body and abiding-places in relation to the system it is situated in.

In this article, the definition of religion is as follows: it is possibly the most comprehensive and superlative inquiry into the main or foundational topics of life and the process of life, and the subsequent theories and explanations advocated or the directions in practice provided. However, there could be thousands of ways to operate religions. The inquiry described above can be called a "religious operation." Therefore, after employing style as a means to categorize vastly different religions, it is then possible to make analyses of "styles of religious operations."

For example, excluding those instances of manipulation, fraud, or embezzlement that involve misuse or abuse, religions can be categorized into the following types according to their different goals: seeking consolation, getting protection, ascending to heaven after death, seeking eternal life, reaching liberation, or achieving enlightenment. If the ways of achieving the goals are by means of categorization, then the following types can be differentiated: sincere religious beliefs, rituals, worship of spiritual entities, cultivation of notions, cultivation of minds, or cultivation of breathing. If the various items in ontology are the criteria for differentiating religions, then the following types can be distinguished: celestial gods as the subject, human beings as the subject, all beings as the subject, nature as the subject, material objects as the subject, or no subject.

In theory, there can be an infinite number of criteria for categorizing different types of religious operations. However, the main point of this section does not lie in making a comprehensive list of all the various ways to formulate categories. Rather, it strives to confirm what "Samanta-mukha-parivarta" advocates, the "universal gateway-ness," and to propagate its message by unfolding religious operations. Therefore, it is necessary to explain the meaning of "unfolding" from the perspective of the differing styles of religious operations, which can be approached in two ways, i.e., conceptual clarification and definition.

First, a clarification of the concept of unfolding reveals its difference from the following four situations. The first possibility is that religion leads to closed, locked, fixed, or unchanging situations. The second possibility is that religion leads to situations such as opposition, resistance, hatred, struggle, or invasion. The third possibility is that religion only stops at the stage of learning, cultivation, and incubation, while the fourth possibility entails one-sided, or uni-directional expectations such as going to heaven, being reborn in Pure Land, or being liberated.

Second, from the perspective of a conceptual definition, there are at least four main points in the so-called unfolding. Firstly through religion, one will remain involved in a space-time continuum that is vast in space and extremely long in time and where various sentient beings keep living and dying. One would not shut oneself outside the world of life , or the space-time continuum of various sentient beings. Secondly, through religion, one will be open to the view of the world of life from the perspectives of perception and consolation. Thirdly, through religion, ontologically, one would not only be opened from a closed or folded state, but would also extend or stretch out to a greater or the fullest length. Fourthly, through religion, from the perspective of function, one would not unfold one single aspect alone but would, at the same time, causeadverse withering or limitations to other aspects. On the contrary, the unfolded aspect will involve and stimulate others to start unfolding, too.

The previous passages have broadly explained the meaning of unfolding from the perspectives of conceptual clarification and definition. In short, if "the relationship between religion and the ultra-long time and vast space of the world of life" is the criterion, then it can be categorized into different types of religious operation, such as unfolding, closed, opposing, cultivating, heaven ascending, Pure Land aiming, or liberating. One of those, the unfolding religious operation, exhibits the comprehensive unfolding or extension in aspects of perception, consolation, ontology, and function through observation, benevolence-compassion and salvation.

As a result, what is involved in unfolding is mainly the "connection" within the world of life which is a continuum of spaceand time. However, this unfolding of the religious operation cannot be achieved in one step. Therefore, it is necessary to reflect on the priority of the foundation of the religious operation. Based on this perspective, "Samanta-mukha-parivarta" could be comprehended as the following four main theses which could serve as the foundation of unfolding reality. First is the "foundation of the worldview:" the world to which Bodhisattva Avalokiteśvara is connected or in which Bodhisattva Avalokiteśvara lives is not limited to an insignificant or enclosed abiding-place or country. Rather, it has to be unlocked in a continuum of space-time of the world of life. Second is the "theoretical foundation:" there does not exist any materialistic or quintessential distinction or opposition among objects in the world of life--such as mind, body, abiding-places, time period, material objects, and sentient beings--it is utterly and thoroughly unimpeded. Third is the "foundation in practice:" It is not limited to individual mind, body, and abiding-places; it is not the life experience caught in the recycling of life and death; step-by-step cultivation of the practice is not the whole spectrum; nor is it fixated in a liberated state. It is beyond the stage of cultivation and practice and it is capable of putting what has been learned into practice in the world of life to a superlative state, all-encompassingly, and infinitely. Fourth is the "foundation of operation:" the so-called unfolding religious operation does not promise aimlessly, nor does it operate without any plan. It highly values *upāya-kauśalya* (skill-inmeans/skilful means) as the criterion for the operation.

4. Unfolding of the Mind, Body and Abiding-Places

One of the chief attractions of philosophical inquiry lies in searching for better perspectives or clues to unveil and further understand this world of life. What "Samanta-mukhaparivarta" is trying to express is the nature of unfolding religious operations. In the same way, topics on mind, body and abiding-places are also unfolding in terms of thinking and practice. Therefore, research into this chapter not only provides an opportunity to learn how to think about these topics in an unfolding sense, but can also help us to expand our vision of these topics. The three sub-sections here will elucidate how topics such as mind, body and abiding-places create unfolding thinking and practice.

4.1. Unfolding the Mind

Mind is the totality of activities of perception, cognition, sentiment, and attitude. Employing the "growth-related world of life" as a criterion, activities of the mind can be divided into different types such as enclosed, ensnared, mediocre, growing, and unfolding. Among them, by contrasting the passive and active sides, the unfolding of mind based on "Samantamukha-parivarta" can bring forth explanations for at least the following five topics: boundaries of perception, the center or base of perception, packaging of recognition, inclination of sentiments, and scale in attitude.

First, "boundaries of perception:" It does not focus on the immediate situation, a specific item, or any particular characteristic in time; it is totally open-minded and it observes a long period of life experiences and the vast world of life.

Second, the "center or base of perception:" It does not establish any centre or subject of perception. It is not a self-centered perception, nor is it a self-based perception. The worldview on which the perception is based is not a dichotomy of any group such as "center vs. peripheral," "foundation vs. auxiliary," "subject vs. object," or "self vs. others." Instead, the structure of the category in-reality is equal and unimpeded. From an equal and unimpeded worldview emerges the equal and unimpeded perception that observes the world of life in all aspects.

Third, "packaging of cognition:" It does not package cognition with concepts nor does it encircle cognition and build walls, thorns, or traps such as *ātma-saṃjñā* (conception or ideation of the self), or *para-saṃjñā* (conception or ideation of the other). Instead, it opens and clears a way through the process of cognition by observing causes and conditions so as to search for proper resolution.

Fourth, "inclination of sentiments:" It does not produce agitated or attached sentiments from a self-centered being; nor does it set up a world on the outside, or another world to create an indifferent or hostile sentiment. It expands sentiments vastly, equally, and thoroughly, and into a universal consolation and compassion regardless of the distance in between.

Fifth, "scale in attitude:" It does not wrap itself into a circumscribed situation and result in negative sentiments such as being penurious, plundering, grasping, feeling lost, having low self-esteem, being too proud of oneself, being dominating, or scolding. Instead, it sends out, contributes, and influences the world of life peacefully. For example, *a-bhayaṃ-dada,* "Bestower or Contributor of fearlessness" never worried about being caught in the whirlpool of terror or fear. Rather, he helped those who were in an agony of terror and fear rescued them using all methods possible. In addition, one would not be enslaved by agitated sentiments such as greed, anger, and delusion, nor be inclined to scold or berate other sentient beings' agitated sentiments. One can in fact employ all possible ways to help sentient beings be free from those agitated sentiments and become their saviour by solving their emotional problems.

To conclude, "Samanta-mukha-parivarta" does not take the general narrow minded views of average sentient beings as granted and accept their viewpoints, nor is it satisfied at being a mediocrity nor is it accustomed to the enclosed and opposing activities of the mind. The style of the enfolding view of mind and mental practice exemplified by Bodhisattva Avalokiteśvara is on the one hand exclusive of all phantasmagoric incongruities. On the other hand, it is premised upon an equal and unimpeded perception and recognition in the world of life, which is a space-time continuum and entails universal observation. In another aspect, in terms of content, studious mental practice entails undiscriminating consolation and limitless benevolence and compassion. He not only can be aware of the causes and conditions of the horror and defilements that vex sentient beings, but can also arrange and make plans for tools and clues to figure out ways to help sentient beings to get out of their mental quagmire. In other words, the unfolding of mind exemplified by

Bodhisattva Avalokiteśvara is universal observation and he provides sentient beings with ways to solve their mental problems.

4.2. Unfolding of Body

How body is perceived and body is formed, the issue of how to operate body and then how the state of body or function of body is formed, are interconnected. The view of body and the function of body as unfolded from "Samanta-mukha-parivarta" provide a stunning religious program in teaching on body.

An unfolding view of body, on a passive level, neither recognizes that a body is an entity that is to be differentiated from others, nor reckons the so-called body as either a fixed or static entity, nor perceives the body as any superficial shape or form, such as female/male, big/small, beautiful/ugly, or black/white, nor identifies with such states as healthy, sick, pleasurable, or suffering, nor comprehends the body as various components such as head, eyes, heart, lung, cell and neurons. It does not identify the so-called body as the self, nor does it identify the so-called self as the so-called body. All these body conceptions or body identities are commonly accepted by average sentient beings or ordinary people. However, they impose tendencies of isolation, fixation, materialization, characterisation, and superficialization on the so-called body. Thus, all these characterestics together construct aconstricted view, which fragments bodies into one black box after another, alienated from the vast and interconnected world of life, from reality. Therefore, it is not recommended that one subscribes to the narrow viewpoint described above.

For an unfolding view of body, on an active level, the key lies in the cognition that the so-called body is "a phantasma that is in relation and connected to the world of life." The term "In relation" means that the so-called body and the world of life are not separate entities, they are interwoven into the process, context, or network of becoming, changing, and fading. While "connected" means that there is nosubstantial dividing wall or obstacle between the so-called body and the world of life, they are inter-linked to each other's process and network of causes and conditions. Moreover, the so-called "phantasma" means that the so-called body as well as the world of life are like illusions which lack a substantive content or shape. In addition, they are like the result of a phantasma, also lacking fixed consistency. Through such recognition, the so-called body can be unfolded in the process and network which are related and inter-connected to the world of life.

After covering both the passive and active aspects of the unfolding view of body, the following will explain the unfolding function of body. As regards how to manipulate body into different states and functions, there is a sharp contrast between two different kinds of operation in "Samanta-mukha-parivarta." One could be named the "closed body function," which usually leads the body to all sorts of quagmires on the part of average sentient beings or ordinary people. The other could be named the "unfolding body function," which can transform into seemingly different bodies as one of the tools to help save sentient beings. Bodhisattva Avalokiteśvara is most famous for performing this sort of task. There is a well-known quote from "Samanta-mukha-parivarta" that best describes the "unfolding body function:"

> *"santi kula-putra loka-dhṃjñātavo, yeṣv Avalokiteśvaro bodhisattvo mahāsattvo buddha-rūpeṇa sattvṃjñānṃjñāṃ dharmaü deśayati. santi loka dhātavo, yeùv Avalokiteśvaro bodhisattvo mahāsattvo bodhisattva-rūpeṇa sattvānāṃ dharmaṃ deśayati. keṣāṃ-cit pratyekabuddha-rūpeṇāvalokiteśvaro bodhisattvo mahāsattvaḥ sattvānāṃ dharmaṃ deśayati. ---śrāvaka-rūpeṇa --- brahma-rūpeṇa ---śakra-rūpeṇa--- gandharva- rūpeṇa ---. yakṣa-vaineyānāṃ sattvānāṃ yakṣa rūpeṇa dharmaṃ deśayati. --- īśvara-rūpeṇa --- maheśvara-rūpeṇa ---cakra varti-rāja-rūpeṇa --- piśāca-rūpeṇa ---vaiśravaṇa-rūpeṇa -- senā-pati-rūpeṇa --- brāhmaṇa-rūpeṇa --- vajra-pāṇi-rūpeṇa ---. evam a-cintya-guṇa-samanvāgataḥ kula-putra Avalokiteśvaro bodhisattvo mahāsattvaḥ."* (pp. 500-502.)

From the perspective of the unfolding body function, there are at least four unfoldings in the passage quoted above. First, there is unfolding in time, not being limited to a brief period. Second, there is unfolding in space, direction, kingdom, and place, not being enclosed in any specific area. Third, there is unfolding in shape, posture, and facial features, not being confined to any particular or fixed representation. Fourth, there is unfolding in target, goal, aim and purpose, not being restricted to any pre-programmed linkage.

However, how is it possible to unfold one's body? After scrutinizing "Samanta-mukhaparivarta," three aspects are likely to be the key answers. First, avoid doing anything that is "anti-unfolding." Second, practice the supreme ability of "transforming the body." Third, the purpose of transforming the body is to save various kinds of sentient beings or practitioners without discrimination.

First , Bodhisattva Avalokiteśvara does not do anything that is "anti-unfolding." Among all possibilities, the following are some examples: (a) never considers notions like "this is my body" thus becoming trapped in banalities such as "body is owned by self," or "my body solely belongs to me;" (b) never thinks that "there is divisibility or opposition between a body itself and others" thus becoming trapped in banalities such as "this is my body," or "that is yours or its body;" (c) never thinks that "there is the sameness, difference or opposition between sameness and difference of body" thus becoming trapped in banalities such as "The body I own is the same all the time," or "I own several different bodies;" (d) never thinks that "concerning the conformation of life, there is divisibility or opposition of body in sex/ gender" thus becoming trapped in banalities such as "my body is female or my body is fixed as a female one," or " your body is male or your body is fixed as a male one;" (e) never thinks that "there is divisibility or opposition of body in age" thus becoming trapped in banalities such as "my body is fixed in a baby's body," or "your body is fixed in the body of a child, a youth, a middle-aged person, or an elder;" (f) never thinks that "there is divisibility or opposition of body in social status" thus becoming trapped in banalities such as "my body is is fixed as a labourer or worker," or "your body is is fixed in a body of an official, a solider, or a priest;" (g) never thinks that "there is divisibility or opposition of the body in religious practice" thus becoming trapped in banalities such as "my body is is fixed in an endeavour towards liberation," or "your body is is fixed in a body of a Bodhisattva practicing Mahāyāna Buddhism." In sum, regardless of the destination, self-or-otherness, sameness-or-difference, confirmation of life, sex/gender, age, social status, or the way of practicing religion of a body, none of the commonplace notions or methods advocating limits, segregation, or opposition will be applied. Therefore, on the one hand, one will not be trapped from the beginning in a mediocre banality of "anti-unfolding body." On the other hand, it will pave a smooth, wide and limitless road for the body to unfold in all aspects.

Second, Bodhisattva Avalokiteśvara cultivates a superlative ability to "transform his body." Due to the fact that there are always things to be dependent on, for example, if even for a short while there is still food to eat, clothes to wear, places to live, and things to enjoy, then one would not necessarily practice or cultivate the ability. Therefore, one would lack the abilities in aspects such as cognition, operation, liberation or salvation appropriate to areas of learning, ways of practice, the world of life, or experience of life. It seems that Mahāyāna Buddhism provides a long-term program for advanced yet arduous practice to progress continuously on the path to enlightenment as well as to acquire the necessary abilities to unfold in the vast world of life. Among those superlative abilities in saving various sentient beings in an unfolding way, the ability to transform into various forms and multiple bodies is certainly a very difficult skill. After Bodhisattva Avalokiteśvara cultivated and acquired the superlative ability to transform his body, he would not easily be trapped in any quagmire such as "incapable of ruling the country," or "incapability of religion."

Third, Bodhisattva Avalokiteśvara transforms his body for the sake of saving various sentient beings or practitioners on an equal basis. If he transforms his body just for the sake of body transformation, then this would be like declaring war for the sake of war, or creating for the sake of creation. Not only would the reason for transforming the body be abruptly impeded, but also the ability to transform one's body would turn into a petty act. In fact, for the purpose of saving the entire spectrum of sentient beings and practitioners, and since all beings possess and expect different bodies in space and time, Bodhisattva Avalokiteśvara needs to manifest all possible representations and meet all possible expectations. Hence, the "universal manifestation" then emerges.

4.3. Unfolding Abiding-places

Since Bodhisattva Avalokiteśvara exemplifies the unfolding view of mind, mental practice, view of body, and body function, when it comes to abiding-places, he still employs the same principle, i.e. unfolding.

From the perspective of living space or place, the so-called abiding-places are no different from any other mundanely conditioned existence that exhibits the process of the four steps of arising, abiding, deteriorating, and becoming empty with little possibility for unfolding. However, the "unfolding of abiding-places" should be based on the general concept of abiding-places or the function of abiding-places. In other words, the unfolding concept of abiding-places and putting the function of abiding-places into practice will entail the further development and unfolding of abiding-places.

There are two aspects as to how the unfolding views of abiding-places are constructed: the passive elimination of obstacles, and the active disentanglement of the "knot."

First, what needs to be eliminated in unfolding views of abiding-places is mainly the views of average sentient beings and ordinary people. For example, (a) the view that all isolated and segregated items existing in time and in space in terms of direction, national territory, and abiding-place exist by themselves, or contain fixed substance, content or features; (b) the view that all the segments isolated from the space element are fixed themselves, and each segment is divisible from and opposed to another; (c) the view that ties certain incidents in a being's life, such as birth, living, and death, to some isolated area where, on the one hand, a specific isolated area is identified or is in the possession of certain beings, certain incidents and/ or certain places, and where, on the other hand, certain sentient beings are identified or in the possession of a certain location; (d) the view that not only a specific sentient being and a certain place are bound together by identity or belonging, and other sentient beings and other places are tied together too, but the resultant grouped bundles are considered divisible from and opposed to each other. In sum, the views described above, that tying up or restricting specific sentient beings and places are the so-called "anti-unfolding views of abiding-places."

Second, in order to formulate the unfolding views of abiding-places, one should avoid being trapped in the banal mediocrity of "anti-unfolding views of abiding-places," and should actively release the unfolding potential of abiding-places. For example: (a) It is necessary to comprehend that all abiding-places are *pratītya-samutpāda* (conditioned co-arising) that experience changes of arising and cessation and they are *svabhāva-śūnya* (empty of own-beings). As a result, they do not possess any self-existing power of confinement. (b) Since all abiding-places are devoid of their own-beings, abiding-places are in fact *a-dvaya* (nondual/non-dualistic), i.e. there is no difference among abiding-places and they are not opposed to each other. Furthermore, they can all be connected to each other through the process, context and network of changes of arising and cessation. (c) The reality that all abiding-places are founded on the conditioned co-arising process of changes of arising and cessation entails their phantasmagoric contents, which can be manipulated and transformed. In other words, the key to the unfolding of abiding-places lies in a clear comprehension that the foundational status is a series of conditioned co-arising, changes of arising and cessation, emptying of own-beings, non-duality, and phantasm.

What Bodhisattva Avalokiteśvara exemplifies through his unfolding views of abiding-places are the unfolding functions of abiding-places. The characteristics can be briefly described as follows: on the one hand, none of the abiding-places will be used for identifying or belonging, nor will any abiding-place become the premise upon which the process of birth, aging, sickness, and death takes place. On the other hand, *"Going throughout countries in the ten directions, He* [Bodhisattva Avalokiteśvara] *manifests everywhere in all places."* Focusing on saving various sentient beings, Bodhisattva Avalokiteśvara emerges in various places of the world, depending on the need of sentient beings, so as to manifest various appearances appropriate to the circumstances. Precisely due to the reality that any abiding-place in the world can be the place to save sentient beings, there is no abiding-place that is not suitable for saving sentient beings. As a result, the unfolding function of abiding-places can be achieved.

In sum, advanced Bodhisattvas eliminate the "anti-unfolding view of abiding-places" at the passive level, and fully comprehend a series of foundational states that an abiding-place is merely a process of conditioned co-arising and transformation. The consequent unfolding view of abiding-places will not employ identity, belonging, or incidents such as birth, aging, sickness, and death to enclose or limit certain abiding-places in their function as abiding-places. Instead, all abiding-places can be thoroughly used in saving sentient beings. Therefore, saving sentient beings can be unfolded, as can abiding-places as a function and concept of abiding-places.

5. Philosophical Reflection on "Possible Superlative Unfolding"

By advocating the "universal gateway" in "Samanta-mukha-parivarta," it is clear that those Bodhisattvas had gone beyond the theoretical stages in

Mahāyāna Buddhism and reached the stage where they were actively putting in practice what they had learnt. What this text conveys is the unfolding religious operation; consequently, topics in mind, body and abiding-places are also unfolding thoughts and applications. Therefore, there are two closely related issues that are worthy of discussion: one is on what kind of unfolding of Bodhisattva deeds Bodhisattva Avalokiteśvara exhibits, and the other is on how one reflects on these Bodhisattva deeds.

5.1. Unfolding Bodhisattva Deeds: "Possible Superlative Unfolding"

There are many aspects to the way that one can approach the unfolding Bodhisattva deeds performed by Bodhisattva Avalokiteśvara. If scope and status are the main concerns, then this can be comprehended as "possible superlative unfolding."

The so-called "possible superlative unfolding" is equivalent to the "advanced unfolding," and "limitless unfolding." Linguistically, it is comparatively different from "initial unfolding," "medium unfolding," and "limited unfolding." The reason for coining the term "possible superlative unfolding" is that on the one hand, this term should not denote immediate opposing meanings. On the other hand, the unfolding Bodhisattva deeds exemplified by Bodhisattva Avalokiteśvara are not in the past tense, nor the present progressive tense, but a forever ongoing future progressive tense. Therefore, in order to express the scope of this egalitarian, active, open, and continuous form, the term "possible superlative unfolding" is coined, However, if one wishes to emphasize that the practitioner is a high-level Bodhisattva, then "possible superlative unfolding by Bodhisattva" can be used.

5.2. How Is the "Possible Superlative Unfolding" Possible?

Once Bodhisattva Avalokiteśvara's actions are understood as "possible superlative unfolding by Bodhisattva," then a philosophical reflection can be undertaken: how is the "possible superlative unfolding" possible?

While most ordinary people try their best to keep their heads above the flow of birth, aging, sickness, and death, it is only a handful of people that are not often beset by vexations or limited by the struggle to survive. It is extremely difficult for practitioners to dedicate their lives to cultivating themselves without retreating from where they are, deviating from the way of practice, or exalting one stage after another by cultivating their own qualities and professional abilities. Unlike those who keep practicing beyond the final stage of cultivation in Mahāyāna Buddhism, to keep advancing toward the unsurpassed goal, and, at the same time, to keep unfolding the Bodhisattva deeds in all directions regardless of distance, these are utterly beyond the imagination or comprehension of most average sentient beings.

Focusing on "Samanta-mukha-parivarta," there are two approaches, theory and practice, to illuminate the question of the possibility of "possible superlative unfolding."

First, the theoretical approach does not have to be overly complex; it can be kept straightforward. When taking the perspective of *a-saṃskṛta-dharmatā* (unconditioned reality/ unconditioned state of being the dharma), then all who are floating in the life experience, cultivating practices arduously, and unfolding in the world of life are nothing but representations of conditioned co-arising. Being influenced due to conditioned co-arising with its unconditioned state of being, the dharma is thoroughly empty and non-dual in its own-being. In other words, limitedness does not exist in its own-being, nor does exist distinctability, opposition, or peripheralness, i.e., there does not exist any thorough form of limitedness.

Second, the Bodhisattvas have been dedicated to the cultivation stages in practice. Focusing on the Bodhisattva deeds of saving various sentient beings, if Bodhisattvas can comprehend the idea of non-conditioned state of dharma and if, fundamentally, there does not exist any form of limitedness, then it is possible to put into practice the idea of non-limitedness; thus, the principle of the Bodhisattva practice of non-limitedness can be acted out. One issue to be clarified here is that the so-called possibility of 'this and that' is not equal to the possibility of the non-conditioned state of dharma, nor is it equal to the thinking that the non-conditioned state of dharma is opposed to real life in this mundane world. In fact, the so-called possibility of 'this and that' are the assertions made up by the arising of the causes and conditions with the help of division by analysis and borrowing in language. It is only suitable to think passively that there limitedness in the non-conditioned state of dharma does not exist; the possibility in ontology cannot be asserted positively. This is because any item in ontology, even if it were only a possibility in ontology, would have violated the emptiness in the state of dharma.

Therefore, the theory is constructed upon the thoroughly non-existing limitedness in any form of the state of dharma. After comprehending the idea that wherever the practice is acted upon, its state of dharma is as ever thoroughly devoid of limitedness in any form, then the unfolded Bodhisattva deeds can exemplify the "possible superlative unfolding" in the context of the ideas constituting Bodhisattva deeds. In other words, it is possible to unfold the theoretical Bodhisattva deed to a superlative state in a feasible chain of reasoning.

5.3. The "Possible Superlative Unfolding": A Feasible Chain of Reasoning

It is necessary to note that the prior discussion in this section is limited to the elucidation of how the "ideas constituting Bodhisattva deeds" are possible and how they unfold. It does not insist that Bodhisattva deeds have already unfolded to a superlative state and in an egalitarian way. Further, as far as the ideas constituting Bodhisattva deeds are concerned, it is not so magical that the Bodhisattvas can achieve anything they wish. On the contrary, they need to follow a feasible chain of reasoning.

This so-called feasible chain of reasoning involves many levels. Initially, there are two major aspects worth emphasising: one is the reasoning for the mechanism of conditioned coarising, and the other is the reasoning for transformation in salvation.

First of all, the reasoning for the mechanism of conditioned co-arising can be further expressed as *"asmin sati, idaṃ bhavaty; asyotpādād, idam utpadyate. asminn asati, idaṃ na bhavaty; asya nirodhād, idaṃ nirudhyate."* (此有故彼有，此生故彼生；此無故彼無，此滅故彼滅。) "When that exists (or is present), this comes to be; from the arising of that, this arises. When that does not exist (or is not present), this does not come to be; from the cessation of that, this ceases." Regardless of what one does, going through birth, aging, sickness, and death, suffering in the cycle of birth and death, proceeding on the path of cultivation, looking for ways out of the cycle of birth and death, developing and enhancing the abilities of life, and committing to save various sentient beings--all these deeds are within the mechanism of conditioned co-arising. At the same time, they cannot be alienated from conditioned coarising. In turn, conditioned co-arising embodies or abides as relationships, aggregates, productions, changes, dismissal, distinguishing, continuum, growth, or unfolding, which not only are traceable in reasoning, but also share the fundamental reasoning, i.e. the common and thorough mechanism of conditioned co-arising. At this point, even though it is possible to unfold the conduct of saving sentient beings theoretically and to a superlative state, it is not omnipotent, nor can it be done totally independently from other entities. On the one hand, Bodhisattvas flexibly adjust to a whole spectrum of different kinds of sentient beings' circumstances and then fine-tune their methods and skills in salvation. On the other hand, Bodhisattvas will actively invest major related items to alleviate the concurrent difficulties, and then reveal to sentient beings the directions, clues, or ways for them to be free from the cycle of birth and death. In short, in order to be able to save sentient beings, there has to be a feasible chain of reasoning that complies with the mechanism of conditioned co-arising.

Among the many examples of the reasoning for the mechanism of dependent-co-arising in "Samanta-mukha-parivarta," only two are listed as follows: (a) What Bodhisattvas offer to sentient beings in need is help that ameliorates immediate suffering or indicates ways out of dire situations. Bodhisattvas will not promise anything that violates the mechanism of conditioned co-arising, such as returning to the original situation, being fixed in the current situation in the mundane world, life without death, or an eternal life after death; and (b) The text repeatedly uses the optative mood of the verb *parimucyeran* or *parimukto bhavet* (might be liberated). This shows that Bodhisattva Avalokiteśvara alone cannot liberate sentient beings; that is, salvation cannot be achieved unilaterally. Therefore, the so-called "Other-Power salvation (*tariki* salvation)" is not part of "Samanta-mukha-parivarta."

The second major aspect is that, reasoning for transformation in salvation can be described as "being compliant with the objects that are receiving guidance in order to manifest the corresponding format to teach the Dharma to them." Irrespective of whether those are the sentient beings pursuing life experience or practitioners already practicing, fundamentally, they are all illusions. They might be trapped in perplexities, be looking for better directions in life, be on the verge of changing lanes in ways of practice, or still have a long way to go on whichever way they are practicing. All these situations are among the possible rescue domains; therefore, there is the possibility for Bodhisattvas to unfold to a superlative state.

However, even though there is the possibility of superlative unfolding, caution should be exercised so that such terminology is not used in an absolute sense or is misused.

According to "Samanta-mukha-parivarta," there are four main arguments in the conduct of egalitarian salvation: (a) It is necessary to recognize that the object of being saved is an illusion, so are the saviour and the act of salvation. If any one of them is not illusory but fixed with substantial content or appearance rather than being the embodiment of changes, then there is no need trying to save anyone because there is no room for salvation; (b) For the sake of egalitarian salvation, it is necessary to perceive various sentient beings' differences and what makes them different. It is then possible to offer appropriate help best suited to all different needs. If one claims to be a saviour yet is not flexible, or can only embody limited appearances, then it will be difficult to offer help to various sentient beings; (c) Not only are there various sentient beings and practitioners, but their past, present, future, environment, superficial levels and levels underneath are also extremely diverse. The most important perspective when offering help lies in the *"x-vaineyānāṃ sattvānāṃ"* to those sentient beings who are to be guided (or instructed) by the form of x. The key word *"vaineya"* can be dissected into *"vai"* (prefix *vi* with a *vçddhi* formation) + *"neya"* (the future passive participle of $\sqrt{}$*nī*). The literal meaning of the word is "to be guided individually or should be guided individually" while it means "what should be directed, guided, instructed, or adjusted." The reason for laying emphasis on "the categories that should be guided" is not so as to dwell only on the past or present, but also that Bodhisattvas should guide them into their own appropriate future; (d) After comprehending the reasons for all different sentient beings, Bodhisattvas should carefully ponder the categories best suitable for guiding them, manifest appropriate appearances to rescue sentient beings from their agonies, and also be able to teach the Dharma to sentient beings *(sattvānāṃ dharmaṃ deśayati)*. As a result, sentient beings can learn, practice, develop capabilities, and cultivate abilities so as to find the ways that are suitable to them or to advance realistically on the ways of practice.

In the final analysis, the unfolding Bodhisattva deeds performed by Bodhisattva Avalokiteśvara can be comprehended as "possible superlative unfolding" from the perspective of the range of styles. Furthermore, how "possible superlative unfolding" can be possible has been expounded from the perspective of theory and practice. Upon further scrutiny at the level of constituting ideas, then the reasoning for the mechanism of conditioned co-arising and the reasoning for transformation in salvation are the two key ingredients to achieve superlative unfolding.

Conclusion

"Samanta-mukha-parivarta" expresses unfolding religious operations as well as related topics, such as mind, body and abiding-places, that are all unfolding thoughts and applications.

On the topic of mind, Bodhisattva Avalokiteśvara embodies the unfolding view of mind and practice of mind. On the one hand, it eliminates all sorts of dividing devices in perception or cognition. On the other hand, relying on the equal and thoroughly unimpeded styles in perception and cognition, universal observation will emerge in this space-time continuum. After studious practice of mind, egalitarian consolation and vast benevolence and compassion can perceive the reason why sentient beings are vexed by horrors or afflictions. Furthermore, Bodhisattva Avalokiteśvara will make arrangement for tools, clues, and ways for sentient beings to be free from all perplexities.

On the topic of body, there are three major points: one should avoid doing anything "antiunfolding;" one should cultivate the supernatural power to "transform body;" and the reason for transforming body is to save various sentient beings and practitioners equally.

On the topic of abiding-places, by eliminating the "anti-unfolding view of abiding-places" passively and comprehending clearly the series from fundamental conditioned co-arising to transformation, the function of the resulting unfolding view of abiding-places does not link tactics such as identity and belonging, or incidents such as birth, aging, sickness and death to specific abiding-places that turn abiding-places into enclosed or limited domains. Rather, all abiding-places can be used as locations for various sentient beings to be rescued from. As a result, the conduct of saving various sentient beings can keep unfolding, and abiding-places can be unfolded into the correct view and function of abiding-places.

In sum, the unfolding Bodhisattva deeds exemplified by Bodhisattva Avalokiteśvara can be comprehended as "possible superlative unfolding" in scope and style. In theory, there does not exist any form of limitedness in reality. In practice, none of the actions exhibits any form of limitedness in their unconditioned state of being the dharma, either. The Bodhisattva deeds unfolded will embody the "possible superlative unfolding" in the "ideas constituting Bodhisattva deeds." In other words, it is possible to unfold the principle of Bodhisattva deeds with a feasible chain of reasoning to a superlative state. In view of the teaching that Bodhisattvas are compliant with "reasoning for the mechanism of conditioned co-arising" and "reasoning for transformation in salvation," these two paths of reasoning are the keys for determining the feasibility of Bodhisattva deeds and the means by which Bodhisattva deeds can be unfolded to a superlative state.

10

Some remarks on the language of Kumārajīva's translation of the Lotus Sūtra

Barbara Meisterernst

1. Introduction

In this paper a few peculiarities of the language of Kumārajīva's translation of the Lotus Sūtra will be discussed. This analysis of the language of the *Miāofǎ liǐnhuā jīng, the Lotus Sūtra (Saddharmapuṇḍarīka-sūtra),* is based on a previous - more general - investigation of the temporal and aspectual structures of Early Buddhist texts. In these texts, the language of the *Miāofǎ liǐnhuā jīng,* a translation text, is particularly compared to the language of the *Gāosēng Fǎxiǎn zhuān*, a text which is originally written in Chinese. This comparative study has revealed that although both texts were written at the same time (at the beginning of the 5th century), the text written by Kumārajīva is evidently more conservative in its grammatical structure than the original Chinese text written by *Fǎxiǎn.*

Although Kumārajīva also regularly employs the newly developed aspectual structures which only emerged after the Han and during the Wei Jin Nanbei chao periods, his translations are to a great extent apparently influenced by his obviously excellent knowledge of the Classical Chinese language. For instance, he frequently employs temporal adverbs which are typical of the Classical Chinese language (600-300 century BCE), rather than employing the typical Han period Chinese (206 BCE -220 CE) or later variants. However, many constructions which are also typical of Han period Chinese are attested in his translation. The paper will present examples for both, the innovative structures employed by Kumārajīva , as also the more conservative structures and it will show that although his language certainly differs from that of the Classical Chinese literature, it is considerably influenced by it.

2. Kumārajīva and his work

Kumārajīva, Jiūmóluóshí 鳩摩羅什 in Chinese, an erudite monk from Kucha, was one of the 'four great translators' of Buddhist texts into Chinese together with Paramārtha of the 6th century, Xuanzang of the 7th century and Amoghavajra of the 8th century (Hureau 2003: 7). In his biography, the *Gāosēng zhuān*, he is praised for his great intelligence. This intelligence is exemplified by the fact that he is said to have already recited a thousand gathas per day, consisting of 32.000 words, at the age of seven, after he left his home and followed his mother who had become a Buddhist nun. Later, at the age of nine, after he followed his mother to Kashmir, he wrote a thousand gathas from morning till noon and recited another thousand from noon till evening. In Kucha he was ordained at the age of twenty, and in Kashgar he converted from Hinayana to Mahayana Buddhism. As the son of an Indian Brahmin and a princess from Kucha he learned Chinese only during his sixteen years as a captive of the General Lü Guang 呂光 who conquered and occupied Kucha in 384. When he finally arrived in Chang'an in the 12th month and on the 20th day of the third year of the era *hongshi* (i.e. in February 402) he became head of a translation project in which he collaborated with around 800 monks (according to Huijiao) in order to translate or retranslate Buddhist texts into Chinese.[1] A similar project had already been established for about three hundred years in Luoyang in the Baima-monastery (Dutt 1962, 1988, p. 303-306 cf. Singh 2008). Besides his translations, Kumārajīva is also reported to have written some genuine Chinese texts.

Although not all of the texts attributed to Kumārajīva have actually been composed by him, yet he was one of the most eminent translators of his time.[2] He was the most productive among a number of translators active during the same period like Fótuóyēshè 佛陀耶舍, Zhú Fóniàn 竺佛念, Dào Luè 道略, Tǐnmóyèshè 曇摩耶舍, Lóngshùpúsà 龍樹菩薩, Típópúsà 提婆菩薩, Hélíbǐmó 訶梨跋摩, Qiúnăbǐmó 求那跋摩, Mămíngpúsà 馬鳴菩薩, Fúruòduōluó 弗若多羅, Tiānjīnpúsà 天親菩薩, Shèngzhělóngshù 聖者龍樹, and Sēngzhào 僧肇. His translations, although having been criticized by some of his contemporaries for their free paraphrases of the original texts (and also for the fact that he was not a native speaker of Chinese)[3] were most influential in later times and

---

1 According to Hui Jiao's *Gāosēng zhuān* 高僧傳, Taisho 50, 2059. See also Lu (2004).

2 For a detailed analysis see Hureau (2003).

3 See Yang Lu (2004:37) who states: "Sengrui, for example, commented on the impact Kumārajīva'a limited ability in the Chinese language had on the quality of his translations in the prefaces to the *Da zhi du lun and Mūlamadhyamakārikā,* both of which were translated by Kumārajīva."

his translation of the Lotus Sūtra remains the source for many translations into other languages such as English. With regard to his translation style, the Digital Dictionary of Buddhism (DDB) notes that it "was distinctive, possessing a smoothness that reflects a prioritization on the conveyance of the meaning as opposed to precise literal rendering. Because of this, his renderings of seminal Mahāyāna texts have often remained more popular than later, more exact translations." (DDB http://www.buddhism-dict.net/cgi-bin/ accessed 20.12.2010). Besides the Lotus-Sūtra he also translated amongst others the Diamond Sūtra *Jīngāng jīng* 金剛經, the Amitâbha-sūtra *Āmítuó jīng* 阿彌陀經, the Vimalakīrti-nirdeśa-sūtra *Wéimó jīng* 維摩經, the Madhyamakakārikā *Zhōng lún* 中論[4] and the Mahā-prajñāpāramitā-śāstra *Dā zhìdù lún* 大智度論.[5]

2.1 A linguistic study of Kumārajīva's Lotus Sūtra

The Wei Jin Nanbei chao period (220-581), i.e. the early Medieval period, is most interesting for diachronic studies in Chinese, since many of the source structures of Modern Chinese grammar have their first regular appearance during that time. The structure of the language of Buddhist texts of the Wei Jin Nanbei chao period also constitutes the basis from which the grammar typical of the Tang period (618-907) Buddhist texts develop, and it is of particular interest linguistically, since it is supposed to reflect the vernacular language of the time in a much higher degree than non-Buddhist Chinese literature. As one of the great translators of this period, Kumārajīva's translations can serve well as an example for a particular variety of the language of the time. In this paper only one aspect of Kumārajīva's language will be elucidated: i.e. the expressions of the categories Tense and Aspect in verbal predicates, and their differences from or similarities with the respective expressions in the Classical and Han period literature.

Verbal predicates refer to events or to situations of different types which are all characterised by an aspectual and a temporal meaning. In the Indo-European languages, and accordingly also in the source languages from which the Chinese Buddhist texts are translated, these meanings are realised in the morphology of the verb. The category Aspect (i.e. grammatical aspect) is defined as indicating the viewpoint from which a situation is presented; this

---

4 The *Zhonglun* 中論 *[Mūla-madhyamaka-kārikā]* T 1564.30 is Nāgârjuna's (2nd – 3rd c.) most important work and has been translated by Kumārajīva's translation who includes a commentary that stays close to the root text, merely unpacking the arguments (see DDB http://www.buddhism-dict.net/cgi-bin/xprddb.pl?9f.xml+id%28%27b9f8d-6a39%27%29 accessed 30.12.2010).

5 The *Dā zhìdù lún* 大智度論 is not supposed to be an authentic text by Nāgârjuna. The DDB states: The *Dazhidulun* contains many elements hard to reconcile with the authentic Nāgârjuna, and, like the *Twelve Gate Treatise*, no mention of it is found anywhere outside Eastern Asia. Some scholars speculate that this may have been Kumārajīva's commentary (DDB http://www.buddhism-dict.net/cgi-bin/xprddb.pl?9f.xml+id%28%27b9f8d-6a39%27%29 accessed 30.12.2010.)

is basically the perfective-imperfective distinction, whereas Tense is defined locating a situation on the time axis. Besides the categories tense and aspect which are usually realised by grammaticalized morphemes, a third category exists which refers to the event structure of a situation; different labels have been proposed for this category, e.g. Lexical Aspect (in contrast to grammatical aspect), Situation type, or Aktionsart. Languages do not need to mark tense or aspect in their verbal systems (and many languages actually do not mark these categories morphologically), but the third category which deals with the structure of the event the predicate refers to is always inherent in the semantics of a verb or predicate, and is accordingly considered basic.

In Chinese, the category tense has apparently at no time been expressed in the morphology of the verb - contrastively to the Indo-European languages; however, it has been assumed that Ancient Chinese had the capacity to mark different verbal categories, including aspectual meanings, by affixation (Sagart 1999). But the evidence provided as yet for this hypothesis is not sufficient to establish a coherent and productive morphological system for the early stages of Chinese, comparable, e.g. to that of the Indo-European languages.[6] Since neither tense, nor aspect, are visibly marked in the morphology of the verb in Classical and Han period Chinese, other grammatical means have to be assumed to indicate temporal and aspectual relations; these are predominantly the semantics of the verb, i.e. the event structure of the predicate, and additional lexical means such as adverbial phrases, sentence-final particles, etc. All these syntactic devices have the capacity to express even subtle temporal and aspectual relations.

In contrast to Classical and Han period Chinese, Modern Chinese exhibits a productive system of aspectual suffixes indicating different aspectual notions. This system starts to develop at the end of the Han and particularly during the Wei Jin Nanbei chao periods and successively gains more prominence in the Buddhist literature during the Tang period. The employment of these suffixes is closely related to the semantics, the event structure of the verb they attach to,[7] as is, in a comparable manner, the employment of adverbs, which is closely connected to the situation type or lexical aspect of the verb or predicate they modify. This relation is in particular relevant for the employment of the

---

6 There is general agreement on the development of the departing tone *qù shēng* 去聲 from a former suffix *–s*, for which many different functions have been assumed (e.g. Downer 1959, Schüssler 2007). One of these functions, i.e. the possible distinction of a perfective from an imperfective variant (Unger ms.) or the indicating of the past/passive (Schuessler 2007: 42), might be relevant in this context, but here again, evidence for a *qù shēng* reading in a predicate at issue is difficult to obtain.

7 Accordingly the different verb classes have been subject to a variety of linguistic studies on Modern Chinese syntax and semantics (e.g. by Tai 1984, Smith 1991, Ross 1995, 2002, Tang 2001, Lin 2003, 2005 and others).

closed class of aspectotemporal adverbs which mark the predicate temporally or aspectually and accordingly serve a similar purpose as the aspect and tense markers of e.g. the Indo-European languages. These adverbs belong to the class of genuine adverbs operating on the level of V which can be separated by the verb only by a small range of syntactic elements, including prepositional phrases, and manner adverbs. But, in contrast to aspectual or temporal markers in the morphology of the verb, the aspecto-temporal adverbs of Chinese are not obligatory.

3. Aspectual structures in early Buddhist Chinese[8]

During the Classical and Han periods, temporal and aspectual meanings are basically expressed by aspecto-temporal adverbs.[9] Many of the adverbs employed during the Han period are still attested more or less unchanged in the early Buddhist Chinese literature in both genuine Chinese and translation texts. However, as an important innovation, the introduction of the source structure of the aspectual suffixes of Modern Chinese, the structure: V_1 (NP) V_2, can be observed during this period. This structure serves to express completion or the resultative, similar to and together with the Classical employment of the aspecto-temporal adverbs *jì* 既 and *yǐ* 已 which serve the same purpose. Within the closed class of aspecto-temporal adverbs, changes are less obvious during the Wei Jin Nanbei chao periods. Some of the Classical and Han period adverbs retain their functions with only minor alterations, but others show semantic changes or are on their way towards disappearing. The position of the aspecto-temporal adverbs with relation to the verb is unchanged, identical to the position of temporal adverbs expressing a point of time (TA) 'at X time' 'from X time on' etc. and the position and syntax of duration phrases 'for X time'. In general, their basic syntactic constraints do not change from Classical to Wei Jin Nanbei chao Chinese despite the changes in the Chinese syntax which have been assumed to develop under the influence of the Buddhist translation literature. In another innovation, additional to the above mentioned innovation VP1 (NPObj) VP2, the occasional employment of two modal auxiliary verbs as markers of the future tense can be observed during the period at issue here. In the following study the conservatism and innovations in the expression of temporal and aspectual meanings in Kumārajīva's translation of the Lotus Sūtra will be presented. With its long narrative passages, this text displays many different grammatical features and is accordingly particularly apt for a linguistic study of temporal and aspectual relation.

8 Some of the material presented in the following has already been discussed in Meisterernst (2011).

9 If any morphological markers of aspectual relations were still present in Classical Chinese, they were certainly not productive anymore.

3.1 Perfective, completive, resultative

In Classical and Han period Chinese, completion and the resultative notions related to the perfective aspect, can only be expressed productively by aspecto-temporal adverbs, i.e. the aspecto-temporal adverbs *jì* 既 and *yǐ* 已 'already'.[10] Contrastively, during the Wei Jin Nanbei chao period, two different structures are available to express these notions: One, the same aspecto-temporal adverbs as in Classical and Han period Chinese, and second, the newly developed construction V_1 + (NP_{obj}) V_2 which exhibits the same functions. In the early stages of the development of this structure, different verbs of which only *liǎo* 了 survives are available for the position of V_2 which all have the common meaning 'to finish'. The different possible syntactic patterns to mark completion or the resultative in Wei Jin Nanbei chao Chinese are exemplified below.

Structure 1a: V_1 (NP_{obj}) V_2

V_2 can be represented by different verbs, the only relevant of which in the *Miàofǎ liǐnhuā* is the verb *yǐ* 已.

(1) 佛見此已便作是念 T09, no.262, p.13a26

Fó jiàn cǐ yǐ biàn zuò shì niàn

Buddha see this finish then make this thought

"... after the Buddha had seen this, he thought to himself ..."

Structure 1b: ADV V_1 (NP_{obj}) V_2

V1 is additionally modified by the aspecto-temporal adverb *jì* 既, never by adverbial *yǐ* 已.

(2) 既得此已，心大歡喜，自以爲足，而便自謂： T09, no.262, p.17b23

Jì dé cǐ yǐ, xīn dà huānxǐ, zì yǐwéi zú, ér biàn zì wèi

Already get this YI, heart great be-happy, self consider sufficient, CON then self say 'After we got this, we were very happy in our hearts and considered it sufficient, and then we said to ourselves:'

Structure 2: ADV V (NP_{obj})

The verb is only modified by one of the aspecto-temporal adverbs *jì* 既 or *yǐ* 已.

[10] Additionally, some of the sentence-final particles have traditionally been assumed to display aspectual functions, in particular the sentence-final particle *yǐ* 矣(Pulleyblank 1994, 1995), but they are not part of the verb phrase.

(3) 既到本國，與八萬四千菩薩圍繞至淨華宿王智佛所，白佛言：

T09, no.262, p.56b22

Jì dào běn guó, yǔ bā wàn sì qiān púsà, wéirǎo

Already arrive origin country, with eight ten-thousand four thousand bodhisattva, encircle

zhì jìnghuāsù wžng zhì fó suǒ, bǎi fó yžn

arrive Pure Flower Constellation King Wisdom Buddha place, talk Buddha say 'After he had arrived in his original country, he went, encircled by 84.000 bodhisattvas, to the place of the Buddha Pure Flower Constellation King Wisdom, and said to the Buddha:'

(4) 父知子心，漸已廣大，欲與財物。 T09, no.262, p.18b2

Fù zhī zǐ xīn, jiàn yǐ gužng dà, yù yǔ cži wù

Father know son heart, gradually already wide great, wish give properties

'The father knew that his son's heart had already gradually become wider and bigger and he wished to give him his properties.'

3.1.1 The structure V_1 NPobj V_2 in the *Miàofǎ ližnhuā jīng*

As the source structure of the aspectual suffix *-le* 了 in Modern Mandarin, the structure V_1 NPobj V_2 has been comprehensively and controversially discussed in the linguistic literature.[11] It has been assumed that the sentence-final position of the second verb (V_2) is due to the fact that in the Chinese Buddhist texts it often serves to translate a sentence-final gerundial verb in Sanskrit (Cheung 1977: 66), but Mei (1981: 70) already provided convincing evidence against this hypothesis based on the general syntactic constraints of Chinese.[12] In the Medieval Buddhist literature, different synonymous verbs can fill the slot of V_2. These are the verbs: *yǐ* 已 'finish, stop, complete', *jìng* 竟 'finish, complete', *qì* 訖 'finish, cease', *bì* 畢 'finish', and *liǎo* 了 'finish, complete' all expressing different notions of 'finish, complete'.[13] Of all these variants *yǐ* 已 is the only relevant V_2 in the *Miàofǎ ližnhuā jīng,* although some of the other variants are occasionally attested in this position in other contemporary Buddhist texts.[14] *Yǐ* 已 appears as both the aspecto-temporal adverb 'already'

[11] It has for instance been studied by Cheung 1977; Zhao 1979; Mei 1981, 1999; Jiang 2001, 2007, Karashima 2007, Meisterernst 2011 among many others.

[12] This argument has been pursued and supported by studies in particular by Jiang (2001, 2007) and by Meisterernst (2011).

[13] The functions of these five verbs have been analysed in Jiang (2001). In Mei (1981: 68) different glosses provided in the early lexicographical literature are presented.

[14] However, all of these verbs can appear as independent predicates. In the *Miàofž liánhuā jīng, ližo* 了 is attested several times in verbal compounds such as *míngližo* 明了 'understand', but it is never attested as V_2 in the construction V_1 NP V_2.

and the V_2 in the construction V_1 NPobj V_2. However, as already mentioned, contrastively to the aspectotemporal adverb *jì* 既, *yǐ* 已 is not attested as an adverb in structure 1b.[15] As a V_2, *yǐ* 已 can combine with verbs of different situation types (Aktionsart), but the predicate it attaches to is predominantly telic or bounded, i.e. it expresses either an accomplishment or an achievement. The V_2 *yǐ* 已 serves to express that the final change of state point of the situation has been obtained and that the situation is completed or terminated. Frequently it attaches to predicates consisting of an activity verb (which is atelic and unbounded), such as *shuō* **說** 'say, recite', or *zuò* 作 'make', with a definite / quantified NP as its inner argument which presents a boundary to the situation and changes the situation type of the entire predicate from atelic to telic, i.e. to an accomplishment.[16] The following verbs are attested in the structure V_1 NPobj V_2 in the texts at issue:

1. V_2 *yǐ* 已

Situation type	*Miàofǎ ližnhuā jīng*
Telic	放；授；令；(知)[17]；滅度；過；盡；見；聞；死；得；拾；具足；破；到;受；起；責；(聽)；持；出；滿；解；饒益；白；畢；散；
Atelic	說；供養；行；知；思維；作；尊；具足；讚；誦；白；讚歎

As the table shows, the predominant number of verbs consist of telic achievement verbs; some of the verbs appear in both categories. However, the following examples will reveal that the predicates built with verbs of the second category as V1, i.e. the atelic verbs, also frequently obtain a telic reading in the structure V1 NPobj V2, since their object-NPs are predominantly definite, which shifts the situation type of the entire predicate from activity to accomplishment as in example (5) with the verb *shuō* **說** 'tell, preach' which is followed by an object NP explicitly marked as definite by the demonstrative pronoun *shì* 是.

(5) 諸比丘尼**說**是偈已，白佛言：「世尊！ T09, no.262, p.36b7

Zhū bǐqiūní shuō shì jì yǐ, bži Fó yžn: Shì zūn

All bhiksunī say this gāthā YI, tell Buddha say: World Honoured

---

[15] Additionally the character *yǐ* 已 writes a variant of the preposition and connector *yǐ* 以 and, if only rarely, the final particle *yǐ* 已.

[16] According to Jiang (2001: 76) the employment in combination with continuous verbs such as *shuō* 說 or *zuò* 作 (持續動詞) can be considered as the original function of *yǐ* 已 as V2 for which a few examples are already attested in Han period Chinese and the second function which expresses completion (with achievement verbs) has been derived from this function. See also Mei (1999). For a further discussion of this topic see Jiang 2007, Meisterernst 2011).

[17] The brackets indicate that these verbs can have both a telic and an atelic reading. Situation type in general is compositional, i.e., it is determined by the verb and its arguments and adjuncts, in particular by the semantics of the inner argument of the verb.

'After all the bhiksunīs had recited this *gāthā,* they said to the Buddha: "World Honoured One!"'

Example (6) with verb *zuò* 作 'make' which is also atelic when isolated, is of the same structure as example (5), again the object-NP is marked as definite by a demonstrative determiner. This verb also belongs to the prototypical verbs to which *yǐ* 已 can be attached. The clause with *yǐ* 已 refers to a telic situation which has come to its natural final point, namely the final point of one particular and quantifiable situation expressed by the predicate. After the final point has been reached, a change of situation takes place.

(6) 作是念已，疾走而去。 T09, no. 262, p.16c21

Zuò shì niàn yǐ, jí zǒu ér qù

Make this thought YI, quick run CON leave 'After he thought that, he left quickly.'

In contrast to the preceding examples in which the verb in isolation is atelic and only becomes telic in combination with its internal argument, the definite object-NP, the verbs in the following examples are genuine telic, i.e. achievement verbs. The verb *dé* 得 'get, obtain' in example (7) represents a prototypical achievement verb. Identical to the preceding examples, the inner argument consists of a definite NP, but with an already telic verb no change of situation type is involved.

(7) 得是六根清淨已，更增壽命二百萬億那由他**歲**, T09, no.262, p.51a6

Dé shì liù gēn qīngjìng yǐ, gèng zēng shòu mìng èr bǎi wàn yì nžyóutā suì,

Get this six sense organ purify YI, otherwise accumulate longevity mandate two hundred ten-thousand hundred thousand nayuta (million) year, …

'After he had obtained the purification of the six sense organs, he once more accumulated his longevity to two hundred ten thousand million nayutas of years...'

In example (8) *yǐ* 已 is attached to a VP composed of the verb of perception *wén* 聞 'hear about' which also usually expresses an achievement and a definite object-NP. The *yǐ* 已 - clause refers to a completed situation, a resultant state in the future, which demonstrates that the construction is not confined to past contexts.

(8) 願爲解**說**，除我等疑，及未來世諸善男子聞此事已，亦不生疑。」 T09, no.262, p.41c27

Yuàn wèi jiě shuō, chú wǒ děng yí, jí wèilži shì zhū shàn nžnzǐ wén cǐ shì yǐ, yì bù shēng yí

With therefore explain say, remove I PL doubt, when future generation all good male hear this affair YI, also NEG grow doubt

'We request you therefore to explain in order to remove our doubts, so that all good men in future generations who will have heard about this affair, will also not develop doubts.'

Besides transitive VPs as in the examples presented above, *yǐ* 已can also attach to intransitive VPs as a V_2, which are passive (or maybe middle) constructions (with a patient subject),[18] or intransitive constructions with an agentive subject. In example (9) the verb *gōngyǎng* 供養 'make offerings' is attested in an intransitive construction, the inner argument is present in subject position, which is not obligatory. The subject in (9) is not marked for definiteness, but it can be assumed to be quantifiable; the situation type of the predicate is telic, but in a passive construction which always represents a situation as completed, rather the resultant state is focussed on; the situation reaches its natural final point when all the flowers available for the occasion have been used up.

(9) 華供養已，各以宮殿奉上彼佛，而作是言： T09, no.0262, p.23b6

Huā gōngyǎng yǐ, gè yǐ gōng diàn fèng shàng bǐ Fó, ér zuò shì yǎn

Flower offer YI, each with palace palace present above that Buddha, and make this word

'After the flowers had been offered, they each presented their palace to the Buddha and made this speech:'

In the following examples the V_1 is additionally marked by the aspecto-temporal adverb *jì* 既 'already'; these examples belong to the structure 1b which is generally confined to achievement verbs.[19] The verbs appearing in this structure are *dé* 得 'get, obtain', *zhī* 知 'recognise', evidently in its achievement reading, and the verb *wén* 聞 'hear' in its achievement reading. Already in Classical and Han period Chinese the aspecto-temporal adverb *jì* 既 by default modifies telic, achievement verbs, and state verbs, focussing either on the final or -with state verbs - the initial point of change. As the following discussion will show, in the texts under investigation, in a manner characteristic for each text, *jì* 既predominantly or exclusively selects achievement verbs. Semantically this structure seems to be redundant, since both *yǐ* 已 as V2 and the adverbial *jì* 既 basically serve the same purpose, i.e. to indicate that the first of two situations has been completed before the next one starts.

[18] In the linguistic literature this constructions can also be referred to as ergative or unaccusative, in contrast to unergative constructions which have an agentive subject.

[19] This structure, which retains Classical characteristics is only very rarely attested in other early Buddhist texts. Only one instance of the structure 1b is attested in the *Fǎxiǎn* and it is not at all attested in the *Zhèngfǎ huā jīng* where the aspecto-temporal adverb *jì* 既 is in general quite infrequent. In the *Zá āhán jīng*, only three identical instances of structure 1b occur.

(10) 既得此已，心大歡喜，自以爲足，而便自謂： T09, no.262, p.17b23

Jì dé cǐ yǐ, xīn dà huānxǐ, zì yǐwéi zú, ér biàn zì wèi

Already get this YI, heart great be-happy, self consider sufficient, CON then self say

'After we got this, we were very happy in our hearts and considered it sufficient, and then we said to ourselves:'

As this example demonstrates, occasionally both structures 1a and 2 are merged which leads to the assumption that the functions of preverbal *jì* 既 and *yǐ* 已and of verbal *yǐ* 已 as V_2 in the structure V_1 (NPobj) V_2 (and the other predecessors of *liǎo* 了 attested in this position) cannot be regarded as completely identical. Nevertheless, in the linguistic literature, predicates modified by preverbal *jì* 既 and *yǐ* 已 are, despite their syntactic differences, regarded as functionally comparable to those marked by the verbal suffix-*le* 了 indicating the perfective aspect in Modern Mandarin. This comparison is based mainly on the similar etymological sources of *jì* 既, *yǐ* 已, and *-le* 了 and the semantic similarities of the predicates modified by one of the Classical morphemes *jì* 既 and *yǐ* 已 and by Modern *-le* 了respectively.[20]

3.1.2 Adverbial modification by the aspecto-temporal adverbs *jì* 既 and *yǐ* 已

In Classical and Han period Chinese the aspecto-temporal adverbs *jì* 既 and *yǐ* 已 are the only lexical means to indicate the perfective, the resultative, and the completive aspect explicitly.[21] They usually select a telic predicate, mainly with an achievement verb, always focussing on the final change of state point and the initial point of the resultant state. According to their capacity to focus on the initial point of a resultant state, they can, in analogy, also focus on the initial point of a genuine state as long as the state is changeable and very occasionally they can also select an activity, always viewing the situation in its entirety from an external perspective. In the *Miàofǎ liánhuā jīng* both aspecto-temporal adverbs are attested mainly with telic, but - as in Classical and Han period Chinese - also with atelic verbs.[22] In general, the adverb *jì* 既 seems to be more confined in its employment with regard to the situation type of the verb than the adverb *yǐ* 已. Additionally, and in contrast to *yǐ* 已, *jì* 既 predominantly

[20] See Pulleyblank (1995:112): "In Modern Mandarin the verbal suffix *–le* is used to indicate perfectivity, that is, that an event is looked upon as complete or a bounded whole. In the Classical language an equivalent role is played by the preverbal particles *jì* 既 and *yǐ* 已. Modern *–le* is derived from the verb *liǎo* 了'to finish, dispose of' and classical perfective adverbs have a similar etymology."

[21] The particular aspectual function of the sentence final particle *yǐ* 矣 will be left out from this discussion.

[22] Contrastively, in the contemporary genuine Chinese text, the *Gāosēng Fǎxiǎn zhuàn*, *jì* 既 and *yǐ* 已 are confined to telic verbs which can be due to the fact that the text is much shorter than the *Miàofǎ ližnhuā jīng*, but also to the fact that it is less conservative than the latter.

appears in subordinate clauses, identical to *yǐ* 已 as V_2, whereas *yǐ* 已 as an aspecto-temporal adverb frequently marks the resultative in matrix clauses. The following verbs are attested with the aspecto-temporal adverbs *jì* 既 and *yǐ* 已.

a) The aspecto-temporal adverb *jì* 既

Situation type	*Miàofā liǐnhuā jīng*
Telic	飽；得；疲；益；聞；出；(知)；入；起；滿；信伏；滅度；見；到；遇
Atelic	遠；讚歎；久；幼稚；長大；知；玄

b) The aspecto-temporal adverb *yǐ* 已

Situation type	*Miàofā liǐnhuā jīng*
Telic	盡；得；具足；知見；從；教化；出；滿足；成；除；(知)；失；燒，救；離；見；通；集；度；聞；成就；辦；斷；起；說；有；信解受持；畢；授；至；死；趣；施；滅度；報；信解
Atelic	供養；具足；知；慇懃；朽邁；廣大；二十年 (NP)；辦；說；有；如；能破；作

The following two examples represent typical achievement verbs modified by adverbial *jì* 既. Examples like these do not differ from the examples in Classical and Han period texts.

(11=3) 既到本國，與八萬四千菩薩圍繞至淨華宿王智佛所，白佛言： T09, no.262, p.56b22

Jì dào běn guó, yǐ bā wàn sì qiān púsà, wéirǎo zhì jìnghuāsù wžng zhì fó suǒ, bži fó yžn

Already arrive origin country, with eight ten-thousand four thousand bodhisattva, encircle arrive Pure Flower Constellation King Wisdom Buddha place, talk Buddha say

'After he had arrived in his original country, he went, encircled by 84.000 bodhisattvas, to the place of the Buddha Pure Flower Constellation King Wisdom, and said to the Buddha:'

(12) 既得阿羅漢道，自謂滅度， T09, n.262, p.29a18

Jì dé āluóhàn dào, zì wèi mièdù, zīshēng jiānnžn, dé shǎo wéi zú

Already get arhat way, self mean extinction, necessities difficult, get few make enough 'When we obtained the way of an Arhat we thought we had gained extinction.'

Both adverbs *jì* 既 and *yǐ* 已 can be combined and modify a verb in a subordinate clause as in example (13), but also in matrix clauses.[23] In this combination the completion of the first situation is emphasized more explicitly than in the examples with *jì* 既 alone. The verbs attested in this combination are all telic achievement verbs, i.e. verbs to which *yǐ* 已as a V_2 can also attach.

(13) 時二使人即求窮子，既已得之，具陳上事。 T09, no.262, p.17a12

Shí èr shì rén jí qiú qióng zǐ, jì yǐ dé zhī, jū chén shàng shì

Time two envoy man then search poor son, already already get OBJ, together explain above affair

'At the time the two envoys were looking for the impoverished son, and when they found him, they together explained the above [mentioned] affair [to him].

In the following examples, the adverb *yǐ* 已on its own modifies the verb indicating completion or the resultative. In contrast to the adverb *jì* 既 which in the analysed texts is confined to the subordinate clause,[24] the adverb *yǐ* 已 predominantly modifies the verb of a matrix clause or of a clausal object following verbs of meaning and saying such as *wèi* 謂'mean' or *yžn* 言 'say'. In example (14) the adverb modifies the typical achievement verb *dé* 得'get, obtain' in a matrix predicate.

(14) 今法王大寶自然而至，如佛子所應得者皆已得之。」 T09, no.262, p.17c9

Jīn fǎ wžng dà bǎo zìržn ér zhì, rú Fó zǐ suǒ yīng dé zhě jiē yǐ dé zhī

Now dharma king great precious naturally CON arrive, like Buddha son REL ought get NOM all already get OBJ

'Now the values of the Dharma king all arrive quite naturally, it is similar to [the fact] that everything the Buddha's sons ought to get, they have already got [it].'

In example (15) the verb *zhī* 知 '(get to) know, recognise' in a matrix clause is marked by *yǐ* 已. Although the verb *zhī* 知can also refer to an achievement 'realize, learn (to know)', in this example the verb is evidently stative, referring to the resultant state of knowing. The employment of *yǐ* 已 in combination with this verb in its state reading is well attested in the Han period literature.

(15) 於無量億劫，行此諸道已，道場得成果，我已悉知見，如是大果報

T09, no.262, 5c22

[23] In *Zá āhán jīng* two instances of the combination *jì yǐ* 既已 in a matrix clause are attested (T02, no.99, p-164b12 and T02, no.99, p.167c07).

[24] See also Gurevič (1974: 95).

Yú wú liàng yì jié, xíng cǐ zhū dào yǐ, dàochǐng

At not-have measure hundred thousand kalpa, got this all way YI, Buddhist rites

dé chéngguó, wǒ yǐ xī zhī jiàn, rú shì dà guǒbào

get achievement, I already completely know see, be.like this great retribution

'In the immeasurable hundred thousands of kalpas, after he had conducted all these ways, he had achieved his goal at the place of enlightenment; I have already completely known and seen those great retributions.'

In example (16) the disyllabic verb *fèngshì* 奉侍 'serve' which by default has an atelic reading is modified by *yǐ* 已, the situation is viewed from an external - perfective - viewpoint as completed.[25]

(16) 前已奉侍億百千佛，從億百千佛發意立願， T09, no.263, p.100b23

Qiǎn yǐ fèngshì yì bǎi qiān fó, cóng yì bǎi qiān fó fāyì lì yuàn

Former already serve hundred-thousand hundred thousand Buddha, follow hundred-thousand hundred thousand Buddha have. intention establish wish

'Formerly, they already served the millions of Buddhas, and according to the millions of Buddhas they have made their intentions and vows …'

The presented examples demonstrate that in the early Buddhist literature the structures representing the resultative, completive and perfective show on the one hand an important innovation with the structure V_1 (NO_{obj}) V_2, but on the other hand - with regard to the employment of the aspecto-temporal adverbs *jì* 既 and *yǐ* 已 - they are most conservative.[26]

However, with the appearance of the structure V_1 (NO_{obj}) V_2 there is an obvious tendency for the aspecto-temporal adverb *jì* 既 to be replaced by the new structure, and for he adverb *yǐ* 已 to appear in a matrix clause for which the new structure is not available.[27]

---

[25] Since the verb *fèngshì* 奉侍 'serve' is attested with a postverbal duration phrase expressing situational duration in T09, no. 263, p.105b09, its default reading is evidently atelic; with a telic achievement verb the duration phrase can only express resultant state duration.

[26] However, it has to be conceded that contrastively to Classical and Han period Chinese sentence with one of the adverbs *jì* 既 and *yǐ* 已 are usually not concluded by the final particle *yǐ* 矣 anymore (there is one instance in the *Zhèngfǎ huā jīng*). In general, this final is only attested very infrequently in the texts at issue.

[27] According to Gurevič (1974: 95) *yǐ* 已 can occur in both independent sentences and subordinate clauses. However, in most of the examples presented it appears in a matrix clause.

3.2 Adverbial modification by aspecto-temporal adverbs indicating past tense

a) The Classical adverb *chžng* 嘗:

In Classical and Han period Chinese the adverb *chžng* 嘗 is usually employed to indicate the singular occurrence of a situation located in the past which can be either atelic or telic. This adverb belongs syntactically to the same category as the adverbs *jì* 既 and *yĭ* 已, but it is less confined with regard to the situation type of the selected verb; i.e. verbs of all situation types can be modified by *chžng* 嘗. Its basic function is evidently to express temporal relations. The temporal analysis can be supported by the fact that sentences with *chžng* 嘗 can be additionally marked by temporal adverbials explicitly locating the situation on the time axis. The adverb *chžng* 嘗 quite early became homophonous with the adverb *chžng* 常 expressing habituality and possibly the two have occasionally been employed interchangeably,[28] but as has been shown in a study on these adverbs (Meisterernst ms.) the two different readings depend on the semantics of the verb and other syntactic evidence. Even if a habitual reading can be assumed for the predicate, *chžng* 嘗always locates the habitual situation in the past.

In the early Buddhist literature *chžng* 嘗is obviously already obsolete; it only appears very occasionally in combination with the aspectual negative marker *wèi* 未;[29] in this combination it is also most frequently attested in the Classical and Han period literature, but only very few instances occur in the *Miàofă ližnhuā jīng* and other Buddhist texts from the same period.

(17) 又見佛子，未嘗睡眠，經行林中，懃求佛道。 T09, no.262, p.3b1

Yòu jiàn fó zĭ, wèi chžng shuìmyžn, jīng xíng lín zhōng, qĭn qiú fó dào

Again see Buddha son, NEGasp CHANG sleep eye, pass go forest middle, diligent seek Buddha way

'Again I see the sons of the Buddha who have never closed their eyes to sleep; they walked around (performed ca kamana) in the forests diligently seeking the Buddha way.'

Example (17) above represents the only instance of *chžng* 嘗 in the *Miàofă ližnhuā jīng*.[30]

---

[28] Dobson (1959: 54), who operates with the category aspect in his analysis of the Chinese verb system, analyses *chžng* 嘗 as an adverb indicating customary aspect: "The act is viewed as being one of habit rather than of a specific occurrence".

[29] See also Gurevič (1974: 109). The particular semantics of this combination are discussed below.

[30] Another instance is attested in the *Zhèngfă huā jīng* T09, no.263, p.115c14. In the *Zá āhán jīng* the combination *wèi cháng* 未嘗 is slightly more frequent.

In general, in the early Buddhist literature *chžng* 嘗 is regularly replaced by the aspectotemporal adverb *céng* 曾 which is attested either independently or in combination with the aspectual negative marker *wèi* 未.

b) The Han period adverb *céng* 曾:

The aspecto-temporal adverb *céng* 曾, which occasionally serves to gloss the adverb *chžng* 嘗 discussed above, has to be distinguished from the adverb *zēng* 曾 'then, even, just' which is frequently combined with a negative marker and which serves to emphasize the negative force of the predicate. The aspecto-temporal adverb *céng* 曾 corresponds to *céngjīng* 曾經 'once' in Modern Mandarin, and to *chžng* 嘗 in Classical and Han period Chinese to which it is synonymous (Pulleyblank 1995: 119); it refers to situations of different types in the past (*Gŭdài Hànyŭ xūcí cídiăn* 2000: 47). It only becomes more frequently attested in the Han period literature -however, in the *Shĭjì* (ca. 100 BCE) it is still very rare - and it obviously replaces *chžng* 嘗 in the early Buddhist literature. In its function as an aspecto-temporal adverb it indicates a singular situation located temporally in the past, independent of the situation type of the verb selected.[31] It is predominantly attested in subordinate temporal clauses which serve to provide background information, but it can also appear in a matrix clause. Identically to *chžng* 嘗, *céng* 曾 also combines with the aspectual negative marker *wèi* 未.

The adverb *céng* 曾 is frequently attested in the *Miàofă ližnhuā jīng,* in the predominant number of instances in combination with the negative marker *wèi* 未: *wèi céng* 未曾, but also on its own.[32] Occasionally it appears in combination with the aspecto-temporal adverb *yĭ* 已 in the order *yĭ céng* 已曾. In the following section a few examples of the aspecto-temporal adverb *céng* 曾 and its respective combinations will be discussed. The first example represents the adverb *céng* 曾 on its own modifying a telic, i.e. achievement verb, referring to a situation in the past.

(18) 佛曾親近百千萬億無數諸佛，盡行諸佛無量道法， T09, no.262, p.5b28

Fó céng qīn jìn băi jiān wàn yì wú shù zhū fó, jìn xíng zhū fó wú liàng dào fă

Buddha CENG personally approach hundred thousand ten-thousand hundred-thousand not, have number all Buddha, completely go all Buddha not. have measure way dharma

'The Buddha has in the past personally approached a hundred, a thousand, ten thousand, a million, a countless number of Buddhas and has completely carried out an immeasurable number of methods to obtain *nirvāṇa.'*

---

[31] See Gurevič (1974: 105) who defines *céng* 曾 as indicating that an action or a fact takes place at some undefined moment in the past.

[32] It is also attested in the the *Zhèngfă huā jīng,* and in the *Zž āhžn jīng* , but not in the *Făxiăn.*

In example (19) and (20) two atelic verbs are modified by *céng* 曾, in example (19) it is the atelic verb *gōngyǎng* 供養 'make offerings' and in (20) the existential state verb *wú* 無 'not have'.

(19) 若人有福，曾供養佛，志求勝法，爲**說**緣覺。 T09, no.262, p.3a02

Ruò rén yǒu fú, céng gōngyǎng fó, zhì qiú shèng fǎ, wèi shuō yužnjué

If man have good.fortune, CENG offer Buddha, intention seek superior dharma, therefore talk *pratyekabuddha*

'If a man has a good fortune and has once made offerings to the Buddha, and with all his will seeks the superior dharma, he preaches therefore the [way of the] *pratyekabuddha*.'

(20) 常演**說**法，曾無他事。 T09, no.262, p.20a16

Chžng yǎn shuō fǎ, céng wú tā shì

Constantly practice tell law, CENG not.have other affair

'I constantly practice and preach the law, and never did I occupy myself with anything else.'

Example (21) shows an irregular word order with regard to the two adverbs: the modal adverb *yì* 亦 which is supposed to precede the aspecto-temporal adverb follows it.

(21) 我在十六數，曾亦爲汝**說**。 T09, no.262, p.26c25

Wǒ zài shí liù shù, céng yì wèi rǔ shuō

I be.at ten six number, CENG also for you tell

'I myself was among the sixteen, and once I also preached for you.'

According to the general rule that aspecto-temporal adverbs follow modal adverbs in Han period Chinese the expected word order would be [modal | aspectual] *yì céng* 亦曾. This word order is attested in a manuscript version of this part of the text on the manuscript Ch 647 from the Turfan collection in Berlin which dates between 300 and 550 (Thilo 1985: 46), i.e. from the time when the *Miàofǎ ližnhuā jīng* had originally been composed. The word order *céng yì* 曾亦 in example (21) is unique in the early Buddhist literature, and accordingly it can be assumed that the word order variant in the manuscript represents the correct order. The regular word order is e.g. attested in the *Zž āhžn jīng* and it is also attested with other modal adverbs such as *bì* 必.[33]

[33] The regular word order is attested in the following example from the *Zá āhán jīng* thus providing more evidence for the irregularity of the word order in the example (21) from the *Miàofǎ liánhuā jīng*:

(i) 『我長夜輪轉生死以來，亦曾更受如是之苦，其數無量，T02, no.99, p.241c16

Wǒ cháng yè lún zhužn shēng sǐ yǐ lái, yì céng gèng shòu rú shì

I long night wheel turn born die CON come, also CENG further receive be.like this

zhī kǔ, qí shù wú liàng

SUB suffer, its number not.have measure

'Since then for long nights I turned the wheel of life and death, I also once additionally received all kinds of bitterness of immeasurable numbers.'

In the following examples *céng* 曾 appears in combination with negative markers, i.e. predominantly with the aspectual negative marker *wèi* 未 in the combination *wèi céng* 未曾; this is the successor of the combination *wèi chǎng* 未嘗.[34] Similar to the aspecto-temporal adverbs *jì* 既 and *yǐ* 已 discussed above, the aspectual negative marker *wèi* 未 'not yet' chooses an event as its complement; it is attested in complimentary distribution with *jì* 既 and *yǐ* 已 and refers to the non-obtainment of a situation.[35] In combination with the aspectotemporal adverbs *chǎng* 嘗 and *céng* 曾, the negative marker *wèi* 未 also selects mainly telic verbs as its complement, but it is not confined to them; i.e. although it is only infrequently attested with state verbs (adjectives), it is regularly attested with the existential verb *yǒu* 有 'there is, have' expressing categorical denial in the past, present, and future. In the combination *wèi céng* 未曾 the semantics of the aspecto-temporal adverb *céng* 曾 adds to the semantics of the negative marker: the predicate refers either to a habitual or continuous situation in the past, which continues up to reference time, or it expresses a categorical denial of the situation referred to by the verb which is valid for all times. However, contrary to a predicate negated by *wèi* 未 alone, which by default denies the existence of an event but usually still anticipates the change of state point the verb refers to, this is not the case when *wèi* 未 co-occurs with the aspecto-temporal adverbs *chǎng* 嘗 or *céng* 曾. Examples such as the following are omnipresent in the early Buddhist literature.

(22) 是諸大眾，得未曾有，歡喜合掌，一心觀佛。 T09, no.262, p0002b16

Shì zhū dà zhōng, dé wèi céng yǒu, huānxǐ hé zhǎng, yī xīn guàn fó

This all great mass, get NEGasp CENG have, happy join palms, one heart look at Buddha

'All these people got what they never had before, they were happy and joined their palms and looked at the Buddha with one mind.'

(23) 我自昔來，未曾從佛聞如是說； T09, no.262, p. 6b09

Wǒ zì xīlži, wèi céng cóng fó wén rú shì shuō

I since ancient.times, NEGasp CENG from Buddha hear be like this talk

'Since ancient times I have never heard such a speech from the Buddha.'

In the following examples the aspecto-temporal adverb *yǐ* 已 is combined with the aspectotemporal adverb *céng* 曾. Like *yǐ* 已alone, the combination *yǐ*

---

[34] Very occasionally, *céng* 曾 is attested in combination with negative markers different from *wèi* 未 in the early Buddhist lituature, i.e. with the negative marker *bù* 不 following *céng* 曾. The combination is not attested in the *Miàofǎ liánhuā jīng* or the *Fǎxiǎn* and in the entire Āgama literature there appear merely four instances.

[35] Jì 既 and *yǐ* 已 refer to the obtainment of the respective situation.

céng 已曾 also predominantly modifies telic verbs; however, it differs from *yǐ* 已insofar as its function is rather temporal than aspectual. Karashima (2001: 329) glosses it as 'formerly, in the past' which suggests a purely temporal interpretation. Most frequently the combination *yǐ céng* 已曾 modifies the verb *gōngyǎng* 供養 'offer' in the Buddhist literature as in the following example, but it is not confined to this verb.[36] *Yǐ céng* 已曾 is apparently the successor of the combination *yǐ chžng* 已嘗 which is occasionally attested in Han period texts. It explicitly locates the completed situation at some point in the past, i.e. both adverbs retain their particular semantics in this combination. Identically to *yǐ* 已alone, the combination of the two adverbs frequently appears in independent sentences or matrix clauses.[37]

(24) 『是十六菩薩沙彌，甚爲希有，諸根通利，智慧明了，已曾供養無量千萬億數諸佛。 T09, no.262, p.25a20

Shì shí liù púsà shāmí, shèn wéi xī yǒu, zhū gēn tōnglì, zhì huì míng liǎo, yǐ céng gōngyǎng wú liàng qiān wàn yì shù zhū fó

This ten six bodhisattva, novice (śrāmanera), very be rarely have, all sense sharp-intelligence, wisdom knowledge bright clear, already once offer not-have measure thousand ten-thousand hundred thousand many all Buddha

'These sixteen bodhisattvas and novices are of a very rare kind, all their sense organs are very sharp and their wisdom is bright and clear, they already offered once to the immeasurable several thousands, ten-thousands, and hundred thousands of Buddhas.'

In example (25), two different predicates are modified by *yǐ céng* 已曾: the first consists of the two verbs *zhī* 知 'know' and *jiàn* 見 'see'; both verbs can have a telic (achievement) and an atelic reading, but modified by *yǐ* 已, the telic reading has to be preferred. In the last clause, the atelic activity verb *zuò* 作 is modified by *yǐ céng* 已曾. As has been shown above in example (6), this verb attains a telic (accomplishment) reading when its inner argument (independently of whether it appears in subject or in object position) is definite. This is not the case in example (25), but since the predicate is modified by *yǐ* 已 the situation is represented as completed from a perfective viewpoint.

(25) 我等已曾於此法如實知見，於六**內**入處觀察無我，我等已曾作如是意解：

T02, no.99, p.74a29

Wǒ děng yǐ céng yú cǐ fǎ rú shí zhī jiàn, yú liù nèirùchǔ guān ch wúwǒ, wǒ děng yǐ céng zuò rú shì yì jiě

---

[36] In the Āgama-literature *yǐcéng* 已曾 is only infrequently attested and never with the verb *gōngyǎng* 供養.

[37] In the *Zhèngfǎ huā jīng* the combination appears in both orders *yǐ céng* 已曾 and *céng yǐ* 曾已. Of the texts at issue here, the *Zhèngfǎ huā jīng* is the only one in which the reverse order is attested, but according to the CBETA search engine (www.cbeta.org), it is also attested in other texts.

I Pl YI CENG at this law be.like reality know see, at six internal.senses watch investigate no-self, I Pl YI CENG make be.like this thought explanation

'When we once with this dharma learnt and recognised according to the facts and with the six internal senses investigated the selflessness, we achieved to make the following explanation:'

c) The adverb *běn* 本The adverb *běn* 本 is listed in Shadick (755ff.) as a PA, a predicate adjunct of quality with the meaning 'originally, really'. It is classified together with a number of other adverbs which can be categorised as modal adverbs according to their position with regard to the verb phrase such as the above mentioned modal adverbs *bì* 必 'necessarily, certainly', and *yì* 亦'indeed, in fact'. In Dobson (1964: 68) it is listed as a late Han replacement of *shǐ* 始 'for the first time, first' "in the aspectual position".[38] The adverbial meaning 'originally' is clearly derived from the nominal meaning *běn* 本 'trunk, base, foundation'. The adverb *běn* 本 is already attested in the *Hǎn Fēi zǐ* and several times in the *Shǐjì*, but in these instances it is evidently not yet grammaticalized as an adverb indicating the past tense comparable to *céng* 曾.[39] In its original meaning the adverb *běn* 本still prevails in the Early Buddhist literature as in example (26). However, according to the examples in the *Zhèngfă huā jīng* (286 CE), the earlier translation of the Lotus Sūtra, *běn* 本 obviously appears higher in the adverbial hierarchy and accordingly differs syntactically from the other aspecto-temporal adverbs discussed above. This can be evidenced by the fact that, when the adverb *běn* 本 is attested in combination with other aspecto-temporal adverbs, it always precedes them. Additionally, it also precedes the modal adverb *yì* 亦, which in its default position is followed by a genuine aspecto-temporal adverb, as has been shown above in example (21) and in note (29).[40] According to the syntactic constraints displayed in the *Zhèngfă huā jīng*, the adverb *běn* 本 in these examples cannot be included into the class of genuine aspecto-adverbs which are located lower in the hierarchy of adverbs; it rather has to be analysed as a sentential, probably a 'subject-oriented', adverb. Unfortunately, in general, combinations with other adverbs - in particular

[38] As has been shown in Meisterernst (ms.) *shǐ* 始 evidently belongs to the aspectual adverbs in Han period Chinese which display a close relation with the verb they modify.

[39] Only one example in the *Shǐjì* shows an employment which might have served as a source for the development of *běn* 本 as marker of the past:
(i) 「君木誅諸呂，迎代王，今又矜其功，受上賞，*Shǐjì*: 10,421
Jūn běn zhū zhū Lyŭ, yíng Dài wáng, jīn yòu jīn qí gōng, shòu shàng shăng
Prince originally punish PL Lyu, welcome Dai king, now again boast his success, receive superior reward 'Once (originally) you punished the Lüs and invited the King of Dai, now you are boastful with your merits and receive the emperor's rewards, …'

[40] In the non-Buddhist literature, instances which exhibit the combination of the two adverbs *běn* 本 and *yì* 亦 are extremely rare. In the only instance in the *Sānguó zhì* the adverbs show the same word order as in the *Zhèngfă huā jīng*, no instances for the reverse order are attested in this text. In the Buddhist literature, according to the CBETA (www.cbeta.org) search engine, both orders are attested. In the *Zhōng āhán jīng* from the end of the 4th century, the reverse order *yì běn* 亦本 is attested which argues for an extension of the function of *běn* 本.

with *yì* 亦 or other modal adverbs -are quite rare in the literature. Accordingly, without any additional syntactic evidence, the exact position of the adverb *běn* 本 in its original function in these texts is difficult to determine, but according to its semantics it can be assumed that in the Pre-Buddhist literature it does not yet function as an aspecto-temporal adverb. However, as the examples demonstrate, there is an obvious extension of the functions of *běn* 本, and in the 5th century texts it can evidently also be employed in theposition as the other genuine aspecto-temporal adverbs, thus functioning as a marker of the past tense. As with the other aspecto-temporal adverbs indicating the past tense, there does not seem to be any constraint on the situation type of the predicate modified by *běn* 本, it can be both atelic and telic.

The following example represents the adverb *běn* 本 in its original meaning. In example (26) the adverb precedes the relativizer *suǒ* 所 as most adverbs do; only very few adverbs including some of the aspecto-temporal adverbs, are licensed in the position following *suǒ* 所.

(26) 諸子各乘大車，得未曾有，非本所望。 T09, no.262, p.13a01

Zhū zǐ gè chéng dà chē, dé wèi céng yǒu, fēi běn suǒ wàng

All son each mount great carriage, get NEGasp CENG have, is.not originally REL look.for 'Each of the sons mounted a large carriage and got what he never had before, and this was not what they originally had hoped for.'

In the following examples, no additional syntactic evidence argues for or against the analysis of *běn* 本 as an aspecto-temporal adverb, but semantically, the original notion is not necessarily present anymore. In all instances the predicate evidently refers to a singular situation in the past. Both atelic (state and activity verbs) and event verbs (achievement and accomplishment verbs) can be selected by *běn* 本.

(27) 我本著邪見，爲諸梵志師， T09, no.262, p.11a10

Wǒ běn zhuó xié jiàn, wèi zhū fànzhì shī

I formerly attack bad view, for PL brahmacārī teacher

'I was formerly attached to bad views and was a teacher for the brahmacārī.'

(28) 其佛本坐道場，破魔軍已，垂得阿耨多羅三藐三菩提，

T09, no.262, p.22b20

Qí fó běn zuò dàochǎng, pò mó jūn yǐ, chuí dé ānòuduōluó sānmiǎo sānpútí

That Buddha once sit site.of.enlightenment, defeat devil troop FINISH, almost get anuttarā-samyak-saṃbodhi

'That Buddha once sat at the place of enlightenment, and after he had defeated the troops of evil and almost attained anuttarā-samyak-saṃbodhi, ...'

The temporal adverb *běn lži* 本來, which is according to Wu (1996) typical for the *Dūnhužng biànwén* literature - together with the adverb *yužnlži* 元來 - is not attested in the *Miàofǎ ližnhuā jīng,* although it is attested with a few examples in other Buddhist texts from the period.[41]

With regard to the aspecto-temporal adverbs indicating the past tense, a change in the lexicon can be observed. The Classical and Han period adverb *chžng* 嘗 has become obsolete and has almost completely been replaced by the synonymous adverb *céng* 曾 which is also occasionally attested in the Han period literature. Additionally, the sentential (and modal) adverb *běn* 本 'originally, really' extends its functions and can be analysed as a marker of the past under the condition that it follows the syntactic constraints for aspecto-temporal adverbs, i.e. that it appears in the position following modal adverbs.

3.3 Adverbial modification by aspecto-temporal adverbs indicating present or simultaneity and future

a) The adverb *fāng* 方 expressing simultaneity in Buddhist texts In Han period Chinese *fāng* 方 can express functions comparable to those of the marker of the continuous aspect *-zhe* 着 and the progressive (or durative) marker *zài* 在 in Modern Mandarin.[42] But in contrast to the two markers of Modern Mandarin which show a different distribution according to the situation type of the verb they select, this is not the case for *fāng* 方 which is not confined in the selection of the situation type of the verb it modifies. However, different parts in the temporal structure of the situation are focussed on according to the situation type of the verb modified by *fāng* 方: with durative verbs (activities and states (and accomplishments)) *fāng* 方 focuses the durative part of the situation and with nondurative verbs, i.e. with achievement verbs, *fāng* 方 occasionally focuses a point imminent to the change of state point, but predominantly it emphasizes a point immediately following the change of state point, i.e. the beginning of a resultant state. One typical example with an activity verb may serve to elucidate the Han period function of *fāng* 方 to focus the ongoing process part of the situation, aspectually comparable to the English progressive form.

---

[41] It is also not attested in the *Fǎxiǎn,* but there are a few instances of *běnlái* 本來 in the *Zhèngfǎ huā jīng* and a single instance in the *Zá āhán jīng.* Other adverbs which indicate past tense in the *Dūnhuáng biànwén,* i.e. the adverbs *zǎogě* 早箇, *zǎoyǐ* 早已, and *zǎoshì* 早是, are not attested in the *Miàofǎ liánhuā jīng* and the other texts mentioned above, although there are a few examples for adverbial *zǎo* 早 – always in the meaning 'early'.

[42] It has to be distinguished from the preposition *fāng* 方 which regularly introduces temporal adverbials in Han period Chinese, but does not seem to be attested in the *Miàofǎ liánhuā jīng.*

(29) 漢王方食，曰：「子房前！ *Shiji*: 55;2040[43]

Hàn wžng fāng shí, yuē zĭ Fžng qižn

Han wang just eat, say zi Fang before 'The king of Han was eating just then and said: "Come in."'

Contrastively to atelic verbs, in most of the examples with telic, i.e. achievement verbs *fāng* 方 rather refers to the point immediately following the change of state, i.e. it refers to the initial point of the state resulting from the preceding change of state as in the following example.

(30) 「天方開楚，未可伐也． *Shiji*: 42; 1769[44]

Tiān fāng kāi Chŭ, wèi kě fž yě

Heaven FANG open Chu, NE$_{Gasp}$ can attack FIN
'Since heaven has just opened for Chu, it cannot be attacked yet.'

In the early Buddhist literature at issue here the aspecto-temporal adverb *fāng* 方 is in general not very frequent and its function as a marker of the continuous or the progressive aspect is obviously obsolete, even if the temporal structure of the verb licenses a progressive reading. Contrastively, the function of *fāng* 方 to refer to the initial point of a resultant state is still productive, although not very frequently attested as in the following example (31). Identical to example (30) *fāng* 方 modifies an achievement verb referring to the beginning of the resultant state of the situation: 'just now, just then'. However, in contrast to example (30), *fāng* 方 modifies the predicate of the matrix clause whereas in the Han period literature it predominantly modifies the predicate of a subordinate clause. But identical to the Han period examples, *fāng* 方 in these instances usually expresses simultaneity.

(31) 而我等不知真是佛子。今我等方知世尊， T09, no.262, p.17c03

Ér wŏ děng bù zhī zhēn shì fó zĭ. Jīn wŏ děng fāng zhī shìzūn

But I PL NEG know really be Buddha son. Now I PL FANG know world. honoured.one 'But we did not know that we were really Buddha sons. Now we just have recognized the World Honoured One.'

This is the only example of the kind in the *Miàofă ližnhuā jīng*. However, depending on the situation type of the verb, different other functions are attested with the aspecto-temporal adverb *fāng* 方 in the early Buddhist literature. Apparently confined to achievement verbs *fāng* 方 can appear in the matrix clause of a complex temporal sentence, meaning 'only then', "emphasising the need for S2 to happen before S1" (TLS, http://tls.unihd.de/home_en.lasso,

[43] The adverb *fāng* 方 is attested in the same phrase, although in a different context in *Hànshū:* 40; 2029.

[44] The same instance is also attested in *Shuō Yuàn:* 12.

accessed 03.05.2010). This function is evidently derived from the function represented by example (30) and is licensed by the change in the syntax of *fāng* 方 from predominantly subordinate to superordinate clauses represented by example (31).[45] Additionally *fāng* 方 is attested with accomplishment predicates in the early Buddhist literature (but not in the *Miàofǎ liǎnhuā jīng*). But, in contrast to the Han period examples in which *fāng* 方 focusses the process part of the situation expressed by an activity or accomplishment predicate, in the instances attested in the Buddhist literature, it focusses on the situation in its entirety excluding its final points. The situation is usually located in the very recent past; it takes place almost simultaneously and is relevant to the main narrative string, and it is represented from an external perspective in a perfective viewpoint.[46]

Occasionally *fāng* 方 is combined with *dāng* 當 which is briefly discussed below as a newly introduced marker of the future in the early Buddhist literature.[47] The combination of both indicates future tense and combines with both telic and atelic verbs. This combination is not attested in the *Miàofǎ liǎnhuā jīng*.[48]

b) The aspecto-temporal adverb *jiāng* 將 expressing future

Both adverbs expressing future in Classical and Han period Chinese *jiāng* 將 and *qiě* 且 are syntactically proper adverbs.[49] In Classical and Han period Chinese they serve to locate a situation to the right of the time conceived as the present time of the narrative on the time axis (or to the right of speech time) and accordingly they are deictic referring to a point of time in the distant, near, or the immediate future; additional modal values depend on the semantic interrelation of the subject and the verb. Predicates modified by *jiāng* 將 and *qiě* 且 serve to predict that an individual situation is expected to take place in the future real world, but they can also -in hypothetical contexts - refer to situations which are supposed to happen or not to happen under particular circumstances. Despite the fact that these adverbs are deictic, referring to a time in the future, they differ syntactically from purely deictic temporal adverbials referring to a point of time and evidently belong to the same category as the other aspecto-temporal adverbs discussed in this paper. Their hierarchical position is identical to that of the other aspecto-temporal

---

[45] In this function it is also attested in the *Zǔtáng jí* (Anderl ms.: 554)

[46] In the TLS (http://tls.uni-hd.de/home_en.lasso, accessed 04.05.2010) this function is probably captured by the gloss 'PRECED, padV, first, just'.

[47] In Karashima (1998:133) the combination *fāng dāng* is glossed 'will, is going to', i.e. as a marker of the future.

[48] It is also not attested in the *Fǎxiǎn*, but a few instances appear in the *Zhèngfǎ huā jīng* and in the Āgama-literature In the TLS (http://tls.uni-hd.de/home_en.lasso, accessed 04.05.2010) is is glossed as 'will, going to V', in the Buddhist literature.

[49] This has already been shown in Meisterernst (2004b).

adverbs, although they are sometimes labelled as modal adverbs which would place them in a higher position in the hierarchy of adverbs.[50] In the *Miàofǎ liǐnhuā jīng*, evidently only one of the two Classical and Han period adverbs is employed on a regular basis to indicate the future tense: this is the adverb *jiāng* 將, although it is supposed to be the older of the two aspecto-temporal adverbs *jiāng* 將 and *qiě* 且.[51] None of the markers expressing future in the *Dūnhuǎng biànwén* according to Wu (1996) are attested in the *Miàofǎ liǐnhuā jīng;* these are: *kān* 看 and several combinations with *kān* 看: *kānkān* 看看, *kānjiāng* 看將, *kānjí* 看即 and *yǎnkān* 眼看. In the following examples (32) and (33) the aspecto-temporal adverb *jiāng* 將 selects a telic, an achievement verb.

(32) 「若說是事，一切世間天、人、阿修羅皆當驚疑，增上比丘將墜於大坑。」
T09, no.262, p.6c16

Ruò shuō shì shì, yīqiè shìjiàn tiān, rén, Āxiūluò jiē dāng jīng yí, zēng shàng màn bǐqiū jiāng zhuì yú dà kēng

If speak this affair, all world deva, man, Asura all will startle doubt, increase above arrogant monk JIANG fall in great pit

'If I speak of this affair, all the devas, human beings and Asuras of the world will all be startled and will doubt, and the most supercilious monks will fall in a great pit.'

(33) 「世尊，爾時長者有疾，自知將死不久。 T09, no.262, p.17a29

Shìzūn, ěr shì zhǎng zhě yǒu jí, zì zhī jiāng sǐ bù jiǔ

World-Honoured-One, that time elder NOM have illness, self know JIANG die NEG long

'World-Honoured-One, at that time the old man was sick and he knew for himself that he was going to die before long.'

c) The aspecto-temporal adverb *qiě* 且 expressing future

In contrast to the adverb *jiāng* 將which in Classical and Han period Chinese is confined to its aspecto-temporal function, the adverb *qiě* 且 is additionally employed in modal contexts, i.e. generally in demands, in optative, hortative, or imperative meanings. In Han period Chinese the adverb *qiě* 且may best be qualified as an aspecto-temporal adverb, also including different modal values, which have in common that they do not refer to a situation in the real world but to situations viewed with different grades of certainty in a prospective or hypothetical world. The categorisation as an aspecto-temporal adverb is

[50] *Jiāng* 將is also occasionally labelled as auxiliary verb, but some of its syntactic constraints argue against this analysis.

[51] This contradicts Gurevič (1974: 163) who states that *jiāng* 將 in this function is only rarely attested in the texts of the 3rd to the 5th century and is replaced regularly by *dāng* 當 as a marker of the future.

mainly based on its syntactic position in the sentence, i.e. the fact that it can be preceded by other modal adverbs; in this function it is employed synonymously with *jiāng* 將.[52] The different (the modal and the aspecto-temporal) readings are closely connected with the situation type of the verb. In the following examples, *qiě* 且expresses hortative or imperative meanings and accordingly it functions as a modal adverb which refers to situations that have not yet taken place in the real world, but are expected or suggested to take place in the future world. This function which is already attested in the Han period literature is evidently the predominant function of *qiě* 且 in the *Miàofǎ ližnhuā jīng* and its still prevails in e.g. in the *Zǔtžng jī* according to one example presented in Anderl (ms: 500). In its purely temporal function *qiě* 且 is apparently obsolete in the Buddhist literature: it is neither attested in the *Miàofǎ ližnhuā jīng*, nor in the *Fǎxiǎn*, or in the *Āgama* literature. Most examples are similar to example (34), i.e., they express a direct command or recommendation to an addressee which is the agent of the prospective situation expressed by the verb and can be represented by a second person pronoun (as in example (34)) or a lexical noun which functions as a term of address.

(34) 釋迦牟尼佛告智積曰：「善男子！且待須臾。 T09, no.262, p.35a20

Shìjiāmóuní fó gào Zhìjī yuē shàn nžnzǐ, qiě dài xūyú

Śākyamuni Buddha tell Zhiji say good man, QIE wait a.while

'*Śākyamuni* Buddha said to *Jñānākara,* "Good man, wait a little while…"'

d) The modal auxiliary verb *dāng* 當 as a future marker

In Classical texts the character *dāng* 當 mainly represents a full verb 'match, correspond to' and a preposition 'at', whereas in the Han period literature it increasingly occurs as a modal auxiliary verb 'ought, should' which is an extension of its meaning as a full verb. The basic meaning of *dāng* is glossed in the *Shuōwén jiězì* as '*tižn xiāng zhí* 田相值' (cf. *GDHYXCCD* 2000: 87) 'fields correspond to each other'. According to Dobson (1962: 280) it is first attested in the *Shāngshū;* and in this instance it is labelled by him as a "the positive injunctive form", i.e. in his terminology as a 'modal determiner' (see also Li 2004: 219). As an auxiliary verb *dāng* 當 expresses root obligation, i.e. root necessity, a necessity according to laws, conventions, agreements etc.[53] It

[52] The syntactic status of *qiě* 且 as an adverb seems to be less controversial than that of jiāng 將. A more comprehensive discussion on the two adverbs and the different functions of *qiě* 且 has been presented in Meisterernst (2004) and Meisterernst (ms.). The modal value as a hortative or optative adverb is presented in Graham as a new development of *qiě* 且 in Han period Chinese (with four instances in the *Shǐjì*) "used to propose a course of action during the immediate future ("Let us for the moment")" (Graham 1960: 179).

[53] According to Anderl (ms: 431) *dāng* 當 (in the *Zǔtáng jí*) represents "obligation, necessity (expresses the speaker's conviction that an event will take place in the future)". In the *Gǔdài Hànyǔ xūcí cídiǎn dāng* 當 is classified as a modal adverb. See also Li (2004: 219) who assumes 'deontic necessity' as the earliest modal meaning of *dāng* 當.\

frequently selects agentive verbs which fits well the constraints proposed by Coates' (1983: 66) for the English modal should in its root meaning. This kind of modality is less strong than the deontic meaning of strict obligation; rather, it usually implies a suggestion than a command.

The predominant function of *dāng* 當 in Han period Chinese to express root obligation (necessity) still prevails in pre-Medieval Chinese,[54] while a new function develops besides the strictly modal values; this is the marking of a situation which is supposed to happen in the future as in example (35) from the *Miàofǎ liǐnhuā jīng*, i.e. a prediction.[55] In this example *dāng* 當 appears in the last of a succession of predicates referring to the past, the present and the future. Past and present are indicated by an aspecto-temporal and a temporal adverb respectively, whereas the future tense is marked by the auxiliary verb *dāng* 當.

(35)「我所說經典無量千萬億，已說、今說、當說，而於其中，

T09, no.262, p.31b17

Wǒ suǒ shuō jīng diǎn wú liàng qiān wàn yì, yǐ shuō, jīn shuō, dāng shuō, ér yúqí zhōng,

I REL tell classic scripture not-have measure thousand ten-thousand hundred thousand, already tell, now tell, should tell, CON at its middle,

'Of all the immeasurable thousands, ten-thousands, hundred thousands sūtras I have recited, which I have already recited, recite now, and will recite, among all these, …'

This new function apparently develops from the basic function of modal *dāng* 當 which is to indicate the strong or weak (subjective) root meaning of obligation (necessity), namely, that a situation has to be realised necessarily in the future world.[56] From this, a function to refer to future contexts in a more neutral way develops. According to Gurevič in texts from the 3rd to the 5th century this function of *dāng* 當 is more frequently attested than the modal function (Gurevič 1974: 119), and it is employed replacing the future marker *jiāng* 將 of Classical Chinese (ibidem: XXI, 110), but she concedes that

[54] Gurevič (1974) lists two different modal values for dāng 當 in 3rd to 5th century Chinese: 1. to express 'necessity' and to express a 'command'.

[55] According to Anderl (ms: 411) *dāng* 當 indicates that a situation *"is bound"* to happen, that "an action or state will certainly take place in the future". According to Meisig (1987: 550) in Buddhist Chinese *dāng* 當 expresses the imperative, the potentialis and the future "sollen, mögen, können", the hortative and/or optative and possibly functions as a 'Temporalpartikel' (Meisig 1988: 215).

[56] Nevertheless occasionally epistemic meanings are also attested usually induced by a particular syntactic context.

it cannot be confined to this function, but displays a wider semantic range (1974: 110, 120).[57] In general, the future tense is closely related semantically to the category of modality, and, as pointed out in Bybee *et al.* (1994:263), modal markers of obligation belong to the lexical sources which have the capacity to develop into markers of the future.[58] In the following a few examples for *dāng* 當 referring to the future will be presented. In example (36) *dāng* 當 serves to predict that a situation will take place in the future. An additional temporal adverbial supports the temporal reading of *dāng* 當. Apparently, a future (prediction) reading is often induced when the subject is represented by a first person pronoun, but not confined to it as in example (36) and (37), whereas the modal reading is often induced when the subject is an addressee, either in the second or third person, with regard to whom the obligation or suggestion is expressed.[59]

(36) 『如來於今日中夜，當入無餘涅槃。』 T09, no.262, p.4b02

Rúlži yú jīn rì zhōng yè, dāng rù wúyú nièpžn

Tathāgata PREP today day middle night, DANG enter not.have.rest nirvāna

'Today, in the middle of the night, the Tathāgata will enter remnantless nirvāna.'

In example (37) and (38) *dāng* 當 appears in the apodosis of a conditional sentence. Frequently modal or temporal markers referring to the future appear in this position, in (37) with a third and in (38) with a first person subject.

(37) 若說是事，一切世間諸天及人皆當驚疑。」 T09, no.262, p.6c8

Ruò shuō shì shì, yīqiè shìjiān zhū tiān jí rén jiē dāng jīng yí

If talk this matter, whole world PL deva and man all DANG startle doubt

'If I talk about this matter, the entire world, all the devas and human beings will be astonished and doubtful.'

(38) 汝今善聽，當爲汝說。」 T09, no.262, p.7a14

Rŭ jīn shàn tīng, dāng wèi rŭ shuō

[57] Gurevič (1974: 120) concludes her comprehensive analysis with the following three basic functions of *dāng* 當 in the Buddhist literature of the 3rd to the 5th century: 1) indicating future, including intention, in a personal clause / sentence; 2) indicating necessity in an impersonal clause / sentence; 3) indicating a command, the imperative in mainly personal, but occasionally also in impersonal clauses / sentences. However, she concludes that the situation is more complicated than this classification shows.

[58] See also Li (2004: 27) who assumes in a table modified from van der Auwera & Plungian (1998: 111) "postmodal meanings coming from either possibility or necessity' (one of these postmodal meanings is future).

[59] See Gurevič (1974: 112, 114) according to whom the future reading with a 2. or 3. person subject is by far less frequent than with a 1. person subject. See also (1974: 120).

You now good listen, DANG for you talk

'If you now listen carefully, I will talk for you.'

In the following example (39) the agentive subject expresses its future intentions. The verb is telic.

(39) 汝等於此火宅、宜速出來，隨汝所欲，皆當與汝。』 T09, no.262, p.12c11

Rŭ dĕngyú cĭ huŏ zhè, yí sù chū lzi, suí rŭ suŏ yù, jiē dāng yŭ rŭ

You PL PREP this fire house, appropriate quick go.out come, then you REL wish, all DANG give you

'You must quickly leave this burning house, and then, whatever you want, I will give it to you.'

e) The modal auxiliary verb *yù* 欲 as a future marker

Another modal verb which occasionally occurs as a future marker in the early Buddhist literature is the modal verb of volition *yù* 欲 'wish to, intend to' which - contrary to *dāng* 當 -is already regularly attested in its modal function in Classical Chinese.[60] This verb has been discussed shortly in Peyraube (2001) where he treats it as an auxiliary verb according to his definition of auxiliary verbs, i.e. if it is followed by a VP, taking the VP as its complement.[61] In the *GDHYXCCD* (2000: 787) it is labelled as an auxiliary verb which originally functions as both a full verb with the meaning 'wish, desire', and an auxiliary verb with the meaning 'need, want', and which further grammaticalizes into a marker of the future '*jiāngyào* 將要'. It is the most frequently attested of all auxiliary verbs of volition (Peyraube 2001: 180), and it expresses an "intention, or the desire to accomplish an action, or a wish" (ibidem); in Classical (Late Archaic) Chinese it is predominantly employed in "affirmative declarative sentences" (Peyraube 2001: 281). According to Peyraube (2001: 180), the future meaning is not present yet in Classical Chinese, and only develops during the Six Dynasties period, i.e. the time at issue in this paper. This development agrees well with cross-linguistic observations according to which a close connection exists between expressions of desire and the marking of future. Many future markers have been derived from expressions of desire, as has already been stated in Lyons (1977: 815) and furthermore in Bybee *et al.* (1994:254) who claim that "A common agent-oriented pathway to future begins with desire." However, in the *Miàofă lĭznhuā jīng,* this new function of *yù* 欲 is rare, and it is

[60] See also Anderl (ms: 423f) who states that in the *Zŭtáng jí* the modal function is predominant, although a few cases of *yù* 欲 in its derived function, "indicating imminent action or near future" are attested in this text, too.

[61] Peyraube concedes that the status of volitives in the linguistic literature has been debated and that in many approaches they are labelled as full verbs (2001: 177).

apparently confined to predicates with a [-human] subject. Additionally these predicates frequently express a non-desirable situation.[62]

(40) 是佛滅後，法欲盡時，有一菩薩，名常不輕。 T09, no.262, p.51b13

Shì fó miè hòu, fā yù jìn shí, yǒu yī púsà, míng Chžngbùqīng

This Buddha extinguish after, dharma YU exhaust time, there.is one bodhisattva, name Changbuqing

'After this Buddha had entered extinction, and when the law was about to expire, there was a bodhisattva named Never Disparage.'

Occasionally, the volitional auxiliary verb is combined with the aspecto-temporal adverb *jiāng* 將 to indicate future.[63] However, in the following example from the *Miàofā ližnhuā jīng* the auxiliary verb *yù* 欲 appears in its modal meaning 'want to, wish to' selected by the aspecto-temporal adverb *jiāng* 將; the subject is evidently [+human] and in this instance an analysis of *yù* 欲 as a grammaticalized future marker can be excluded.

(41) 「爾時長者將欲誘引其子而設方便，密遣二人 , T09, no.262, p.17a07

Ĕr shí zhăng zhĕ jiāng yù yòu yĭn qí zĭ ér shè fāngbiàn, mì qiăn èr rén,

That time elder NOM FUT want entice draw his son CON establish expedient.means, secrete send two man

'At that time, since the old man wanted to entice his son and draw him [near again], he employed an expedient means, and sent two men in secret, ...'

Of the two aspecto-temporal adverbs of Classical and Han period Chinese marking future *jiāng* 將 and *qiĕ* 且, the younger one, the adverb *qiĕ* 且 has become obsolete as an aspectotemporal adverb and has only prevailed as a modal adverb in the early Buddhist literature, whereas the older of the two adverbs, the adverb *jiāng* 將 is still productively employed. As an innovation, the two modal auxiliary verbs *dāng* 當, expressing obligation and necessity, and *yù* 欲, expressing volition, are - under particular syntactic constraints - starting to develop as markers of the future tense.[64] The adverb *fāng* 方 which

[62] As for *dāng* 當 and for modal auxiliary verbs in general comprehensive studies of their exact semantic and syntactic constraints and their diachronic development are still a desideratum, and many of the hypotheses stated here have to be confirmed by more detailed investigations.

[63] This is the case in the following example from the *Făxiăn*:
(i) 日將欲中眾僧則出鉢。與白衣等種種供養。 T51, no.2085, p.858b28
Rì jiāng yù zhōng zhòng sēng zé chū bō, yù băiyī dĕng
Sun JIANG YU middle all monk then go.out bowl, participate layman PL
zhŏngzhŏng gōngyăng all.kind offer.sacrifice
'When the sun is coming up to midday all monks bring out the bowl and participate in the different kinds of offerings of the laymen.'

[64] The analysis of the exact syntactic and semantic constraints and the diachronic development of these modal auxiliary verbs is still a desideratum and has been postponed to separate studies.

among other functions expresses the continuous or progressive aspect in Han period Chinese when it selects activity or state verbs has become obsolete in this function in the early Buddhist literature even if the selected verb licenses a progressive or continuous reading. Apparently, it has not been replaced by another construction to express the same functions. It is still attested in combination with atelic and telic verbs, but changes in its syntax and its semantics can be observed.

4. Conclusion

The preceding discussion on the central temporal and aspectual markers in the *Miàofǎ liǎnhuā jīng* demonstrates that the language of Kumārajīva's translation of the Lotus Sūtra is evidently strongly influenced by the Classical Chinese language. Additionally, a comparison with other contemporary Buddhist texts has shown that Kumārajīva's language is syntactically more conservative than the language of the genuine Chinese text *Gāosēng Fǎxiǎn zhuàn*.[65] On the basis of the preceding analysis and on comparative material from the same period it can be stated that except for the one innovation of the construction V1 (NP) V2, and a few lexical innovations or reanalyses of existent function words, the temporal and aspectual system displays an evident continuation of the temporal and aspectual structures in Classical and Han period Chinese. No real paradigmatic change from this period can be detected in the language of the 5th century represented here by the *Miàofǎ liǎnhuā jīng* by Kumārajīva. Although not all of the predominant aspecto-temporal adverbs are still employed to the same degree or in exactly the same function, the system of aspecto-temporal adverbs as such does not exhibit any substantial changes, e.g. no changes in the basic word order of adverbs occur. Yet, it has to be conceded that the category of 'progressive', or 'simultaneity' regularly expressed by *fāng* 方 in the *Shǐjì* and in Modern Mandarin by the aspectual suffix *-zhe* 着 or the marker *zài* 在 does not seem to be marked explicitly even if the situation type of the verb licenses a progressive reading. Only the function *fāng* 方in combination with achievement verbs seems to have survived and extended to a certain extent to activity verbs.[66] Besides some lexical innovations, with regard to the aspectotemporal adverbs, apparently modal auxiliary verbs start to be employed as markers of the future tense in addition to and occasionally in combination with the aspecto-temporal adverb *jiāng* 將 of the Classical Chinese language. In general the syntactic and semantic constraints of the closed class of aspecto-temporal adverbs did not change in early Medieval

[65] This corresponds well to the assumptions on the development of a *gǔdài báihuà wén* presented by Zhu Qingzhi in this volume.

[66] A close study of the least 'Classical' text of the three texts at issue, the *Gāosēng Fǎxiǎn zhuàn* did not display any obvious alternative constructions on the level of V to express the progressive.

Chinese and provides some evidence for the conservatism of a basic system of the Chinese language, the adverbial system, in a period of linguistic changes. But since the *Miàofǎ liǎnhuā jīng*, and a few other contemporary Buddhist texts analysed for comparison, only represent a small part of the literature at the time, no final conclusions can be drawn yet.[67]

(80) Tables of the aspectual system in Early Medieval Chinese in comparison to Han period Chinese

Table 1: The aspecto-temporal system in Han period Chinese

Temporal and aspectual categories in Han period Chinese	**Syntactic category: Adverb**	**Syntactic category: verbal construction**	**Syntactic category: auxiliary verb**
completion, resultative	既, 已	-	-
past	嘗,曾	-	-
progressive	方	-	-
simultaneity	方	-	-
future	將, 且	-	-

Table 2: The aspecto-temporal system in Early-Medieval Chinese

Temporal and aspectual categories in Early Medieval Chinese	**Syntactic category: Adverb**	**Syntactic category: verbal construction**	**Syntactic category: auxiliary verb**
completion, resultative	既, 已	V1 (NPObj) V2 (almost exclusively 已)	-
past	曾, 本	-	-
progressive	-	-	-
simultaneity	方	-	-
future	將	-	當, 欲 (only under particular syntactic conditions)

[67] A more comprehensive analysis of the aspectual and temporal system at the time has been presented in a paper on "Verb classes and aspectual marking in early Buddhist Chinese texts" (Meisterernst ms).

BIBLIOGRAPHY

Anderl, Christoph. 2004. *Notes on the development of modal verbs and their functions in Late Middle Chinese texts*. Ph.D. Dissertation, Oslo.

Cao Guangshun 曹廣順. 1986. ""Zutangji" zhong de "di (di)" "que (le)" "zhe" 《祖堂集》中的《底 (地)》《卻(了)》《著》〉", *Zhongguo yuwen* 1, pp.192-202.

Cao Guangshun 曹廣順. 1999. "Shilun Hanyu dongtai zhuci de xingcheng guocheng 試論漢語動態助詞的形成過程", In Peyraube, Alain; Sun Chaofen, eds. *In Honor of Mei Tsu-Lin. Studies on Chinese Historical Syntax and Morphology*. Paris: École des Hautes Études en Sciences Sociales, pp.19-32.

Cheung, Samuel Hung-nin. 1977. "Perfective Particles in the Bian-Wen Language". *Journal of Chinese Linguistics* 5,1, pp.51-74.

Coates Jennifer. 1983. *The semantics of the modal auxiliaries.* London and Canberra : Croom Helm.

Comrie, Bernard. 1976 *Aspect*. Cambridge: Cambridge University Press.

Gudai Hanyu xuci cidian 古代漢語虛詞詞典. 1999, 2000. (*GDHYXCCD*). Beijing: Shangwu yinshu guan.

Gurevič, I.S. 1974. Očerk Grammatiki kitajskogo jasyka III.-V. BB, Moskau: Nauka.

Harbsmeier, Christoph. 1981 *Aspects of Classical Chinese Syntax*. London; Malmö: Curzon Press.

Harbsmeier, Christoph. 1989. "The Classical Chinese Modal Particle *YI* 已". In: *Proceedings on the Second International Conference on Sinology*. Taipei: Academia Sinica.

He Leshi 何樂士. 1992. "Cong "Guan Han qing xiqu ji" yu "Dunhuang bianwen ji" de bijiaokan Yuan Zaju yufa de ruogan tedian 從《關漢卿戲曲集》與《敦煌變文集》的比較看元雜劇語法的若干特點", In: Cheng 程湘清. *Song Yuan Ming Hanyu yanjiu* 宋元明漢語研究. Shangdong: Shandong Jiaoyu chubanshe.

He Leshi 何樂士. 1992. "Cong "Zuozhuan" yu "Shiji" de bijiao kan "Shiji" ruogan tedian 從《左傳》與《史記》的比較看《史記》若干特點", In: Cheng Xiangqing 程湘清. *Liang Han Hanyu yanjiu* 兩漢漢語研究. Shangdong: Shandong Jiaoyu chubanshe.

Hureau, Sylvie. 2003. Kumārajīva (env. 344-413), Conseiller des Princes, Traducteur et Instigateur d'une Orthodoxie Bouddhique en Chine. Ph.D. thesis, Paris 2003.

Jiang Shaoyu 蔣紹愚. 2001. ""Shishuo xinyu", "Qimin yaoshu", "Luoyang qielan ji", Xianyu jing", "Bai yu jing" zhong de *'yǐ', 'jìng', 'qì', 'bì'* 《世說新語》，《齊民要術》，《洛陽伽藍記》，《賢愚經》，《 喻經》，中的《已》，《竟》，《訖》,《畢》", *Yuyan yanjiu* 1,42, pp. 73-78.

Jiang Shaoyu 蔣紹愚. 2007. "Yi yuyan jiechu de yige an li ---zai tan 'V (0) 已已 語言接觸的一個案例 -再談《V (O) 已》", *Yuyanxue luncong* 36.

Karashima, Seishi. 1998. *A Glossary of Dharmaraksa's Translation of the Lotus Sūtra* 正華經詞典. Bibliotheka Philologica et Philosophia Buddhica IV. Tokyo: The International Institute for Advanced Buddhology Soka University.

Karashima, Seishi. 2001. *A Glossary of Kumārajīva's Translation of the Lotus Sūtra* 妙法蓮華詞典. Bibliotheka Philologica et Philosophia Buddhica IV. Tokyo: The International Institute for Advanced Buddhology Soka University.

Krifka, Manfred. 1998. "The Origins of Telicity". In: Rothstein, Susan, ed. *Events and Grammar*. Dordrecht: Kluwer Publ., pp.97-134.

LI Renzhi. 2004. *Modality in English and Chinese. A typological perspective.* Boca Rota (Florida): Dissertation.com.

Lu Yang. 2004. "Narrative and Historicity in the Buddhist Biographies of Early Lu Medieval China: The Case of Kumārajīva ", *Asia Major*, 17,2, pp. 1-43.

Lyons, John. 1978 (reprint). *Semantics*. Vol. 2, Cambridge : Cambridge Universtiy Press.

Ma Qingzhu 馬慶株. 1992. *Hanyu dongci he dongci xing jiegou* 漢語動詞和動詞性結構. Beijing: Beijing Hanyuxueyuan.

Mei Zulin 梅祖麟. 1981. "Xiandai Hanyu wancheng mao ju shi he ciwei de laiyuan 現代漢語完成貌句式和詞尾的來源", *Yuyan yanjiu* 1, pp. 65-77.

Mei Zulin 梅祖麟 (1999). "Xian-Qin liang Han de yi zhong wancheng mao ju shi 先秦兩漢 的一種完成貌句式", *Zhongguo yuwen* 4, pp. 285-294.

Meisig, Konrad. 1987. *Das Śrāmanyaphala-Sūtra.* Wiesbaden: Harrassowitz.

Meisig, Konrad. 1988. *Das Sūtra von den Vier Ständen.* Wiesbaden: Harrassowitz,

Meisterernst, Barbara. 2004. "The Future Tense in Classical and Han period Chinese", In: Takashima Ken'ichi and Jiang Shaoyu (eds.). *Meaning and Form: Essays in Pre-Modern Chinese Grammar*, München: Lincom, pp. 121-146.

Meisterernst, Barbara. 2005. "Some remarks on the syntax and the semantics of the so-called aspectual markers *ji* and *yi*". *Journal of Chinese Linguistics* 33,1, pp. 68-113.

Meisterernst, Barbara. 2008. "The negative *wei* in Han period Chinese".*Journal of Chinese Linguistics*, 36,1 , pp.121-154.

Meisterernst, Barbara (ms.) Temporality in the *Shiji*: tense, aspect and situation type in a Han period text.

Meisterernst, Barbara. 2010. "Aspectual structures in Buddhist Chinese texts", presented at the 3rd International Conference on Chinese Buddhist Literature and Linguistics. Taipei: Zhengzhi daxue, 31.10.-02.11.2008, Taiwan: Academic Publishing, Dharma Drum Buddhist College.

Meisterernst, Barbara. (ms.) 2009. "Verb classes and aspectual marking in early Buddhist Chinese texts".

Peyraube, Alain. 2001. "On the modal auxiliaries of volition in Classical Chinese", In : Chappell Hilary (ed.). Sinitic grammar: Synchronic and diachronic perspectives. Oxford : Oxford University Press.

Pulleyblank, Edwin G. 1994. "Aspects of Aspect in Classical Chinese", In: Gassmann, Robert and He Leshi, eds. Papers of the First International Congress on Pre-Qin Chinese Grammar, Yuelu shushe.

Pulleyblank, Edwin G. 1995. *Outline of Classical Chinese Grammar*. Vancouver: UBC Press.

Sasse, Hans-Jürgen, ed. 1991. *Aspektsysteme*. Köln: Institut für Sprachwissenschaft, Universität Köln.

Singh, Upinder, *A history of ancient and medieval India: from the Stone Age to the 12th century*. Delhi: Dorling Kindersley, 2008.

Smith, Carlota. 1991, 1997. *The Parameter of Aspect*. Dordrecht; Boston; London: Kluwer Academic Publishers. Tai, James H.-Y. 1984. "Verbs and times in Chinese: Vendler's four categories in Lexical Semantics", In: Testen, D., Mishra, V., and Drogo, J., eds. Chicago: Chicago Linguistic Society, pp. 289-296.

Thilo, Thomas. 1985. *Katalog chinesischer buddhistischer Textfragmente*. Bd. 2. Berlin: Akademie Verlag.

Unger, Ulrich. 1987-97. *Grammatik des Klassischen Chinesisch*. Münster (unpublished).

Vendler, Zeno 1967. *Linguistics and Philosophy*. Ithaca: Cornell University Press.

Wang Haifen *et al.* 王海棻等. 1996. *Gu Hanyu xuci cidian* 古漢語虛詞詞典. Beijing: Beijing daxue chubanshe.

Wang Li 王力. 1992. *Wang Li wen ji*, vol. 8. Shandong: Shandong jiaoyu chubanshe.

Wu Fuxiang 吳福祥. 1996. *Dunhuang bianwen yufa yanjiu* 敦煌變文語法研究. Yuelu shushe.

Wu Fuxiang 吳福祥. 1998. "Chong tan "dong+le+bin" geshi de layuan he wancheng ti zhuci "le" de chansheng 重談《動+了+賓》格式的來源和完成體助詞《了》的產生", *Zhongguo yuwen* 6, pp.452-462.

Wu Fuxiang 吳福祥. 2004. *Dunhuang bianwen 12 zhong yufa yanjiu* 敦煌變文12种語法研究. Henan daxue chubanshe.

Yang Bojun, He Leshi 楊伯峻, 何樂士. 1992. *Gu Hanyu yufa ji qi fazhan* 古漢語語法及其發展. Beijing: Yuwen chubanshe.

Yang Yonglong 楊永龍. 2002. "'Yijing' de chu jian shidai ji cheng ci guocheng 已經的初見時代及成詞過程", *Zhongguo yuwen* 1, pp.41-49.

Online resources:

Chinese Buddhist Electronic Text Association: http://www.cbeta.org/.
Digital Dictionary of Buddhism: http://www.buddhism-dict.net/ddb/.

TLS Thesaurus Linguae Sericae: http://tls.uni-hd.de/.

11

The added topic-shift markers in the Chinese translatitons of Buddhist scriptures: a Sanskrit-Chinese comparative analysis of the Lotus Sūtra

Jiang Nan

Based on a Chinese-Sanskrit comparative analysis of the Lotus *Sūtra* and a comparison between its Chinese translations by Dharmarakṣa and Kumārajīva, this paper reports on a structural feature of topics in the Chinese translations of Buddhist scriptures. Topic markers such as *"ershi* (尔时)" *"jin(zhe/ri)* (今者/今日)" *"fuci/cifu* (复次/次复)", and *"(fu)you* (复有/复)" were always added at the beginning of a sentence to initiate a new topic even though there was no counterpart in the original text, which was a practice increasingly favored by the translators because it made an obvious boundary between sentences or clauses. As a topic-prominent language, Chinese has an intrinsic demand for projecting the topic in discourse. Adding topic-shift markers in the translations highlight the typological property of Chinese.

1. It is well-known that there is a huge discrepancy in linguistic structure between Sanskrit and Chinese languages. Sanskrit is rich in inflection such as gender, number, case, person and so on, which not only enables the subject to charge its predicate within a sentence, but also can manifest the topical transition between sentences or clauses. However, the Chinese language is lacking analogous inflection and rarely employs syntactic markers. As a result, Chinese sentences or clauses are usually banded together without any obvious boundary, especially in ancient times, and the relationship between topic and statement mainly depended on the semantic abountness. So, as typical translated works, the enormous quantity of Chinese Buddhist scriptures

contained many linguistic features that are different from cotemporary Chinese literature. The high-frequency of the topic-shift markers is a case in point. The purpose of this paper is to reveal the deep-seated typological correspondence of this phenomenon through the method of the Sanskrit-Chinese comparative analysis and the comparison among different Chinese versions of *Saddharmapuṇḍarīkasūtra*[1]. There are three integrated Chinese versions of this Sūtra in existence, in the following chronological order :

西晋·竺法护 (Dharmarakṣa) 译《正法华经》十卷27品，286年译出。姚秦·鸠摩罗什(Kumārajīva) 译《妙法莲华经》七卷28品，406 年译出。隋·阇那崛多共笈多(Jñānagupta and Dharmagupta) 译《添品妙法莲华经》8卷27品，601 年译出。

Tenpin is just a revision of Kumārajīva's version, so most scholars paid more attention to the other two versions translated by Dharmarśa in the 3rd century and Kumārajīva in the 5th century. Both of them are great translators in Chinese history, creating the most popular and influential translations. As a result, their translations could reflect the real state of Buddhist Chinese at that time. Furthermore, the interval of more than 100 years between these two versions also provides us more concrete observations on the language evolutionary process over this period.

First, many topic-shift markers were used in both Chinese versions. Sometimes there were counterparts in the original text, including some functional particles such as *atha khalu, punar api, tatra* etc., or some temporal words indicating topic transition, which were accordingly translated into Chinese as temporal nouns, conjunctions or adverbs at the head of sentences, such as *ershi* 尔时, *yushi* 于是, *fuci/cifu* 复次/次复 etc. For example:

(1) *anusmarāmy aham kula-putrā atīte 'dhvany asaṅkhyeyaiḥ kalpair asaṃkhyeyatarair vipulair aprameyair acintyair aparimitair apramāṇais tataḥ pareṇa parataram yad'āsīt / tena kālena tena samayena candrasūryapradīpo nāma tathāgato 'rhan samyak-sambuddho loka udapādi vidyā-caraṇa-sa ṃpannaḥ sugato loka-vid anuttaraḥ puruṣa-damyasārathiḥ śāstā devānāṃ ca manuṣyāṇāṃca buddho bhagavān*

护：又念往故無央數劫，不可思議，無能度量，時有如來，號日月燈明、至真、等正覺、明行，成爲善逝、世間解、無上士、道法御、天人師，爲佛、世尊。什：諸善男子！如過去無量無邊不可思議阿僧祇劫，爾時有佛，號日月燈明如來、應供、正遍知、明行足、善逝世間解、無上士、調御丈夫、天人師、佛、世尊。

The lineation denotes the Sanskrit-Chinese corresponding words. The temporal nouns at the head of the sentence, i.e., *shi* 时 in Dharmarakṣa's

[1] *Saddharmapuṇḍarīka-sutra, Romanized and Revised Text of the Bibliotheca Buddhica Publication by Consulting a Sanskrit Ms. and Tibetan and Chinese Translations,* U.Wogihara and C. Tsuchida, The Sankibo Buddhist Book Store, Hongo, Tokyo, Japan, 1934-35. In the aspect of Chinese translations: "护" indicates the Dharmarakṣa's version, T9, No.263. "什" indicates the Kumārajīva's version, T9, No.262.

version and *ershi* 尔时 in Kumārajīva's version are both direct translations of *tena kālena tena samayena* a temporal phrase of the singular, instrumental form in the original text.

(2) *te ca deva-putrās tasyām velāyām imā gāthā abhāṣanta*

护：時諸天子讚頌曰: .. ..

什：爾時諸天子欲重宣此義，而說偈言：.. .. ..

The temporal nouns at the head of the sentence, i.e., *shi* 时 in Dharmarakṣa's version and *ershi* 尔时 in Kumārajīva's version were both directly translated from *tasyām velāyām*, a temporal phrase of the singular, locative form in the original text.

(3) *atha khalv āyuṣmāñ śāriputro bhagavantam etad avocat*

护：於是舍利弗白世尊曰：.. .. ..

什：爾時舍利弗白佛言：.. .. ..

Both the conjunction *yushi* 于是 in Dharmarakṣa's version and the temporal noun *ershi* 尔时 in Kumārajīva's version at the head of the sentence directly correspond to *atha khalu*, a particle with the function of shifting topic in the original text.

(4) *tasya khalu punaḥ kula-putrś candrasūryapradīpasya tathāgatasya-arhataḥ samyak-sambuddhasya pareṇa parataram candrasūryapradīpa eva nāmnā tathāgato ærhan samyaksambuddho loka udapādi*

护：又族姓子！其日月燈明如來滅度之後，次復有佛，亦號日月燈明

。什：次復有佛，亦名日月燈明。次復有佛，亦名日月燈明。

The adverbs *you* 又 and *cifu* 次复 in Dharmarakṣa's version and the two cifu 次复 in Kumārajīva's version at the head of the sentence both directly correspond to *khalu punaḥ* and *pareṇa paratara*, particles with the function of shifting topic in the original text.

Nevertheless, in many cases the topic-shifts are not indicated in the original text by concrete words, but by means of inflection. In traditional Chinese literature,although the boundary between sentences or clauses could be distinguished with the help of reliable textual or semantic clues, it is difficult for most translators who are not native speakers. In addition, considering that they made a direct connection with the original text, they were liable to be impacted and inspired by the Sanskrit grammatical features, among which the well-marked topical transition by temporal words, particles or inflections is a case in point. This might drive them to add topic-shift markers at the head of sentences even in optional circumstances by analogizing those sentences already have topic markers, in order to build a deep typological correspondence between Sanskrit and Chinese. For example (the signals in the parenthesis represent gender, person, number and case):

(5) *(m.sg.G.→) atha khalu maitreyasya bodhisattvasya mahāsattvasya etad abhūt (m.sg.I.û) mahā-nimitta prātihāryam bata idam tathāgatena kṛtam*

护：於是彌勒菩薩心自念言。| 今者世尊如來至真等正覺，

……現大感變。什：爾時彌勒菩薩作是念。| 今者世尊現神變相。

The underlined Chinese temporal noun *jinzhe* 今者 has no corresponding word in the original text. The topic of the first sentence is *maitreyasya bodhisattvasya mahāsattvasya* (masculine, singuilar,genitive), and the topic of the second sentence is *athāgatena* (masculine, singuilar, instrumental). This topical transfer is conveyed by the difference of cases. So both translators intended to supplement *jinzhe* 今者 at the head of the second sentence as a marker to begin a new topic as well as to switch topics.

(6) (*pers.1.sg.N.* →) *yan nv aham mañjuśriya kumāra-bhūtam etam arthamṃ pariprccheyamṃ (f.pl.G. →) tāsām catasṛṇām parṣadām bhikṣu-bhikṣuṇy-upāsaka -upāsikānām bahūnām adeva-nāga-yakṣa-gandharva-asura-garuḍa-kiṅkara-mahoraga-manuṣya-amanuṣyāṇām imam evam-rūpam bhagavato mahā-nimitta prātihāryāvabhāsam dṛṣṭv′ ācarya-prāptīnām adbhuta-prāptānām kautūhala-prāptānām etad abhavat.*

护：欲請問之。| 時四部眾比丘、比丘尼、清信士、清信女、諸天、龍、神、揵沓惒、阿須倫、迦留羅、真陀羅、摩休勒，志懷猶豫，得未曾有，見斯大聖無極威曜神足變化，各各發意，欲問世尊，決散疑網。

什：我今當問。 | 爾時比丘、比丘尼、優婆塞、優婆夷，及諸天、龍、鬼神等，咸作此念："是佛光明神通之相，今當問誰？"

The underlined "*shi* 时", "*ershi* 尔时" also had no corresponding words in the original text, but translators still supplemented temporal nouns as topic markers according to the different appearance in person, number and case.

Secondly, the comparison of different Chinese versions further shows that the later translation by Kumārajīva more consciously supplemented topic-shift markers than the version of Dharmarakṣa. A typical case lay in the exceeding narration at the beginning of the first chapter:

(7) *evam mayā śrutam ekasmin samaye* |*(m.sg.I.→) bhagavān rājagṛhe viharati sma gṛdhakūṭe parvate mahatā bhikṣu-saṅghena sārdham* ‖ *(n.pl.I.→) dvādaśabhir bhikṣu-śataiḥ sarvair arhadbhiḥ ...(n.du.I.→) anyābhyām ca dvābhyām bhikṣu-sahasrābhyām śaikṣāaikṣābhyāmā(n.pl.I.→) mahāprajāpatī-pramukhais ca ṣaḍbhis bhikṣuṇī-sahasrais* ‖ *(f.sg.I.→) yaśodharayā ca bhikṣuṇyā rāhula-mātrā saparivāray* ‖ *(n.pl.I.→) aśītyā ca bodhisattva-sahasraiḥ sārdham sarvair avaivartikair eka-jāti-pratibaddhair yad utānuttarāyām samyak-sambodhau ...* ‖ *(m.sg.I.→) śakreṇa ca devānām indreṇa sārdham vimāati-devaputra-sahasra-parivāreṇa* ‖ *(m.sg.I.→) tadyathā candreṇa ca*

devaputreṇa sūryeṇa ca devaputreṇa samatagandhena ca devaputreṇa ratnaprabheṇa ca devaputreṇa-avabhāsaprabheṇa ca devaputreṇa evam pramukhair viṁśatyā ca devaputrasahasraiḥ ‖ *(m.pl.I.→) caturbhiś ca mahā-rājaiḥ sārdham triṁśad-devaputra-sahasraparivāraiḥ* ‖ *(m.sg.I.→) īśvareṇa ca devaputreṇa maheśvareṇa ca devaputreṇa triṁśaddevaputra-sahasra-parivārābhyām* ‖ *(m.sg.I.→) brahmaṇā ca sahām-patinā sārdham dvādaśa-brahmakāyika-devaputra-sahasra-parivāreṇa* ‖ *(m.sg.I.→) tadyathā śikhinā ca brahmaṇā jyotiṣprabheṇa ca brahmaṇā evam pramukhair dvādaśabhiś ca brahmakāyikadevaputra-sahasraiḥ* ‖ *(m.pl.I.→) aṣṭābhiś ca nāga-rājaiḥ sārdham bahu-nāga-koṭī-śata-sahasra-parivāraiḥ ...* ‖ *(m.pl.I.→) caturbhiś ca kinnara-rājaiḥ sārdham bahu-kinnara-koṭī-śata-sahasra- parivāraiḥ* ‖ *(m.pl.I.→) caturbhiś ca-gandharva-kāyika-devaputraiḥ sārdham bahu-gandharva-śata-sahasra-parivāraiḥ ...* ‖ *(m.pl.I.→) caturbhiś ca-asurendraiḥ sārdham bahv-asura-koṭī-śata-sahasra-parivāraiḥ ...* ‖ *(m.pl.I.→) caturbhiś ca garuḍendraiḥ sārdham bahu-garuda-koṭī-śata-sahasra-parivāraiḥ ...* ‖ *(m.sg.I.→) rājñā ca-ajātaśatruṇā māgadhena vaidehī-putreṇa sārdham.*

护：一時 ǀ 佛游王舍城靈鷲山。‖與大比丘眾复。‖比丘千二百一切無著。……‖（缺譯）‖菩薩八萬皆不退轉，堅住無上正真之道。……‖爾時天帝釋與二萬天子复。‖日天子與無數眷屬复；月天子以寶光明普有所照；寶光天子光耀天子复。‖四大天王與萬天子复。‖[火*僉]明大梵自在天子與三萬天子复。‖梵忍跡天子與三萬二千天子复。‖飾幹大梵與無數天子。又梵名[火*僉]光與無數大眾复。來詣佛所，稽首畢，退坐一面。ǀ有八龍王與無央數千諸龍眷屬复。‖四真陀羅王（名號略），各與營從來詣佛所，稽首畢，退住一面。‖淨身四天子（名號略），复來詣佛所，前稽首畢，退坐一面。‖四阿須倫王（名號略），與無央數百千阿須倫人民复，來詣佛所，前稽首畢，退坐一面。‖ 四金翅鳥王（名號略），复來詣佛所，稽首畢，退住一面。‖摩竭國王阿闍世與十子並諸營從，來詣佛所，稽首畢，退坐一面。諸天龍神世人莫不歸命奉敬侍坐。

什：一時ǀ佛住王舍城耆闍崛山中。‖與大比丘眾萬二千人复，皆是阿羅漢。……‖復有學無學二千人。‖摩訶波闍波提比丘尼與眷屬六千人复。‖羅睺羅母耶輸陀羅比丘尼亦與眷屬复。‖菩薩摩訶薩八萬人皆于阿耨多羅三藐三菩提不退轉。……‖爾時釋提桓因與其眷屬二萬天子复。‖復有名月天子、普香天子、寶光天子。‖四大天王與其眷屬萬天子复。‖自在天子、大自在天子與其眷屬三萬天子复。‖娑婆世界主梵天王（名號略），與其眷屬萬二千天子复。‖屍棄大梵光明大梵等。‖有八龍王（名號略），各與若干百千眷屬复。‖有四緊那羅王（名號略），各與若干百千眷屬复。‖有四阿修羅王，名號略），各與若干百千眷屬复。‖有四迦樓羅王（名號略），各與若干百千眷屬复。‖韋提希子、阿闍世王與若干百千眷屬复，各禮佛足，退坐一面。

In the original text, the sentence possessed a long instrumental modifier in which topic alteration took place many times: 比丘众>学无学>摩诃波阇波提比丘尼>.. .. .. but every alteration was concomitant with the obvious inflection in number (sg.du.pl.). Accordingly in the Chinese versions, Kumārajīva supplemented more markers like *ershi* 尔时, *(fu)you*（复）有 than Dharmarakṣa. Other examples are as follows:

(8) *(n.pl.N.→) tasyṣṭau śatāny ante-vāsinām abhūvan* ǀ *(m.sg.N.→) sa ca*

bhagavāṃs tataḥ samādher vyutthāya

护：侍者十八人。丨佛三昧正受。從三昧起。

什：有八百弟子。丨是時日月燈明佛從三昧起。

In Kumārajīva's version, *shishi* 是时 was added with intent in front of the new topic as a topic transfer marker to correspond with the different inflection in gender and number in the original text.

(9) (*pers.1.sg.N.→*) *mayā pūrvakānām tathāgatānām arhatām samyak-saṃ buddhānām idam evaṃ-rūpam pūrva-nimittam dṛṣṭam abhūt* 丨 (*m.sg.N.→*) *tathāgataḥ kartu-kāmo mahādharma-śravaṇam śrāvayitu-kāmo yathedam eva -rūpaṃ pūrva-nimitta prāduṣkṛtavān*

护：乃從過去諸佛世尊見斯像瑞……。丨諸如來至真等正覺欲令眾生聽無極典，故現斯應。什：我於過去諸佛曾見此瑞……。 丨 今佛現光亦復如是，欲令眾生咸得聞知一切世間難信之法，故現斯瑞。

in Kumārajīva's version, *jin* 今 was also appended with intent as a topic transfer marker to correspond with the different inflection in person in the original text.

It is proved by the examples above that more skillful translations lead to more accurate reflections of typological discrepancy between the source language Sanskrit and the target language Chinese and the more systematical correspondence, which is a deep typological correspondence. Generally speaking, the inflection in Sanskrit is equivalent to the lexical or functional elements on the linear sequence of Chinese.

A similar tendency is also displayed by another narrative Såtra called Vimalakīrtinirdeśa[2]. For example:

(10) (*m.sg.N.→*) *evam mayā śrutam ekasmin samaye bhagavan vaiśālyā viharati sma* ..丨 (*n.pl.N.→*) *dvādaśa ca śakra-sahasrāṇy anyānyobhyaś catumahādvīpakebhyo abhyāgatāni tatra-eva parṣadi sannipatitāny abhūvan*

支：聞如是，一時佛游於維耶離奈氏樹園 ……｜彼天帝萬二千釋從四方來。

什：如是我聞，一時佛在毘耶離庵羅樹園

……｜復有萬二千天帝，亦從餘四天下來在會坐。玄：如是我聞，一時薄伽梵住廣嚴城庵衛林……｜復有萬二千天帝，各從余方四大洲界亦爲瞻禮供養世尊及聽法故，來在會坐。

[2] *Vimalakīrtinirdeśa, Transliterated Sanskrit Text Collated with Tibetan and Chinese Translations*，Study Group on Buddhist Sanskrit Literature, The Institute for the Comprehensive Studies of Buddhism, Taisho University, 2005. In the aspect of Chinese translations: "支" indicates Zhiqian's version，T14，No.474. "什""什" indicates the Kumārajīva's version,T14, No.475. "玄" indicates Xuanzang's version, T14, No.476.

The lined part represents the Sanskrit-Chinese correspondence, and we can see the additional translated noun *"fuyou* 复有" as a topic transfer marker in the version of Kumārajīva and Xuanzang in order to deliver the topic variation by different genders and numbers.

(11) *(pers.1.sg.N.→) tatrāhamsaparivāro dharmaśravaṇāya-upasaṅkrāmiṣyāmi* .. .. | *(m.sg.N.→) evam ukte bhagavāṃc chakram devānām indram etad avocat sādhu sādhu*

支：吾與官屬共詣其所……。| 佛言：善哉善哉。

什：我亦與諸眷屬，聽受法故共到其所……。| 佛言：善哉善哉。

玄：我亦與一切眷屬，爲聞法故共詣其所……。| 爾時世尊告天帝釋：善哉善哉。

Similarly, as a topic transfer marker *"ershi* 尔时" was translated additionally in the version of Xuanzang to express the topic variation by different persons.

2. Zhou Yilang(1964) has related the frequent utilization of *"fuci* 复次" at the head of sentences as a feature of Chinese translated Buddhist scriptures, never seen in the traditional writings of native Chinese literati. Surely, *fuci* 复次, *ershi* 尔时 are new words first appearing in Buddhist scriptures, but they play the same function as other topic markers at the head of sentences to switch topics as well as begin a new topic, which was already quite popular in Chinese, long before the translation of Buddhist scriptures.

In old Chinese, the temporal nouns such as *shishi* (是)时, *jin* 今 had already been used at the head of sentences to mark a new topic. For the following examples:

是時孔子當厄，主司城貞子，爲陳侯周臣。（《孟子·萬章上》）| 時吳政峻急，莫敢宣也。（《搜神記》卷八）| 爾時吳興沈充爲縣令，當送客過浙江。（《世說新語·雅量》）| 今商王受，弗敬上天，降災下民。（《尙書·泰誓》）| 今王與百姓同樂，則王矣。（《孟子·梁惠王上》）| 今夫性惡之人，使與性善者同類乎？（《論衡·命義篇》

Pulleybank (1995) has pointed out that *jin* 今 at the head of sentences is used just as an introducing particle with no relation to the temporal factor. In complete agreement with his viewpoint, I further assert that *shishi* (是)时 should own the same property.

The non-subject sentence beginning with *you* 有 is also an inherent sentence pattern of Chinese, such as:

有女懷春，起士誘之。（《詩經·召南·野有死麇》）| 有鰥在下，曰虞舜。（《尙書·堯典》）| 子貢曰：有美玉於斯，韞櫝而藏諸，求善賈而沽諸？（《論語·子罕》）| 我明告子：有楚大夫于此，欲其子之齊語也。（《孟子·滕文公下》）| 有鳥止於南方之阜，三年不動不飛不鳴，是何鳥也？（《呂氏春秋·重言》）| 禮還，復有詔責數諸葛瑾、复騭、朱然、呂岱等。（《三國志·吳書·吴主傳》）| 有人從長安來，元帝問洛下消息，潸然流涕。（《世說新語·夙惠》）| 須臾，復有一婢來，問曰：……（《世說新語·文學》）| 有癡婿，婦翁

死，婦教以行吊禮。（《古小說鈎沉·笑林》）｜有一類人家兒子，不行。（《敦煌變文·父母恩重經講經文》）｜有個髯鬚將軍，匹馬單鞭，要見元帥。（《水滸傳》64回）｜有一個沒理的村牛打我來。（《朴通事》）

Jerry Norman (1995) calls it a non-subject type of existential sentence, Cao Fengpu (1990) calls it an introducing sentence. Judging from the numerous instances of this kind of sentences at the beginning of a text or paragraph in old Chinese, Li Zuofeng(1994) considers that you 有 has an introducing function to introduce a new topic in the discourse.

Besides, there are many other topic markers in old Chinese, including particles such as *fu* 夫, *ruofu* 若夫, *qiefu* 且夫, *wei* 唯(惟、维、隹) etc. before the topic:

夫戰，勇氣也。（《左傳·莊公十年》）｜若夫豪傑之士，雖無文王猶興。（《孟子·盡心上》）｜且夫暴國之君，將誰與至哉？（《荀子·宥坐》）｜夫八萬人奔散，非八千人所能縛。（《三國志·魏書·武帝紀》裴注）｜夫陵者，高大之象也。（《搜神記》卷六）｜夫無者，誠萬物之所資。（《世說新語·文學》）｜維予小子，未堪家多難。（《詩經·閔予小子之什》）

and particles *zhe* 者, *ye* 也 etc. after the topic such as:

信者，言之瑞也，善之主也。（《左傳·襄公9年》）｜此二君者，異於子幹。（《左傳·昭公13年》）｜寡人之于國也，盡心焉耳矣。（《孟子·梁惠王上》）｜是鳥也，海運則將徙於南冥。（《莊子·逍遙遊》）｜是月也，雷將發聲。（《論衡·命義》）

So it is obvious that as a topic precedence language, Chinese has an inherent demand to make a topic prominent within a discourse. Mainly due to the special style of Chinese translated Buddhist scriptures, translators gave up some old markers and tended to employ those before the topic; yet the driving force came from a definite expression of topic transfer though abundant particles and inflections as markers in the original text which result in more frequent utilization of topic transfer markers in Chinese translated Buddhist scriptures than contemporary Chinese traditional literature. The table below provides a simple evidence:

Items Texts	夫-	-也	今（也/者）	(是)时	尔时	（复）有-	复次-	合计
《搜神记》	10	2	13	29	0	86	0	**140**
《世说新语》	3	4	14	24	4	45	0	**94**
《法华经》	0	0	42	103	149	75	6	**375**

However, rather than running against the Chinese structural and organizational principle itself, these additional translated topical transfer markers reinforce Chinese typological characteristic instead, and to a certain extent they speed up the Chinese topicalization towards the discourse configurational language. As to whether these pre-added elements had grammaticalized to syntactic topic markers like those mood particles *ba* 吧, *ma* 呢, a 啊, *dehua* 的话 etc. as suffixed topic markers, this still needs further discussion. Above all, the translators' strong inclination to add topic transfer markers made a great contribution to Chinese topicalization through widespread publication of their translations. This highly-frequent additional translation once again testifies that despite the languages of the world looking very different on the surface, they share a universal and deep logical structure. This comparative research can help us to discover the respective organizational principles of languages and provide a new perspective to explore the grammatical evolution of Chinese accompanied by the influence of the translation of the Buddhist scriptures as well.

Abbreviations

du. dual
f. female
G. genitive
I · instrumental
m. masculine
N. nominative
n. neuter
pers.1. first-personal
pl. plural
sg. singular

BIBLIOGRAPHY

Bell, R.T. 1989. *Translation and Translating: Theory and Practie*, rendered by Qin Hongwu, Foreign Language Teaching and Research Press. 2005.

Cao Fengpu. 1977. *A Functional Analysis of Topic in Chinese— The First Step toward Discourse Analysis*, rendered by Xie Tianwei, Language and Literature Press, 1995. ----1990. *Sentence and Clause Structure in Chinese: A Functional Perspective*）, rendered by Wangjing, Beijing Language and Culture University Press. 2005.

Jerry Norman. 1995. *Chinese*, Language and Literature Press.

Li, Charles N. & Sandra A.Thompson. 1976. *Subject and Topic:A New Typology of Language*, in C.Li,ed, *Subject and Topic*. New York: Acdemic Press. Li Zuofeng. 1994. *Wenyan Shici* (文言实词). Language and Literature Press.

Pulleybank. 1995. *Outline of Classical Chinese Grammar*, rendered by Sun Jingtao, Language and Literature Press. 2006.

Xu Liejiong & Liu Danqing. 1998. Huati de Jieguo yu Gongneng (话题的结构与功能). Shanghai Education Press.

Zhou Yiliang. 1963. Lun fodian Fanyi Wenxue, Zhou Yiliang Ji 3 (论佛典翻译文学, 周一良集<第三卷>). Liaoning Education Press. 1998.

12

Kumārajīva and Abhidharma

Charles Willemen

Kumārajīva (Qiuci 龜茲，i.e. Kucha 庫車, 344 A.D.- Chang'an 長安, i.e. Xi'an 西安, 413 CE[1]) is, together with Xuanzang 玄奘 (602-664 CE), the most important translator of Indian Buddhist literature in China. One may even say that his Chinese works (*Lotus Sūtra; Vimalakīrtinirdeśa; Prajñāpāramitā* literature; *Smaller Sukhāvatīvyūha* etc..) are more influential in China and Japan than the monumental work of Xuanzang. Xuanzang knew the work of Kumārajīva well. For e.g. *Fazhi* 發智 in Xuanzang's Chinese title of the *Jñānaprasthāna*, the 'body, *śarīra*' of Vaibhāṣika 'orthodoxy", is Kumārajīva's terminology[2]. Although Xuanzang often just "improves" Paramārtha's (499-569CE) work and terminology, he was also very familiar with Kumārajīva's work. Kumārajīva precedes Xuanzang by more than two centuries. The information given in his "encyclopedia", the *Da zhidu lun* 大智度論 *Mahāprajñāpāramitopadeśa* T.XXV 1509, is much older than Xuanzang's information, as we find it in his works and in the work of his disciples, e.g. Puguang 普光.

Kumārajīva introduced a different Chinese terminology. An important reason for this was the fact that the original Indian language had changed from Prakrit to mainly Sanskrit. Kumārajīva's Kucha was mainly Sarvāstivāda, specifically Sautrāntika, of Gandhāran origin. This can be seen in the stories depicted on the walls of the famous Kizil caves[3]. He went to study in *Jibin* 罽賓, i.e. Northwestern India, which in the 4th century included Kaśmīra, the area of Sanskrit Vaibhāṣika "orthodoxy". *Jibin* originally -first two centuries BCE -was

---

1 Other dates given: Ca. 350-409 A.D.. Upon his arrival in China he resided in the *Xiaoyao* 逍遥 Garden, but he soon moved to the *Caotang* 草堂, a pavilion in the *Da Si* 大寺. Today this is located in the Hu 户 district of Xi'an.

2 T.XXV 1509: 70a12. Kumārajīva calls this *śāstra sūtra*,, because it was considered Buddha's word in Kaśmīra.

3 See Ghosh, Rajeshwari 2010:Passim.

Uḍḍiyāna[4] and Gandhāra, but early on Bactria was included in the Gandhāran cultural area. Kaśmīra became part of *Jibin* from ca. 200 CE onwards, but the Indians who kept arriving in Chang'an hardly ever came from the Kāśmīra area. The western Sarvāstivādins, called Sautrāntikas at the time of Kaniṣka's synod, ca. 170 CE, slowly adapted to the Kāśmīra "orthodoxy".

At the end of the 7th century, between Xuanzang's and Yijing's 義淨 (635-713 CE) travels in India, non-Vaibhāṣika Sarvāstivādins were united with the Vaibhāṣikas, and all were called Mūlasarvāstivādins. Kumārajīva was familiar with the Sanskrit Vaibhāṣika *vinaya*, as his participation in the translation of T. XXIII 1435 *Shi song lṃ* 十诵律 *Daśabhāṇavāra* shows. When he arrived in Chang'an on February 8, 402CE, he was immediately asked by Sengrui 僧叡 (371-438 CE) for a meditation manual, and he composed the *Zuochan sanmei jing* 坐禪三昧經, T. XV 614[5]. Kumārajīva himself was much more interested in Mādhyamaka, but the Chinese were apparently more interested in *vinaya* to organize the *saṅgha*, and also in meditation techniques. Kumārajīva knew the path of preparatory application, *prayogamārga*, the exercises expounded by Sautrāntikas leading to the first *dhyāna*. This path is also known as "five gates *dhyāna, wu men chan* 五门禪" in China. These exercises allow a common person with dull faculties to attain the first *dhyāna*, to become an *ārya*, noble one, *sheng* 聖. Later in e.g. Tiantai 天台 the term *xian* 賢, sage, is used for someone who practices these preparatory exercises, before he becomes a noble one, *sheng*. Kumārajīva's meditation manual consists of a Gandhāran style Sarvāstivāda first part, and a second "Mahāyāna" part. Kumārajīva considered himself to be a disciple of Nāgārjuna's Mādhyamaka. While he was on his way back home from *Jibin*, he was converted by a Mahāsāṅghika scholar in Kashgar. He became convinced that Nāgārjuna was right. Nāgārjuna, the founder of Mādhyamaka, founded this group, *pai* 派, within the Mahāsāṅghika *nikāya, bu* 部, in Andhra. Mādhyamikas and Vaibhāṣikas are contemporary, both using Sanskrit but holding opposite views. Upon his arrival in Chang'an, Kumārajīva immediately began teaching Nāgārjuna's ideas. With the help of disciples his *Da zhidu lun* was brought out on February 1st, 406 CE

[4] The *Mahāvaṇija Jātaka* (Book XIV 493) makes it clear that *Ji* means *kambala*, and that *Uḍḍiyāna* is famous for this fabric. It reads: *Kāsikāni ca vatthāni Uddiyāne ca kambale*. Just as *Kāśī* was famous for its silk, so *Uḍḍiyāna* was famous for its blankets *(ji)*. Willemen, Charles 2011.

[5] Yamabe, Nobuyoshi, and Sueki, Fumihiko 2009.
Kumārajīva is said to be the author of more meditation manuals. T.XV 616 Chanfa yao jie 禪法要解, composed between 402 and 405 A.D., Summary Explanation of the Way to Meditate, can be considered an addition to T. 614. T. 613 may well be Dharmamitra's work, not Kumārajīva 's. T.617 is not Kumārajīva's. A study of this last text is now being undertaken. Many of the erroneous attributions are caused by Fei Zhangfang's 費長房 (often erroneously transcribed Fei Changfang) catalogue of 597 A.D., Lidai sanbao ji 歷代三寶紀, T. XLIX 2034.

The *Upadeśa:*

This "encyclopedia" contains information known to Kumārajīva at the time. The text informs us about Sarvāstivāda, and about Mahāsāṅghika "*abhidharma*". We now know two *nikāyas* whose *abhidharma* is *buddhabhāṣita*, proclaimed by Buddha. The Theravāda school, having added the *Kathāvatthu*, finalized its *abhidhamma* in Śrīlaṅkā. A. Hirakawa proposes that this happened at the end of the 2nd century BCE. Theravāda thus established its "orthodoxy" against dissenting *Sthaviras*, against Mahīśāsakas[6], and against continental Mahāsāṅghika influence. The second school with such an *abhidharma* is known as Vaibhāṣika. They are the new Sarvāstivāda "orthodoxy" in Kaśmīra, at the end of the 2nd century CE. At that time, the time of Kaniṣka's synod, a modern, brief *vinaya* was established, but also a new *abhidharma* of seven texts was established. The new "orthodoxy" was established against several kinds of Gandhāran Sarvāstivādins, and against the ever popular Mahāsāṅghika "Mahāyāna" ideas.

Non-Vaibhāṣika Sarvāstivādins, also called Sautrāntikas from the time of Kaniṣka, also had an *Abhidharmapiṭaka*. It contained such texts as the *Abhidharmahṛdaya*, T.XXVIII 1550, composed by the Tokharian Dharmaśreṣṭhin. The purpose of this *abhidharma* is to teach how to attain arhatship, or how to attain the first *dhyāna*. This *abhidharma* is "practical". It will save us. It, of course, uses elements which can be found in *sūtras*. It agrees with the teaching as found in sacred texts. It teaches us about the *dharma (abhidharma)*, and its practice. It does not just offer "theology", but the practice of *yoga*. All Sarvāstivāda schools, except Vaibhāṣikas and Theravādins, seem to have had practical *yoga* texts as *abhidharma*. These texts, commonly known as *yogācārabhūmi*, were in China at the time of An Shigao 安世高 (Ashkani, active in Loyang 洛陽 ca. 148-170CE)[7]. The texts remove ignorance or delusion, *avidyā* or *moha*, and develop knowledge, *jñāna*. The rival Mahāsāṅghikas developed wisdom, *prajñā*, insight, the most important one of the six perfections, *pāramitās*. The oldest Chinese text of this literature is the *Aṣṭasāhasrikā*, called *Daoxing* 道行 *(yogācāra) bore* 般若 *(prajñā) jing* 經, T. VIII 224, of 179 CE. It is the work of a Tokharian (Zhi 支), known as Loujia Chen 婁迦讖, also called Zhi Chen. The Chinese is usually said to mean Lokakṣema. The earlier part(s) of the text may date as far back as the 1st century B.C., to the Gandhāran cultural era. The Chinese title shows that it was introduced in Loyang as an alternative kind of *yogācāra*, different from the Sarvāstivāda *jñānayoga*. It is quite likely that Mahāsāṅghikas in the Gandhāran cultural area, seeing the success of the *yogācāra* of their rivals, also developed comparable texts.

[6] Willemen, Charles 2011.

[7] See T. XV 607 Dao di jing 道地經, Saṅgharakṣa's *Yogācārabhūmi*.

Kumārajīva is an early witness of developments in *Jibin,* and also in Kucha, but his spiritual master was Nāgārjuna. He informs us about *abhidharmic* traditions in his *Da zhidu lun* T. XXV 1509: 70 a 6-22, b 8-11; and also in 192a 28-194b1[8].

It should be remembered that Kumārajīva -like other translators in China -used existing terminology, existing Chinese translations. For example, the language of Saṅghabhadra's *Vibhāṣā* T. XXVIII 1547, may have been a Gāndhārī Prakrit, but Kumārajīva still uses this text, even though he mainly bases himself on Sanskrit. Kumārajīva knew Saṅghadeva's recent *Aṣṭagranthaśāstra, Ba jiandu* 八犍度 *lun* 論, T. XXVI 1543, originally a Gandhāran Prakrit text. This being the only available Chinese version at the time, Kumārajīva uses its terminology, even when mentioning the Vaibhāṣika *Jñānaprasthāna.* Kumārajīva says that Kātyāyana made the eight *granthas,* compositions, of the *Jñānaprasthānasūtra.* We know that the eight *skandhakas* of the *Jñānaprasthānaśāstra* are meant. Kumārajīva informs us that Śāriputra is the ultimate authority of *abhidharma,* and that the Vātsīputrīyas, i.e. the original Pudgalavādins, recited his *abhidharma.* Brahmins seem to have had a problem with *anātmaka.* So they seem to have called *ātman* by another name, i.e. *pudgala*[9]. Kumārajīva also informs us that another of Buddha's ten great disciples, Mahākātyāyana, made a *Peṭaka,* which was used by the *upadeśācāryas* in Southern India. He means Mahāsāṅghikas in Andhra. *Peṭaka* means: *About the (Sūtra) piṭaka.* So, Mahāsāṅghikas seem to have had a *Peṭaka,* not "*abhidharma*" about the *Sūtrapiṭaka.* They had *upadeśas,* explanatory discourses. An explanatory discourse in such *Peṭaka* is called *Peṭakopadeśa.* Kumārajīva mentions three kinds of "*abhidharma*": 1. *Jñānaprasthāna* corpus and its *Mahāvibhāṣā.* 2. Six parts, *pāda.* The Kāśmīra texts seem to be meant, but the Gandhārans eventually seem to have had a comparable collection[10]. 3. *Peṭaka,* most probably the Mahāsāṅghika exegetical tradition, which, strictly speaking, is not called *abhidharma.*

In his *Da zhidu lun,* p 192a28 -b7, Kumārajīva explains three "gates of the law". 1. The *Peṭaka* gate. 2. *Abhidharma* gate. 3. Gate of emptiness. The last one is Nāgārjuna's teaching. The second one is the Sthaviravāda, i.e. Sarvāstivāda *abhidharmic* analysis. In the first one, the *Peṭaka* gate, *upadeśas* are very numerous. They explain several methods. Kumārajīva gives two examples: The method based on characteristics, and the method by opposition. S. Zacchetti

---

[8] Willemen, Charles 2008. 57-58; 66; etc.

[9] Vātsīputrīyas, Sāṃmitīyas seems to have been quite popular in Bactria early on. This can be seen in Saṃghadeva's work: T.XXV 1506 Tridharmakhaṇḍa (ka)? This work inspired Huiyuan's 慧遠 San bao lun 三報論, On the Three Kinds of Retribution (T.LII 2102: 34b3-c25). Sarvāstivādins seem to have had quite some links with Pudgalavādins in the Bactrian area. It was even considered meaningful to add a chapter about the refutation of the pudgala to the *Abhidharmakośabhāṣya,* a text which traces its origin to the Bactrian Abhidharmahṛdaya.

[10] Willemen, Charles 2008: 55-57.

has established that the contents of the explanations largely agree with the *Lakkhaṇahāra* and with the *Āvattahāra* of the Pali *Peṭakopadeśa*[11]. This Pali text is not in the Pali *Tipiṭaka*, most probably because it has a Mahāsāṅghika origin. So, Mahāsāṅghikas had *Peṭakopadeśas*. They presented methods for interpretation, exegesis. By the way, the *Abhidharmakośabhāṣya* says that an Upagupta made a *Netrīpada*. This Upagupta may have been a northwestern Mahāsāṅghika teacher, who made a text with a title to match the six Sarvāstivāda *abhidharma* parts, "feet". I am quite convinced that the Sthaviravāda versus Mahāsāṅghika dynamics are more important than the Hīnayāna-Mahāyāna divide. The Sthaviras had *śāstras* and their rivals had *upadeśas*. Both sides constantly tried to use the useful ideas of their antagonists. This reminds me of the nine or twelve *aṅgas*, members, of Buddha's teaching. It is just possible that the nine (five plus four?), as found in the Mahāsāṅghika *vinaya* and in Pali, are the oldest set. The Mahāsāṅghikas had *upadeśa* in their *Peṭaka*, and Sautrāntikas had a long *vinaya*, containing many *avadāna* and *nidāna*, stories. This long *vinaya* is the reason why they are also known as Dārṣṭāntikas. Sautrāntikas may have added *nidāna, avadāna,* and *upadeśa* to the set of nine, establishing a set of twelve. Mahāsāṅghikas, who ever since the early centuries CE were doctrinally hardly different from the Sarvāstivādins[12], had the same set of twelve, and so had their offshoot, the Dharmaguptakas. Mahāsāṅghikas may later have adopted the set of twelve too, because the *Da zhidu lun* has the set of twelve.

Kumārajīva seems to have expounded his "encyclopedia" in Ch'ang-an wanting to convince China of the superiority of Mādhyamaka. He seems to have orally expounded his knowledge and ideas. I would be very surprised if we will ever find a Sanskrit original text, because Kumārajīva did not translate a text. Chinese disciples wrote down a Chinese text, based on Kumārajīva's explanations. Kumārajīva does not inform us about *Tathāgatagarbha* or about *ālayavijñāna*. *Tathāgatagarbha* was popular in Mahāsāṅghika circles in Andhra. This is obvious in Guṇabhadra's (394-468 CE) *Shengman jing* 勝鬘經, T. XII 353, of 436 CE in Southern China. But Gandhāran *Sthaviras* became interested too. For instance, Buddhabhadra from Nagarahāra, contemporary of Kumārajīva, brought out XVI 666 in Southern China. Also, Paramārtha was a firm believer, as seen in his *Dasheng qi xin lun* 大乘起信論, T. XXXII 1666, of 553 CE. *Ālayavijñāna*, an "existing" *vijñāna,* seems to be of Sarvāstivāda origin. Asaṅga, although a Mahāsāṅghika monk, and Vasubandhu continued the Gandhāran Sarvāstivāda *yogācāra* tradition, forming a new *yogācāra* group, taking in the successful Madhyamaka ideas about emptiness. Sautrāntikas had already been using successful Mahāsāṅghika ideas in their *yoga*. This time a new group, *pai*

[11] Willemen, Charles 2008: 67

[12] Willemen, Charles 2011.

派, was formed within the *Jingliang bu* 經量部, Sautrāntika *nikāya,* i.e. Gandhāran Sarvāstivādins, Dārṣṭāntikas, Sautrāntikas. The oldest Chinese *Laṅkāvatāra sūtra,* Guṅabhadra's *Lengqie jing* 楞伽經, T. XVI 670, of 443 CE, comes too late for Kumārajīva[13]. Kumārajīva never makes a clear distinction between Western Sarvāstivādins and Vaibhāṣikas. Kucha was an area of Sautrāntikas. Is that the reason why he does not stress the Vaibhāṣikas "orthodoxy"? He also clearly mentions the seven *abhidharma* texts as two equal, separate groups. On the one hand there is the *Jñānaprasthāna* (body, *śarīra)* and its new *Mahāvibhāṣā*. On the other hand the six parts, "feet", are mentioned as a separate collection (*kāya*). Kumārajīva leaves no doubt about the *Peṭaka,* going back to Mahākātyāyana. The *upadeśas* of this *"abhidharma"* are most likely Mahāsāṅghika. Even Kumārajīva's own *Da zhidu lun* is an *upadeśa.*

BIBLIOGRAPHY

Demiéville, Paul. 1978. *Répertoire du canon bouddhique Sino-Japonais Fascicule annexe* du *Hōbōgirin*. Paris-Tōkyō: Maison Franco-Japonaise.

Ghosh, Rajeshwari. 2010. *"The Alluring Mysteries of the Kizil Caves: The Interface between Literary Sources and Iconography"*. In S.Rai (ed.) *Buddhist Culture in Asia: Unity in Diversity.* Vol.1:67-90. Mumbai-New Delhi: Somaya Publications. Willemen, Charles. 2008. *"Kumārajīva's Explanatory Discourse about Abhidharmic Literature"*. *Journal of the International College for Postgraduate Buddhist Studies* 12: 37-83 (156-110).

Willemen, Charles. 2011.*"Mahāsāṅghika. Some New Ideas"*. Forthcoming in *Dharmapravicaya. Vol. in Honor of N.H.Samtani.* Delhi: Buddhist World Press.

Yamabe, Nobuyoshi, and Sueki, Fumihiko. 2009. *The Sūtra on the Concentration of Sitting Meditation.* BDK English Tripitaka Series. Berkeley: Numata Center for Buddhist Translation and Research.

[13] Bodhidharma (in China ca. 479 û died ca. 534 A.D.), is said to be from Xiangzhi 香至, Gandhavatī, i.e. Gandhāra, in the Zutang ji 祖堂集 (Sodō shū) of 952 A.D., and in the Jingde chuandeng lu 景德傳燈錄 (*Keitoku dentō roku*), T. LI 2076: 217a9, of 1004 A.D.. He is said to be the third son of royalty from Gandhāra, in southern India. As is widely known, his practice is closely linked with the *Laṅ kāvatāra* sūtra. Here I would like to mention that the nuns from Śri Laṅkā, who arrived in southern China early in the fifth century, may well have been Mahāsāṅghika nuns who left their homeland for a welcoming South China. The Mahāvihāra monks were very powerful at the time, antagonizing i.a. Mahāsāṅghikas.

13

Kumārajīva and Prajñāpāramitā in China*

Bill M. Mak

Introduction

As the carrier of ideas and religious values, sacred texts provide the religious institution identity as well as continuity and are thus of great importance. In the case of Buddhism which flourished outside its homeland, the translation of the Buddhist scriptures played a particularly important role. Kumārajīva 's Chinese translation of the Prajñāpāramitā (PP) texts is one of such examples, of which many had surpassed their parallel translations/ retranslations. Some of his works such as the Chinese translations of the Lotus Sūtra and the Diamond Sūtra are recited daily by East Asian Buddhists up to this day, over 1500 years after their creation. These works have taken an incredibly strong root in the East Asian cultures and continue to show vitality not only as translations transmitting religious ideas, but also as works of great philosophical as well as literary values.

In this paper, I would like to examine the relationship between Kumārajīva, the PP texts and their Chinese translations during the crucial and formative period of East Asian Buddhism, namely the Six Dynasties from 3rd to 6th century C.E. By examining the circumstances in which Kumārajīva produced these important translations, I hope to answer the following questions - What motivated Kumārajīva to undertake the retranslation of such voluminous texts which occupied nearly half of the translator's total output? And furthermore, what are the reasons which make these translations last for such a great span of time up to the modern age?

* I thank Prof. Funayama Tōru for his valuable comments and corrections while I was preparing a draft of this paper. Needless to say all errors remain mine.

1.0 Prajñāpāramitā in China prior to Kumārajīva

1.1 The translations of Smaller and Larger PP and other philological works

By the designation "Prajñāpāramitā texts", we refer to a body of texts which took up Prajñāpāramitā, one of the six *pāramitā*-s or Perfections in Mahāyāna Buddhism, as its main subject-matter, reflected through their titles as well as their contents.[1] Though there are no clear evidences as to when and where these text were composed and/or compiled, archeological findings suggest that Prajñāpāramitā texts were in circulation in Northwest India and subsequently in Central Asia by the 1st century C.E.[2] During the 1st and 2nd century when Buddhist missionaries from India and Central Asia entered China, PP texts were amongst the earliest Buddhist texts introduced to the Chinese. In 179 C.E., the Yuezhi monk Lokakṣema 支婁迦讖 translated *Daoxing bore jing* 道行般若經, known later as the Smaller PP. Subsequently, a number of retranslations were made on the same text, each time supposedly an improvement of the previous ones in terms of accuracy or style.[3] As Lokakṣema's translation was the first and had apparently the widest circulation, never supplanted by other retranslations before Kumārajīva 's arrival in Ch'ang-an, *Daoxing* became synonymous with the Smaller PP.

Despite the apparent success of Lokakṣema's *Daoxing*, Chinese Buddhists from a very early age were well aware of the existence of a "larger" PP text of which the Smaller PP was believed to be an abridgement. Demands for a "true" and more complete PP manuscript in the legendary "West" continued to grow.[4]

---

1 For the most comprehensive, though somewhat outdated, survey of PP literature, see Conze 1978. Amongst Kumārajīva's PP-related outputs are the Larger PP 大品般若, the Smaller PP 小品般若, the Diamond Sūtra *(Vajracchedikā-prajñāpāramitā)* 金剛般若經, the Heart Sūtra 般若波羅蜜多心經 *(Prajñāpāramitāā-hṛdayam)* and the Commentary to the Larger PP大智度論 *(*Prajñāpāramitopadeśa)* attributed to Nāgārjuna. Furthermore, the Mādhyamika treatises translated by Kumārajīva belong also to the PP system of thoughts.

2 According to the Indian tradition as it was known to Kumārajīva through his translation of **Prajñāpāramitopadeśa (Daizhidu lun)*, PP was preached by the Buddha himself in the second turning of the Dharma Wheel: 諸天聞般若，大歡喜踊躍…作是言：我等於閻浮提見第二法輪轉。《大智度論》卷65〈43 作實相品〉T(1509)25.517a. Modern scholars however see the PP as a key work of the Mahāyāna movement which emerged gradually out of the older Original Buddhism. Conze gave the date of "the elaboration of a basic text" of PP as "ca. 100 B.C. to 100 A.D." (Conze 1978:1). The earliest fragments of PP manuscript to date belong to the first and fifth *parivarta-s* of the Gāndhārī *Aṣṭa* in the "Split-collection", carbon-dated to 1st or early 2nd century (Falk 2009:7).

3 The *Damingdu jing* 大明度經 was the first retranslation of the same text based on the same manuscript but in a more colloquial language, made by Zhi Qian 支謙 in 225 C.E. According to the *Chu sanzang jiji*出三藏記集 (CSZJJ), at least three more translations of the Smaller PP, none of which extant, were made by Zhu Shuofo 竺朔佛, Wei Shidu 衛士度 and Dharmarakṣa 竺法護.

4 One should bear in mind that to the Chinese mind of 2nd or 3rd century C.E., the idea of the "West" was still somewhat nebulous despite Zhang Qian's 張騫 renowned exploration of Central Asia in 2nd century B.C.E. Beyond the Jade Gate 玉門關 (near today's Dunhuang), the entire landmass of Eurasia together with India was known as the *Xiyu* 西域 or the Western Region. The idea of a sacred text in the "West" had undoubtedly inspired dedicated Chinese Buddhist to seek out the true text as well as stimulated public imagination.

In 257 C.E., the Chinese monk Zhu Shixing 朱士行 obtained the Larger PP in Khotan, which was eventually partially translated by Dharmarakṣa as *Guangzan jing* 光讚經 in 286 C.E.[5] Five years later, in 291 C.E., the text was translated in its entirety by *Mokṣala 無叉羅 as *Fangguang jing* 放光經, which was extremely well received and was widely preached by Chinese monks in the subsequent decades. *Fangguang jing*, more expansive in contents, was believed to be a more complete version of the shorter *Daoxing jing*, which was often criticized for its obscure, and by then archaic language.[6] The availability of the translations of the Larger PP together with the older Smaller PP translations in the early years of the 4th century offered the opportunity of comparative analyses.[7] In 382 C.E., a translation team consisting of Dharmapriya, Buddharakṣa and Zhu Fonian prepared a "critical edition" of the Larger PP through comparison of the Sanskrit manuscript with the two, by then most authoritative PP texts, viz., Lokakṣema's *Daoxing* and Mokṣala's *Fangguang*.[8] The result was essentially a retranslation of the parts which were found missing or different, together with notes on variations. Such meticulous philological works reflected the intense interest in these texts leading up to the end of the 4th century.[9] Yet the ultimate solution would be a complete retranslation of the two texts, a task which awaited Kumārajīva seventeen years later when he was brought to the capital of China in 402 C.E.[10]

1.2 Popularization and indigenization of Prajñāpāramitā thoughts

To fully appreciate the atmosphere of the Buddhist community in Chang'an before Kumārajīva's arrival in 402 C.E., one should bear in mind that starting from the early 4th century, Chinese Buddhism underwent rapid indigenization through a process known as *geyi* 格義. Though often criticized as misconstruction of Buddhist ideas as a result of misleading translation, and that the discussion contained therein was driven by concerns of indigenous

---

5 As Tang had noted, Dao'an insisted on recording all translations even if they were incomplete, which is the case of *Guangzan*, a partial translation of Larger PP of which Dao'an received a copy only years after he received *Fangguang* (Tang 1938:208-9).

6 See Dao'an's preface to the *Daoxing jing* in the CSZJJ. T(224)8.425a.

7 As Zhi Daolin 支道林 did in his *Daxiaopin duibi yaochao* 大小品對比要抄. Only the Preface of this work by the author himself survived and was recorded in the CSZJJ. T(2145)55.55a.

8 The traditional attribution of this edition, titled 摩訶鉢羅若波羅蜜經抄, to T226 has been disputed, see Kajiyoshi 1944:77-87; Yinshun 1981:602.

9 For a comprehensive review of the Chinese translation of PP texts, especially those prior to Kumārajīva, see Kajiyoshi 1944:1-87, Yinshun 1981:591-619.

10 Or more precisely, the priority would be given a more thorough translation of the Larger PP which was at any rate thought to be the basis of the Smaller PP. Kumārajīva did exactly just that or possibly at the request of his patron, and only 4 years after the retranslation the Larger PP was completed (in tandem with the translation of DZDL) did he begin on the retranslation of the Smaller PP at the request of prince Yao Hong 姚泓. CSZJJ T(2145)55.54c.

scholars of Dark Learning 玄學 rather than genuine Buddhist concerns,[11] *geyi* was nonetheless an important bridge that connected the Chinese intellectuals to the foreign religious philosophy. With respect to the PP, this transitional stage of indigenization was evinced by the emergence of the so-called Six Branches and Seven Schools 六家七宗 who proposed different interpretations of the philosophy of the PP.[12] As the Buddhist community continued to mature, *geyi* gradually phased out, and there was a greater desire to understand the original texts and what they truly meant, thus demanding a more sophisticated way of reading the texts. Amongst the most influential proponents of this idea was Dao'an 道安, who besides being a seminal figure in the history of Chinese Buddhism, was also a lifetime preacher of PP texts. Dao'an was remembered in particular for his observations through his long career working with the translations of PP texts, of the "five losses and three things ought not to be changed" 五失本三不易.[13] Up to the end of Dao'an's life (c. 385), there was a feeling within the Buddhist community that there was still much to be desired with regards to the Chinese translation of PP texts. Besides the lingering problems of *geyi*, the relation among the texts of different Buddhist schools was never clear to the early Chinese Buddhist, in particular, the position of Mahāyāna. In that regard, the obscure language of the early PP translations certainly did not help. Doctrinally speaking, many of Kumārajīva 's translations have a clear Mahāyāna orientation, which laid the foundation as well as some of the subsequent development of Mahāyāna Buddhism in China.[14]

2.0 Kumārajīva and Prajñāpāramitā

According to his biography in Huijiao 慧皎's *Gaoseng zhuan* 高僧傳 (GSZ), Kumārajīva , who had an illustrious career as a learned monk and preacher prior to his arrival in China, was well trained in the Āgamas and Abhidharma during his stay at various monasteries in Kashmir and Kashgar. Sometime during his teenage years (c. 355-363 C.E.), Kumārajīva was converted to Mahāyāna after his encounter with the monk Sūryasoma, a prince of Shache 莎車.[15] Subsequently, he returned to his native Kucha 龜茲 and received his full

[11] Zhou 1990:255ff.

[12] On the doctrines of the various indigenous schools, see Tang 1938:229-277.

[13] For a long time, this set of observations noted in his preface to *Lokakṣema's Daoxing* was understood by both traditional Chinese and Western scholars as the "Five Losses and Three Difficulties". I have adopted Ōchō's suggestion that yi 易 should be interpreted verbally as "change" (Ōchō 1958:251; see discussion in Hurvitz/Link 1974:426) since it fits better to the context of the preface.

[14] One of the main contributions of Kumārajīva's translations from a doctrinal point of view is that for the first time, Chinese Buddhists saw the difference between the Mahāyāna and the Theravāada from the point of view of the former. Subsequently, Buddhist polemics no longer followed the indigenous paradigm of the Dark Learning but rather directly from the Buddhist perspective (Zhou 1990).

[15] *Shache* 莎車 was first mentioned in Han records and has been identified by scholars as Yarkhänd. Pelliot reconstructed *Shache* as *Sāka/Săka (Pelliot 1963:879).

ordination at the age of twenty. For some years, Kumārajīva stayed in Kucha and began his career as a preacher. It was during his twenty-six years' stay in his native land that a miraculous event concerning a manuscript of the Larger PP took place:

於是留住龜茲，止于新寺。後於寺側故宮中，初得放光經。始就披讀，魔來蔽文，唯見空牒。什 [3] 知魔所為，誓心踰固。魔去字顯，仍習誦之。復聞空中聲曰：” 汝是智人，何[4]用讀此？” 什曰：” 汝是小魔，宜時速去，我心如地，不可轉也！” 停住二年，廣誦大乘經論，洞其祕奧。龜茲王為造金師子座，以大秦錦褥鋪之，令什升而說法。

[After being prompted by his mother to preach in China prior to her departure to India, Kumārajīva] rested in Kucha, staying at **Navavihāra*. Later, inside a former palace next to the *vihāra*, he received *Fangguang jing* [i.e., the Larger PP] for the first time. As soon as he started reading it, the Māra concealed the text, causing him to see only a blank manuscript. Kumārajīva knowing that it was the doing of Māra, resolved to overcome the challenge. The letters appeared after Māra departed and he continued to study and recite it. [Some time later,] again he heard a voice from the sky saying, "You are a genius. Why would you need to read this?" Kumārajīva answered, "You petty Māra, begone without delay. My mind is imperturbable like the earth!" During his sojourn of two years, he extensively preached the Mahāyāna sūtras and commentaries, making their mysterious and profound meanings clear. The King of Kucha made a Lion's Seat in gold, covered with fine Roman textile and made him ascend on it to preach.[16]

With regard to the actual source of Kumārajīva's PP manuscripts, there is very little we can say for certain since they were apparently already in circulation

[16] While we do not doubt that the account given in GSZ was based on elements of historical veracity, Sengrui's CSZJJ offered us a slightly different reading:
於龜茲帛純王新寺得放光經。始披讀。魔來蔽文。唯見空牒。什知魔所為。誓心逾固。魔去字顯。仍習誦之。後於雀梨大寺讀大乘經。忽聞空中語曰。汝是智人。何以讀此。什曰。汝是小魔。宜時速去。我心如地。不可轉也。停住二年。
Sengrui's passage presented to us a number of key differences: Firstly, the passage preceding the miraculous event recounting Kumārajīva's mother's bidding to his son is missing; secondly, the miraculous event consists in fact of two parts which took place in two different places; thirdly, the laudatory passage following the miracles is also missing. Though CSZJJ and GSZ were composed roughly at the same time in early 6th century, considering Huijiao was still in his twenties when he worked on GSZ while Sengyou was fifty two years older than the former, GSZ is likely the one to have borrowed its materials from CSZJJ. As CSZJJ was a work concerning translations and their translators while GSZ focused on the monks as eminent figures, it is understandable that GSZ would want to highlight to its readers the remarkable events concerning the individual. If this was indeed the case, GSZ had very likely deliberately conflated the events presented in CSZJJ and turned them into a dramatic series of interconnected events, showing the connection between Kumārajīva, PP and the arrival of both into China. In connection with Kumārajīva, it may also be noted that miracles were associated not only with the Larger PP, but also the Smaller PP (T2145.55.54c; Chen2001:51). For further remarks on the difference between the two narratives, see Lu 2004:18-21.

in Central Asia in the early 2nd century C.E., particularly in places like Khotan where Mahāyāna Buddhism flourished as a new religious movement.[17] From a textual point of view, of great interest and importance was Kumārajīva's translation of **Mahā Prajñāpāramitāopadeśa/ Daizhidulun* 大智度論 (DZDL), a commentary to the Larger PP attributed to Nāgārjuna. According to Sengrui and also an anonymous postscript in the tenth fascicle of CSZJJ, the hundred fascicles of Kumārajīva's translation of DZDL amounted only to less than a tenth of original of 100,000 *ślokas*.[18] The extensiveness of this commentary suggested a strong tradition of PP scholarship up to 4th century C.E. in India.[19]

3.0 Kumārajīva's translation of Prajñāpāramitā Texts

On 8th February, 402 C.E., through the arrangement of Yao Xing 姚興, the Later Qin King, Kumārajīva arrived in Ch'ang-an, after having been captured by Lü Guang 呂光 almost twenty years earlier when Fu Jian 苻堅 attacked Kucha. Kumārajīva was in his late fifties then and was almost immediately sent to work as the chief translator at Ximingge 西明閣 of Xiaoyaoyuan 逍遙園 in the capital Chang'an. Kumārajīva examined the existing Chinese translations of various Buddhist texts against the Sanskrit texts he had access to. The result was that many discrepancies were found and new translations were deemed urgently needed.

During the first year of his stay in Ch'ang-an, Kumārajīva was apparently still improving his Chinese.[20] As much as he wanted to be engaged in the translation of more challenging works, he completed only a handful of shorter texts, including *Zuochan sanmei jing* 坐禪三昧經[21], *Amituo jing* 阿彌陀經[22] and *Xianjie*

---

17 As pointed out earlier, Khotan was where Zhu Shixing found a copy Larger PP. For the development of Mahāyāna in Central Asia, see Hirakawa 699-704.

18 See Sengrui's preface to DZDL. T(2145)55.74c. For a detailed studies on this preface as well as its background, see Shih 1980.

19 Amongst the most widely accepted theory concerning the authorship of DZDL was Lamotte's claim - "D'après les indications fournies par l'auteur, il semble avoir exercé son activité au début du IVe siècle de notre ère, dans le Nord-Ouest de l'Inde… en égard à son époque et aux sources qu'il utilize, il semble que l'auteur du *Traité* fut un sarvāstivādin acquis peut-être tardivement au Mahāyāna." (Lamotte 1970:IX-XIV). For an alternative view which disputed the concept of authorship and suggested to approach the issue as a "historical event", see Chou 2004.

20 Sengzhao's 僧肇 account of Kumārajīva's Śataśāstra suggested that an earlier translation (402 C.E. or before) was deemed unsatisfactory due to his lack of mastery of Chinese, but by 404 C.E. Kumārajīva and his team were able to revise the text to make satisfactory T(2145)55.77b. The account suggested the rapid improvement of Kumārajīva's Chinese and/or the proficiency of his translation team. See also Jizang's 吉藏 account T(1827)236a.

21 In three fascicles by *Saṅgharakṣa. According to LDSBJ, Kumārajīva's translation was completed on the 5th day of the 1st month of Hongshi 弘始 (402 C.E.) - T(2034)49.78a.

22 **Sukhāvaty-āmṛta-vyūha-sāstra,* also known as *Wuliangshou jing* 無量壽經 in one fascicle. According to LDSBJ, it was translated by Kumārajīva on the 8th day of the 2nd month of Hongshi 弘始 (402 C.E.) and was thought to be the same text as translated by Saṅghavarman in the 4th year of Jiaping 嘉平 252 - T(2034)49.78a.

jing (**Bhadrakalpasamādhi-sūtra*) 賢劫經[23], before he started translating the monumental DZDL of a hundred fascicles in the summer of the same year. The translation lasted three and a half years and was completed toward the end of 405 C.E. Shortly after the translation of DZDL began, Kumārajīva started translating the Larger PP (403-404 C.E.) concurrently, revising it against DZDL in tandem. During all this time, Kumārajīva was engaged in the translation of other texts as well, most notably the Sarvastivāda vinaya and Āryadeva's Śataśāstra (402/404 C.E.). After completion of the content of DZDL and the Larger PP, Kumārajīva translated a number of shorter, but important sūtras, namely the *Vimalakārtinirdeśa* 維摩所說經 of three fascicles and the *Saddharmapuṇḍarīka* 法華蓮花經 of eight fascicles. He then made a revision of the meditation text *Zuochan sanmei jing* before he spent about three months in 408 C.E. retranslating the Smaller PP. According to CSZJJ, Kumārajīva completed in total the translation of thirty-five titles, amounting to 294 fascicles, almost half of which were the PP or related commentaries.

Year (C.E.)	Title	No. of fascs.	Translation (months)	Revision (months)	Team members
402/404	百論 *Śataśāstra*	2			
402-405	大智度論 DZDL	100	42		c. 500
403-404	大品般若 Larger PP	24	8	4	c. 500
408	小品般若 Smaller PP	8	3		?[24]
409	十二門論 Dvādaśamukha-Śāstra	1			
409	中論 **Mūlamādhyamaka - kārikā**	1			
40?	金剛般若 Vajr. PP	1	?		

Kumārajīva's translation of PP texts and other Mādhyamika commentaries

One should bear in mind that PP was, by far, not Kumārajīva's only specialization as demonstrated by the great variety of texts he had translated, encompassing the entire range of Buddhist literature - śàstra, vinaya and

[23] First translated by *Dharmarakṣa as Xianjie jing* 賢劫經 in seven fascicles in the 1st year of Yuankang 元康 (300 C.E.) - T(2145)55.7b. According to LDSBJ, the Kumārajīva's retranslation of *Yanjie jing* in ten fascicles was completed on the 5th day of the 3rd month of 4th year of Hongshi 弘始 (402 C.E.) - T(2034)49.40a. By the time of Sengyou (c.510 C.E.), this retranslation, which was marked as having only seven fascicles, was no longer extant - T(2145)55.10c.

[24] One may expect the translation team of these smaller works be significantly reduced. In 406 C.E., Kumārajīva moved from Xiaoyaoyuan to Dasi to continue his translation work. In that year, according to Sengrui's account the Lotus Sūtra was translated with the help of General Yao Song 姚嵩 and preached to over 800 monks.

commentarial works.[25] Nonetheless, PP-related texts did occupy a significant place in Kumārajīva's career as a translation, in terms of time spent on the translation as well as actual output. In particular, DZDL and the translation of the Larger PP might be considered Kumārajīva's first major achievement as a translator. His retranslations of the PP-texts were seen as a solution to long-standing textual problems of the Larger vs. Smaller PP. Perhaps even more importantly, his translation of the commentarial works including DZDL[26] as well as Śataśāstra, *Dvādaśamukhaśāstra* and *Mūlamadhyamakakārikā* were seen as important contributions to what was believed to be the true understanding of Mahāyāna philosophies.[27] Bearing this in mind, as far as the technical side of these new translations were concerned, Kumārajīva's main objective was to bring out what he believed to be the intended meanings of the original text through careful reading, which contrasted with the more literally minded Xuanzang two centuries later. But more important, as pointed out earlier, the translation of these PP and Mādhyamika texts was part of Kumārajīva's effort to establish "true" Mahāyāna Buddhism in China through "correct" translations.

4.0 Characteristics of Kumārajīva's translations

Given the historical background of the translation of PP texts in China prior to the arrival of Kumārajīva, it is not surprising to see that both King Yao Xing and the Chinese Buddhist community in the early 5th century had very high expectations of Kumārajīva's retranslations, together with the new translation of works such as the Mādhyamika commentaries. Yao Xing supported a large team of scholarly monastics during Kumārajīva's sojourn in Ch'ang-an, as King Fu Jian did during the time of Dao'an, heralding a new age of state-sponsored translation.[28] The scale of Kumārajīva's translation team was however unprecedented, with over five hundred monks collaborating on the translation of DZDL alone. As a result, the final products of some of the best minds and most educated elites in Ch'ang-an were of much higher quality in various aspects than the earlier works, which were expected then to be replaced.

---

[25] In fact as Kamata has pointed out, Kumārajīva's translations gave access to the Chinese Buddhists for the first time the comprehensive outlook of the Tripiṭaka - sūtra, vinaya and abhidharma (Kamata 2004: 35).

[26] As Chou pointed out, "the exposition of the DZDL put the Chinese Buddhists' groping for the meaning of *prajñāpāramitā* to an end. Whatever later Chinese Buddhists were baffled about what the mind in the enlightened state is like, they just read the DZDL. The DZDL became the solely authoritative work to answer this religiously ultimate question in Chinese Buddhism." (Chou 2004:326).

[27] Before all the Mādhyamika commentaries were translated into Chinese, we have an account of Jizang 吉藏 that in 405 C.E., an Indian Kṣatriya 刹利 arrived in Ch'ang-an through the sea route, examined Kumārajīva's understanding of Mahāyāna doctrines utilizing Śataśāstra and Mūlamadhyamakakārikā, and was thoroughly impressed. According to the account, these two commentarial works were extremely important to Kumārajīva 何故羅什如朗月之照無所愧？以其善解中百故。T(1824)42.4c.

[28] T'ang 1938:219-227; Zürcher 1972:200-204; Hurvitz/Link 1974:407.

To examine the characteristics of Kumārajīva's translation of PP texts, I would like to follow the tripartite standard of translation, viz., 1) Faithfulness 信; 2) Intelligibility 達; 3) Style 雅.[29]

4.1 Faithfulness

A large part of what motivated the retranslation of PP texts during Kumārajīva's time was the inadequacy deemed of the earlier translations. Other attempts at retranslating the Larger and Smaller PP texts were made but were either considered unsuccessful or unable to reach a wide audience and subsequently became lost. Decades before Kumārajīva's arrival in Ch'ang-an, as summarized by his view of the "five losses and three changes-ought-not-be", Dao'an's advice to his disciples concerning the need for better and more accurate translations was undoubtedly a response to not only Dao'an's personal conviction, but also to the demands of a growingly sophisticated audience.[30] At any rate, the conditions where these new translations were produced were by far more favorable than before. To start with, Kumārajīva himself had an excellent training in Buddhist texts of different schools and even non-Buddhist texts in Sanskrit. Secondly, Kumārajīva was able to make use of the extensive commentary of DZDL to verify and edit the content of the Larger PP, which in turn served as a basis to his later translation of the Smaller PP. Thirdly, with a large team of collaborators who served to cross check the translations against the old ones, Kumārajīva strived to clear all possible doubts which might arise from discrepancies with either the Indic original or the earlier translation. Thus, according to Sengrui, his disciple:

法師手執[1]胡本。口宣秦言。兩釋異音。交辯文旨。秦王躬[2]覽舊經。驗其得失。諮其通途。坦其宗致。與諸宿舊義業沙門釋慧恭、僧䂮、僧遷、寶度、慧精、法欽、道流、僧叡、道恢、道[3]欞、道恒、道悰等五百餘人。詳其義旨。審其文中。然後書之。(CSZJJ)

[1]胡K：梵YM [2]覽SYM：攬K [3]欞T：㯳K

The Dhrama Master [Kumārajīva] with the Indic text held in his hand, spoke in Chinese. Going back and forth between the two languages, he examined the meaning of the text. The King of Qin [Yao Xing] read the old [translation of the] sūtra to determine its merits and demerits. By inquiring its way of interpretation, its meanings were made plain. Together with over five hundred people, including those senior śramaṅa -s who were experienced with doctrinal matters, such as Shi Huigong, Senglue, Sengqian, Baodu, Huijing, Faqin, Daoliu, Sengrui, Daohui, Daobiao, Daoheng, Daozong, [Kumārajīva]

[29] Though considered by many as clichŗ amongst Chinese scholars, the three difficulties in translation (譯事三難) proposed by Yan Fu 嚴復 (1854-1921) in the preface of his Chinese translation of *Evolution and Ethics* in fact overlaps with the concerns of Dao'an and Kumārajīva without the specific religious ones.

[30] See Hurvitz/Link 1974:427-30.

thoroughly examined its meaning according to the text before committing it into writing.

While a detailed comparison of Kumārajīva's translations and the older ones or the extant Sanskrit versions would be beyond the scope of this paper, suffice it to say that from a text-critical point of view, these different translations should not be construed as similar. For both the Larger and Smaller PP, chaptering and even the contents of Kumārajīva's translations and the earlier ones reveal significant differences, suggesting that the exemplars they were based on were not the same to start with.[31] Earlier in 382 C.E. Dharmapriya's translation team had no doubt noted the problem of textual discrepancies and took the more scientific approach of separating out minor variants (wordings) from the major variants (passages);[32] Kumārajīva on the other hand took a bolder approach, presented what he believed to be correct and judged the works of his predecessors as inaccurate, or in some cases, simply as wrong.

At any rate, the Indic PP texts in Kumārajīva's possession were taken as definitive, as his treatment on the discrepancies in chaptering would indicate:

[1]胡本唯序品、阿鞞跋致品、[2]魔事品有名。餘者直第其[3]事數而已。法師以名非佛制。唯存序品。略其二目。(CSZJJ)

[1]胡K：梵YM [2]魔事K：魔T：事SYM [3]事K：品SQYM

In the Indic text, only the prefatory chapter, the chapter of *Avaivartika* and the chapter of *Māra* contain the name [of the chapter], while the rest gave its chapter number only.[33] Dharma Master [Kumārajīva] believed that the names were not given by the Buddha, therefore beside the title of the prefatory chapter which he kept, the other two titles were eliminated.[34]

---

31 In the case of the last three chapters of the Smaller PP, viz., the story of Sadāprarudita and Dharmodgata, as Lancaster noted, a significant different plotline was presented in Lokak÷ema/Zhi Qians' translation, which differed from all subsequent translations (Lancaster 1968:220). In the Appendix sample (2), one can see the description of *dhyāna* varies from the fourth and the third in the Chinese translation, while the Sanskrit recension, clearly the latest one, gives the reading of the first *(prathama)*. Kumārajīva obviously had not taken into consideration the possibility of such textual development.

32 Commenting on a certain abridged (re)translation of PP by Dharmapriya et al, Dao'an wrote, "...as for the parts whose meanings diverged, not knowing which one is correct, both were kept in parallel against each other, with notes frequently made underneath. This amounted to four fascicles. In case when there are differences of one sheet [or] two sheets, [such passages] were translated separately as one fascicle, totaling thus in five fascicles.".. .. 其義異不知孰是者，[1]輙併而兩存之，[2]往往為訓其下。凡四卷。其[3]一紙二紙異者，出別為一卷。T55(2145).52b. [1]輙KJ：輒Q(T)(TZ) [2]往往Q(T) (TZ)：徃徃KJ [3]一紙二紙異者出別為一卷SZQYM(TZ)：一紙二異者出別為一卷K1：一經JK2(T)

33 Amongst the PP mss. extant which belong to the Large PP system, there is none which contains heading titles for each chapter. Conze reconstructed the headings based on Tibetan translation (Conze 1978:41-45).

34 In the current Chinese canon, however, heading titles are given to each chapter, which according to this description, could only be a later addition.

Given our knowledge of the Indic PP texts, the textual variants contained in Kumārajīva's manuscripts must be considerable, as shown by the fact that Kumārajīva himself found it necessary to modify his translation of the Larger PP on the basis of the commentary DZDL.[35]

4.2 Intelligibility

One of the greatest criticism Dao'an directed toward the older translations, *Daoxing* and *Guangzan*, was their awkward phrasing and obscure choice of words. Kumārajīva was undoubtedly trained in traditional Indian linguistics and was thus made aware of the importance of the unity of word (*śabda*) and meaning (*artha*). His concern with faithfulness was nonetheless predicated upon this belief in word-meaning unity and that the ultimate acid test being the intelligibility of the final product:

> 其事數之名與舊不同者。皆是法師以義正之者也。如陰入持等。名與義乖。故隨義改之。陰為眾。入為處。持為性。解脫為背捨。[1]陰入為勝處。意止為念處。意斷為正勤。覺意為菩提。直行為聖道。諸如此比。改之甚眾。[2]胡音失者。正之以天竺。秦[3]名謬者。定之以字義。不可變者。即而書之。是以異名斌然。[2]胡音殆半。斯實匠者之公謹。筆受之重慎也。(CSZJJ)
>
> [1]陰入K：除入T [2]胡K：梵YM [3]名KT：言SYM

As for doctrinal and numerical items which did not match the older version[36], all were corrected by the Dharma Master based on their [true] meanings. For example, for terms such as *yin* 陰, *ru* 入, and *chi* 持, where words and meanings diverged from each other, they were amended based on the meaning. *Yin* 陰 became *zhong* 眾 (*skandha*); *ru* 入 became *chu* 處 (*āyatana*); *chi* 持 became *xing* 性; *jietuo* 解脫 became *beishe* 背捨 (*vimokṣa*); *yinru* 陰入 became *shengchu* 勝處 (*abhibhvāyatana*);[37] *nianzhi* became *nianchu* 念處 (*smṛtyupasthāna*); *yiduan* 意斷 became *zhengqin* 正勤 (*samyagvyāyāma*); *jueyi* 覺意 became *puti* 菩提 (*bodhi*); *zhixing* 直行 became *shengdao* 聖道 (*āryamārga*). Besides these, there were many such changes. When the [correct] Indic sound was lost [in the translation], one corrected it with the correct Indian [sound]; when the Chinese word was

---

35 Though the text was roughly settled, when it was examined with the commentary, there were still places requiring improvement. Therefore, as one translated the commentary, one corrected [the translation of the sūtra] at the same time (CSZJJ).文雖粗定。以釋論撿之。猶多不盡。是以隨出其論。隨而正之. Given the above example, however, it is conceivable that there are considerable amount of variants among even the source texts.

36 I took shishu 事數 as expressing two concepts, namely, doctrinal items and numerical items.

37 The Taishō reading churu 除入 is not found in either Guangzan or Fangguang. On the other hand, yinru 陰入 is noted in Guangzan : 倚著諸種諸陰入 T(222)8.174a. The here does not however agree with Kumārajīva's translation of abhibhvāyatana as shengchu 勝處 as in "eight controls of perceptions". The only item associated with eight in the list of dharma in Guangzan and Fangguang were youxing 由行/ daoxing 道行 and 正行/賢聖八品道 respectively which are the translations of *aṣṭamakamārga*. As far as I can tell, abhibhvāyatana was either not translated or not found in the manuscript which *Guangzan* and *Fangguang* were based on. Sengrui's understanding could therefore possibly be incorrect.

wrong, one corrected it with the [actual] meaning of the word. Those which could not be changed were written out [as it sounded]. Therefore new words appeared in great number, over half of which were of Indic phonetic origin. That was in fact due to the strictness of the craftsman and the consideration of the scribe.

The examples given in Sengyou's Preface illustrated Kumārajīva's organic approach toward intelligible translation delivering the intended meaning: *yi* 義. Therefore, while a word like *skandha* (lit., "sheath") being translated as *yin* 陰 ("shade", "hidden") in the older translations should not be considered wrong, for Kumārajīva, *zhong* 眾 ("collection", "aggregate") accorded better to the doctrinal interpretation. In the case of proper names, phonetic transcriptions were chosen for *ānanda, Gaṅgadeva, Akṣobhya,* while translation was given *Suvarṇapuśpa.*[38] As for technical terms, phonetic transcription was given to *anuttarā samyaksambodhi,* while literal translation was preferred in the case of *āryamārga*. These examples reveal that Kumārajīva did not have a single strategy to achieve his goal of intelligibility; instead he carefully evaluated his choice of words on a case-by-case basis as any translator would do under the best circumstances.[39]

4.3 Style

With a highly qualified translation team supporting Kumārajīva's work, his translations strove to be not only faithful and intelligible representation of Buddha's words, but also products of literary merit. Given the highly affected formalism (e.g., *pianli* 駢儷) which dominated the literary world during Kumārajīva's time,[40] his translation free of stylistic verbiage must have been perceived as a major innovation.[41] As the main purpose of religious texts in a foreign land is to proselytize and is therefore functional, the main criterion for the success of Kumārajīva's translations is their intelligibility. Prior to Kumārajīva, Dao'an in his observation of "five losses", had noted that Chinese translations turned the prosaicness of the Indic text into something elaborate,

[38] Appendix sample (1).

[39] Critics would naturally say that Kumārajīva's style is inconsistent. Thus, Xuanzang over two hundred sixty years later would choose a more literal approach, placing more emphasis on form than to meaning.

[40] Pianli is a style which pairs up sentences which show near-symmetry in terms of content and parts of speech. Hu Shih described the style as the most "superficial, unnatural and incorrect style" ever created in Chinese literature. As it was impossible for translated literature to fit in such literary mold, these new works had no choice but to adapt a freer form (Hu 1927:229).

[41] For discussion of the impact of Kumārajīva's impact to Chinese colloquial literature, see Hu 1988:229-243.

resulting in some inevitable "loss".[42] Kumārajīva was aware of his limitation[43] and took a pragmatic approach by striking a balance between literality and artistry.[44]

At any rate, the translation was a collaborative effort[45] and the final products, in particular, his translation of the PP texts turned out to be highly successful due to their stylistic traits.[46] Despite the prosaicness of these translations, they were readily received by the Chinese readers for a number of reasons as pointed out by earlier scholars including Chen Yinke, Hu Shih and Jin Kemu. First, the largely dialogical framework adopted by the PP texts was analogous to didactic works like Analects and Mencius which had a long tradition in China. Secondly, it reminded the Chinese audience of a form of dramatic prose known as *fu* 賦 which the literate Chinese were already familiar with.[47] Such works contained distinct elements such as characters, dialogues, setting and a plot, dramatic elements not unlike the PP texts. In particular, this literary form contained a lot of repetition as narrative effects, a noteworthy trait of Mahāyāna literature in general as well. Finally, the content of Mahāyāna texts themselves was fascinating to the Chinese readers - drama filled with witty dialogues interspersed with miraculous episodes. Thus, with literary prototypes to model upon and contents which captivated the imagination of

---

42 "Secondly, the Indic sūtra has preference over prosaicness while Chinese prefers an elaborated style." 二者胡經尚質。秦人好文。傳可眾心。非文不合。斯二失本也。An example would be Zhi *Qian's Damingdu jing*, which is essentially a retranslation of Lokak÷ema's *Daoxing* using the same manuscript but with a new literary language.

43 Thus in CSZJJ, Kumārajīva described translation as "chewing up rice to offer to others, which lost not only its original flavor but also induced disgust." 但改梵爲秦，失其藻蔚，雖得大意，殊隔文體。有似嚼飯與人，非徒失味，乃令歐穢也。T(2145)55.101c.

44 The balance between the two styles are well known in Chinese literature as noted in the Analects 質勝文則野，文勝質則史《論語•雍也》. In a well known anecdote in GSZ, Kumārajīva once commented Dharmarakṣa's translation of a passage in the Lotus Sūtra as too literal and approved Sengrui's proposal of a more eloquent expression 昔竺法護出 《正法華經•受決品》 云：" 天見人，人見天"。什譯經至此，乃言：" 此語與西域義同，但在言過質。" 叡曰：" 將非人天交接，兩得相見。" 什喜曰　"實然，其領悟標出，皆此類也。"T(2059)50.364b. Though the alleged passage was not attested in the extant translation of Dharmarakṣa, it nonetheless reflected the attitude of Kumārajīva and his disciples concerning style (see Hu 1928:242 and also comments in Yoshigawa/Funayama 2009-10 II:284 fn2).

45 From various passages, Sengrui appeared to be one of the main embellishers of Kumārajīva's translation (See T(2145)55.101c; T(2059)50.364b). The large assembly of monks, as many as five hundred during the translation of DZDL and the Larger PP, must have played an important role as well. The lack of division of labor and a clear workflow resulted however in various pre-approved versions of the Greater PP "leaking out" before the final proofreading took place - T(2145)55.53b.

46 One may detect a somewhat apologetic tone of Sengrui in his preface to Kumārajīva's Larger PP in CSZJJ - "We hope that the wise [readers] who believed in faithfulness toward the original text would evaluate carefully to realize its [true meaning] and not to be misled at the prosaicness of the translation, or to become annoyed by the textual variations and become intimidated." 幸冀遵實崇本之賢，[1]推而體之，不以文撲見咎，煩異見[2]慎也。[1]推Z(T)：椎K [2]慎KZ：情SYM - T2145.55.52c.

47 *Fu* emerged during the late Warring State Period (3rd century B.C.E.) and continued to be developed throughout the Three Kingdom Period (3rd century C.E.) An example of works quoted by Prof. Jin Kemu included Song Yu's 宋玉 Gaotang fu《高唐賦》, Sima Xiangru's 司馬相如 Zixu fu《子虛賦》, Mei Cheng's 枚乘 Qifa《七髮》and Cao Zhihi's 曹植 Luoshen fu《洛神賦》(Jin 1982:134).

the audience, Kumārajīva's new translations must have struck the audience at that time as something both new and strangely familiar. Unremarkable as they are in the vast world of Indian narrative literature, the translations of Mahāyāna texts, especially those of Kumārajīva's, opened up a new genre in Chinese literature characterized by romantic fantasy, dramatic plots and dialogue and elegant prose - a genre which continued to thrive throughout the subsequent ages, harking back constantly to their foreign prototypes.[48]

5.0 Legacy and Influences

Due to the great fame and achievement of Kumārajīva, his translations had undoubtedly gained popularity even during his lifetime, and had spread through his disciples to the rest of China. A further thrust of the popularization of these works took place a century later when Emperor Liang (reigned 502-549 C.E.) converted practically his entire kingdom into Buddhism. Amongst the Mahāyāna texts which Emperor Liang preached personally was the PP, to which he wrote a lengthy preface. By the time of the T'ang Period, Kumārajīva's translation of Vajracchedikā PP had become widely popular among the Chinese gentry.[49] Like his predecessors, Xuanzang found discrepancies between the older translations and the latest Sanskrit manuscripts he brought with him from India and justified to the emperor of the time the need for retranslation.[50] Despite Xuanzang and his contemporaries having the opinion that Kumārajīva sacrificed accuracy for the sake of style, Xuanzang's retranslations never superseded Kumārajīva's with the sole exception of his retranslation of the Heart Sūtra which remains probably the only widely known translation of Xuanzang.

---

48 Cf. classical fantastic works such as *Liexian zhuan*《列仙傳》, *Xiyou ji*《西遊記》and *Fengsehn zhuan*《封神傳》(Hu 1928:248).

49 The traditional account of Huineng the Sixth Patriarch of Chan attaining Enlightenment through hearing Kumārajīva's translation of the Vajracchedikā-PP attests to the popularity as well as sanctity attributed to his works.

50 Xuanzang's criticism toward Kumārajīva's translation of the Vajracchedikā PP as noted in his biography *Datang daci'ensi sazang fashi zhuan*大唐大慈恩寺三藏法師傳 is mainly toward the missing words/phrases. Emperor Tai's criticism of "distortion of meaning through embellishment" is also of interest and such sentiment was also echoed in other supporter of Xuanzang's new translation (See next note). 帝又問:《金剛般若經》一切諸佛之所從生，聞而不謗，功逾身命之施，非恒沙珍寶所及。加以理微言約，故賢達君子多愛受持，未知先代所翻，文義具不？法師對曰：此經功德實如聖旨。西方之人咸同愛敬。今觀舊經，亦微有遺漏。據梵本具云『能斷金剛般若』，舊經直云『金剛般若』。欲明菩薩以分別為煩惱，而分別之惑，堅類金剛，唯此經所詮無分別慧，乃能除斷，故曰『能斷金剛般若』，故知舊經失上二字。又如下文，三問闕一，二頌闕一，九喻闕三，如是等。什法師所翻舍衛國也，留支所翻婆伽婆者，少可。帝曰：師既有梵本，可更委翻，使眾生聞之具足。然經本貴理，不必須飾文而乖義也。故今新翻《能斷金剛般若》，委依梵本。奏之，帝甚悅。T50(2053)259a. Xuanze 玄則 in his preface to the second division of Xuanzang's "Great PP of sixteen parts" made the following comparisons between the three versions of the Greater PP: "Though [Kumārajīva's] *Greater* [PP] when compared to [*Dharmarakùa's] *Guangzan [jing,* may be considered] as much more beautiful as enriched by great degrees in terms of diction然《大品》之於《光讚》，詞倍豐而加美，即明此分之於《大品》，文益具而彌正，攢輝校寶，豈不盛歟。T(220)7.220.1a

After Kumārajīva had passed away, his three thousand disciples, including Sengzhao 僧肇 and others continued to preach Mādhyamaka philosophies based on Kumārajīva's translation of PP texts and commentaries. Subsequent to the political turmoil toward the end of the Six Dynasty Period, Mādhyamaka teachings continued to spread throughout China and in the Sui Dynasty, the School of Three Treatises 三論宗 was founded by 吉藏 (549-623 C.E.) with the support of various emperors. The school continued to grow throughout the T'ang Dynasty until Emperor Wu's destruction of Buddhism (841-846 C.E.). Nonetheless, Kumārajīva's translations became firmly established as part of the tradition, absorbed into all indigenous Buddhist schools including Tiantai, Pure Land and Ch'an.

Conclusion

Though Kumārajīva's contribution to Chinese Buddhism was multifaceted and the Buddhist texts he brought to China were of a great variety, ranging from sūtra to vinaya, and from dhyāna-texts to abhidharma, PP and Mādhyamika texts held a special position in terms of his personal history, his career as a translator, as well as a legacy to Chinese Buddhism and society. The large success of Kumārajīva's translation of PP texts was closely connected to the development of Chinese Buddhism when new translations of PP texts and a more refined hermeneutical language were urgently sought after by the increasingly sophisticated Chinese converts and gentry audience. With royal patronage, Kumārajīva and his large team of collaborators produced some of the finest prose translations of his time, half of which turned out to be PP-related texts and Mādhyamika commentaries.

From a more personal point of view, Kumārajīva from a very early age took a keen interest in Mādhyamika commentaries as a basis of his Mahāyāna faith and philosophy. The miraculous incident associated with Larger PP and not other texts during Kumārajīva's earlier years in Kucha, though somewhat exaggerated in the hands of Chinese writers, pointed nonetheless to his close relationship with the PP. Kumārajīva's new translations, done in an innovative, colloquial yet artistic style, were well received by the Chinese readers and remained unrivalled by the subsequent retranslations. These texts were subsequently absorbed into all schools of Chinese Buddhism in the following 1500 years and became part of not only Chinese Buddhist tradition, but also the wider Chinese literary tradition whose impact continues to be felt.

ABBREVIATIONS

AP	Aṣṭasāhasrikā Prajñāpāramitā
AdP	Aṣṭādaśasāhasrikā Prajñāpāramitā
CSZJJ	*Chusanzang jiji* 《出三藏記集》 by Sengyou 僧祐 (T2145). Early 6th c. (51? C.E.)
DDJ	*Daodejing* 《道德經》
DZDL	*Daizhidulun* 《大智度論》 attributed to Nāgārjuna, trans. by Kumārajīva (T1509)
GSZ	*Gaosengzhuan* 《高僧傳》 by Huijiao 慧皎 (T2059). Early 6th c. (519 C.E.+)
KYK	Kokuyaku issaikyō 国訳一切経
KYSJL	*Kaiyuan shijiao lu* 《開元釋教錄》 by Zhisheng 智昇 (T2154). 730 C.E.
LDSBJ	*Lidai sanbao ji* 《歷代三寶紀》 by Fei Changfang 費長房 (T2034). 597 C.E.
PP	Prajñāpāramitā
T	Taishō shinshū daizōōkyō ō大正新脩大藏經
X	Wanxuzang 卍續藏
XGSZ	*Xu gaosengzhuan* 《續高僧傳》 by Daoxuan 道宣 (T2060). Mid 7th c. (645 C.E.+)
Z	Zürcher (see below)
ZZML	*Zhongjing mulu* 《眾經目錄》 by Fajing et al. 法經等 (T2146). 594 C.E.

BIBLIOGRAPHY

Chen Yinke 陈寅恪. 2001. *Chen Yinke ji - dushu zhaji sanji* 陈寅恪集-读书札记三集. Beijing: Sanlian shudian.

Chou Po-kan. 2004. "The Problem of the Authorship of the *Mahàpraj¤àpàramitopade÷a*: A Re-examination." 臺大歷史學報 34:281-327.

Conze, Edward. 1978. *The Prajñāpāramitā Literature.* Tokyo: Reiyukai.

Falk, Harry. 2009. *The 'Split' Collection of Kharoṣṭhī Texts.* Unpublished manuscript.

Harrison, Paul. 1993. "The Earliest Chinese Translations of Mahāyāna Buddhist Sūtras: some notes on the works of Lokakṣema." *Buddhist Studies Review* 10 (2): 135-177.

Hikata Ryusho. 1958. *Suvikrāntavikrāmi-paripṛcchā-Prajñāpāramitā-sūtra.* Fukuoka: Kyushu University.

Hirakawa Akira平川彰. 1978. *Daijō bukkyōōto-wa nani ka*大乘佛教とは何か. Tokyo: Shunjåsha.

Hu Shih 胡適. 1928. *Baihua wenxue shi* 白話文學史. Shanghai: Xinyue shudian. Reprinted in *Hushi xueshu wenji* 胡适学术文集. 1988. 129-396. Beijing: Zhonghua shudian.

Hurvitz, Leon and Arthur E Link. 1974. "Three Prajñāpāramitā Prefaces of Tao-An." In M,langes de Sinologie offerts … Monsieur Paul Demiéville, vol. 2. Bibliothèque de L'Institut des Haûtes Ètudes Chinoises volume XX. Paris. 403-470.

Jin Kemu. 1982. "Zenyang du hanyi fojing - luejie Jiumoluoshi jiantan wenti"怎样读汉译佛典——略介鸠摩罗什兼谈文体." *Dushu* 读书 2:127-135.

Kajiyoshi Kōun 梶芳光運. 1944. *Genshi hannyakyō no kenkyū* 原始般若経の研究. Tokyo: Sankibō.

Kamata Shigeo 鎌田茂雄. 1994. *Jiumoluoshi dui dongyafojiaoshi de yingxiang* "鸠摩罗什对东亚佛教史的影响." Trans. by Liu Jian 刘建. 《世界宗教研究》第二期. 第五次中日佛教学术会议专辑.

Karashima Seishi. 2010. *A Glossary of Lokakśema's Translation of the Aṣṭasāhasrikā Prajñāpāramitā.* Tokyo: International Research Institute for Advanced Buddhology, Soka University.

Lancaster, Lewis. 1968. *An Analysis of the Aṣṭasāhasrikā Prajñāpāramitā from the Chinese Translations.* PhD Thesis. Wisconsin University.

Lamotte, Ètienne. 1970. *Le Trait, de La Grande Vertu de Sagesse, Tome III.* Louvain: Institut Orientaliste.

Lu, Yang. 2004. "Narrative and Historicity in the Buddhist Biographies of Early Medieval China: The. Case of Kumārajīva ." *Asia Major (Third Series)* 17 (2): 1-43.

Lu Yang 陸揚. 2005. "Jiedu Jiumoluoshi: Jietan Zhongguo zhonguzongqi de fojiao wenhua yu shixue" 解讀《鳩摩羅什》: 兼談中國中古早期的佛教文化與史學." *China Scholarship* [Zhongguo Xueshu] 中國學術 6 (3).

Nakajima Ryūzōō 中嶋隆蔵. 1997. *Shutsusanzōki Shū Jokan Yakuchū* 出三藏記集序巻訳注. Kyoto: Heirakuji Shoten.

Ōchō Enichi, 横超慧日. 1958. *Chūkoku bukkyō shoki no honyakuron* "中国仏教初期の翻訳論." In *Chūkoku bukkyō* no *kenkyū* 中國佛教の研究. Kyoto: Hōzōkan.

Pelliot, Paul. 1963. *Notes on Marco Polo II.* Paris: Imprimerie Nationale.

Robinson, Richard. 1967. *Early Mādhyamika in India and China.* Madison: University of Wisconsin Press.

Shih, Robert. 1980. "La préface du Ta tche che louen par Seng-Jouei." In *Indianisme et bouddhisme : mélanges offerts* à *Mgr Ètienne Lamotte.* Louvain-la-Neuve: Universit, catholique de Louvain, Institut orientaliste. 313-328.

Tang Yongtong 湯用彤. 1938. *Hanwei liangjin nanbeichao fojiaoshi* 漢魏兩晉南北朝佛教史. Changsha: Shangwu yinshuju.

Yinshun印順. 1981. *Chuqi dacheng fojiao zhi qiyuan yu kaizhan* 初期大乘佛教之起源與開展. Taipei: Zhengwen.

Yoshikawa Tadao and Funayama Tōru 吉川忠夫, 船山徹. 2009-2010. *Kōsōden* 高僧伝. Vol. 1-4. Tokyo: Iwanami Shoten.

Ui Hakuju 宇井伯壽. 1956. *Shaku dōōan kenkyū* 釋道安研究. Tokyo: Iwanami Shoten.

Zacchetti, Stefano. 2005. In Praise of the Light : A Critical Synoptic Edition with An Annotated Translation of Chapters 1-3 of Dharmarakśṣa's Guang Zan Jing. Vol. 8 of Bibliotheca philologica et philosophica Buddhica. Tokyo: International Research Institute for Advanced Buddhology, Soka University.

Zürcher, Erik. 1972. *The Buddhist Conquest of China.* Leiden: E. J. Brill.

APPENDIX

	Sample	(1)
Larger PP	*Mokṣala T221	佛告阿難：是恒加調弟，當來之世當作佛，號名金華如來，無所著，等正覺。畢女人身，受男子形，後當生於妙樂佛國，於彼國修梵行。是菩薩摩訶薩在所生國，常有金華名號。
	Kumārajīva T223	佛告阿難：是恒伽提婆姊，未來世中當作佛，劫名星宿，佛號金華阿難。是女人畢是女身，受男子形，當生阿閦佛阿鞞羅提國土，於彼淨修梵行。阿難，是菩薩在彼國土，亦號金華。
	Xuanzang T220-2 (cf. T220-3/T220-4)	爾時世尊告慶喜曰：今此天女於未來世，當成如來應正等覺，劫名星喻，佛號金花。慶喜當知，今此天女，即是最後所受女身，捨此身已，便受男身。盡未來際，不復為女。從此歿已，生於東方不動如來，應正，等覺，甚可愛樂佛國土中，於彼佛所勤修梵行。此女彼界，便號金花。
	Sanskrit (Kimura ed.)	*evam ukte bhagavān āyuṣmantamānandam etad avocat: iyam ānanda gaṅgadevā bhaginī anāgate 'dhvani suvarṇapuṣpo nāma tathā gato ærhan samyaksambuddho loke bhaviṣyati tārakopame kalpe æyam ānanda etasyā gaṅgadevāyā bhaginyāś caramaḥ strāībhāvo bhaviṣyati. iyam ānanda gaṅgadevā bhaginī strībhāvam vivarjya puruṣabhāvaṃ pratilabhyākśobhyasya tathāgatasyārhataḥ samyaksaṃbuddhasya buddhakśetre upapatsyate abhiratyāṃ lokadhātau, sa tatra brahmacaryaṃ cariṣyati.*
Smaller PP	*Lokakṣema T224	佛言：是怛竭優婆夷，却後當來世，名星宿劫。是中有佛，名金華佛。是優婆夷後當棄女人身，更受男子形，却後當世阿閦佛剎。
	Zhi Qian T225	佛語阿難：是恒竭清信女，却後當來劫，劫名星宿。中有佛名金花，是清信女後於此時，棄女為男，後當生無怒佛剎，從一剎生一佛剎。
	Kumārajīva T227	佛告阿難：是恒伽提婆女人，當於來世星宿劫中而得成佛，號曰金花。今轉女身，得為男子，生阿閦佛土，於彼佛所常修梵行。
	Xuanzang T220-4	爾時世尊告慶喜曰：今此天女於未來世，當成如來應正等覺，劫名星喻，佛號金花。慶喜當知，今此天女，即是最後所受女身，捨此身已，便受男身，盡未來際，不復為女。從此歿已，生於東方不動如來可愛世界，於彼佛所勤修梵行。此女彼界，便字金花。
	*Dānapāla T228	佛言：阿難，今此昂誐禰嚩女人，終此身已，轉生當得男子之身，生於妙樂世界阿閦佛剎中，於彼如來，應供，正等正覺所，恭敬供養修持梵行。於彼沒已，復生他方諸佛剎中，如是從一佛剎至一佛剎，世世所生不離諸佛，常得瞻禮親近供養。譬如轉輪聖王尊貴自在，從一宮殿至一宮殿，自生至終足不履地，今此女人亦復如是。從一佛剎至一佛剎，不離諸佛，乃至於未來世星宿劫中當得成佛，號金華如來，應供，正等正覺，明行足，善逝，世間解，無上士調御丈夫，天人師，佛，世尊，出現世間。
	Sanskrit (Ghoṣa ed.)	*evam ukte bhagavān āyuṣmantamānandam etad avocat: iyam ānanda gaṅgadevā bhaginī anāgate ædhvani suvarṇapuṣpo nāma tathā gato bhaviṣyati arhan samyaksambuddho vidyācaraṇasampannaḥ sugato lokavid anuttaraḥ puruṣadamyasārathiḥ śāstā devānām ca manuṣyāṇām ca buddho bhagavāṁlloka utpatsyate, tārakopame kalpe ænuttarāṃ samyaksambodhimabhisambhotsyate. seyam ānanda gaṅgadevā bhaginī strībhāvamṃvivartya puruṣabhāvam pratilabhya itaś cyutvā akśobhyasya tathāgatasyārhata samyaksambuddhasya buddhakśetre abhiratyām lokadhātāv upapatsyate.*

	Sample	(2)	(3)
Larger PP	*Mokṣala T221	持是勇進之意從是東行。去是二萬里。國名香氏。	復遙見其城中央法上菩薩。與諸大眾數百千萬圍遶說法。遙見是已甚大歡喜。其身安隱譬如比丘得第四禪。又自念言：我今不可於車上載當下步耳。
	Kumārajīva T223	善男子。汝以是勤精進愛樂法故。從是東行。去此五百由旬。有城名眾香。	薩陀波崙菩薩見曇無竭菩薩時。心即歡喜。譬如比丘入第三禪攝心安隱。見已作是念：我等儀不應載車趣曇無竭菩薩。作是念已下車步進。
	Xuanzang T220-2 (cf. T220-3/ T220-4)	(*220-1) 又，善男子！汝以如是勇猛精進愛樂恭敬求法之心，從此東行過於五百踰繕那量，有大王城名具妙香。	(*220-1) 爾時，常啼菩薩摩訶薩最初遙見法涌菩薩摩訶薩故，身心悅樂，譬如苾芻繫念一境忽然得入第三靜慮。既遙見已，作是念言：我等不應乘車而趣法涌菩薩摩訶薩所。作是念已，即便下車整理衣服。
	Sanskrit (Kimura ed.)	-	-
Smaller PP	*Lokakśema T224	善男子。當作是守念。從是東行索般若波羅蜜。去是間二萬里。國名揵陀越。	是時薩陀波倫菩薩及五百女人。皆遙見如是。見已皆大歡欣踊躍。自念言：我曹義不可於車上載。當下步入國耳。
	Zhi Qian T225	當隨經教殖志守淨。從是東行去是二萬里。國名香淨。	闓士及諸女。遙見如斯。欣豫無喻。念曰：吾等義當下車。步行入城。
	Kumārajīva T227	是故善男子。 汝以是勤行精進。愛樂法故從是東行。去此五百由旬有城名眾香。	心即歡喜。譬如比丘得第三禪。見已作是念：我等不應載車趣曇無竭菩薩。即皆下車步進。薩陀波崙與五百侍女恭敬圍繞。各持種種莊嚴諸物。俱詣曇無竭菩薩所。
	Xuanzang T220-4	–	–
	* Dānapāla T228	是故汝應益加精進勇猛堅固。從此東行五百由旬。有一大城名曰眾香。	如是見已。常啼菩薩摩訶薩。心生慶快踊躍歡喜。譬如苾芻得第三禪樂。一心專注尊重恭敬。即謂長者女言：此城名為眾香。彼菩薩者。是謂法上菩薩摩訶薩。我等今時不應乘車前詣其所。發是言已即各下車。歡喜肅恭步進於前。
	Sanskrit (Ghoṣa ed.)	*tena hi tvam kulaputra etenaiva vīryeṇa etenaivotsāhena etayaivārthikatayā etayaiva cchandikatayā anubadhya pūrvām eva diśammgaccha. asti kulaputra itaḥ pañcabhir yojana-śatair gandhavatī nāma nagarī*	*saha darśanenaiva ca tasyaivaṃrūpam sukhamṃ sampratilabhate sma. tadyathāpi nāma prathama-dhyāna- samāpanno bhikśur ekāgreṇa manasikāreṇa dṛṣṭvā cāsyaitad abhūt. na mama pratirūpam etad bhaved, yad ahamṃrathagata eva dharmodgataṃ bodhisattvaṃ mahāsattvam upasaṃkrāmeyaṃ yan nv aham rathād avatareyaṃ sa tato rathād avātarat.*

14

Two traditions of Śrāvaka meditation: Kumārajīva's Zuo chan san mei jing and Buddhaghoṣa's Visuddhimagga

Kin-Tung Yit

Background of the transmission of the *Zuo chan san mei jing*

According to the preface, the *Guan zhong chu chan jing xu* (關中出禪經序 Preface to the Meditation Sūtra transmitted in the Guan Zhong Area) written by Sengrui (僧叡), the *Zuo chan san mei jing* (坐禪三昧經, *Sitting Meditation Samādhi Sūtra*, henceforth ZCSMJ) was transmitted into China in 402 by Kumārajīva, probably six days after he arrived at Ch'ang-an. The text was revised by Sengrui later, and the final version was completed in 407.[1] According to Sengrui, this text consists of materials representing "five gates" (五門 = "five means") of mediation practices that come from a number of famous mediators or commentators, such as Upagupta, Pārśva, Vasumitra, Kumāralāta, Aśvaghoṣa, Saṅgharakṣa and Saṅghasena.[2] Unfortunately, we do not have a definite description from Sengrui to indicate what portion of the five particular meditation practices belong to or was transmitted by which one of the above seven persons; this is awaiting further investigation. However, by looking at the background and the life of most of these seven mediators or commentators, there is little doubt that this kind of meditation practices can be traced back from the 1st to the 4th century CE. They were developed in North-

1 Cf. Chu san zang ji ji (《出三藏記集》), T55, 65a19-b2: 究摩羅法師，以辛丑之年十二月二十日，自姑臧至常安。予即以其月二十六日，從受禪法；既蒙啓授，乃知學有成准，法有成條。…出此經後，至弘始九年閏月五日，重求撿挍。懼初受之不審，差之一毫，將有千里之降。詳而定之，輒復多有所正，既正既備，無間然矣。

2 Ibid.: 其中五門是婆須蜜、僧伽羅叉、漚波崛、僧伽斯那、勒比丘、馬鳴、羅陀禪要之中，抄集之所出也。

Western India and Central Asian areas,[3] and therefore can be considered as belonging to the "northern tradition".

The background of the *Visuddhimagga*

The *Visuddhimagga* (henceforth VISM)[4] is probably one of the most comprehensive meditation guide books for Theravāda Buddhism. According to the records in chapter 37 of the *Mahāvaṃśa* and the *Visuddhimagga* itself,[5] this monumental work was written by the great commentator Buddhaghoṣa, who was born in North India and came to Sri Lanka in the period of King Mahānāma (409-431). In order to pass the test requested by the monks who belonged to Mahāvihāra lineage in Anurādhāpura, he finished the work by following the doctrinal thinking system of the Mahāvihāra lineage, and gained the trust of the monks there, who later offered him many commentaries. Modern scholars have pointed out that the core content of the *Visuddhimagga* is similarly found in the other work, the *Vimuttimagga*, which only exists in the Chinese translation (*Jie tuo dao lun* 解脫道論, T32n1648).[6] Its author is known as Upatissa (優波底沙), whose period was about 200 years earlier than Buddhaghoṣa's. Therefore, the source of the *Visuddhimagga* might go back to the 2nd or 3rd century CE.

The five gates of Śrāvaka meditation in the *Zuo chan san mei jing*

The content of the ZCSMJ is mainly contained in three parts: detailed description of the Śrāvaka path and the Bodhisattva path, and a brief description of the Pratyekabuddha path in between. In the śrāvaka path, five kinds of meditation (literally "five gates of meditation methods" 五門禪法) are explained, and by practicing these methods practitioners are able to attain four dhyānas, five supernatural powers, four stages before the first fruit, and eventually the completion of all four fruits (stream-entrant, once-returner, non-returner and arhat) as signifying the highest goal of liberation. In a later section of bodhisattva path, these five methods were mentioned again, and they were transformed into Mahāyanic form of meditation practices.

---

3 Some useful information is seen in Yin Shun (1968, 1992) *A Study of the Śāstras and Ācāryas of the Sarvāstivāda and Other Schools* (說一切有部為主的論書與論師之研究), Taipei: ZhengWen Pub. Especially chs. 6 and 12. A brief description is also seen in Yamabe, Nobuyoshi & Sueki, Fumihiko (2009) *The Sutra on the Cencentration of Sitting Meditation,* BDK English Tripitaka Series, Berkeley: Numata Center for Buddhist Translation and Research, xv-xvii.

4 *Visuddhimagga.* 1950 ed. H. C. Warren. revised D. Kosambi. Harvard. Cf. Ñāṇamoli, Bhikkhu (1956) *The Path of Purification,* Colombo. (An English translation of the *Visuddhimagga*)

5 Mhv XXXVII 225-37; VISM 711-3.

6 G. P. Malalasekera 1928. *The Pali Literature of Ceylon.* Kandy. 79-101; Ñāṇamoli (1991)*The Path of Purification,* Kandy, xxviii-xl; Norman, K. R. (1983) *Pāli Literature: Including the Canonical Literature in Prakrit and Sanskrit of all the Hīnayāna Schools of Buddhism.* Wiesbaden. 120-130.

The meditation framework in the *Visuddhimagga*

The meditation framework in the *Visuddhimagga* follows a scheme of seven purifications[7] under the structure of *sīla*, *samādhi* and *paṭṭā*. Most of the concentrative meditation practices are recorded in the division of *samādhi* (*citta-visuddhi*), especially 40 subjects for calming meditation (*samatha kammaṭṭhāna*). In contrast to the five independent meditation methods as categorized by the ZCSMJ, the VISM has a different method of sorting: the meditation of mindfulness on breathing and contemplation of the Buddha are put under the context of ten *anussati*, the meditation of the observation on the impurities is found in the context of ten impurities, the cultivation of compassionate mind appears in the context of four *brahmavihāra*, and the meditation of dependent origination is not an individual subject among forty *kammaṭṭhāna*, but is seen in chapter seventeen of the division of *paṭṭā*.

The comparison of the observations on the impurities (不淨觀)

The ZCSMJ mentions that the practice of observation of the impurities is to counteract desires or lust. The method of this practice includes observation of impurities filled in the body, and ten stages of the corpse corruption.[8] Following this, the text mentions three levels of practitioners: the beginner, the intermediate, and the advanced (初習行、已習行、久習行). The beginner is taught to think of broken skin (作破皮想), the intermediate, the thinking of removing the skin and flesh (想却皮肉), and the advanced, the thinking of further removing the skin and flesh (身中一寸，心却皮肉). In fact, the whole process refers to the completion of the so called "white bone contemplations" (白骨觀),[9] which will be elaborated later.

The VISM also has detailed description of the observation of the impurities. In Chapter 6, ten impurities of corpse corruption are mentioned,[10] and five kinds of proper methods in observing the phenomena of each impurity are emphasized. The text further discusses the specificity of each impurity and the principle to obtain the five factors for gaining the first *jhāna* through this practice.[11]

---

7 Namely: *sīla, citta, diṭṭhi,* kaṅkhāvitaraṇa, maggāmaggañāṅadassana, paṭipadāñāṇadassana and ñāṇadassana.

8 T15, 271c11-12: 青瘀、膖脹、破爛、血流、塗漫、臭膿、噉食、不盡、骨散、燒焦。Yamabe & Sueki (2009) reads nine stages, by combining the words 噉食 and 不盡 as one item. This is perhaps supported by the ZCSMJ itself, as in later section in the bodhisattva path, the term 九想不淨 is seen. Here I temporarily keep it as ten items, as in the above sentence it seems to use two words to refer to one item; the other reason is that in the VISM and *the Jie tuo dao lun* we also see the expression of ten items.

9 T15, 271c6-272a29.

10 VISM 178: uddhumātaka, vinīlaka, vipubbaka, vicchiddaka, vikkhāyitaka, vikkhittaka, hata-vikkhittaka, lohitaka, puḷuvaka and aṭṭhika.

11 VISM 178-196.

Both ZCSMJ and VISM have mentioned the impurities in terms of the corpse corruption, and the function of counteracting desires according to different types of corruption characteristic.[12] The differences between the ZCSMJ and the VISM are summarized as follows:

1. The ZCSMJ includes 36 impurities in the body (presumably present in a living person, not in the corpse), but the VISM regards the same practice (with 32 impurities) as another independent meditation object, the mindfulness of the body (*kāyagatasati*), which is explained in Chapter 8.

2. The ZCSMJ explains in detail about the "white bone contemplations", and applies the result of this practice to the gaining of three "pure signs" (淨觀).[13] These are significant signs of meditation accomplishment. This is not seen in the VISM, which is probably one apparent difference between the two traditions.

3. The VISM elaborates five kinds of proper ways to do the practice, regarding the many steps and details of gaining the sign of impurities, which are probably valuable experiences that were developed by the Theravāda tradition, which is not mentioned by the ZCSMJ.

4. The identification of *jhāna/dhyāna* attainment is mentioned by the VISM as gaining five factors and the appearance of two signs: 'sign of upholding' (*uggaha-nimitta*) and 'the counterpart sign' (paṭibhāga-nimitta), while the ZCSMJ applies the idea of "pure sign".

Comparison of cultivation of compassionate mind (慈心觀)

The ZCSMJ mentions that the practice of cultivation of compassionate mind is to counteract hatred or anger, and this is also the case for the VISM. The ZCSMJ continues to apply three methods for three levels of practitioners in respect of this practice: the beginner shall cultivate a strong sharing sense: by gaining personal happiness, he wishes that the people whom he likes, of being able to obtain it (慈及親愛). The intermediate one further extends the sense whereby he wishes that neutral people can also acquire the same happiness (慈及中人); and at the advanced level even hostile people are included as his object for sharing this happiness (慈及怨憎).[14] In addition, the ZCSMJ mentions that the final result of this practice is to accomplish the so called "*maitrī* (mind) *samādhi*" (慈心三昧).

The VISM expounds the same practice in Chapter 9, in the context of

12 The ZCSMJ mentions seven types of desirous attachment (多婬人有七種愛), while the VISM mentions ten.

13 若得禪定，即有三相：身體和悅，柔軟輕便；白骨流光、猶如白珂；心得靜住，是爲淨觀。

14 T15, 272b1-c9.

four "divine abidings" (*brahmavihāra*). Four methods are referred to: loving kindness (*metta*), compassion (*karuṇa*), gladness (*pīti*) and equanimity (*upekhā*). They are all operated in a similar process: observation of the faults of hatred or anger, the advantages of being patient, five objects to be encountered with (oneself, loved one, very loved one, neutral person, enemy) in order to cultivate loving kindness, compassion, gladness, and equanimity being the final stage of the practice. The VISM has a long description of explaining the standard formulations of the *brahmavihāra* as seen in the canonical texts, and analyzing the merits of this practice, as well as its relationship with *jhāna*s in the form realm and ten *pāramīs*.[15]

The similarities in the ZCSMJ and the VISM are: both point out different types of people as becoming objects of cultivating compassionate mind; the ZCSMJ indicates three types and the VISM mentions five, all of which are placed in the same sequence: easy type, neutral type and difficult type. Both texts denote a number of reasons for "positive thinking", explaining why hatred or anger should be eliminated, and a number of stories are taken as exemplars.

The main differences between the ZCSMJ and the VISM are as follows:

1. The ZCSMJ mentions the practice as "giving or sharing happiness" and resources or happiness comes from one's psychophysical happiness;[16] the VISM does not emphasize this idea, but only cultivates a sense of "maintaining sentient beings' happiness" or "strongly wishes that they are having no anger or hatred".

2. The ZCSMJ extend the objects to unlimited number of people in ten directions of the world, and the VISM sticks only to the fixed description of the standard formulae.

3. The VISM has many descriptions that are not found in the ZCSMJ, such as how to avoid improper objects (e.g. opposite gender, deceased person), 11 kinds of merits for cultivating compassionate mind, and some other foundations for the right direction of this practice.

4. The VISM mentions all four *brahmavihāra*s as a set of practices to gain four *jhāna*s, but the ZCSMJ only mentions one: *maitrī/metta*.

Comparison of contemplation of dependent origination (因緣觀)

The ZCSMJ mentions that the contemplation of dependent origination is to counteract ignorance. Based on three levels of practice, the beginner shall

15 VISM 295-314.

16 寒時得衣，熱時得涼；飢渴得飲食；貧賤得富貴；行極時得止息。

contemplate the meaning of "birth is the condition for ageing and death, ignorance is the condition for volitional actions", which are the first and the last phrases of the formulation of twelve links of dependent origination. The intermediate one shall further contemplate the other eight phrases in the formulation (from "volitional actions is the condition for consciousness" to "grasping is the condition for existence"), and the advanced one shall be able to contemplate the whole process in a concrete and complete way, to attain the state of *samādhi*.[17] The VISM does not regard this practice as one of the calming meditation objects; in other words, this is not regarded as practice that leads to the attaining of *jhāna* state. However, the description of dependent origination is not missing, and it is placed in the context of wisdom (*paññā*). In fact, the VISM elaborates almost all details of the meaning of dependent origination in Chapter 17, with over 80 pages of explanation.[18]

From the above explanation, it is quite clear that both texts have given the status and function of dependent origination in different ways; therefore it is difficult to do a comparison in the same context. Nevertheless, it is worth noting that the fact that the ZCSMJ takes the content of dependent origination as one particular meditation practice to counteract ignorance is perhaps one specific development in the northern tradition. Why does VISM not take it in the same way? And what sort of practice is to be used in order to counteract the ignorance in the VISM? The answer may be found in the analysis of the six characteristics of practitioner as especially emphasized by the VISM, that "ignorance type" is identical to the "speculative temperament type". This means that the suitable meditation object for counteracting ignorance is the same for both types of practitioners, which is the *ānapānasati* (數息觀), and hence the VISM may take *ānapānasati* as being the object to counteract ignorance.

Comparison of mindfulness on breathing (數息觀)

The ZCSMJ mentions that the contemplation of mindfulness on breathing is to counteract speculative temperament. For the beginner, the main point of practice is to "count" the breathing in and breathing out actions from numbers one to ten. The intermediate practitioner pays his attention on "follow", by following the breath coming in and out, and the advanced one should complete six methods (六種門: counting, following, fixing, contemplating, shifting and purifying; 數、隨、止、觀、轉觀、清淨) and sixteen aspects (十六分).[19] Both, the six methods and sixteen aspects are described by the ZCSMJ in detail, being the longest segment explained among all other meditation methods. (See the tables in the appendix)

[17] T15, 272c10-273a11.
[18] VISM 517-597.
[19] T15, 273a12-276a5.

The VISM also contains detailed and comprehensive description of the practice of mindfulness on breathing in Chapter 8.[20] It lists out the complete formulation of *ānapānasati* which occurs many times in the Pāli canon, and the meaning of the key words and sentences in the formula is explained comprehensively. The VISM also applies the category of sixteen aspects (soḷsavatthu)[21] which is the same as the ZCSMJ, and eight kinds of attention *(manasikāravidhi)*[22] which is similar to the six methods in ZCSMJ.

There are many differences in these two texts, but if we list out all of them then many trivial points will have to be included. Therefore, three main issues are chosen here to illuminate significant distinctions between the two traditions:

1. The items of six methods in the ZCSMJ and the items of eight attentions in the VISM are more or less the same, though two extra items are seen in the VISM: touching and looking back on the previous seven steps. One apparent difference in the process of these practices is that the ZCSMJ mentions observation of breathing process from the navel, chest to the nose in the third stage: 'fixing'; while the VISM mentions this in its second stage: 'following'. Furthermore, the VISM indicates that the stage of fixing is in fact equivalent to the stage of "absorption concentration" (*appaṇā-samādhi*), one important goal of accomplishing the calming meditation. Unfortunately there is no further explanation for the rest of the four items after the fixing stage in the VISM, and it is difficult to see if they are identical to the latter three items of the six methods in the ZCSMJ. For the ZCSMJ, these latter three items are referred to a level higher than calming meditation: the "insight meditation" (觀法) that is conducive to the purification and "path of no defilements" (無漏道). A similar arrangement is only seen in the latter four purifications in the context of seven purifications in the VISM.

---

[20] VISM 266-293.

[21] S V 310, 321: (1) So satova assasati, satova passasati. Dīghaṃ vā assasanto 'dīghaṃ assasāmī'ti pajānāti, dīghaṃ vā passasanto 'dīghaṃ passasāmī'ti pajānāti; (2) rassaṃ vā assasanto 'rassaṃ assasāmī'ti pajānāti, rassaṃ vā passasanto 'rassaṃ passasāmī'ti pajānāti; (3) 'sabbakāyappaṭisaṃvedī assasissāmī'ti sikkhati, 'sabbakāyappaṭisaṃvedī passasissāmī'ti sikkhati; (4) 'passambhayaṃ kāyasaṅkhāraṃ assasissāmī'ti sikkhati, 'passambhayaü kāyasaṅkhāraṃ passasissāmī'ti sikkhati; (5) 'pītippaṭisaṃvedī assasissāmī'ti sikkhati, 'pītippaṭisaṃvedī passasissāmī'ti sikkhati; (6) 'sukhappaṭisaṃvedī assasissāmī'ti sikkhati, 'sukhappaṭisaṃvedī passasissāmī'ti sikkhati; (7) 'cittasaṅkhārappaṭisaṃvedī assasissāmī'ti sikkhati, 'cittasaṅkhārappaṭisaṃvedī passasissāmī'ti sikkhati; (8) 'passambhayaṃ cittasaṅkhāraṃ assasissāmī'ti sikkhati, 'passambhayaṃ cittasaṅkhāraṃ passasissāmī'ti sikkhati;(9)'cittappaṭisaṃvedī assasissāmī'ti sikkhati, 'cittappaṭisaṃvedī passasissāmī'ti sikkhati; (10)'abhippamodayaṃ cittaṃ assasissāmī'ti sikkhati, 'abhippamodayaṃ cittaṃ passasissāmī'ti sikkhati;(11) 'samādahaṃ cittaṃ assasissāmī'ti sikkhati, 'samādahaṃ cittaṃ passasissāmī'ti sikkhati; (12) 'vimocayaṃ cittaṃ assasissāmī'ti sikkhati, 'vimocayaṃ cittaṃ passasissāmī'ti sikkhati; (13) 'aniccānupassī assasissāmī'ti sikkhati, 'aniccānupassī passasissāmī'ti sikkhati; (14) 'virāgānupassī assasissāmī'ti sikkhati, 'virāgānupassī passasissāmī'ti sikkhati; (15) 'nirodhānupassī assasissāmī'ti sikkhati, 'nirodhānupassī passasissāmī'ti sikkhati; (16) 'paṭinissaggānupassī assasissāmī'ti sikkhati, 'paṭinissaggānupassī passasissāmī'ti sikkhati.

[22] gaṇanā, anubandhanā, phusanā, ṭhapanā, sallakkhaṇā, vivaṭṭaṇā, pārisuddhi and tesañ ca paṭipassanā.

2. What is the relationship between the six methods and sixteen aspects in the ZCSMJ, and the sixteen aspects and eight kinds of attention in the VISM? The VISM simply puts the description of eight kinds of attention after the first tetrad of sixteen aspects without any further explanation about their relationship. The ZCSMJ mentions that the first three tetrads are not "purification" (the sixth method); although it mentions that six methods are practiced in the *kāya-anusmṛti*, it does not indicate the relationship of six methods with other *anusmṛti* practices. Therefore, we can only infer that these might be two related and parallel but independent practices.

3. How are the sixteen aspects distributed with the standard four satipaṭṭhāna? The VISM applies the pattern of four tetrads as a standard way of distribution, which allocates each set of four aspects to one specific satipaṭṭhāna in a regular sequence.[23] The ZCSMJ has a different allocation: the first five aspects belong to *kāya-satipaṭṭhāna*, the next three are *vedanā-satipaṭṭhāna*, followed by three items for *citta-satipaṭṭhāna* and the last five for *dhamma-satipaṭṭhāna*. Apparently, compared to the VISM, the first and the last *satipaṭṭhāna* each have one extra item, while the second and the third each have a missing one. The description of the ZCSMJ is rather distinctive, as this is not seen in many other commentarial texts (e.g. Abhidharma traditions).[24] The only evidence for supporting the arrangement of the ZCSMJ is seen in the *Da zhi du lun* (大智度論), which has exactly the same distribution of 5-3-3-5 model.[25] Interestingly, this reading has been influential in later Chinese interpretation, such as meditation texts in *Tian tai* school.[26]

Comparison of contemplation of the Buddha (念佛觀)

The ZCSMJ mentions that the contemplation of the Buddha is to counteract the problem of having equally distributed defilements, that is to say, the practitioner is not having a particular defilement that is especially graver than others. The other function is to diminish the karmic effects of grave transgression (除重罪). The ZCSMJ emphasizes three kinds of engagement in

---

[23] See the formulation listed in note 21, the items of (1) to (4) being the first set of four items or the first tetrad as representing *kāya-satipaṭṭhāna*, (5)-(8) as the second tetrad representing vedanā- satipaṭṭhāna, (9)-(12) as the third tetrad representing *citta-satipaṭṭhāna* and (13)-(16) for *dhamma-satipaṭṭhāna*.

[24] Cf. KL Dhammajoti, "The Sixteen-mode Mindfulness of Breathing", *Journal of Buddhist Studies (JCBSSL)*, Vol. VI, Centre For Buddhist Studies, Sri Lanka, 2008, 251-288. Dhammajoti has done a wonderful job for the comparison of mindfulness of breathing in many texts.

[25] T25, 138a10-15: 出入息中復有十六行：一、觀入息，二、觀出息，三、觀息長息短，四、觀息遍身，五、除諸身行，六、受喜，七、受樂，八者、受諸心行，九、無作喜(or心作喜)，十、心作攝，十一、心作解脫，十二、觀無常，十三、觀散壞，十四、觀離欲，十五、觀滅，十六、觀棄捨。

[26] E.g. *Shi chan po luo mi chi di fa men* (釋禪波羅蜜次第法門) from 天台智者大師: 十六特勝者，一知息入，二知息出，三知息長短，四知息遍身，五除諸身行，六受喜，七受樂，八受諸心行，九心作喜，十心作攝，十一心作解脫，十二觀無常，十三觀出散，十四觀欲，十五觀滅，十六觀棄捨。(T46, 525b23-27)

the practice; the beginner contemplates on the Buddha statue(s) to produce mental images (觀佛像相好); the intermediate one contemplates the 32 major marks (三十二大人相) and 80 minor marks (八十種小相) of the Buddha and the story of the life of the Buddha (佛(生)身); and the advanced one contemplates the qualities of the Buddha, such as his ten titles and their representative profound meanings (念佛功德法身). The VISM has simply mentioned the contemplation of the Buddha in Chapter 7, in the light of his ten titles. An important view point about the accomplishment of this practice is that the ZCSMJ asserts that this practice can lead to the Buddha-anusmṛti-samādhi (*nien fo san mei* 念佛三昧), and the VISM assumes that only "access concentration" (upacāra-samādhi) is obtained due to the profoundness of the qualities of the Buddha being contemplated. Additionally, both texts mention a lot of other merits that are also obtained during this practice. Significant differences between these two texts is that the ZCSMJ has developed a systematic way of practice, including many experiences of how to attain *nien fo san mei*. The goal is not only to reach the state of samādhi, but also to act as a foundation to develop wisdom: while encountering the Buddha who appears in the practitioner's deep meditation state, the Buddha's teaching will dispel the practitioner's doubt (既得見佛，又聞說法言、或自請問，佛爲說法，解諸疑網). The description of the *nien fo san mei* is in fact very rich in the ZCSMJ; for instance, it is mentioned that practitioners are able to see one Buddha, two Buddhas, and up to ten directions of incalculable Buddhas (見一佛、二佛，乃至十方無量世界諸佛色身). This is obviously a Mahāyanic concept, which follows the system of Mahāyanic Buddha-anusmṛti-samādhi ideas found in a number of Mahāyanic meditation texts. The methods transmitted by Kumārajīva in the ZCSMJ are no doubt representing important cases for actualizing these ideas. This can be seen as one significant achievement in the "northern tradition" of meditation system that is significantly different from "southern tradition". However, this issue needs further comprehensive research, and cannot be discussed here.

Concluding remarks

It appears that both ZCSMJ and the VISM have preserved abundant sources of meditation practices for the southern tradition as well as northern tradition respectively. Moreover, it is worth noticing that these two texts have also kept distinctive records of meditation methods and experiences that were coming from different areas or lineages. We have tried to point out some of the significant differences, and distinctive methods developed in each tradition. In sum, other than standard formulation occurring in canonical texts, living inheritance of meditation methods among practitioners from the past can reveal useful information of why differences exist in different traditions. Kumārajīva has no doubt played an important role in decoding this matter. The next step of research is perhaps to put forward questions about the origin of these practices. To find out this, real entities relevant to these practices will need to be examined carefully; for example, the background of named meditators, together with evidence such as information coming from the meditation caves, etc.

APPENDIX:

The six methods and sixteen aspects of mindfulness on breathing in the ZCSMJ

六種門 **six methods**

	Main points of practice	**Attained states**
數 counting	一心念入息，入息至竟數一，出息至竟數二。若未竟而數爲非數，若數二至九而誤更從一數起。	1. 入息出息生滅無常，易知易見故。 2. 斷諸思覺故，得一心故。 3. 餘觀法寬難失故，數息法急易轉故。…數息心數不得 少時他念，少時他念則失數，以是故初斷思覺應數息。
隨 following	已得數法當行隨法，…入息至竟當隨，莫數一；出息至竟當隨，莫數二。…知入息異、出息異…出息暖、入息冷。	知入出息因緣，而有虛誑不真、生滅無常…思惟：出息從口鼻因緣引之，而有入息因緣，心動令生。而惑者不知，以爲我息。息者是風，與外風無異。地水火空，亦復如是。是五大因緣合故生識，識亦如是，非我有也。五陰、十二入、十八持，亦復如是。
止 fixing	已得隨法當行止法。止法者，數隨心極住意風門，念入出息。…知息出時，從臍心胸咽，至口鼻，息入時，從口鼻咽胸心，至臍，如是繫心一處，是名爲止。	何以故止？斷諸思覺故、心不散故。數、隨息時，心不定、心多劇故止，則心閑少事故，心住一處故念息出入。
觀 contemplating	心止法中住觀，入息時五陰生滅異，出息時五陰生滅異。	如是心亂便除却，一心思惟，令觀增長，是名爲觀法。
轉觀 shifting	捨風門住，離麁觀法。離麁觀法，知息無常。…觀五陰無常，亦念入息、出息生滅無常。見初頭息，無所從來。次觀後息，亦無跡處。因緣合故有，因緣散故無，是名轉觀法。	除滅五蓋及諸煩惱，雖先得止觀，煩惱不淨，心雜，今此淨法，心獨得清淨。

清淨 purifying	復次，前觀異學相似行道，念息入出，今無漏道相似行善有漏道，是謂清淨。	初觀身念止分，漸漸一切身念止。次行痛、心念止，是中非清淨、無漏道遠，故今法念止中，觀十六行，念入出息。得煖法、頂法、忍法、世間第一法，苦法忍、乃至無學盡智，是名清淨。

十六分 **sixteen aspects**

	Main points of practice	**Attained states**
身念止 Body-mindfulness	1. 初入息分，六種安那般那行； 2. 出息分亦如是； 3. 一心念息入出，若長、若短…是故言息 長、息短，是中亦行安那般那六事。 4. 念諸息遍身，亦念息出入，悉觀身中， 諸出息入息。息出覺知遍至身中，乃至 足指遍諸毛孔，如水入沙。 5. 除諸身行，亦念入出息。初學息時，若 身懈怠、睡眠體重，悉除棄之。身輕柔 軟，隨禪定心受喜，亦念息入出。…入 身念止中竟。	3. 譬如：人怖走上山，若擔負重，若上氣，如是比是 息短，若人極時，得安息歡喜。又如得利，從獄中出， 如是爲息長。一切息隨二處：若長、若短處。 4. 息出覺知從足至髮，遍諸毛孔，亦如水入沙。口鼻 風入出亦爾，觀身周遍，見風行處。復心非獨口鼻， 觀息入出，一切毛孔及九孔中，亦見息入息出，是故 知息遍諸身。 5. 除懈怠、睡眠、心重，得心輕、柔軟，隨禪定心 喜。

Sensation- mindfulness 痛念止	6. 已得身念止，實今更得 痛念止，實受喜。	6. 次已知身實相，今欲知心、心數法實相。是故受喜，亦念息入出；
	7. 受樂，亦念息入出。	7. 是喜增長，名爲樂。…初心中生悅，是名喜；後遍身喜，是名樂。 初禪、二禪中，樂痛名喜；三禪中 樂痛名受樂。
	8. 受諸心行，亦念息入 出。	8. 諸心生滅法、心染法、心不染法，心散法、心攝法，心正法、心邪 法，如是等諸心相，名爲心行。
Mind-mindfulness 心念止	9. 心作喜時，亦念息入出。…是 念法心 作喜，若心不悅，勸勉令喜。	9. 先受喜自生不故作，念心故作喜。問曰：何以故故 作喜？答曰：欲治二種心：或散心、或攝心，如是 作心，得出煩惱。
	10. 心作攝時，亦念息入出。設心不定， 強伏令定。	10. 如經中說：「心定是道，心散非道。」
	11. 心作解脫時，亦念息入出。若意不解，強伏令解。…是名心念止作解脫。	11. 譬如羊入蒼耳。蒼耳著身，人爲漸漸出之，心作解 脫諸煩惱結，亦復如是。
Dharma-mindfulness 法意止	12. 觀無常，亦念息入出。觀諸法無常、 生、滅、空、無吾我。	12. 生時諸法空生，滅時諸法空滅。是中無男、無女、 無人、無作、無受，是名隨無常觀。
	13. 觀有爲法出散，亦念息入出，無常，是名出散。	13. 諸有爲法，現世中出。從過去因緣和合故集，因緣 壞故散，如是隨觀是名出散觀。
	14. 觀離欲結，亦念息入出。心離諸結，是法第一，是名隨離欲觀。	14. 心離諸結，是法第一，是名隨離欲觀。
	15. 觀盡，亦念息入出。	15. 諸結使苦，在在處盡，是處安隱，是名隨盡觀。
	16. 觀棄捨，亦念息入出。…如是觀，是 名隨法意止觀。	16. 諸染愛、煩惱、身心五陰、諸有爲法棄捨，是第一安隱。

15

Kumārajīva and early Cave-temples of China: The case of the Dhyāna-sūtras

Chongfeng Li

Kumārajīva [鸠摩罗什, 344-413 C.E. or 350-409 C.E.[1] was a great scholar of the Buddhist Tripiṭaka [三藏] and an eminent translator of the Buddhist scriptures. His teaching and translations exerted a far-reaching influence on Buddhism as well as Buddhist art in China. Therefore, Kumārajīva occupies a pivotal position in the history of Sino-Indian cultural relations.

According to *Weishu: Shilaozhi* [魏书·释老志, *A History of the Wei Dynasty: Treatise on Buddhism and Taoism*] by Wei Shou [魏收], at that time there was in the Western Regions a foreign śramaõa by the name of Kumārajīva [鸠摩罗什] who was eager of spreading the Dharma (Buddhism). The eminent Chinese monk, Dao'an [道安, 312-385 C.E.][2] was much greatly interested to have discussions with Kumārajīva and often urged Fu Jian [符坚], founder of the Former Qin kingdom [前秦, 351-394 C.E.], to send for him. Kumārajīva, in his turn, having heard of Dao'an's noble reputation, called him the Saint of the East. At times he paid him his respects by bowing to him from afar. Some twenty years after Dao'an's death, Kumārajīva arrived in Ch'ang-an [长安, present-day Xi'an]. He regretted not finding Dao'an and was deeply sorrowed by his loss. The ideas in the texts corrected by Dao'an and the versions translated by Kumārajīva are in complete harmony and entirely free from disagreement. Through Kumārajīva's work, the content of the Dharma was made widely known throughout Central China [中原][3].

---

[1] Lü, Cheng 1979: 87.

[2] Dao'an was also a great scholar of the Buddhist *Tripiṭaka* and an eminent translator of Buddhist scriptures in the 4th century C.E. in northern China; cf: Tang, Yongtong 1982: 133-163.

[3] Wei, Shou 1974: 3025-3062, esp. 3029-30; James R. Ware 1930: 100-181, esp. 125-126; Leon Hurvitz 1956: 23-103, esp. 50.

When Kumārajīva arrived in Ch'ang-an in 401 C.E. at the invitation of Yao Xing [姚兴], ruler of the Later Qin kingdom [后秦, 384-417 C.E.], he was given the position of National Preceptor [国师, purohita][4]. At the Caotang Temple [草堂寺] in Ch'ang-an, 800 students gathered together to interpret or retranslate the scriptures under his guidance. The eloquent and great thinker Kumārajīva knew both Chinese and the vernacular languages of the Western Regions. At that time śramaṇas such as Daorong [道肜], Senglue [僧略], Daoheng [道恒], Daobiao [道檦], Sengzhao [僧肇], Tanying [曇影] and others, along with Kumārajīva, helped one another to elucidate what was very obscure. They altered and fixed the composition of ten odd works consisting of long, profound sūtras and śāstras, so that the text might be clear and intelligible. Down to this day these works are taken as models by all śramaṇas in their studies[5]. According to *Jinshu: Yaoxing zaiji* [晋书·姚兴载记, *A History of the Jin Dynasty: Biography of Yaoxing*] by Fang Xuanling [房玄龄], about five thousand śramaṇas and monks from far away areas gathered at the capital (Ch'ang-an), a stūpa was built at Yongguili [永贵里] and a prajñā platform [般若台] was set up in the palace [中宫]. The śramaṇas who practiced dhyāna numbered in the thousands, and all counties and prefectures were influenced by Kumārajīva's teaching and translations with the result that nearly ninety per cent of the people in the kingdom converted to Buddhism[6].

During this period, regions and territories occupied by the Han nation lacked Sūtra and vinaya texts in the vernacular language; they were, thus, inaccessible to the masses, Kumārajīva, consequently, was immersed in the translation of Buddhist scriptures. On the basis of a conversation between Kumārajīva and Vimalākṣa [卑摩罗叉], most of the new scriptures on the Buddhist Sūtra [经, the Buddha's doctrinal teachings], vinaya [律, rules of the monastic discipline] and śāstras or abhidharma [论, commentaries on sūtras and vinaya] were reinterpreted or translated into Chinese by Kumārajīva, and more than three thousands students of the Dharma studied with him[7]. According to *Chu sanzang ji ji* [出三藏记集, *A Collection of Records concerning the Tripiṭaka*] by Sengyou, Kumārajīva continuously produced or translated 35 Buddhist texts into Chinese in 294 fascicles. Among them were *Emituo jing* [阿弥陀经, *Sukhāvatīvyūha, Amitābha-Sūtra*], *Fahua jing* [法华经, *Saddharma-puṇḍarīka-sūtra, Lotus Sūtra*], *Weimojie jing* [维摩诘经, *Vimalakīrti-nirdeśa-Sūtra*], *Shizhu jing* [十住经, *Daśabhūmikā Sūtra, Sūtra on the Ten Stages*], *Yijiao jing* [遗教经, *The Buddha's Legacy Teachings Sūtra*], *Mile xiasheng jing* [弥勒下生经, *Maitreyavyākaraṇa, Advent of Maitreya Sūtra*], *Foshuo mile chengfo jing* [佛说弥勒成佛经, *Sūtra of Maitreya becoming a Buddha*], *Shisong lü* [十诵律, *Sarvāstivādavinaya,*

[4] Sengyou *Taishō* 55: 100-102, esp. 101b.
[5] Wei, Shou 1974: 3031; cf: James R. Ware 1930: 130-131; Leon Hurvitz 1956: 54.
[6] Fang, Xuanling et al 1974: 2975-3006, esp.2985.
[7] Sengyou *Taishō* 55: 102a.

Ten Divisions of Monastic Rules], *Dapin bore* [大品般若, *Mahāprajñāpāramita-Sūtra, Larger Wisdom Sūtra*], *Xiaopin bore* [小品般若, *Smaller Wisdom Sūtra*], *Bailun* [百论, *Treatise in One Hundred Verses*], *Zhonglun* [中论, *Mādhyamika-śāstra, Treatise on the Middle Way*], *Shi'ermen lun* [十二门论, *Treatise on the Twelve Gates*], *Dazhidu lun* [大智度论, *Mahāprajñāpāramitā-śāstra, Treatise on the Great Perfection of Wisdom*] and *Chengshi lun* [成实论, *Satyasiddhi-śàstra, Treatise on the Establishment of Truth*]. In addition, Kumārajīva translated and compiled some sūtras on dhyāna such as *Chanfa yaojie* [禅法要解, *Interpretation of the Dhyāna-discipline* or *Essential Explanation of the Way to Meditate*], *Chanjing* [禅经, *Dhyāna-sūtra or Dhyāna-meditation-Sūtra*]/ *Zuochan sanmei jing* [坐禅三昧经, *Dhyāna-samādhi-Sūtra, Sūtra on the Concentration of Sitting Meditation*]/ *Guanzhong chanjing* [关中禅经, *Dhyāna-sūtra translated in the Central Shaanxi Plain*] and *Chanfa yao* [禅法要, *Essentials of the Dhyāna-discipline*]/ *Chanmi yaofa jing* [禅密要法经, *Secret Essentials of the Dhyāna-discipline* or *Sūtra about the Secret Essence of Dhyāna*][8].

Undoubtedly, it is clear that Emperor Xiaowen [孝文帝, 471-499 C.E.] of the Northern Wei Dynasty was honoring Kumārajīva as a Saint who had attained the Mahāyāna enlightenment of the bodhisattva stage and who had been active in converting the people. According to *Weishu: Shilaozhi* (*A History of the Wei Dynasty: Treatise on Buddhism and Taoism*), in the fifth month of the twenty-first year (497 C.E.) of Emperor Xiaowen, the following imperial order was issued: "Whereas the Master of the Law (dharmācārya) Kumārajīva may be called a man who has quit the world like a divinity and who resolutely entered upon the Four Practices; and whereas the monastery which he constantly inhabited still has surplus land; and whereas we respect and take pleasure in the traces of his practices, and deeply regret the master's demise; permission is granted to erect in memory of him a three-storied stūpa on the site of the old building which he inhabited"[9].

According to *Lüxiang gantong zhuan* [律相感通传, *Responses to Dreamlike Dialogues with Devas*] by Daoxuan [道宣], Kumārajīva thoroughly understood Mahāyāna enlightenment, fully comprehended the Buddha's preaching and freely translated the scriptures on the Sūtra, vinaya and śāstra. Kumārajīva's translations have brought honor to his ancestors and prosperity to his descendants, an achievement which most others aspire to but cannot attain. Because his versions are faithful to the originals of the Tripiṭaka, they have been chanted and studied by Buddhist followers since they were translated into Chinese and were not replaced by others at least until the early 7th century C.E[10].

---

8 Sengyou *Taishō* 55: 10c-11a, 101b.

9 Wei, Shou 1974: 3040; cf: James R. Ware 1930: 156; Leon Hurvitz 1956: 82-83.

10 Daoxuan *Taishō* 45: 874-882, esp. 877a.

With respect to the various versions of the Buddhist Tripiṭaka in Chinese, only those translated by Kumārajīva continued to be popular through the centuries all over China, a trend which exists even up to modern times. Kumārajīva's translations and interpretations were prized by later generations for their excellence and clarity and were without parallel, in terms of technique and correction; they ushered in a new epoch in the history of the translation of the Buddhist Tripiṭaka and greatly impacted development of Buddhism in China[11].

Dhyāna or meditation is a practice that focusses the mind on one point in order to purify the spirit, thereby eradicating illusions and perceiving the truth. Dhyāna was widely practiced in India before Śākyamuni was born, and was incorporated into Buddhism later, which developed its own forms and approaches. "When the Chinese were first brought face to face with Indian Buddhism with its rich and elaborate imagery, concepts, and modes of thinking, they were fascinated at first and finally overwhelmed and conquered. After a few centuries, however, the practical nature of the Chinese began asserting itself; it began to search for certain features within Buddhism which it could understand and practice, and in this search it soon picked on the dhyāna exercise as the essence of Buddhist discipline"[12].

In fact, ways of practicing meditation and stages of attainment began to be transmitted side by side after Buddhism spread in China, but there was no regular method or pattern of meditation-practice before the late 4th century C.E. The monk Sengrui [僧叡], who was one of the disciples of Monk Dao'an and later became an assistant of Kumārajīva, was filled with emotion and stated that "the heart cannot be laid at any place, because the way of dhyāna discipline has not been introduced yet"[13], or, in other words, the heart of dhyāna discipline had not been understood at that time. Sengrui was taught and given instruction in dhyāna-discipline by Kumārajīva, only six days after Kumārajīva had arrived in Ch'ang-an. On the basis of *Guanzhong chu chanjing xu* [关中出禅经序, *Preface to the Dhyāna-sūtra translated in the Central Shaanxi Plain*] by Sengrui, "*dhyāna* is the ABC to the mārga (way of Buddhism) and a ferry crossing to the nirvāṇa (enlightenment)[14]. In addition, the contemporary Buddhist scriptures in the region of the Yangtze at the time, according to *Chu sanzang ji ji* (*A Collection of Records concerning the Tripiṭaka*) by Sengyou, were mostly incomplete; the dhyāna method was unheard of, and the available collection of monastic rules (vinaya-piṭaka) was also fragmentary. Huiyuan [慧远], a great master of Chinese Buddhism in Southern China, was saddened by

[11] Lü, Cheng 1979: 86-99.
[12] Kenneth Ch'en 1973: 350.
[13] Huijiao *Taishō* 50: 364a.
[14] Sengrui *Taishō* 55: 65a.

the incompleteness of the Buddhist doctrine and ordered his disciples Fajing [法净] and others to go a far distance in search of Buddhist scripture[15]. These records indicate that not only dhyāna scriptures were lacking or incomplete in Northern China before the 4th century C.E., but Sūtra texts were also less translated during the initial stage of dissemination of Buddhism in Southern China. Dhyāna was unknown to the public and vinaya texts were incomplete or with parts missing even in the same region during the same period[16]. After Kumārajīva came to Ch'ang-an, key dhyāna-sūtras, besides various scriptures on the Sūtra, vinaya and śāstra, were reinterpreted or translated into Chinese by him along with his brilliant disciples. As a result, Huiyuan "expresses his joy at the translations made by Kumārajīva in this field"[17] and said that Kumārajīva had opened up a realm of dhyāna-discipline[18].

With regards to Kumārajīva's translations, *Chanjing (Dhyāna-Sūtra)*, namely, *Zuochan sanmei jing* (*Dhyāna-samādhi-sūtra, Sūtra on the Concentration of Sitting Meditation*) or *Guanzhong chanjing* (*Dhyāna-sūtra translated in the Central Shaanxi Plain*) in two fascicles[19], which explains the method of dhyāna practice in detail, was compiled and produced on the basis of seven sūtras on dhyāna discipline in 402 C.E. This work was simultaneously the outcome of both interpreting and editing sūtras on dhyāna[20]. Later, *Chanfa yaojie* (*Interpretation of the Dhyāna-discipline* or *Essential Explanation of the Way to Meditate*) in two fascicles[21] was compiled according to *Chishi jing* [持世经, *Upholder of the Age Sūtra*] in the same year.[22] This work is similar to general practice of Hīnayāna Buddhism. Since he was not satisfied with what he had translated or compiled before, Kumārajīva checked up his previous versions carefully and re-edited what he had previously done; he also worked on some other sūtras about the dhyāna-discipline. As a result, *Chanfa yao* (*Essentials of the Dhyāna-discipline*) viz. *Chanmi yaofa jing* (*Secret Essentials of the Dhyāna-discipline* or *Sūtra about the Secret Essence of Dhyāna*) in three fascicles[23] finally came out in 407 C.E.[24] It considers contemplation of filthiness [不净观, *aśubhā-smṛti*][25] as the dominant factor and elaborates on the dhyāna discipline belonging to Hīnayāna

---

15 Sengyou *Taishō* 55: 110a.
16 Sengyou, *ibidem.*
17 E. Zürcher 1972: 223.
18 Huiyuan *Taishō* 55: 66a.
19 Kumārajīva *Taishō* 15: 269-286.
20 Sengrui *Taishō* 55: 65a-b.
21 Kumārajīva *Taishō* 15: 286-297
22 Sengrui *Taishō* 55: 65b.
23 Kumārajīva *Taishō* 15: 242-269
24 Sengrui *Taishō* 55: 65b.
25 The contemplation of filthiness (aśubhā-smṛti) is also called meditation on the vileness of the body or meditation on the impurity of the body. The practice of meditation or contemplation on the inherent impurity of the human body is to overcome craving and greed, that is, it is aimed at stemming desire and quieting the mind.

Buddhism. In addition, Kumārajīva used to translate *Guanfo sanmei jing* [观佛三昧经, *Buddha-dhyāna-samādhī-sūtra*] into Chinese, but it was unfortunately lost[26]; *Siwei lueyao fa* (*An Outline of Meditation* or *Outlining the Way to Reflect*), which records ten kinds of contemplation and wholly belongs to Māhayāna Buddhism, seems to have also been translated by Kumārajīva[27]. These versions of the dhyāna-sūtras fully testify that Kumārajīva taught and gave instruction in dhyāna-discipline immediately after he came to Ch'ang-an. In conclusion, he carefully reinterpreted and edited the dhyāna scriptures[28].

As a matter of fact, Kumārajīva's mother had a strong interest in dhyāna and devoted herself to practicing the dhyāna-meditation. According to *Gaoseng zhuan* (*Biographies of Eminent Priests*) by Huijiao, when she travelled out of the city, she saw a cemetery with bare bones between the tombs scattered around randomly. She was deeply moved by the thought of suffering and its origin and she vowed to become a nun. She said that if her hair were not cut to become a nun, then she would not drink or eat. After going hungry for six days and nights, her energy and strength were exhausted and it was doubtful that she would live until the morning. Her husband became frightened, and allowed her to become a nun under the circumstances. However, without shaving her hair, she would not eat. Thereupon, by an imperial order, her hair was cut. After that, she began to drink and eat. Then the next morning she received the precepts and happily did her meditation practice as before[29] . On his way back from Jibin [罽宾, greater Gandhāra or Gandhāran cultural area][30], Kumārajīva also stayed in Ush-Turfan [温宿) for a while. The king of the Kucha kingdom personally went to Ush-Turfan and welcomed Kumārajīva to return to his native country to preach widely on various sūtras, since the whole world admired his school of thought as nothing could compare with it. At that time the Princess of Kucha had already become a Buddhist nun whose secular name was Ajieyemodi [阿竭耶末帝, Akāyamatī][31]. She was widely learned in many sūtras and she was especially proficient in dhyāna-discipline[32].

---

[26] 1) Fei, Zhangfang *Taishō* 49: 78c; 2) Daoxuan *Taishō* 55: 253b; 3) Zhisheng *Taishō* 55: 513b.

[27] As for *Siwei lueyao fa (An Outline of Meditation or Outlining the Way to Reflect),* Sengyou put it under the translations of An Shigao [安世高], but Fei, Zhangfang, Daoxuan and Zhisheng listed this text as Kumārajīva's translation. However, Lü, Cheng argues that its translator was mislabeled as Kumārajīvaby Zhisheng and Charles Willemen infers this Chinese text was probably established in the early 5th century in Jiankang by Chinese monks using popular ideas of the time. If an Indian dhyāna master was involved in the compilation, it may have been someone like Dharmamitra, ca. 430-440 C.E. See 1) Sengyou Taishō 55: 6a-b; 2) Fei, Zhangfang Taishō 49: 78c; 3) Daoxuan Taishō 55: 253b; 4) Zhisheng Taishō 55: 513b, 668b, 721b; 5) Lü, Cheng 1980: 90; 6) Charles Willemen 2012: 15-17.

[28] Lü, Cheng 1979: 75-76.

[29] Huijiao *Taishō* 50: 330a; cf: Marylin M. Rhie 2002: 389.

[30] 1) Richard Salomon 1999: 3; 2) Charles Willemen 2008: 39 (154), 69 (124); 3) Charles Willemen 2012: 16; 4) Li, Chongfeng. "Jibin and China as seen from Chinese Documents", in: *Archaeology of Buddhism in Asia*" ed. by B. Mani. New Delhi: Archaeological Survey of India (in press).

[31] Here, Akāyamatī should be the mother of Kumārajīva; cf: Tang, Yongtong 1982: 201.

[32] Huijiao *Taishō* 50: 330c-331a; cf: Marylin M. Rhie 2002: 391.

On the basis of what he had learned from greater Gandhāra as well as the Western Regions, Kumārajīva, whose thinking and ideology had very likely been influenced by his mother's dhyāna-discipline, not only translated and edited dhyāna sūtras, but also fostered five thousand disciples and directed most of them to practice dhyāna at Ch'ang-an. For instance, according to the *Weishu: Shilaozhi* (*A History of the Wei Dynasty: Treatise on Buddhism and Taoism*), when Shizu [世祖, i.e., Emperor Taiwu 太武帝, 424-452 C.E.] of the Northern Wei Dynasty defeated Helianchang [赫连昌] in 426 C.E., he captured a master monk by the name of Huishi [惠始] who, hearing that Kumārajīva had translated some new sūtras, went to Ch'ang-an to interview him. Directing his attention to the learning of Sūtra, he sat in meditation north of the White Canal [白渠]. During the day he entered the city to listen to the expositions, but at night he returned to his abode to sit quietly'. When Tongwan [统万] had been conquered, Huishi went to the capital (Pingcheng 平城, present Datong). He gave much instruction and guidance, but his contemporaries could not fathom his manner. Shizu of the Northern Wei valued him greatly and often paid him homage. Huishi who practiced dhyāna-meditation from that time, up to his death, said that for fifty odd years he never layd down to sleep even once,[33].

After the dhyāna-sūtras were translated into Chinese by Kumārajīva, the practice of dhyāna became progressively regular in Northern China and the procedure of practicing dhyāna-meditation was also standardized in this vast region. Therefore, Kumārajīva, who not only produced dhyāna-sūtras, but also gave instruction in dhyāna practice, did all he could in regard to this discipline. He is, thus, regarded as the great master of the dhyāna-discipline in Northern China[34].

Besides Kumārajīva, some other Buddhist masters also translated sūtras on dhyāna-discipline into Chinese, such as *Damoduoluo chanjing* [达摩多罗禅经, *Dharmatara dhyāna-sūtra* or *Yogācārabhūmi*], i.e., *Lushan chanjing* [庐山禅经, *Dhyāna-sūtra translated at Mt. Lu*][35] and *Foshuo guanfo sanmeihai jing* [佛说观佛三昧海经, *Buddha-dhyāna-samādhisāgara-sūtra, Sutra on the Sea of Mystic Ecstasy Attained by Visualizing the Buddha* or *Ocean of Meditation on the Buddha Sūtra*][36] by Buddhabhadra [佛驮跋陀罗, 359-429 C.E.], among others. Buddhabhadra arrived in Ch'ang-an around 410 C.E. and at first assisted Kumārajīva in the translation of Buddhist scriptures. They often had discussions together

33 Wei, Shou 1974: 3032-33; cf: 1) James R. Ware 1930: 135-136; 2) Leon Hurvitz 1956: 63.

34 1) Tang, Yongtong 1982: 210, 213, 218-219; 2) Liu, Huida 1996: 332.

35 *Taishō* 15: 300-325. Hui-yuan wrote a preface to this sūtras, namely, Huiyuan *Taishō* 55: 65-66.

36 *Taishō* 15: 645-697. The text, generally called as *Sea Sūtra*, belongs to a category of *Kuan Sūtras* on visualizing Amitayus. Kuan was a systematic system of building visual images through different steps, advancing from simple to complex. *Kuan Sutra* refers to the images and statues as a first step towards visualizing the beauty of the divinity. The mental pictures were formed with help of images that took the practitioner to the ecstatic vision.

and mutually explored some of the abstruse implications of canonical texts. Nevertheless, they breathed a different intellectual atmosphere later, as their scholastic lineages apparently derived from separate origins. The lectures on dhyāna by Buddhabhadra at Ch'ang-an, however, seem to be very different from what was taught by Kumārajīva. Kumārajīva devoted himself to disseminating the teachings of sūtras, particularly the Mahāyāna doctrine of Nāgārjuna, and was favorably recognized by Yao Xing, ruler of the Later Qin kingdom. Moreover, Kumārajīva and his disciples, more than three thousand in number, could freely go in and out of the palaces and courts. Buddhabhadra, however, strictly adhered to the modes of teaching of the Sthaviravāda of the Śrāvakayāna, cultivating meditation and concentration, living a plain and simple life without any display or show. Owing to such divergences, gradually there arose a discord between the disciples of the two great masters. In the 17th year of the Yixi [义熙] era (411 C.E.) of the Eastern Jin Dynasty [东晋], some disciples of Kumārajīva blamed Buddhabhadra as being guilty of telling a lie — thus breaking a fundamental commandment — and relying upon the support of the masses. This compelled Buddhabhadra to leave Ch'ang-an, and he went southward to Mt. Lu where he was welcomed by Huiyuan, who had heard of Buddhabhadra's fame. During his residence at Mt. Lu, Buddhabhadra, at the request of Huiyuan, lectured on the doctrine of meditation and translated a special work on dhyāna, *Yogacaryā-bhūmi-sūtra,* and thus gave him great help in his meditation and contemplation[37].

According to Lü Cheng's study, though Buddhabhadra's translations touched upon different aspects of Buddhism, his special attention was concentrated on the methods of meditative contemplation. Buddhabhadra had translated the works of both Dharmatrāta and Buddhasena on the methods of dhyāna. Of course, Kumārajīva also taught methods of contemplation; but he recommended only some essentials of dhyāna of the old masters of the Sthaviravāda of the Śrāvakayāna without giving them an orderly and systematic formulation. Buddhabhadra's methods, however, were those handed down from master to disciples for generations and therefore kept their purity intact[38].

Chanfa yao (Essentials of the Dhyāna-discipline)/ Chanmi yaofa jing (Secret Essentials of the Dhyāna-discipline or Sūtra about the Secret Essence of Dhyāna), Zuochan sanmei jing (Dhyāna-samādhi-Sūtra, Sūtra on the Concentration of Sitting Meditation)/ Guanzhong chanjing (Dhyāna-sūtra translated in the Central Shaanxi Plain), Chanfa yaojie (Interpretation of the Dhyāna-discipline or Essential

[37] 1) Sengyou *Taishō* 55: 103b-104a; 2) Huijiao *Taishº* 50: 334b-335c; 3) Lu, Chêng 1971: 382-384; 4) Tang, Yongtong 1982: 218-219.

[38] 1) Lü, Chêng 1971: 382-384; 2) Li, Chongfeng. "Jibin and China as seen from Chinese Documents. "*Archaeology of Buddhism in Asia*" ed. by B. Mani. New Delhi: Archaeological Survey of India (in press).

Explanation of the Way to Meditate) and *Damoduoluo Chanjing (Dharmatara dhyāna-sūtra or Yogācārabhūmi) / Lushan chanjing (Dhyāna-sūtra translated at Mt. Lu)* are all sūtras on mental dharmas, which explained the established dhyāna practice to the followers; they were held up as models by the devotees who intended to practice dhyāna[39]. The lost *Guanfo sanmei jing* (*Buddha-dhyāna-samādhī-Sūtra*) translated by Kumārajīva and extant *Foshuo guanfo sanmeihai jing* (*Buddha-dhyāna- samādhisāgara-Sūtra, The Sūtra on the Sea of Mystic Ecstasy Attained by Visualizing the Buddha* or *Ocean of Meditation on the Buddha Sūtra*) translated by Buddhabhadra, as the titles indicate, are mainly devoted to the contemplation of the Buddha (*buddhānusmṛti-samādhi*), precisely the kind of mental concentration which was much in vogue among the followers of Huiyuan. Thus, it can be inferred that the pursuit of dhyāna-discipline was a matter of philosophical discussion in the 5th century C.E. In the early 5th century, Kumārajīva in the north and Buddhabhadra as well as Huiyuan in the south disseminated dhyāna discipline and enabled Indian dhyāna to become progressively popular in China[40].

The aim of dhyāna-meditation is to free oneself from worldly worries and to become a Buddha; in other words, this is a meditative practice for the Buddhists who were eager to attain enlightenment. An ideal place for dhyāna practice should be both monasteries and araṇya (forest hermitages), as is often the case. According to dhyāna sūtras, the practice of dhyāna meditation needs to take place in extremely quiet surroundings. A place suitable for meditation must be extremely peaceful, such as forest land, places between tombs, under trees, and *araṇya*. Therefore, it tends to be found in mountains, forest, marshes, or near streams; dhyāna practice should be carried out in places far from cities and towns, and in locations where people rarely go[41].

Originally, caves in different areas were used by monks as places of meditation where they could discipline themselves in order to rid their hearts of any vestiges of worldly thoughts, such as Buddha allowing bhikṣus to walk around (经行, caṅkramaṇa) and to dwell in chanku [禅窟, meditation-cave][42], Mahākāśyapa used to sit in meditation in a cave named Pippala [宾鉢罗窟] near Gṛdhra-kūṭa [耆闍崛山, Vulture-mountain][43]. According to *Faxian zhuan* [法显传, *Travels of Faxian*], when Faxian arrived at the Vulture-mountain, three *li* from the summit he found a cave in the rock, facing south, where Buddha used to sit in meditation. Thirty paces to the North-West there is another such cave, in which Ānanda used to sit in meditation when Māra-pāpmen or Pāpīyas

[39] Tang, Yongtong 1982: 552.

[40] Hu, Shih 1997: 42.

[41] 1) Kumārajīva Taishō 15: 270c; 2) Kumārajīva *Taishō* 15: 252a, 269b.

[42] Kumārajīva *Taishō* 9: 45c.

[43] Kinkara, Tanyao *Taishō* 50: 298c; cf: 1) Faxian 1985: 114; 2) H. A. Giles 1972: 52; 3) Xuan Zang 1985: 730; 4) Samuel Beal 1980: 374-375, footnote 53.

[魔波旬] changed himself into a vulture and stood before the cave in order to frighten Ānanda. Nevertheless, the Buddha by his divine power pierced the rock and stretched out his hand to stroke Ānanda's shoulder, so that his fear was allayed. The tracks of the bird and the hole for Buddha's hand are both still to be seen; hence the name Vulture-cave Mountain. In front of the cave is the place where the four Buddhas sat down, and also the caves where each one of arhats sat in meditation, several hundred in all[44].

At that time, these caves were natural ones and many Buddhist monks went to the forest and lived in natural caves to meditate. Usually, forests and caves were associated with meditation as there were no people living there and there was less disturbance.

There were certainly rock shelters used by ascetics of many creeds in the times before Aśoka, but no ruler or king ever thought of furnishing them with permanent settlements chiselled out of solid rock. It was Aśoka, king of the Maurya Empire, who initiated cutting living rocks into architectural forms. As proof of his tolerance towards all religious sects, he had caves built in the Barābār hills in Gayā and presented them to the jīvikas [邪命外道] in 257 B.C; one of his successors donated three caves at Nāgārjuna hills to the same Ājāvikas as well[45]. Sometime in the post-Aśoka period, the activity of hewing out an abode in the living rock spread to the Deccan under the patronage of the Buddhists of the Theravāda school. Some irregularly open or single monastic cells at Bhājā, Kanheri and other sites may be regarded as the earliest examples of rock-cut architecture on the Western Deccan. With liberal donations by the public and preserving efforts made by the Buddhist monks, more and more cave-temple complexes came into existence in India[46].

This custom spread to China along with the transmission of Buddhism, and dhyāna was the only activity practiced by Buddhist monks in Northern China from the late 4th to the early 7th centuries C.E.[47]. Construction of Buddhist rock-cut temples in China as well as arrangement of the Buddhist images inside seem to be closely related to dhyāna-discipline.

On the basis of *Weishu: Shilaozhi* (*A History of the Wei Dynasty: Treatise on Buddhism and Taoism*), when Gaozu [高祖, i.e. Emperor Xiaowen] ascended the throne in 471 C.E., Xianzu (显祖, i.e. Emperor Xianwen/献文帝465-471 C.E.) went to live in the Chongguang Palace [崇光宫] in the Northern Park [北苑], where he was said to always read books on the Mystery. Xianzhu ordered construction of a Deer-park Temple [鹿野佛图, Mṛgadāva stūpa] on the Western mountain within the park, about 10 *li* to the right of Chongguang Palace, with

[44] Faxian 1985: 2, 113; cf: 1) H. A. Giles 1972: 50; 2) Xuanzang 1985: 727-728; 3) Samuel Beal 1980: 373.

[45] Harry Falk 2006: 255-279.

[46] Li, Chongfeng 2003: 2-4.

[47] Tang, Yongtong 1982: 570-572.

meditation-cells hewn into the rock, and monks who practiced dhyāna dwelt therein[48]. Therefore, Gao Yun [高允] who was a famous scholar of the Northern Wei Dynasty said: "To carve or hew out a celestial cave in the rock is to supply a place for a monk sitting in meditation"[49]. The remains of a rock-cut temple found in 1987 in a mountain valley near Xiaoshi village [小石寺村] at Datong, moreover, tallies with the record in *Wei Shu* (*A History of the Wei Dynasty*) and is considered to be a component part of the ruined Deer-park Temple[50].

Buddhism was formally disseminated to the interior of China in the middle of the Yongping era [永平, 58-75 C.E.] of Emperor Ming [明帝] of the Later Han Dynasty [后汉, 25-220 C.E.], which had a strong influence on Chinese culture and ideology from the 3rd century onwards[51]. The Buddhist temples or monasteries and images, however, most likely made their debut somewhat later. The cave-temples were but a special kind of temple. Therefore it is reasonable to suppose that they appeared in China only after some time, evolving from the more common types of temple building and image making.

The cave-temple complex at Mogaoku [莫高窟], Dunhuang, according to a stone tablet named *Dazhou lijun mogaoku fokan bei* [*大周李君莫高窟佛龛碑, A Tablet Commemorating a Buddhist Cave built by an Individual named Li at Mogao in the Great Zhou Period*] and dated to 698 C.E, was started in 366 C.E. by a hermit monk named Lezun [樂僔] and continued by another hermit monk named Faliang [法良], to be developed later by Prince Dongyang [东阳王] and Lord Jianping [建平公]. Both Lezun and Faliang were monks who practiced meditation[52]. There is reason to believe that each of these men came from Central China, east of Dunhuang[53]. Hence it would appear that the history of the Mogaoku caves can only be understood as a part of the history of Central China.

The cave-temple complex at Binglingsi [炳灵寺] in Yongjing, which was also known as Mt. Tangshu [唐述山] or Mt. Jishi [积石山] in historical records, became an integral part of the religious activities of the Western Qin kingdom [西秦, 385-431 C.E.][54]. According to an inscription found at niche 6 in cave 169, construction of the cave-temples at Binglingsi (fig. 1) was initiated around 420 C.E.[55]. Although we do not know who was the first to hew out a temple in the rock there, we do know that the dhyāna-discipline was very popular in Western Qin kingdom and Monk Tanwupi [昙无毗, Dharmapriya?] who

[48] Wei, Shou 1974: 3038; cf: 1) James R. Ware 1930: 149-150; 2) Leon Hurvitz 1956: 75.

[49] Gao, Yun *Taishō* : 52: 339b.

[50] 1) Li, Zhiguo & Liu, Jianjun 1991: 212-215; 2) Liu, Jianjun 2010: 1-9.

[51] Tang, Yongtong 1982: 1-21.

[52] Liu, Huida, "op cit.: 331-348, esp. 332

[53] Su, Bai 1996: 262-269, 355-356, esp. 265, 355.

[54] 1) Li, Daoyuan 1989: 138-40; 2) Daoshi *Taishō* 53: 595a-b.

[55] Cave 169 at Binglingsi is a large natural cave, the Buddha images made in clay sculpture and Buddhist motifs or subjects represented on the mural were added around 420 C.E. According to the Buddhist tradition, monks usually went to the forest and lived in natural caves to meditate in the early period. In this way, cave 169 probably used to be a place for monks to practice dhyāna meditation and contemplation.

came from a foreign country taught dhyāna-discipline and led the followers to practice meditation in the kingdom[56]. Monk Tanwupi's portrait was even painted in the mural of cave 169 at Binglingsi (fig. 2). Moreover, Xuanshao [玄绍], who was one of the disciples of Monk Xuan'gao [玄高], devoted himself to dhyāna discipline and went to Binglingsi to practice meditation later. Binglingsi was, for this reason, an important place where meditating monks gathered and learned dhyāna discipline during the period of the Western Qin kingdom.

The cave-temple complex at Maijishan [麦积] in Tianshui, wherein many meditation monks such as Xuan'gao, Tanhong [昙弘] withdrew from society and lived in seclusion, accommodated more than one hundred hermit monks who practiced dhyāna. Xuan'gao, who was a great master of dhyāna-discipline in Northwest China at that time, used to have three hundred disciples who dwelt in the rock-cut dhyāna-cells at Mt. T'ang [堂山] in Linyang [林杨][57]. Xuan'gao was later invited as a teacher of Prince Huang [太子晃] of the Northern Wei Dynasty after 439 C.E.[58] Yu Xin [庾信], who was a famous scholar in the Southern and Northern Dynasties period, called Maijishan the "Vulture-island [鹫岛][59] where meditation monks dwelt as hermits"[60]. This indicates that Maijishan used to be another important place in which meditating monks gathered and practiced dhyāna-discipline.

The cave-temple complex at Yungang [云冈] in Datong is believed to have been constructed on the initiative of Monk Tanyao [昙曜], who seems to have been one of Xuan'gao's disciples and was also famous for his dhyāna-discipline in Northern China[61]. According to *Weishu: Shilaozhi* (*A History of the Wei Dynasty: Treatise on Buddhism and Taoism*), in the first part of the reign period of Heping [和平, 460-466 C.E.] of Emperor Wencheng [文成帝, 452-465 C.E.], śramaṇa Shixian [师贤][62] died; Monk Tanyao succeeded him and changed his title to Shamentong [沙门统, Chief of the Śramaṇas]. As a result, Buddhism

---

56 Huijiao *Taishō* 50: 397-398, esp. 397a.

57 Huijiao *Taishō* 50: 397a-b.

58 Tang, Yongtong 1982: 353-357.

59 The term Vulture-island should originate from the Indian Gṛdhra-kūta (Vulture-mountain) where, according to various sūtras and historical records, the Buddha, Mahākāśyapa, Ānanda and a lot of bhikṣus used to sit in meditation in the caves over there.

60 Yu, Xin 1966: 4149-4150, esp. 4149.

61 1) Huijiao *Taishō*, 50: 398b; 2) Daoxuan *Taishō* 50: 427c-428a.

62 Śramaṇa Shixian (Siṃhabhadra? ?-460C.E.), who was a relative of the King of Jibin and entered the Buddhist order at young age, came east to Liangzhou [凉州], a Buddhist center of then northern China. After Liangzhou was subdued by the Northern Wei Dynasty in 439 C.E., Siṃhabhadra went on to its capital (Pingcheng). While Buddhism was forbidden by Emperor Taiwu of the Northern Wei in 444 C.E., Siṃhabhadra, who disguised himself as a medical practitioner, reverted to the lay life but observed the doctrine without alteration. On the very day of the restoration of Buddhism by Emperor Wencheng of the Northern Wei Dynasty in 452 C.E., Siṃhabhadra became a śramaṇa again. The emperor personally performed hair-cutting ceremony for Siṃhabhadra and his associates, altogether five men, and Śramaṇa Siṃhabhadra was appointed Daorentong [道人统, Chief of the Clerics, in Control of the Religious], as before, by the emperor in the same year. Wei, Shou 1974: 3036; cf: 1) James R. Ware 1930: 145; 2) Leon Hurvitz 1956: 71.

became the official religion of the Northern Wei Dynasty in 452 C.E, having being restored after the persecution, and Tanyao was ordered to come from Zhongshan [中山] to the Capital Pingcheng. When he met the Emperor on the road, who had come to welcome him, one of the horses (of the Emperor's chariot) advanced and took Tanyao's robe in his teeth. This event was deemed to be auspicious as it was believed that even the horse recognized a good man. The Emperor afterwards respected him as a teacher. Monk Tanyao humbly begged the Emperor to chisel out the rocky wall of the mountain of Wuzhou pass [武州塞], west of the capital, open up five caves and carve out an image of the Buddha in each one. The tallest image was seventy feet high, the next tallest sixty feet high, with superb carvings and decorations , a crowning glory to the world[63].

The rock-cut caves at Wuzhou hills [武州山, an old name of Yungang] and those at the Deer-park Temple in Datong were opened up simultaneously or successively, and both of them are located in the suburbs of Pingcheng. The rock-cut caves at the Deer-park Temple were hewn out to create a space for meditating-monks[64] and those at Wuzhou hills too may have been set up for the hermit monks who practiced dhyāna[65].

When an Indian monk named *Fotuochanshi* [佛陀禅师, Buddha-dhyāyin?], who was a famous master of dhyāna as his name implies, arrived in the capital, Emperor Xiaowen requested the building of an appropriate grove and a rock-cut niche, which were suitable for this hermit monk and convenient for him to gather followers and to practice dhyāna-meditation[66]. Therefore, it is very clear that to hew out a cave in the rock is mostly to provide a place for monks to practice dhyāna-meditation[67].

The cave-temples carved out in the region around the capital Ye [邺城, present-day Linzhang][68] in the second half of the 6th century C.E., such as those at Xiaonanhai [小南海], Xiangquansi [香泉寺], Daliusheng [大留圣] and Xiangtangshan [响堂山], were also closely related to the monks who practiced dhyāna.[69]

After fall of the Western Jin Dynasty [西晋, 266-316 C.E.) in 316 C.E., a large number of Northern literati migrated to Southern China and brought the

---

[63] Wei, Shou 1974: 3037; cf: 1) James R. Ware 1930: 146-147; 2) Leon Hurvitz 1956: 72.

[64] Gao, Yun *Taishō* 52: 339, esp.339b.

[65] Tang, Yongtong 1982: 558.

[66] Daoxuan *Taishō* 50: 551, esp. 551a.

[67] Tang Yongtong 1982: 559.

[68] Capital Ye used to be successively capitals of the Wei [曹魏, 221-265 C.E.], Former Yan [前燕, 337-370 C.E.], Later Zhao [后赵, 319-350 C.E.], Eastern Wei [东魏, 534-550 C.E.] and Northern Qi [北齐, 550-557 C.E.] kingdoms or dynasties.

[69] Li, Yuqun 2003: 234.

Xuanxue school [玄學, metaphysics][70] to the south. It later flourished in Southern China, especially in the area around Jiankang [建康, present-day Nanjing]. The southern style of Buddhism began to take its inspiration from Xuanxue and had a strong philosophical aspect to it, which emphasized discourse and theory. In this way, Buddhism in Southern China came to be very different from that in Northern China which emphasized dhyāna practice[71]. Therefore, Buddhists in Northern China not only built free-standing temples, but also carved out caves in which monks meditated. In the south, however, Buddhists tended to emphasize temple ceremonies and to discourse on theory[72]. Should they meditate, it would be in a temple, not in a cave, that is, a devotee would sit in meditation in fatang [法堂, the chief temple or main hall] of a monastery, cleansing his heart and mind[73]. In other words, in Northern China dhyāna was following the Indian tradition of moving away from the secular world but in Southern China dhyāna was influenced by Xuanxue, where religious life was closely associated with meditation and philosophical discussion. The Buddhist monks in Southern China preferred a free-standing temple to a rock-cut cave.

A relation between a rock-cut cave and dhyāna or dhyāna-practice, however, can be also found in *Song Shu* [宋书, *A History of the Song Dynasty*] by Shen Yue [沈约]. In fascicle 97, it records that the meditation monks from Northern China all gathered in the free-standing Douchang Temple [斗场寺][74] after they moved to Jiankang. For this reason, the common saying that "Douchang Temple is a cave for the meditation monks"[75] was born in the capital, which indicates that the "rock-cut cave" had a close relation with dhyāna and even the people who lived in Southern China had such a judgment.

It is noteworthy that a number of hermit monks gathered to meditate at Mt. She [攝山, old name of Qixiashan 棲霞山] near Jiankang at the end of the 5th century C.E., and it is only at this time that we begin to find cave-temples in this region. These rock-cut caves are the Buddhist cave-temple complex at Mt. Qixia near Nanjing (fig. 3), which was designed by Fadu [法度], a hermit monk known for meditation, along with Ming Sengshao [明僧绍] and his son Ming

[70] Xuanxue was a mystical school in the realm of philosophy, which developed in the 3rd and 4th centuries C.E., characterized by metaphysical speculations seeking to adapt Daoist theories to a Confucian milieu. Bai, Shouyi 1982: 177-178.

[71] Tang, Yongtong 1982: 350-394.

[72] Shenqing *Taishō* 52: 573-636, esp. 596c.

[73] Huiyuan *Taishō* 52: 351, esp. 351c.

[74] Douchang Temple was named after Douchang Alleye [斗场里]. It was called Daochang Temple [道场寺] in the Biographies of Eminent Priests by Huijiao, who seems to think that meaning of "斗 (dou, fight)" was not suitable for a Buddhist temple, so he changed it to "道 (dao, way)" whose tone sounds like "斗 (dou)". Douchang Temple was a very important temple in southern China during the Southern Dynasties period, where eminent monks such as Buddhabhadra and Huiyuan used to stay there for a while. Sun, Wenchuan and Chen, Zuolin 2008: 139-285, esp. 188-190.

[75] Shen, Yue 1974: 2391-2392.

Zhongzhang [明仲璋], both of whom were devout secular Buddhists[76].

In addition, Monk Senghou [僧侯, 395-484 C.E.], a native of Xiliangzhou [西凉州, present-day Zhangye], who devoted himself to reciting *Fahua* (*Lotus Sūtra*) and *Weimo* (*Vimalakīrti-nirdeśa*) as well as *Jinguangming* [金光明, *Suvarṇaprabhāsottama-sūtra*], came to Jiankang around 454 C.E. Later, Senghou was invited by Xiao Huikai [萧惠开, 423-471 C.E.] to go to Sichuan for a while. When Senghou returned to the capital (Jiankang), he requested that a cave should be carved in the rock at Hougang [后冈] for the practice of dhyāna meditation[77].

With respect to study of the cave-temple, however, not only a comparison and analysis of its images should be made, but special attention should be paid to its contents. The contents of the cave-temple may be viewed from two aspects: on the one hand, it caters to the wishes of four kinds of the Buddhist followers (catasraḥ pārṣadaḥ) and, on the other, it appeals to the tastes of secular people. Concerning the monks' demands and secular tastes, there are some matters of common concern, but there are also some differences in their interests and views. The common interests of monks and secular people include making offerings and worshipping images as well as some of the worldly requirements, but the different interests lie in the monks' demand for religious practice or activity. The only activity of the monk who lived from the 4th to the early 7th century C.E. in Northern China, as it has been demonstrated, was to practice dhyāna.

On the basis of form and structure, many extant caves in China can be classified according to the nature or functions for which they were originally designed. Therefore, any cave which was made expressly for meditation is called a meditation-cave. Some meditation-caves are single cells, while the others form part of a group (fig. 4). There were also some caves designed as living quarters or habitation so that monks may actually live there, and these of course were larger than a normal meditation-cave. The latter is called sengfangku [僧房窟, habitable cave or dwelling cave], which is similar to the Indian lēṇa[78].

It is known from sūtras that monks need to contemplate on the Buddha during meditation. Therefore, prior to engaging in dhyāna-meditation they must first carry out ceremonies of worship before an image of the Buddha[79]. For

---

[76] Jiang, Zong [江总, 519-594 C.E.], Jinling sheshan qixiasi bei [金陵摄山棲霞寺碑, A Tablet on the Qixia Temple at Mt.She, Jinling]; cf: Su, Bai 1996: 176-199, esp. 177-178.

[77] Huijiao *Taishō* 50: 408, esp. 408c.

[78] In this article, I sometimes use lēṇa as a convention for the characteristic cave structures of China which was used for dwelling. The term is known from Prākrit or Prākrīta inscriptions from the Buddhist caves of the Western Ghats, and has been popularized since the time of colonial Indology. See H. Lüders 1912: Nos. 998-1002, 1005-1007, etc.

[79] 1) Kumārajīva *Taishō* 15: 297-300, esp. 298a, 299a; 2) Kumārajīva *Taishō* 15: 242-269, esp. 258b.

this reason we find a Buddhist rock-cut temple in the vicinity of the meditation-caves. In the early period of cave-temples we generally find a stūpa in the centre of a cave (fig. 5), a feature in keeping with the fact that Buddhist sūtras often mention "going into a stūpa to view the image of the Buddha"[80]. This kind of cave is to be distinguished from the previously mentioned meditation-caves and habitable caves, and is known as tamiaoku [塔庙窟, stūpa-cave] or zhongxinzhuku [中心柱窟, central pillar cave], which is analogous to the Indian chaityaghara both in form and nature[81]. Later there appeared some caves especially designed for displaying Buddhist images and for contemplation of Buddha. This kind of cave is called zunxiangku [尊像窟, Buddha-image cave or Buddhist icon cave] or fodianku [佛殿窟, Buddha-hall cave]. Sometimes a master monk would attract a number of disciples around one of these cave-temples. Naturally, the master monk had to lecture or held discussions on the sūtras, and for this purpose jiangtangku [讲堂窟, lecture-hall or preaching hall cave] was constructed in some sites of the rock-cut cave-temples. Sometimes the lecture-hall cave has an image in it, in which case the cave could serve both as a Buddha-hall and as a lecture-hall.

In some places, where numerous caves were set up, we can truly speak of a Buddhist cave-temple complex. Not all the caves we discuss necessarily merit the label of cave-temple complex, but for the sake of convenience we shall refer to all of them as cave-temples[82]. It is not the number that should matter but whether the basic requirement of a monastery was respected.

The remains of the cave-temples in Xinjiang are all to be found in the northern belt of the Tarim basin. Both Hīnayāna and Mahāyāna Buddhism were transmitted into Xinjiang through the Silk Road. Along the northern route, however, east of Kashgar, Hīnayāna Buddhism was more popular, which emphasizes meditation even more than Mahāyāna, so to this extent, one can understand why many cave-temples were carved out. The earliest caves in Xinjiang are mostly single meditation caves and habitable caves with a long foyer. Before long we begin to find rectangular stūpa-caves with a Kucha-style stūpa inside, and later we also find lecture-hall caves. Before the construction of lecture-hall caves became the fashion, there was also a period in which a complex consisting of several kinds of caves such as meditation-caves and stūpa-caves seem to have flourished. This kind of cave group gets

---

[80] Buddhabhadra *Taishō* 15: 645-697, esp. 655b, 688c-689a.

[81] In this article, I sometimes use chetiyaghara as a convention for the characteristic cave structures of China with a central cetiya/stūpa surrounded by an open circumambulatory passageway. The term is known from Prākrit inscriptions from the Buddhist caves of the Western Ghats, and has been popularized since the time of colonial Indology. See H. Lüders 1912: No. 1050, 1058, 1140, 1141, 1153, 1178, 1179, 1183, etc.

[82] Su, Bai 2010: 7.

more complicated over time. In the later period it developed to such a degree that the rock-cut caves were combined with surface constructions outside the caves. Therefore, it became a Buddhist temple with the cave itself serving as the main hall[83].

In addition, *Shier yinyuan jing* [十二因缘经, *Twelve Nidānas*] inscribed on votive stone stūpa found at Jiuquan and Turfan, the term dhyāna-cave [定窟] in the tablet commemorating a monastery set up by Juqu Anzhou [沮渠安周, 444-460 C.E.] of the Northern Liang kingdom unearthed in Turfan, and representations of monks practicing dhyāna meditation and contemplation in cave 42 at Toyuk all seem have a close relation with the dhyāna sūtras produced by Kumārajīva[84].

As one of the four prefectures in the Hexi Corridor [河西走廊][85], Liangzhou [凉州, present-day Wuwei] was both a political and Buddhist centre of the corridor, especially during the period of the Northern Liang kingdom. According to *Weishu: Shilaozhi* (*A History of the Wei Dynasty: Treatise on Buddhism and Taoism*), Liangzhou had believed in Buddhism from the time of Zhang Gui [张轨, 313 C.E., founder of 前凉/Former Liang kingdom] onward for generations. When Juqu Mengxun [沮渠蒙逊] ruled over Liangzhou, he also had a liking for Buddhism. At that time there was a śramaṇa by the name of Tanmochen [昙摩谶, Dharmarakṣa, 385-433 C.E.] who came to Liangzhou from Central India in 412 C.E. Dharmarakṣa, who was familiar with the sūtras and śāstras and translated at least ten sūtras including *Daboniepan jing* [大般涅槃经, *Mahāparinivāṇa sūtra*], was skilled in fortune-telling and magic, predicting in detail the events which took place in other kingdoms or states and which came to be true. Juqu Mengxun often consulted him on affairs of the kingdom[86]. It is said Juqu Mengxun sponsored the making of a sixteen-feet stone Buddha image for his mother[87] and he also had a cave-temple carved out in a mountain about one hundred *li* to the south of Liangzhou around 397 C.E, that is, the cave-temple complex at Tiantishan [天梯山][88]. While the dhyāna-master Dharmamitra [昙摩蜜多, 356-442 C.E.] stayed in Liangzhou before 424 C.E., his disciples and followers were numerous and the practice of dhyāna meditation was very earnestly pursued[89]. It is noteworthy that the Buddhism of Liangzhou was famous not only for translation of the scriptures, but also for dhyāna-discipline. For instance, Juqu Jingsheng [沮渠京声], a young cousin

[83] Su, Bai 2010: 11.

[84] Jia, Yingyi 1999: 146-158.

[85] Hexi or Gansu Corridor is located in northwestern Gansu, it is so called because it lies to the west of the Yellow River.

[86] Wei, Shou 1974: 3032; cf: 1) James R. Ware 1930: 133-134; 2) Leon Hurvitz 1956: 57-61.

[87] Huijiao *Taishō* 50: 335-337, esp. 336b.

[88] Daoxuan *Taishō* 52: 404-435, esp. 417c-418a.

[89] Sengyou *Taishō* 55: 105, esp. 105a.

on the paternal side of the Nothern Liang ruler, was a monk who practiced dhyāna-meditation in Liangzhou[90]. Monks Xuan'gao, Xuanshao and Tanyao, who all practiced dhyāna-meditation and supported the activity of opening up rock-cut temples, did have a close relation with the dhyāna-discipline of Liangzhou. Therefore, any place with a rock-cut temple was created for hermit monks to practice dhyāna-meditation; any devotee who practiced dhyāna-meditation must have had ties with Liangzhou, because dhyāna-meditation needed instruction from others and could not be studied independently. A monk or a lay devotee, without the guidance or supervision of a dhyāna-master, was unable to learn art of concentration, he/she would perform heterodox and false contemplation and would not be able to achieve proper dhyāna-meditation[91].

In 439 C.E., the Northern Wei Dynasty conquered the Northern Liang kingdom and occupied Liangzhou. Immediately they deported Juqu Maoqian [沮渠茂虔, or Juqu Mujian/沮渠牧犍, ruler of then Northern Liang, 433-439 C.E.] and his clans as well as all the elites and many commoners from Liangzhou to Pingcheng, about 100,000 families in all[92]. According to *Weishu: Shilaozhi* (*A History of the Wei Dynasty: Treatise on Buddhism and Taoism*),"Liangzhou was conquered and the people of the kingdom moved to the capital". The śramaṇas and Buddhist paraphernalia as well as practices all came to East, and Xiangjiao [象教 image-religion, viz. Buddhism][93] prospered more and more and increased far and wide"[94]. The focus of temple building activity had definitely shifted to the vicinity of the political center of gravity, i.e., Pingcheng. Not long after the Buddhist craftsmen were moved to Pingcheng, a number of eminent monks followed, some of them coming from Liangzhou during the emigration[95]. If we look at the individual Buddhist images remaining from before and after the restoration of Buddhism during the Northern Wei Dynasty in 452 C.E., we can

---

[90] Huijiao *Taishō* 50: 337a.

[91] Tang, Yongtong 1982: 278-283.

[92] Cui, Hong 1960: 603.

[93] As for term xiangjiao [象教or 像教], some scholars believe it is the equivalent of the Sanskrit pratirūpakadharma or saddharma-pratirūpaka [像法], the second period in the teaching of the Good Law. According to an explanatory note of Toutuosi beiwen [头陀寺碑文, Inscription on the Tablet of Dhūta Temple] in Wen Xuan [文选, Anthology Through the Ages], however, we are told by Li Zhouhan [李周翰] that "xiangjiao means to use the image to teach people". Here, the Chinese character xiangjiao was composed of two characters, "xiang[像]" and "jiao[教]", the former signifies image and the latter religion, compounded together as image-religion, which indicates or implies Buddhism, because Buddhist followers all worship the image of Buddha. From the late Northern Wei Dynasty onwards, Buddhism was often called image-religion by Chinese, the Buddha image became the most important means for the dissemination of Buddhism, and the idea that "to erect the image is to establish the religion" was deep-rooted in medieval China. Li, Shan et al 1987: 1089.

[94] Wei, Shou 1974: 3032; cf: 1) James R. Ware 1930: 135; 2) Leon Hurvitz 1956: 61.

[95] For instance, Xuangao went to Pingcheng during this time and became a teacher of Prince Huang. He used to stay in a dhyāna-cave and carried forward dhyāna-practice in the capital. Huijiao *Taishō* 50: 397c-398a.

see that in subject matter, style and clothing, the images of Buddha all reflect the earlier traditions popular under the Northern Liang. These factors, taken together with records of forced immigrations to the Northern Wei capital, lead us to conclude that the early Buddha images of the Northern Wei Dynasty are closely related to those of the Northern Liang[96]. In short, Buddhism of the Northern Wei Dynasty definitely followed that of the Northern Liang[97]. In addition, from 409 to 469 C.E., for a period of about 60 years, the Northern Wei Dynasty made it a policy to gather the combined expertise of the major talents in all trades and professions in Northern China in the area around the capital. With the accumulation of talent and the restoration of Buddhism, the Northern Wei Dynasty, under the direction and guidance of Monk Tanyao who came from Liangzhou[98], had the means to construct the mammoth-scale cave-temples at Wuzhou hills, west of the capital[99].

Because of such patronage by the Northern Wei imperial house and other ruling groups, Buddhist cave-temples were carved out in various sites in Northern China beginning with the latter half of the 5th century C.E. and continued to be patronized by the ruling families of the Sui (581-618 C.E.) and T'ang (618-907 C.E.) dynasties all the way to the mid 8th century in China[100].

Within this development, we only find three types of rock-cut caves in the cave-temple complex set up from the latter half of the 5th century to the early 6th century, namely meditation-caves, stūpa-caves and Buddha-hall-caves. As for the rock-cut caves hewn out in the early 6th century, the number of meditation-caves and stūpa-caves are relatively small, while Buddha-hall-caves became predominant at this stage. The types of rock-cut caves opened up during the mid-late 6th century remain virtually the same, but at this time a stūpa was often carved out on the open face of the cliff above the entrance of the caves as in Xiangtangshan. If a devotee enters this kind of cave to worship the Buddha image, the point of this may well be to represent the idea expressed in sūtras that a devotee "enters a stūpa to view the Buddha image"[101]. This is a necessary requirement for monks carrying out meditation. From this, we may infer that up to this period the caves carved out in Northern China still included the provision of a space for monks carrying out dhyāna[102].

In addition, some reliefs or murals depicting monks in dhyāna-meditation can also be found in cave-temple complexes such as those in Yungang Caves. 7, 8, 12 and Mogaoku Cave 285 (fig. 6), which provide us the visual evidence

96 Tang, Yongtong 1982: 359.
97 Tang, Yongtong 1982: 557.
98 Tang, Yongtong, *ibidem.*
99 Su, Bai 1996: 114-144.
100 Su, Bai 2010: 16-18.
101 Buddhabhadra *Taishō* 15: 645-697, esp. 656b, 665b, 681c, 688c-689b, 694c.
102 Su, Bai 1996: 16-20.

that "to carve a celestial cave in the rock is to supply a place for a monk sitting in meditation".[103] The cave-temple complexes constructed from the 4th to the 6th century C.E. in Northern China, with respect to function and nature, were mostly to provide a place for monks practicing dhyāna meditation and contemplation.

The method of meditation was earlier found in the practice of "remembrance (念, anusmçti)" of Buddha Amitàbha as described in *Bozhou sanmei jing* [般舟三昧经, *Pratyutpanna-buddha-sammukhāvasthita samādhi-sūtra, Sūtra of Meditation to behold the Buddhas,*] by Lokakṣema [支娄迦谶, 147 C.E.-?] in 179 C.E.[104] The subject of this important sūtra is a form of mental concentration which enables a devotee to behold all Buddhas as if they were standing before his eyes[105]. The object of the meditation is to cause the spirit to liberate itself from the cycle of birth and death, pain and trouble, and to achieve a state of nirvāṇa. The method of this meditation is to concentrate mentally on one particular object, thought, etc., thereby creating conditions favourable to acquiring the power of vision. In practice, a devotee could concentrate on anything at all, but the most important object of early Chinese Buddhism was to concentrate with his/her whole heart on the image of Buddha[106]. This is to say, a devotee was thought to be able to achieve a mental state in which he/she could not distinguish between himself/herself and Buddha by concentrating his/her thoughts entirely upon the image of Buddha. The practitioner can eventually become a Buddha himself/herself. A devotee must faithfully observe all rules of religious life; then he/she must go to a secluded spot and there concentrate his/her mind upon the Buddha, for one day and one night, or for a whole week, continuously, until he/she is able to achieve his/her objective. Having achieved this concentration, Buddha will manifest himself before the devotee's eyes and preach the doctrine to the latter, like an image in a dream or a shape reflected in a mirror[107]. According to *Yu yinshi liu yimin deng shu* [与隐士刘遗民等书, A Letter to Hermit Liu Yimin and others] by Huiyuan, when Liu Yimin had spent just half a year concentrating his thought and sitting in meditation, he saw in samàdhi the Buddha. Whenever he met a Buddhist image on the way, the Buddha would manifest himself in the air, his halo illuminating heaven and earth all bathed in a golden color, and again he would see himself wearing a kāṣāya and bathing in the jewel pond of Sukhāvatī. When he had come out of samādhi, he asked the monks to recite the sūtra[108].

---

103 Gao, Yun *Taishō* : 52: 339, esp.339b.

104 *Taishº* 13: 902-919.

105 E. Zürcher 1972: 220.

106 Kumārajīva *Taishō* 15: 269-286, esp.276a.

107 E. Zürcher 1972: 221.

108 Huiyuan *Taishō*: 52: 304, esp.304b.

The content of a monk's meditation inside a cave, however, is mainly to practice remembrance of the Buddha. According to *Siwei lueyaofa* (*An Outline of Meditation* or *Outlining the Way to Reflect*), "Buddha is the king of the law. He can let one obtain all kinds of good qualities. That is why someone who practices meditation should first be mindful of Buddha"[109]; to be precise, a devotee who desires to attain enlightenment should practice the remembrance of Buddhas in ten directions (daśa diśaḥ) and the Buddhas of the past, present and future (trayo-dhvanaḥ) before entering dhyāna[110]. According to *Chanmi yaofa jing* ((*Secret Essentials of the Dhyāna-discipline* or *Sūtra about the Secret Essence of Dhyāna*), Buddha told Nandhi [难提 or 禅难提] and Ānanda to teach, in the future, to all human beings who had committed many sins in , to practice the remembrance of Buddha in order to put an end to their faults, vexations or retributions in this life for the sins of previous existence. A devotee who intends to practice the remembrance should first of all sit up straight, with his hands crossed, eyes closed and tongue touching the palate. Once he is calmed down by this posture, the devotee should be totally absorbed in remembrance, his attention completely concentrated. Before carrying on the remembrance, the devotee should sit in front of an image and practice the contemplation of Buddha. After Buddha's parinirvāṇa, bhikṣu [比丘], bhikṣuṇī [比丘尼], upāsaka [优婆塞] and upāsikā [优婆夷] should be yearning to contemplate on Buddha, seek peace and quietness, and if they repent their faulty behaviour, to confess their sins[111]. In the light of the same text, Buddha told Ānanda that if a bhikṣu desires licentious passion he should be taught to contemplate on the Buddha; this contemplation will help him to move away from faults and sins. Then, he might be taught to practice the remembrance of Buddha with his whole heart or mind[112]. According to *Siwei lueyaofa* (*An Outline of the Meditation* or *Outlining the Way to Reflect*),"mindfulness of Buddha makes one's serious wrongs of immeasurable eons trifling, and one may reach concentration". If one is earnestly mindful of the Buddha, Buddha is mindful of you too. Just as enemies and creditors do not dare to approach him who is held dear by the King, any remaining evil factor will not come to disturb the person who is mindful of the Buddha. If one is mindful of the Buddha, Buddha is always present. How must one be mindful? One's confidence must not go beyond ones' eyes. One should visualize a fine image to be like the real Buddha. One should descend to the feet from the cranial knot and from the white tuft of hair between the eyebrows, and from the feet one should again reach the cranial knot. When the characteristics are thus carefully grasped, one should turn to a tranquil place. Reflecting with eyes closed, one should be concentrated on the image, so that

109 Kumārajīva *Taishō* 15: 297-300, esp. 299a; cf: Charles Willemen 2012: 31.

110 Kumārajīva *Taishō* 15: 269-286, esp.281a.

111 Kumārajīva *Taishō* 15: 242-269, esp. 255a-256a.

112 Kumārajīva *Taishō* 15: 242-269, esp. 258b.

one does not think of anything else. If one thinks of another object, one should control one's thoughts and make them return. If one observes with one's mental eye, seeing as one wishes, this is the concentration attaining visualization of the image. One should perform this mindfulness: "I will not go to it, and the image will not come either, but what I have seen will dwell in my thoughts because of my mental concentration'".[113] The process of contemplation entails observing the sitting Buddha first, then the standing Buddha and finally the Buddha in parinirvāṇa[114]. The contemplation of Buddha's physical features and characteristics (相好, lakṣaṇa and vyañjana) as well as that of the seated Buddha, standing Buddha and the Buddha in parinirvāṇa are called Guanfo sanmei [观佛三昧, Buddha-dhyāna-samādhi, contemplation of Buddha][115]. After the contemplation of the image, the devotee should continue to examine shengshen [生身, the body of birth], such as his previous life and present life, and fashen [法身, the body of qualities or dharma-kāya], such as the maṇi [摩尼] pearl[116]. Then, the devotee has to contemplate on the Seven Buddhas[117], who would be witnessed to the devotee's practice of dhyāna-meditation[118].

By this time, the devotee, having seen all the Buddhas to whom he had contemplated, is aware that one Buddha is the equivalent of all the Buddhas and all the Buddhas are of one Buddha[119]. If the devotee returns to the cave and fails to meditate on the Buddha whom he had contemplated on, or what he meditated on, or differs from what he contemplated on, then the devotee has to enter a stūpa to contemplate on the Buddha again[120]. If he succeeds, it means that the devotee has escaped from the bonds of various cravings or secular life and obtained the freedom from transmigration, from *karma*, from illusion and from sufferings. At this point the devotee needs to worship Maitreya, the future Buddha, because he will meet Maitreya during dhyāna meditation and contemplation[121]. The contemplation of Maitreya is based on the versions written by Kumārajīva, such as *Mile xiasheng jing* (*Maitreyavyākaraṇa, Advent of Maitreya Sūtra*)[122], *Foshuo mile chengfo jing* (*Sūtra of Maitreya becoming a*

113 Charles Willemen 2012: 31; cf: Kumārajīva*Taishº* 15: 297-300, esp. 299a.

114 Kumārajīva *Taishō* 15: 242-269, esp. 255a-256a.

115 Kumārajīva *Taishō* 15: 242-269, esp.255a-256c.

116 1) Kumārajīva *Taishō* 15: 242-269, esp. 265b; 2) Kumārajīva *Taishō* 15: 297-300, esp. 299a-c.

117 The term "Seven Buddhas" means seven Buddhas of the past, that is, Śākyamuni [释迦牟尼佛] and six Buddhas said to have preceded him. The six Buddhas are Vipaśyin [毗婆尸佛], Śikhin [尸棄佛], Viśvabhū [毗舍佛], Krakucchanda [拘留孙佛], Kanakamuni [迦那含牟尼佛] and Kāśyapa [迦叶佛]. Among them, the first three Buddhas appeared in the past Glorious Kalpa, while the other four Buddhas including Śākyamuni appeared in the present Wise Kalpa; cf: Kumārajīva *Taishō* 15: 242-269, esp. 254a.

118 1) Kumārajīva *Taishō* 15: 242-269, esp. 254a; 2) Buddhabhadra *Taishō* 15: 645-697, esp. 693a.

119 Kumarajıva *Taishō* 15: 269-286, esp.277a.

120 Buddhabhadra *Taishō* 15: 645-697, esp. 665b, 681c.

121 Kumārajīva *Taishō* 15: 242-269, esp. 268a.

122 *Taishō* 14: 423-425.

Buddha)[123] and *Chanmi yaofa jing* (*Secret Essentials of the Dhyāna-discipline* or *Sūtra about the Secret Essence of Dhyāna)*[124]. In terms of the content of contemplation, furthermore, *Fahua sanmei guan* [法华三昧观, *Saddharma-puṇḍarīka-samādhi, Samādhi of the Lotus of the Law,*][125] is one of the most important contemplations[126] as it enables a devotee to worship Śākyamuni and Prabhūtaratna [释迦、多宝] together. They are recorded in detail in *Fahua jing* (*Saddharma-puṇḍarīka-sūtra, Lotus Sūtra)*[127] which was translated into Chinese by Kumārajīva in 406 C.E. Kumārajīva's version was regarded as the best among the Chinese translations and was widely read and quoted[128] and it exerted a great influence on Buddhism in medieval China[129].

In short, if we consider the content and meaning of the above described contemplation and meditation activity, it really identifies with or corresponds to that of the cave-temples carved in China from the 4th to the 6th century C.E. A small cave was hewn out of living rock for the meditation, a big Buddha-hall-cave was designed for contemplation, and a stūpa-cave was especially carved for a devotee who had to enter the cave again to practice contemplation and meditation, besides circumambulation of the stūpa.

This phenomenon is reflected most clearly among the cave-temple complex at Yungang and becomes even more pronounced over time[130]. The huge Buddha images carved out in the cave-temples of the first period at Yungang present the notable marks or features and physical characteristics of the Buddha before our eyes, which are recorded in detail in the dhyāna sūtras translated by Kumārajīva. For instance, most of the thirty-two features [三十二相, *dvātriṃśan mahā-puruṣa-lakṣaṇāni*] and some of the eighty characteristics [八十种好, *aśīty-anuvyañjanāni*] of Buddha, which are recorded in detail in *Chanmi yaofa jing (Secret Essentials of the Dhyāna-discipline or Sūtra about the Secret Essence of Dhyāna)*[131] and regarded as necessary for image contemplation [观像法], are the most important part of the monks' dhyāna-contemplation[132]. The features and characteristics of Buddha recorded in the text are as follows: the *uṣṇīṣa*, a knot of flesh on the head like a topknot or cranial knot; hair on the head is dark purple, one hair grows from each pore and total number of the hairs is 84000, each graceful hair became a dextro-curl, stretching for 13 *chi* (about 318 cm)

123 *Taishō* 14: 428-434.

124 Kumārajīva *Taishō* 15: 242-269, esp. 254c, 268a

125 Kumārajīva *Taishō* 15: 297-300, esp. 300b-c; cf: Charles Willemen 2012: 45-47.

126 Liu, Huida 1996: 339.

127 *Taishō* 9: 1-62, esp. 32b-34b.

128 Among various translated versions of the Lotus Sūtra, as Daoxuan pointed out, only the version produced by Kumārajīvawas taken as the model and widely quoted by Buddhist followers. Daoxuan *Taishō* 9: 1, esp. 1b.

129 Su, Bai 1996: 39-51, esp. 50; 76-88, esp. 83.

130 1) Su, Bai 1996: 76-88; 2) Su, Bai 2010: 34-35.

131 Kumārajīva *Taishō* 15: 269-286, esp. 276a-c.

132 Kumārajīva*Taishō* 15: 242-269, esp. 256a.

when it was uncurled; the round face like a full moon, having an impressive bearing and a commanding presence; the *ūrṇā*, a white tuft of hair between the eyebrows, curling to the right, like a white glass pearl; the nose like the beak of an eagle-king; the mouth and lips are red-coloured, in them it appears the shape of the *bimba;* the even teeth number forty, close, white and regular; the neck like a glazed tube, showing a golden color; the śrīvatsalakṣaṇa (卐) on the chest is very clear and obvious among other marks; arms look like the trunk or proboscis of an elephant-king, extremely flexible, soft and lovely; the pliant hands grow hair, with fingers uneven and golden coloured; the finger was connected by pearl-net shaped membrane, just like the feet of a goose king; body seated steady like a golden hill, properly dignified and straight; the calf of the lower leg looks like the calf of a antelope or deer king, straight and round; the level feet stood or seated on the lotus, with a thousand-spoke-wheel-sign on the soles and toes; base of the toes was connected by a pearl-net shaped membrane, like the feet of a wild goose, and so forth. In addition, Buddha has an aureole and nimbus around his body, Nirmāṇa-Buddhas [化佛], bhikṣus and Bodhisattvas can be seen in the light radiating from the body. If a devotee contemplates the Buddha from *uṣṇīśa* (cranial knot) to feet, it is called favorable contemplation, if done in reverse order it is called inverse contemplation[133].

Such notable features and physical characteristics of the Buddhas were fully represented in the early cave-temples at Yungang (fig. 7)[134]. If a devotee carries on the contemplation in such a way or sits in meditation, his/her heart will be perfectly clear[135]. Consequently, a devotee can eventually come to think that there is no distinction between Buddha and himself/herself. In short, a kind of hallucination or mirage in which one beholds the Buddha will appear in the end[136]. For Buddhist adepts or monks, an act of worshipping Buddha is the same as concentrating their mind on the image of Buddha. During meditation, if a devotee fails to see the real Buddha, then he/she must enter the caves again and again to view the image of Buddha and to meditate. However, if, after a long time a devotee still fails to see Buddha, then the devotee may begin to have doubts. When this happens he/she must seek the aid of Maitreya, who stays in our world to help him/her in his/her crisis of the faith[137]. But how can a devotee approach Maitreya? Simply by worshipping

133 Kumārajīva *Taishō* 15: 242-269, esp. 255b-c.

134 Liu, Huida 1996: 335-36.

135 Kumārajīva *Taishō* 15: 242-269, esp. 255b-c.

136 A monk named Shijiong [释冏] used to have such a dreamland when he practiced dhyāna-meditation. Daoshi *Taishō* 53: 785a.

137 Kinkara and Tanyao *Taishō* 50: 297-322, esp.320a.

before the image of Maitreya, the image of Maitreya will appear (fig. 8)[138]. The most important Buddhist images of the first period at Yungang, moreover, are the Buddhas of the three existences [三佛][139], which were not only especially emphasized by Monk Tanyao[140], but also recorded in dhyāna-sūtras translated by Kumārajīva[141]. These of course include Śākyamuni and Maitreya[142].

The subject matter of the second period at Yungang is more complex. Apart from Śākyamuni, scenes from the life of the Buddha, jātaka stories and stūpas which naturally represent Śākyamuni, we also find Śākyamuni and Prabhūtaratna in pairs (fig. 9), Thousand Buddhas [千佛, Budhasahasra] in large scale, the seven Buddhas as well as Samantabhadra [普贤] riding on an elephant, etc.[143]. In addition, the importance of Maitreya becomes more and more obvious. The variety of images to be found in these later cave-temples has expanded to include the rather extraordinary phenomenon of two Maitreyas together. This evidence points out that monks carrying on meditation at that time were seeking ever more images and ways of imagining the Buddha image, in order to free themselves from the cycle of rebirth. This may also reflect the boredom and vexation of monks resulting from constant meditation[144]. Since dhyāna-sūtras deal especially with the methods employed in meditation and the ways of contemplating the Buddha image, as a result only the objects that monks should contemplate on are pointed out. Details of specific stories such as the life of the Buddha and jātaka stories were not mentioned.

The cave-temples of the third period were carved out after the move of the capital from Pingcheng to Luoyang in 494 C.E. The cave-temples at Yungang in this period clarify several important points worth noting in this context. For instance, middle and small sized caves became especially numerous. There are quite a number of caves that are so small as to "allow room for only one

138 *Foshuo mile xiasheng chengfo jing (Sūtra of Maitreya becoming a Buddha)* was produced by Kumārajīva in 402 C.E., who was requested to translate and to meet the need of the Buddhist followers in the Later Qin kingdom. Su, Bai 1996: 176-199, esp. 190-191.

139 The Buddhas of the three existences [三佛, or the Buddhas of the three epochs], which mean the Buddha in past existence, the Buddha in present existence and the Buddha in future existence, are used to indicate all of time, from the eternal past, through the present, to the eternal future. In the Buddhist sūtras, expressions such as "the Buddhas of the three existences [三世佛]" and "the Buddhas of the three existences and ten directions [十方三世诸佛]" indicate all Buddhas throughout eternity and boundless space. The subject of "the Buddhas of the three existences" was in full vogue after the restoration of Buddhism in 452 C.E. in the northern China, because Monk Tanyao, by translating Fu fazang yinyuan zhuan (A History of the Buddha's Successors), demonstrated that Buddhism has an extremely long, long history.

140 Tang, Yongtong 1982: 357-360.

141 1) Kumārajīva *Taishō* 15: 242-269, esp.267c; 2) Kumārajīva*Taishō* 15: 269-286, esp.281a.

142 Liu, Huida 1996: 340-341.

143 Liu, Huida 1996: 339-342.

144 Su, Bai 2010: 34-35.

seated person"[145]. From this we can deduce that a great many of the caves that were opened up during this period were intended as cells for the meditation of individual monks. This kind of cave is exemplified by cave 38. Since the sidewall of this cave are covered with images of monks meditating and since this cave also displays the story of Śākyamuni comforting Ānanda (Fig. 10)[146], such images speak eloquently of the nature and function of such a cave.[147]

BIBLIOGRAPHY

Bai, Shouyi 白寿彝. ed. 1982. *An Outline History of China*. Beijing: Foreign Languages Press.

Beal, Samuel. 1980. *Si-Yu-Ki—Buddhist Records of the Western World; Chinese Accounts of India,* translated from the Chinese of Hiuen Tsiang. London: Trubner, 1884. rep. Delhi: Bharatiya Publishing House.

Buddhabhadra 佛驮跋陀罗 (359-429 C.E.). *Damoduoluo Chanjing* 达摩多罗禅经 (*Dharmatara dhyāna-sūtra* or *Yogācārabhūmi*) / *Lushan chanjing* 庐山禅经 (*Dhyāna-sūtra translated at Mt. Lu*). *Taishō* 15: 300-325.

Buddhabhadra. *Foshuo guanfo sanmeihai jing* 佛说观佛三昧海经 (*Buddha-dhyāna-samādhisāgara-sūtra, The Sūtra on the Sea of Mystic Ecstasy Attained by Visualizing the Buddha* or *Ocean of Meditation on the Buddha Sūtra*). *Taishō* 15: 645-697.

Ch'en, Kenneth. 1973. *Buddhism in China: A Historical Survey*. Princeton: Princeton University Press.

Cui, Hong 崔鸿 (478-525 C.E.). 1960. *Shiliuguo chunqiu: Beiliang lu* 十六国春秋：北凉录 (*Annals of the Sixteen Kingdoms: the Northern Liang*). *Taiping yulan* 太平御览 (*Taiping Reign-Period Imperial Encyclopedia*) compiled by Li, Fang 李昉 et al in 984 C.E. facsimile edition. Beijing: Zhonghua Book Company.

Daoshi 道世 (596-683C.E.). *Fayuan zhulin* 法苑珠林 (*The Forest of Gems in the Garden of the Law*) in 668 C.E. *Taishō* 53: 269-1030.

Daoxuan 道宣 (596-667 C.E.). "*Miaofa lianhuajing hongchuan xu* 妙法莲花经弘传序 (Preface to *Dissemination of the Saddharma-puṇḍarīka-sūtra or Lotus Sūtra of the Wonderful Law*)." *Taishō* 9: 1.

Daoxuan. *Lṃxiang gantong zhuan* 律相感通传 (*Responses to Dreamlike Dialogues with Devas*) in 667 C.E. *Taishō* 45: 874-882.

Daoxuan. *Xu gaoseng zhuan* 续高僧传 (*Continued Biographies of Eminent Priests* or *The Tang Dynasty Biographies of Eminent Priests* or *A Continuation of the Memoirs of Eminent Monks*) in 665 C.E. *Taishō* 50: 425-707.

Daoxuan. *Ji shenzhou sanbao gantong lu* 集神州三宝感通录 (*Collection of the Strange and Extraordinary Deeds of the Buddhist Triratna in China*). *Taishō* 52: 404-435.

Daoxuan. *Datang neidian lu* 大唐内典录 (*The Great Tang Dynasty Catalogue of Buddhist Scriptures* or *A Catalogue of the Buddhist Canon compiled under the Tang Dynasty*) in 664 C.E. *Taishō* 55: 219-341.

145 Daoxuan *Taishō* 50: 557, esp. 557c.

146 1) Faxian 1985: 113; 2) H. A. Giles 1972: 50; 3) Xuan Zang 1985: 727-728; 4) Samuel Beal 1980: 373.

147 1) Su, Bai 1996: 76-88; 2) Su, Bai 2010: 34-35.

Falk, Harry. 2006. *Aśokan Sites and Artefacts: a source-book with bibliography*. Mainz am Rhein: Verlag Philipp von Zabern.

Faxian 法显 (?-423 C.E.). 1985. *Faxian zhuan* 法显传 (*The Travels of Faxian*). collated and annotated by Zhang, Xun 章巽. Shanghai: Shanghai Classics Publishing House.

Fang, Xuanling 房玄龄 (579-648 C.E.) et al. 1974. *Jinshu* 晋书 (*A History of the Jin Dynasties*) in 646 C.E. punctuated edition. Beijing: Zhonghua Book Company.

Fei, Zhangfang 费长房. *Lidai sanbo ji* 历代三宝记 (*Record of the Triratna through the Ages* or *Record concerning the Triratna under Successive Dynasties*) in 597 C.E. *Taishō* 49: 22-127.

Gao, Yun 高允 (390-487 C.E.). "*Luyuan fu* 鹿苑赋 (*Rhapsody on the Deer-park*)" in: *Guang hongmingji* 广弘明集 (*Further Anthology of the Propagation of Light*) in 664 C.E. by Daoxuan. *Taishō* : 52: 339.

Giles, H. A. 1972. *The Travels of Fa-hsien (399-414 C.E.) or Record of the Buddhistic Kingdoms*. Cambridge: Cambridge University Press, 1923. rep. Varanasi: Indological Book House.

Hu Shih 胡适. 1997. "*Chanxue gushi kao* 禅学古史考 (On the History of the Dhyāna-discipline)." *Hushi xueshu wenji: Zhongguo foxueshi* 胡适学术文集：中国佛学史 (*Collected Works of Hu Shih: A History of Chinese Buddhism*). Beijing: Zhonghua Book Company. 38-54.

Huijiao 慧皎 (ca.495-554 C.E.). *Gaoseng zhuan* 高僧传 (*Biographies of Eminent Priests* or *The Liang Dynasty Biographies of Eminent Priests* or *Biographies of Eminent Monks* or *Memoirs of Eminent Monks*) in 519 C.E. *Taishō* 50: 322-424.

Huiyuan 慧远 (334-416 C.E.). "*Yu yinshi liu yimin deng shu* 与隐士刘遗民等书 (A Letter to Hermit Liu Yimin and others)" in: *Guang hongmingji* (*Further Anthology of the Propagation of Light*) by Daoxuan. *Taishō* 52: 304.

Huiyuan. "*Nianfo sanmei shiji xu* 念佛三昧诗集序 (Preface to *A Collection of Poems on Buddhānusmṛti-samādhi*)" in: *Guang hongmingji* (*Further Anthology of the Propagation of Light*) by Daoxuan. *Taishō* 52: 351.

Huiyuan. "Lushan chu xiuxing fangbian chanjing xu 庐山出修行方便禅经序 (Preface to *Dhyāna-sūtra of Buddhasena / Dharmatara Dhyāna-sūtra translated at Mt. Lu* or General Introduction to *Dhyāna Scriptures produced on Mt. Lu as Means to Religious Cultivation*)" in: *Chu sanzang ji ji* (*A Collection of Records concerning the Tripiṭaka*) by Sengyou. Taishō 55: 65-66.

Hurvitz, Leon. 1956. tr. *Treatise on Buddhism and Taoism* by Wei Shou. in: *Yun-kang; The Buddhist Cave-monasteries of the Fifth Century C.E. in North China; detailed report of the archaeological survey carried out by the mission of the Tōhōbunka Kenkyūsho 1938-45* by S. Mizuno & T. Nagahiro. vol. xvi. Supplement and Index. Kyoto: Jimbunkagaku Kenkyūshū, Kyoto University. 23-103.

Jia, Yingyi 贾应逸. 1999. "*Jiumoluoshi yijing he beiliang shiqi de gaochang fojiao* 鸠摩罗什译经和北凉时期的高昌佛教 (Kumārajīva's translated versions of the *sūtras* and the Turfan Buddhism in the Northern Liang Kingdom)." *Dunhuang Research* No.1: 146-158.

Kinkara 吉迦夜 & Tanyao 昙曜. *Fu fazang yinyuan zhuan* 付法藏因缘传 (*A History of the Buddha's Successors*) in 572 C.E. *Taishō* 50: 297-322.

Kumārajīva 鸠摩罗什. *Miaofa lianhua jing* 妙法莲花经 (*Saddharma-puṇḍarīka -Sūtra* or *Lotus Sūtra of the Wonderful Law*). *Taishō* 9: 1-62.

Kumārajīva. *Chanfa yao* 禅法要 (*Essentials of the Dhyāna-discipline*) / *Chanmi yaofa jing* 禅密要法经 (*Secret Essentials of the Dhyāna-discipline* or *Sūtra about the Secret Essence of Dhyāna*). *Taishō* 15: 242-269.

Kumārajīva. *Zuochan sanmei jing* 坐禅三昧经 (*Dhyāna-samādhi-sūtra, Sūtra on the Concentration of Sitting Meditation*)/ *Guanzhong chanjing* 关中禅经 (*Dhyāna-sūtra translated in the Central Shaanxi Plain*). *Taishō* 15: 269-286.

Kumārajīva. *Chanfa yaojie* 禅法要解 (*Interpretation of the Dhyāna-discipline* or *Essential Explanation of the Way to Meditate*). *Taishō* 15: 286-297.

Kumārajīva? *Siwei lueyao fa* 思惟略要法 (*An Outline of Meditation* or *Outlining the Way to Reflect*). *Taishō* 15: 297-300.

Li, Chongfeng 李崇峰. 2003. *Zhong yin fojiao shikusi bijiao yanjiu: Yi tamiaoku wei zhongxin* 中印佛教石窟寺比较研究：以塔庙窟为中心 (*Chētiyagharas in Indian and Chinese Buddhist Cave-temple Complexes: A Comparative Study*). Beijing: Peking University Press.

Li, Chongfeng. "Jibin and China as seen from Chinese Documents." *Archaeology of Buddhism in Asia*". ed. by B. Mani. New Delhi: Archaeological Survey of India (in press).

Li, Daoyuan 郦道元 (466 or 472-527 C.E.). 1989. *Shuijing zhu* 水经注 (*Commentary on Waterways Classic*). sub-commentated by Yang, Shoujing 杨守敬 and Xiong, Huizhen 熊会贞. Nanjing: Jiangsu Classics Publishing House.

Li, Shan 李善 (630-689 C.E.) et al. 1987. *Liuchen zhu wenxuan* 六臣注文选 (*Annotations to Anthology Through the Ages* compiled by Xiao, Tong 萧统, 501-531C.E.) in 718 C.E. facsimile edition. Beijing: Zhonghua Book Company.

Li, Yuqun 李裕群. 2003. *Beichao wanqi shikusi yanjiu* 北朝晚期石窟寺研究 (A Study on the Cave-temples of the Late Northern Dynasties Period). Beijing: Cultural Relics Publishing House.

Li, Zhiguo 李治国 & Liu, Jianjun 刘建军. 1991. "*Beiwei pingcheng luyeyuan shiku diaocha ji* 北魏平城鹿野苑石窟调查记 (A Survey of Rock-cut caves at the Deer-park Temple of the Northern Wei Dynasty at Pingcheng)." *Zhongguo shiku: Yungang shiku* (*The Cave-temples of China: Yungang Caves*). Beijing: Cultural Relics Publishing House. I: 212-215.

Liu, Huida 刘慧达. 1996. "*Beiwei shiku yu chan* 北魏石窟与禅 (Dhyāna and the Cave-temples of the Northern Wei Dynasty)." *Zhongguo shikusi yanjiu* 中国石窟寺研究 (*Studies of the Cave-temples of China*) by Su, Bai 宿白. Appendix I. Beijing: Cultural Relics Publishing House. 331-348.

Liu, Jianjun. 2010. "*Luyeyuan shiku diaocha baogao* 鹿野苑石窟调查报告 (A Report on Rock-cut caves at the Deer-park Temple at Datong)." *Shikusi yanjiu* 石窟寺研究 (*Studies of the Cave-temples*). Beijing: Cultural Relics Publishing House. I: 1-9.

Lü, Cheng. 1971. "Buddhabhadra." *Encyclopaedia of Buddhism*. ed. by G. P. Malalasekera. Colombo: The Government of Ceylon. III: 382-384.

Lü, Cheng 吕澂. 1979. *Zhongguo foxue yuanliu luejiang* 中国佛学源流略讲 (*Origin and Development of the Chinese Buddhism: An Outline*). Beijing: Zhonghua Book Company.

Lü, Cheng. 1980. *Xinbian hanwen dazangjing mulu* 新编汉文大藏经目录 (*A New Catalogue of the Chinese Versions of the Buddhist Tripiṭaka*). Ji'nan: Qilu Publishing House.

Luders, H. 1912. "A List of Brāhmī Inscriptions from the earliest times to about A.D.400 with the exception of those of Aśōka." Appendix to *Epigraphia Indica and Record of the Archaeological Survey of India*. Calcutta: Superintendent Government Printing, India.

Rhie, Marylin M. 2002. *Early Buddhist Art of China & Central Asia*. vol. 2. Leiden: Brill.

Salomon, Richard. 1999. *Ancient Buddhist Scrolls from Gandhāra: The British Library Kharoṣṭhī Fragments,* Seattle: University of Washington Press.

Sengrui 僧叡. "*Guanzhong chu chanjing xu* 关中出禅经序 (Preface to *Dhyāna-sūtra translated in the Central Shaanxi Plain*)" in: *Chu sanzang ji ji* (*A Collection of Records concerning the Tripiṭakas*) by Sengyou. *Taishº* 55: 65.

Sengyou 僧祐 (445~518 C.E.). 1995. *Chu sanzang ji ji* 出三藏记集 (*A Collection of Records concerning the Tripiṭakas* or *A Collection of Records of Translations of the Tripiṭaka*). *Taishō* 55: 1-114.

Shenqing 神清. *Beishan lu* 北山录 (*Buddhism recorded at the Northern Mountain*) in 806 C.E. *Taishō* 52: 573-636.

Shen, Yue 沈约 (441-513 C.E.). 1974. *Song Shu* 宋书 (*A History of the Song Dynasty*) in 488 C.E. punctuated edition. Beijing: Zhonghua Book Company.

Su, Bai 宿白. 1996. *Zhongguo shikusi yanjiu* 中国石窟寺研究 (*Studies of the Cave-temples of China*). Beijing: Cultural Relics Publishing House.

Su, Bai. 2010. *Zhongguo fojiao shikusi yiji* 中国佛教石窟寺遺迹 (*The Buddhist Cave-temples of China*). Beijing: Cultural Relics Publishing House.

Sun, Wenchuan 孙文川 (1822-1882 C.E.) & Chen, Zuolin 陈作霖 (1837-1920 C.E.). 2008. *Nanchao fosizhi* 南朝佛寺志 (*Record of the Buddhist Monasteires of the Southern Dynasties*) in: *Jinling suozhi jiuzhong* 金陵琐志九种 (*Nine Annals of the Local History of Jinling*). Nanjing: Nanjing Publishing House. 139-285.

Taishō shinshū daizōkyō 大正新脩大藏經 (*Taishō Tripiṭaka*). 100 volumes. ed. by Junjirō, Takakusu 高楠順次朗 and Kaigyoku, Watanabe 渡邊海旭. Tokyo: Taishō Issaikyō Kankōkai. 1924-1934. abbreviated to *Taishō.*

Tang, Yongtong 汤用彤. 1982. *Han wei liang jin nanbeichao fojiao shi* 汉魏两晋南北朝佛教史 (*A History of Buddhism from the Han down to the Southern and Northern Dynasties*). Shanghai: Commerce Press, 1938. 2nd ed. Beijing: Zhonghua Book Company.

Ware, James R. 1930. "Wei Shou on Buddhism." *T'oung Pao* 30: 100-181.

Wei, Shou 魏收 (506-572 C.E.). 1974. *Weishu: Shilaozhi* 魏书·释老志 (*A History of the Wei Dynasty: Treatise on Buddhism and Taoism*) in 554 C.E. punctuated edition. Beijing: Zhonghua Book Company. 3025-3062.

Willemen, Charles. 2008. "Kumārajīva's "Explanatory Discourse about Abhidharmic Literature." *Kokusai Bukkyōgaku Daigaku-in Daigaku Kenkyū Kiyō* 国際仏教大学院大学研究紀要第12号(平成20年)/ *Journal of the International College for Postgraduate Buddhist Studies.* XII: 37-83 (156-110).

Willemen, Charles. 2012. *Outlining the Way to Reflect/* 思维略要法 (T. XV 617), Mumbai: Somaiya Publications Pvt Ltd.

Xuanzang 玄奘 (ca. 602-664 C.E.). 1985. *Datang xiyu ji* 大唐西域记 (*Record of the Western Regions of the Great Tang Dynasty*) in 646 C.E. collated and annotated by Ji, Xianlin 季羡林 et al. Beijing: Zhonghua Book Company.

Yu, Xin 庾信 (513-581 C.E.). 1966. "*Qinzhou tianshuijun maijiya fokan ming bing xu* 秦州天水郡麦积崖佛龛铭并序 (Preface and Epigraph to the Buddhist Niches at Maijiya, Tanshui District, Qinzhou Prefecture)." *Wenyuan yinghua* 文苑英华 (*The Best Works in the Literary and Art Circles*) compiled by Li, Fang 李昉 et al in 987 C.E. facsimile edition. Beijing: Zhonghua Book Company. 4149-4150.

Zhisheng 智昇. *Kaiyuan shijiao lu* 开元释教录 (*The Kaiyuan Era Catalogue of the Buddhist Canon* or *A Catalogue of the Buddhist Sacred Books of the Kaiyuan Period* or *A Catalogue of the Buddhist Canon compiled in the Kaiyuan Period*) in 730 C.E. *Taishō* 55: 477-723.

Z rcher, Erik. 1972. *The Buddhist Conquest of China: The Spread and Adaptation of Buddhism in Early Medieval China*. Leiden: E. J. Brill.

ILLUSTRATIONS

Fig. 1 Amitabha niche dated to 420 C.E., north wall of cave 169 at Binglingsi, Yongjing (from *The Cave-temples of China: The Binglingsi Caves of Yongjing, op cit.*: pl.21)

Fig. 2 Portrait of Monk Tanwupi (Dharmapriya), mural painting, north wall of cave 169 at Binglingsi, Yongjing (from *The Cave-temples of China: The Binglingsi Caves of Yongjing, op cit.*: pl.25)

Fig. 3 The cave-temple complex at Qixia, Nanjing

Fig. 4 Lēṇa, plan and longitudinal section, cave 285 at Mogaoku, Dunhuang (from *The Cave-temples of China: The Mogaoku Caves of Dunhuang, op cit.*: 225)

Fig. 5 Stūpa-cave, viz, *chētiyaghara*, cave 2 at Yungang, Datong (from *The Cave-temples of China: The Yungang Caves*, compiled and edited by Yungang Caves Depository for Cultural Relics, vol. 1, Beijing: Cultural Relics Publishing House, 1991: pl. 11)

Fig. 6 Monk in dhyāna meditation, mural painting, ceiling of cave 285 at Mogaoku (from *The Cave-temples of China: The Mogaoku Caves of Dunhuang, op cit.*: pl. 146)

Fig. 7 Main Buddha, cave 20 at Yungang

Fig. 8 Maitreya image, cave 13 at Yungang, Datong (from *The Cave-temples of China: The Yungang Caves*, compiled and edited by Yungang Caves Depository for Cultural Relics, vol. 2, Beijing: Cultural Relics Publishing House, 1994: pl. 111)

Fig. 9 Śākyamuni and Prabhataratna, northern face of the stūpa in cave 6 at Yungang, Datong (from *The Cave-temples of China: The Yungang Caves*, compiled and edited by Yungang Caves Depository for Cultural Relics, vol. 1, Beijing: Cultural Relics Publishing House, 1991: pl. 62)

Fig. 10 Śākyamuni comforting Ānanda, relief, south wall of cave 38 at Yungang (from *Zhongguo shikusi yanjiu (Studies of the Cave-temples of China* by Su Bai, Beijing: Cultural Relics Publishing House, 1996: 87, fig. 4).

16

Kumārajīva's influence on humanistic Buddhism from Yin Shun's conversion

Liu Cheng-you

Yin Shun in Brief

From CE 1840, being faced with the so-called "the greatest crisis of Chinese history and civilization in the millennia", Chinese intellectuals strived hard for the reconstruction of social order and cultural values. Especially after the initial reform in CE 1898 and the founding of the Republic of China in 1912, their inner spirituality was emphasized on "refreshing the Chinese morality". Against this background, the traditional religion cultures, such as Confucianism and Buddhism, had been revived. Moreover, foreign trends and ideas were introduced into China – Christianity was one of them.

A particularly interesting phenomenon was that some intellectuals with a Buddhist background were later converted to Christianity, while some with Christian backgrounds later became Buddhists. In both cases, they had studied Confucian writings in their earlier years. What is the reason for their conversion? They gave reasonable explanations for their doings. What is the theoretical value? They also were able to speak on and write some works that had great influence on the whole of society. Therefore, to some extent, it is valuable to analyze their religious ideas in order to identify the Chinese intellectuals' group consciousness.

During the Republican period (1912-1949), some intellectuals encountered an unavoidable contradiction. Which religion should they decide to choose as their basic belief, Christianity or Buddhism? Even the foreign preachers encountered questions for such a choice . We can find related materials from some famous writers, such as Wang Zhi-xin, Xie Fu-ya, Zhang Chun-yi,

Zhao Zi-chen, Wei Zhuo-min, Xu Song-shi, Karl Ludvig Reichelt (a preacher from Norway), Miao-Ji, the Christians, , the Buddhists etc. Two initial works studying the ideas of the figures mentioned above have been published. One, edited by Lai Pan-chiu, is entitled *Buddhist-Christian Encounter in Modern China* (To Fung Press, 2003). Another is *Zhang Chun-yi's Buddhist-Christian Theology* by So Yuen-tai (To Fung Press, 2007). But, their research did not refer to the monk Yin Shun's religious conversion.

In fact, Yin Shun is also a representative figure. Yin Shun (1906-2005, his name was Zhang Lu-qin before becoming a monk), diligent in thinking and writing, had finished a great number of works with more than 7 million words in his life time. His major works, the Miaoyun collections (Miaoyunji, Miaoyun means auspicious clouds, which can bring luck through reading his Buddhist works.), were edited in 24 books, and were usually called the smaller Tripiṭaka (Xiao Zang Jing). One of his works, *History of Zen in China,* also attracted the attention of Japanese Buddhists. In 1973, he was granted a Doctorate in Literature (not honorary) by the Dazheng University in Japan. In Taiwan's Buddhist circle, Yin Shun was regarded as a spiritual tutor, "Sower of Humanistic Buddhism" and "the greatest figure after Xuan Zang". Among the so-called Four Buddhist Sects in Taiwan, except for monk Wei Jue in Zhong Tai Mountain, the remaining are related to to Yin Shun's Humanistic Buddhism. They are Ciji Merit Charity Association set up and led by Zheng Yan, Fo Guang Mountain set up by Xing Yun, and Fa Gu Mountain set up by Sheng Yan. Actually, the development of the entire Chinese Buddhist Concept in the 20th century would not be so splendid without Yin Shun's Humanistic Buddhist idea. So, I think that it is very representative and significant to study Yin Shun's views on Christianity and Buddhism.

Yin Shun's ideas before converting to Buddhism

When he was a child, Yin Shun began to read many books; he got enlightened education in Kai Zhi (it means enlightment) Senior Primary School in Haining, Zhejiang province. He was taught writing by the famous teacher, Zhang Zhong-wu. Among the students who were trained by the latter, Xu Zhi-mo became a great poet later. After finishing primary school at thirteen, Yin Shun started to study Chinese medicine. He preferred essential medical principles to medical technology. At sixteen, his father was worried about his obsession and ceased his medical learning. Then, he became a teacher in the local primary school. In the process of teaching, he had more time to study a variety of ideas and kept thinking about the significance of life.

Understanding the Theories of Lao Tzu and Chuang Tzu

Because Chinese traditional medicine has something in common with Taoism and its academic school, in the beginning Yin Shun chose some classic books by Lao-tzu and Chuang-tzu, as his reading, attempting to find a base for his own studies. However, he found that Lao Tzu and Chuang Tzu's theories could not solve one's psychological confusions in a short time. In his opinion:

> *The philosophic theory in Lao-tzu and Chuang-tzu is profound argument, but it fails to compass its own limits. Their thought did not fit into human nature because they put nature before humanity. Their ideal was to go back to the natural state in which everything would be simple, including human life. The well-known social psychology seems to be reasonable, while it lacks the spirit of actively going forward. Living alone far away from society always brings a negative life view. Although the theories of Taoism, to some degree, inspired me to enter the Buddhist world, the philosophy of Taoist Academics and the ways of their cultivating oneself got my partial sympathy. I was determined not to be a Taoist and to wake up from the virtual dream.* [1]

His basic understanding of the philosophy of Taoism was not only expressed by his mature thinking, but also provided theoretical support for his awareness. The style of Taoist academics was more suitable for the aged or the hopeless in life. At that time, the social requirement was to save the nation and the poor people.

Confucian Academics Upbringing

After a while, he picked up the Confucian Academics Scriptures that he had read in his childhood in private school. Although the slogan "Batter down the bastion of the old ethics- Confucianism" was prevalent in society, Confucian Academics had a series of fine Kong Fu and ambitions, and were full of passion for real life. The Four Books (Si Shu) are fundamental classics of Confucianism. San Gang (three main headings) and Ba Mu (eight items) in the Great Learning are usually regarded as the Confucian core. The San Gang include lighting your virtue by yourself (Ming Ming De), reforming the people's unreasonable habit and life worth (Xin Min), and pursuing the best moral target (Zhi Yu Zhi Shan). Lighting the virtue by oneself belongs to individual moral culture. Reforming the people's unreasonable habits and life worth belongs to one's duty for his society. Pursuing the best moral target is one's end-result, just as a bird knows how to go home when night comes. Ba Mụ includes practice (Ge Wu), knowledge which comes from one's practice

---

[1] Yin Shun, my view on religion , Miao Yun Colections, Zhengwen press,Taibei, 2000. P P. 302-303.

(Zhi Zhi), sincerity which fits into the law of nature (Cheng Yi), correcting one's mind (Zheng Xin), cultivating one's morality (Xiu Shen), keeping a family in order (Qi Jia), managing state affairs (Zhi Guo), making peace in our world (Ping Tian Xia). Its simple and practical features, without doubt, could guide people's life according to Yin-Shun's views at that time. Its social concern is totally different from the negative and self-closing Taoism.

However, the philosophy of the Confucian Academics was still unable to reach his requirement. In his mind:

> *Common, practical, people-esteem and reason are exactly the mainstream of Chinese national culture. I can pay sympathy to it and speak highly of it. Anyway, it could not release my sense of emptiness and confusion. People thought of me as over-practical, while I just felt much more confused.*[2]

In his eyes, Confucian thinking was not only over-worldly, but also imperfect in itself, and lacking something, similar to Taoism's compass.

When his thinking was set later, Yin Shun analysed this realization systemically. He argued that Confucius, as the founder of the Confucian Academics School, put too much emphasis on practical politics and education, which are considered as non-religious elements. Hence Confucius was attached to sacrificing ceremony, but never referred to the existence of God (Ji Ru Zai, Ji Shen Ru Shen Zai). Yin Shun said:

As Confucian thinking goes, all that is related to religion, such as origin of the universe, the fate of after-life, ghosts and mysterious phenomena etc., were all set aside without argument. "To respect ghosts and gods but keep distance" (Jing Gui Shen Er Yuan Zhi) had been exactly the spirit of Confucian academics since Confucius founded it. "Sages arrange culture and education through setting up some church and other temples" (Shen Ren Yi Shen Dao She Jiao) clearly indicated that the ancient Chinese did not know what exactly religion was, but they were quite sure about making use of it as a controlling tool for people.[3]

In addition, Confucian scholars from the Song Dynasty to Qing Dynasty followed this tradition and gradually developed into rejecting religion. If there is some value in religion, that must be its ethical significance. This thinking had been broadcast widely so that many later scholars formed a strong concept that people would link the errors of superstition with religion. After the Song Dynasty, Cheng Zhu Li Xue, which was usually called Neo-Confucianism, gradually became the State ideology. Buddhism and Taoism turned into minority beliefs and flew into folklore. Many religious rites such as releasing

---

[2] Ibid., p.303.

[3] Ibid., p.33.

souls from purgatory and attending funeral ceremonies (Chao Wang Song Si) seemed to be the symbols of Buddhism and Taoism. This reinforced the Confucianists to misunderstand that religions like Buddhism and Taoism were superstition.

Yin Shun did not think that Confucian academic culture, lacking life-encompassing qualities, was a blessing for the Chinese nation. In the book *Chinese Religion Ups and Downs and Confucianism Academic School,* he wrote:

> *Time has changed greatly, western civilization is following the step of their strong and sharp weapons. Confucian academic culture failed to adapt to this situation, so it fell behind rapidly. The so-called normal Chinese culture was so vulnerable that it could not afford a strike. It seems to be ridiculous and incredible. All Confucian temples changed overnight without reason. Compared to Buddhism and Taoism's protesting against breaking temples and disfiguring icons, Confucianism is worth nothing. This is obvious and strongly proved that upper-class culture without religion and belief is unavailable.*[4]

According to Yin Shun's view, there are two aspects which were not emphasized enough in Confucianism. One, it was short of reaching religion. Secondly, it did not emphasize the compatibility between religion and society. Therefore, Confucianism was lacking in society's critical spirit. He thought that this feature may be an important reason why Confucianism was on the decline in the Qing Dynisty and could not establish itself. In other words, Yin Shun could not accept Confucianism on the whole.

Learning Christianity for 2 Years

During the summer vacation in 1926, a teacher at a church primary school in Yin Shun's hometown was sick. The founder of the school came to know that Yin Shun would come back to his hometown. So the founder invited him to teach elementary students in his church school. Yin Shun agreed. The church service caught Yin Shun's attention while teaching. Under a friend's recommendation, he came to know Christianity and became more interested in it.

At this time, Yin Shun found that the theories of the Tao and Confucian academic schools were both short of religious emotions. One was too weak, and the other was too secular, while Christianity was different from them. It was sociable and one could feel the devout and pure religious confidence. Yin Shun who had been focusing on life-encompassing, now seemed to find what he needed from Christianity with confidence, hope and love. Thereby, he devoted himself to Christianity with great enthusiasm, praying, reading the Bible and some magazines such as *True Light, Spiritual Light* and *Christian* etc. He once even joined the Spiritual Revival Conference (SRC).

[4] Ibid., p.51.

The full name of SRC is Spiritual Evangelical Meeting, Serving as Primary Preaching Means by Spiritual Party of Christianity. In its system, all participants could feel completely at ease. It was founded in America and Britain in the 19th century. The purpose was to encourage common people to preach the doctrine, motivate religious appeal and re-establish the authority of the church. From 1875 to 1915, the American evangelist Mody started this spiritual movement with the support of parties. This movement soon spread to places all over the world. Without information, it is not clear how Yin Shun joined the party and whether this was a sign of his baptism. But it is quite certain that at the age of 21 or 22, Christianity shocked him. The key was that he had matured physically and spiritually. After the initial fascination, he must have done some calm thinking combined with excellent theoretical judgment.

Yin Shun's View on Christianity

1. On Missionaries and Mission

At the end of 1927, as he acquired more knowledge of Christianity and the higher degree of the research he did, he finally got to know that Chinese anti-Christianity movement had nothing with the doctrine itself, but with the suspicion of a "cultural invasion" because of the western background of Christianity. People disliked the manner of some missionaries' in that period: knocking at the gates of China with weapons disagreeing with the traditions of Chinese courtesy. That may be why so many Chinese people continually rejected Christianity in their minds.

This basic conclusion is drawn from Yin Shun's readings when he was in the small church primary school in his hometown. Zhang Chun-yi, another active figure in Christian circles, working in Gguangxue Association in Shanghai during the period of 1909-1920, had initially expressed dissatisfaction with foreign Christian missions. In his opinion, most Christians and priests did not know the truth of God, so Christianity had nothing to be worshipped by the Chinese. He said, "Many missionaries have no true knowledge of Christianity, even its shortcomings. Therefore, what they said is not only useless but also misunderstanding Jesus' real idea."[5] Yin Shun also saw that the priests returned to Europe and killed countless people during the four-year European War. After all those crimes, they came to China again and went on to preach the doctrine. The so-called wise man always taught the people ridiculous, even wrong doctrines.[6] In fact, the missions in China, both the Beijing Christianity Ally in the passing years and the Shanghai Christianity Mission did not appear to be any good. They were just a diplomatic tool.[7]

[5] Zhang Chun-yi, true Christianity is not different form Buddhism, if not it's not true Christianity, world Buddhists in-home in Shanghai, 1921, vol.1, p.4.

[6] Yin Shun, my view on religion, the Miao Yun Colections, pp. 303-304.

[7] Ibid.

Could these Christian priests or their mission save people from suffering? He therefore put forward the definition "true Christianity" according to the Buddhist doctrines. In 1923, he finally raised his Buddhist-Christian Theology. He said, "True Christianity is not different from Buddhism. If not, it's not true Christianity". In 1926, he finished the book, *The Secret of Gospel,* which systematically explained his theology. Hence, Chun-yi Zhang's thinking, during this period, was deeper than Yin Shun's.

2. On Christian Doctrine

Surely, the basic factor causing Yin Shun's conversion in belief lay in his understanding of the Christian doctrine itself. He acknowledged that he could not accept some of the Christian doctrines. He said:

> *For example, believing or not will lead to eternal life or eternal death. Obeying me, survive; rebelling against me, die. The standard is only belief, without human behavior. This concept is much too exclusive according to his opinion. All will be damaged except for God and God's believers. Under God's love, we feel more cruelty and hatred, like a feeling of opposite class. Another reason is the soul coming from God. If the soul comes from God, meets together anew, one person will be coming. According to the doctrine (only rebirth can save), most people will go to hell.*[8]

We will not comment on his understanding as true or false. What we are interested in is that the understanding resulted in his religious conversion. Of course, Yin Shun's understanding of Christianity may not be correct enough, while Zhang Chun-yi who indulged himself in Christianity for many years, once had similar thinking when he put out "True Christianity". Zhang considered that the Christianity which was in fashion despises humanity: "Only God is kind and a human cannot become God forever". It is unfair. Seen from this point, Buddhism, especially Māhayāna, shows more equality in argument, that everyone equally possesses Buddhahood and has the possibility to be Buddha. Zhang Chun-yi also holds that the Christianity in fashion was not as broad as Buddhism. He thought the main reason was that the present doctrine was not the true one.[9] In his opinion, people should embrace both Buddhism and Christianity, because the doctrine of Christianity is similar to the Pure Land Sect or the Flower Garland Sect, factually Māhayāna Buddhism.[10] Even

---

[8] Ibid.

[9] Zhang Chun-yi, About the Relation between Moism and Christian, Reseaching Collections on Mo Tzu, Beijing Library Press, vol.28, p. 713.

[10] Zhang Chun-yi, true Christianity is not different form Buddhism, if not it's not true Christianity, world Buddhists in-home in Shanghai, 1921, vol.1, p.9.

the definition "Śūnyatā" (creative void), is regarded by Zhang as the core of "true Christianity". He said that only three characters, including Jesus, John and Paul, knew the truth of emptiness. He said, "For example, Jesus said that who could extend his life a moment because of thoughtfulness? Physical body was endless. And Jesus told his disciples to give up their body with the Cross. John said that only one who detested and loathed one's life could keep his life and obtain eternal of life in the world. Paul said that he regarded a great number of eras or worlds as dung earth. This is true Christianity."[11] So, Zhang Chun-yi and Yin Shun hold similar viewpoints on Christian doctrine.

As for Yin Shun, after 30 years, his view on Christian doctrine still did not change. When his new pulpit which was named Hui Ri (the first Chinese character means wisdom, the second means sun. When combined together, it means that wisdom has great power like the sun) was completed in 1961 in Taipei city, a Christian invited him to give a Bible. He took advantage of this chance and wrote an article entitled "God Loves World". This article drew the attention of priest Wu (Wu Enpu) of Hong Kong and Gong (Gong Tianmin) of Taiwan and led to a hot debate. In this background, Yin Shun wrote another thesis *"Further Discussion on God Loves World"*. Yin Shun explained his view on Christianity and Buddhism and gave some personal reasons on why he left Christianity for Buddhism.

In these articles, he clearly pointed out that in his view the basic standing of Christianity is a master-slave relationship and its main method is to make people strangers and divide them.[12] According to his own experience of reading scriptures, Yin Shun thought that God Jehovah possesses powers of life and death over all things including human beings because God created them. Once those created by God ate the Knowledge Apple, they could understand good and evil. Then God would force the persons to leave the Garden of Eden. Why does the God do that? Yin Shun wrote:

> *If a human being has judgment, and then has eternal life as God does, his wisdom will become stronger day after day. What if he were God? God could not bear with such a thought. So God drove him out before he became strong enough and ordered Death to fall on people. However, Death could not stop the intelligence of human beings. The development of human beings continue from generation to generation not only by relying on the experience of ancestors, but also by charting their own progress. When God wanted to change a human being's ascent, he passed on from an era of agriculture into that of industry – people can make bricks, build a city and wished to set up soaring towers towards heaven. .. .. If people can make everything they want, would the glory still belong to God? This makes God seriously worried. After all God's astuteness is great! He thinks*

[11] Ibid., p.5.

[12] Ibid. , p.218.

out a wonderful idea to create confusion through languages. Different kinds of languages will mean different nations and different cultures. The diversity of languages not only formed different nations and cultures, but also brought about conflicts, clashes and fighting, which could weaken the power of human unity and progress. That is why God divided human languages."[13]

Depending on this understanding, he continued to say:

> *In short, knowing nothing is a kind of cheating-the-citizen policy. The purpose is to blind people, control their mind and finally form a strong faith. Dispersion without organization would lead to argument, conflicts, revenge, fighting and so on. This is a policy of dispersion. These means can weaken the power of unity among people and make God unique gradually.*[14]

3. On Religious conversion

The Christian scriptures and related readings inspired him to deeply think about his faith. Christianity believes in truth without any questioning, while, Yi Shun who once worshiped Lao Tzu, Chuang Tzu, Confucius and Mencius, he didn't believe: "God Loves Us". Therefore, he made a claim firmly: "I am a Chinese. I have no idea how to make myself to be a slave by God's will. I have never thought to be a master, or a slave. Here I have to say sorry to God: I will leave you and follow Buddha."[15]

Yin Shun's View of Buddhism

1. Comparative Advantage of Buddhism

After reading Buddhist sūtras for a few years, Yin Shun gradually realized:

Buddha judges somebody whether he is a layman or a sage, by his deeds, not only by one's belief or wishes. Buddha does not simply put emphasis on self enlightenment, but on benefit for everyone. Buddha pays more attention on 'thorough awareness'. Thorough awareness means thorough freedom. Buddha is the sum of conviction, intellect and charity. The cultivation of heart and soul not only takes advantage of Confucianism and Taoism but also develops it further. Christianity believes in the confession and correction of guilt, so does Buddhism. Buddhism possesses the merits of all religions, including basal principle and flexible methods. It is tolerant so that it can adapt to various situations.[16]

---

[13] Ibid., pp.205-207.
[14] Ibid., pp.214-216.
[15] Ibid., p.191.
[16] Ibid., pp.305-306.

Yin Shun is sure that the ideas about the three periods (San Shi) are most reasonable which will guide people to be kind and thus can elevate a person to be a sage. Even though he cannot enlighten or even degrade himself, he will make progress and free himself at the end. It is not just the absolute destination but also the process that can encourage, comfort and guide us to go through the journey with hope.[17]

Under these circumstances, Yin Shun devoted himself to Buddha in 1930. He became a monk in Putuo Moutain, Zhejiang province when he was twenty five years old andlived as a Buddhist up to the age of 75. During this period, wherever he was, whether at Zhengjiang, Chongqing, Hong Kong and Taiwan, he sought learning, reading a great numbers of scriptures, taught and explained Buddhist sūtras, and wrote books. In this long journey, his knowledge of Buddhist theoretical systems became much clearer. He also attained great success.

2. Setting up the Humanistic Buddhist Thought

Based on the life of a Buddhist monk Tai Xu, Yin Shun had gradually developed a Buddhist life style. The Humanistic Buddhist thought took shape in the mind of Yin Shun, at last.

However, overall, there are four kinds of shapes in modern Chinese Buddhism :

A. The expression of traditional Buddhism by living life away from this world (Chu Shi): Under this expression, Buddhists live in the temples. They cultivate themselves and are not worried about any human affairs.

B. The expression of traditional Buddhism lies in deterioration: Under this expression, some people living in the temples want to take advantage of Buddhism to pursue money and power. Other monks focus on rituals such as funeral or burial ceremonies. They do not care for the meaning of life.

C. The Buddhist life as advocated by monk Tai Xu: He said that the Buddhists should play a role in society and think of the meaning of life while he recognizes the existence of external Gods.

D. The Humanistic Buddhism preached by Yin Shun: He placed emphasis on the human world and stressed vigorously on a human being's role in creating an ideal society (This was named as Pure Land). However, he admitted that there were six kinds of life in the world (Six States of Existence). 1. Naraka, i.e. Hell (Di Yu); 2. Preta, i.e. Hungry Ghosts (E Gui); 3. Tiryagyoni, i.e. Animal (Chu Sheng); 4. Asura, i.e. spirits with malevolent nature (E Xiu Luo); 5. Manuśya, i.e. Human Existence (Ren); 6. Deva, i.e. Heavenly Existence (Tian).

[17] Ibid.

The Humanistic Buddhist thought was preached during the War of Resistance against Japan. Buddhist activities in the shadow of the war was criticized by the famous scholar, Liang Shu-ming. Yin Shun then began to think deeply of the Buddhist social influence. According to Liang's opinion, Buddhists were not concerned for the real society and human life. He named this feature of Buddhism "carelessness on this time, this place and this person". (Ci Shi, Ci Di, Ci Ren)

When Yin Shun read in 1940 that the Buddha was successful in our world, not in the Kingdom of Heaven in the Ekottarāgama-sūtra, he suddenly had an idea that Buddha was neither a deity nor an angel. Buddha successfully obtained the truth of universal and human life merely in our world. Therefore, he thought that only the lives that are born in our world could receive the Buddhist doctrine, practice these doctrines and go a step further to the real freedom, Nirvāṇa. So, this idea that "Buddha was successful in our world" is an important thought. It makes clear that Buddhist enlightenment is the realistic road along which everybody will understand the truth in universal and human life. Meanwhile, one can also make other people understand it (Zi Jue Jue Ta). Therefore, the Buddhist doctrine is "the Humanistic Buddhism". Buddhism should not be regarded as the ghost deified Buddhism! Yin Shun thought that this sentence may completely dispel Liang's misunderstanding of Buddhism. The connection between Buddhist thought and a realistic society is closely related. Buddhism may definitely take this significant function for the future ideal form of society. From then on, he further gradually cleaned up the social concerns of Buddhist history, and raised the essential meaning of Humanistic Buddhism and the Pure Land in our society.

3. Features of Humanistic Buddhist Thought

As a whole, there are two core ideas in Humanistic Buddhism and its Pure Land: The first is people-oriented thought. A human being is most important in the world. He thought that human society was open. Therefore, Buddhism is the original human religion in the world. The Buddhists should make all sorts of altruistic enterprises so long as some people live in some place.

The other is the creative thought that puts emphasis on enterprise and awareness creation by people themselves. He thought that the Pure Land (ideal world) was the universal desire for almost all people. The Pure Land includes not only nature, but also society. Therefore, the Buddhists who practice Pure Land shall understand correctly its true meaning – to purify the world, not to enjoy that ideal world without being hard-working. Therefore, besides wanting to go to the Pure Land, Buddhists shall intensively ask the question about the source of the Pure Land in this belief. Amitābha said clearly in the *Amitābha Sūtra* that the people with a little good behaviour would not go to the

Western Pure Land of Ultimate Bliss. Its meaning is that people's behaviour is the most important. If one only wants to go to the Pure Land after death without caring to dignify the world and to create the Pure Land, it would amount to the Pure Land being regarded as a kind of heaven in Christianity. Yin Shun firmly criticized firmly this Buddhist thought.

Kumārajīva's Influence on Humanistic Buddhism

Yin Shun is always regarded as a famous thinker for the intermediate perspective. He advocated that there are three parts in Mahāyāna Buddhism. They are Emptiness sect, Yogācāra sect, and Tathāgata-garbha sect (the natural spatial nominalism; vij¤apti-mātratā theory and Really often idealism). In his words, the Emptiness sect is legitimate. What is more, his standpoint in Humanistic Buddhism is also the Emptiness sect. As we had known, the Emptiness sect founded by Nāgārjuna, is a common source of Eight Sects in Chinese Buddhism. Most of Nāgārjuna' works were translated by Kumārajīva. The main works of Emptiness sect which were read by Yin Shun was one of these. It can be said that Yin Shun was affected profoundly by Kumārajīva.

On the basis of the above mentioned simple examination, we think that there are some significant concepts that can be summarized as follows:

1. There exists a close relation between the religious function and "society is the Nirvāṇa"

After 1840, the Chinese people faced a real crisis which made almost all Chinese intellectuals pay attention to the path of saving the nation and rescuing people from suffering at that time. Their ideals of hard-work were embodied mainly in the Westernization Movement, the Political Reform in 1898 (WuXu Bian Fa) and the New Cultural Movement. These movements belonged to one of the social ideological trends. They believed, at first, that the value of every thought, including all kinds of religion, should relieve the Chinese people's misery. This demand from religion by both Yin Shun and Zhang Chun-yi who too voiced similar concerns. At that time, the ultimate question which the Buddhist paid attention to, was that religion ought to have a close connection with the realistic society. This initiated the thought that society was Nirvāṇa. More or less, Nāgārjuna's idea of Nirvāṇa has profoundly affected Chinese Zen. Asking the Bodhi without the world is similar to looking at the rabbit's horns. This is nearly a classical language. This is also one of the reasons that the Chinese accepted Bodhisattva thought. Su Yuan-tai pointed out in his research that the idea mentioned above was an important feature in Zhang Chun-yi's thought. [18]

[18] So Yuen-tai, ZHANG Chun-yi's Buddhist-Christian Theology, To Fung Press, Hong Kong, 2007, PP.124-125.

2. The Influence of Both Confucian Thinking Mode and Dependent Origination of Eight-Non

It is usually difficult for Chinese intellectuals not to be influenced by the traditional thinking mode. When they discussed the usefulness of something (Yong), they must get involved in the thing-in-itself (Ti) which is behind the thing. If the body is inalienable, the Chinese would understand immediately and intuitionally that it is without logic. This thinking mode was Eight-Non origins in Nāgārjuna's books. This thinking mode was called Li Shi Wu Ai in the Flower Garland sect (one sect of Chinese Buddhism) in T'ang Dynasty, while it was also called Ti Yong Yi Yuan in Neo-Confucianism. The thinking mode was also called Yue Yin Wan Chuan or Li Yi Fen Shu. What's the meaning of these set phrases? There is only one moon in the sky, but we can see many moons in the sea or river. According to Zhu Xi, the common principle of all things is like the moon in the sky while the innate character of a special thing is like the inverted reflection of the moon in water. The principle is only one. It is the essence of myriad things while being the only principle embodied in the myriad things. The essence of myriad things is not the division of the common principle, but the common principle that is in everything completely. Thus there is a unity and equivalence between the concrete things and the final main body. The final main body has no similar concept like "the creator".

Based on the analogous thinking mode, Yin Shun naturally regarded that the relation between God and person was similar to the connection between master and servant. Zhang Chun-yi also regarded God thus, as the concept was similar to the law of nature in his so-called True Christianity. They did not accept the concept of God in the fashion of Christianity.

3. About Individual Extrication and Bodhi Thought

Correspondingly, Yin Shun and Zhang Chun-yi hold the opposite standpoint on external redemption. Whether somebody would attain Buddhahood in the society or the "Christ from the heart"[19], they emphasized on the intrinsic consciousness within. Actually, it is an important view that human beings will become sages depending on their thinking and hard-work in real life. The sage of Confucianism or the immortal of Taoism achieved their goals by the manner mentioned above in the realistic life. Buddhism had been an important part of the world of the Chinese mind since it was introduced into China. I think that one of the reasons lies in the similarities between Buddhism

[19] Zhang Chun-yi, true Christianity is not different form Buddhism, if not it's not true Christianity, World Buddhists in-home in Shanghai, 1921, vol.1, p.6. "佛经者，白纸耳，黑墨耳，与新约等，决不能挽回社会。在善读者，以自心之佛，自心之基督，在在期与经义相应而实现之，始足以晚会社会。

and Confucianism. As we know, both the Bodhisattva spirit in the Māhayāna Buddhism, especially Nāgārjuna's Bodhi and the Confucian's concern about society, for example, managing state affairs, making peace in our world may reach the same goal or conclusion from different approaches.

Certainly, there is also the concept of God-like in Chinese traditional culture but this idea is mainly popular in common society. It is not easy for almost any intellectual of China to pay attention to the concept of God. It is well illustrated that Taoism and the Pure Land belief had only been popular in the common society for more than 2000 years. Today, China's objection to the dissemination of Christianity and the follower's distribution are also reflecting the same phenomenon. It is estimated that 80% of the Chinese Christian population is in the countryside today. These followers still constitute the so-called "three-more"— the old persons, the women, and the illiterates, as they are the main believers. There is a massive Chinese traditional folk belief ingredient inside their mind. Christianity has in fact become the substitute of the populace's original belief.

Xiao Zhi-kuo thought: "They had found the original religious consciousness as a new home from Christianity. They did not change their belief from atheism into theism."[20] Wang Wei-fan also said, "In fact, it is one kind of shift or extreme transference for universal Chinese common people to change their belief object from the ghosts to God".[21] In the eyes of many followers, God is only the substitute for the deities of the original faith, such as supernatural beings, Bodhisattva, etc. Therefore, the followers always think that God is unable to say 'no' when they seek help, particularly when they want to be relieved from the pain of a lingering disease. Because of this, in many places, so long as an original disease-healing miracle occurs to a Christian believer, his whole family, the clansmen, and even his area's people will adhere to Christianity.[22] According to some statistics, in the countryside above 60% of Christian followers had adopted Christianity due to sickness.[23] Under this kind of influence, almost all Chinese Christians in the countryside neither understand the religious doctrine nor pay great attention on the religious doctrine generally. What they care about is only the curative function of Christianity and the miracles that may occurr.

However, the Chinese intelligentsia who have read the Four Books have ingrained the thought as Confucius once said about respecting the ghosts and gods but keeping a distance (Jing Gui Shen Er Yuan Zhi). Moreover, becoming

[20] Xiao Zhi-tian, Thinking about Modern Religion Question in China, Shanghai, 1994, p. 164.

[21] Wang Wei-fan, About the Current Situation of Christian, Religion, 1991, vol. 1.

[22] Deng Zhao-ming, Receiving and holding: the Gospel Torch in China, Chinese Christianity Culture Research, Hong Kong, 1998.

[23] Liang Jialin: Reform and open policy Chinese Countryside Church, p.418.

a Saint and practicing moral culture is also a subconscious-like life pursuit in their minds.

Preliminary Conclusion

Although Yin Shun's views on Christianity, Confucianism and Buddhism may be subjected to various appraisals, his manner of thinking about the question has obviously been of Chinese character. Just like the Buddhist-Christian theology of Zhang Chun-yi, we may regard Humanistic Buddhism as the Confucian-Buddhist Theory. What is expressed in their thought is not completely the religious believer's characteristic. Here, we have no intention to appraise which is right or which is wrong. What we want to know is whether their manner of thinking is particular or universal? In other words, does their thinking merely have individual significance or universal significance? In my opinion, a similar thinking mode will continue to exist in China in the future.

17

Defining a new road for Mahāyāna Buddhism in China

Pokan Chou

Recent research on the origins of Mahāyāna Buddhism strongly suggests that early Mahāyāna Buddhists in India were actually "a small, isolated and embattled group" who lived "in [Indian] periphery and marginal areas."[1] Through the study of inscriptions and of early Buddhist texts of the 2nd/ 3rd centuries in their Chinese translations, the term "Mahāyāna," though not very distinctive, already appeared, even though it was embedded within complex doctrines pointing to a currency, no matter whether it is conscious for a self-identity, underwent with a group of forest-dwelling, radical ascetic monks, scattered in various Buddhist communities.[2] New findings certainly revise the already established pattern of Indian Buddhist development (1) in a lineal conception that periodizes Buddhism in India into Śākyamuni's Buddhism, Sectarian Buddhism and Mahāyāna Buddhism, and (2) that the origin of Mahāyāna Buddhism was initiated by laity as suggested by Lamotte and Hirakawa, and in association with the worship of stūpa, as suggested by Hirakawa.[3] For this revision, Gregory Schopen claims, "the history of Mahāyāna in China may well have been the single most powerful determining force in how the history of Mahāyāna in India was perceived and reconstructed."[4] His insightful observation, unfortunately does not come

1 Grogory Schopen, "The Mahāyāna and the middle period in Indian Buddhism: through a Chinese looking-glass," *Eastern Buddhist* (Kyoto) 32, 2 (2000): 1-15

2 Paul Harrison, "Who gets to ride in Mahāyāna Buddhism?" *Journal of International Association of Buddhist Studies* 10,1 (1987):67-89

3 To see the criticism of the conventional view, one can see Jonathan A. Silk, "What, if anything, is Mahāyāna Buddhism," *Numen* 49,4 (2002): 355-405.

4 Grogory Schopen, ibid, p.1.

with supportive arguments. This paper will strengthen his view, but retrace his refutation of Hirakawa's argument with a modification in this study of Kumārajīva's Buddhism: laity is indeed the main driving force of Mahāyāna Buddhism, but in China rather than in India. On the other hand, "Mahāyāna" was mainly defined by the *Lotus Sūtra*, rather than any other Buddhist texts in China.

Eric Zürcher's study of the Western Region of Han China (206 BCE-220 CE) reminds us that at least by the early 3rd century CE, Buddhism was absent in today's Tarim Basin. Pioneering monks who brought Buddhism into Han China were from areas west of the Pamir Mountains, that is, today's Central Asia and Kashmir.[5] Taking into consideration all the accounts together about the hazards of travelling through the Pamir Mountain in Chinese travelogues, monks who advanced with Central Asian caravans into Tarim Basin and further arrived in China[6] must have been a few brave ones. Considering that Indian Brahmanism and Mainstream Buddhist Saṅgha were hostile to Mahāyāna Buddhists and their scriptures[7], the difficult situation must have forced Mahāyāna monks in India to give up their homeland and to migrate into what they perceived to be "borderland." In spite of the fact that we are far from a panoramic understanding of Mahāyāna Buddhism in Central Asia and Tarim Basin, their religious zeal must have driven Mahāyāna Buddhist missionaries to translate Buddhist texts into local languages,[8] to propagate Mahāyāna doctrines. Being in the political and the economic influence sphere, monks in Tarim Basin were inclined to migrate to China and finally further translated Buddhist texts into Chinese. What Buddhist texts were translated by linguistically talented Dharmarakṣa (active 265-316) must be representative of the earliest Buddhist thoughts in Tarim Basin. Among them, the *Prajñāpāramitā* literature penetrated into the circle of Chinese cultural elites, and the *Lotus Sūtra* appealed to Chinese Buddhist communities.[9] Yet, the low quality of

---

5 W. Idema & E Zürcher, ed., *Thought and Law in Qin and Han China*, 1990, Leiden UP.

6 James Heitzman,"Early Buddhism, Trade and Empire," in *Studies in the Archaeology and Paleoanthropology of South Asia*, New Delhi: Oxford & Ibh Publishing Co.; and Liu Xinru, *Ancient India and Ancient China: Trade and Religious Exchange, AD 1 – 600*, Delhi: Oxford University Press, 1988.

7 In regard to how the mainstream Buddhist Sangha institutionally rejected newly emerged Mahāyāna Buddhist scriptures, see R. Gambrich, "How MahāyānaMahāyāna began," *Journal of Pali and Buddhist Studies* 1 (1988):29-46.

8 Of course, that does not mean that Sanskrit Buddhist texts ceased being used by local Buddhists. Kumārajīva himself is a good example who mastered Sanskrit and regarded Sanskrit texts to be better than those in the translation of local languages in terms of faithfulness of doctrinal and literary expression. Archaeological findings of a number of manuscripts of Sanskrit texts in Tarim Basin also attest this.

9 According to his biography in *Biographies of Eminent Monks*, he mastered thirty-six languages. It is said "the credit that Buddhist scriptures and Dharma could be widely disseminated in China must be attributed to him." See the *Gaosheng Zhuang* 高僧傳, T 50, 326c-327a.

his translation of these two texts proved difficult for Chinese Buddhists to understand their doctrines.[10] Based on the way he had paved, Kumārajīva came to re-translate these two texts but with the translation of a commentarial work on the *Pañcaviṁśatisāhasrikā Prajñāpāramitā*, the *Mahāprajñāpāramitopadeśa*, and three Mādhyamika works, the *Mādhyamikacārikā* and the *Śataśāstra*, the *Dvādaśamukha-śāstra*.

As we have known, the *Prajñāpāramitā* literature is precursory and foundational to Nāgārjuna's Mādhyamika Buddhism.[11] From Kumārajīva's biography in the *Biographies of Eminent Monks*, Mādhyamika philosophy must have been brought into Tarim Basin just before his birth.[12] He was excited about this new philosophical thought, with which he wished to follow suit Nāgārjuna to revive the glory of Buddha's *Saddharma* (right and wonderful Truth) in the world (actually in China, as his unexpected captive life occurred later.) Yet, Nāgārjuna himself must not have known the *Lotus Sūtra*. All his works available either in Sanskrit or in the Chinese translation now have no trace of the noted doctrine of *ekayāna* of the *Lotus Sūtra*. Actually, Mādhyamika's dialectical discourse of *reductio ad absurdum* does not require a positive discourse to the mysterious existence of *ekayāna*, which subsumes the three vehicles, wravaka-yāna, pratyeka-buddha-yāna, and bodhisattva-yāna. In addition, the *Lotus Sūtra* relegates the three doctrinal characteristics of the *Prajñāpāramitā* literature, emptiness (*śūnyatā*), signlessness (*nimitta*), and wishlessness (*apranihita*), to be of the beginning stage toward Mahāyāna's ultimate state. By means of prophesying one to attain Buddhahood in the future because of one's earnest adoption of the behavior of dharma-preacher, the *Lotus Sūtra* is more inclined to religious practice than to intellectual sublimation to

[10] Seishi Karashima, *A glossary of Dharmarakṣa's translation of the Lotus Sūtra*, Tokyo: The International Research Institute for Advanced Buddhology, Soka University, 1998. D. Boucher, "Gāndhārī and the Early Chinese Buddhist Translations Reconsidered: The Case of the Saddharmapuṇḍarīkasūtra," *Journal of the American Oriental Society* 118, 4 (Oct. - Dec., 1998): 471-506. Actually, Huiguan 慧觀, one of Kumārajīva's Chinese disciples attested how misleading the Dharmarakṣa's translation had been. "[Hui-] Guang learnt the doctrine of returning to the One-[vehicle] when young. As growing, I was appealed to by its hidden secret of unifying various doctrines. However, the more hard I thought it over, the more difficult the mysterious idea was comprehended. I often faced Mt. Gṛdhrakūṭa to ponder it over; yet, as reading words and sentences, I only had more and more doubts. It was simply caused by the misleading translation that distorted the writing, and absurd expressions that led the right understanding astray." The *Chu Sanzhang Jiji* 出三藏記集 (as abridged as *CSZJJ* hereafter), T55, p. 57 b.

[11] T. R. V. Murti *The central philosophy of Buddhism : a study of the Mādhyamika system*, London; Boston : Unwin Paperbacks, 1955.

[12] When Nāgārjuna lives is controversial among scholars. Lamotte demonstrates that according to Chinese sources, Kumārajīva believed that Nāgārjuna lived in the third century. See his *The Teaching of Vīmalakīrti*, London: Routledge & Kegan Paul, 1976, 14-17. The Chinese accounts of Kumārajiva's view of Nāgārjuna's life being in the third century, See Sengrui's essay, "The Prolegomenon to the Mahāprajñāpāramitodeśa," *CSZJJ*, T 55, 74c-75a, and his "A Clarification of Doubts," *CSZJJ*, T 55, 41c.

attain the perfect enlightenment (*anuttara-samyak- sambodhi*). Moreover, those who attain the perfect enlightenment are not limited to forest-dwelling, radical ascetic monks; instead, they are extended to the four assemblies including devotional laity who wanted to hold, study, chant, transcribe and explain the *Lotus Sūtra*. What the *Lotus Sūtra* shaped Mahāyāna Buddhism lays down is a (Chinese) Buddhist infra-structure wherein to absorb all kinds of Buddhist thoughts and practices.

It is interesting to see how Kumārajīva, essentially as a Mādhyamika advocator, translated and explained two kinds of Buddhist works, the *Prajñāpāramitā* literature and its commentary, and the *Lotus Sūtra*, having different intellectual penchants to the same Chinese audiences, in a short period (401-405 CE) without feeling any doctrinally interpretative inconsistency in them. His acute Chinese disciples certainly noticed it in such blended Buddhism. On being asked questions as to how everyone who is without "essence" can become Buddha as asserted by the *Lotus Sūtra* in the dialectical thought of *Prajñāpāramitā*, he answered them in an ambivalent and unassertive way. That gave way to the rise of the doctrine of *Tathāgata-garbha* in the next stage of Buddhist development in China which is by no means distinctive in Indian Buddhism.[13]

The mission of Kumārajīva's translation and propagation of what he believed in Mahāyāna Buddhism is to disentangle the confusion of his contemporary Chinese Buddhists about the doctrine of *Prajñāpāramitā.* While he successfully completed this mission by the introduction of Indian Mādhyamika Buddhism into China through translation and preaching, the soteriologically mysterious, or the doctrine of *ekayāna*, that every one, regardless of one's status, can attain Buddhahood in the *Lotus Sūtra*, which is more advanced than the intellectual dialectical in the Mādhyamika Buddhism, becomes enigmatic to Chinese Buddhists. With Mādhyamika works alone, an Indian Mahāyānist would argue that one with a dialectical mind, in and of oneself, attains the perfected enlightenment (*anuttara-samyak-sambodhi*) without further ado with doctrines like *ekayāna*. The combination of these two texts, as a result, forms an internal intension and problem–why is the doctrine of Prajñāpāramitā lower than the doctrine of ekayāna in terms of attainment of Buddhahood? Kumārajīva's missionary undertaking in China of the early 4th century had a two-fold effect for the Buddhist development in this critical time. On the one hand, it not only released Chinese Buddhists' understanding of Mahāyāna Buddhism from the trap of the previous indigenous "concept-matching" method, but also cut off their association of Mahāyāna Buddhism with Sarvastivādin Buddhism. On the other hand, it posited a new problem

[13] In spite of the fact that the present textbook of Mahāyāna Buddhism, such as Paul Williams', adds a chapter on *Thatāgata-garbha,* Yi-jing (635-713) noticed that this thought was negligible in India.

from the tension of the *ekayāna* and the *Prajñāpāramitā*. The solution of this problem gave rise to the study of the doctrine and its related texts of *Tathāgata-garba*. Since then, the Buddhist development in China ran in another direction, unlike its Indian counterpart.

To review this process, the paper is divided into three sections highlighting (1) Chinese Buddhists' misperception of Mahāyāna Buddhism with the "concept- matching" method, (2) Kumārajīva's rectification of it with Mādhyamika philosophy and the *Lotus Sūtra* as well and (3) the religious impasse that gave way to the rise of the doctrine of *tathāgata-garbha* in Chinese Buddhism.

1. Chinese misperception of "Mahāyāna" before Kumārajīva

As disclosed by Paul Harrison, the earliest Buddhists who identified their belief with Mahāyāna could be a group of forest-dwelling, radical ascetic monks. Chinese Buddhist elites of the 3rd and 4th centuries who embraced the doctrine of *Prajñāpāramitā* certainly were not of that type. They were inherent aristocracies well-educated with traditional Confucianism and possessed large properties and fortunes.[14] What appealed to them in the idea of *Prajñāpāramitā* was its intellectual "congeniality" with Chinese Metaphysical Learning, i.e., that the enlightened mentality of the Buddha is similar, and thereby instilled ideas, to a then fervent issue under discussion–what the ultimately sublimed knowledge in sage hood was like. In the mode of thinking called "concept-matching" in which "mahā" as the "Great" is referred to the metaphysical vis-a-vis "Hīna" as the "little" as referred to the verbal or the elementary, "Mahāyāna" used in this Chinese sense is not equivalent to the specific meaning of "Mahāyāna Buddhism" in India. As a result, "Mahāyāna"大乘 could be applied to Sarvastivādin Buddhist monk Saṅghabhadhra,[15] and "Great law" or "*dafa*" 大法 to Sarvastivādin Abhidharma works.[16] Chinese "Mahāyāna" Buddhists were neither concerned about the specific meanings of elementary Buddhist terminologies such as *skandha* (aggregate), *āyatana* (entrance), *dhātu* (hold), etc. (the learning of them appeared to be of "Hīnayāna,") nor about its transcendent practices such as abiding to moral precepts and bearing patience.[17]

---

[14] Eric Zurcher calls them "gentry Buddhists." *Buddhist Conquest of China*, Leiden: E. J. Brill, 1959.

[15] When a Sarvāstivādin monk came to Ch'ang-an, Chinese Buddhists in the city thought that he Buddhism which he was preaching was MahāyānaMahāyāna. GSZ, T 50, 328b. In addition, Dao'an "praised" *Agāmas* for being "*hīnayāna*." He also "praised" the meditational practice of *ānāpāna* to be of Mahāyāna. See my paper, "Early Chinese Buddhist Conception of Hīnayāna." *Taiwan Daxue Lishixi Xuebao* 16 (1991): 63-79.

[16] See Dao'an stated about Abhidharma. "The Abhidharma means the "the great law," *dafa* 大法 in Chinese, The Buddha wanted something through which one could see what the ultimate achievements of the way are, what they appear to be, and what characters they hold, In this sense of transcending, Abhidharma is called "great"." *CSZJJ*, T 55, 72a.

[17] Beidu 杯度, a Mahāyāna monk, was indulgent in hunting and drinking, *GSZ*, T 50, 390b. Even Kumārajīva himself could not keep himself from drinking, which resulted in his abandonment of the priestly life.

However, the close reading of Buddhist texts disturbed Chinese monks about misreading Mahāyāna Buddhism, but they were unable to find a right way out. Dao'an, the most learned monk, for example, associated the *Jñānaprasthāna*, a main Sarvastivādin abhidharmic work, with the *Prajñāpāramitā Sūtra*, which probably is the oddest case in the history of Buddhism. As he said,

> The *Abhidharma[-jñānaprasthāna]* is the garden of dharmas. In Kapilavastu, there were no erudite scholars who did not study the Abhidharma. The boat to be made for crossing the great ocean must be sturdy of structure. Likewise, the text to be formed by exhausting every dharma must be grand in its composition. Therefore, from the beginning, the *Prajñāpāramitā Sūtra* is the voice of all scriptures, the core of the Way. How can one not study it hard! How can one not study it hard! [18]

He even strongly recommended that every Buddhist student carry the *Abhidharmavibhāśā* with him as the primary reference book when reading Buddhist scriptures[19], without knowing that Sarvāstivāda is philosophically incompatible with the dialectical doctrine of *Prajñāpāramitā*.[20]

Kumārajīva's Rectification

To rescue Chinese Buddhists from being trapped in the indigenous concept-matching mode of thinking, Kumārajīva re-translated the *Pañcavimśasāhasṛkā Prajñāpāramitā* and the *Aṣṭasāhasrikā prajñāpāramitā* into Chinese, and along with the translation of the *Pañcaviṁśāhasṛkā Prajñāpāramitā*, its commentarial work, the *Mahāprajñāpāramitodeśa*, on the claim that the work was written by Indian Buddhist saint, Nāgārjuna. Without repeating what I have stated in my previous study on this enormous Buddhist commentarial work (almost a total of one million Chinese characters),[21] I highlight some crucial findings of mine here. (1) The commentary proceeds in Mādhyamika interpretative discourse, therefore the claim of its author as Nāgārjuna has no doctrinal contradiction with Mādhyamika philosophy at all, especially since Nāgārjuna's *Madhyamikakārikā* was cited in it and translated into Chinese later. (2) The work actually is a recording of Kumārajīva's translation and interpretation of the original Sanskrit text and of his answers to attendants' questions. (3) The present work was the final product that had undergone editing by Sengrui, the contemporary amanuensis to the translation, following the Chinese division of the previous *Pañcavimśasahasrikā Prajñāpāramitā* with their titles of chapters (in a moderate revision), and the conventional Chinese commentarial

---

18 *CSZJJ*, T 55, 70a

19 Ibid, 367b.

20 See Paul Williams, "On the Abhidharma Ontology," Journal of Indian Philosophy, 9 (1981):221-57.

21 Pokan Chou, "The Problems of the Authorship of the *Mahāprajñāparamitodeśa: a Re-examination," Taida Lishi Xuebao* 台大歷史學報 34 (Dec., 2004): 281-327.

textual format, in which the exposition was put underneath the text of being exposited. (4) The work is very much like a vibhāśā style. It may explain that Kumārajīva intended to correct the previous Dao'an mistake of associating Sarvāstivādin abhidharmic works with the *Prajñāpāramitā Sūtra*. (5) The detailed explanations of Mahāyāna Buddhist doctrines are given through the textual comparison with the previous Chinese translations, the *Fangguang* 放光 and the *Guangzan* 光讚, of the *Prajñāpāramitā Sūtra* in order to make the, Mahāyāna doctrines stand in their own right while sweeping out the previous mistranslations as well as the previous misunderstanding in the mode of concept-matching thinking. The best witness is Sengzhao's essay "Prajñā has no knowing," which was completed in 404 CE.

Prajñā, as the abridgement of *Prajñāpāramitā* is called, stood for the act of knowing of the Enlightened one, or "Holy Knowledge" *shengzhi* 聖智 in Chinese. In the realization that the knower, the known and the knowing are empty in and of itself, and the constitution of them is in constant change, the knowing of the enlightened one is dynamic without grasping, or being grasped with, a name (or a conceptualized entity). Moreover, in the realization that the knower, the known and the knowing are designated with names for the sake of cognition and communication in the worldly linguistic world, a name in such conventional usage limits the nature of a thing which is named; and, thereby, it is perceived to be what a name stands for and what a name does not stand for. What a thing really is, in the constant flux of factors (or dharmas), internally and externally, is always missed by humanly constructed names or concepts. All these are realized, and thus not hindered, by the Holy (i.e. the Buddha's) Mind (*shengxin* 聖心 in Chinese), which is like a mirror always reflecting a thing as it is in any mode. It dialectically stands between/ beyond "there is" and "there is not" of a thing on its linguistic level and intuits its essentially illusive nature on the ontological level, without being one-sided with the conventional cognition of it. None of languages can apply to how *Prajñā* dialectically acts to know a thing in any mode, and how *Prajñā* is acquired in a certain way. Yet, such holy knowledge must exist and illuminate this deluded world.[22] The essay beautifully grasps the dynamic and dialectical meaning of *pra-* (forward), *-jñā-* (to know), *-pāram-* (over/beyond), and *-itā* (to have gone [the limited scope of designated dharmas or concepts]).[23]

After the publication of the *Mahāprajñāpāramitodeśa* in 405, Chinese

[22] Otherwise, there is the inexistence of the Buddha, which is impossible. Richard Robison translated this essay into English in his *Early Mādhyamika in India and China,* Madison : University of Wisconsin Press, 1967, 212-221. His translation needs re-do.

[23] I completely agree with Xuanzhuang's idea that the five kinds of Sanskrit words are un-translatable into Chinese, or in any language; one of them is this. In English, *prajñāpāramitā* usually is translated to be "transcendent wisdom." However, such English translation loses its dynamic and dialectical dimension.

Buddhists ceased various (mis-)interpretations of *prajñāpāramitā*, i.e. previously called "the five schools and the seven theses." They have since disappeared forever. Yet, in the next year when the *Lotus Sūtra* was (re-)translated into Chinese, Kumārajīva's Order in Chang'an advanced into another doctrinal problem, which lasts in the consequent Chinese Buddhist history.

2. The Place of the doctrine of *Prajñāpāramitā* in the *Lotus Sūtra*

The dynamic and dialectical doctrine of the *prajñāpāramitā* is disclosed in the dialogue between the Buddha and his disciples, Śāriputra, Subhūti, Mahākātyāyna, Mahākaśyapa and Mahāmaudgalyāyana. The teaching in the meeting was finally entrusted by the Buddha to Ānanda, and those who heard the Buddha's teaching. One question arises here.

Though the doctrine of *prajñāpāramitā* is set for bodhisattvas, those who heard the Truth from Buddha are actually śrāvakas in status. To embrace this Mahāyāna Buddhist doctrine as the main theme, the *Lotus Sūtra* contrives the soteriological doctrine of *ekayāna*, while extending the life of Śākyamuni Buddha to be immeasurable, who addresses this salvific doctrine to bodhisattvas of this land and other lands in the past incalculable *kalpas*.[24] As a result, while all these *śrāvakas* were merely "outwardly shown," but "inwardly concealed with bodhisattva-conduct;"[25] they are indeed bodhisattvas in their very nature. Hence, they, like all who heard the Buddha preaching the *Lotus Sūtra*, are prophesied eventually to become buddhas.

Moreover, there is one more doctrinal problem in the *Lotus Sūtra* that has to be settled in relation to the Mahāyāna Buddhist idea of *prajñāpāramitā*. Before the four great śrāvakas–Subhūti, Mahākātyāyna, Mahākaśyapa and Mahāmaudgalyāyana–illustrated their understanding of the doctrine of *ekayāna* as the mysterious, the deepest meaning of the Buddha's teaching with the parable of the Poor Son, they confessed:

"We are the seniors of the saṅgha, old and feeble. We considered ourselves to have attained nirvāṇa and to be incapable of further seeking highest, complete enlightenment, so we did not do so.

It has been a long time since the Bhagavat taught the Dharma in the past. Now we sit with weary bodies and only contemplate emptiness, signlessness, and wishlessness. Neither the bodhisattva teaching, nor the carefree sporting with transcendent powers, nor the pure buddha worlds, nor helping sentient

---

[24] See Chapters XV "Bodhisattvas Emerging from the Earth," and XVI "The Life Span of Tathāgata" of the sūtra.

[25] Leon Hurvitz, tr., *Scripture of the Lotus Blossom of the Fine Dharma*, New York: Columbia UP, 1976, p. 160.

beings attain enlightenment produced any eager desire in us.

Why is this? Because the Bhagavat caused us to leave the triple world and to attain Nirvāṇa. But now we are old and feeble. We did not take even a single thought of pleasure in the Buddha's inspiration of the bodhisattvas to highest, complete enlightenment". [26]

The doctrinal characteristics of *Prajñāpāramitā*—emptiness, signlessness, and wishlessness—are repeated in the *Prajñāpāramitā* literature. They are very similar to the nature of the act of knowing in the enlightened state, as demonstrated in the above-mentioned Sengzhao's essay: how is it possible now to be told that hearers "did not take even a single thought of pleasure in the Buddha's inspiration of the bodhisattvas to highest complete enlightenment?" Here we see a critical and subtle doctrinal switch occuring in Kumārajīva's preaching.

First, Dharma in the above citation is referred to as the doctrine of *ekayāna* subsuming the three vehicles of śrāvaka, pratyekabuddha and bodhisattva. That the *Prajñāpāramitā* literature only discloses the doctrine of bodhisattva is not sufficient.

Second, the main protagonist of the *Lotus Sūtra* is the dharma-preacher who is not inclusively ascribed to Buddhist monks and nuns, or forest-dwelling, radical ascetic monks, but rather to the four devoted assemblies who hold, read, recite, and study the Sūtra, and explain it to everyone. They should worship the Sūtra "with various offerings of flowers, perfumes, necklaces, scented powders and ointments, burning incense, canopies, flags, banners, clothing, or music."[27] Such enthusiastic devotion qualifies them to be "the ambassadors of the Tathāgata," "dispatched by the Tathāgata and carry out the Tathāgata's work."[28] What dharma-preachers need to do after Buddha's parinirvāṇa is "wherever this Sūtra is taught, read, recited, copied, or wherever it is to be found," they "should build a seven-jeweled stūpa of great height and width and richly ornamented. There is no need to put a relic inside,"[29]simply "because...these places are the terraces of enlightenment where all the Buddhas have attained the highest, complete enlightenment, where all the Buddhas have turned the wheel of the Dharma."[30] Mahāyāna Buddhism might have been initiated by a group of sharp-minded, and as suggested by Prof. Paul Harrison, forest-dwelling, and radical ascetic, monks

---

[26] Hereafter I adopt Tsugunari Kubo's and Akira Yuyama's translation of the *Lotus Sūtra* (Berkeley: Numata Center for Buddhist Research and Translation, 2007), since it is closer to traditional Chinese (East Asian) understanding. The translation as cited above is seen its page 79.

[27] Chapter X "The Expounder of the Dharma," ibid., pp. 157-58.

[28] Ibid., p. 158.

[29] Ibid., p. 161.

[30] Ibid., p. 273.

who intended to make knowledge and practice of Mainstream Buddhism more dynamic and dialectic. However, the *Lotus Sūtra* fuels this religious determination by extending to the four assemblies of all social strata a newly claimed doctrine of ekayāna as "the hidden secret of all buddhas" subsuming all kinds of Buddhist gnosis and practices.

Third, the words and expressions of the *Prajñāpāramitā* literature are too illusive and dialectical for readers to grasp the exact meaning of the doctrine. Though the doctrine of *ekayāna* is said to be so mysterious that "no one but the Buddhas can completely know,"[31] the *Lotus Sūtra* cryptically switches the certification of the realization of the mysterious to the cultivation and accomplishment of the four types of religious practice in Chapter 14 "Ease in Practice," in which practitioners, monastics or laity, earnestly tread the bodhisattva discourse, bodily, orally, mentally, and volitionally. As a result, the *Prajñāpāramitā* literature, an intellectually orientated text which gave rise of Mādyamika philosophy in India, makes a concession to the *Lotus Sūtra*, an ecumenically orientated text which powerfully stimulates the Buddhist spread in China. Stūpa as the simultaneous symbol containing buddha's (or buddhas') śarīra and dharmakāya was widely erected in China. Without relegating the doctrine of *Prajñāpāramitā* to be the inferior vehicle, it turns to be "primary," rather than "ultimate," of "Chinese" Mahāyāna Buddhism.

Now let us review the noted event in the recent study of Buddhism whereby Hirakawa's view of the origin of Mahāyāna Buddhism as the result of laity's worship of the stūpa is refuted by Gregory Schopen who argues that the origin of Mahāyāna Buddhism should be attributed to the continued Buddhist tradition of the worship of the book (or in a more precise expression, the Buddhist knowledge). It is only in the *Lotus Sūtra* that the stūpa becomes the worshipped object incorporating *śarīra* and *dharmakāya*.[32] Hirakawa recognizes that his ignorance of the excellence of the doctrine of *Prajñāpāramitā* over the worship of stūpa in the comparison of these two in the *Prajñāpāramitā* literature, makes his advocacy of the worship of stūpa by the laity as the origin of Mahāyāna to be insufficient.[33]

As I said in the beginning of this paper, Schopen, by adopting E. Zürcher's research, figures out that our perception of the origins of Mahāyāna Buddhism might have been effected by Chinese Buddhist conception and reconstruction. As is widely known, Zürcher's, and other Japanese scholars', like Tsukamoto Zenryū's, systematical research on the Buddhist development in China in English stopped at Huiyuan (334-416)[34]. Kumārajīva's Buddhism has not been

---

[31] Ibid., p. 23.

[32] Gregory Schopen, "The phrase 'sa pṛthivipradeśaś caityabhūto bhavet' in the Vajracchedikā: notes on the cult of the book in Mahayana," *Indo-Iranian Journal* 17, 3-4 (1975): 147-181.

[33] Hirakawa Akira, *A History of Indian Buddhism*, tr. by Paul Groner, Honolulu: University of Hawaii Press, 1990, p. 340. Hirakawa's admittance is not in his Japanese original work.

[34] Tsukamoto Zenryū, *A History of Chinese Buddhism: from its introduction to the death of Hui-yüan*, Tokyo: Kodansha, 1979.

systematically studied yet. Questions as to whether Buddhist texts translated and propagated by him were his own, locally popular in Tarim Basin, and the extent to which they were related to the early Mahāyāna Buddhism in India or in Central Asia, are far from a clear understanding up to now. What is known, as far as I know, is that Kumārajīva defined a new road to Mahāyāna Buddhism in China. If, as Gregory Schopen suggests, our perception of the origin of Mahāyāna Buddhism was through the lens of Chinese Buddhism, Hirakawa's view may not be entirely wrong—he only misplaced the worship of stūpa and its related religious practice in the *Lotus Sūtra* from China after the 4th century to India. The main mistake Hirakawa committed, I think, is essentialist. He relied upon later translated Chinese Buddhist materials to "reconstruct" the origin of early Mahāyāna Buddhism. History shows that what emerged in earlier Indian Buddhism would not invariably develop in China, nor what was active in Chinese Buddhism can be traced back to India. The agent, i.e. missionary, as well as his Chinese followers, play a tremendous role in the Buddhist transmission from India to China. Such transmission, unfortunately, is missing with the linkage of what actually occurred in Central Asia and Tarim Basin, whose traces have been almost buried in the past one thousand years during the domination of Muslims over this vast area. The case of Kumārajīva's Buddhism is such a good example . In the next section, I will further reveal the reaction of Chinese Buddhists to the doctrinal tension between *Prajñāpāramitā* and *ekayāna* that Kumārajīva himself hardly resolved. As a result, the Buddhist development in China runs in its own way of selecting doctrines in relation to its concerned issues, but is still within the infra-structure built by Kumārajīva.

3. Harbinger to Further Development of Mahāyāna Buddhism in China

The *Lotus Sūtra* gives an equal opportunity to the monastics and the laity in any social stratification to become Buddhas in the future, as long as they stick to the unific idea of *ekayāna* and the four kinds of bodhisattva's practice. One question arises here: if one is inspired to look for the attainment of buddhahood, such inspiration is a kind of "seed" which is eventually nurtured through various practices to maturation, i.e. to attain buddhahood, or is it simply a sentient feeling in which one tries to avoid suffering? The former is predisposed with a positive cause, and the latter is not.

Sengrui, one of the best disciples of Kumārajīva's and his amanuensis to the translations of many Buddhist scriptures, pressed questions of this kind in Chang'an in retrospect after he read the *Nirvāṇa Sūtra* in Jiankang, the capital of the South Dynasties.

If Kumārajīva could have heard [the Nirvāṇa Sūtra] that the Buddha possesses true self and that all sentient beings are Buddhas by nature, he would surely have felt as if the rays of the sun entered his breast, or as if nectar flowed through his limbs. How do I know? Because (during the sessions in the academy at Ch'ang-an) he was hard pressed with questions, such as: "If the Buddha in and of itself is illusory, who else will be the Founder who teaches knowledge of enlightenment and of meritorious practice of accumulating good karmas?" Or he replies in a roundabout way: "If the Buddha is really illusory, who else is real? If he is really illusory, in what (or whom) does one result, as accumulating good karmas and merits in practice?".. ...

> When (Kumārajīva) was asked, "How is it explained that in this country there was a sūtra previously saying that all sentient beings will become Buddhas?" he answered: "The *Lotus Sūtra* is aimed to demonstrate Buddha's knowledge and insight. Its teaching can be implied that all sentient beings have Buddha nature. Yet, if it indeed states that all sentient beings have Buddha nature, why does it not explicitly state that everyone can become Buddhas? What the *Lotus Sūtra* demonstrates is that there exists the One way (to salvation), which is the Buddha Vehicle, not two or the three vehicles. It does not say that all sentient beings shall become Buddhas. I have neither read such words, nor be positive that it does not occur (in its implication.)[35]

We can see that Kumārajīva was cautious in answering Sengrui's questions, lest he fell into the substantialist error as attacked by dialectical Mādhyamika philosophy. Yet, such an ambivalent and unassertive attitude by him failed to explicitly maintain (1) that there is essence in human nature that will eventually be matured to have one attain buddhahood, (2) whether everyone, including Icchāntikas, those who do not have, or have lost, desire to attain perfect, complete enlightenment (anuttara-samyak-sambodhi), can become a Buddha in the future, (3) what if someone, if any, was not prophesied by Śākyamuni Buddha to become a Buddha? All these questions are not expected in the *Lotus Sūtra* which runs its soteriological parables along with the Buddhist literary traditions of avadāna and vyākaraṇa. Actually, Kumārajīva's ambivalent and unassertive attitude indeed shows him to be a true Mādhyamika follower. However, because of this very intellectual position, he did not directly answer the doctrinal problems in relation to the Lotus Sūtra that inspired his missionary passion to disseminate Buddha's teaching in the world.

If there exists someone who cannot be saved by *dharma* preachers, as stated in the *Lotus Sūtra,* who shall imitate Śākyamuni Buddha to save all

[35] CSZJJ, T55, p. 42, a18-b1. Walter Libenthal once translated this essay, "A Clarification," of Sengrui's into English. See *Sino-Indian Studies,* Vol. V., pt., 2, 1956, 88-99. However, his translation is full of mistakes. I re-translate the relevant passages here.

sentient beings in suffering, then the *Lotus Sūtra* is not a final teaching of Mahāyāna. As Prof. Lopez points out that the *Lotus Sūtra* probably is the most powerful one disseminating Buddhism by a story-telling linkage of parables to Buddhist philosophy,[36] to make intelligible between its fictitious parables and Kumārajīva's detouring rhetoric in the Mādhyamika discourse, that became the undertaking of Chinese Buddhists of successive generations. Not surprisingly, right after the death of Kumārajīva, the *Parinirvāṇa Sūtra* came to the forefront with its doctrine of *Tathāgata-garbha* to explain parables in the *Lotus Sūtra*. The episode in the parable of the Poor Son, "while he [the poor son] was wandering about he gradually started back to his native country,"[37]was precisely explained in this way. What causes the poor son to "start back" to "his native country," i.e. the Mahāyāna state, is his innate Buddha nature.[38]

The positivist belief in the universal and the innate existence of the Buddha seed in the human nature now strengthens, and, of course, twists, absolute devotion in which to propagate Mahāyāna Buddhism that Kumārajīva conceived.

BIBLIOGRAPHY

Ben-ami Scharfstein. eds. *Myths and Fictions,* Leiden. Brill.

Chou Pokan. 1991. *Early Chinese Buddhist Conception of Hīnayāna. Taiwan Daxue Lishixi Xuebao* 16 --*The Problems of the Authorship of the Mahāprajṭāparamitodeśa: a Re-examination," Taida Lishi Xuebao* 台大歷史學報 34 (Dec., 2004)

D. Boucher. 1998. *Gāndhārī and the Early Chinese Buddhist Translations Reconsidered: The Case of the Saddharmapuṇḍarīkasūtra. Journal of the American Oriental Society* 118, 4 (Oct. - Dec., 1998).

Donald Lopez, Jr. 1993. *The Institution of Fiction in Mahāyāna Buddhism*. Schlomo Biderman and

Eric Zürcher. 1959. *Buddhist Conquest of China.* Leiden. E. J. Brill.

Fayun 法雲. *Exposition of the Lotus Sūtra.* 法華經義記. T33,

Gregory Schopen. 1975. *The phrase 'sa prthivipradesas caityabhuto bhavet' in the Vajracchedika : (notes on the cult of the book in Mahayana," Indo-Iranian Journal* 17, 3-4

Grogory Schopen. 2000. *The MahāyānaMahāyāna and the middle period in Indian Buddhism: through a Chinese looking-glass.* .Kyoto. Eastern Buddhist.

Hirakawa Akira. 1990. *A History of Indian Buddhism.* tr. by **Paul Groner.** Honolulu. University of Hawaii Press.

Jonathan A. 2002. *Silk, "What, if anything, is Mahāyāna Buddhism, Numen.*

Lamotte. 1976. *The Teaching of Vīmalakīrti,* London. Routledge & Kegan Paul.

Leon Hurvitz. 1976. tr., *Scripture of the Lotus Blossom of the Fine Dharma.* New York. Columbia UP.

---

[36] Donald Lopez, Jr. argues that Mahāyāna uses parables and philosophy side by side to disseminate Buddhism. See his "The Institution of Fiction in Mahayana Buddhism." In Schlomo Biderman and Ben-ami Scharfstein, eds. *Myths and Fictions,* Leiden: Brill, 1993, 355-388.

[37] Kubo and Yuyama, ibid., p.8. with my modification.

[38] See Fayun's 法雲 explanation in his *Exposition of the Lotus Sūtra,* 法華經義記, T33, p. 634 b.

Paul Harrison. 1987. *Who gets to ride in MahāyānaMahāyāna Buddhism? Journal of International Association of Buddhist Studies* 10,1:67-89.

Paul Williams. 1981. *On the Abhidharma Ontology," Journal of Indian Philosophy*. Tr. Richard Robison. 1967. *Early Mādhyamika in India and China*, Madison. University of Wisconsin Press.

R. Gambrich. 1988. *How MahāyānaMahāyāna began. Journal of Pali and Buddhist Studies.* Seishi Karashima. 1998. *A glossary of Dharmarakṡa's translation of the Lotus Sūtra*, Tokyo. The International Research Institute for Advanced Buddhology, Soka University.

Sengrui. *The Prolegomenon to the Mahāprañṭāpāramitodeśa," CSZJJ*, T 55, 74c-75a, --A Clarification of Doubts. *CSZJJ*, T 55, 41c.

T. R. V. Murti. 1955. *The central philosophy of Buddhism : a study of the Mādhyamika system*, London; Boston. Unwin Paperbacks.

Tsugunari Kubo and Akira Yuyama. 2007. Tr. *Lotus Sūtra.* Berkeley. Numata Center for Buddhist Research and Translation.

W. Idema & E Z rcher, ed.. 1990. *Thought and Law in Qin and Han China.* Leiden. UP.

James Heitzman,"Early Buddhism, Trade and Empire," in *Studies in the Archaeology and Paleoanthropology of South Asia*, New Delhi: Oxford & Ibh Publishing Co.; and Liu Xinru, *Ancient India and Ancient China: Trade and Religious Exchange, AD 1 — 600*, Delhi: Oxford University Press, 1988.

Tsukamoto Zenryū. 1979. *A History of Chinese Buddhism: from its introduction to the death of Hui-yüan.* Tokyo. Kodansha.

Walter Libenthal. 1956. Tr. *A Clarification," of Sengrui's.* Sino-Indian Studies. Vol. V., pt., 2.

18

Kumārajīva: A great contributor to the creation of Chinese Buddhism and the Chinese culture*

Zhu Qingzhi

Introduction

It is well known that the cultural development in ancient China from the Eastern Han 東漢 Dynasty (25-220 CE) to the Northern Sòng 北宋 Dynasty (960-1127 CE) was directly and deeply influenced by Indian culture and civilization. The impact was largely achieved through the dissemination of Indian Buddhism. Without this magnificent religious medium, it is hard to imagine that a foreign culture with a considerably different character could have had such a great influence on the already highly developed and extremely secularized Chinese culture. For this reason, Chinese scholars tend to apply Indian Buddhism to refer to Indian culture or civilization when discussing its influence on Chinese culture. As Professor Ji Xiānlin 季羨林 (1988) once said, "Without studying the impact of Buddhism on Chinese culture, it is impossible to write an authentic history of Chinese culture, Chinese philosophy, or even a history of China." The term "Buddhism" mentioned here does not only refer to the religion *per se*, but to the whole complex of ancient Indian culture and civilization that had been brought by Buddhism into China.

People may wonder: how did Buddhism, the carrier of Indian culture, find its way into China? The languages used for the transmission of Indian Buddhism and Indian culture are mostly from the Indo-European language

* The work described in this paper was fully supported by the grant from the Research Grants Council of Hong Kong Special Administrative Region, China (HKIEd844710/H).

family, while the Chinese language as the essential vehicle of Chinese culture belongs to the Sino-Tibetan language family. The huge typological gap between the languages used in ancient India or Central Asia and Chinese reflects the great underlying difference between Indian and Chinese cultures. Anyone with a little knowledge about this difference will be astonished by the tremendous achievements accomplished by the communication between these two cultures in ancient times. A substantial part of the achievements, fairly speaking, is owed to the enterprise of translating Buddhist texts into Chinese, which lasted for about a thousand years. This enterprise perhaps serves as one of the most spectacular examples of intercultural exchange in human history. During nearly ten centuries, from the Eastern Han 東漢 to the Northern Sòng 北宋, hundreds of Buddhist masters coming from India or Central Asia to China, along with their Chinese assistants, translated thousands of Indian Buddhist scriptures into Chinese. Thereby, they made known to the Chinese people not only Buddhist teachings, but also an extensive and rich set of Indian cultural information, which finally even had effects on their daily life. In this sense, it is reasonable to say that without the translation of Buddhist texts into Chinese, there could have neither been the widespread dissemination of Buddhism in China, nor the establishment of Chinese Buddhism, not to mention the profound influence of Indian culture on Chinese popular culture. Among those honourable Buddhist masters, the most outstanding one is Kumārajīva (344-413 CE) whom we commemorate today.

Chinese Translations of Buddhist Scriptures and their Value for the Studies of History of Chinese Buddhism and Chinese Culture

In order to appreciate the value of Chinese translations of Buddhist scriptures on the history of Chinese Buddhism and Chinese culture, it is necessary to understand firstly the features of these scriptures and secondly the nature of such translation activity.

In comparison to the sacred texts of other religious traditions, the Jewish Torah, the Islamic Qurán and the Christian Bible for example, Buddhist scriptures distinguish themselves by their tremendous quantity, dynamic formats and heterogeneous contents. They cover various domains of knowledge, including philosophy, literature, linguistics, arts, medicine, geography, astronomy, mathematics, engineering, physical education, etc. It can be said that, for the sake of promoting the greatness, boundlessness and all-encompassing nature of Buddha's Dharma, ancient Indian Buddhists transferred almost all the knowledge available to them to illustrate and interpret the doctrines of Buddhism. Since Buddhist scriptures represent a synthesis of the achievements of Indian civilization and cultural development in certain historical periods, their translation into Chinese therefore introduced to the Chinese people not just religious doctrine, but also the civilization and culture of ancient India.

Obviously however, it was not an easy task to translate Indian Buddhist scriptures into Chinese. When Buddhism first arrived in China around the beginning of the Common Era, China herself was already a highly civilized nation, possessing long-established cultural traditions which are supposed to have originated from areas around the Yellow and Yangtze Rivers. The indigenous Chinese culture diverged considerably from the Indian culture in both concepts and language forms. More importantly, in contrast to the ancient Indian culture which was deeply steeped in religious traditions and ascetic practices, the Chinese culture was innately endowed with a secular ethos and comparatively lacking in religious elements from the very start. By the time of the advent of Buddhism, China had witnessed a long period of contention among the so-called "hundred schools of thought" and finally Confucianism, whose emphasis was primarily on social-ethical principles and political orders, had become the orthodox ideology. It is not difficult to imagine how immensely demanding it would have been for the early Buddhist missionaries, who came from Central Asia and India, to carry out their translation activities under such circumstances.

In order to make the Buddhist scriptures comprehensible to the Chinese people, these eminent monks, one after another over generations, endeavoured not only to coin a large number of new words and expressions to render the non-Chinese (Indian) elements in original texts, but also to employ various translation techniques or policies to ensure the level of accuracy of their works. It can be said that if there had been no translation of Buddhist scriptures or widespread dissemination of Buddhism in China, there would neither have been any Buddhist "conquest" of China nor an "Indianization" process of Chinese culture in a later period (see Zücher 1959).

The translation of Buddhist texts into Chinese represents one of the most glorious chapters in the history of cultural exchange between ancient China and the outside world. According to incomplete statistics, the translation process lasted almost one thousand years from the beginning of the Eastern Han 東漢 to the mid-Sòng 宋, and produced more than 2,000 works, altogether over 60 million Chinese characters. Almost no activity in the cultural history of ancient world–except perhaps the translation of the Christian Bible–could be compared with this process. The huge amount of Indian Buddhist scriptures, which contain an extensive body of new knowledge about Indian civilization, covering humanities, social sciences and natural sciences, came into China and greatly transformed the contours and contents of Chinese culture.

In sum, traditional Chinese culture is a pragmatically-orientated one, with predominant emphasis on active engagement in worldly affairs; indigenous Chinese philosophy and worldview are based on the primacy of the material world with relatively few religious elements. The translation of Indian

Buddhist scriptures into Chinese introduced to the Chinese people a brand new outlook which is primarily concerned with salvation and release from the mundane realms (that is, the realms of *saṃsāra*), and therefore totally opposed to its traditional one. The first significant fruit of the interaction between Buddhism and indigenous Chinese ideological traditions was to strengthen the mystery of Taoist philosophy and encourage the metaphysics (*xuanxue* 玄學) to produce around the Wei-Jin 魏晉 period (220-420 CE) as a new philosophical trend. Immediately following this period, Chinese Buddhism, the variant of Indian Buddhism in China, appeared in the Northern and Southern Dynasties (420-589 CE). At the same time, Taoism, a local Chinese religion, became more mature when it came into contact with Buddhism. These developments greatly enriched the spiritual world of Chinese people.

Chinese Buddhism and Indian Buddhism differ clearly from each other as the former is a localized variant of the latter. The differences were mainly caused by the translation of Buddhist scriptures. Tibetan Buddhism, being also a variant of Indian Buddhism, tried to promote the Buddha Dharma in a faithful manner by translating Buddhist texts as Chinese Buddhism did. Yet, Tibetan Buddhism adopted completely different translation strategies by using *zhiyi* 直譯 "metaphrase" or "literal translation" method with much more borrowings from the source language such as loan translations and transliterations, while Chinese Buddhism was inclined to adopt *yiyi* 意譯 "paraphrase" or "free translation". In comparison, the former could maximize the "fidelity," and the latter would inevitably lead to some "distortion,"[1] and thus Chinese Buddhism was the result of this "distortion." Tinted distinctly with secular colours, Chinese Buddhism was the compromising product of salvation-oriented Indian Buddhist philosophy and secularism-oriented traditional Chinese philosophy. Its greatest impact on Chinese culture was to give birth to *Lixue* 理學 in the Sòng Dynasty, which was a newly developed philosophical thought composed of traditional Confucianism, Taoism and Buddhism. In replacement of Confucianism, *Lixue* eventually became a new orthodox thought in China from the Ming 明 Dynasty (1368-1644 CE).

The impact of Chinese translations of Buddhist scriptures on Chinese culture are comprehensive and far-reaching. Previous studies in this area have already shown relevant evidences from different perspectives including philosophy, literature, linguistics, art and medicine. Instead of repeating the familiar examples, in the following paragraphs, I would like to offer a few interesting cases based on my own research.

---

[1] This is due to the differences in the written scripts and the underlying cultural psychologies of the two languages.

Lóng 龍

Lóng 龍, the Chinese "Dragon," has a long history in Chinese culture; recent archaeological discoveries have shown that its existence can be traced back as early as the Hongshān Culture 紅山文化 (fl.4,000-3,500 BCE). The word *lóng* can also be found in *Jiăgŭ wen* 甲骨文 "oracle bone inscriptions" (1,200 BCE). In Xŭ Shen 許慎 (58-147 CE)'s *Shuowen jiĕzi* 說文解字 *"Explaining [Single-Component] Graphs and Analyzing [Compound] Characters,"* the first Chinese character dictionary published in the Eastern Han Dynasty, the explanation for "dragon" reads: "龍，鱗蟲之長。能幽能明，能細能巨，能短能長。春分而登天，秋分而潛淵。" (Roughly it means that a dragon is the king of the scaly species, which can change its appearance in an unpredictable manner.) It was not a real creature, but a cultural totem based on imagination, and as such, the *lóng* 龍 became a symbol of royal or imperial power. From the Wei-Jin 魏晉 period, the cultural image of "dragon" underwent a significant change and entered into people's daily life. In particular, the personification of "dragon" came into use for the first time, appearing in such new images as *elóng* 惡龍 "rampaged or wicked dragon," *lóngw'ang* 龍王 "dragon king" or *hăi-lóngw'ang* 海龍王 "sea dragon king," and *lóngn* 龍女 "daughter of dragon" in Chinese. These new images are all from Chinese translations of Buddhist scriptures. People may wonder: why the unique "Chinese dragons" appeared in Indian works? Or is there the same image in Indian language and culture? It can be traced back to the very beginning that when translating Buddhist texts into Chinese, translators used the indigenous term *lóng* 龍 to correspond with the Indian word *nāga*, "a serpent in general, or especially the spectacled snake, or cobra capella" (Wilson 2011), a image that does not exist in Chinese language and culture. As a result, Indian *nāga* greatly enriched the cultural connotations of the Chinese word "dragon."

The image of "rampaging dragon" can be found in the Chinese translations produced as early as the Three Kingdoms era 三國時代 (220-280 CE). A proper example could be found in *Pusā benyuan jing* 菩薩本緣經 *"Scripture on the Story of His Present and Past Lives of the Bodhisattva"* volume 2, which is traditionally attributed to ZhiīQian 支謙, a master from the tribe of the Greater *Yuezhi* 大月氏 (*Ta Yueh-chih* "Ywati"):

> 譬如惡龍放雹殺穀、如金剛杵摧破大山、如阿修羅王遮捉日月、猶如暴雨漂沒村落、猛盛大火焚燒乾草。是婆羅門，亦復如是，持是惡心，往迦尸城月光王所。(CBETA, T03, no. 153, p. 63, b18-21)[2]

Just like rampaging dragons pouring down hail to ravage grains, the *vajra* destroying great mountains, the king of *asuras* covering the sun and the moon, rainstorms flooding villages, or great fires consuming dry grass, in the same

[2] CBETA stands for the Chinese Buddhist Electronic Text Association, Taipei.

way, this Brahmin, with the evil mind, went to the residence of the Moonlight (*candraprabha*) King in the city of Kāśī.

The earliest occurrence of "dragon king" (*nāga-rāja*) can be found in translations from the Eastern Han Dynasty. In volume 2 of *Xiuxing benqi jing* 修行本起經 *"Scripture on Former Events of the Self-Cultivation [of the Buddha]"* translated by an Indian monk Tan Guo 曇果 and Kang Mengxiang 康孟詳, an immigrant from Kangju 康居, the Sogdian land was described as:

> 國中人民，男女大小，見太子者，或言天人，或言帝釋梵王、天神龍王，歡喜踊躍，不知何神。(CBETA, T03, no. 184, p. 468, b7-9)
>
> People in the country, young or old, male or female, who saw the prince, either said that he was like a god, or said that he was Indra, king of the Brahma-heaven, celestial deity, or dragon king. They were all joyful but did not know what kind of god he actually was.

The image of "a sea dragon king (*sāgara-nāgai-rāja*)" can be initially found in the translations from the Western Jin Dynasty. For instance, in volume 1 of the work *Sheng jing*生經 *"Scripture on the [Previous] Lives [of the Buddha]"* translated by an Indo-Scythian monk named Dharmarakṣa (Zhu Fahu 竺法護), it is said:

> 時，五百人心獨堅固，便望風擧帆，乘船入海，詣海龍王，從求頭上如意之珠。龍王見之用一切故，勤勞入海，欲濟窮士，即以珠與。(CBETA, T03, no. 154, p. 75, c13-16)
>
> At that time, five hundred people were determined to voyage. They sailed into the ocean and visited the sea dragon king, earnestly asking him for the wish-granting pearl. The king was moved because they had reached him by all means, with hearts to help the poor people, and thus he granted their request and gave the Pearl to them.

The image of "daughter of dragon" can be initially found in the translated scriptures in the Three Kingdoms era, such as the word *lóngn* 龍女in volume 3 of the afore-mentioned work *Pusā benyuan jing* 菩薩本緣經. The paragraph is:

> 菩薩往昔，以恚因緣墮於龍中，受三毒身：所謂氣毒、見毒、觸毒。……常爲無量諸龍所遶，自化其身而爲人像，與諸龍女共相娛樂。(CBETA, T03, no. 153, p. 68, b29-c5)
>
> In the past, the bodhisattva fell amid the dragons in consequence of his hatred, and suffered from the three basic evil afflictions.. .. .Often surrounded by the unlimited dragons, he transformed himself into a human form and rejoiced with the female dragons.

Afterwards, these new and plebeian figures became the co-stars, even the leading characters in Chinese folklore, popular narratives, paintings, dramas and so on and accompanied the Chinese people in their history even till today.

The Peacocks Fly to the Southeast 孔雀東南飛

"The peacocks fly to the southeast" is the first verse of *Gushī wei Jiāo Zhòngqīng qī zuò* 古詩爲焦仲卿妻作"*An ancient poem written for* Jiāo Zhòngqīng 's wife,"[3] a famous long narrative folk song in Chinese literature history, and has the function of *qixing* 起興" suggestive of "The poem tells a tragic love story of a young couple, Jiāo Zhòngqīng 焦仲卿, a minor official of local government in Southeast China, and his wife Liu Lanzhī 劉蘭芝. After marrying Zhòngqīng and living with the Jiao family, Lanzhi did very hard housework day after day. But unfortunately her contribution was not recognized by her mother-in-law, who later forced her to return to her parent's home. Lanzhi's mother and elder brother proposed to arrange another marriage for her but she refused it. After discussion, and out of desperation the young couple determined to commit suicide for love; and they were transformed into a pair of mandarin ducks (*yuanyang* 鴛鴦) after death. This poem is believed to be composed in the Wei-Jin period. It left us a few questions: Peacocks did not originate in China, but why did they appear in the Chinese folk song? Why would a couple who committed suicide for love be transformed into a pair of mandarin ducks? And more importantly, why was this love story so similar to an Indian one that appears many times in the Buddhist scriptures? The following is the brief version of this story found in *Zhong be nqi jing* 中本起經 volume 2 translated by Kang Mengxiang 康孟詳 in the Eastern Hān Dynasty. The context of the story is as follows: there were countries arguing endlessly with one another about the theory of "Love is the root of all evil" put forward by Śākyamuni. As far as this matter was concerned, the king sent the officers to visit Śākyamuni who then told them a story:

> [佛告大臣：] "譬如有人，父母終亡，妻子死盡，財沒縣官。此人憂惱，可堪勝不？"大臣對曰："審如尊教。"又言大臣："古昔有人居貧窮困，而其娶婦得富家女，嬾墮無計，日更貧乏。家困餉饋，欲奪更嫁。妻聞家議，便以語夫：'我家勢強，必當奪卿，當作何計？'夫聞婦言，將共入房：'今欲與汝共死一處。'即便刺婦，還復自刺。"佛告那利繩："恩愛相殺，何但憂悲？"(CBETA, T04, no. 196, p. 160, a23-b5)

> [The Lord told the minister,] "For example, if a man lost his parents, wife and fortune, would he be worried and annoyed?" The officer replied, "Yes, as what you said." Śākyamuni went on telling the minister, "Once upon a time there was a poor man who married a rich girl. He was too lazy to make a living and eventually could not support the family. Without other choices, the girl's family wanted to get the girl back and select another husband for her. When she learnt about their plan, the girl said to her

[3] Another English title of the poem is "The southeast fly, the peacock."

husband, "My family is so powerful that I will definitely be taken away from you, what shall we do?' Hearing what she said, the man holding her went to the room and said, 'I will die with you together.' As soon as he finished talking, he stabbed his wife to death and then committed suicide." The Buddha then said, "Isn't it terribly sad that people kill each other because of love?"

Peacocks and mandarin ducks as symbols of love or reincarnation of lovers were frequently used in Buddhist Scriptures at that time.

As everyone knows, after the Han Dynasty, when Buddhism was introduced to China, the Chinese people often drew some narrative motifs from the stories in Indian Buddhist scriptures. Therefore, we have reason to suggest that this poem may have been profoundly influenced by the Buddhist scriptures (see Zhū 1994).

Jinlian 金蓮

In feudal China, women had the custom of foot binding. The small feet after binding were known as *jinlian* 金蓮 "golden lotus" or *sāncùn-jīnlián* 三寸金蓮 "three-inch golden lotus." The direct source of the term *jinlian* is believed to come from a story recorded in *Nanshā* 南史 *"History of the South Dynasties"*: The sixth Emperor Xiao Baojuān 蕭寶卷 of Qi 齊 Dynasty (479-502 CE) covered a floor with blossoming lotuses made of gold. As he watched his beloved Concubine Pan (潘妃) stepping on it and walking back and forth, he explained, "This is that [at] every step grows a lotus" (此步步生蓮華也). What did he mean? The fact was that Emperor Xiao was a fanatical Buddhist, and he was portraying a story of the Buddha's mother, Māyā, being a daughter of a deer in her past life. This story is commonly seen in Chinese translations of Buddhist scriptures, and the following is the version in *Liudu ji jing* 六度集經 *"Sūtra on the Collection of the Six Perfections"* traditionally ascribed to Kāng Senghui 康僧會 in the Wu 吳 of the Three Kingdoms era.

.. .. .. 母終神遷，應爲梵志嗣矣。其靈集梵志小便之處，鹿舐小便，即感之生。時滿生女，梵志育焉。年有十餘，光儀庠步，守居護火。女與鹿戲，不覺火滅。父還恚之，令行索火。女至人聚，一躇步處一蓮華生。火主曰："爾遶吾居三匝，以火與爾。"女即順命。華生陸地，圍屋三重。行者住足，靡不雅奇。斯須宣聲聞其國王，王命工相相其貴賤。師曰："必有聖嗣，傳祚無窮。(CBETA, T03, no. 152, p. 14, b3-11)

...After the mother passed away she was to be reincarnated as the child of a Brahmin. Her soul convened at the place where the Brahmin urinates. A deer came to lap up the urine and immediately got pregnant. Then, she gave birth to a girl who was later raised by the Brahmin. When the girl was in her teens, she was asked to guard the kindling. One day, she played happily with the deer and did not notice that the fire had gone out. Upon knowing this, her father was furious and sent her out to collect fire. As she walked to the village, at every step she took, a lotus grew under her feet. The owner of the tinder said to her, "If you circle my house three times, I will give you the kindling." The girl agreed, and when she finished, there were three layers of blossoming lotuses around the house. The passersby stopped and were amazed by what they saw. Shortly afterwards, the king learnt about the miracle and asked the fortuneteller to predict the girl's future, and the fortuneteller professed, 'She will give birth to a majestic son, and the reign could last endlessly.'"

From then on, *jīnlián* 金蓮 "golden lotus" was often used to represent beautiful women or their dainty bound feet in Chinese literature (See Zhu 1992b).

I. Kumārajīva's Translations and His Major Contributions Towards Chinese Buddhism

In the Chinese Buddhist tradition, the history of translation of Buddhist scriptures is usually divided into three stages: *Guyi* 古譯 "Ancient Translation", which generally covers the period of Late Han, Three Kingdoms and the Western Jin Dynasty *Jiuyi* 舊譯 "Old Translation", which was during the period of Eastern Jin, Northern and Southern Dynasties and Sui 隋 Dynasty; and *Xinyi* 新譯 "New Translation", which was during the T'ang and Sòng period. The translators who named their stage as *Xinyi* and others as *Guyi* and *Jiuyi*, claimed that this was the most contributive one among the three; however, this viewpoint needs to be re-examined today.

Guyi is the preliminary stage of Buddhist scripture translation. In this period, the translators, most of whom were foreign monks coming from Western Region, in general were not proficient in Chinese, and they were not able to present unique Buddhism or Indian concepts into appropriate Chinese expressions. The translators applied relatively "primitive" or "literal" translation techniques, and the scripture translation is rather rough and unrefined. As a result, on the one hand, in the translation works there was a great quantity of transliterations, calques, expressions, and even sentences (or sentence structure) coming from the source languages which were very difficult to understand for native Chinese people; on the other hand, in the translation texts there were so many vernacular elements which are traditionally only appropriate for use in the spoken language than in written language. Besides, the scripture's content were not fully translated: only excerpts of chapters, sections (such as *Jātaka*), or sometimes anthologies (e.g. Ān Shigao 安世高's works T150 and T101 as Paul Harrison 1997 and 2002 has observed) from the original texts were translated.

Jiuyi appeared three hundred years after Buddhism came to China. More shortcomings were found in the ancient translations, and the old translation style did not suffice to meet the increasing demands for dissemination of Buddhism. A new translation style developed due to practical needs. Based on paraphrasing, the scripture translation of *Jiuyi* became smoother and more refined than *Guyi*. Instead of extraction, completeness became one of the aims of translation, and more texts were translated in full versions.

The latest generation of translators, with Xuanzang 玄奘 as the most famous representative, believed that *Jiuyi* was just another extreme of *Guyi*. While *Jiuyi* overemphasized the writing fluency, it adversely affected the translation accuracy. These translators combined three criteria (*xin* 信 "accuracy," *da* 達 "comprehensibility," and *ya* 雅"elegance") into a new translation style which they called *Xīnyi*. Undoubtedly, this new style fostered the development of translation theory. *Xinyi* required that translated scriptures should conform to the originals in content and presentation format. In both, the translating process and its results, the translation of Buddhist scriptures became well-organized and programmed. The translated texts should be capable of being re-worked into the original writings and thereby fulfill the requirement of *xin* "accuracy"; however, it lost the natural beauty and vitality of *Jiuyi* due to the mechanical nature of translation. The Buddhist scriptures translated in the *Xinyi* stage were so refined (or rigid) and mechanical that it went beyond the comprehensibility and aesthetics of the general public. Although Buddhist scripture translations with the largest proportion, an expanded content, and the widest scope (including scriptures like realism from Mahāyāna and Yogācāra, and scriptures of Vajrayāna Buddhism) were among the three stages produced during the period of *Xinyi*, perhaps it brought the least influence to the development of Chinese Buddhism and culture. To the current and future generations, the impact of the scriptures translated by Xuanzang and his followers was much lesser than those of the *Jiuyi* stage, and furthermore, there obviously is some clear link between the stylized and aristocratic *Xinyi* and the complete development of *Chán* School 禪宗 in Chinese Buddhism, which is characterized by the exclusion of scriptures and pursuit of the Sudden Enlightenment. This indicates the beginning of the declining tendency of Chinese Buddhism.

To conclude, a huge amount of scriptures were translated in both the *Jiuyi* and the *Xinyi* stages; in terms of the transmission of Buddhism and Indian culture in China, and the influence of Buddhism on Chinese culture, the period of *Jiuyi* is considered to be the most important and contributive stage. During this period, the translation method of paraphrase, that was much more suitable to the Buddhist text translation than metaphrase, was completely mature and commonly adopted by translators. More and more new words and expressions corresponding to Chinese language structure and usage were created; translations of the unique elements in Indian original scriptures were more vivid and fluent. With the improvement of translation techniques and strengthening of translation ability, some important Buddhist scriptures were for the first time translated in full version. These bulky scriptures include the *Cháng āhán jīng* 長阿含經 *"Dīrghāgama-śāstra"* (T1, 22 volumes), the *Zhōng āhán jīng* 中阿含經 *"Madhyamāgama-śāstra"* (T26, 60 volumes), the *Zōng āhán jīng* 增壹阿含經 *"Ekottarāgama-śāstra"* (T125, 51 volumes), and the *Zōng āhán jīng* 雜阿含經 *"Saṃyuktāgama-śāstra"* (T99, 50 volumes) from Mainstream Buddhist traditions; early scriptures from the *Mahāyāna* tradition like the *Dā fangguangfo huayan jāng* 大方廣佛華嚴經 *"Buddhāvataṃsaka-mahāvaipulya-sūtra"* (T278, 60 volumes), the *Dā banniepan jīng* 大般涅槃經 *"Mahāparinirvāṇa-sūtra"* (T374, 40 volumes), the *Moh banruo boluomi jīng* 摩訶般若波羅蜜經 *"Mahā-prajñā-pāramitā-sūtra"* (T223, 27 volumes), the *Dàfandeng Dā ji jīng* 大方等大集經 *"Mahā-saṃnipāta-sūtra"* (T397, 60 volumes), the *Zhengfa niānchu jīng* 正法念處經 *"Saddharma-smṛty-upasthāna-sūtra"* (T721, 70 volumes), and the *Fó běnxīng ji jīng* 佛本行集經 *"Abhiniṣkramaṇa-sūtra"* (T190, 60 volumes); important *vinaya* texts of different Buddhist schools like the *Sìfēn lü* 四分律 *"Dharmagupta-vinaya"* (T1428, 60 volumes), the *Wǔfēn lü* 五分律 *"Mahàsàsaka-vinaya"* (T1421, 30 volumes), the *MóhēSēngqī l* 摩訶僧祇律 *"Mahāsaṅgha-vinaya"* (T1425, 40 volumes), the *Shīsóng l* 十誦律 *"Sarvastivāda-vinaya"* (T1435, 61 volumes); and other important commentarial texts like the *Dāzhīdù lùn* 大智度論 *"Mahāprajñāpāramitā-śāstra"* (T1509, 100 volumes), and the *Āpīt'n pīpḍshā lùn* 阿毘曇毘婆沙論 *"Śāriputrābhidharma-śāstra"* (30 volumes), etc. In these translated scriptures, Buddhist doctrines and philosophy, as well as Indian culture and civilization, are presented in a more complete and comprehensive manner. Most translated passages were smooth, fluent and authentic, with many vernacular elements, as well as literary flavour. The translation was welcomed by the common or less-educated Chinese people; it was widely disseminated in Chinese society, and eventually influenced the Chinese culture while indeed they were comparatively lacking in accuracy.

The success of *Jiuyi* was accomplished with various trials of exploration and practice, which occurred during the *Guyi* stage from which the method of *yiyi* "paraphrase" was developed with various experiments. Based on the previous experience, initiators and leaders of *Jiuyi* proposed a new set of translation techniques and methods, and put them into practice, therefore developing a new stage of translation. One of them is Kumārajīva, the greatest Indian Buddhist master of the stage coming from Kucha 庫車 (*Kucāna*).

Kumārajīva, known as the Jiomu Luoshi 鳩摩羅什 in Chinese, was born in Kucha on the northern branch of the Silk Road in 344. His father (Kumārāyaṇa) was a Buddhist priest, and his mother was the princess of the nation. Kumārajīva followed his mother to renounce the secular life *(pravrajyā)* at the age of seven, studied with local Buddhist scholars in Kapisi at nine, and discussed with scholars of various nations in the Western Regions and learned from each other at twelve. Being a learned Buddhist, Kumārajīva returned to Kucha and preached sermons for over twenty years. Kumārajīva came to China in 385, first reaching Liángzhou 涼州 (today's Wuwei 武威 City of Gansu 甘肅 Province in Northwestern China) and lived there for the next seventeen years. During his stay in Liángzhou, Kumārajīva acquired knowledge of the Chinese language and culture. This established the fundamentals for him to become a great scholar in languages and cultures of India and China, and in the history of Buddhist scripture translation as well.

In 401, Kumārajīva came to Ch'ang-an 長安 on the invitation of the King Yáo Xing 姚興 from the Kingdom of Late Qin 後秦 (384-417 CE). He started translating Buddhist scriptures in the following year. According to the *Taishō Shinshū Daizōkyō* from Japan, Kumārajīva worked on the largest quantity of translations at his time: he translated a total of 51 scriptures, 278 volumes, altogether about 2,224,000 Chinese characters (previously, Dharmarakṣa from the Western Jin Dynasty translated a total of 93 scriptures, 197 volumes, about 1,576,000 characters). One of his significant contributions towards Chinese Buddhism was that he proposed paraphrase as the main translation method of Buddhist scriptures and developed the new translation stage. In addition, he opened the era of the Buddhist localization, nurturing local Chinese scholars with Indian Buddhist knowledge.

As mentioned above, the translated scriptures were rough and unrefined in reading at the stage of *Guyi* for two reasons: (1) translation method; and (2) translators' Chinese competence. Translators from various nations in the Western Regions adopted the existing translation techniques of Buddhist scriptures, and worked on the translation mostly with the method of transliteration. The process involved switching between the languages in the same family or group (e.g. Indo-European languages or Indo-Iranian languages), which usually shared similar phonological system, words and structure of sentences as well as similar alphabetic writing and cultural background. Thus, those special conceptual terms were handled with transliteration in most cases, or in other words, the target language is used to borrow those specific words and expressions, even sentences from source languages easily and directly. However, this method did not work when dealing with Chinese translations. Besides, there were two aspects regarding the Chinese proficiency of foreign translators. The first aspect was concerned with the difficulties in translating Buddhist scriptures into Chinese. The difficulties came from the cultural differences between India and China, as the Chinese expression tools had not been well-developed to translate the Buddhist scriptures and cultural meanings accurately. Another aspect is that translators in general were not very proficient in Chinese: they were not familiar with the characteristics of Chinese, and they did not comprehend the mentality of Chinese-speaking people (in comparison with their native languages). The foreign translators did not understand that Chinese was a typical analytical language without the inflected nature of their mother tongue; they did not understand that Chinese words were a form of ideogram with both audio and visual codes. Therefore, the amount of Chinese Buddhist translations was comparatively small in the period of *Guyi*, and also the translation quality was relatively poor.

Paraphrase method was adopted as early as in Kang Mengxiáng 康孟詳's translation more or less from the late Eastern Han Dynasty. Zhi Qian 支謙 and Kang Senghuii 康僧會 from the Three Kingdoms period, and Dharmarakṣa and Faju 法炬 (*Dharmōlkā) from the Western Jin Dynasty (especially in the translation of the *benyuán* 本緣 "*Avadāna*" scriptures), also adopted the paraphrase method and even presented the translated scriptures in a literary style. As the next generation of immigrants from the Western Regions, these translators studied both Indic languages and Chinese from the time they were born. They were able to adopt the paraphrase method sometimes because of their high proficiency of Chinese language and mastery of Chinese cultural knowledge. However, the entire style of these translators maintains the metaphrase tradition of An Shihkao 安世高 and Lokakṣema.

The greatness of Kumārajīva is that he was the first person who adopted the paraphrase consciously. Kumārajīva addressed the principle of 曲從方言而趣不乖本 "[language should] submit to the local one (namely Chinese), but meaning preserves to originals" (see the Fahua zongyāo-xu 法華宗要序 "Preface of *The Essentials of Fahua Sect or Tien Tai Sect*" written by Huiguan 慧觀, a student and assistant of Kumārajīva, T2145, p. 57, b8-9) and applied this principle to his translation work, thereby exerting influences on translators of the same period and subsequent generations. "Submission to local language" requires translators to follow the structure and usage of Chinese language, bringing in Hàn cultural characteristics and reading fluency simultaneously, but not solely to reflect characteristics of the original scriptures in the stage of *Guyi*. "Preservation to originality" requires translators to retain the main points of the original scriptures. Kumārajīva applied this principle into the translations of the scriptures not only like the *banyuán* 本緣 division (e.g. *Dā Zhuāngyánlṣn-jing* 大莊嚴論經 "**Sūtrālaṅkāra-śāstra*" and *Zhòngjīng zhuān Zápīyú* 眾經撰雜譬喻 "*Avadāna*," etc.) which is considered to belong to the Classical Indian literature, but also like the *bānruò* 般若 "*Prajñāpāramitā*" division of *sūtra-piṭaka* (e.g. the *Móhē bānruò bōluómì jāng* 摩訶般若波羅蜜經 "*Mahā-Prajñāpāramitā-sūtra*," *Jīngāng bānruò bōluómì jīng* 金剛般若波羅蜜經 "*Vajracchedikā-prajñāpāramitā-sūtra*" and *Āmítuó jīng* 阿彌陀經 Shorter *Sukhāvatīvyūha-sūtra*, etc.) and the *abhidharma-piṭaka* (e.g. the *Zhōng-lùn*, "*Mūlamadhyamaka-kārikā*," the *Bi lùn* 百論 "*Śata-śāstra*," and the *Shī'èr mén lùn* 十二門論 "*Dvādaśamukha-śāstra*," etc.) In addition, he also revised the existing translated scriptures, such as the *Miāof liánhuā jīng* 妙法

蓮華經 *"Saddharma-puṇḍarīka-sūtra"* (previously translated by Dharmarakṣa) and *Wéimójié su shuō jīng* 維摩詰所說經 *"Vimalakīrti-nirdeśa-sūtra"* (previously translated by Zhi Qian), and announced paraphrase as a breakthrough and the most advanced method of Buddhist scripture translation history.

Why did Kumārajīva stand out among various eminent Buddhist priests and scholars, and become the greatest master at the time? There were a lot of factors to explain this phenomenon. Most importantly, as a foreign priest from the Western Regions and being knowledgeable in original Buddhist scriptures, Kumārajīva had acquired an admirable mastery of Chinese language, and discovered the most scientific and efficient methods of Sanskrit-Chinese code switching.

Kumārajīva left Liángzhou in 401, came to Ch'ang-an 長安, capital of the Kingdom of Late Qin 後秦, and presided over the first official translation centre of Buddhist scriptures in Chinese history. As the second important contribution to Chinese Buddhism, he put translation into practice, and taught a number of gifted disciples well-versed in both Chinese and Indian Buddhist lore. These scholars are Dāoshēng 道生, Sēngzhāo 僧肇, Sēngruì 僧叡, Dāohéng 道恒, Tányāng 曇影, Huìguān 慧觀, Huìyǎn 慧嚴, Dāoróng 道融, Sēngqì 僧契, Sēngqiān 僧遷, Fǎqīn 法欽, T'an Wúchèn 曇無讖, Sēngdǎo 僧導, Sēngyè 僧業, and Sēngsōng 僧嵩, etc. generally named as *Shímén Bājùn* 什門八俊 (eight intellectuals of Kumārajīva School), *Shímén Sìshèng* 什門四聖 (four saints of Kumārajīva School), and *Shímén Shízhé* 什門十哲 (ten philosophers of Kumārajīva School). As the first generation of Buddhist scholars receiving local education, these disciples took an active role in disseminating Buddhism in China (for example, Sēngzhāo published a series of important commentaries and treatises including *Zhù wéimójiéjāng* 注維摩詰經 *"Annotation to the Wéimójié jāng [Vimalakīrti-nirdeśa-sūtra],"* *Jāngāngjāng zhù* 金剛經注 *"Annotation to the Jāngāng jāng [Vajracchedikā-prajñāpāmitā-sūtra],"* *Bǎzāng lùn* 寶藏論 *"On the treasure of Buddha's law,"* *Zhào lùn* 肇論 *"The theory of Sēngzhào,"* etc.) and fostering localization of Indian Buddhism in China. Applying paraphrase into the translated scriptures, their works contain Chinese local style and laid the foundation of Chinese Buddhism or even East Asian Buddhism.

The dialogue between Dāoxuān 道宣 and Lù Xuanchàng 陸玄暢 from the T'ang Dynasty may help us to understand the contribution of Kumārajīva's translations to the transmission of Buddhism in China:

> 南山律師嘗問天人陸玄暢云："什師一代所翻之經，至今若新，受持轉盛，何耶？"答云："其人聰明，善解大乘；已下諸人，並皆俊乂，一代之寶也。絕後光前，仰之所不及。故其所譯，以悟達爲先，得佛遺寄之意也。"

> The *Vinaya* Master of Nánshān (viz. Dāoxuān) asked Lù Xuánchāng who was a celestial being, "Master Kumārajīva's translations had been

circulated since long time ago; why are his works still in fashion until now? For what reasons is the number of readers still increasing?" Lù replied, "He was intelligent, and well comprehended the theories of *Mahāyāna*. His students were all famous scholars and elites of the time who ranked at the top of society. Their achievements are unprecedented and unrepeatable. I respect him and his followers, and I can never go beyond their scholarship standard. Therefore, the priority of their translating is to express clearly and correctly the ideas of Buddha which are conserved in the original Buddhist scriptures [without textualism]."

II. The Contribution of "Old Translations" towards Chinese Culture under the Leadership of Kumārajīva

The stage of *Jiuyi* "old translations" is the golden period in the history of translation of Buddhist scriptures into Chinese, and also the period which witnessed the most significant influence of Buddhism in China. It boosted the localization or indigenization of Buddhism and laid the foundation of Chinese Buddhism. It was during this time that the influence of Buddhism on Chinese culture started to yield tangible fruits and had more concrete representations. The establishment of the *gŭdài báihuà* 古代白話"ancient written Vernacular Chinese" and *gŭdài báihuàwén* 古代白話文 "ancient written Vernacular Chinese writing," is one of the examples that illustrate how the stage of *Jiuyi*, with Kumārajīva as its representative, contributed to the development of Chinese culture.

The earliest history of script and script writing in China can be traced to the Shāng 商 Dynasty (fl.1,600-1,100 BCE), where the augurs kept the divination records with the *jiăgŭ wénzì* 甲骨文字 (lit. "script or character written on oracle bone"). The demand for script and script writing led to the development of a literary language. Based on the colloquial language from the Zhōngyuán 中原 (lit. "Centre Plains," the area centered by Xiányáng 咸陽 of Shūnxī 陝西Province and Luòyán 洛陽 of Hénán 河南 Province in North China), literary language was established in the *Chūnqiū* 春秋 "Spring and Autumn Periods" (770-256 BCE). Until the *Zhànguó* 戰國 "Warring States Period" (255-221 BCE), books of philosophy, history, and literature were mostly written in this language. However, most books were burned and destroyed during the United War for the establishment of the Qín 秦 Dynasty (221-206 BCE) under the order of Emperor Qín shĭhuáng 秦始皇 (lit. Qín's first emperor). When the Hān 漢 Dynasty (206 BCE-220 CE) began, people's daily life returned to peace. The intellectuals were filled with nostalgic emotions, and they tried to restore the ancient culture. Scriptures from the past were re-discovered, re-recorded[4], and became classics; their language became the standard of literary writing

[4] Scriptures in the Hān Dynasty is divided into two kinds, *gūwén* 古文 "documents written in ancient characters" and *jīnwén* 今文 "documents written in current characters."

language. During the establishment period of classics, namely the Warring States Period, literary language and colloquial language were reputed to be closely related to each other: the development of literary language correlates with that of colloquial language. The separation of literary language and colloquial language lasted from the Hān Dynasty to the May Fourth Movement in 1919. No matter how colloquial language changes and develops, literary language is still retained with the basic characteristics from the pre-Qín 先秦 period. This kind of literary language is called *wény'an* 文言 (lit. "writing's language" or "language used in writings"), the language in which most official documents and scholastic writings were composed along the Chinese history, and the writings in *wr̄ny'an* 文言 is called *wény'an-wr̄n* 文言文 (lit. "article written in *wény'an* 文言). In the May Fourth Movement, a leader of the Movement, Hú Shì 胡適 and other intellectuals opposed the *wény'an-wén*, as it brought about a huge increase of illiterate population, blocked the transmission of knowledge, and hindered the development of Chinese society. They proposed reform with the idea of *wǒshǒu xiě wǒkǒu* 我手寫我口 (lit. "[with] my hand [I] write [what] my mouth [says])." *Wény'an* was then replaced by a kind of literary language closer to the colloquial language, that is, the *báihuà* 白話 (lit. "verbally unrefined language"), literary language derived from the colloquial language, which is called *xiàndài-báihuà* "modern written vernacular Chinese" in order to distinguish it from *gūdài-báihuà* 古代白話 "ancient vernacular Chinese". Further, *wény'an-wén* was also replaced by *xiāndāi báihuā-wén* (lit. "article written in *xiāndāi báihuā-wén*), a new form or style of Chinese writing.[5]

As a form of writing, the written vernacular Chinese was not created only during the May Fourth Movement. Before the time, as agreed by most modern scholars, another kind of literary language was already developed no later than the Late T'ang 晚唐 period (fl.836-907 CE); however, this kind of literary language was mainly used in the folk literature, such as popular narratives, known as *biànwén* 變文 (lit. "transformation texts"), in the Late T'ang and the Five Dynasties, as well as fiction and *xìqǒ* 戲曲 "Chinese dramas" in the Sòng and Yuán Dynasties. In Míng and Qīng Dynasties, the acceptance of such a kind of written Vernacular Chinese increased and more and more intellectuals wrote their works in the Vernacular Chinese. However, this language was only used in popular literature (see Mair 1988a, b) and that is why this kind of literature is called *báihuà-wénxué* 白話文學 (lit. *báihuà* literature) in China.

The Vernacular Chinese and its writing before the May Fourth Movement is usually regarded as *gūdai-báihuà* 古代白話 or *gū-báihuà* 古白話, and *gūdài báihuà-wén* 古代白話文 (both hereinafter referred to as the AWVC) by modern

[5] As Vernacular Chinese modifies according to the colloquial language, this literary language is more easily acquired and understood by illiterates or semi-literates. On the contrary, Classical Chinese rejects against the literary language, resulting in a long period of language acquisition or incapability of understanding. In reality it is a language adopted by minority.

scholars.[6] There is no doubt at all that the *xiàndài-báihuà* and *xiàndài báihuà-wén* (both hereinafter referred to as the MWVC) are relatively closely related with the AWVC. The difference between them is very clear, that the former is rather loosely related to *wény'an-wén*, while the latter is related to it much more closely and directly (see Norman 1988: 109). The MWVC is the written form of modern Chinese, that is, its basis is current spoken Chinese, especially *Pūtōnghuà* 普通話 (lit. common speech) or *Guóyū* 國語 (lit. national language).[7] If *wény'an* in the post-Hàn period is regarded as a kind of "dead language," the MWVC belongs to a kind of "living language." It is "living" because almost of all the grammatical elements of the language are living in spoken Chinese. In contrast, the AWVC is very different although both share the same word *báihuà*. To all appearances it mixes the characteristics of *wény'an* with those of vernacular spoken Chinese (namely *wén bái jiāzá* 文白夾雜 in Chinese) in vocabulary and grammar. It contains elements of current colloquial language, and grammar and vocabulary which have disappeared in current conversations. The traditional elements, however, were not temporarily acquired by the writers but from the literary language, i.e. *wény'an-wén* of the time. As a result, the AWVC is not a completely "living" language but a mixture of colloquial language and *wény'an*. To make a further deduction, I would like to say that the basis of the AWVC is not any kind of spoken languages but *wény'an*, a dead language. To put it another way, it is not a written form of the spoken language of a certain period, but a vernacularized form of *wény'an* or *wény'an-wén*.[8] It is very important to understand this feature of the AWVC.[9]

The next question is: under the cultural environment of Classical Chinese being the standardized literary language, how was the AWVC formed with the mix of Classical Chinese and Vernacular Chinese elements? Or more simply, how did the mixture of Classical Chinese and Vernacular Chinese

---

6 In the ancient times, different from the *wényán-wén*文言文 "Classical Chinese" with the characteristic of inner unity, AWVC was not a uniform one, in other words, there were many varieties. In regions with a relatively large population and advanced economy and culture, local written language developed based on the local dialect in most cases. These written languages were mainly used in composing local folk literatures. On the other hand, with the most influential power, the written language popularized in the capital region possibly served as the "common language" of AWVC, and might be used in the whole country.

7 *Pūtōnghuà* is defined as "the common language of China, based on the northern dialects, with the Peking phonological system as its norm of pronunciation and the canonic modern vernacular literatures as the model of grammar." (Ref. Norman 1988:135)

8 *Gūdài báihuà-wén* is almost sharing the same writing system or Hànzì 漢字 (Chinese character) system with wényán wén "Classical Chinese writing."

9 Some researchers wrongly equate or contrast *gūdài báihuà-wén* with *xiàndài báihuà-wén*. Let me clarify once more: Vernacular Chinese writing is divided into ancient and modern times. *Gūdài báihuà-wén* is actually a revision of Classical Chinese writing, and a colloquial version of Classical Chinese writing. This implies that Vernacular Chinese writing is not a new creation, but a development and refinement of originally poor-quality Classical Chinese writing.

characteristics come into being? Given that *wény'an-wén* is based on the language of traditional Classics as the standard, one may also wonder whether the AWVC had such a standard or not?

Most scholars believed that the AWVC was first adopted in folk or popular literature. However, this was not the case. The AWVC first emerged in the stage of *Guyi* "ancient translation" of Buddhist scriptures, and then came to its maturation in the stage of *Jiuyi* "old translations." The representative works like *Būiyù jāng* 百喻經 (T209), *Xián yú jāng* 賢愚經 (T202) and *Zá būozàng jāng* 雜寶藏經 (T203) essentially share the same linguistic and stylistic features with the *Dūnhuáng biànwén* 敦煌變文 "Transformation Texts from Dūnhuáng Manuscripts."

Biànwén is the script of *biàn* 變 (lit. "transformation"), a kind of popular folk performance in the North during the Five Dynasties of Late *Tang*. Somehow the *biànwén* failed to be handed down. Some *biànwén* manuscripts were discovered by the Dūnhuáng archeological activities in the 1920s and 1930s (therefore also known as *Dūnhuáng biànwén*). In *biànwén*, there is a major section of Buddhist narratives known as *Jiūngjāng-wén* 講經文 (lit. "exegetical texts of Buddhist scripture"), illustrating the close relationship among *biàn*, *biànwén*, Buddhism, and Buddhist scripture translation (see Mair 1988b). My research in 1990 argued for the close relationship between the vocabulary systems of *biànwén* and Buddhist scripture translation, based on the fact that a great number of lexical items in *biànwén* could be traced to Buddhist scriptures in pre-T'ang period. Hence, the translation of Buddhist scriptures facilitated the earliest development of the AWVC (see Zhū 1990/1992). Meanwhile, Professor Victor H. Mair from the University of Pennsylvania supported this statement in his paper published in 1994: he related Buddhism to the origins of vernacular writing in China and other East Asian ethnic groups (see Mair 1994). However, at that time, neither of us was clear about the notion about how and when the AWVC was created by Buddhist scripture translation, or which language forms in Buddhist scripture translation had already been the AWVC afterwards.[10]

As mentioned above, literary written Chinese had already been developed before Indian Buddhism was introduced into China. All literary writings at the time were based on the language of traditional classics which was later named as *wény'an-wén*. After the introduction of Buddhism, the tradition was broken by the translation of Buddhist scriptures.

---

[10] Professor Mair 2003 had highlighted the decisive impact of the Buddhist translation to the emergence of so-called *Vernacular Sinitic*, he, however, did not discuss how it was happened.

Indian Buddhism was introduced to China by monks from Central and Western Asia and India. At the beginning (that is, the early stage of *Guyi*),[11] "translation" basically refers to a form in which monks verbally preached to the Chinese people. In order to do so, these monks had to learn Chinese and acquire certain language proficiency. Undoubtedly, these foreign monks had only obtained basic speaking skills without writing skills. They did not know that a person without writing ability is regarded as illiterate by the Chinese people.[12] This is one main reason that no Buddhist scripture was translated into *wény'an-wén*. Another reason is that the audience receiving the preaching was mostly the general public at the beginning; they came from the lower class and they were illiterate. This required foreign monks' oral practice of preaching in Buddhism. Later, Chinese participants recorded these orally-preached "scriptures" in written form. One might suspect that using *hànzì* 漢字 "Chinese character" to record oral content led to the creation of a new different written form. Of most significance is that it would break the tradition of Chinese culture, although oral content in written form is actually a different concept from literary language[13] and it brought little influence on the Chinese tradition at this time.

In the middle stage of *Guyi*, the descendents of Central and Western Asian immigrants, who were either born or dwelt in China, participated in Buddhist scripture translation, such as Kāng Mèngxiáng 康孟詳, an offspring of an immigrant family from Kāngqú 康居in the Late Hàn Dynasty, Zhī Qiān 支謙, an offspring of an immigrant family from Yuèzhī月氏and Kāng Sēnghuì 康僧會, also an offspring of an immigrant family from Kāngqú in the Three Kingdoms. These translators received a better training of Chinese culture and produced scriptures like *Zhōng běnqū jāng* 中本起經 (T196), *Xīngqū xíng jīng* 興起行經 (T197), *Liùdù jí jīng* 六度集經 (T152), and *Tàizū rèiyìng běnqī jīng* 太子瑞應本起經 (T185).[14] Their translation style was different from that of Ān Shìgāo 安世高 and Lokakṣema 支婁迦讖 which was mainly based on colloquial language. The best example is *Liùdù jí jīng* 六度集經, a wonderful work written in Classical Chinese. Compared to other Classical Chinese writings from the same period, the afore-mentioned translated scriptures were not in a purely indigenous style but a hybridization of Classical Chinese, colloquialisms, and foreign items, such as loanwords, loan translations or calques, and Indo-Europeanized expressions and sentences. While some of these translated scriptures contain a higher

---

[11] Gùyì can be divided into 3 sub-periods with different representatives: (1) Ān Shìgāo and Lokakṣema; (2) Kāng Mèngxiáng, Zhī Qiān, and Kāng Sēnghuì; and (3) Dharmarakṣa.

[12] Among ten named translators In the East Hàn Dynasty, Kāng Mèngxiáng is an exception.

[13] Although literary language comes from colloquial language, it is not a mere written form of colloquial language. Contrary to colloquial language, literary language is added with a certain level of refinement and standard.

[14] There are some un-translated classics during the period, such as Dàfāngbiànfó bào'ēn jīng 大方便佛報恩經.

proportion of oral language (e.g. Zhī Qiān and Kāng Mèngxiáng's translation), some contain a smaller proportion (e.g. Kāng Sēnghuì's translations). These works were not appropriate and suitable from the viewpoint of traditional Chinese writing standards because the language of these translations may have been regarded as some kind of "breakthrough" at the time,[15] given that it probably sounded awkward to the contemporary Chinese literati when they studied, listened to, or read out these texts. Nevertheless, this was a great effort of translating Buddhist scriptures into *wény'an-wén*. Though being unsuccessful, this early effort laid the foundations and also set up basic characteristics for Vernacular Chinese writing of the next period: the period of *Jiuyi* "Old translations" as represented by Kumārajīva.[16]

Why are the translations of Kāng Mèngxiáng and Kāng Sēnghuì not to be considered as vernacular Chinese writings? There are three main reasons. First of all, the mixture of *wén* 文 (lit. "refined") and *bái* 白 (lit. "vernacular") is still not "organic" and "natural" in their translation. That is to say, the refined and vernacular qualities of their translation had not been well-balanced. While some of their works were over-refined and undistinguishable from Classical Chinese writing, others were over-vernacular and similar to colloquial language in a written form. Neither of them was naturally and fluently presented with the literary language. Secondly, there were a lot of "loan" elements from the source language in their works, lexical and grammatical, which affect reading fluency and sentence structure. Finally, translation in such style can only be seen in the literature-oriented scriptures (e.g. *Jātaka*); translated scriptures of other genres were all based on colloquial language. Mixing Classical and Vernacular Chinese was still not a common and conscious choice adopted by most translators due to the following: (1) the translators' Chinese language proficiency; (2) restrictions of Chinese language, both colloquial and literary, in presenting the contents of Buddhist texts; and (3) application of inappropriate translation methods.

The AWVC had been developed in the stage of *Guyi* under the following circumstances. As translators gave up metaphrase and adopted paraphrase, transliterated words, as well as Indo-Europeanized sentences affected by grammatical structure of Indic originals, were reduced in number. The Chinese language skills of translators generally improved, and their translated

---

15 This is an argument by Japanese scholar Shimura Ryoji 志村良治 (1984). General intellectuals claimed that translated scriptures contained too many colloquial and foreign words. The vulgar nature of colloquial words had destroyed the sophistication and classical style of Classical Chinese writing; the breakthrough of applying foreign words was inappropriate for Chinese writing style.

16 In between the period of Kāng Mèngxiáng and Kāng Sēnghuì and *Jiùyì*, there is the third stage of *Gùyì*. The stage's representatives (e.g. Kumārajīva and Kāng Mèngxiáng) are sharing the same cultural background as immigrants from the Western Regions, and they obtained a better training of Chinese culture.

scriptures became more sophisticated and fluent. With advanced Chinese language skills, these translators were able to supervise the translation quality; meanwhile, the Chinese assistants to the translators, compared with their predecessors, gained a better knowledge of Buddhism and therefore more actively engaged themselves in the polishing of the translations. With the establishment of translation system, translation processes became organized and methodology-oriented. After several hundred years, the practice of mixing Classical and Vernacular Chinese had been accepted by the general public; it even paved the way for substituting paraphrase for metaphrase.

As the leader of *Jiuyi*, Kumārajīva developed the AWVC in mixing the characteristics of Classical and Vernacular Chinese with the basis of *wény'an-wén*. First, with every effort he promoted the translation method of paraphrase and put it into practice, reducing the foreign influence caused by the source language. For example (Jiāng 2011:219), there is a paragraph in *Saddharma-puṇḍarīka-sūtra*:

> *samam asmābhiḥ kula-putrā eka-kṣaṇa eka-muhūrte mayā c' ānandena ca anuttarāyāṃ samyak-saṃbodhau cittam utpāditaṃ dharma-gaganābhyudgatarājasya tathāgatasya arhataḥ samyak-saṃbuddhasya saṃmukhaṃ /*
>
> Young men of good family, I and Ananda have in the same moment, the same instant conceived the idea of supreme and perfect enlightenment in the presence of the Tathagata Dharmagahanabhyudgataraga, the Arhat, &c. (*The Lotus of the True Law*, IX, Translated by H. Kern. In *the Sacred Books of the East* vol. XXI, Oxford 1884, p.208)

Among various words and phrases, *kula-putrā*, son of good family, is an independent vocative case being inserted in the sentence. Dharmarakṣa metaphrased the paragraph in *Zhèng fǎhuá jīng*正法華經 as following:

> 佛法 平等 族姓子 適 發 無上 正真 道意
>
> Fó-fǎ píngděng zúxìng-zǐ shì fā wúshàng zhèngzhēn-dàoyì
>
> Buddha-law harmony son-of-good-family just arise greatest correct enlightenment
>
> 前 於 超空 如來 至真
>
> qián yú chāokōng rúlái zhìzhēn
>
> approach into absolute-emptiness thus-come absolute-truth
>
> 等正覺 所 (T09/263/p98/b12-14)
>
> děngzhèngjué suǒ
>
> perfect-supreme-enlightenment place

The Chinese translated word of *kula-putrā* is *zúxìng-zǐ,* which was inserted as its Sanskrit parallel. From the perspective of Chinese understanding, this translation has not only broken the sentence structure and speech fluency, but also become difficult to identify and misunderstood as subject in the sentence.

Kumārajīva paraphrased in *Miàofǎ liánhuā jīng* 妙法蓮華經the same paragraph as follows in which the word *shànnánzǐ* 善男子 "good son" was moved to the beginning of the sentence to meet Chinese grammar:

諸善男子， 我與 阿難 等 於空王 佛 所 同時

zhū shàn-nánzǐ wǒ yú Ā'nán děng yú Kōngw'ang Fó suǒ tóngshí

Good sons, I with ānanda etc. in Emptiness-King Buddha house at-same-time

發 阿耨多羅 三藐三菩提 心 (T9/262/p30/a2-4)

fā ānuòduōluó-sānmiǎosānpútí xīn

arise unexcelled-complete-enlightenment thought

Secondly, Kumārajīva rejected the over-colloquial nature of translation language in *Guyi*. There is a section in *Volume 7: Sēngruì-zhuàn* 僧叡傳 (lit. "Biography of Sēngruì") of *Gāosēng-zhuàn* 高僧傳 ("Biographies of Eminent Monks"). Sēngruì is Kumārajīva's student and translation assistant:

弘始七年冬，更譯《法華》。興執法護經相挍，什誦梵本，僧叡等筆受。至於"五百弟子授記品"，什曰："昔護譯云 '天見人，人見天'，此語與西域義同，但在言過質。"叡應聲曰："將非 '人天交接，兩得相見'乎？"什大喜。

At the seventh *Hóngshǐ* 弘始 era [of King Yáo Xīng's reign], Kumārajīva re-translated *Saddharma-puṇḍarīka*. Yáo Xīng checked with Dharmarakṣa's translated version (named as the *Zhèng fǎháu jīng* 正法華經), Kumārajīva read aloud the Sanskrit original, and Sēngruì and other students took record. When they went through one chapter (the chapter of *Wūbǎi dìzǐshòujì-pǐn* 五百弟授記品), Kumārajīva said, "In the past, Dharmarakṣa translated [this Sanskrit sentence] into *'tiān jiàn rén, rén jiàn tiān'* [17] (lit. "the Heavenly-beings, *deva,* see the Human-beings, the Human-beings

[17] In modern edition of *Zhèng fǎhuá jīn,* the relevant sentence is much different: "爾時江河沙等三千大千世界爲一佛土，七寶爲地，地平如掌，無有山陵、丘墟谿谷、荆棘礫石，重閣精舍周匝普滿，而用七寶，猶如諸天宮殿麗妙，遙相瞻見，天上視世間，世間得見天上，天人世人往來交接。"At this moment, three thousands of *mahāsāhasra-lokadhātu,* which were more than the amount of sands of the river *(gaṅgā),* were united in a single Buddhist region. In this region, the land was consisted of the "Seven jewels *(sapta-ratnāni)",* and was flat as human's palm, with no mountains, hills or valleys, thorns or gravels on it. Cascading temples with many layers spread all over the region and also built with the "Seven jewels", gorgeous and splendid as the palaces in Heaven. In these temples and palaces, human-beings and the Heavenly-beings meet each other and both of them are able to see each other. (CBETA, T09, no. 263, p. 95, c24-29) which indicates that the modern edition is not the one of

see the Heavenly-beings"). This phrase fulfils the original meaning, but its language is too vulgar." Sēngruì replied immediately, "Should we change it to *'rén-tiān jiāojiē, liăng dé xiāngjiàn'*? (lit. 'the Human-beings and the Heavenly-beings meet each other and both of them are able to see each other.')" Kumārajīva was very much delighted.

In this narrative, Kumārajīva commented on the Dharmarakṣa's translation of *Saddharma-puṇḍarīka* about the over-colloquial nature of the language. He agreed to change the colloquial phrase - *"tiān jiàn rén, rén jiàn tiān"* into the literary phrase *"rén-tiān jiāojiē, liăng dé xiāngjiàn."* Kumārajīva's translation was not the standardized Classical Chinese.[18] In order to improve the elegance level of translation, he adopted the mixture of Classical and Vernacular Chinese, mixed both characteristics in a fluent and natural manner, and established the standard of the AWVC.

Although we cannot simply conclude that the MWVC and the AWVC are directly related to each other, the AWVC has its own historical significance. The AWVC enhanced the development of traditional folk literature since the T'ang 唐 Dynasty (618-907 CE), enabling it to be an important stage in the history of Chinese literature. In the Sòng 宋 and Yu'an 元 Dynasties, literature of the AWVC and that of Classical Chinese differentiated between one another, enriching Chinese literature with its achievements. The AWVC is only a transformation of Classical Chinese: its nature is based on unofficial Classical Chinese writing, its acquisition and writing are much easier than those of standardized Classical Chinese, and it is widely accepted by the general public. The AWVC is an important path for a "living" colloquial language changing to a literary language. In omission of its vulgar nature, the colloquial style of the AWVC had been transformed into standard Classical Chinese writing style which had been adopted for 2000 years. In both cultural and linguistic perspectives, the AWVC gave adequate preparation for the establishment of the MWVC.

Kumarajiva's time. Cf. *Miàofă liánhuā jīng:*
"其佛以恒河沙等三千大千世界爲一佛土，七寶爲地，地平如掌，無有山陵谿澗溝壑，七寶臺觀充滿其間，諸天宮殿近處虛空，人天交接，兩得相見。" The Buddhist created the single Buddhist region with the thousands of *mahāsāhasra-lokadhātu,* which were more than sands in *gaṅgā.* In this region, the land was consisted of the "Seven jewels", and was flat as human's palm, with no mountains, hills or valleys on it. Cascading temples built up with the "Seven jewels" were spread all over the region. The palaces of heaven were so near in the sky, in which the human-beings and the Heavenly-beings meet each other and both of them are able to see each other. (CBETA, T09, no. 262, p. 27, c21-25)

[18] While some scholars regarded competition of *wén* and *bái* as competition of paraphrase and metaphrase, other scholars referred it as stylistic competition. Combining two statements, *wén* and *bái* contain both ideas translation methods and stylistic nature (Please refer to Mèng Zhāolián 2009 a, b for details). However, one should be reserved about the reference of *wén* and *bái* to Classical and Vernacular Chinese respectively.

Conclusion

In this paper we try to highlight the contributions of Kumārajīva to the creation of Chinese Buddhism and Chinese culture in his time at least in three aspects:

a) Consummating and choosing the *yìyì* 意譯 "paraphrase" as the mechanism of Chinese Buddhist translation which is the only suitable method for Chinese.

b) Training Chinese Buddhist scholars consciously and massively the first time in history.

c) A new written vernacular Chinese and its writing were created under the leadership of Kumārajīva by which popular literature can be recorded from then on. It was a significant advancement of Chinese culture.

BIBLIOGRAPHY

CBETA. 2011. *CBETA Chinese Electronic Tripiṭaka Collection* (version 2011). Taipei.

Harrison, Paul. 1997. "The *Ekottarikāgama* Translations of An Shigao." In Petra Kieffer-Pülz and Jens-Uwe Hartmann (eds.). *Bauddhavidyāsudhākaraḥ: Studies in Honour of Heinz Bechert on the Occasion of His 65th Birthday* (*Indica et Tibetica*, 30.). pp. 261–284. Swisttal-Odendorf.

Harrison, Paul. 2002. "Another Addition to An Shigao's Corpus? Preliminary Notes on the Early Chinese *Saṃyuktāgama* Translation." In Sakurabe Ponshu Committee (ed.), *Studies in Honour of Dr. Sakurabe Hajime on the Occasion of His Seventy-seventh Birthday*. pp. 1-32. Kyoto: Heirakuji Shoten.

Jì, Xiànlín季羡林. 1988. "Wǒ hé Fójiào Yánjiū" 我和佛教研究 (My Research on the Buddhism). In editorial office of *Wén Shǐ Zhīshí* 《文史知識》 (ed.), *Fójiào yǔ Zhōngguó Wénhuà* 《佛教與中國文化》 (Buddhism and Chinese Culture), pp.16-21. Běijāng: Zhōnghuá Shūjú.

Jiāng, Nán 姜南. 2011. *Jīyū Fàn Hàn Duìkān de Fǎhuájīng Yǔfǎ Yánjiū* 《基於梵漢對勘的〈法華經〉語法研究》 (*A Comparative Study on the Grammar of Lotus Sutra of Chinese translation and its Sanskrit parallel*). Ph.D. dissertation of Peking University (2008). Běijīng: Shāngwù Yìnshū Guǎn [Commercial Press]商務印書館.

Mair, Victor H. 1988a. *Painting and Performance: Chinese Picture Recitation and Its Indian Genesis*. Honolulu: University of Hawaii Press.

Mair, Victor H. 1988b. *T'ang Transformation Texts: A Study of the Buddhist Contribution to the Rise of Vernacular Fiction and Drama in China*. Cambridge: Harvard University Press.

Mair, Victor H. 1994. "Buddhism and the Rise of the Written Vernacular in East Asia: The making of National languages." In *Journal of Asian Studies* 53, no.3, pp. 707-751.

Mair, Victor H. 2003. "Buddhist Influences on Vernacular Literature in Chinese." In R. E. Buswell (ed. in chief), *Encyclopedia of Buddhism*, pp.154-157. New York: Macmillan Reference USA.

Mèng, Zhāolián孟昭連. 2009a. "Hànyì Fójāng Yǔtǐ de Xíngchéng"漢譯佛經語體的形成 (On the forming of the writing style of Chinese translation of Indian Buddhist sutras). In *Zhōngnán Mínzú Dàxué Xuébào*《中南民族大學學報》, no. 2, pp. 155-161. Wǔhàn 武漢: Zhongnan Minority University.

Mèng, Zhāolián孟昭連. 2009b. "Wén Bái zhī Biàn: Yì Fó Shǐ Shàng Wén Zhì zhī Zhēng de Shízhì" 文白之辯—譯佛史上文質之爭的實質 (On the difference between *wén* and *bái*: the substance of the discussion on the *wén* and *zhì* in history of Chinese Buddhist translation). In *Nánkāi Xuébào* 《南開學報》, no. 3, pp. 130-140. Tiānjīn: Nankai University.

Norman, Jerry. 1988. *Chinese*. Cambridge: Cambridge University Press.

Shimura, Ryoji志村良治. 1984. *Chugoku chusei gohoshi kenkyu*《中国中世語法史研究》(*A Historical Grammar of Middle Chinese*). Tokyo: Santosha. Chinese version translated by Jiāng Lánshēng江藍生 and Bái Wéiguó白維國. Běijīng: Zhōnghuá Shūjú, 1995.

Wilson, H. H. 2011. *Wilson Sanskrit-English Dictionary (2011)*. Digital version of *A Dictionary in Sanskrit and English*, 2nd ed., Calcutta, 1832.

Zhū Qìngzhī朱慶之. 1992a. *Fódiǎn yǔ Zhōnggǔ Hànyǔ Yǔhuì Yánjiū*《佛典與中古漢語語匯研究》(*Study of the relationship between Buddhist scriptures and the vocabulary of medieval Chinese*). Ph.D. dissertation of Sichuan University (1990). Taipei: Wénjīn Chūbǎnshè 文津出版社.

Zhū Qìngzhī朱慶之. 1992b. "Jīnlián Yǔshì Kǎoyuán" 金蓮語事考原 (The origin of the word and story of the golden-lotus). In *Wén Shǐ* 《文史》, vol. 34, pp. 311-314. Běijīng: Zhōnghuá Shūjú.

Zhū Qìngzhī朱慶之. 1994. "Fódiǎn yǔ *Kǒngquè Dōngnán Fēi*" 佛典與《孔雀東南飛》(The relationship between Buddhist literature and the narrative poem *The Southeast, the Peacock*). In Chén Shǎofēng 陳少峰(ed.), *Yuán Xué*《原學》, vol. 1, pp. 1-25. Běijīng: Zhōngguó Guǎngbō Diànshì Chūbǎnshè 中國廣播電視出版社.

Zücher, Erik. 1959. *The Buddhist Conquest of China: The Spread and Adaptation of Buddhism in Early Medieval China*. Leiden: Brill.

19

Kumārajīva's visibility: research in translation studies

Paula Tizzano Fernandez

Key words: Kumārajīva, Buddhist Translation, Translation Studies.

To my mentor Daisaku Ikeda,
who opened up and showed me
the path of my own mission
as a translator, proposing Kumārajīva
as a model and a living example.

A life fully devoted to translation
is an adventurous journey
through mountains and rivers.
But what a breathtaking view!

Introduction

According to authoritative voices in the fields of history, Buddhist studies and Chinese culture, Kumārajīva (344-413), was one of the foremost translators in the history of humanity.

A study in context

I must say I am not a completely detached researcher. My initial interest in Kumārajīva developed hand in hand with my personal Buddhist practice and my activities as a Buddhist translator for the last 29 years. I had the good fortune to become a translator in response to the personal encouragement of Buddhist philosopher and peace-builder Daisaku Ikeda, who inclined me toward a life of mission, helping to transmit Buddhist teachings for the benefit of humanity. In fact, it was through one of his books, *The Flower of Chinese*

Buddhism (Ikeda 1986)(, 1986 #1), which is one of my precious sources, that I learned to value Kumārajīva as a true master of translation.

Among other commendable Buddhist initiatives in the field of translation deserving open recognition, the unprecedented efforts of the lay Buddhist organization Soka Gakkai International (SGI) have to be acknowledged and credited for making the Lotus Sūtra and Mahāyāna Buddhism widely known and actively practiced in 192 countries and territories, with their respective languages, including distant Argentina. In my native country, so far away from Kucha and so unrelated to Eastern tradition, there are thousands of people who enact in their daily lives the spirit of the teachings which Kumārajīva translated 1600 years ago, and who revitalize themselves with the vibrant practice of the Lotus Sūtra as promoted by SGI. The fact that millions of people having different types of lives and cultures are now reading and practicing the Lotus Sūtra both in the East and the West is something which, I am sure, would make Kumārajīva immensely happy and constitutes a retrospective proof of the validity of his work.

New trends in Translation History

In his innovative book, *Method in Translation History,* Anthony Pym (Pym) offers four guiding principles for historical research in Translation Studies:

1) Translation history should explain why translations were produced in a particular social time and place; that is, aim to explain social causation.
2) The central object of historical knowledge should not be the text of the translation, nor its contextual system or its linguistic features, but the human translator, since only humans have the kind of responsibility appropriate to social causation.
3) If translation history is to focus on translators, it must organize its world around the social contexts where translators lived and worked (interculturality).
4) The reasons for doing translation history exist in the present, in connection with our problems and situations here and now.

Pym comments: "I am in favour of serious subjective involvement in translation history. If humans are to stand at the centre of our object, then our historiographical subjectivity must also be humanized" (Pym 1998: ix-x).

I came across this book when my work was well in progress, and I was surprised to find out that my research on Kumārajīva was proceeding more or less along the same lines. My interest and focus are placed on Kumārajīva the human being, Kumārajīva as a wise, focussed and compassionate man who chose translation as his own life-path, Kumārajīva as a milestone in human history showing how much a simple person can accomplish by devoting every aspect of his life and circumstances to the commitment of a cherished, exciting, self-chosen vision.

In terms of cognitive processes, we translate today much in the same way as our predecessors did forty-thousand years ago (Muṭoz MartḬn 2009). What Kumārajīva may show us is absolutely relevant to each and every translator who seeks a life of meaning and contribution.

In our translational activity as well, technology has developed at an unprecedented, fast pace, but human spirit has not progressed at the same dizzying speed. In fact, it is very difficult to signal out any other translator in the last sixteen centuries whose influence and effects have been as widespread, lasting and epochal as those of Kumārajīva.

We are exploring Kumārajīva's life because it has everything to do with our world and work, and the more we research, the more sources of inspiration, advice and reference we will tap to create value in modern translation practice and teaching.

Food for research from an eightfold approach

I will now mention eight perspectives which I personally consider relevant to our age and deserving close scrutiny by contemporary scholars for their links to current issues:

1. *From a historical and global approach*, now that the importance of multiethnic values is being revisited in our globalized world, we suggest that Kumārajīva, as a representative of "interculturality" (Pym 1998), can offer a living model to explore the potential of crossroads societies in the fostering of constructive global attitudes and open-minded citizens.

   We tend to think that the feared globalization is a one-sided imposition of Western values and interests, but from an ethical perspective, just as implied in the Lotus Sūtra (Watson 1993), it could mean the ability to take the well-being and safety of all humanity as a standard for our personal behavior. Amartya Sen (Sen 2002) comments that the printing of the first book in history was a globalized initiative with which the West had nothing to do, but where Kumārajīva was a main character. As he elaborates, printing was a Chinese technology and invention; the object of the publication was the Diamond Sūtra, a Sanskrit Buddhist teaching coming from India; and Kumārajīva, who translated it to Chinese, was a half Turkish, half Indian man. Sen proposes that this story involving China, India and Turkey in a cultural breakthrough was a model of a non-Western globalized effort with positive, lasting influence and value for the whole world.

So it is pertinent to ask how this ability to work with a global view, creating global effects, relates to his upbringing in a crossroads society. To which extent will multicultural and multilingual environments help instill in their inhabitants capacities that are useful assets, not only for the acquisition of translation competence, but also in the execution of diplomacy, commerce, cultural management and other human activities? Can this be measurable and objectively proved, and can Kumārajīva, as we suggest, be examined as a representative case study in this regard?

2. *From a psychological standpoint*, Kumārajīva can help us study the role of multiethnic and bilingual homes in the cognitive acquisition of early translation competence and the development of intellectual skills. Kumārajīva was the son of a highly intelligent and independent Kuchan mother, endowed with courage and sincere spiritual values, and an Indian father with diplomatic and political skills, trained in peace-work and in royal counselling, who embraced faith as a deliberate choice (Ikeda 1986). Their son developed and enhanced all these traits, in a complex bilingual matrix which activated his potentialities.

   There is much research currently taking place in Translation Studies, particularly from the constructivist approach, about the influence of bilingual childhoods in cognitive acquisition (Tse 1996). The extra effort these children have to make in their daily life is often rewarded by a more developed performance in what we call "natural translation". It must not be hastily concluded that children who perform language brokering at home are necessarily better translators; they need to acquire additional competences and metacognition to become accomplished professionals (Muṭoz Martn 2009). But the fact that Kumārajīva's parents were linguistically diverse and that he was raised in a bilingual affective environment is a major element to consider in the making of his abilities as a gifted translator.

3. *From a political point of view*, Kumārajīva can help us gauge the role of secular powers in the sponsorship and promotion of highly valuable civilizational projects. Kumārajīva's team was the first scripture translation team in China that was directly supported by the Emperor (Sai 2008).

   Although his work suffered a major delay due to the authoritarianism and political ambition of his captor Lü Kuang, at the same time he also benefitted from the generous and unrestricted support of Yao Hsing, the Emperor of the Later Qin who went to all lengths to support his work. So Kumārajīva's life is instrumental in observing through a looking glass both the negative and the positive effects of political power in cultural advancements of historical import.

Despite his resolute patronage, Yao Hsing did not impose his own views, nor forced Kumārajīva to make compromises or created pressures as a benefactor (Sai 2008). Yao Hsing's strategies and criteria as a statesman show that he did not put his selfish interest or his personal need of recognition in the centre; he created the best possible material environment so that Kumārajīva could produce his superb translations for the sake of humanity.

This is food for thought in our present world, where "resource allocation" for cultural projects is the object of a very tense power dynamics, possibly much more complex than in the times of the Qin dynasty.

Can Kumārajīva be studied from this perspective as a model case highlighting the all-important role of benefactors, patrons and governments in the creation of cultural and educational breakthroughs? Can we show, through Kumārajīva's case, to what extent the presence of highly accomplished people and highly useful projects can be enhanced by the existence of courageous policies of cultural promotion sustained by decision-makers, and propose model frameworks in this regard?

4. *From a sociological point of view*, Kumārajīva is the best example to reveal the role played by skilled translators in the building of diplomatic and friendly international relationships among cultures, as relevant actors in the process of peace, culture and education. He can even lead us to appreciate how decisive and influential translators and their contributions can be in the shaping of civilizations.

   There are two sides to this: how society sees translators, and how we translators see ourselves. Many scholars in our discipline have examined the socio-cultural aspects of translation, such as Schffner (2007), Venuti (1995) (1998) or Tymoczko (Hermans 2006); the conceptual propositions by French sociologist Pierre Bourdieu have led others to suggest that by paying close attention to the living practices of translators — their "*habitus*"— (Bourdieu 2007), it is possible to understand how they influenced the development of culture (Cronin 2006).

   Kumārajīva's achievements and his living practices show us why it is so important to include these dimensions in the syllabi and training of professional translators focusing on the 21st century and its global issues. If these links with our important role and responsibility are left unnoticed in translation courses and policies, and we see translators as mere information brokers, a grave disservice to civilization is being done.

   From the 5th century to our present age, Kumārajīva's translations have nurtured lasting developments and international movements focused on human rights, mutual friendship, and a sustainable view of happiness for all human beings as equals. There hasn't been a single century or decade in the last 1600 years in which his translations were not treasured by the common people, studied in the context of intellectual pursuits, or practiced as a source of hope, courage and compassionate love, particularly his version of the Lotus Sūtra (Watanabe 2005).

This perdurability, of which his unburned tongue is a symbol (Ikeda 1986), is related to a deep awareness of his mission and role, which in turn acted as a catalyst for his skills. How can this awareness be reinforced and instilled in today's translators' training? Which representations and values about translation underpin society and in which ways are these replicated by the educational system? Perhaps by making Kumārajīva a more active presence in translation courses in the West, we could help highlight the importance of ethics and the translators' sense of identity in the promotion of global values and in the solving of critical collective issues.

5. *From the standpoint of translation studies*, a deep and extensive survey of Kumārajīva's work would be a necessary act of balance in the West, to counteract its ethnocentric pervasive view and include important knowledge, now regrettably excluded.[1]

   From a descriptive standpoint, I have summarized the following ten aspects in which Kumārajīva's translations are remarkable. These are concomitant with Prof. Ocho's, Pres. Ikeda's and other experts' points of view:

   a) They were exact and accurate in meaning and essence.
   b) They were beautiful, compelling and fluent in style.
   c) They were produced at a very fast and driven pace.
   d) They were intended for eternity and posterity.
   e) They convey an all-encompassing understanding of the Sūtras, not limited only to its religious value.
   f) Their context was a strict hermeneutic questioning by Kumārajīva and his disciples.
   g) They became a nurturing field for the training of youthful successors and disciples.
   h) They were the reflection of Kumārajīva's personal sense of mission in life.
   i) They were the spiritual fruit of his Buddhist faith and practice.

[1] See Hermans 2006 and Tymoczko 2006.

j) They promoted a wide flourishing of civilization, peace and human development in all ages and continents.

All these aspects deserve detailed examination in the context of Translation Studies. How could this be promoted?

While there are many excellent works about Kumārajīva written by Eastern scholars — some of which are fortunately translated into English and are treasured as indispensable sources in my work —, the fact remains that Kumārajīva is an under-researched character in Western Translation Studies. To amend this unfair omission, I would like to make more specific proposals:

On the one hand, any systematic approach of this subject in a university context would require collective action; at the same time, a short mention in the syllabus of "History of Translation 101" would not suffice, as it would reduce Kumārajīva's contributions to a mere Encyclopedia entry or a short section at best.

To address this need, I would like to propose, as a first stage, the creation of a Kumārajīva Research Group at the Translation Studies Department of a university or across universities, led by senior researchers and formed by Translation Studies students and graduates. A Research Group like this could include interdisciplinary voices and dialogic exchanges. Several research questions and goals could be defined, such as the ones I have been outlining here and, mainly, the Spanish and English translations of Eastern academic articles which would increase our knowledge and insight.

6. *From the perspective of translators' pedagogy*, one of the most important contributions by Kumārajīva is his successful Translation School, which stands foremost in the world's translation history.

Based on the existing platform of the State School of Translation at Ch'ang-an, and invited by Emperor Yao Hsing and by Tao'an, who was regarded as the most eminent Buddhist at that time, Kumārajīva fostered a highly specialized translation team (Zhong 2003). He did not translate in isolation or in an individualistic way as we generally do in the West, but was surrounded by a multitude of editors, sub-editors, proofreaders and scribes (Tan 2004) —between 800 and 2000 (Ikeda 1986)—, who jotted down his oral translation, listened to his doctrinal explanation about Buddhism, and absorbed the translation strategies involved in each rendering. The trainees, on their part, commented on them, asked questions and proposed alternatives, helping to edit the final versions (Watson 1993) and creating an organic, dynamic workshop. In other words, Kumārajīva developed a combined method consisting of oral translation, master class about

Buddhist doctrine, and didactic explanation of translation strategies, paired with a collective edition and revision work.

I suggest that this teaching methodology can be an advantageous paradigm for the training of specialized translators and for the production of specialized translations, not only in the field of religion, but also in other disciplines in which translation requires a sensitive and sensible understanding of complex concepts.

In which conditions could Kumārajīva's forerunning method be reinstalled in our contemporary world as an innovative framework? This is a most interesting question which I suggest could be developed in the frame of an "action-research" project led by a specific study group, focused on Translation Teaching and Training Planning in our discipline.

7. *From the ethic standpoint,* Kumārajīva can teach us invaluable lessons about his sense of mission as a Buddhist translator, a value which probably needs to be reinstated and reinforced in our civilization, particularly in young people and students.

   Kumārajīva never set his mission aside or forgot it, even when imprisoned, or forced to violate the precepts. His honesty and courage about his chosen mission were so amazing, that he offered his own body as a proof of truthfulness, because every translated word issued by his voice had been precise, earnest and faithful (Nichiren 1275). This episode serves to underscore that Kumārajīva translated with body and soul, putting at stake the whole of his being in the fulfillment of his purpose.

   What do we mean when we speak of the sense of mission? Where does it lie? Is this a universal constant in all great people who opened up new developments in history?

   The initial attempt to define 'sense of mission' has shown a surprising lack of academic work, with the scarce materials available being centered on strategic corporative marketing or in a narrower religious evangelism. However, while examining the sense of mission in Kumārajīva's context, we have seen the connections with several human qualities and attributes of his, such as his spiritual independence, the ability to live with clear intentionality, a correct understanding of life and death, a solid life-philosophy as a source of resilience, an optimistic approach to one's own possibilities of action, a persevering and patient long-term view, and a fighting spirit to challenge hindrances. All this, and much more, is connected to the sense of mission, and it is a field for further and necessary research.

8. *Finally, from the philosophical and hermeneutic perspective,* Kumārajīva can offer yet another very rich lesson about the inseparability or oneness

between master and translator-disciple, which is a unique and core Buddhist concept. Kumārajīva's first and primary source of knowledge about language was the Buddha himself. He applied in his translation work exactly what Gautama had revealed, warned and shared about the power of words and the relation between the Law, which is beyond language, and speech, which is the only way to express the Law, as human beings are structurally language-bound. In this regard, Kumārajīva and the Buddha shared one same view about discursive practices to spread philosophical concepts for the universal enlightenment and empowerment of people. They both were masters of language.

Works by Bakhtin (1982), Gadamer (Dostal 2002), or Derrida (1985) in the fields of dialogics, hermeneutics or deconstructivism have made us rethink our ideas about the dichotomy between "original" and "translation", in the sense that all originals are translations of translations of textual knowledge embodied by human subjects across cultural interfaces (Vidal Claramonte 1995) (Hermans 2006). A translation can also be seen as an original, as it carries the subjective marks of the translator's intervention on a text, and some scholars even point out that a translation is a text enhancer, "as the mirror which not only reflects but also generates light" (Steiner 2000). Though this may initially provoke hard frowns in the religious believer, I think Kumārajīva's translations can be thought of as originals, as texts produced by Kumārajīva him upon reading the Sūtras with his own life, holding a responsive and dialogic alterity, and rephrasing the exact message in Chinese with absolute faithfulness to the core of Śākyamuni's spirit, explicit or implicit in words. He did not interfere with his own personal opinions, as Nichiren clarified (Nichiren 1275-b); instead, he rewrote the Sūtras in Chinese based on the essential Buddha's will and intention, which he could grasp through his own struggle in faith.

Faith, as espoused in the Lotus Sūtra which Kumārajīva translated and lived by, is not a blind belief or the mere observance of precepts. It is a demanding, self-motivated process of human revolution, an honest all-out spiritual effort to express human potential to the utmost, in symbiotic harmony with the world and with other beings.

From the Buddhist standpoint, the personal mission can be specific and different among individuals, but the sense of responsibility and the commitment to a common purpose can be equally shared by people united with the same mind. As Petrilli (2008) observes, "translation implies [...] the highest levels of dialogism, responsiveness, amorous and participative interpretation which most contributes to the text's resurrection, to its life in the great time".

In this sense, Siddhartha was a Buddha, and Kumārajīva was a translator monk, but they both can be thought of as one and the same entity, inseparable as master and translator-disciple, on an equal basis of pledge to the spiritual empowerment of all human beings. This oneness, which takes place beyond language and is based on the shared vow to save all living beings, is what, perhaps once in many ages, blossoms like the *udumbara* flower and creates the magic of a vibrant, luminescent, everlasting translation.

BIBLIOGRAPHY

Bajtin, Mijal. 1982. *Esttica de la creacin verbal*. Trans. Tatiana Bubnova. Mxico: Siglo XXI Editores.

Bassnett, Susan. 1998. "The Cultural Turn in Translation Studies." In *Constructing Cultures: Essays on Literary Translation*, ed. Susan y Lefevere Bassnett, Andr. Clevedon, Buffalo, Toronto: Multilingual Matters. 123-139.

Bourdieu, Pierre. 2007. *El sentido práctico*. Trans. Ariel Dilon. Buenos Aires: Siglo XXI Editores.

Cronin, Michael. 2006 Review. Moira Inghilleri (Guest editor), The Translator, vol. 11, n. 2, 2005, Special Issue on Bourdieu and the Sociology of Translation and Interpreting. *JosTrans - The Journal of Specialised Translation* (6): 4.

Chan, Wing-tsit. 1963. *A Sourcebook on Chinese Philosophy*. Princeton: Princeton University Press.

Chandra, Lokesh. 1998. "India and China: Beyond and within." In *Across the Himalayan Gap*, ed. Chung Tan. New Delhi: Gyan Publishing House. 553 + xxvi.

Derrida, Jacques. 1985. *The Ear of the Other*. New York: Schocken Books.

Dostal, Robert (ed.). 2002. *The Cambridge Companion to Gadamer*. of *Cambridge Companions to Philosophy*. Cambridge: Cambridge University Press.

Fox, Alan. 1995. "Jizang, disciple of Kumārajīva." In *Great Thinkers of the Eastern World*, ed. Ian McGreal. New York: HarperCollins Publishers. 84-88.

Hermans, Theo (ed.). 2006. *Translating Others I*. Manchester: St. Jerome Publishing.

Hinüber, Oskar von. 2006. Everyday Life in an Ancient Indian Buddhist Monastery. *ARIRIAB* IX (March 2006): 29.

Hua, Tripitaka Master. 1983. *Records of High Sanghans*. Edited by Dharma Realm Buddhist University. Vol. 1. Trans. Heng Chia. Malaysia: Buddhist Text Translation Society.

Ikeda, Daisaku. 1986. *The Flower of Chinese Buddhism*. Trans. Burton Watson. New York: Weatherhill.

Lḍpez-Gay, Jesús. 1995. El Buda como Padre en el Hokekyo. *Revista de Estudios Budistas* (8).

Muṭoz Martn, Ricardo. 2009. "Nomen mihi Legio est. A cognitive approach to Natural Translation." Presented at the 10th Symposium on Translation and Interpretation, Castellón.

Nichiren. 1275. "The Selection of Time." In *The Writings of Nichiren Daishonin*. Tokyo: Soka Gakkai.

Nichiren. 1275-b. "Attaining Buddhahood in One's Present Form." In *The Writing of Nichiren Daishonin*. Tokyo: Soka Gakkai.

Petrilli, Susan. 2008. "Bakhtinian Dialogics in Translation Theories." Presented at the 13th International Conference on Mikhail Bakhtin, London, Canada.

Pym, A. 1998. *Method in translation history*. St. Jerome.

Runyan, Mary Edith. 1972. Beginning and Spread of Buddhism in China to the T'ang Dynasty. *Chung Chi Journal* 11 (2): 11.

Sai, Seong Siu. 2008. Theorizing Buddhist Scripture Translation as an Act of Giving: a Buddhist Perspective. *New Voices in Translation Studies* 4: 14.

Schffner, Christina. 2007. "Politics and Translation." In *A Companion to Translation Studies*, ed. Piotr y Littau Kuhiwczkaw, Karin. Clevedon, Buffalo, Toronto: Multilingual Matters. 134-147.

Sen, Amartya. 2002. How to Judge Globalization. *The American Prospect*, (Winter 2002).

Steiner, George. 2000. "The Hermeneutic Motion." In *The Translation Studies Reader*, ed. Lawrence Venuti. New York: Routledge. 186-191. Original edition, 1975.

Tan, Piya. 2004. *The Spread of Buddhism: A strategic analysis Buddhist history in East Asia.* of *Buddhism in China: Tradition and Innovation*. Singapore: Singapore Buddhist Federation.

Tse, Lucy. 1996. Language brokering in linguistic minority communities: The case of Chinese- and Vietnamese-American students *The Bilingual Research Journal* 20 (3 & 4): 485-498.

Venuti, Lawrence. 1995. *The Translator's Invisibility: A History of Translatioon*. Edited by Susan Bassnett and Andrŗ Lefevere of *Translation Studies*. New York: Routledge.

Venuti, Lawrence. 1998. *The Scandals of Translation: Towards and Ethics of Difference*. New York: Routledge.

Vidal Claramonte, África. 1995. *Traduccin, manipulacin, desconstruccin*. Salamanca: Ediciones del Colegio de Espaţa.

Watanabe, Hoyo. 2005. "The Tradition of the Lotus Sūtra Faith in Japan." Presented at the XIVth Conference of the International Association of Buddhist Studies, London University.

Watson, Burton (trad.). 1993. *The Lotus Sūtra*. New York: Columbia University Press.

Zhong, Weihe. 2003. An Overview of Translation in China: Theory and Practice. *Translation Journal* 7 (2).

Zurcher, Eric. 1959 / 2007. *The Buddhist Conquest of China: The Spread and Adaptation of Buddhism in Early Medieval China*. Edited by Barend Ter Haar. Vol. 11 of *Sinica Leidensia*. Leiden: Brill.

20

Kumārajīva and his translation of Buddhists Classics viewed through the Chinese literature of 13th and 14th century

Liu Yingsheng

The former researches on Kumārajīva in China have been more concentrated on the period of his life, i.e. 344-413 CE., or evaluation of his translations from modern viewpoints.[1] The sources describing the life of Kumārajīva and his activities of translation of Buddhist classics are the main historical documents written in the pre-T'ang period, or the Buddhist classics written in Chinese. A limited number of Few scholars have noticed that Kumārajīva was continuously mentioned in the sources compiled after the T'ang period.

Source 1, Chen Suo 陈栎, a Yüan author, mentioned that Yao Xing 姚兴, the King of Hou Qin 后秦, offered Kumārajīva the title Guoshi 国师, meaning the 'Adviser of Empire', and he translated more than 300 juan of Buddhist classics into Chinese under the order of Yao Xing.[2] 300 juan of the Chinese translation works of Buddhist classics finished by Kumārajīva was first mentioned in

[1] See the recent researches like Fang Litian's paper entitled *Chang'an Fuojiao de Lishi Diwei* (方立天：《长安佛教的历史地位》， *the Historical Position of Ch'ang-an Buddhism*) in *Zhongguo Zongjiao* 《中国宗教》，*China Religion)*, no.8, 2008, pp. 30-36; Guo Ying-jie & Zhao Qing's paper *Jiumoluoshi he Sheng Aogusiding de Fanyi Yishu Bijiao*(郭英杰、赵青：《鸠摩罗什和圣奥古斯丁的翻译艺术比较》, *Comparison of Translation Styles of Kumrājīva and Aurelius Augustinus)*, in Journal of Luoyang Normal University 《洛阳师范学院学报》, 2009, 29(3).

[2] Yao Xing 乃以胡僧鸠摩罗什为国师，命译经三百余卷, see Chen Suo, *Lidai Tonglue*, juan 1, Sikuquanshu edition [元]陈栎：《历代通略》卷一，清文渊阁四库全书本. Chen Suo was born in 12.of the Chunyiu period of the Song (1252). Except *Lidai Tonglue*, he wrote *Qinyiutant Suilu* 《勤有堂隨録》，*Dingyu Ji* 《定宇集》 *and Shangshu Jichuancuan Shu* 《尙書集傳纂疏》 as well.

the book entitled *Shiliu Guo Chunqiu*《十六国春秋，*Histories of the 16 Kingdoms* written by Cui Hong 崔鸿 (AD 478-525CE) at the end of the Northern Wei (北魏，AD 386-557 CE) period.[3] Shortly thereafter, this story was copied by Hui Jiao 慧皎（497-554 CE.), a monk of the Southern Liang (南梁，502-557CE.), in his *Gaoseng Zhuan*《高僧传》, *Biographies of the Famous Monks)*.[4] We are still not sure yet if Chen Suo's narrative was based on Cui Hong or on Hui Jiao.

Source 2, in juan 4 and juan 5 of Luo Daxiang's (骆大骧) *Leibian Ch'ang-anzhi*《类编长安志》, *A Classified Gazetee of Ch'ang-an,* there are texts related to Kumārajīva's activities in Ch'ang-an, like Chengxuan T'ang (澄玄堂，Chengxuan Hall) and Cao T'ang Chansi (草堂禅寺, Cao T'ang Buddhist Temple). Chengxuan Hall was the place where Yao Xing, the King of Qin led his monks to listen to Kumārajīva's introduction of Buddhist classics.[5] The author cited this paragraph from a book entitled *Jianwenlu*《见闻録》, written by Wang Yan (王演). This book does not exist aynow and our information about it is not substantial, although Luo Daxiang 骆大骧 used this source three times in his book.

In the text of Cao T'ang Chansi (草堂禅寺, Cao T'ang Buddhist Temple), Luo Daxiang 骆大骧 has said that it is was situated at the foot of Gui Feng (圭峯, Gui Mount) of Yusuchuan 御宿川, formerly it had been the Cao T'ang Xiaoyaoyuan (草堂逍遥园, CaoT'ang Xiaoyao Garden) of the King Yao Xing, where Kumārajīva translated Buddhist classics. After he died, while his body was cremated, his tongue did not burn. His stūpa existed at the time when Luo Daxiang 骆大骧 wrote his book.[6] Meanwhile, there is another text entitled Cao T'ang 草堂 in juan 9 of the same book giving a similar description. The author Luo Daxiang 骆大骧 said that his source about the history of Cao T'ang was a book entitled *Ch'ang-an Zhi*《长安志》, *Gazettee of Ch'ang-an*. We know Song Mingqiu 宋敏求, ADCE 1019--1079 wrote *Ch'ang-an Zhi*《长安志》, *Gazettee of Ch'ang-an,*[7] but the paragraph cited by Luo Daxiang 骆大骧 could not be traced.

---

[3] Juan 57 of Shiliu Guo Chunqiu, edition of the Lanhui Tang of the Tu family 屠氏兰晖堂刻本 of the 37th year of the Wanli 万历 period(1609) of the Ming, Nanjing Library.

[4] Juan 2 of Gaoseng Zhuan《高僧传》by Hui Jiao, ms of the Ming edition, Shanghai Library.

[5] 姚兴引诸沙门于澄玄堂，听鸠摩罗什演说佛经, juan 4 of Luo Daxiang, *Leibian Changanzhi* (骆大骧《类编长安志》, *A Classified Gazeteer of Ch'ang-an)*, ms. of the Ming(ADCE 1368-1644) period, in *Songyuan Fangzhi Congkan,* facsimilie published by Zhonghua Shuju, 1990, book 1《宋元方志丛刊》，中华书局，1990年，第一册.

[6] Cao t'ang Buddhist Temple 在御宿川圭峯下， 本姚兴草堂逍遥园， 鸠摩罗什译经是园。 什死焚之，其舌不坏， 塔今存焉, juan 5 of Luo Daxiang's *Leibian Changanzhi(A Classified Gazetee of Changan),* ms of the Ming(1368-1644 A.d.) period, in *Songyuan Fangzhi Congkan,* facsimilie published by Zhonghua Shuju, 1990, book 1 骆大骧：《类编长安志》卷五， 明抄本， 收于《宋元方志丛刊》， 中华书局， 1990年，第一册).

[7] Also facsimile published in *Songyuan Fangzhi Congkan* by Zhonghua Shuju, 1990, book 1. The narative of Chengxuantang (澄玄堂，Chengxuan Hall) can be found in this book.

Source 3, in juan 226 of Ma Duanlin's *Wenxian Tongkao* 马端临：《文献通考》, it was mentioned that Dao An 道安, a famous monk, was highly respected by Fu Jian 符坚, the emperor of the Former Qin 前秦 (ADCE 350-395). He heard about of of Kumārajīva's knowledge of Buddhism and asked Emperor Fu Jian to invite him. Kumārajīva received this news and expressed his regards to Dao An as well. In the 2nd year of the Hongshi period 弘始 of the Later Qin (后秦，AD 384-418CE), it was in the year ADCE 400CE, when Kumārajīva arrived in Ch'ang-an 长安, the capital of the then empire, Dao An had passed away 20 years ago. Kumārajīva was very sad about this. He started his translation of Buddhist classics in Ch'ang-an, and his translations were the same as what was corrected by Dao An. At that time, among many foreign monks in Ch'ang-an, Kumārajīva was the best. His translation of *Wei Mo*《维摩》, namely *Weimoji Jing*《维摩诘经》, *Vimalakīrti-nirdeśa)*，*Fahua Jing* 《法华》, *Saddharmapuṇḍarīka-sūtra*，Chinese transcription (萨达磨奔茶利迦素怛缆) *Chengshi Lun* 《成实论》 *(Satyasiddhi āstra)* and *Shisong Lu*《十诵律》 were the important documents of Mahāyāna [8]. The above mentioned description of Kumārajīva in Ma Duanlin's book was copied from the juan 35, namely the chapter of bibliography of the classics of Taosim and Buddhism of the *Shuishu*《隋书》, *History of the Sui Dynasty*, 581-618 CE.) written by Wei Zheng 魏征, 580-643 CE.), a famous high ranking official of the T'ang period.

Ma Duanlin has also mentioned the titles of the Chinese translations of Buddhist classics translated by Kumārajīva, like *Jingang Banruo Jing*《金刚般若经》,[9] *Weimoji Suoshuo Jing*《维摩诘所说经》[10] and *Miaofa Lianhua Guanshiyin Pumenping*《妙法莲华经观世音普门品》[11].

For the *Jingang Banruo Jing*《金刚般若经》*Vajracchedika-prajñāpāramitā-sūtra)*, Ma Duanlin cited the words of Chao 鼂氏 stating that 5 personages, monk Zhong Mi 宗密 and Zhi En 知恩 of the T'ang, Si Yuanren 思元仁, Mei Changchao 思元仁 and Wang Anshi 王安石 of the Royal Dynasty, Huang Chao 皇朝, namely the Song, annotated this sūtra.[12] This Chao 鼂氏 should be Chao Gongwu 晁公武, ca. 1105-1180. The sentence cited by Ma Duanlin can be found in the 2nd part of juan 3 of the book entitled *Zhaode Xiansheng Junzai Dushu Zhi* 《昭德先生郡斋读书志》written by Chao Gongwu 晁公武, ca. 1105-1180.[13] Fang Hui 方回, a Yuan author commented that Kumārajīva's translation of

8 Ma Duanlin: Wenxian Tongkao, juan 226, Xihu Shuyuan edition of 1324, Nanjing Library 马端临：《文献通考》卷二百二十六，元泰定元年西湖书院刻元明递修本,[清]丁丙跋,南京图书馆藏).

9 ibid.

10 ibid.

11 Ma Duanlin: *Wenxian Tongkao*, juan 227, Xihu Shuyuan edition of 1324, Nanjing Library 马端临：《文献通考》卷二百二十七，元泰定元年西湖书院刻元明递修本,[清]丁丙跋,南京图书馆藏.

12 Ma Duanlin: *Wenxian Tongkao*, juan 226, Xihu Shuyuan edition of 1324, Nanjing Library 马端临：《文献通考》卷二百二十六，元泰定元年西湖书院刻元明递修本,[清]丁丙跋,南京图书馆藏

13 Sibuchangkan 四部丛刊三编 edition.

Vajracchedika-prajñāpāramitā-sūtra was the easiest one.[14] Ma Duanlin also called this translation of Kumārajīva as *Liuyi Jingang Jing(*《六译金刚经》, *6 Translations of Vajracchedika-prajñāpāramitā-sūtra)* as it was translated 6 times into Chinese till then.[15]

Weimoji Suoshuo Jing 《维摩诘所说经》translated by Kumārajīva, should be *Wei Mo* 《维摩》, *Vimalakīrti-nirdeśa)* as mentioned above. Meanwhile *Miaofa Lianhua Guanshiyin Pumenping* 《妙法莲华经观世音普门品》should be the already discussed *Fahua Jing* 《法华》, *Saddharmapuṇḍarīka-sūtra)* mentioned by Ma Duanlin.

Source 4 and 5 are the *Zhiyuan Fabao Kantong Zonglu* 《至元法寶勘同总録》, *A General Catalogue of the Precious Buddhist Classics Identified in the Zhiyuan Period*) compiled by Qing Jixiang 庆吉祥, a Yuan Monk.

According to the preface of the book, long before the period of Qubilay Qa'an, Buddhist sūtras had spread into China. As translation was a special kind of work, and he ordered Khitay Sari 合台萨里, an Uigur monk[16] and the chief official of Buddhist Affairs of the Empire, to invite Tibetan Lama hPhags-pa, the teacher of the Emperor, and other Tibetan, Uigur and Han Chinese monks at to Xingjiaosi 兴教寺, a Buddhist temple in Daidu (Beijing). They worked there for more than two years, between 1285 and 1287, where they examined and checked the Buddhist sutras collected till then.[17]

---

14 "最简者鸠摩罗什之《金刚经》"， see Fang Hui''s (方回) Huizhou Dongmen Guanyintang Ji (《徽州东门观音堂记》), in juan 2 of Tongjiang Ji (《桐江集》), Wan Weibie''s collection of the Jiaqing period of the Qing.

15 Ma Duanlin: Wenxian Tongkao, juan 226, Xihu Shuyuan edition of 1324, Nanjing Library (马端临：《文献通考》卷二百二十六，元泰定元年西湖书院刻元明递修本,[清]丁丙跋,南京图书馆藏).

16 He was also called Qitai Sali (乞台薩理) in Yuan sources. The text of the tomeestone of his son, A Lu Hun Sa Li (阿鲁浑萨理, Ar γ un Sali) was written by Zhao Mengfu（ 赵孟頫）, stating that Qitay Sali was a Uyigur of Beiting (北庭, Bešbalïq). His son Ar γ un Sali (阿鲁浑萨理) had learned Esoteric Buddhism from hPhags-pa Lama and after several months, he understood Tibetan scripts and Chinese and other languages. Qubilayi QKha''an ordered him learn written Chinese and Chinese classics. Later, when hPhags-pa returned to Tibet, he followed him. hPhags-pa introduced him to prince Jinkim, the son of Qubilayi QKha''an, —Qitay Sali Shendaobei(《乞台萨理神道碑》, the text of the tomeestone of Qitay Sali)，in Songxuezai Ji(《松雪斋集》)，juan 7. Sibucongcan (四部丛刊) edition. Ar γ un Sali has an biography in juan 130 of Yuanshi(《元史》) based on the text of this tomestone. She Nianchang''s (釋念常) Fuozu Tongzai(《佛祖通載》) copied the text of the tomestone, meanwhile misunderstood Ar γ un Sali and his father Qitay Sali—see the edition of 7 th year of Zhizheng 至正 period (1347).

17 The text states the identification of Buddhist classic was headed by Hetay Sali. Other Uyigur monks mentioned in the text are Zaiya Dasi (斋牙答思) , Danyasun (旦压孙) whose official position was Hanlinyuan Chengzhi (翰林院承旨) and Anzang (安藏).
In juan 7 of Songxuezai Ji(《松雪斋集》) of the above mentioned Zhao Mengfu, a Danya Gong, namely Mr. Danya (旦牙公) working in Xuanzhengyuan(宣政院), an institution responsible for the administration of the affairs of Buddhism, was mentioned. He should be Danyansun. Meanwhile in the Gazettee of Zhenjiang (《至顺镇江志》) compiled in the Zhishun period (1330-1332) a Danyadasi（旦牙答思） with the same position was mentioned. Cheng Jufu, an Yuan author mentioned that Anzang was an Uyigur whose hometown was Beübalnq...—see the Text of the Tomestone of Qingguo Wenjin Gong (秦國文靖公神道碑), Xuelou Ji (雪樓集), juan 9, edition of the Hongwu period (1368-1398).

This work mentioned 52 Buddhist classics translated by Kumārajīva, and out of them those which can be identified and are collected in juan 1, are as follows:

1. *Xiaoping Banruo Bolomito Jing*《小品般若波罗蜜多经》, *Prajñāpāramitā-hṛdayasūtra)*
2. *Jingan Banruo Bolomito Jing*《金刚般若波罗蜜多经》, *Vajracchedikā-prajñāpāramitā-sūtra)*
3. *Renwang Huguo Banruo Jing*《仁王护国般若经》*Kāruṇika-rāja Prajñāpāramitā-sūtra)*
4. *Mohe Banruo Bolomi Daming Zoujing*《摩诃般若波罗蜜大明呪经》, *Sūtra of the Great Illumination Mantra of Mahā-prajñā-pāramitā)*
5. *Xumoti Shanlong Jing*《须摩提善隆经》, *Sumagadhi)*

Those collected in juan 2 which can be identified are as follows:

6. *Zhuangyan Puti Xin Jing*《庄严菩提心经》, *The Sūtra on the Magnificent Bodhi*
7. *Shiwei Jing*《十位经》, *Daśabhūmika sūtra),* which is the same sutra entitled *Jianbei Yichie Zhide Jing*《渐备一切智德经》
8. *Xiaofa Lianhua Jing*《妙法莲华经》, *Saddharmapuṇḍarīka-sūtra*)
9. *Weimoji Suoshuo Jing*《维摩诘所说经》, *Vimalakīrti-nirdeśa*. These two have been discussed.

Those collected in juan 3 which can be identified are as follows:

10. *Amito Jing*《阿弥陀经》*Amitāyurdhyāna*
11. *Huashu Jing*《华手经》*Kuśala-mūla-saṅgraha*

    Those collected in juan 8 which can be identified are as follows:

12. *Fanwang Jing*《梵网经》, *Brahmajāla-sūtra*
13. *Da Zhidu Lun*《大智度论》, *Mahāprajñāpāramitāśāstra, Great Treatise on the Perfection of Wisdom* by Nāgārjuna 龙树菩萨

Those collected in juan 8 which can be identified are as follows:

14. *Zhong Lun*《中论》, *Mūlamādhyamakakārikā* by Nāgārjuna 龙树菩萨
15. *Shier Men Lun*《十二门论》*Dvādaśanikāya-Śāstra)* by Nāgārjuna 龙树菩萨
16. *Shizhu Biposha Lun*《十住毗婆沙论》, *Daśabhūmika-vibhāṣā* by Nāgārjuna 龙树菩萨
17. *Da Zhuangyan Jing Lun*《大庄严经论》, *Mahāyāna-sutrā-laṅkara* by Aśvaghoṣa 马鸣菩萨造
18. *Chengshi Lun*《成实论》, *Satyasiddhi-śāstra* by Harivarman 诃梨跋摩
19. *Zuochan Sanmei Jing*《坐禅三昧经》, *Dhyānā-dhiṣṭhita-samādhi-dharmaparyāya-sūtra*

The other Buddhist classics translated by Kumārajīva mentioned in this book which have not yet been identified are as follows:

1. *Fulouna Huishuo*《富楼那 *(Pūrṇa)*会说》
2. *Shanbi Pusa Huishuo*《善臂菩萨会说》
3. *Zhizaiwang Pusa Jing*《自在王菩萨经》
4. *Dashu Ji Naluowang Suowenjing*《大树祭那罗王所问经》
5. *Ji Yichie Fude Sanmei Jing*《集一切福德三昧经》
6. *Siyi Fantian Suowen Jing*《思益梵天所问经》
7. *Chishi Jing*《持世经》or *called Queying Jing*《誵印经》
8. *Zhufa Wuxing Jing*《诸法无行经》
9. *Mile Chengfuo Jing*《弥勒成佛经》
10. *Mile Xiasheng Jing*《弥勒下生经》
11. *Wenshu Shili Wen Puti Jing*《文殊师利问菩提经》
12. *Shou Lenyan Sanmei Jing*《首楞严三昧经》
13. *Qianfuo Yinyuan Jing*《千佛因緣经》
14. *Fashang Lu*《法上録》
15. *Kongquewang Zou Jin(*《孔雀王呪经》or called *Da Jinse Kongquewang Jing*《大金色孔雀王经》
16. *Fangniu Jing*《放牛经》
17. *Hai Bade Jing*《海八德经》
18. *Chan Biyao Fa Jing*《禅秘要法经》
19. *Dengzhi Yinyuan Jing*《灯指因緣经》
20. *Fuozang Jing*《佛藏经》 *or called Xuanze Zhufa Jing*《选择诸法经》
21. *Ye Fangguang Jing*《耶方广经》
22. *Shisong Biqiu Jieben*《十诵比丘戒本》or called *Shisong Buoluo Tiliancha Jie*《十诵波罗提栋叉戒》
23. *Shisong Biqiuni Jieben*《十诵比丘尼戒本 or called *Shisong Biqiuni Buoluo Tibencha Jie*《十诵比丘尼波罗提本叉戒》
24. *Bai Lun*《百论》by Deva
25. *Fa Putixin Lun*《发菩提心论》
26. *Pusahe Seyu Fa*《菩萨诃色欲法》
27. *Chanfa Yaojie Jing*《禅法要解经》or called *Chanyao Jing*《禅要经》
28. *Siwei Yaolue Fa*《思惟要略法》
29. *Zhongjing Xuanchu Za Biyu Jing*《众经撰出杂譬喻经》
30. *Biography of Aśvaghoṣa*《马鸣菩萨传》
31. *Biography of Nāgārjuna*《龙树菩萨传》

32. *Biography of Deva*《提婆菩萨传》

33. *Notes on Vimalakīrti-nirdeśa*《注维摩诘经》

The work done by the monks gathered in Beijing under the regime of Qubilai Qa'an, who were Uigur Buddhists, Tibetan Lamas and Han Chinese monks, has great importance. It is the first time that Buddhist monks of different ethnic origins worked together, checked and compared the translations of Kumārajīva with those Tibetan translations translated from Sanskrit, and registered each version passed by Kumārajīva and its parallel Tibetan versions.

Before the Yuan period Kumārajīva was mainly known by the people of the interior of China, namely, the Han Chinese. During the Mongol-Yuan period, through the interchange between Buddhists of different nations, the translations of Kumārajīva of Buddhist classics became the common treasure of Buddhists all over China, no matter what their ethnic background was. In other words, the name of Kumārajīva and his work was known by the inhabitants of the mainland of China as well as by the people settled in Mongolia and Tibet.

21

Kumārajīva in 18th century Tibetan Sources

Guilaine Mala

Introduction

The beginning of the 5th century CE may be regarded as a decisive turning point in the history of Buddhism in China, especially because of the work of two eminent monks, the Chinese Huiyuan (慧遠:334-417) in Southern Yangzi region of China,[1] and more particularly because of the extensive translation work of the Kuchean monk, Kumārajīva (Ch. Jiumoluoshe 鳩摩羅什: 350-409?) in Chang'an, Northern China, under the patronage of the proto-Tibetan Emperor Yao Xing (姚興: 384-417) of the Later Qin Dynasty (Hou Qin 後秦).[2]

Kumārajīva was not the first Kuchean monk to go to China. Before him, two or three others had gone. But it is the special life of Kumārajīva due to the intense political instability and turmoil during his lifetime which made all the difference. Having been a prisoner in Liangzhou for 17 years, he mastered the Chinese language well enough to be able to pass on the real meaning of Buddhist scriptures.

Thanks to the range and the quality of his translations, Kumārajīva helped Chinese Buddhism to free itself of the theories and methods of the "Dark Learning" (*Xuanxue* 玄學) and the "Pure Conversations" (*qingtan* 清談), as well as the method of *Ge Yi* (格義, lit. "Matching the Meaning [of a Sanskrit term with one of a Chinese expression already existing in traditional philosophy]"), which had caused numerous misinterpretations. Moreover, Kumārajīva was

---

1 See Huiyuan's biography in

2 See Yao Xing's biography in *Jinshu* 晉書 by Fang Xuanling (578-648) et al., Beijing, Zhonghua shuju, 10 vols, 1974, vol.

responsible for introducing into China the *Madhyamaka* school (Ch. *Zhonglun* 中論) or Middle Path, which was founded in India by Nāgārjuna (c. CE 150-250).

Kumārajīva's biography is to be found at least in the annals of the Jin dynasty (*Jinshu, j.*95), in the *Gaoseng zhuan* (T. no 2059), the *Chu sanzangji ji* (T. no 2145], the *Guang hongming ji* (T. no.2103), as well as in the prefaces to some *Sūtras* he translated into Chinese; moreover, some further information can be collected from biographies of his disciples and other famous monks of his lifetime.[3]

Mention of Kumārajīva is also to be found in some 18th century Tibetan sources written by Tibetan and Mongol authors. In Tibetan, Kumārajīva is named Ku-mā-ra-shri or "The Glorious Kumāra".

However, it is important to state that Kumārajīva has not left any imprint on Tibetan Buddhism, and therefore his name is only known to Tibetan scholars and researchers, who have an interest in Chinese Buddhism and who are acquainted with a specific genre of Tibetan literature. It may also be noted that Kumārajīva's fame has been eclipsed in Tibet by that of the Chinese pilgrim Xuanzang (玄奘: 662-664) of the Tang dynasty because there exists in Tibetian several summarized accounts of the travels of Xuanzang to India.

Many earlier Tibetan chronicles include a chapter on China, but these chapters deal with royal genealogies, that is the history of the succession of Chinese dynasties. If we examine the best known Buddhist chronicles, which include a Chapter on China, such as the *rGyal-rabs gsal-ba'i me-long* (1328), *Deb-ther dmar-po* (1346), *rGya-Bod yig-tshang* (1434), *Deb-ther sngon-po* (1476-1478), *Deb-ther dmar-pogsar-ma* (1538), *Chos-'byung mkhas-pa'i dga'-ston* (1545-1564), we see that they all begin the history of the royal genealogies of China with "the first emperor of China named Ci'u" (rendering of Zhou 周). This is because their authors follow a well-known Chinese tradition based on forged texts, which assign the Buddha's birth to the wood-tiger (*jiayin* 甲寅) year (Tib. *shing-pho-stag lo*, wood-male-tiger year), that is the 24th year of the reign of

[3] See *Jinshu* 晉書 by Fang Xuanling (578-648) et al., Beijing, Zhonghua shuju, 10 vols, 1974, vol. 8, *juan* 95, pp.2499-2502; *Gaoseng zhuan* 高僧傳, *Taishō* 50, no. 2059, *j.* 2, pp. 330a-333a; *Chu sanzangji ji* 出三藏記集 , *Taishō* 55, no. 2145, *j.* 14, pp. 100-102a; *Guang hongming ji* 廣弘明集, *T.* vol. 52, no. 2103, *j.* 23, pp. 264b-265b. See French translation of Kumārajīva's biography in SHIH Robert, *Biographies des Moines Eminents (Kao Seng Tchouan) traduites et annotées*, University of Leuven, Institut Orientaliste, Bibliothèque du Muséon, Vol. 54, Leuven, 1968, pp. 60-81.

King Zhaowang of the Western Zhou dynasty (i.e. 1029 BCE according to the traditional chronology.[4] And that is why the history of China really begins with this dynasty, which is particularly meaningful for these Buddhist historians.

However, one of the most renowned Tibetan sources mentioning Kumārajīva does not belong to the historical genre but to the so-called "doctrinal literature" (*grubmtha'*, Sk. *siddhānta*) of Tibet, an important genre of Tibetan literature which seeks to clarify the classification of Buddhist and non-Buddhist schools , and expound the doctrinal position of each of these schools. It is the *Grub-mtha' shel-gyi me-long* ("The Crystal Mirror of Doxographies"), which was written in the period 1801-1802 by Thu'u-bkwan Blo-bzang chos-kyi nyi-ma (lit. "Noble-Minded Dharma-Sun":1737-1802), a native of Eastern Tibet and a Khutugtu ("Holy"), one of the highest ranking Lamas of the dGe-lugs-pa Order also known as "Yellow Hats", who spent several years at the Manchu Court, at a time when the Manchu Emperors of China converted to Tibetan Buddhism, and the Tibetan dGe-lugs-pas were linked by a relation of patron-chaplain.

The full title of Thu'u-bkwan's *Grub-mtha'* is *Grub-mtha' thams-cad-kyi khungs dang 'dod-tshul ston-pa legs-bshad shel-gyi me-long* or "The Crystal Mirror of Aphorisms which Expound the Origins and Assertions of All Doctrinal Systems".

It is unique in its genre for its author did not treat only the philosophical systems of India and Tibet, but also of China, Mongolia, Khotan and even the hidden kingdom of Sambala. It was intended to serve as Thu'u-bkwan's testament, his spiritual legacy for generations to come. Among all his works, which fill ten volumes, it is the most renowned. One of its chapters in particular offers an invaluable testimony to his perception of Chinese religions.[5]

---

[4] This is the case in chronicles such as: 1) the *rGyal-rabs gsal-ba'i me-long* (1328) by Saskya-pa Bla-ma dam-pa bSod-nams rgyal-mtshan (1312-1375), transl. by P.K. Sorensen, pp. 77-84; the 'Red Annals', *Deb-ther dmar-po*, also known as *Hu-lan deb-gter/ther* (1346), by 'Tshal-pa Kun-dga' rdo-rje, Beijing edn. 1981, chapter four, pp. 11-12; 3) *rGya-Bod yigtshang* (1434) by dPal-'byor bzang-po, Chengdu edn. 1985, pp. 99, 101; 4) the 'Blue Annals', *Deb-ther sngon-po* (1476-1478) by 'Gos-lo gzhon-nu-dpal (1392-1481), who quoted the *Debdmar*, Chengdu edn. 1987, I, pp. 73-81, transl. by G.N. Roerich, pp. 47-57; 5) the New Red Annals, *Deb-ther dmar-po gsar-ma* (1538) by the Panchen bSod-nams grags-pa, transl. by G. Tucci, p. 175; 6) the Scholars' Feast, *Chos-'byung mkhas-pa'i dga'-ston* (1545-1565) by dPa'-bo gtsug-lag phreng-ba, Beijing edn. 1986, vol. 2, p. 1389, etc.

[5] Thu'u-bkwan Blo-bzang chos-kyi nyi-ma (1737-1802), *Grub-mtha' shel-gyi me-long;* complete title: *Grub-mtha' thams-cad-kyi khungs dang 'dod-tshul ston-pa legs-bshad shel-gyi me-long,* Lhasa Zhol edition, volume 2 (KHA, pp. 5-519) of the Collected Works of Thu'ubkwan blo-bzang-chos-kyi-nyi-ma edited and reproduced by Ngawang Gelek Demo with an Introduction by E. Gene Smith, New Delhi, 1969; and vol. 2 of the Thu'u-bkwan *gSung-'bum* (Blockprint in 10 vols.) acquired in 1963 by the Bodleian in Oxford (see *rJe-btsun bla-ma dam-pa Thu'u-bkwan blo-bzang chos-kyi nyi-ma dpal-bzang-po'i gsung-'bum,* Tib. Block book a.47, vol. 2 KHA).; modern edition of Lanzhou, Kan-su'u mi-rigs dpe-skrun-khang, 1st edn.1984, 2nd edn. 1986, 3rd edn. 1989.

Characteristics of the Chapter on Chinese Religion contained in the 'Crystal Mirror of Doxographies'

Thu'u-bkwan's Chapter on Chinese religions is entitled "History of [Confucian] Learning and [other] Doctrinal Tenets in the Country of Great China" (*Ma-hā Tsi-na'i yul-du rig-byed dang grub-mtha' byung-tshul*). [6]

This Chapter provides an introduction to non-Buddhist religions as understood by a Tibetan scholar whose mind was entirely immersed in the realm of Buddhist thought.

Now, if one wonders whether non-Buddhist Chinese religions could have any real influence on the thought of a 18th century Tibetan scholar, Thu'u-bkwan gives the key from the start by opening his chapter with a poem stating that all religions, like Buddhism, were similarly planned by the Jina (an epithet for Buddha meaning "Victorious"). Thu'u-bkwan's view is perfectly logical in the context of *Mahāyāna* Buddhism, according to which the Buddha is perceived as an eternal presence, appearing simultaneously under many forms in multiple universes for the benefit of all sentient beings. In conformity with this belief, non-Buddhist systems were taught through the empowering blessings of the *buddhas*, and were diffused as necessary stratagems, convenient methods adapted to the faculties of those who were not able to grasp directly the true essence of Buddhism.Therefore, all doctrines have their validity within the Buddhist point of view, so far as the *Mahāyāna* key device of "skilful means" (*upāyakauśalya*) is applied to them.

Moreover, in this Mahayanist perspective, Thu'u-bkwan expounded Chinese religions in a specific way, which does not conform to the orthodox opinion. Although Thu'ubkwan also examined briefly the fate of Hinduism in China and more substantially that of Islam, the doctrines which are examined principally by him, are the main three doctrines prevailing in China, namely Confucianism, Taoism and Buddhism, which are known collectively as the Three Teachings (*bstan-pa gsum, sanjiao* 三教).

His Chapter comprises four parts, which are respectively devoted to the history of:

1] Confucian Learning, which is compared to the stars;

2] Taoism, which is named *Bon*, and which is compared to the moon (*Bon* was the pre-Buddhist religion in Tibet, which managed to survive until

[6] See Chapter on Chinese Religions in modern edn. Lanzhou 1989, pp. 391-446; Lhasa Zhol edition (chapters 10 and 11, volume 2 (KHA) of the Collected Works of Thu'u-bkwan Blo-bzang-chos-kyi-nyi-ma edited and reproduced by Ngawang Gelek Demo with an Introduction by E. Gene Smith, Gedan Sungrab Minyam Gyunphel Series, New Delhi, 1962, vol. 2, folios 421-482); and vol.2 (KHA), pp. 212-242, of Thu'u-bkwan *gSung-'bum* (Blockprint in 10 vols.) acquired in 1963 by the Bodleian in Oxford (Tib. Block book a.47).

this day, after having transformed itself and adapted to the Buddhist milieu. Tibetan scholars often identify Shenrab, the founder of *Bon* according to the tradition with Laozi, thus making *Bon* a derivative of Taoism);

3] Hinduism and Islam, which are qualified as "traditions of limited scope"; and

4] Buddhism, which is compared to the sun.[7]

The treatment accorded to the Three Teachings (*sanjiao* 三教) appears to follow a Chinese syncretic tradition that can be traced back to the 6th century CE.[8]

References to this syncretic tradition can be found in a number of Chinese sources from the 7th century to the 17th century, in Chinese Annals of the Sui and that of Northern Dynasties, and in Buddhist compilations of the Song and Yuan dynasties, where the metaphor of the Three Luminaries (*Sanguang* 三光) –the stars, the moon and the sun–symbolizing the unity of the Three Teachings is progressively distorted to demonstrate the superiority of Buddhism.[9]

Kumārajīva' legacy to Chinese Buddhism according to the *Grub-mtha' shel-gyi me-long*

It is in the section on Indian Buddhism introduced into China that mention of Kumārajīva is to be found. His Indian legacy in China is described in the following way: (p. 426: l.2) "The Buddha's Teaching spread in the country of

[7] 1]"History of the tradition named Confucian Learning, which is similar to the stars" (*sKarma lta-bu she'u zhes-bya'i lugs-srol byung-tshul*);
2] "History of the *Bon* doctrine, a religious tradition, which is named Taoism and which is similar to the moon" (*Zla-ba lta-bu chos-lugs dou'si zhes-pa Bon-gyi grub-mtha' byungtshul*).
3]"History of some 'minor' traditions (*Lugs-srol nyi-tshe-ba 'ga'-zhig byung-tshul*), namely Hinduism and Islam, both being treated as regards to their fate in China and then for Islam in particular, its ultimate fate according to the Tibetan beliefs.
4]"History of the religious tradition of the Buddhist Insiders (*Nang-ba Sangs-rgyas-pa'i choslugs byung-tshul*), this last section being itself composed of two parts, which are: a) History of the introduction of Indian Buddhism into China, and b) "History of the introduction of Tibetan Buddhism into China".

[8] Among the various attempts to harmonize the Three Teachings in China, it appears that one of the earliest references to the reconciliation of the Three Teachings is this argument in favour of the unity of the Three Teachings compared to the Three Luminaries which is attributed to Li Shiqian (李士謙:523-588 according to the *Annals of the Sui Dynasty*), a scholar, a poet and a military administrator, native of Hebei province. Concerning his biography and the transmission of his argumentation, see G. Mala, "Perception of Chinese Religions in Eighteenth-Century Tibet: A Study of Thu'u-bkwan's *Grub-mtha' shel-gyi melong* and Related Tibetan Works Written by Mongol Authors", doctoral thesis, University of Oxford, 2006, pp. 83-99.

[9] Li Shiqian's argumentation is to be found at least in the following sources:
1] *Suishu* 隋書 by Wei Zheng (魏徵:580-643) and others, 77. 1754: 3-4;
2] *Beishi* 北史 by Li Yanshou 李延壽 and others (before 601 to after 675 CE.), 33. 1234:12;
3] *Sanjiao pingxin lun* (三教平心論, "Treatise [viewing] the Three Teachings with a Balanced Mind"), written by Liu Mi (劉謐:13th cent.), *T.* 2117, A. 781c16-17;
4] *Fayun zhilüe* (法運志略, "A Concise Record on the Fate of the Law"), part of the *Fozutongji* (佛祖統記, "A General Record on the Patriarchs of Buddhism": 1269), by Zhipan (志磐:actif: 1258-1269), *T.* 2035, 39.360a13; 44. 405b24-25; 54. 472a16-17;

China through what are known as the five distinct lineages (Tib. *brgyud-pa rnam-pa lnga*, Ch. *wuzhong chuancheng* 五種傳承), [which are respectively]: [1] the lineage of *Vinaya* or Discipline (Tib. *'dul-ba'i brgyud-pa*, Ch. *lüchuancheng* 律傳承 or *Lüzong* 律宗), [2] the lineage of *Tantras* (Tib. *gsang-sngags-kyi brgyud-pa*, Ch. *Mizong* 密宗), [3] the lineage of Vast Conduct (Tib. *rgya-chen spyod brgyud*, Ch. *Guangdaxingzong* 廣大行宗 or *Faxiangzong* 法相宗), [4] the lineage of the Profound View (Tib. *zab-mo lta brgyud*, Ch. *Shenshenguangpai* 甚深觀派 or *Faxingzong* 法性宗), and [5] the lineage of the Quintessential Meaning (Tib. *snying-po don brgyud*, Ch. *Chanzong* 禪宗). (Lanzhou edn., 1989, p. 426:5) 'Concerning the first [of these lineages, the *Vinaya*]: It seems that a transmission of a lineage from *Arhat* Ma-tanggi [for ga] existed for a while, but later came to an end. A *Vidyādhara* (*rig-'dzin*, lit."Knowledge-holder") named Ku-mā-ra-shri (Kumārajīva), who was learned in all sciences and had clairvoyance and magical powers, came to China.

The Jo-bo Sandal-wood Statue (*tsandan Jo-bo*) was brought at that time also. The King named Hung-shi (Hongshi 弘始 reign title of Yao Xing 姚興: 384-417 of the Later Qin, Houqin 後秦) honoured [Kumārajīva] greatly, and, together with the monk Ce'u (Ce'u hwa-shang, Zhu *heshang* 竺和尚, lit. "Monk disciple of an Indian Master") and another eight hundred learned disciples, [Kumārajīva] translated many *sūtras* and *śastras*. By his explanations, he widely promulgated the *Mahāyāna* Teaching, and in particular gave many monks vows (*dge-slong-gi sdompa*) and *bodhisattva* vows (*byang-chub sems-dpa'i sdom-pa*). From that time there was the tradition of taking *bodhisattva* vows after the full ordination. Three [masters], i.e. the *Vinayadhara* (*'dul-'dzin*) named Buddha-dznyā-na (Buddhajṭāna, Fozhi 佛智), Bi-ma-la-tsaskṣu (Vimalākṣa, Bimoluocha 卑摩羅叉) and Dha-rmā-rutsi (Dharmaruci, Tanmoliuzhi 曇摩流支), together with Ku-mā-ra, translated much of the *Vinaya* (*'dul-ba'i skor*) such as the "Four Sections of Statements" [of the *Sarvāstivāda Vinaya*] (*lung-sde bzhi, Sifenlṃ* 四分律), and they gave direct instructions on the monastic training (*dge-slong-gi bslab-bya*). Also, the *Sthavira* named dGe-'dun-go-cha (Saṁghavarman, Sengqiebamo 僧伽跋摩) came [to China], and propagated the *Vinaya*'s transmission of vows and the training. From him and Kumārashrī there came a transmission of the

5] [*Lidai biannian*] *Shishi tongjian* (歷代編年釋氏通鑑, "Complete Guide / Universal Mirror Chronicling the **śā**kya clan through the Ages': 1270), by Benjue 本覺, in *Dai Nihon zokuz***ō** *ky***ō**, vol. 131, 6. 436ro b10-11;

6] *Fozu lidai tongzai* (佛祖歷代通載, "A General Record of the Patriarchs of Buddhism through the Ages": 1333), by Nianchang (念常:d. 1341), *T*. 2036, 10. 559b 28;

7] [*Lichao*] *Shishi zijian* (, "Well-documented Guide/Mirror by Periods of the Sakya Clan"; 1336), by Xizhong, in *Dai Nihon zokuz***ō** *ky***ō** , vol. 132, 7.7ro 15;

8] *Shishi jigu lüe* (, "Outline of the Ancient Records of the Sakya Clan": 1354), by Jue'an, T. 2037, 2. 808b 13;

9] *Sanjiao huibian yaolüe* (, "Compendium on the Three Teachings": 1562), by Lin Zhaoen (: 1517-1598), a great syncretist of the Ming dynasty, in Linzi quanji, XI: 1.1a.

[vows or teachings of] individual liberation [from cyclic existence] (*so-thar*, Sk. *pratimokṣa*) and *bodhisattva* [precepts] (*byang-sems-kyi rgyun*) that still exists [in China].[10] (427:1) There is an account of a [party of] ten nuns including the Ceylonese nun De-ba-sa-rā (Therī Triśāraṇa, Tie-sa-ra, Ch. Tiesaluo 鉄薩羅) coming from India to China, but it is not known if there was a transmission of *Bhikṣuṇīs* precepts (*dgeslong-ma'i sdom-rgyun*) [conferred in] their lineage originating from them.[11] From the Four Root Precepts (*rtsa-ba bzhi*) up to the Seven Rules [given for] settling disputes [among the monks] (*rtsod-pa zhi-bar byed-pa'i chos-bdun*), [the Chinese *Vinaya*] is no different from the Tibetan. However, it is said that concerning the numerous point of the training (*bslab-pa'i chos*), [some] were adopted from other classes (*sde-ba gzhan-nas*) which were in agreement with the customs of the country. They do not eat meat, they do not ride horses, they carry a begging bowl even smaller than the smallest size, and the pieces forming the monk's robe are like the successive layers of bird's feathers (*bya-spu yas-non-gyi tshul*). There is no more than one class [of Buddhists] (*sde-ba*) in this country, and therefore there is no need to fear mistaking [the order they belong to], and perhaps that is why the custom of [displaying regulation] signs [on the monk's robe] does not exist. According to the Chinese Law (*rGya'i khrims-lugs-la*), yellow is the colour reserved for the Emperor and red is for the ministers. The emperor [reigning] at that time

[10] Transliteration of this passage: (426:2) *rGya'i yul-du dar-ba'i Sangs-rgyaskyi bstan-pa-la brgyud-pa rnam-pa lngar grags-te / 'dul-ba'i brgyud-pa / gsangsngags-kyi brgyud-pa / rgya-chen spyod brgyud / zab-mo lta brgyud / snying-don brgyud dang lnga'o //* (426:5) *dang-po-ni / dgra-bcom-pa Ma-tanggi-las brgyud-pa'i sdom-rgyun rezhig-gi bar-du byung yang phyis-su rgyun chad-pa 'dra-la / rig-'dzin Ku-mā-rashri zhes-bya-ba rig-gnas mtha'-dag-la mkhas-shing mngon-shes dang rdzu-'phrul mnga'-ba zhig rGya-yul-du byon / 'di phebs dus-su tsandan jo-bo yang gdandrangs/ rgyal-po Hung-shi bya-bas bkur-sti chen-po byas-te Ce'u hwa-shang gtsospa'i slob-ma mkhas-pa brgyad-brgya dang bcas-pas bka' bstan-bcos mang-du bsgyur / bshad-pa'i sgo-nas kyang theg-chen-gyi bstan-pa rgya-cher spel / khyadpar-du dge-slong-gi sdom-pa dang / byang-chub sems-dpa'i sdom-pa mang-du gnang / 'di-nas bzung hwa-shang-rnams bsnyen-rdzogs-kyi rjes-la byang-sdom len-pa'i srol dang / 'dul-'dzin Buddha-dznyā-na dang / Bi-ma-la-tsakṣu dang /Dha-rmā-ru-tsi bya-ba gsum yang / Ku-mā-ra dang mnyam-du byung-bas lung-sde bzhi sogs 'dul-ba'i skor mang-du bsgyur-cing dge-slong-gi bslab-bya mdzub-khriddu bstan / gzhan-yang gnas-brtan dGe-'dun go-cha bya-ba byon-nas kyang 'dulba'i sdom-rgyun dang bslab-bya dar-bar mdzad-pas Ku-mā-ra-shrā dang 'di gnyislas brgyud-pa'i so-thar dang byang-sems-kyi rgyun-ni deng-sang-gi bar-du gnas-so//* (427:1) *Singgha-la'i dge-slong-ma De-ba-sa-rā sogs rGya-gar-nas dge-slong-ma bcu-phrag-gcig rGya-yul-du byon-pa'i lo-rgyus 'dug kyang/ de-dag-las brgyud-pa'i dge-slong-ma'i sdom-rgyun byung ma-byung ma-shes-so // rtsa-ba bzhi-nas rtsodpa zhi-bar byed-pa'i chos bdun-gyi bar-ni Bod dang khyad-par med-la / bslab-pa'i chos mang-po'i skor-la yul lugs dang bstun-nas sde-ba gzhan-nas blangs-pa'ang yod zer / sha mi-za-zhing / bzhon-pa mi-zhon-pa dang / lhung-bzed chung-tshadlas kyang chung-ba 'chang-zhing / snam-sbyar-gyi tshal bu ni bya-spu yas-non-gyi tshul dang / yul 'dir sde-ba gcig-pu-las med-pas 'khrul-dogs mi-dgos-pas yin-nam grwa rtags-kyi srol med-do // rGya'i yul lugs-la/kha-dog ser-po rgyal-po dang / dmar-po blon-po'i tshos skal yin-cing / de-dus-kyi rgyal-pos kha-dog de-gnyis rab-byung-la dmigs-bsal-gyis gnang-ba ma-ster-zhing / rGya'i yul lugs-la lus-kyi sha rjen-par mngon-pa ngo-tsha'i gnas-su byed-pa'i dbang-gis hwa-shang-rnams gos-phu-thung-ma smug-po gyon-pa'i srol dar-la / phyis-su Bod-kyi bla-ma byonpa-rnams-kyis Bod lugs-kyi rab-byung-ba'i gos gyon kyang / Hor-gyi rgyal-po'i dus yin-pas dmigs-bsal gnang-bar brten da-lta'i bar-du hwa-shang-rnams smug chas dang / Bod-kyi dge-'dun-rnams gos dmar ser gyon-pa'i lugs so-sor byung-bar snang-ngo /*

[11] See *Biqiuni shou jie lu* 比丘尼受戒錄 in one juan by Hong Zan 弘贊 of the Qing dynasty, in *Dai Nihon zokuzō kyō* 大日本續藏經, vol. 107, 93Ro

did not give permission for these two colours to be used by the monks, and as uncovered flesh is considered shameful in the Chinese tradition, the Buddhist monks established the custom of wearing dark robes with [long] sleeves (*gos-phu-thung-ma smug-po*). Later, when the Tibetan Lamas went [to China], even though they wore the Tibetan monastic robes, as that was at the time of the Hor kings (the Mongol Yuan dynasty), they were given the permission to do so. Due to this there developed the different traditions of the Chinese monks wearing dark robes and the Tibetan monks wearing yellow and red robes.

[These customs remain unchanged] until this day." Kumārajīva is mentioned briefly a second time (p. 428) in the paragraph concerning the second lineage, that of the *Tantras*:

"The *Vidyādhara* Ku-mār-shrī did not bestow [his tantric knowledge] to many, [but] only to one or two worthy recipients (*snod-ldan*)."[12]

Concerning Kumārajīva's doctrinal contribution to Chinese Buddhism, we know that through his translations of the [*Mūla*]-*Madhyamaka śāstra* (*Zhonglun* 中論, *T*. 1564), the *Dvādaśanikāya śāstra* (*Shi'ermenlun* 十二門論, *T*. 1568) and the *śataśāstra* (*Bailun* 百論, *T*. 1569) in particular, he was responsible for introducing into China the "Three Treatises School" (*Sanlun zong* 三論宗); these three texts were the basic texts of that school, which was the Chinese form of the *Madhyamaka* school (Ch. *Zhonglun* 中論) or Middle Path, which was founded in India by Nāgārjuna (c. CE 150-250). The first patriarch of the *Sanlun zong* is traditionally considered to be Jiaxiang Dashi (嘉祥大師:549-623) because he refined the exposition of the doctrinal system. Therefore, why is Kumārajīva considered as one of the patriarchs of the Chinese school of *Vinaya* (Ch. *Lüzong* 律宗) in this Tibetan source? The real founder of the school of *Vinaya* was Daoxuan (道宣:596-667).

It may be that Kumārajīva was considered a marking figure in an earlier lineage of teaching transmission of the *Vinaya* rather than a patriarch of the so-called *Lüzong* school. However, to answer this question, one has to identify Thu'u-bkwan's main source for his Chapter on Chinese Religions.

The Main Tibetan Source Used by Thu'u-bkwan for his Chapter on Chinese Religion: *the rGya-nag chos-'byung* (1736) by the Duke mGon-po-skyabs

Now, even before Thu'u-bkwan's "Crystal Mirror of Doxographies" was conceived, a similar treatment of Chinese Buddhism within the same Chinese syncretic view of the Three Teachings and the distorted egalitarian argumentation could be found in at least two other chronicles written in Tibetan by Mongol authors.

[12] Transliteration of this passage: */rig-'dzin Ku-mā-ra-srīs kyang snod-ldan regnyis tsam-las byings-la ma-gnang* /

These are the *rGya-nag chos-'byung* or "The Chronicle of Buddhism in China", which was written in 1736 by mGon-po-skyabs (c.1690-1750)[13], and the chapter on China contained in the *dPag-bsam ljon-bzang* or "The Wish-fulfilling Tree", which was written in 1748 by Sum-pa mKhan-po Ye-shes dpal-'byor (1704-88), an Oirat Mongolian historian.[14]

A comparative study of the three texts reveals that Thu'u-bkwan's exposition is mainly based on the setting described in the *rGya-nag chos-'byung*, while the *dPagbsamljon- bzang* appears to be a shortened version of *the rGya-nag chos-'byung*.[15] The *rGya-nag chos-'byung* being the most ancient and the most developed, prime attention is given here only to the latter.

These three sources, contrary to earlier chronicles, do not begin the history of China with King Zhaowang of the Zhou dynasty, but identically go back much further in time, to the highest antiquity, the epoch of the mythical founders of civilization, beginning with hPhu-ṣi (Fuxi 伏羲: accession to the throne: 2952 B.C.E. according to the traditional chronology) as the first king of China. This last point seems to mark rupture with, or a change, from the earlier Tibetan sources dealing with the history of China, and it seems that this second type of account has originated from the earliest of these three texts, the *rGya-nag chos-'byung*, The fact that Thu'u-bkwan relied principally on mGon-

---

[13] mGon-po-skyabs (Mong. Gombojab or Gombujab, Ch. Gongbu Zhabu 工布查布: c. 1690-1750?), *rGya-nag chos-'byung*; complete title: *rGya-nag-gi yul-du dam-pa'i chos dartshul gtso-bor bshad-pa blo-gsal kun-tu dga'-ba'i rna-rgyan*, Chengdu, 1983.

[14] Sum-pa mKhan-po Ye-shes dpal-'byor (1704-88), *dPag-bsam ljon-bzang*; complete title: *rGya-gar 'Phags-pa'i yul / rGya-nag chen-po / Gangs-can Bod-yul / Sog-yul-rnams-su damchos rin-chen byung-tshul dPag-bsam ljon-bzang*, in Lokesh Chandra (ed.), *dPag-bsam-ljonbzaṅ of Sum-pa-mkhan-po Ye-ś es-dpal-ḥ byor, Part III: containing a history of Buddhism in China and Mongolia, preceded by the Re'u-mig or chronological tables, with a Foreword by G. Tucci and a preface by L. Petech, śata-piṭ aka*, Indo-Asian Literatures, vol. 8, *Bhoṭ a-piṭ aka* vol.3, New Delhi, 1959.
See Chapter on China by Sum-pa mKhan-po Ye-shes dpal-'byor in Lokesh Chandra, *dPag-bsam-ljon-bzaṅ , part III, śata-piṭ aka* Series vol. 8, New Delhi, 1959, pp. 61-133.

[15] The full title of this chronicle, which is his most famous work, is *rGya-gar 'Phags-pa'i yul / rGya-nag chen-po / Gangs-can Bod-yul / Sog-yul-rnams-su dam-chos rin-chen byungtshul dPag-bsam ljon-bzang* or "The Wish-fulfilling Tree [on] the Origin of the Precious holy *Dharma* in Ōryadeś a [India], Great China, Tibet the Land of Snows and Mongolia".
This chronicle consists of four parts dedicated to the history and the spread of Buddhism in these respective countries. The chapter on China (pp. 61-133) is entitled *Mahā-Tsi-nar gragspa'i rGya-nag chen-por chos rgyal-bstan-'dzin bstan-pa grub-mtha' sogs byung-tshul bshadpa*, "Exposition on the History of the Dharma-rājas, the holders of the Jina's Teaching, the Buddhist doctrinal tenets and others in Great China renowned as Mahā-Tsi- na". It is divided into two major parts: 1] the history of China from the first Sovereign Fuxi until Qianlong's accession to the throne in 1736 (pp. 61-107); 2] the history of the diffusion of Buddhism in China, this second part being in two sections, a] the history of different doctrines (*grub-mtha' mi-'dra-ba*), not only Taoism and Confucianism but also Islam in China and others (pp. 107-109); and b] the history of the Jina's Teaching (*rGyal-bstan*) culminating with the vast spread in China and Mongolia of the dGe-lugs-pa tradition which enjoyed the exclusive favour of the Manchu Emperors; after a review of the diffusion of the Doctrine in China through five distinct lineages of transmission, it gives the description of a comparative Catalogue, which is *the Zhiyuan Fabao kantong zonglu*, for which interest and fame were revived under the Qing (pp. 109-133).

po-skyabs' "Chonicle of Buddhism in China" for his Chapter on Chinese religions and copied many passages from it is quite understandable, for the *rGya-nag chos-'byung* is the only work so far in Tibetan historical literature that is entirely devoted to the history, both religious and worldly, of China. In Tibet, this habit of borrowing and copying is not considered plagiarism; it is rather a recognition that [the imitated author] had reached so perfect a style and had such sound information that it was not possible to differ from him. Whole passages are borrowed from him to honour him and at the same time to give a solid foundation and authority to the new written text.

The *rGya-nag chos-'byung* (lit. "The History of [the origin, growth, and development] of the Buddhist Doctrine in China") is indeed a very special work, which was written in 1736 by the "Duke" (Gung, Ch. *gong* 工) mGon-po-skyabs, most certainly one of the best polyglots and polymaths of his time. He belonged to the clan Üjümücin from the easternmost part of Mongolia. Officially appointed head of the Tibetan School (Xifan xue 西藩學) in Beijing, he was responsible for Tibetan Studies and translations of Tibetan and Mongol texts.

The full title of this chronicle is *rGya-nag-gi yul-du dam-pa'i chos dar-tshul gtsobor bshad-pa blo-gsal kun-tu dga'-ba'i rna-rgyan* or "The Delightful Earring of clear understanding, which explains principally how the Holy Dharma spread in the country of China". On the back of the last page of the modern Sichuan edn. or sDedge edn. (Chengdu 1983), which is used for the present work, the title is rendered as *Hanqu Fojiao yuanliu ji* (汉去佛教源流).

This chronicle is formed of three chapters (*sa-bcad*), which are devoted to: 1] the cosmological and physical geography of China (qualified as supports of the country, *rten*), and the history of its royal genealogies (the supported or entrusted by the country, *brten-pa*) until the end of the Ming dynasty (pp. 3-61); 2] the history of Buddhism in China through that of the successive upholders of the Teaching (pp. 62-175); 3) a descriptive catalogue of the *Dharma* Texts which were written or diffused in succession by these Doctrine-Holders. Remarkably, this last chapter appears to bethe Tibetan translation of the *Zhiyuan Fabao kantong zonglu* (至元法寶勘同總錄), a catalogue which was compiled during the Yuan dynasty in 1285-87 by Qing Jixiang (慶吉祥), a Chinese monk who worked in Peking with the Tibetan 'Phags-pa (Basiba 八思八, var. 巴思巴: 1239-1280). This catalogue, whose preface was written by Khubilai himself, is the result of Tibeto-Chinese collaboration, and it is a comparative catalogue of the Chinese and Tibetan *Tripiṭaka*, in which differences between the two are pointed out. It is preserved in *Taishō* vol.99, no. 25 (in Taibei edn. 1973, *Fabao zongmulu* 法寶總目錄 vol. 2, pp. 179-238).

The montage in the *rGya-nag chos-'byung* is very original, for mGon-poskyabs manages to encompass the whole of his exposition, which is dedicated to Mañjuśrī, the bodhisattva of wisdom, within Tantric prophecies and Indo-Buddhist doctrinal patterns to transform and re-interpret the history of China in the light of his own Buddhist beliefs. Clearly inspired by Chinese Buddhist apologists and syncretists of the past, he makes a deliberate use of religious syncretism to Buddhicize and even Tibetanize the whole Chinese culture. His chronicle, filled with numerous prophecies, is a reflection of his own conception of history, which is the verification and realization of the Buddha's prophecies. mGon-po-skyabs' *rGya-nag chos-'byung* became and remains the reference par excellence for Mongol historians.

Kumārajīva's summarized biography in the *rGya-nag chos-'byung*

It is indeed in mGon-po-skyabs' 'Chronicle of Buddhism in China' that a summarized biography of Kumārajīva is to be found, in the second Chapter, which describes in chronological succession the work of all foreign Buddhist scholars who went to China.

(Chengdu edn., p. 73) "The Chinese King hPhu-ki-yan of Hor (Mongol) race heard of the fame of a *Vidyādhara* (rig-'dzin, lit."Knowledge-holder") named Ku-mār-shrī (Kumārajīva), who had perfected the five sciences and was endowed with clairvoyance and unobstructed magical powers. Not long after, as [Fu Jian] was asking the reason why an auspicious star had arisen, a minister soothsayer prophesised that a great being from the border land would come in to accomplish the welfare of beings. Incidentally, as [Fu Jian] was eager to obtain some parts of the Indian country, he dispatched [to Kashgar] the General Lu'i-kwang with a vast army, and the Paṇḍit [Kumārajīva] was invited together with the Tsandan Jo-bo /sandal statue. I have already explained the greater part of that in my story of the Tsandan Jobo.

[However,] due to [political] circumstances, sixteen years elapsed without any Buddhist activities in the place of Li'ang-ṭe'u (Liangzhou, present Wuwei). Then, during the third year of Hung-shi of [the reign of] the Chinese King Yo'u-ṣing (Yao Xing), this king [happened] to have a tree which grew up to a notable tree of more/ than one *'li'* in height and all seedlings[*rtsang-'bras*] which had been sown in the pleasure-grove named ṣi'o'u-yo'u-yu'an (Xiaoyao yuan 逍遙園) turned into fragrant grass named "cha'i".[16] The soothsayer prophesied like before [that this was an auspicious sign of the coming of a wise man]. Subsequently, [Kumārajīva] was invited from Liangzhou to the fortified city of Chang'an and he was granted the title of *Guoshi* (國師"National Preceptor"). (p. 74) [The King] honoured [Kumārajīva] greatly, and requested him to teach and to make translations of the Holy Dharma. [Kumārajīva], together with eight hundred learned disciples headed by the monk Ce'u (Ce'u hwa-shang, Zhu

[16] See Taishō, vol. 50, p. 332 a.

heshang 竺和尚, lit. "the Monk disciple of an Indian Master") , translated [into Chinese] the *Sūtras* such as the *Vajracchedikā prajñāpāramitā*, the *Prajñāpāramitā in 8000 Verses*, the *Daśabhūmika*, the *Saddharma-puṇḍarīka*, the *Vimalakīrtinirdeśa*, the *Sūraṃgamasamādhi*, the *Vasudhara*, the *Buddhapiṭakaduhsilanirgraha*,[17] the *Bodhisattvapiṭaka*,[18] etc., and *śāstras* such as "the Commentary on the Bodhisattva precepts" (*Byang-sdom 'grel-pa, Pusa jie shu* 菩薩戒疏)[19] and "The 112 Gates" (*sGo brgya dang bcu-gnyis-pa*), in total more than 300 chapters (*juan* 卷). His revisions and corrections were numerous, and by his explanations, he widely promulgated the *Mahāyāna* Teaching. He thought carefully of the best way to spread the Doctrine for the benefit of all beings in this country as it was, and that is why he stated that he would not bestow his Tantric knowledge. He gave monks' vows (*dge-slong-gi sdom-pa*) to some people only. However, it is from that time that the tradition of taking *bodhisattva* vows after the full ordination was established.

There is a story according to which Kumārajīva had ten spiritual consorts [female partners for Tantric practice], and because of that, the monks were dissatisfied, so Kumārajīva took a bowl filled with needles and [ate them]. After that, those who had lost faith changed their mind [and did not doubt him any longer]. However, Kumārajīva then left and it is Ce'u Hwa-shang (Zhu Heshang) who took the Seat.

Kumārajīva passed away at the age of forty-two and when his body was burnt, his tongue [did not burn] and remained untouched."[20] ... (p. 75, l. 11-15)"The great *Vinayadhara* (*'dul-'dzin*) named Sangs-rgyas ye-shes (Buddhayaśas, Fotuoyeshe 佛陀耶舍), Bi-ma-la-tsakṣu (Vimalākṣa, Bimoluocha 卑摩羅叉) and Dha-rmā-ru-tsi (Dharmaruci, Tanmoliuzhi 曇摩流支) arrived at the same time as Ku-mā-ra, and together they translated much of the *Vinaya* (*'dul-ba'i skor*) such as the "Four Sections of Statements" [of the *Sarvāstivāda Vinaya*] (*lung-sde bzhi, Sifenlü* 四分律). They gave direct instructions on the monastic training and they widely promulgated the *Vinaya* Teaching."

It is clear that mGon-po-skyabs followed the text of the *Gaoseng zhuan*, changing a few details to fit better Tibetan taste and customs. What is emphasized here is Kumārajīva's important role as a translator, a wise man, a magician and a master of *Vinaya*.

---

[17] lit. *bDe-gshegs snying-po*, (Sk. *Tathāgatagarbha*), designates the *Fozang jing* 佛藏經, *T*. 653.

[18] *Byang-chub-sems-dpa'i mdzod* (*Pusa zang* 菩薩藏), see Robert Shih, p. 76, n. 65.

[19] *T*. 1500 and 1501 were not translated by Kumārajīva.

[20] Transliteration of this passage: (73:4) Rig-'dzin Ku-mār-shrī zhes-pa rig-pa'ignas lnga mthar-son cing mngon-shes dang rdzu-'phrul thogs-med mnga'-ba de'igrags-pa Hor rigs-kyi rGya rgyal hPhu-ki-yan-gyis thos-pas mi-ring-ba zhig na blonpo ltas-mkhan-gyis bkra-shis-pa'i skar-ma shar-ba'i rgyu-mtshan zhu-barmtha'-'khob-pa chen-po zhig phan-grogs-su 'byung-bar lung-bstan-pas/ zhor-la rGyagar-gyi yul khams 'ga'-zhig 'thob-tu 'dod-pas dmag-dpon Lu'i-kwang dpung chen-podang-bcas btang-bas paṇḍita dang Tsandan Jo-bo gdan-drangs-pa sogs phal-cher bdaggis Tsandan Jo-bo'i lo-rgyus-su

The five lineages of transmission (*rGya-nag chos-'byung*, Chengdu edn., 1983 pp. 171-175) Concerning the classification in five distinct lineages of transmission of Buddhist teachings in China, the same classification is to be found in the *rGya-nag chos-'*byung (pp. 171-175). The passage mentioned by Thu'u-bkwan concerning Kumārajīva and the lineage of *Vinaya* is to be found p.171.

The five distinct lineages of transmission/traditions described in the 'Chronicle of Buddhism in China':

Tib. *brgyud-pa rnam-pa lnga*, Ch. *wuzhong chuancheng* 五種傳承:

[1] the lineage of *Vinaya* or Discipline (Tib. *'dul-ba'i brgyud-pa*, Ch. *lüchuancheng* 律傳承 or *Lüzong* 律宗),

[2] the lineage of *Tantras* (Tib. *gsang-sngags-kyi brgyud-pa*, Ch. *Mizong* 密宗),

[3] the lineage of Vast Conduct (Tib. *rgya-chen spyod brgyud*, Ch. *Guangdaxingzong* 廣大行宗 or *Faxiangzong* 法相宗),

[4] the lineage of the Profound View (Tib. *zab-mo lta brgyud*, Ch. *Shenshenguangpai* 甚深觀派 or *Faxingzong* 法性宗),

and [5] the lineage of the Quintessential Meaning (Tib. *snying-po don brgyud*, Ch. *Chanzong* 禪宗).

It is clear that mGon-po-skyab's analysis of the formation of Chinese Buddhism is not orthodox. It seems that he gave his personal interpretation by using Indo-Tibetan concepts that he applied to Chinese Buddhist concepts. He thus gives a specific designation to a school because that school seems to emphasize a particular aspect :

'dul-ba'i brgyud-pa, discipline, moral code *gsang-sngags-kyi brgyud-pa*, Secret Mantra Lineage *rgya-chen spyod brgyud* (Sk. *udārācārya paramparā*), the

bshad zin-la/ dus-kyi dbang-gis Li'ang-ṭe'u'i gnas-su bstan-pa-la bya-ba med-par lo bcu-drug thogs/ de-nas rGya rgyal Yo'u-ṣing hungshi'i lo gsum-pa rgyal-po de yin-par ra-ljon-shing chen-po le-dbar lhag-pa'i yal-'dabcan zhig skyes shing/ ṣi'o'u-yo'u-yu'an zhes-pa'i skyed-tshal na rtsang-'bras btab-pa/cha'i zhes-pa'i dri-zhim-pa'i rtswar bsgyur-bar ltas-mkhan-gyis snga-ma ltar lungbstan-pas/ Li'ang-ṭe'a [for: ṭe'u] nas Chang-an mkhar-du spyan-drangs/ ka-shi'i (74:1) mtshan gsol/ bkur-sti chen-po byas te dam-pa'i chos 'chad-pa dang bsgyur-bar snyangsan phab-pas/ Ce'u hwa-shang-gis gtsos slob-ma mkhas-pa brgyad-brgya bcas rDorgcod/brGyad-stong-pa/ Sa-bcu-pa/ Pad-dkar/ Dri-med grags-pas bstan-pa/ dPabar 'gro-ba'i ting-nge-'dzin/ 'Jig-rten 'dzin-gyis zhus-pa/ bDe-gshegs snying-po/Byang-chub-sems-dpa'i mdzod la-sogs-pa'i bḳa' dang/ Byang-sdom 'grel-pa/ sGo brgya dang bcu-gnyis-pa sogs bstan-bcos khyon-bsdoms bam-po sum-brgya lhag-par bsgyur/ 'gyur bcos kyang shin-tu mang/ bshad-'grel-gyi sgo-nas kyang theg-chen rgya-cher spel/ yul-phyogs 'dir ji-ltar-gyis bstan 'gro-la phan-thogs che tshul brtagspas/gsang-sngags byings-la mi-gnang-bar bka'-yis bcad/ 'ga'-zhig-la sdom-pa dngossu gyur-pa dang/ de min kyang bag-chag 'jog-pa sogs don mang-po la dgongs zer tegang-ltar kyang bsnyen-rdzogs-kyi rjes-su byang-sdom len-pa'i srol da-lta'i bar khyab-che'o/ rig-ma bcu yod-par dge-'dun-rnams ma-rangs-pas khab sder-gan bzhes-nas ma-dad-pa ldog-pa'i lo-rgyus yod/ 'on-kyang de-nas khri zur-pa mdzad-nas Ce'u hwa-shang gdan-sar bzhag dgung-lo zhe-gnyis-par zhi-bar gshegs-pa'i spur sbyangs-pas ljags ma-nyams-par byon-no/

lineage of extensive deeds; the lineage of teaching and practice coming from Maitreya, Asaṅga and Vasubhandu mainly emphasizing the method aspect of Buddha's teachings *zab-mo lta brgyud* (Sk. *gaṃbhīradarśanatantra*), the lineage of profound view; lineage of teaching and practice coming from Mañjuśrī, Nāgārjuna and Candrakīrti which mainly emphasises the wisdom aspect of the teachings. snying-po don brgyud, an expression very unusual in Tibetan Buddhism.

Why Brahmanism was never introduced into China: Shi Daorong (釋道融), Kumārajīva's disciple

[see *rGya-nag chos-'byung* p. 84-85; *Gaoseng zhuan*, *Taishō* vol. 50, no. 2059, *juan* 6, p.363 b-c]:

"Da'u-bzhung (Daorong) was an outstanding expert in Sanskrit and totally self- 13 reliant. At that time, a non-Buddhist (*phyi-rol-pa*, lit. "Outsider") Paṇḍit named Great Brahman (*Bram-ze chen-po*, Ch. Da Poluomen 大婆羅門) from Ceylon (Sing-ghala'igling, Sk. Singhala-dvīpa) arrived in China, with Vedic texts loaded on a camel.

He informed the Chinese King Yo'u-chang [in fact Yao Chang's son, Yao Xing :384-417 according to the *Gaoseng zhuan*] that it was necessary to introduce also [into China] the doctrines [proper] to the country of India. The King, being in doubt, was unable to take a decision and asked Kumāraī [jīva] his opinion. The latter replied that although this Brahman had not come in order to [provoke] a debate, however, in the future, his tradition would progressively inflict a great harm to the Buddhists (*nang-pa*, lit. "Insiders"), and for that reason, it would be good to oppose him to a Chinese Buddhist monk. Da'u-bzhung (Daorong) was appointed as his opponent. As they started to debate in the centre of an assembly formed by the King, his Ministers and many monks and laymen, the Brahman became more and more agitated and protested: "I did not come here to provoke debates and make controversies; it is because I thought that China is a great country and that if I introduce our religious tradition, it will become similar to India."

The Chinese Monk replied: "All the Vedic texts that exist in your country, we have them already in China" and he recited in Sanskrit the [titles of] the *Vedas* known in China, and in addition numerous other Vedic texts. Having enumerated three times more [texts] than the [Brahman], the latter was dismayed and gave a salutation [to the Chinese Monk].

After that, Kumāra said that the Brahman should be expelled back to his country, and the King sent him off, after having granted him a few gifts. That is why, thanks to that Master's kindness, [the wrong views] of eternalism and nihilism of the unreflective Tīrthikas (*rtag-chad smra-ba'i mu-stegs-pa rang-ga-ba*) from India are not to be found in the country of China until now. "

Conclusion:

We saw the description of Kumārajīva as a scholar, a seer, a magician, and translator in 18thcentury Tibetan Sources. Although the primary source is the *rGya-nag chos-,gyung*, Thu'u-bkwan's *Grub-mtha'* will remain the most widespread source.

Thu'u-bkwan devoted the last two years of his life to the writing of his *Grubmtha'*, and he stopped correcting it only two days before his death. Having been sick for a long time, he warned that some mistakes in his text still needed to be corrected. The *Grub-mtha' shel-gyi me-long* became not only the model of the dGe-lugs-pa lore for later Tibetan scholars, but also one of the usual sources of study for Chinese disciples converted to Tibetan Buddhism. The Chinese *Dharma* Master Fazun (Fazun Fashi 法尊法师: 1901-1981 or 1902-1980), who mastered Tibetan religious Studies in Drepung Monastery in Lhasa, and became in 1956 the Vice-President of the Chinese Institute for Buddhist Studies (*Zhongguo Foxue yuan* 中國佛學院) in Beijing, devoted his life to spreading Tibetan Buddhism in China by giving and translating into Chinese dGe-lugs-pa teachings. In his "Political and Religious History of the Tibetan People" (*Xizang minzu zhengjiao shi* 西藏民族政教史) in six volumes (*ce* 冊), it is the *Grub-mtha' shel-gyi me-long* that he mentioned as his main source for the doctrinal study of the religious Orders of Tibet.[21]

I would like to add that the study of the story of Kumārajīva's life and work emphasizes the crucial role played by the ruler Yao Xing in developing Buddhism in China, and as Yao Xing was a Qiang 羌, and therefore a proto-Tibetan, his deeds seem to symbolise the destiny of Tibet which is to preserve and diffuse the Buddha's Teaching for the benefit of all living beings. Moreover, as these 18th century texts were written in a spirit of dialogue and reconciliation, I wish that this commemoration of Kumārajīva similarly paves the way for a better understanding between India and China by nurturing a reflection on Buddhist thought. Its message of tolerance, wisdom and compassion due to the Buddhist view of interconnection of all beings is more than ever useful to our modern world, which is still torn apart by savage capitalism, social injustice, racial hatred, tribal mentality, and religious tensions.

[21] See Xizang Minzu Fojiao shi, Beijing, Xinhua shudian, 1991, 6. 39, and Appendix, p. 9

22

Kumārajīva's translation of Vimalakīrtinirdeśa and its contribution to Chinese literature

Fan Jingjing

In medieval China, literature underwent a considerable change, largely because of the translations of Buddhist scriptures. Now, many scholars agree that the most important translator in this period was Kumārajīva, whose translations were widely read and commented not only by his contemporaries but also by later generations. Among the numerous Buddhist scriptures translated by him, one of the most popular is *Vimalakīrtinirdeśa*. It has exerted a great influence on Chinese literature since the Six Dynasties.

According to Buddhist bibliographies, there had been several different translations of *Vimalakīrtinirdeśa* before Kumārajīva, of which only one is extant till today. That is Zhiqian's 支謙 translation. After Kumārajīva, Xuanzang 玄奘, a monk who has made a great contribution to the cultural exchange between ancient India and ancient China, translated this sūtra again. Therefore, we have three different Chinese translations of *Vimalakīrtinirdeśa* at our disposal. Besides, the Sanskrit manuscript of this sūtra has also been found at the Potala Palace. Although this manuscript is said to have been written after the 7th century and is not the same source text from which Zhiqian, Kumārajīva and Xuanzang made the Chinese translation, it is still of great value to help improve our research. At least, it can be used as a parallel text while analyzing the different Chinese translations.

However, the intriguing question is that although there are three Chinese translations of *Vimalakīrtinirdeśa*, the most widely read and quoted is Kumārajīva's translation. In this paper, I will first make a close reading of the Sanskrit manuscript and the three Chinese translations to figure out Kumārajīva's unique translation strategies, so as to answer why his translation is the most popular. One of the possible answers is the eclectic nature of Kumārajīva's translation; in other words, Kumārajīva consulted both previous translations and Chinese monks who were members of his workshop while translating. The other is that Kumārajīva was not only a technician on translation but also a Buddhist philosopher and preacher, which helped to make his translation more accessible and acceptable to the literati in China. This will be explained in the paper in detail. Then I will continue to explore how Kumārajīva's translation affected the Chinese literati's writings. As far as I am concerned, there are at least two aspects to this question. On the one hand, the imagery in Chinese literature is largely enriched by borrowing materials from Kumārajīva's translation. On the other hand, the style of Kumārajīva's translation has also been imitated by Chinese writers.

The Eclectic Nature of Kumārajīva's Translation

In the process of translation, Kumārajīva not only made use of the previous translations, but also discussed difficult problems with Chinese monks who worked as his assistants. In this way, his translations gained a high quality which contributed to their popularity among both higher intellectuals and lower common people.

When Kumārajīva retranslated *Mahāprajñāpāramitā* whose previous translations were said to be flawed, the Later-Qin king Yao Xing 姚興 who sponsored the translation activity read the previous translations while listening to Kumārajīva's new interpretation. He made a comparison between the new and the old versions and then demanded of Kumārajīva to explain and justify his new translation.[1] Thus Kumārajīva's translation had a nature of synthesis. In other words, it kept the virtues of previous translations while avoiding their defects. In *Annotations to Vimalakīrtinirdeśa*, Sengzhao 僧肇 recorded Kumārajīva's commentaries on previous translations and his explanations of the revision, which takes up half the space of the book. These commentaries and explanations show that Kumārajīva was very careful about the choice of words.

For example, let us take one of Kumārajīva's revisions of previous translations. A case which can illustrate his translating techniques is his retranslation of the Sanskrit original "triratnava śānupacchet bhi". Before him, Zhiqian translated this as "[t]hey ensured the prosperity of the Three Treasures, making certain that these never expired" 興隆三寶，能使不絕. However, Kumārajīva was not satisfied with this translation. He revised Zhiqian's words

---

1 Huijiao 1992: 52.

as "[t]hey ensured the continuance and prosperity of the Three Treasures, making certain that these never expired" 紹隆三寶，能使不絕. After Kumārajīva, Xuanzang's translation is "[t]hey ensured the continuance of the seeds of the Three Treasures, making certain that these never expired" 紹三寶種，能使不絕. [2] From these three different versions, we can see that Kumārajīva paid special attention to the Sanskrit word "vaṃśa" while Zhiqian did not translate it into Chinese. However, Zhiqian added a new meaning to his translation which was not present in the original; and that is "the prosperity of the Three Treasures". Then Xuanzang just left out this information while Kumārajīva preserved it in his translation. [3] According to the analysis above, we can safely conclude that Kumārajīva's translation was rather flexible. On the one hand, he corrected the mistakes of previous translations and thus made his own translation more accurate. On the other hand, he took in some elements which were not in the original, but created by previous translators, in order to make his new translation more acceptable to readers who had already got used to the expressions of the older versions.

At the same time, while referring to previous translations, Kumārajīva also listened to the advice of his Chinese assistants while translating. His translation workshop was the largest among the three sponsored by government. (The other two were led by Boddhiruci in Northern Wei and Xuanzang in Tang dynasty respectively.) To some extent, Kumārajīva's translations were the products of cooperation among many people. In Sengzhao's preface to *Vimalakīrtinirdeśa*, there is a brief description of the process of the translation of this sūtra:

"[Yao Xing] ordered the General Duke Changshan and the General Duke Ancheng with 1,200 monks who had a good command of Buddhist doctrines to help Kumārajīva retranslate this sūtra in the big temple of C'hang-an. ... Kumārajīva held the original Sanskrit manuscript and interpreted the text. The monks and laymen who were present at this occasion listened to Kumārajīva's

---

[2] Study Group on Buddhist Sanskrit Literature, The Institute For Comprehensive Studies of Buddhism, Taisho University, ed. *Vimalakīrtinirdeśa: Transliterated Sanskrit Text Collated with Tibetan and Chinese Translations.* 2004. p.4-5. And I have consulted Burton Watson's The *Vimalakīrti Sūtra* for the English translation.

[3] During the seminar, some scholars reminded me that Kumārajīva's change of the Chinese character "興" to "紹" might had another reason, a particular taboo. That is to say, because "興" is the name of the king, Kumārajīva should avoid it in translation. I really appreciate their kindness and would like to extend my gratitude to them here. However, after the seminar, I have checked *Vimalakīrtinirdeśa* and found that Kumārajīva actually used "興" once in his translation. So it can be safely concluded that Kumārajīva's choice between the two words is because of his understanding of the original meaning, not the taboo of avoiding mentioning a king's name.

interpretation attentively; and they discussed the translation eagerly in order to make sure that the Buddha's teaching be transmitted correctly and clearly."[4] From this description, we can see clearly that there were a number of people who contributed to Kumārajīva's translation, which promoted its circulation more widely.

Kumārajīva as a Faithful Translator or a Creative Preacher?

While translating the Attic orators, Cicero had a famous saying "I did not translate them as an interpreter, but as an orator"[5]. By this confession, Cicero justified his adaptation of the original text. Therefore, we may ask a similar question: how did Kumārajīva regard his own translating job? Was he satisfied to be just a faithful translator or did he have any higher ambition? In Huijiao's *Biographies of Eminent Monks*, there is a paragraph which can help us better understand this question:

"Kumārajīva has always been a disciple of Mahāyāna Buddhism; and he aims at preaching the doctrines to people. He keeps sighing: 'If I had the opportunity to write Mahāyāna *Abhidharma*, I would do better than Kātyāyana. Now that I am here in China, nobody can understand me. My talent is wasted; and what can I do about this!"[6]

Through this narrative, we can infer that he was very disappointed to be just a translator and not a śāstra master, although his role as a remarkable translator had won him much fame. So there was a conflict between the reality of being a passive translator and the ideal of being a creative philosopher and preacher. However, he actually did try his best to reconcile the two. In his translations, he went farther than only strictly obeying the original. He had some creative thoughts about Buddhist philosophy and he then inserted these into his translation. As a preacher who was eager to make Mahāyāna Buddhism popular among Chinese people, he adapted some doctrines while translating, in order to make them more acceptable in the background of Chinese culture.

Moreover, Kumārajīva also took the unique historical circumstances into consideration when he undertook his translations. At that time, China was torn apart by wars. As a result, people were experiencing a hard life and struggling for survival. In this situation, a saviour or a bodhisattva who had mercy for the common people was badly needed, which was a good opportunity to disseminate Mahāyāna Buddhist philosophy. Kumārajīva made best use of this advantage and preached about the possibility of the commoners being saved from their miserable everyday life and being enlightened. Besides, in his translation, he showed much concern for secular life, as Nakamura Hajime

[4] Sengyou 1995: 310.
[5] Munday 2008: 19.
[6] Huijiao 1992: 53.

has pointed out in his paper titled "Thoughts based on the reality of life: one characteristic of Kumārajīva's translation".[7] The following argument has benefited a lot from Nakamura's insightful discovery.

In chapter four "The Bodhisattvas", there is a Sanskrit sentence which is "tat kasmād dheto sarvasatvānubodho hi bodhir"[8]. Kumārajīva's translation is "Why? Because all living beings in truth bear the marks of bodhi."[9] 所以者何？一切眾生即菩提相 While Zhiqian translates it as "Why? Because all living beings should follow the way of the Enlightenment" 所以者何？一切眾生當從覺道故; and Xuanzang tranaslates it as "Why? Because bodhi is what all living beings are equal to follow to be enlightened" 所以者何？夫菩提者，一切有情，等所隨覺. Thurman translates this sentence from the Tibetan version as "Why? Enlightenment consists of the realizations of all living beings".[10] Compared to the others, Kumārajīva's translation speaks highly of the common people and strongly approves their potential for becoming an enlightened Buddha themselves. Moreover, this statement would greatly encourage the disciples to pursue the Buddhist truth, since it guaranteed a bright future for them.

Another convincing example of Kumārajīva's emphasis on common life is his translation of "sarvakleśapraśamanamaṇḍa eṣa"[11] as "[e]arthly desires are the place of practice"[12] 諸煩惱是道場. It is obvious that he omitted the Sanskrit keyword "praśamana" in his translation, which means to extinguish, to pacify. Zhiqian's translation is "[t]o pacify all kinds of worries is that (the place of practice)" 眾勞之靜是. And Xuanzang's translation has also included the word "praśamana", which is "[t]o extinguish earthly desires is bodhi" 息諸煩惱是妙菩提. According to Thurman, the Tibetan translation is "[i]t is the seat of eradication of all passions"[13]. Among the four different translations, only Kumārajīva's contradicts the Sanskrit original. However, what is ironic is that Kumārajīva's unfaithful translation was appealing to Zen masters and become a famous saying in the Zen school, and which prevailed among the Chinese literati even in later generations.

Since Kumārajīva adapted Indian Buddhist doctrines according to the needs of Chinese people, it is no wonder that his works are widely read. In this sense, he was successful both as a translator and a preacher.

---

7 Hajime 1994: 6-10.

8 *Vimalakīrtinirdeśa: Transliterated Sanskrit Text Collated with Tibetan and Chinese Translations.* p.140

9 Watson 1999: 53.

10 Thurman 1991: 34.

11 *Vimalakīrtinirdeśa: Transliterated Sanskrit Text Collated with Tibetan and Chinese Translations.* p.150

12 Watson 1999: 56.

13 Thurman 1991: 36.

Up until now, I have attempted to answer the question why Kumārajīva's translation of *Vimalakīrtinirdeśa* won such popularity in ancient China, though it is not the most faithful to the Sanskrit original. I have found two factors which are attributable to this phenomenon. One is Kumārajīva's open mind to accept both previous translation traditions and Chinese monks' opinions. The other is that he pays special attention to the cultural and historical background of China during his time while translating; and that he is not hesitant to express his own ideas in translation, even at the expense of distorting the original, since he does not only regard himself as a translator but also as a preacher. However, there are also other possibilities which need further exploration in the future.

The Imagery Borrowed from Kumārajīva's *Vimalakīrtinirdeśa* in Chinese Literature

That *Vimalakīrtinirdeśa* has exerted a great and long-lasting influence on Chinese literature has been recognized by most scholars in this field and the significance of this influence cannot be overestimated. The well-known Chinese writer and scholar Lu Xun 魯迅 (1881-1936) claims that "since Jin dynasty on, the upper-class literati (in Six Dynasties) have always taken three books with them, *Analects, Lao tze* and *Vimalakīrtinirdeśa*."[14] Although we do not exactly know whether it refers to Kumārajīva's translation, since Zhiqian's version was also in circulation at that time, what we can ascertain is that Kumārajīva's translation had been much more popular than both Zhiqian's and Xuanzang's from the Tang dynasty onwards. When Li Shan 李善 (ca. 630-689) annotated the *Anthology of Literature* 文選, he made many references to Kumārajīva's *Vimalakīrtinirdeśa*. That is also the case with Prince Li Xian 李賢 (ca. 652-684) when he annotated the *Book of the Later Han* 後漢書. In the works of the great poets Wang Wei 王維 (ca. 701-761) and Bai Juyi 白居易 (ca. 772-846), there are large numbers of quotations from this sūtra as well. On the contrary, Zhiqian's and Xuanzang's translations have almost disappeared into oblivion. After the Tang dynasty, with the development of the Zen school, Kumārajīva's *Vimalakīrtinirdeśa* has been mentioned more frequently since it is one of the major source texts of the Zen sect.

Because of their great fondness for this sūtra, the Chinese literati liked to allude to it in writing. One of the characteristics of Kumārajīva's *Vimalakīrtinirdeśa* is the abundance of beautiful imagery pregnant with meaning, which has largely enriched Chinese literature. The most famous ten similes in this sūtra are as follows:

"This body is like a cluster of foam, nothing you can grasp or handle. This

[14] Lu Xun. *The Complete Works of Lu Xun.* Vol. 5

body is like a bubble that cannot continue for long. This body is like a flame born of longing and desire. This body is like the plantain that has no firmness in its trunk. This body is like a dream, compounded of false and empty visions. This body is like a shadow, appearing through karma causes. This body is like an echo, tied to causes and conditions. This body is like a drifting cloud, changing and vanishing in an instant. This body is like lightning, barely lasting from moment to moment."[15]

The prominent poet Xie Lingyun 謝靈運 (ca. 385-433) wrote a group of poems titled "Praise unto the ten similes in *Vimalakārti sūtra*" 維摩經十譬贊 based on this paragraph, only eight of which are extant today.[16] Since then, these ten similes have been widely employed in Chinese literature. In particular, the image of the plantain enjoys a high frequency of appearances.

In addition, "the silence of Vimalakīrti" is another metaphor which attracted much attention from the literati in ancient China. There are still a number of cases of this kind, but I cannot list them all due to the constraints of space of this paper.

Impact of Kumārajiva's *Vimalakīrtinirdeśa* on the Style of Writing in the Chinese Literature

Kumārajīva's *Vimalakīrtinirdeśa* was warmly welcomed by the Chinese literati because of its daring imagination and hyperbolic descriptions which were foreign to indigenous Chinese literary tradition. By assimilating these writing techniques, the writers could produce more lively and enjoyable works. The six Pienwen 變文 texts adapted from *Vimalakīrtinirdeśa* found in Dunhuang can best support this point . In one of the manuscripts, there is a long paragraph depicting the beauty of the twelve thousand heavenly maidens who are sent by the devil King Papiyas 波旬 to disturb the practice of the bodhisattva Upholder of the Age 持世菩薩. The author employs many similes to illustrate the maidens' attractiveness. For example, he compares them to fresh flowers and magnificent jewellery. He describes their clothes and faces in detail; and he makes an exaggeration of their gorgeousness. The whole paragraph has more than three hundred Chinese characters only to tell us that the maidens are exceptionally good looking, which is a rare case in indigenous Chinese literature.[17] However, this overly elaborate and highly exaggerated narrative helps the readers form a vivid picture in their mind and enjoy their reading more.

---

15 Watson 1999: 34-35

16 From the image "炎" in the second poem, we can know that what he reads is Kumārajīva's translation, since Zhiqian uses the phrase "野馬" instead.

17 Wang 1957: 620.

More importantly, Chinese literati imitated the structure and advocated the style of *Vimalakīrtinirdeśa* in writing. As early as in the Song dynasty, Li Tu 李塗 (ca. 1147) had already pointed out that it could teach people how to compose a good essay.[18] The literary critics in the Ming and Qing dynasties continued to appreciate the high writing skills of this sūtra. Both Wang Shizhen 王世貞 (ca. 1526-1590) and Qian Qianyi 錢謙益 (ca. 1582-1664) admitted that they learned a lot from *Vimalakīrtinirdeśa* on how to write a poem.[19] In the 19th century, the erudite scholar and writer Gong Zizhen 龔自珍 (1792-1841) expressed his enthusiasm for *Vimalakīrtinirdeśa* in one of his famous poems "Song of the fallen flowers in western countryside" 西郊落花歌: "I have finished reading the tripiṭaka, but my most favorite is *Vimalakīrti* since it has beautiful and light words." Interestingly, this poem is also full of grand sceneries and daring imagination which can be seen as parallels of the sūtra itself.

In short, there is a long tradition of Chinese literati appreciating the literary value of Kumārajīva's *Vimalakīrtinirdeśa* and then setting it as an example to follow in writing. This sūtra has become a treasure which they resorted to now and then in their writing career.

BIBLIOGRAPHY

Hajime, Nakamura. 1994. "Thoughts based on the reality of life: one characteristic of Kumarajiva's translation". *Journal of Research on World Religions.*

Huijiao ed. 1992. *Biographies of Eminent Monks*. Beijing: Zhonghua Books House.

Munday, Jeremy. 2008. *Introducing Translation Studies: Theories and Applications*. London and New York: Routledge.

Sengyou ed. 1995. *Chusanzangjiji*. Beijing: Zhonghua Books House.

Study Group on Buddhist Sanskrit Literature, The Institute For Comprehensive Studies of Buddhism, Taisho University, ed. 2004. *Vimalakīrtinirdeśa: Transliterated Sanskrit Text Collated with Tibetan and Chinese Translations*. Tokyo: Taisho University.

Sun, Changwu. 1996. *Vimalakīrti and Avalokiteśvara in Chinese Literature*. Beijing: Higher Education Press.

Thurman, Robert. tr. 1991. *The Holy Teaching of Vimalakīrti*. Delhi: Motilal Banarsidass.

Wang, Zhongmin. ed. 1957. *Anthology of Dunhuang Pienwen*. Beijing: People's Literature Publishing House.

Watson, Burton. tr. 1999. *The Vimalakīrti sutra: From Chinese Version by Kumārajīva*. Delhi: Motilal Banarsidass.

[18] Sun 1996: 390-391.
[19] Sun 1996: 391-392.

23

The third case unearthed Kokera Sūtra copy of Diamond Wisdom Sūtra translated by Kumārajīva excavated at Tenjinnbata historic site, Shiga prefecture

Yu Inoue

Kokera Sūtra Copies:

The Sūtra Copies written with Chinese ink brush on thin wooden pieces called Kokera. A few of them were found being included within the offerings to the temple but most of them have been found as unearthed objects from different historical sites. According to some studies, the Kokera Sūtra Copies were first made in the Kinki area in 12th century (around the end of Heian era). Those pieces were mostly made as offerings of copying sūtras. It seems that twenty to forty pieces were put together into a bundle and fastened with a paper string or a thin rope. Many of them were unearthed from the places which functioned as a water filled basin such as rivers, ditches, or ponds.

Objects discovered from the above historical complex site include those made between Jomon period (8000 to 200 BCE) and medieval centuries. The excavation started in 2008 while redirecting and recovering the extended area of the river of Kamogawa (Aoi river). A canal that used to wind its way within the subject area was 2.5m in depth. Its width is unknown, as the banks of the river have not yet been excavated so far. However, it is estimated to be being over 30 metres. This river must have functioned as a canal for a long time until it sank around the beginning of the modern ages. The Kokera sūtra copies, almost in a bundle, were unearthed in February 2009 underneath the accumulated layers of earth . The era of the accumulated earth layers was considered to be the latter half of the medieval period. The Kokera copies of the sūtra could have been placed in the gentle stream to be honoured.

The era to which the unearthed sutras belong is the latter half of the medieval period (15th to 16th centuries). The number of these Kokera sheets is 115 (excluding the pieces which could not be identified as a part of any sūtra or some insignificant small pieces which are detached from other recognizable parts).

Size, Shape and Condition: Length: 298mm, Width: 21mm, Thickness: less than 1mm. planed, thin sheet-like boards of the needle pine tree family. The thinner parts are somewhat transparent. The Chinese characters were written only on one side with black China Ink. Each line generally consists of 17 letters. There are many sheets which have the middle part missing. It could be assumed that the middle part was put together and fastened tightly as a bundle.

"Kokera" sūtra copies are thin boards or wooden sheets (Kokera) on which sūtras were written with black China ink. Most of them have been unearthed at historic sites. According Ms. Rie Fujiwara (2006), they were unearthed from 102 historic sites. In the past, the majority of Kokera sūtra copies were the copies of myouhourenge-kyō, Hokke-kyō –Lotus Sūtra, some others were Amida-kyō–Amitābha Sūtra, Prajñāpāramitā Sūtra, and Blood Pool Hell Sūtra and so on but the number of cases were very small.

Thirty eight pieces out of the 115 Kokera sūtra copies which were excavated at this time at the Tenjinnbata Historical site and those which could be identified were of the Diamond Wisdom Sūtra. This discovery was the third case of excavation of a Diamond Wisdom Sūtra in the whole nation. In 2009, 14 pieces of Kokera Sūtra copies of the 14th century were unearthed at the Yanagi historical site in Kusatsu city, Shiga Prefecture. Other than that, there was a case of the 16th century which was unearthed in Kiyosujouka-machi, of Aichi Prefecture.

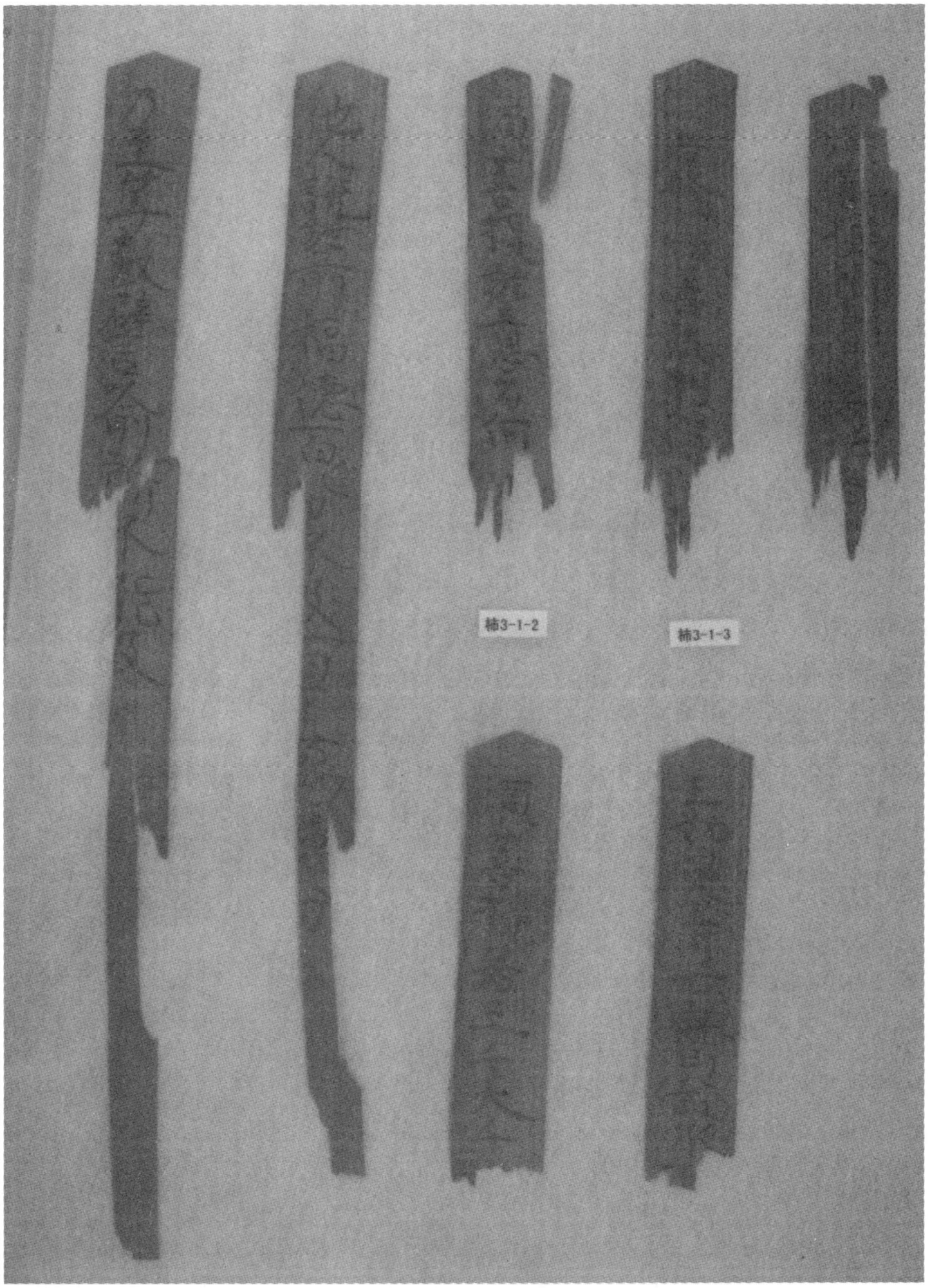

Those were seemingly isolated cases and could not be positioned in a proper historical context. However, the meaning of the second and third discovery which happened within the same Prefecture, Shiga, is quite interesting and significant.

The geographical aspect of the Kokera Sūtra copies:

Diamond Wisdom Sūtra[1] is an old sūtra translated by Kumārajīva. It has been treated as an important sūtra especially by the Zen sect of China. Most of the copies were done by Chinese monks who immigrated to or visited Japan, and by Japanese Zen monks who studied in China and came back to Japan. The Ohmi area in medieval Japan was prepared and ready to accept new trends in Buddhism from China. For example, a monk who studied in China, Genkou Jakushitsu (1290-1367) came back and established a new school called Rinzai sect Eiheiji School at the newly built Eigenji Temple. The unearthed objects from the Ohmi area could imply a profound influence of Chinese Buddhism around that time.

When re-examining the contents of the Kokera Sūtra copies to compare them with copies from other areas, the Kokera sūtra copies which were unearthed from the residential ruins in Tokushima Prefecture in Shikoku had Prajñā Prakara copied on them. The Shikoku area was strongly influenced by the Shingon (True Words) sect and Prajñā Prakara had been one of the core sūtras for the sect. Based on that, it may be inferred that the unearthed sūtra copies could imply characteristics of the belief of the people in the area much more than what was first expected. The latest addition of the Kokera Sūtra copies of Diamond Wisdom Sūtra unearthed from the Tenjinbata area could add interesting information to the study of the Kokera Sūtra copies.

The details of the 115 pieces of Kokera Sūtra Copies unearthed from Tenjinnbata historical site are as follows:

Lotus Sūtra of the Exquisite Dharma	69 pieces
Diamond Wisdom Sūtra	38 pieces
Ryo Dynasty Fudaishiju Diamond Sūtra	3 pieces
Prajñā Pāramitā Sūtra	2 pieces

[1] Diamond Wisdom Sūtra
A sūtra translated by Kumarajiva (344 413). The title means the Complete Attainment of Wisdom by cutting off attachments, earthly desires. The content is an explanation about how not to be preoccupied by anything. It became popular in India, Tibet and Central Asia. It is said that the sixth patriarch of the Chinese Zen school, Eno (638-713) attained enlightenment when he heard one line of the Sūtra, which means that having no dwelling (or attachment) gives a birth to an enlightened heart, he attained enlightenment. Since then that part of the Sūtra has been considered especially important. The old copies of the sūtra are mostly done by monks who immigrated to Japan from China and by Japanese monks who had studied in China and came back. The sūtra has been a favorite of the monks of Tendai and Shingon sects and of Confucians, who have been teaching and interpreting the sūtra.

Great Prajñā Pāramitā Sūtra	1 piece
Indication of Lotus Sūtra	1 piece
Treatise on the Twelve Gates	1 piece

Among these, there are some Sūtras which had never been publicly announced as unearthed objects before. Taisho-shinnshuu-daizoukyou (Index of Buddhism Sūtras compiled in Taisho era) was referred to, in order to find the names of the sūtras. As it was compiled in Taisho era, some names which had existed as different versions of the same sūtras during certain eras before Taisho, are all included. For example, some different versions of Diamond Wisdom Sūtra copies include exactly the same line as in the Ryou-chou-fudaishi-jukonngou-kyou. Therefore, some of the pieces could belong to either one of the above and at this point of investigation, there are still some pieces which cannot be identified definitely. After all, we could say that there has not been any other case in which the Kokera Sūtra copies belonging to such a wide variety of sūtras has been found as this case.

Misekechi (corrections without erasing the original mistakes):

There are corrections made on the Kokera sūtra copies. The mistaken Chinese character has a mark on its left side saying "error". The correct Chinese character was "other" but a wrong character "Buddha" was written. A mark which indicates that it was a mistake and should be corrected is shown on the left side of the Chinese character and the correct letter is written on the right side. This is a correcting method called Misekechi (corrections without erasing the original mistakes). This is the first time throughout the country that Kokera Sūtra copies which used this particular correcting method were unearthed.

As these copies have a wide variety of contents, they are a valuable addition to related studies such as the history of Buddhism in Japan, categorization of the sūtras and linguistics of Japanese.

24

The influence of Sūtras translated by Kumārajīva on the development of Mahāyāna Buddhism in Japan

Gensei Ito

Buddhism, which sprung up from the earth with a history of two thousand years in India, reached China, which has as long a history as India. Buddhism in China then spread to the Korean Peninsula. Thus, from the neighboring Paekche Kingdom of the peninsula, which was separated from Japan by a narrow sea, Buddhism officially arrived in Japan in 538 CE (but, according to another theory, in 552). A political delegation from Paekche brought a bronze Buddha image, some sūtras and a few religious objects. It was recorded in "Emperors in Ancient Japan".

However, there were two influential families around the time, who were rivals, and honouring Buddha created a great controversy. Then, coincidentally, an epidemic ravaged the land. The clan opposed to Buddhism interpreted it as the wrath of the indigenous deities. This led to the objects being thrown into a canal and the temple being burnt down. The oldest sūtras which were formally brought to the Emperor Kinmei were thus ruined. However, soon after that Buddhism was established firmly and the sūtras were considered as objects to be treated with honour. At the same time, copying sūtras became one of the important Buddhists routine practices.

Some decades later, the clan that supported Buddhism prevailed and the first Empress of Japan, Suiko was enthroned. Shotokutaishi (Sacred Prince, Prince Shotoku, 574-622) was appointed as Regent by the Empress (603 CE). He succeeded in establishing a centralized government for the first time in the land of Japan. The Prince was an ardent Buddhist and promulgated a seventeen-article Constitution based on Buddhist concepts given in the Lotus

Sūtra, translated by Kumārajīva. He employed the newly imported Buddhism which was not well known till then even among his nobles , till then. According to Hajime Nakamura, one of the renowned Japanese Buddhist scholars, Prince Shōtoku intended to soften the antagonistic atmosphere among different tribes and to raise the standard of the commoners' ethical code of conduct based on the teachings of the Lotus Sūtra. The Prince studied under two teachers from Korea and he authored his own book on the interpretation of the Lotus Sūtra, which is considered to be the first book in Japan.

Thus, the Lotus Sūtra translated by Kumārajīva in the beginning of the 5th century reached Japan only a century later to become the main spiritual basis in governing the people of Japan through its introduction in the form of a Constitution by Prince Shōtoku.

He commissioned the Shitenno-ji Temple and Hōryuji Temple, both of which are considered great temples in the history of Japanese Buddhism. The Hōryuji Temple especially was considered to be the institution for Buddhist studies, including all the theologies of different sects which were imported directly from Sui Dynasty and later from T'ang Dynasty as well as from the Paekche, Koguryo, and later from Silla on the Korean Peninsula. All the Buddhist sūtras of the Ssix Chinese schools including San-ron, Joujitsu, Kusha, Hossou, Kegon and Ritsu were imported and studied by the Japanese aristocrats. This era was called the "Era of Copying Sūtras" and there had not been any schools started by Japanese as yet.

Another dedicated Buddhist appeared soon after Prince Shōtoku in the imperial family, i.e.,-- Empress Komyo (701 to 760). She practiced Buddhism doing as much as she could in her capacity as Empress throughout her life for saving her people. She was called the Living Buddha and her reputation reached as far as India.

A king in India, contemporary with Empress Komyo, who was also a dedicated Buddhismt, one day had a dream in which he was told that if he wanted to see a living Buddha, he should meet Empress Komyo of Japan. Therefore, he ordered his Buddhist sculptor to visit Japan and make a Buddha statue which would resemble Empress Komyo. He made three Buddha statues resembling Empress Komyo and left one at her place (present Hokkeji temple), took one back to India, and the location of the third one has no record. The image in Japan is called the 11 face Kannon Boddhisattva, which is declared as a National Treasure. When Indian Prime Minister Nehru visited Japan in 1957, he visited Hokkeji Temple privately to see the 11 face Kannon Boddhi Sattva and was amazed by the look of the statue as it so closely resembled the one he saw in India.

Empress Komyo, who was filled with compassion, established an orphanage, Hiden-in, and a hospital, Seyaku-in, where poor sick people were treated with medicines. She was known as a miraculous healer, treating those people with her own hands. The Empress launched a great national project of copying sūtras in 733 CE. About 7000 sūtras were copied and about 1000 copies of them still exist. 750 copies out of the existing ones are stored in the Shosoin (a storage facility was specially designed and built at that time so that the horizontally assembled wooden pieces would expand or shrink depending on the weather in order to control the air flow within the facility to keep the stored objects well protected from a changes of climate).

One of those stored in Shosoin is a copy of Daichido-ron (Mahāprajñāpāramitā-śāstra) written by Nāgārjuna and translated by Kumārajīva. It is entered in the index compiled in the Tasho era.

Empress Komyo had a comprehensive understanding of Theravada and Mahānāya Sūtras (according to the index of her selection of all the sūtras copied.). She, along with her husband, Emperor Shōmu, adapted the Lotus Sūtra translated by Kumārajīva for salvation of her people and built temples especially for atonement called "Lotus Atonement Temple—Kokubunji Temple, and Kokubunniji Temple" in each region.

The Lotus Sūtra translated by Kumārajīva firmly established its status as the most significant sūtra in the Buddhism of Japan when Saicho, who had studied the Tendai sect in China, came back to establish the first sect by a Japanese monk in Japan. It was the beginning of the 9th century. He called the sect "Tendai Lotus Sect" (it became Tendai later) based on the Lotus Sūtra translated by Kumārajīva. Until then, the existing sects in Japan were brought by foreign monks or by laymen delegations to the T'ang Dynasty.

The two major sects newly established in this era, Tendai Lotus Sect and Shingon Esoteric Sect, became the two original points of the wide spectrum of Japanese Mahāyāna Buddhism which developed later. The two founders of those sects were both Japanese monks who studied in China and created their own sects when they came back to Japan. Tendai Sect is the origin of the wide variety of esoteric Buddhist line and Shingon Sect is the origin of the traditional exclusive esoteric Buddhist line.

Tendai Sect in Japan branched out with the 'One-vehicle Teachings' with Lotus Sūtra as their basis, and the emphasis was directed more and more towards "Absolute Entrustment". The Tendai Sect kept to itself its supremacy as the guardian temple of the Emperor's family.

However, at the time when the Lotus Sūtra started flourishing among commoners, the power of the Emperor started diminishing and the warriors of different clans started fighting with each other to rule all of Japan and establish the Shogunate era. While those clans were fighting to gain power, the helpless commoners were unwillingly involved in the conflicts and despaired of guarding their own lives. The commoners were not equipped to read and understand any of the sūtras. Those monks who established new sects for the commoners had studied the Lotus Sūtra translated by Kumārajīva at the headquarters temple of Tendai Sect, including the founder of Jodo (Pure land) Sect, Honen, the founder of Jodo-Shin (Pure land True) Sect, Shinran, the founder of Yuuzuu Nenbutsu Sect, Ryounin, and the founder of Nichiren Sect, Nichiren.

While the commoners were depending on the Lotus Sūtra, the warriors were also exposed to death as their profession was to fight. However, they were too proud of themselves to surrender to untimely death. They preferred being stoic and to attain enlightenment through realizing that life on earth is changing and nothing is absolute or unchanged. Thus, they found the Zen sect based on Diamond Wisdom Sūtra translated by Kumārajīva to be a dependable source for their spiritual training.

While the popularity of the Lotus Sūtra is evident and many related old objects have been found everywhere, not much proof of spreading of the Diamond Sūtra has been unearthed. The copy of Diamond Sūtra excavated in Takashima city, Shiga prefecture, is the 3rd case of an old unearthed copy of Diamond Sūtra, which was made public on March 5th, 2010.

Thus, since the beginning of the time when Japan was first unified till the peaceful 300 years of the Edo era, Mahāyāna Buddhism in Japan has been greatly influenced and shaped by the sūtras translated by Kumārajīva. On the introduction of Buddhism to Japan, the sūtra was selected to be a tool for the governing class of the country and gradually spread to the rest of the Japanese people. While the spread of Buddhism among the governed was underway, another ruling class (Samurai-warrior era) picked up another sūtra translated by Kumārajīva.

Zen was imported from China during the 13th century (Kamakura era) to become a popular sect. The Zen sect reached Japan earlier, but became Japanese when Japanese monks who studied in China came back to establish their own sects in Japan. The Rinzai Sect in Japan was established by Eisai who studied it in Southern Song, in China. The Sodou Sect in Japan was established by Dogen who studied it in China and came back to Japan to establish his own sect. Zen sects spread among the warriors first, then to the commoners. During the Kamakura era (starting in ADCE 1192) many Zen temples were built.

Unlike the Zen Sects developed in China, the Japanese Zen sects considered their theology as important as their practice, as the founders had been deeply influenced by the Tendai sect in Japan. As a result, Japanese Zen reached more people and was more widely known all over the world than the original Chinese Sects. Daisetsu Suzuki did what Kumārajīva had done, for the US and European audiences, through writing in English about Japanese Zen in the 20th century.

According to recent statistics compiled by the Agency for Cultural Affairs, Government of Japan, out of 75,000 existing Buddhist temples in Japan, 62,000 belong to the sects which are based on the Sūtras translated by Kumārajīva. These 62,000 temples belong to the Tendai Sect and its offshoots (Jodo category, Zen category and Nichiren category).

After 300 years of the peaceful Shogunate Edo era, the Emperor was restored as the ruler of Japan formally, which is called "Restoration of the Imperial Rule" and Shintoism replaced Buddhism as the spiritual guardian of the ruler. Buddhism in Japan lost its patron government and the Japanese Buddhist world began working on rebuilding the religion through strengthening its theology. The movement began in the Taisho era and the study of the original sūtras written in Sanskrit has been greatly enhanced as Information Technology (IT) provides much more access to those original sūtras and the like. So the trend continues, as contemporary Japanese people seek the re-evaluation of Buddhism as they feel they need spiritual aspiration in this complex, fast paced world.

25

Kumārajīva and Mādhyamaka school of thought

Bachchan Kumar

Introduction

The present paper discusses the early life of Kumārajīva, as a great translator of the Buddhist texts in China and his Madhayamaka school of thought in China. The Chinese records throw much light on Kumārajīva's ancestors, His biography is well recorded in the Chinese account *Kao seng tehoam* (ch. II) dated 519 C.E., *Tch'ou san tsang ki si* (520 C.E.) and *Chi-mo-lo-shi.* He set a new path of Mahayanist Buddhism in China through the Mādhayamaka philosophy enunciated by Nāgārjuna.

Early Life of Kumārajīva

Kumārajīva's father, Kumārāyaṇa (in Chinese: *Kiu-mo-yen*), belonged to a Brahmin family of Kashmir (Ch'en 1964:.81; Dutt 1962:301)). Descended from an honourable line of Prime Ministers of a kingdom in Kashmir, his grandfather Ta-to was a reputed person. Though, Kumārāyaṇa had a claim to become Prime Minister, he renounced his hereditary claim and became a Buddhist monk. Eventually, he set out along the Silk Route, which threaded its way across the mighty Pamirs and into the Takla Makan desert and Central Asia. Following the northern route, he arrived in Kucha on the northern rim of the great Tarim River basin. Chinese historians write of this area as wealthy and culturally well advanced (Grousset 1932:53). On perceiving knowledge and brightness on his face, the Kuchan king welcomed him in the court and made him a trusted adviser. Soon he was elevated to the position of kuo-shih, 'Teacher of the Nation', a privileged position, which entailed political and cultural duties as well as religious functions.

Jīvā (or Jīvaka), the king's younger sister, had grace, wit, will and an exceptional intelligence. It was said that she had only to glance at a written passage to comprehend it, and only to hear something once to repeat it from memory. She had politely rejected a number of eligible suitors from the neighboring kingdoms, but when she saw Kumārāyaṇa she expressed the desire to become his wife. The king was delighted and insisted that Kumārāyaṇa should accept the proposal. Later, Kumārāyaṇa disrobed himself from monkhood and married Jīvā. In the year 344 C.E., Jīvaka gave birth to a son in Kucha in Central Asia (today, Sinkiang region, China). The child was named partly after the father and the mother, and thus was called Kumārajīva. After the birth of Kumārajīva, Jīvā wanted to become a nun but her husband did not allow her for sometime. (Ch'en 1964:81)

Childhood and Education

At the age of six, Kumārajīva's mother became a Buddhist nun and joined Tsio-li nunnery. Even as a child, Kumārajīva had extraordinary qualities and he committed to memory many Buddhist texts and sūtras. Recognizing his intelligence, his mother became determined to give him the best available philosophical and spiritual training. When he was nine years old, mother and son undertook the arduous journey to India, eventually reaching the Kashmiri kingdom known to the Chinese as Chi-pin, which was his father's native home. Bandhudatta, a renowned Buddhist teacher and cousin of the king, instructed Kumārajīva in the *āgamas* (the *nikāyas* of the Theravāda tradition). Kumārajīva spent the next two years mastering these texts and was recognized by the king. After he defeated several non-Buddhist teachers in a debate held before the ruler, his reputation preceded him wherever he traveled. In addition to learning the scriptures and treatises of the Sarvāstivāda school, Dīrghāgama and Madhyāgama, Kumārajīva took the opportunity to study Indian medicine, astronomy and astrology, exegetical and hermeneutical methods of exposition, logic and the applied sciences.

Three years later he returned with his mother to Kucha. On their journey via Tokharestan and Kashgar, an *arhat* predicted that he had a bright future and would introduce many people to Buddhism. The *arhat* guided him and said:

> *"You must watch over and protect this novice. If by the time he reaches the age of thirty-five he has not abandoned the rules of religious discipline, he will become a great propagator of buddhadharma, enlightening countless people, and he will be the equal of Upagupta (the fourth Indian patriarch after Buddha, who converted the emperor Ashoka to Buddhism)."*

Kumārajīva and his mother spent a year in Kashgar, a Buddhist kingdom known for its excellent teachers and libraries, where he completed his studies of the Abhidharma and the texts revered by the Sarvāstivadins under the Kashmirian Buddhayaśas. During this time he studied Vedic literature and the most important systems of chanting the Vedas, focusing on the power of sound to open the consciousness to transcendental truths. This knowledge later inspired his translations of sūtras and texts into Chinese. He also expanded his knowledge of Sanskrit, Pāli and the languages of Central Asia. On one occasion, a monk recommended that the king of Kashgar invite Kumārajīva to expound a sūtra to a prestigious assembly which included the king himself. After he did this, the monks of Kashgar were indirectly compelled to reform their lax monastic disciplines. The king of Kucha, hearing of the high regard in which Kumārajīva was held in Kashgar, sent a delegation to confirm friendly relations between the two kingdoms.

While in Kashgar, Kumārajīva met Sūryasoma, a prince of Yarkand (So-ch'e), who had renounced his royal inheritance and become a revered teacher. Kumārajīva held that the dharmas, or ultimate constituents of existence, are eternally real, while empirical phenomena, which arise out of the momentary confluence of dharmas under *karma*, are unreal. Suryasoma adhered to the Mahāyāna view that all dharmas are themselves unreal; ontologically, dharmas are like empty space and assume distinct existence only in their momentary, ever-changing combinations. Suryasoma's more universal application of Buddha's doctrine of impermanence won Kumārajīva over to the Mahāyāna school of Buddhism. He felt that he had been emancipated, declaring that he had been like a person who, not knowing what gold was, had previously taken brass for something wonderful. Kumārajīva studied the doctrines of the Madhyamika schools, memorized treatises by Nāgārjuna and Āryadeva, and rapidly assimilated Mahāyāna teachings. He insisted that Bandhudatta, his first teacher in India, come to Kashgar, and eventually won him over.

In 379 C.E, the fame of Kumārajīva reached China through the report of the Chinese monk, Seng-ch'un, who had travelled to Kucha. Immediately, efforts were made by Fu Chien, ruler of the Former Ch'in Dynasty, to get Kumārajīva to the capital in Ch'ang-an. The efforts were to be frustrated for almost two decades, mainly because of the activities of one Lü Kuang, the General send by Fu Chien to subdue the Kucha kingdom. Being a non-Buddhist, Lü Kuang treated Kumārajīva with all kinds of indignities and kept him in Liang-chou in northwestern China for seventeen years in spite of repeated pleas from the Yao family in Ch'ang-an to send him east. Finally in exasperation Yao Hsing dispatched armies to Liang-chou to defeat Lü and bring Kumārajīva to Ch'ang-an in 401 C.E (Wright 1959:62).

Ch'ang-an, under the patronage of the ruling Yao family, was a flourishing centre of Buddhist activities, with the famous monks of the realm congregated there. The Hsiao-yao Garden was placed at the disposal of Kumārajīva and his fellow monks, and here, with a thousand monks sitting in daily sessions, he carried on his translation activities. Sometimes the ruler, Yao Hsing, personally participated in these proceedings by holding the old translations which were used by Kumārajīva as the basis for comparison. During his long sojourn in Liang-chou, Kumārajīva had undoubtedly learned Chinese very well, so that as soon as he arrived in Ch'ang-an he was able to plunge into his work. He was honoured with the title Kuo-shih (National Preceptor) and from 402 to his death, he and his colleagues poured forth a steady stream of translations, which included some of the most important items in the Chinese canon. Later, Kumārajīva had a number of disciples in China adhering to his Madhyamika school.

In the official history (*Shu*) of the Chin dynasty in the 95th chapter, there is a life sketch of Kumārajīva. Sukumar Dutt (1962:305) has also written a biographical his biography in sketch of Kumārajīva. According to one legend, an imperial patron sent him ten glamorous ladies from his court to select as his consort. He renounced monkhood and selected one of them as his wife and entered into a worldly life. He soon realized his mistake. It is reported that he always used to start his preaching's with the apologetic exordium: 'Follow my work, but not my life which is far from ideal. The lotus grows out of mud. Love the lotus, do not love the mud.'

The Great Translator "Kumārajīva"

Kumārajīva was the world's greatest translator. He translated important Mahāyānist Buddhist texts into Chinese. The translated books that go to his credit are 300 in number; out of which many were included in the Chinese *Tripiṭaka* (Nanjio's Catalogue, Appendix II, p. 59). The text "Life of Aśvaghoṣa", was also translated from Sanskrit into Chinese. With the assistance of a number of Chinese collaborators, he made a fresh translation of the voluminous work (*Mahā*) *Prajñāpāramitā-sūtra.* Important texts translated by him in Chinese are *Daśabhūmivibhāṣā, Dvādaśa-nikāya* (*Mukha*) (Murti 1955:91) and *Śataśāstra* (Murti 1955: p. 93). His chief translated *śūnyavādin* works were *Pañcavimśati* (T.D. No. 223), the *Aṣṭasāhasrikā* (T.D. No. 227), the *Vimalakīrtinirdeśa* (T.D. No. 475), the *Vajracchedikā* (T.D. No. 235), and the *Prajñāpāramitāhṛdaya* (T.D. No. 250). He also translated the three Mādhyamaka treatises that form the basis for the San-lun school in China and Japan. The major Vinaya works that were translated by Kumārajīva are *Sarvāstivāda Prātimokṣa-sūtra* and according to tradition the *P'u-sa-chieh-pen* (*Bodhissattva-prātimokṣa*). His pietist translations include the *Saddharmapuṇḍarīka* (T.D. No. 262), the smaller *Sukhāvatīvyūha* (T.D. No. 366) and two Maitreya texts (T.D. No. 286) in collaboration with his friend from Kashgar, Buddhayaśas. The Central Buddhist philosophy of China is based on all these texts. It is said that a number of scholars assisted him in his exacting job. They consisted of specialists of all levels: those who discussed doctrinal question with Kumārajīva; those who checked the new translation against the old and imperfect ones; hundreds of editors, sub-editors and copyists *(Wright* 1959:63). About him, it is said that even at the age of sixty he was engaged in translating the Buddhist texts and continued this hard work till the end of his life. He also revised the earlier Chinese translations which were in crude or even incoherent versions. His translation is considered to be the authentic translation in China.

According to *Kao-seng chuan,* Kumārajīva took his last breath on September 15, 413 in Ch'ang-an (Seng-chao's obituary).

The Mādhyamaka School

Mādhyamaka (Sanskrit: *Mādhyamika,* traditional Chinese: 中觀派, Pinyin: *Zhōng guān bāi;* also known as *Śūnyavāda*), a Mahāyāna Buddhist philosophy, orginated in India in 2nd century CE. This philosophy was developed mainly by a saint āchārya Nāgārjuna on the basis of original teaching of the Buddha Śākyamuni. Nāgārjuna may have arrived at his position from a desire to achieve a consistent exegesis of the Buddha's doctrine as recorded in the āgamas. To Nāgārjuna, the Buddha was not merely a forerunner, but the very founder of the Mādhyamaka system. The tradition and its subsidiaries are called "Mādhyamaka"; those who follow it are called "Mādhyamikas". According to Jaidev Singh (1968:11), three stages of the development of the philosophy of this Mādhyamaka school can be easily distinguished. In the first stage, there was a systematic formulation of the Mādhyamaka philosophy by Nāgārjuna and Āryadeva. The second stage is one of division of the system into two schools the *Prāsaṅgika* and the *Svātāntrika.* The third stage is one of re-affirmation of the *Prāsaṅgika* school.

According to the Mādhyamakas, all phenomena are empty of "substance" or "essence" (Sanskrit: *svabhāva*), meaning that they have no intrinsic, independent reality apart from the causes and conditions from which they arose.

Mādhyamaka is a rejection of two extreme views, and therefore represents the "middle way" between externalism 'the view that something has an objective existence (i.e., its existence does not depend on external objects)' and nihilism. The term *nihilism* is used here in the sense that it is used in Indian philosophy, which differs from that used in Western philosophical *nihilism.* The sense used here denotes either an assertion that all things are intrinsically already destroyed or rendered nonexistent, or a denial of the existence of something that actually exists.

The striking features of Mādhyamaka philosophy is *Śūnya-śūnyatā.* It is also generally known as *Śūnyavāda* i.e. the philosophy that asserts *Śūnya* as the character of Reality. Etymologically, the word *Śūnya* is derived from the root '*śvi*' which means 'to swell, to expand'. Curiously, the word *Brahman* is taken from the root `*brah*' which also has the meaning `to swell, to expand'. It seems that the word is derived from the stage of Buddha, who is is said to be seated in `*Śūnya tattva*, in the *Śūnya* principle.' According to Jaidev (1968:36) "the word *Śūnya* seems to have been used in an ontological sense in this context. In the ontological sense *Śūnya* is the void which is also fullness. It is nothing in particular, it has the possibility of everything. It has been identified with *nirvāṇa*, with the absolute, the supreme Reality, with *Tattva* (Reality).

Mādhyamaka is also a source of the methods for approaching *Prajñāpāramitā*, or "perfection of wisdom", the sixth of the Six Perfections of the Bodhisattva path. The term is used as the collective title of key Mahāyāna sūtras. It explains the teaching on śūnyatā or emptiness. All things are causally interdependent and hence are empty. The Mādhyamaka doctrine of emptiness brought about a change from the ideal of personal salvation to that of universal salvation of all beings. Since all things are empty, nothing, according to Mādhyamaka, has a determinate and self-abiding nature or character which cannot be changed. In principle, all men can be converted to Buddhism and enter into *nirvāṇa*. The teaching of emptiness encourages everyone to transcend himself and thereby attain transcendental wisdom. It also posits the potential to obtain perfect freedom and unconditional liberation from attachment, desire and ignorance. Salvation is not just for the select but for all and one can help others in gaining enlightenment. The goal of salvation is not merely to become an *arhant*, a venerable person who obtains his salvation through effort, but a bodhisattva, an enlightened being who postpones his entrance into *nirvāṇa* for the purpose of helping other creatures, and eventually becomes a Buddha, a man of perfect wisdom. The Mādhyamaka theory of salvation developed by Kumārajīva gave rise to the Sun-lun sect in China and was also much popularized in Tibet.

The San-lun Sect in China

The San-lun sect of China originated from the Mādhamika School of India. This sect is known as the classic sect of China. The characteristic of the teaching in San-lun Sect is no-mark and no-attachment. This sect can be traced back to Lokakṣema, the great translator of the Han Dynasty who is known to be the founder of Mahāyāna Buddhism in China. However, San-lun sect was first introduced by Kumārajīva in China who translated the Three Śāstras. According to Fitzgerald, Kumārajīva worked, taught and spread the doctrines of a new sect of Buddhism in China (1942:pp. 275-276). Later, this text was organised by Master Tao-sheng (360-434 CE) and instituted by Master Chia-hsiang. San-lun is a pronunciation of the Chinese words which means Three Śāstras, or Three Treatises, so this sect is also known as Three Śāstra Sect, or

Three Treatise Sect. The three Śāstras are:

(1) Mādhyamika-kārikās Śāstra or simply Mādhyamika Śāstra or Middle treatise written by Nāgārjuna.

(2) Dvādaśanikāya Śāstra or Twelve Gate treatise also written by Nāgārjuna.

(3) Śata Śāstra, a one hundred verses treatise, written by Āryadeva.

The San-lun sect focuses on emptiness (*K'ung*), the Middle way (*chung-lao*), the twofold truth (*erh-t'i*) and the refutation of erroneous views as the illumination of right views (*p'o-hsieh-hsien-cheng*). These doctrines are interrelated and aim at showing that all things are empty. According to San-lun masters, the refutation of erroneous views is the illumination of the right view; it is not necessary to present other's views but simply to discard false views. The more wrong views one refutes, the closer one is to liberation. In other words, the absence of wrong views is itself the right view. Therefore, to say that all things are empty is not to argue for new metaphysics. Once this is realized, one discovers that even truth should be discarded.

Tibetan Mādhyamikas

There is currently no evidence that the historical Mādhyamikas divided themselves into distinct schools, but later Tibetan scholars, in particular the 11th-century Tibetan translator Patsap Nyima Drak did categorize their views. According to the Tibetan view, the sub-divisions of Mādhyamaka are: the *Prāsaṅgika* and *Svātāntrikas*. Yogāchāra and Mādhyamaka synthesis, sometimes rendered as *Yogācāra-Svātāntrika-Mādhyamaka*. Both *Prāsaṅgikas and Svātāntrikas* cited material in the āgamas in support of their arguments.

The Prāsaṅgika

The *Prāsaṅgika* Mādhyamaka is to show by *prāsaṅga* that any positive assertion (such as "*asti*" or "*nāsti*", "it is", or "it is not") or view regarding phenomena must be regarded as merely conventional (*saṃvṛtti or lokavyavahāra*). No position, therefore, constitutes the ultimate truth (*paramārtha*), including the views and statements made by the Prāsaṅgikas themselves, which are held to be solely for the purpose of defeating all views. The Prāsaṅgikas also identify this to be the message of the Buddha who, as Nāgārjuna put it, taught the Dharma for the purpose of refuting all views.

Buddhapālita and Candrakārti are noted as the main proponents of this approach. Tibetan teacher Longchen Rabjam noted in the 14th century that Candrakīrti favored the *Prāsaṅgika* approach when specifically discussing the analysis for ultimacy, but otherwise he made positive assertions. His central text, *Mādhyamakāvatāra*, is structured as a description of the paths and results of practice, which is made up of positive assertions. Therefore, even those most attributed to the *Prāsaṅgika* view make positive assertions when discussing a path of practice but use *prāsaṅga* specifically when analyzing the ultimate truth.

The Svātāntrika

The *Svātāntrika* Mādhyamaka differs from the *Prāsaṅgika* in a few ways. Conventional phenomena are understood to exist conventionally without existing ultimately. In this way they can make positive or "autonomous" assertions using syllogistic logic, and their name comes from this quality of autonomous statements. *Svātāntrika* in Sanskrit refers to autonomy and was translated back into Sanskrit from the equivalent Tibetan term. They also draw a distinction between the final ultimate truth and approximate or enumerative ultimate that describe the ultimate but are not the true ultimate. Bhāvaviveka is the first person to whom this view is attributed, as they are laid out in his commentaries on Nāgārjuna and his critiques of Buddhapālita.

Conclusion

Concluding this paper, Kumārajīva's contribution to Buddhism, especially to Chinese Buddhism has been exemplary. His translation works are the basis of Buddhism in China. His San-lun sect of Buddhism and his propounded theory of emptiness, the middle way, the twofold truth and refutation of erroneous views as the illumination of right views have been well absorbed into Zen teachings and practices.

BIBLIOGRAPHY

Fitxgerald (1942), *China: A Short Cultural History*, The Cresset Press, London.

Chang, Man-tao (ed.) (1978), *San-lun-tsung-chih-fa-chan-chi-ch'i-ssu-hsian*, (The Development of San-lun School and Its Thought), Taipei: Ta-chen-wen-hua Publishing Company.

---- (1978), *Chung-kuan-ssu-hsian-lun-chi* (The Collection of Essays on San-lun Thought), Taipei: Ta-chen-wen-hua Publishing Company.

---- (1979), *San-lun-tien-chi-yen-chiu* (Studies in San-lun Documents), Taipei, Ta-chen-wen-hua Publishing Company.

Cheng, Hsueh-li (1981), "Nāgārjuna, Kant and Wittegenstein: The San-lun Madhyamika Exposition of Emptiness," *Religious Studies*, No. 17, March, pp. 67-85.

---- (1981), Truth and Logic in San-lun Madhyamika Buddhism," *International Philosophical Quarterly*, No. 21, September, pp. 260-276.

---- (1991), *Empty Logic: Madhyamika Buddhism from Chinese sources*, Delhi.

Ch'en, K. S. (1964), *Buddhism in China: A Historical Survey*, Princeton, New Jersey, USA.

Chatterjee, Heramba Nath (1957), *Mula-Madhyamika-Karika of Nāgārjuna*, Calcutta.

Gregory, Peter N. (1987), *Sudden and Gradual Approaches to Enlightenment in Chinese Thought*,

University of Hawaii Pess, Hawaii.

Grousset (1932), *In the Footsteps of the Buddha*, London.

Murti, T. R. V.(1955), *The Central Philosophy of Buddhism: A Study of the Madhyamika System*, London.

Nanjio's Catalogue of Chinese Tripitaka, Appendix II.

Robinson, R. H. (1976) *Early Madhyamika in India and China*, Delhi.

Santina, Peter Della (1986), *Mādhyamaka Schools in India,*, MLBD, Delhi.

Seng-chao's obituary (*Kuang hungming, chi* 23), May 28, 413.

Singh, Jaidev (1968), *An Introduction to Madhayamaka Philosophy*, Delhi.

Streng, F. (1967), *Emptiness: A Study in Religious Meaning*

Sukumar Dutt (1962), *Buddhist Monks and Monasteries of India: their History and their Contribution to Indian Culture*, London.

Suzuki, D. T. (1963), *Outlines of Mahāyāna Buddhism*,

Wright, Arthur F. (1959), *Buddhism in Chinese History*, OUP, London.

26

Kumārajīva : his connections with Kashmir and the development of Buddhist lore

Advaitavadini Kaul

Overview of Buddhism in Kashmir

The Mūla Sarvāstivādavinaya records the Buddha's forecast to Vajrapāṇi that Mādhyandina - a disciple of Ānanda would propagate his religion in Kashmir, the land of Blue forests - and that he would subdue the malevolent Haluta Nāga and extend the seat on which he would sit cross-legged to miraculously cover the whole of Kashmir, thereby ousting the Nāgas from their habitation and making the vast country of sixty thousand villages an abode for meditating monks[1]. Embellished with legendary colouring, the above description finds unanimity in attributing the introduction of Buddhism in Kashmir to Arhat Majjhāntika/Mādhyandina – a direct disciple of Ānanda, in Pāli[2], Sanskrit[3] and Chinese[4] sources. There is some evidence, according to

---

1 *Bhaiṣajyavastu,* Gilgit Mss, p.1sq: adrākṣit bhagavān dūrād eva nīlanīlaṁ vanarājim/dṛṣtvā ca punar vajrapāṇi yakṣamāmantrate/paśyati tvam vajrapāṇe nīlanīlametāni vanarājim/paśyāmi bhādanta eṣa vajrapāṇe kāśmīra maṇḍalaṁ mama varṣaśataparinirvṛtasya mādhyandina nāmo bhikṣur bhaviṣyati yānandasya bhikṣo sārdham vihārisa halutam duṣṭanāgam vi(neṣoyati) atho paryaṇkam baddhvā samagre kāśmīra-maṇḍala-sāsanaṁ praveśayiṣyati................ pāśānukūlam sayanasanam yadut kaśmira-maṇḍalam ṣaṣṭigrāmasahasrāṇi ṣaṣṭigrāmaśatāni ca, ṣaṣṭigrāmastraya grāma hyetat (ka) śmīramaṇḍalam

2 *Mahāvaṁṣa* XII 834-836 :
thero moggali putto so jina sāsana jotako/niṭhāpetvān saṇgītiṁ pekhamāno anāgataṁ// sāsanassa patiṭṭhānaṁ paccantesu apekkhiyā/pesesi kattike māse te te there tahiṁ tahiṁ// theraṁ kasyīra-gandhāraṁ majhantikam pesayi/apesayi mahādevat theraṁ mahiṣa maṇḍala//

3 *Avadānakalpalatā* of Kṣemendra chapter 70 :
mādhyantikābhindhyo bhikṣorānandasya gurorgirā/buddha śāsanamādhātuṁ yayau kāśmīra-maṇḍala//

4 Watters, Thomas, 1904, p.267

On the banks of River Vitasta (Jehlum) in Kashmir stood many Buddhist viharas. Photo by Kapil Kaul

which Buddhism existed in Kashmir even before its formal introduction by Mādyandina under King Aśoka's patronage. As per the Divyāvadāna[5], several monks of Tāmasavana in Kashmir were invited by King Aśoka to attend the third Buddhist Council that was held at Pāṭaliputra. Again, Kalhana[6] describes the establishment of several vihāras in Kashmir during the reign of King Surendra, the predecessor of King Aśoka.

Aśoka (c 273-236 BCE), whose sway extended to Kashmir, is described by Kalhaṇa[7] as a king of Kashmir and the follower of Jina, i.e. Buddha. He is credited with the establishment of several stūpas and vihāras in the valley. A caitya of amazing height was built by him in the town of Vitastātra[8]. Xuanxang noticed four stūpas set up by Aśoka in the valley, containing a portion of the relics of the Buddha[9]. The Tibetan historian Tārānātha speaks of

[5] *Divyāvadāna*, p.399 :
vasanti kāśmīrapure suramye ye cāpi dhīrās tāmasa vanes'min/mahāvane revatake raye'ryā anugrahārthaṁ mama te'bhyupeyuḥ//

[6] *Kalhana's Raājataraṅgiṇī* (hence forth KRT) I.94, 98
tena sva maṇḍale khanda yaśasā puṇya karamaṇā /vihāraḥ sukṛtodāro nirmitaḥ saurasābhidhaḥ // tat sūnur janako nāma prajānāṁ janakopamāḥ/vihāram agrahāraṁ ca jālorākhyaṁ ca nirmame//

[7] KRT I. 102 : yaḥ śānta vṛjino rājā prapanno jina śāsanam/śuṣkaletra vitastatrau tastāra stūpa maṇḍalaiḥ//

[8] KRT I 103 : dharmāraṇya vihārāntar vitastatra purebhavat/yat kṛtaṁ caityamutsedhāvadhi prāptyakṣame kṣaṇam//

[9] Watters, p.261

Buddhist site, Harwan, Kashmir also known as Ṣaḍarhadvana, 1-2nd cen. CE Photo - IGNCA Collection

King Aśoka as having bestowed lavish gifts on several Buddhist saṁghas in Kashmir[10].

After Aśoka, Buddhism was re-established by the Indo-Scythian rulers particularly Kaniṣka around 1st century CE. The sitting of the fourth Buddhist Council, creation of the famous commentaries and the appearance of distinguished Buddhist masters[11] were some of the important events that occurred in Kashmir during Kaniṣka's reign. According to the Chinese tradition, Vibhāṣā Śāstra denotes a commentary or discussion on an Abhidharma treatise i.e. the Sarvāstivāda Abhidharma. This treatise was written by the masters, chiefly of Kashmir, and those who attached themselves to the Sarvāstivāda school. These masters were called Vibhāṣā shi and sometimes also Kashmir shi. Saṅghabhadra, Dharmatrāta, Vimalamitra etc. were some of the noteworthy Kashmiri masters. Subsequently we find quite a number of masters who went outside Kashmir as missionaries to propagate Buddhism. Many masters who went to Central Asia, China and Tibet, translated Sanskrit texts into the native languages. Also, many Buddhist adherents visited Kashmir to receive firsthand information from the Buddhist masters of Kashmir[12].

[10] Chattopadhyaya, Debiprasad, 1970, p.65

[11] Watters, pp.270-71; Chattopadhyaya, p.91, also ref. Nalinaksha Dutt, 1939, vol. I, p.22

[12] Ref. for details : Kaul, Advaitavadini, *Buddhist Savants of Kashmir - their contribution Aborad,* 1987

Buddhism suffered a reverse after the Kushanas and later in the 5th century CE it was nearly wiped out from the valley by the Huna ruler Mihirakala[13]. Thereafter, under Meghavāhana, Buddhism flourished again[14]. His queens built several vihāras and embellished them with special adornments[15]. Subsequently, Buddhism is seen co-existing alongside other faiths in the valley almost till the advent of the medieval period[16]. However, Buddhism has left deep roots in Kashmir and the traces can be identified even till now.

Moreover, the earliest existing source on Kashmir the *Nīlamata Purāṇa (NP)* which is dated between the 6th-7th century CE refers to the people of Kashmir as engaged in self study and contemplation *(svādhyāya dhyāne niratai)*[17]. It also describes the Buddha as an incarnation of Viṣṇu and prescribes in detail how to celebrate the birthday of the Buddha in the month of Vaiśākha. It describes cleaning of the caityas and the dwelling places of the Śākyas; bathing the images of the Buddha with the water rendered holy with herbs, jewels and scents. Interestingly it also prescribes decorating the caityas with paintings and gifting clothes, food and books to the Buddhists and celebrating the festival with the performance of dancers and actors[18].

In addition to the above discussions, the recent discoveries fully tally with the known facts and is confirmed by the following statement "That Kashmir and the north western areas of peninsular India have played an extraordinarily important role in the history of South and Central Asian Buddhism is nothing that would stand in need of proof. Recent discoveries such as the Buddhist scroll from Gandhāra, now in the British Library, and a considerable number of Buddhist manuscripts from Bāmiyān, now in the (Norwegian) Schoyen collection, to mention only the most spectacular finds, fully tally with the known facts. Influential scholastic traditions such as the (Mūla) Sarvāstivāda, an enormous number of great scholars and a high standard of learning have

---

[13] KRT I.289-325

[14] KRT III.4,7

[15] KRT III.9-15

[16] Ref. Kaul, Advaitavadini, 2005, pp. 165-169.

[17] *Nīlamata Purāṇa*, 14:
Śālimālākulaṁ sphitaṁ satphalādyaiḥ samanvitam/svādhyāyadhyāne niratair yajñaśilair janairyutam//

[18] *Nīlamata Purāṇa*, 709-714:
viṣṇu devo jagannātho braman prāpte kalau yuge/aṣṭāviṁśattame bhāvī buddho nāma jagad guruḥ// puṣpa yukte niśānāthe vaiśākhe māsi kāśyapa/tasmāt kālād athārabhya kāle bhāvinyataḥ param// śukle sampūjanaṁ tasya yathā kāryaṁ tathā sṛuṇu/sarvauṣadhaiḥ sarva ratnaiḥ sarva gandhais tathaiva ca// buddhārcā snāpanaṁ kāryaṁ śākyoktair vacanais tathā/sudhāsitāsca kartavyā śākyāvāsai prayatnataḥ // kvacitcitrayutā kāryā caityā devagṛhāstathā/utsavaṁ ca tathā kāryaṁ naṭa nartaka saṇkulam// śākyānāṁ pūjanaṁ kāryaṁ cīvarāhārapustakai/sarvaṁ etad bhavet kāryaṁ yāvat prāptā bhaven maghā//

always been considered a hallmark of Kashmiri Buddhism right until the beginning of the second millennium AD."[19]

Buddhist site, Parihāspura, Kashmir (8th cen. CE) about 25 kms towards north of Srinagar. Photo - IGNCA collection

Development of Mahāyāna

From Madhyadeśa, where the teaching of the Buddha found its first audience among the general masses during his life-time and immediately afterwards, Buddhism thereafter reached out in the direction of Mathura and Kashmir through the first missionary activity[20]. Both Mathura and Kashmir were the centres of two powerful Hindu cults. Also, the serene atmosphere of Kashmir is said to have been praised by the Buddha himself. In the *Samyuktavastu* the Buddha is represented as saying that Kashmir is the best land for meditation and for leading a religious life[21]. The learned pandits imbued with the spirit of tolerance and ever ready to investigate and learn every new thought, received the canon with all respect. After critical and analytical study they gave it a new interpretation, suiting the time and the aspirations of the people. Thus, the Mahāyāna - the great vehicle, was also developed further as a result of the contemplating mind. The Hīnayāna laid stress on an individual's self efforts for personal salvation. But, to the saints and scholars of Kashmir who were deeply learned in more subtle and higher philosophies, this doctrine seemed incapable of keeping the masses attached to it for long. Therefore, while coming into contact with masterminds, the

[19] Slaje, Walter 2004, p.185
[20] *Mahāvaṁśa* XII. 836
[21] *Samyuktavastu* ch XI translation in Journal Asiatique Nov.-Dec. 1914; Naudon, Jean, 1980, p.1

Buddhist site, Parihāspura, Kashmir(8th cen. CE) about 25 kms towards north of Srinagar. Photo - IGNCA Collection

simple creed of early Buddhism got permeated with their refined ritualistic and philosophic teachings.

The philosophy developed chiefly on the lines of the Sarvāstivāda (realist) school belonging to the Hīnayāna, and Kashmir was the stronghold of this school in Northern India[22]. Nāgārjuna - a contemporary of Kaniṣka[23] is known as the founder of the Mādhyamika school of Buddhist thought[24]. Kaniṣka mentions one Nāgārjuna who resided at Ṣaḍarhadvana, the modern Harwan[25] in Kashmir. Later, Asaṅga and Vasubandhu both stayed and studied in Kashmir, and laid the foundation of a third school i.e. the Vijñānavāda, holding that all phenomena is illusion – it is nothing but thought[26].

Though the early Buddhist doctrine had been carried to China through Indian missionaries in the 2nd century CE, it could not take firm roots there as yet. It was, however, later on that the Mahāyāna, after gaining strength and popularity and attaining the status of a State religion was carried to Central Asia and China with great success. The Kashmiri missionaries played a great role in the dissemination of the Buddhist lore around this period both at home and in neighbouring countries[27]. The interesting aspect of this development is that we get this information from foreign sources.

---

22 Bagchi, Prabodh Chandra, 2008, p.37

23 Watters, p. 245

24 ref. Kaul Advaitavadini, 2003, pp.181-186

25 KRT I. 173 : bodhisattvaṣca deśesminneko bhūmīśvarobhavat/ sa ca nāgārjunaḥ śrīman ṣaḍarhadvana sansrayī//

26 Ref. Kaul, Advaitavadini, 2003, pp.188-189

27 Ref. Kaul, 1987, chapters II & III.

Kumārajīva and his connections with Kashmir

Seen in the background discussed above, the biographical details[28] of the renowned Buddhist scholar Kumārajīva provide many clues that make it possible to reconstruct certain lost links. First of all, his biological link. His father Kumārāyana, it is said, belonged to a royal family of Kashmir. It is not possible to identify this royal family for lack of evidence from the other side. Renouncing the world, it is recorded that Kumārāyana became a monk and proceeded to Kucha in Central Asia. Here he later got married to the princess of Kucha. Her name was Jīva. A son was born to this couple who was given the name Kumārajīva combining the names of his parents.

Soon after Kumārajīva's birth, his mother became a nun. She herself took charge of the upbringing of her son. In this way Kumārajīva received the first training in Buddhist lore in the monasteries of Kucha. Thereafter Kumārajīva was taken to Kashmir by his mother for further studies. This indicates the importance of Kashmir for acquiring higher knowledge. Here, he studied the Tripiṭaka and other Hīnayāna texts thoroughly under a teacher named Bandhudatta. Kumārajīva, having memorised tsu-tsang (Samyukta piṭaka sūtra), Chung-e-hau (Madhyamāgama) and Chang-e-hau (Dīrghāgama), his sharp memory won him the respect of his teacher. He also received favours from the King of Kashmir who appointed five monks and ten novices at his service.

After three years of stay in Kashmir for acquiring knowledge in the Buddhist lore, Kumārajīva started back for Kucha along with his mother. They stopped at Kashgar in between. Here Kumārajīva studied Sarāstivāda Abhidharma with Buddhayaśas, again a renowned Abhidharma teacher from Kashmir. He also studied Ekottarāgama-sūtra here. Most importantly, he is also said to have made an extensive study of the four Vedas, five sciences and allied subjects. It was in Kashgar itself that he got introduced by one Sūryasoma to the Mahāyāna doctrine. Thus, he made a thorough study of the Mādhyamika treatises. It may be noted here that one Sūryasome or Sūryasena is also referred as the propagator of Nāgārjuna's theory in Kashmir[29]. It remains to be investigated if both were the same. However, being impressed by the Mahāyāna doctrine, Kumārajīva returned to Kashmir to explain the inner meaning of Ekayāna to his teacher Bandhudatta in great detail. Bandhudatta

---

[28] Kumarajiva's biography is based upon two Chinese works :

(i) The biography section of *Chu-san-tsang-chi-chi* (collection of the Records of the Translation of the Tripiṭaka) translated in *Lives of Early Buddhist Monks : The Oldest Extant Biographies of Indian and Central Asian Monks,* Saroj Kumar Chaudhuri 2009 pp.96-109.

(ii) *Kāo Seng Chuan (Lives of Eminent Monks)* compiled by Hui-Chiao in 519 CE. Translated into German by Johannes Nobal and published in the Sitzungsberichte der Preussischen Akademie der Wissenschaften xx, Berlin, in 1927. Translated from German into English through IGNCA by Anya Malhotra and published in *Kumārajīva -- The Transcreator of Buddhist Chinese diction,* 2011, pp. 115-132.

[29] Panikkar, K.M.,1957, p.30

realising the truth, submitted to Kumārajīva by saying – I was your teacher in Hīnayāna and you are now my teacher in Mahāyāna – this speaks volumes about the level of interaction and understanding between the great minds.

On returning to Kucha, Kumārajīva was introduced to Sarvāstivāda Vinaya by another Kashmiri master. His name was Vimalākṣa. In this way Kumārajīva acquired great proficiency in all branches of Buddhist learning and his fame spread far and wide. Later on, when Kumārajīva was in China (Kuan-Chang) he came to know about the arrival of his teacher Vimalākṣa there. He was overjoyed and paid due respects to his teacher.

Development of Buddhist Lore

Kumārajīva devoted himself to the propagation of Buddhist teachings with his deep knowledge of all branches of learning. He translated the Buddhist sūtras in Chinese by becoming the chief of the translation bureau to which a large number of Indian and Chinese associates were attached. Here too, there were a large number of Buddhist monks and scholars from Kashmir associated with him. Punyatrāta, Buddhayaśas and Vimalākṣa were the most prominent amongst them all.

Kumārajīva's translations of some fundamental Mahāyāna texts are noteworthy. These include *Sūtrālaṅkāra-śāstra* of Aśvaghoṣa, *Daśabhūmi-vibhāṣā-śāstra* of Nāgārjuna, *Śatasāstra* of Āryadeva and *Tattvasiddhi-śāstra* of Harivarman.

Satyasiddhi (Tattvasiddhi or Bhūta Siddhi) is known as one of the ten schools of Chinese Buddhism. It is based upon the *Satyasiddhi Śāstra* that was composed by one Harivarman in Kashmir around 3rd-4th century CE[30]. Regretting the wrong interpretations, Harivarman made an attempt to return to the basic tenets of the real teachings through his composition of the Śāstra. This became a source of inspiration and right knowledge. Unfortunately, the original text is lost. But Kumārajīva translated this important Śāstra into Chinese. This translation is the only existing version available today. So great was the impact of this Śāstra that Kumārajīva is said to have established a school based upon this Śāstra in China wherefrom it was also introduced in Korea and Japan. It has been pointed out[31] that the six principles of Chinese paintings are based upon this Śāstra. This is a very interesting statement that invites further examination in the direction of locating the traces of the *Nāṭya Śāstra* of Bharata that was very much rooted in Kashmir.

It may be concluded that Indian tradition has been an open stream and a continuous process on the path of realising the ultimate goal. Kumārajīva

[30] *Satyasiddhi Śāstra* of Harivarman, vol. I edited by N. Aiyaswami Sastri, Review in Journal Asiatic Society of Bengal vol.52/53, 1977-78 (new series) p.393; Bagchi, 2008, p. 134.

[31] Ref. Lokesh Chandra's Foreword to *Kumārajīva - The Trancreator of Buddhist - Chinese diction*, p.16

was one of the illuminating torch bearers of this illustrious tradition. He imbibed knowledge from many Kashmiri scholars, not only in Kashmir that was considered an important seat of learning at that time, but he studied under many Kashmiri teachers outside Kashmir as well, as many scholars had already left Kashmir to spread the Buddhist lore in Central Asian States and China under the influence of the political developments taking place in Kashmir. He had many Kashmiri associates working with him in China. Thus, the biography of this renowned Buddhist Philosopher and Seer uncovers the lost links that he had with Kashmir and Kashmiri scholars.

To sum up ".... the translations which Kumārajīva directed at Ch'ang-an, and still more the personal comments sometimes therein mingled, contribute in an interesting manner toward acquainting us with the state of Buddhism in Kāśmīr in the 4th century : for it is his personal Buddhism, all impregnated yet with the teaching of his Kaśmīri masters, that the Koutchean used to comment upon in front of his Chinese listeners[32]".

BIBLIOGRAPHY

Texts

Divyāvadāna edited by E B Cowell & R.A. Neil, Cambridge University Press, 1896.

Kalhaṇa's Rājatraṅgiṇī, A chronicle of the Kings of Kaśmir, translated, with Introduction, Commentary & Appendices by M A Stein, Motilal Banarsidas, Delhi vols. I & II, 1989, vol.III 1988.

Kṣemendra, *Avadānakalpalatā* edited by S.C. Dass, Bibliotheca Indica Series, 1818.

Mahāvaṁsa edited by N.N. Bhagawat, Bombay 1936.

The *Nīlamata Purāṇa* text with translation by Ved Kumari, Vol.II, Jammu and Kashmir Academy of Art Culture and Languages, Srinagar, 1994.

Translations and Studies

Bagchi, Prabodh Chandra 2008, *India and China – A Thousand years of Cultural Relations* (*Zhong-yin Qiannian Shi*), (Revised & Edited) Haraprasad Ray, Munshiram Manoharlal Publishers Pvt. Ltd.

Chattopadhyaya, Debiprasad (ed. & tr.)1970 *Tārānātha's History of Buddhism in India*, Indian Institute of Advanced Studies, Simla.

Chaudhuri, Saroj Kumar, 2010 *Lives of Early Buddhist Monks – The Oldest Extant Biographies of Indian and Central Asian Monks*, Abha Prakashan, New Delhi.

Dutt, Nilinaksha (ed.), 1939 *Gilgit Manuscripts*, Vols. I, II, & III, Research and Publication Department of J & K Govt. Srinagar.

[32] Naudou, 1980, p.3.

Kaul, Advaitavadini 2003 "Bearing of Kashmir in the Development of Buddhist Thought" in *Kalākalpa* (Journal of the Indira Gandhi National Centre for the Arts) Vol. I, No.I, pp. 179-191.

Kaul, Advaitavadini 2005 "Buddhism in Kashmir" in *Indologica Taurinensia* (official organ of the International Association of Sanskrit Studies) Vol XXXI, pp.159-171.

Kaul, Advaitavadini 1987 *Buddhist Savants of Kashmir – Their contribution Abroad,* Utpal Publications, Srinagar.

Naudou, Jean, 1980 *Buddhists of Kashmir,* Agam Kala Prakashan, Delhi.

Pannikar, K.M. 1957 *India and China,* Asian Publishing House.

Sharma, Nirmala, 2011 *Kumārajīva – The Transcreator of Buddhist Chinese diction,* Niyogi Books, New Delhi.

Slaje, Walter 2007 "The Last Buddhist of Kashmir as Recorded by Jonarāja" in Wagish Shukla (ed) *Sanskrit Studies* Vol.2 Special Centre for Sanskrit Studies, Jawaharlal Nehru University and D.K. Printworld, New Delhi, pp.185-193.

Watters, Thomas (tr.)1904 *On Yuan Chwang Travels in India, 629-645 AD* Vol I & II edited by TWR Dawids, London.